16e

Business Communication

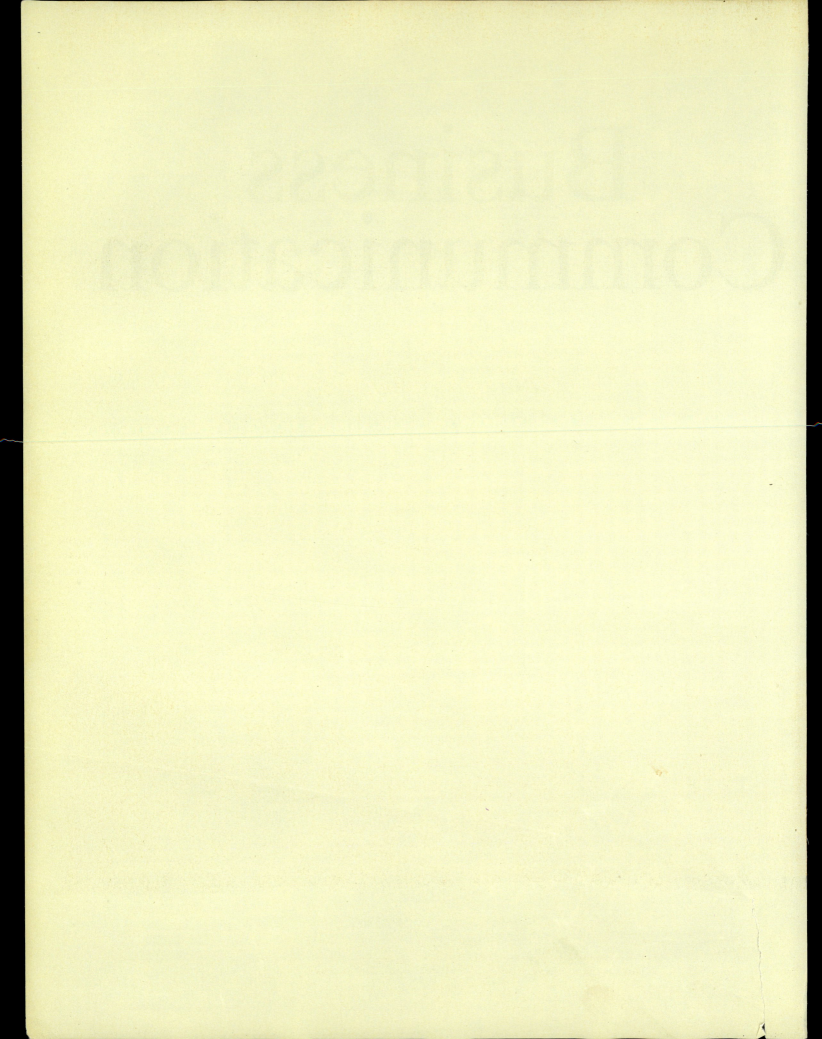

16e

Business Communication

CAROL M. LEHMAN
Professor of Management
Mississippi State University

DEBBIE D. DUFRENE
Professor of Business Communication
Stephen F. Austin State University

Australia • Brazil • Japan • Korea • Mexico • Singapore • Spain • United Kingdom • United States

Business Communication,
Sixteenth Edition
Carol M. Lehman, Debbie D. DuFrene

Executive Vice President and Publisher, Business & Computers: Jonathan Hulbert

Vice President of Editorial, Business: Jack W. Calhoun

Editor-in-Chief: Melissa Acuña

Sr. Acquisitions Editor: Erin Joyner

Developmental Editor: Julie Klooster

Vice President of Marketing, Business & Computers: Bill Hendee

Marketing Coordinator: Shanna Shelton

Sr. Marketing Communications Manager: Sarah Greber

Content Project Manager: Holly Henjum

Media Editor: John Rich

Print Buyer: Miranda Klapper

Production Service/Compositor: S4Carlisle Publishing Services

Sr. Art Director: Stacy Jenkins Shirley

Sr. Image Rights Acquisitions Account Manager: Deanna Ettinger

Photo Researcher: Terri Miller

Sr. Text Rights Acquisitions Account Manager: Mardell Glinski Schultz

Text Permissions Researcher: Karyn Morrison

Internal Designer: KeDesign, Mason, OH

Cover Designer: KeDesign, Mason, OH

Cover Image: © Getty Images/Digital Vision

Interior Design Photos: PDA: © iStockphoto.com/Nadezda Firsova; coffee: © Martin Poole/Stockbyte/Getty Images; blueprints: © Rubberball/Getty Images; magnifier: iStockphoto.com/Emrah Turudu; laptop: © iStockphoto.com/René Mansi

Library of Congress Control Number: 2009942930

Student Edition ISBN 13: 978-0-324-78218-9
Student Edition ISBN 10: 0-324-78218-7
Instructor Edition ISBN 13: 978-0-324-78230-1
Instructor Edition ISBN 10: 0-324-78230-6

South-Western Cengage Learning
5191 Natorp Boulevard
Mason, OH 45040
USA

Cengage Learning products are represented in Canada by Nelson Education, Ltd.

For your course and learning solutions, visit **www.cengage.com**

Purchase any of our products at your local college store or at our preferred online store **www.ichapters.com**

Printed in the United States of America
1 2 3 4 5 6 7 13 12 11 10 09

Brief Contents

Appendices A-1

Contents

4 Preparing Spoken and Written Messages 120

Part 3 Communication Through Voice, Electronic, and Written Messages 153

5 Communicating Electronically 154

6 Delivering Good- and Neutral-News Messages 186

7 Delivering Bad-News Messages 226

8 Delivering Persuasive Messages 268

Part 4 Communication Through Reports and Business Presentations 309

9 Understanding the Report Process and Research Methods 310

10 Managing Data and Using Graphics 348

11 Organizing and P reparing Reports and Proposals 376

12 Designing and Delivering Business Presentations 420

"Powerful communicators are able to communicate strategically, think critically, write and speak proficiently, and interface effectively in a high-tech world."

Communicators Highly Demanded in Challenging Times

One thing that managers can count on is change—constant change . . . change in technology, organizations, the business marketplace, and the economic environment. A key challenge in this world of ever-present change is how to effectively communicate with multiple audiences. *Business Communication, 16e,* leads the way with a learning experience designed to prepare our students and yours for today's dynamic workplace.

As business communication professors in accredited business schools, we know the challenges you face in preparing today's student for the ever-changing workplace and now a recovering economy. A result of our ongoing research with instructors and students, *Business Communication, 16e,* provides the comprehensive coverage that you expect and accreditation requires. An interactive design moves the student easily from text to technology, with a variety of meaningful assessment tools to provide you with measurable learning outcomes. Our commitment through this text and its ancillaries is to share updates, research findings, and ideas to make teaching and learning with *Business Communication, 16e,* a rewarding experience.

We are eager for you to examine *Business Communication, 16e*, an innovative text based on the way today's students learn and today's instructors teach. You've probably already noted some significant changes in the look of the text:

- more inviting and reader-friendly look and feel
- workable blend of text and web
- streamlined design that retains a comprehensive coverage of vital topics

This preface provides an overview of other research-driven shifts in *16e* along with a preview of some of the new and revised content and features. We hope this preview will be useful as you envision ways to adapt your course coverage and ensure that your students enjoy the benefits of the latest information and most effective tools for learning.

Best wishes for a rewarding course as you guide your students in reaching their career potential. Please contact us or visit us at upcoming business communication conferences to share your comments, questions, and successes.

Carol

Carol M. Lehman
Professor of Management
Mississippi State University

Debbie

Debbie D. DuFrene
Professor of Business Communication
Stephen F. Austin State University

Reader-Friendly Design Reflects Sound Pedagogy

Just as change permeates the business environment, it also impacts our classrooms. Today's students are different, and bring to the learning arena unique cognitive styles and particular experiences that shape their expectations for learning. *Business Communication, 16e,* was written with today's student, and their instructors, in mind.

Reader-Friendly Design and Comprehensive Coverage Ensure Success

As in previous editions, *Business Communication* models the concise, coherent writing style demanded in business today. Revisions in *16e* apply cognitive theory principles to maximize learning and minimize the mental effort needed to process information. Note the following text visual that combats cognitive overload by integrating key concepts with an appealing image. See for yourself the appeal of the streamlined format (less reading for your students) and increased learning potential achieved through integrated visuals:

FIGURE 1-5
Levels of Communication
© IMAGE100/JUPITER IMAGES
© DIGITAL VISION/DIGITAL VISION/ GETTY IMAGES
© IT STOCK FREE/JUPITER IMAGES
INTRAPERSONAL
• Communication within oneself
• Not considered by some to be true communication as it does not involve a separate sender and receiver
Examples: Individual reminding himself of tasks to complete or daily schedule
INTERPERSONAL
• Communication between two people
• Goals are to (1) accomplish the task confronting them (task goal), and (2) feel better about themselves and each other because of their interaction (maintenance goal)
Examples: Supervisor and subordinate, two coworkers
GROUP
• Communication among more than two people
• Goal of achieving greater output than individual efforts could produce
Examples: Committee or college class

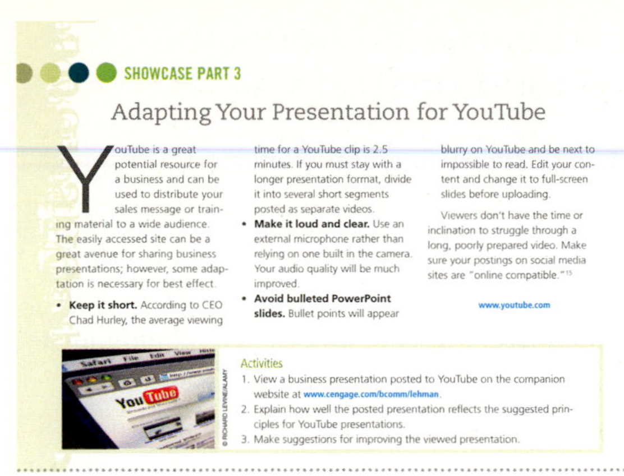

SHOWCASE PART 3

Adapting Your Presentation for YouTube

YouTube is a great potential resource for a business and can be used to distribute your sales message or training material to a wide audience. The easily accessed site can be a great avenue for sharing business presentations; however, some adaptation is necessary for best effect.

- **Keep it short.** According to CEO Chad Hurley, the average viewing time for a YouTube clip is 2.5 minutes. If you must stay with a longer presentation format, divide it into several short segments posted as separate videos.
- **Make it loud and clear.** Use an external microphone rather than relying on one built in the camera. Your audio quality will be much improved.
- **Avoid bulleted PowerPoint slides.** Bullet points will appear blurry on YouTube and be next to impossible to read. Edit your content and change it to full-screen slides before uploading.

Viewers don't have the time or inclination to struggle through a long, poorly prepared video. Make sure your postings on social media sites are "online compatible."[15]

www.youtube.com

© RICHARD LEVINE/ALAMY

Activities

1. View a business presentation posted to YouTube on the companion website at www.cengage.com/bcomm/lehman.
2. Explain how well the posted presentation reflects the suggested principles for YouTube presentations.
3. Make suggestions for improving the viewed presentation.

In response to feedback, *16e* continues to address major business topics in 14 chapters, corresponding well with the weeks in the semester. Areas of expanded and updated coverage include the following:

- Contemporary technology for business business communication uses including:

  Instant messaging and text messaging as appropriate.

  Value of wiki, blogs, and microblogs such as Twitter to the public and to organizations.

  Development of web pages that are compliant with Web Content Accessibility Guidelines.

  Text messaging and permissions email marketing as persuasive communication tools.

  Value and limitations of social networking sites, such as Facebook and MySpace.

  Benefit of social bookmarking sites such as Del.icio.us and Digg for managing web sources and facilitating collaboration.

  Preparation of presentations and video résumés (vésumés) for posting to YouTube and other sites.

  Development of effective virtual teams.

  Legal and ethical issues arising with current technologies, including smartphones.

  Other timely technology issues emphasized in the Electronic Café feature and the holistic assessment case in each chapter.

- Expanded negative organizational news to include strategies for breaking bad news and responding to crises.
- Condensed discussion of presentation design principles with a new poor and good example illustrating key concepts.
- Addition of proofreading procedures and rough draft illustrations that reflect use of on-screen proofreading track changes.
- Streamlined discussion of electronic résumé submissions to include both electronic postings and scannable resumes.
- Updated Appendix A, Document Format and Layout Guide, with new model documents that reflect contemporary word processing formatting styles.
- NEW The updated long formal report at the companion website reflects changes in referencing style required in the recently released *APA Publication Manual,* 6th edition.
- New examples throughout the text using real people and timely events that reinforce important ideas and keep content relevant for students.
- More updates integrated in the strategic forces feature boxes.

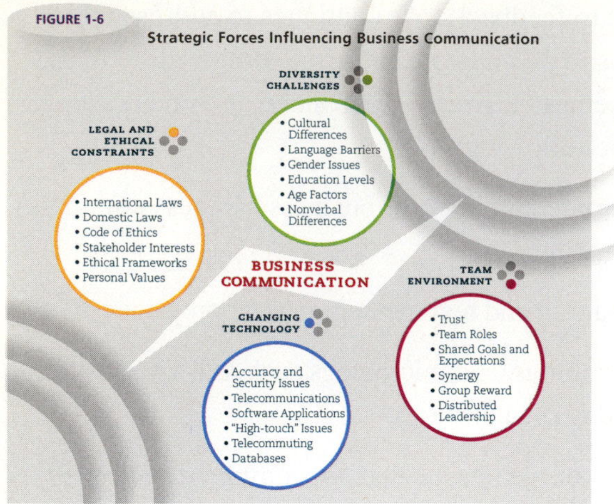

Strategic Forces Model Reflects Communication Constraints

A keystone since the 12th edition, the Strategic Forces model introduced in Chapter 1 and integrated through all remaining chapters makes it easy to weave contemporary topics into traditional subject matter. The strategic model reflects four forces that have an inherent impact on business communication effectiveness: **diversity challenges, legal and ethical issues, changing technology,** and the **team environment.** Students who understand the interrelationships of this model will be able to analyze business communication situations to design effective workplace communications.

- Two strategic forces feature boxes in each chapter and an extended case at the end of the chapter address pertinent strategic forces issues.

  Changes to *16e* include:

  - Persuasive Communication via Text Messaging
  - Improving Your Writing with the Computer (discusses powerful functionality of current software)
  - Significant updates related to becoming generationally savvy, speaking to diverse audiences, graphic design, international market research, inflated résumés, diversity issues affecting employability, and many more

CHANGING TECHNOLOGY

STRATEGIC FORCES

Persuasive Communication via Text Messaging

A line from Disney's *Little Mermaid* sums up the technology scene today: "I've got gadgets and gizmos aplenty."[12] With cell phones, laptops, and smartphones, many people stay perpetually connected electronically. In 2007, more than 363 billion text messages were sent annually, but only 1 percent of all advertisements were sent via text message.[13] Tremendous growth is expected in the use of text messaging for marketing messages.

The United States Air Force uses mobile communication to help potential recruits make their decision about the branch of service where the sharpest technology minds belong.[14]

A growing number of people use their mobile devices to purchase and pay for items. In the first quarter of 2008, nine million mobile subscribers say they used their mobile devices to pay for goods or services.[15] Pappa John's Pizza accepts text message ordering at of its more than 2,700 stores. After first registering on Papa John's website with their payment and delivery preferences, customers can use their cell phones to text message orders. The store then text messages back requesting order confirmation.[16]

© CHRISTINA LICHTI/ALAMY

transactions will be a safe, affordable, and efficient complement to other shopping options. The Telephone Consumer Protection Act restricts unsolicited text messages, as well as phone calls. Various state laws also limit mobile advertising.

In addition to federal and state statutes, industry organizations have developed their own best-practice guidelines to aid consumers and advertisers alike. Two prominent sets of standards were developed by the Mobile Marketing Association (www.mmaglobal.com) and the Cellular Telecommunications & Internet Association (www.ctia.org). Guidelines are available on the two websites that provide valuable information, such as opt-in and opt-out rights. Following best practices helps assure marketers that their promotions and ads are

- Distinctive margin icons focus students' attention on the strategic forces as they relate to chapter content

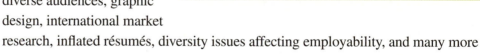

Your Turn 1-4
Assessment

Our nation and economy will demand an expanded and educated workforce to replace the large number of retiring "baby boomers" who will vacate jobs crucial for the nation to maintain its preeminence especially in research, technology, science, and engineering. Many businesses recognize the significant advantage of integrating workers from culturally diverse backgrounds. To realize these benefits, workers must understand and embrace differences.

TAKE ACTION:

- Take the Cultural Awareness Quiz located at www.ethnoconnect.com/html/quiz.asp, or go to your companion website (www.cengage.com/bcomm/lehman) for updated links.
- Prepare a short written summary of what you learned from taking the quiz and how your future attitudes and actions might be impacted.

Barriers to Intercultural Communication

Give several examples of stereotypes that prevail concerning certain cultural groups.

Because cultures give different definitions to such basics of interaction as values and norms, people raised in two different cultures may clash in various ways.

- **Ethnocentrism.** Problems occur between people of different cultures primarily because people tend to assume that their own cultural norms are the right way to do things. They wrongly believe that the specific patterns of behavior desired in their own cultures are universally valued. This belief, known as ***enthnocentrism***, is certainly natural; but learning about other cultures and developing sensitivity will help minimize ethnocentric reactions when dealing with other cultures.
- **Stereotypes.** We often form a mental picture of the main characteristics of another group, creating preformed ideas of what people in this group are like. These pictures,

Chapter 1 *Establishing a Framework for Business Communication* 25

Learner-Inspired Pedagogy Promotes Active Learning

Business Communication, 16e, continues to offer a unique information delivery system that involves your students in an active way by seamlessly integrating text and web. The popular Your Turn features chunk chapter content by providing regular reaction points that invite student involvement. Chapter reading becomes interactive, as the student encounters frequent Your Turn opportunities to apply, practice, and assess learning.

The following five Your Turn elements in each chapter draw the student into active learning. A list of the communication concepts applied in the Your Turn features can be found in the Instructor's Resource Guide and at the companion website.

Miscue

Miscommunications occur in the real world, often with embarrassment or even disastrous results. The Miscue feature enforces the seriousness of these occurrences and asks students to think about prevention strategies.

You're the Professional

Students find themselves in the driver's seat as they justify their responses to a variety of business scenarios. Is it ethical to. . . . ? Should I. . . .? What about . . .?

Career Portfolio

Documenting one's communication abilities is becoming more important to the hiring process as employers look for evidence beyond the résumé. The Career Portfolio feature guides students through the creation of various documents that illustrate their business communication competencies.

Assessment

Instructors, institutions, and accrediting bodies want to know that students have achieved learning objectives. Each Assessment is designed to reflect student knowledge and application of a core course concept, including cultural awareness, understanding of technology, ethical thinking, and various other essential areas.

Electronic Café

Technology is integral in business communication course content. Electronic Cafés enable students to use various technologies to apply their understanding of key topics such as instant and text messaging, discussion boards, intranets, and web pages. An abbreviated preview of each chapter's feature appears in the text, with students referred to the companion site for the continuation.

Real-World Communication Engages Students

A variety of chapter content, cases, applications, and photo essays and thumbnails in every chapter capture student interest by bringing real-world organizations and successful professionals into the discussion of communication principles and practices.

Chapter 6
Delivering Good- and Neutral-News Messages

"Customer service isn't just a department—it is the entire company" CEO Tony Hsieh

SHOWCASE PART 1

Zappos: Customer Service at the Heart of Attitudes and Actions

- ▶ **Organizational ShowCASE feature highlights real companies.** Each chapter showcases the communication challenges and dilemmas of a real-world successful organization and provides users with an in-depth, multi-part experience. The chapter opens with an organization's response to a contemporary communication issue, continues with highlights of the communication strategies of a professional affiliated with the organization, and ends with a case inviting further exploration and successful application of communication concepts highlighted in the featured organization.

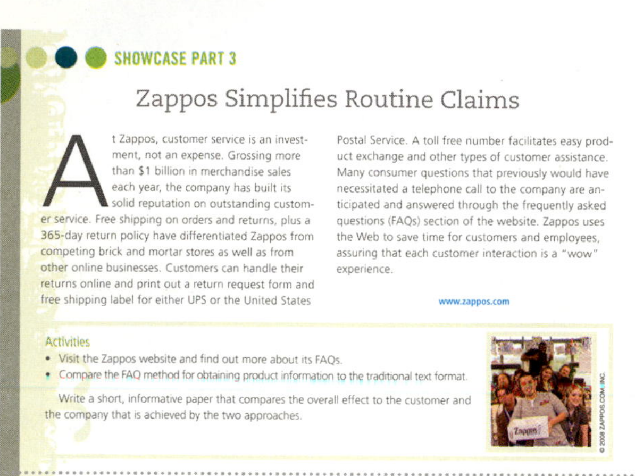

SHOWCASE PART 3

Zappos Simplifies Routine Claims

At Zappos, customer service is an investment, not an expense. Grossing more than $1 billion in merchandise sales each year, the company has built its solid reputation on outstanding customer service. Free shipping on orders and returns, plus a 365-day return policy have differentiated Zappos from competing brick and mortar stores as well as from other online businesses. Customers can handle their returns online and print out a return request form and free shipping label for either UPS or the United States Postal Service. A toll free number facilitates easy product exchange and other types of customer assistance. Many consumer questions that previously would have necessitated a telephone call to the company are anticipated and answered through the frequently asked questions (FAQs) section of the website. Zappos uses the Web to save time for customers and employees, assuring that each customer interaction is a "wow" experience.

www.zappos.com

Activities

- Visit the Zappos website and find out more about its FAQs.
- Compare the FAQ method for obtaining product information to the traditional text format.

Write a short, informative paper that compares the overall effect to the customer and the company that is achieved by the two approaches.

© 2008 ZAPPOS.COM, INC.

In *16e*, your students will learn how

- ▷ **WellPoint**'s diversity focus is central to their meeting health care needs (Chapter 2).
- ▷ **Zappos** uses its website to simplify handling of routine claims (Chapter 6).
- ▷ **Habitat for Humanity** persuades potential donors (Chapter 8).
- ▷ Research and development strategies have been revolutionary for **Novartis** (Chapter 9).
- ▷ **YouTube** allows people and organizations to express their views and talents to a wide audience (Chapter 10).
- ▷ Obama-appointed director of the **Centers for Disease Control**, Dr. Thomas Frieden (Chapter 1), and Mary Schapiro, the first woman to head the **Securities and Exchange Commission** (Chapter 4) use communication to manage their governmental agencies effectively.

NEW

Spotlight Communicators in *16e*, Spotlight Communicator features are previewed in the text, with students led to the companion website for further reading and application.

SHOWCASE PART 2

"Broadcast Yourself"

© CHRISTOPHE MORIN/MAXPPP/LANDOV

SPOTLIGHT COMMUNICATOR CHAD HURLEY

"YouTube and other sites will bring together all the diverse media which matters to you, from videos of your family and friends to news, music, sports, cooking and much, much more."

YouTube's motto "Broadcast Yourself" emphasizes the digital media revolution where everyone can be a star. According to Chad Hurley, CEO, "Our goal is to allow every person on the planet to participate . . .

this new vi on any scr your devic other sites media whi of your far sports, coc Go to your .cengage.cor about Hurl

SEE SHOWCASE PART 3, ON PAGE 368 TO LEARN MORE ABOUT HOW TO ADAPT PRESENTATIONS FOR YOUTUBE.

SHOWCASE PART 2

Showcase Communicator: Chad Hurley, CEO of YouTube

© AP IMAGE/CHRIS PIZZELLO

Spelling Matters. If you're going to impersonate Rachael Ray, be sure you can spell her name. In a Yahoo! blog post allegedly written by media celebrity and cookbook author Rachael Ray, the author misspelled Ms. Ray's first name as Rachel a dozen times.[16]

In a related snafu, Robert Whitney could probably die of embarrassment. A recurring spelling error led police to connect him to holdup notes used in a string of bank robberies in Florida. A note used in one robbery read: "If a die [dye] pack blows, so do you." Finding the same mistake in two other holdup notes, investigators collected forensic evidence linking Mr. Whitney to the crimes.[17] Spelling matters and should be an absolute priority for business writing.

COURTESY OF TWITTER, INC.

Twittering the Internet. Email links, chat rooms, and bulletin boards on corporate websites foster dialogue that leads to strong relationships. In addition to hosting various information exchange methods on corporate websites, an increasing number of business people are participating in social exchange networking and blogging services such as the award-winning Twitter (www.twitter .com). Businesses such as Apple, Dell, CNN, JetBlue, and, Zappos use Twitter to provide updates to customers. "Tweet" postings must be brief, as messages cannot exceed 140 characters.[7] Such forced brevity may be one reason for the service's popularity. If customers are invited to talk, companies must be prepared to respond with timely, effective—even if brief—messages.

NEW

Photo essays convey contemporary topics. In each chapter, you will find mini essays to accompany photos. This highly visual content entices students to consider how communication effectiveness relates to contemporary events and issues. Among the timely issues covered are social bookmarking, microblogging, scrutinizing word usage, making a first impression in interviews, preparing for international travel, avoiding cultural faux pas, looking at plagiarism by a rock band, and considering the least-liked form report—the IRS tax return.

Periodic thumbnail photos draw students' attention to timely content and to bonus content available at the companion website. Featured photos include Bernard Madoff that refers students to the web for more information on communicating ethically and responsibly, former governor Eliot Spitzer that refers students to additional information on apologies, and Simon Cowell with a reference to information about effective delivery of constructive criticism.

© FRANK MICELOTTA/GETTY IMAGES

Applications pose real-world communication challenges. Extended cases at the end of chapters are based on actual events and problems faced by real organizations. Students are asked, for instance, to consider the challenges associated with Mattel's recall of popular toys containing toxic materials and the opportunities associated with volunteerism at Deloitte & Touche. Consider the communication implications of these real-world cases listed by chapter:

- Cynthia Cooper's whistle-blower story: Ethics Put to the Test (Chapter 1)
- NetApp: Boosting Employee Morale in Uncertain Economic Times (Chapter 2)
- Tackling the Challenge of Age Diversity at FedEx (Chapter 3)
- Health Information: Misunderstandings Can Be Costly (Chapter 4)
- Podcasting to Employees: Kraft Re-invents the Nutrition Wheel (Chapter 5)

CASES

© GIL FORD PHOTOGRAPHY

1. Ethics Put to the Test
(Obj. 4)

How brave are you? Are you brave enough to stand up for what you know is right even when what is right is not what is popular? Cynthia Cooper never intended to go public about the drama that resulted in the collapse of a hometown company she loved. As vice president of internal audit at WorldCom in 2002, her curiosity changed to discomfort and then to suspicion based on accounting entries she and her team identified and the curious responses given by financial executives. No one wanted to believe the CFO was perpetuating a multi-billion-dollar fraud.

Cooper and her team of auditors worked together, at night and in secret, to investigate and unearth $3.8 billion in fraud at WorldCom. At the time, this was the largest incident of accounting fraud in U.S. history. Several company officers received prison sentences; and the company, once the United States' second-largest long distance phone company, went through bankruptcy and was eventually sold to Verizon in 2006. On a broader scale, Cooper's actions are also credited as a catalyst for passage of Section 404, an addition to the Sarbanes-Oxley Act that addresses assessment of internal controls.

Cooper was named one of three "People of the Year" by *Time* magazine in 2002. Speaking about the WorldCom scandal and other related cases, Cooper says, "Frauds typically start small and then they begin to grow. People rationalize their decisions." When asked how she found the fortitude to stand up to company executives, Cooper said she had to dig down and find courage, which isn't always easy. She remembered the deeply ingrained advice of her mother: "Don't ever allow yourself to be intimidated." Cooper's book about her experiences at WorldCom, *Extraordinary Circumstances: The Journey of a Corporate Whistleblower,* was published in 2008. Profits from the book were given to universities for ethics education.

Required: As directed by your instructor, read the story of Cynthia Cooper, WorldCom whistleblower:

Cooper, C. (2008). *Extraordinary circumstances: The journey of a corporate whistleblower.* Hoboken, NJ: John Wiley & Sons.

Katz, D. M., & Homer, J. (2008, February 1). WorldCom whistle-blower Cynthia Cooper. *CFO Magazine.* Available at www.cfo.com/article.cfm/10590507

Ripley, A. (2008, February 4). Q & A: Whistle-blower Cynthia Cooper. *Time.* Available at www.time.com/time/arts/article/0,8599,1709695,00.html

Write a two-page report summarizing the ethical struggles Cooper faced and her insights related to ethical leadership and responsibility.

© COURTESY: EVERETT COLLECTION

2. Video Case: The Office: Office Humor and Layoffs: A Bad Combination

In this clip, Manager David succeeds in making Malcolm feel worse about his job security by discounting his concerns and making light of past and future layoffs. David's cheeriness appears in direct contrast to Malcolm's concern and the seriousness of the situation.

Complete the following activities as directed by your instructor after the class has viewed the video:

1. In small groups, discuss how the communication process between David and Malcolm breaks down. Where do the barriers begin and how could these barriers have been avoided?
2. In what type network flow are David and Malcolm participating?
3. How do David's gestures, tone of voice, facial expressions and use of personal space impact the interaction? How should David change in these areas?
4. As a group, write a script for an alternate way to conduct this conversation with the appropriate characters included. Be prepared to present your script as a short skit to the class.

© DAWN HUDSON/SHUTTERSTOCK.COM

3. Inside View: Corporate Diversity

Thanks to the General Motors minority dealer development program, Harlem celebrated the grand opening of its first auto dealership in 40 years. The 300,000 square-foot multilevel auto mall, expected to bring nearly 200 new jobs to Harlem, is boosting the local economy. This project is one example of how smart companies recognize the importance of serving the needs of their important minority customer base and the commitment to diverse markets. Diversity within a company also can pay off, as Henry Ford showed many years ago when he pioneered equal pay for black workers.

How can encouraging minority enterprise development benefit a company's diversity efforts? Companies that invest their resources in minorities are supporting a very important segment of the population and may realize tremendous sales potential from diverse markets.

40 **Part 1** Communication Foundations

Customer Communication: Kindle Propels Popularity of Ebooks (Chapter 6)
Damage Control at Mattel (Chapter 7)
UPS: Getting Paid to Volunteer Time and Talent (Chapter 8)
SurveyMonkey: Survey Research Is Not Just Monkey Business (Chapter 9)
Dove: "Real Beauty" Not So Real (Chapter 10)
Hoover's Online: Financial Reporting Goes Multimedia (Chapter 11)
Learning from Steve Jobs' Life Stories (Chapter 12)
CareerBuilder, Monster.com and Others: Avoiding Online Job Scams (Chapter 13)
Deloitte & Touche: Volunteerism Is Alive and Well in Corporate America (Chapter 14)

New Video Segments from *The Office* Make Learning Fun

Short video cases at the end of each chapter refer students to view clips from the popular television program *The Office.* These clips humorously illustrate communication faux pas in the workplace and guide students in responding to reflective questions and writing applications. Timely business communication issues depicted include "Office Humor and Layoffs: A Bad Combination" (Chapter 1), "Persuasion: It's Not All About Me" (Chapter 8), and "Delivering Bad News at a Team Briefing? NOT" (Chapter 11). A complete list can be found in the Instructor's Resource Guide and at the companion website.

Inside View video cases available for each part of *16e* provide updated reflection and application of timely issues. Issues include corporate diversity (Chapter 1), power of language (Chapter 4), customer service (Chapter 8), presentation anxiety (Chapter 12), and interviewing strategies (Chapter 14).

Sound Pedagogy Leads to Favorable Results

Integration throughout the text of written, spoken, and electronic communication concepts prepares students for communicating expertly through an ever-expanding number of channels. This sample annotated visual reinforces the concept that communication involves a variety of spoken, electronic, and written messages.

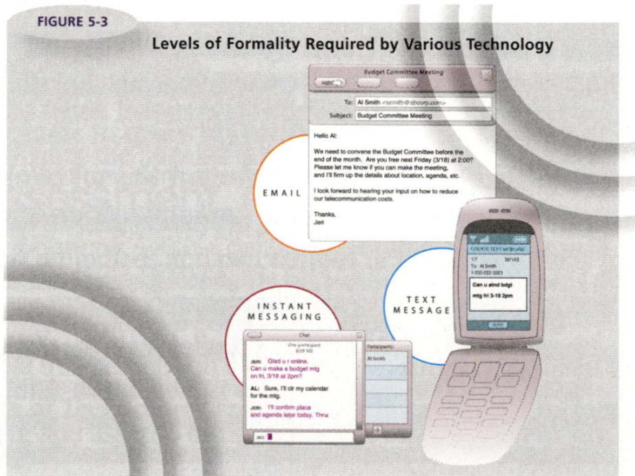

FIGURE 5-3 Levels of Formality Required by Various Technology

Numerous poor and good examples illustrate communication related to a variety of print and electronic documents. To emphasize negative effect, poor examples annotations now reflect the receiver's likely reaction in informal language that captures students' attention and emphasizes potential damage to goodwill (Chapters 5–8). You'll find many new examples, including a letter report, proposal, long formal report, and more.

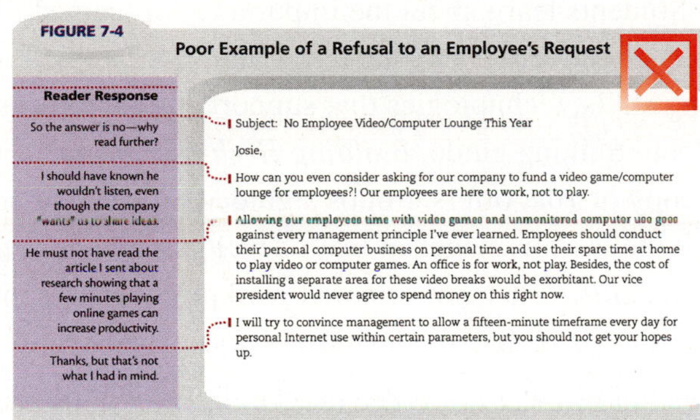

FIGURE 7-4

Poor Example of a Refusal to an Employee's Request

Reader Response

So the answer is no—why read further?

I should have known he wouldn't listen, even though the company "wants" us to share ideas.

He must not have read the article I sent about research showing that a few minutes playing online games can increase productivity.

Thanks, but that's not what I had in mind.

Subject: No Employee Video/Computer Lounge This Year

Josie,

How can you even consider asking for our company to fund a video game/computer lounge for employees?! Our employees are here to work, not to play.

Allowing our employees time with video games and unmonitored computer use goes against every management principle I've ever learned. Employees should conduct their personal computer business on personal time and use their spare time at home to play video or computer games. An office is for work, not play. Besides, the cost of installing a separate area for these video breaks would be exorbitant. Our vice president would never agree to spend money on this right now.

I will try to convince management to allow a fifteen-minute timeframe every day for personal Internet use within certain parameters, but you should not get your hopes up.

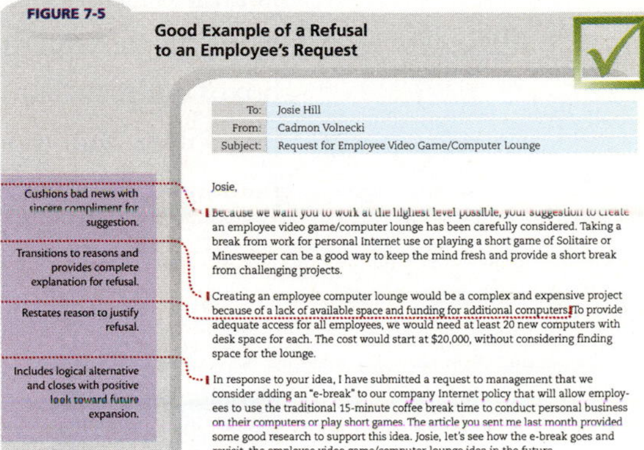

FIGURE 7-5

Good Example of a Refusal to an Employee's Request

Cushions bad news with sincere compliment for suggestion.

Transitions to reasons and provides complete explanation for refusal.

Restates reason to justify refusal.

Includes logical alternative and closes with positive look toward future expansion.

To: Josie Hill
From: Cadmon Volnecki
Subject: Request for Employee Video Game/Computer Lounge

Josie,

Because we want you to work at the highest level possible, your suggestion to create an employee video game/computer lounge has been carefully considered. Taking a break from work for personal Internet use or playing a short game of Solitaire or Minesweeper can be a good way to keep the mind fresh and provide a short break from challenging projects.

Creating an employee computer lounge would be a complex and expensive project because of a lack of available space and funding for additional computers. To provide adequate access for all employees, we would need at least 20 new computers with desk space for each. The cost would start at $20,000, without considering finding space for the lounge.

In response to your idea, I have submitted a request to management that we consider adding an "e-break" to our company Internet policy that will allow employees to use the traditional 15-minute coffee break time to conduct personal business on their computers or play short games. The article you sent me last month provided some good research to support this idea. Josie, let's see how the e-break goes and revisit the employee video game/computer lounge idea in the future.

Evaluative checklists enable students to evaluate their own communication.

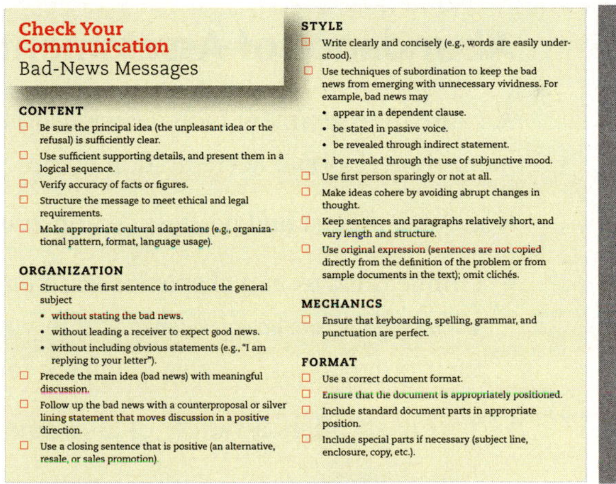

Check Your Communication
Bad-News Messages

CONTENT

- ☐ Be sure the principal idea (the unpleasant idea or the refusal) is sufficiently clear.
- ☐ Use sufficient supporting details, and present them in a logical sequence.
- ☐ Verify accuracy of facts or figures.
- ☐ Structure the message to meet ethical and legal requirements.
- ☐ Make appropriate cultural adaptations (e.g., organizational pattern, format, language usage).

ORGANIZATION

- ☐ Structure the first sentence to introduce the general subject
  - without stating the bad news.
  - without leading a receiver to expect good news.
  - without including obvious statements (e.g., "I am replying to your letter").
- ☐ Precede the main idea (bad news) with meaningful discussion.
- ☐ Follow up the bad news with a counterproposal or silver lining statement that moves discussion in a positive direction.
- ☐ Use a closing sentence that is positive (an alternative, resale, or sales promotion).

STYLE

- ☐ Write clearly and concisely (e.g., words are easily understood).
- ☐ Use techniques of subordination to keep the bad news from emerging with unnecessary vividness. For example, bad news may
  - appear in a dependent clause.
  - be stated in passive voice.
  - be revealed through indirect statement.
  - be revealed through the use of subjunctive mood.
- ☐ Use first person sparingly or not at all.
- ☐ Make ideas cohere by avoiding abrupt changes in thought.
- ☐ Keep sentences and paragraphs relatively short, and vary length and structure.
- ☐ Use original expression (sentences are not copied directly from the definition of the problem or from sample documents in the text); omit clichés.

MECHANICS

- ☐ Ensure that keyboarding, spelling, grammar, and punctuation are perfect.

FORMAT

- ☐ Use a correct document format.
- ☐ Ensure that the document is appropriately positioned.
- ☐ Include standard document parts in appropriate position.
- ☐ Include special parts if necessary (subject line, enclosure, copy, etc.).

Extensive Technology Coverage

Technology coverage is contemporary—including the uses in business communication of text messaging, instant messaging, blogging, wikis, microblogging, social media, social bookmarking, virtual collaboration, and more.

- Electronic Café in each chapter allows students to use various technologies to apply their understanding of key technology topics.
- Holistic assessment case in each chapter (the Case Analysis in the *15e*)

CHANGING TECHNOLOGY

STRATEGIC FORCES
Persuasive Communication via Text Messaging

A line from Disney's *Little Mermaid* sums up the technology scene today: "I've got gadgets and gizmos aplenty."[12] With cell phones, laptops, and smartphones, many people stay perpetually connected electronically. In 2007, more than 363 billion text messages were sent annually, but only 1 percent of all advertisements were sent via text message.[13] Tremendous growth is expected in the use of text messaging for marketing messages.

The United States Air Force uses mobile communication to help potential recruits make their decision to enlist. The Air Force invites contacts to download wallpaper, ringtones, and custom content to their mobile phones. Attendees at recruiting fairs who have special software on their phones can snap a picture of a bar code that provides direct access to promotional material. The Air Force hopes to not only share its informational message, but to convince tech savvy 18-year-olds that it is the high-tech branch of service where the sharpest technology minds belong.[14]

A growing number of people use their mobile devices to purchase and pay for items. In the first quarter of 2008, nine million mobile subscribers say they used their mobile devices to pay for goods or services.[15] Pappa John's Pizza accepts text message ordering at of its more than 2,700 stores. After first registering on Papa John's website with their payment and delivery preferences, customers can use their cell phones to text message orders. The store then text messages back requesting order confirmation.[16]

Messages offering coupons and specials can be sent quickly to a vast audience who will likely see the message nearly instantly. The cost to send text messages is fractional as compared to the cost of a flyer or direct mailing.

Security remains a primary concern of mobile device users who do not participate in online transactions. They want proof that their mobile transactions will be a safe, affordable, and efficient complement to other shopping options. The Telephone Consumer Protection Act restricts unsolicited text messages, as well as phone calls. Various state laws also limit mobile advertising.

In addition to federal and state statutes, industry organizations have developed their own best-practice guidelines to aid consumers and advertisers alike. Two prominent sets of standards were developed by the Mobile Marketing Association (www.mmaglobal.com) and the Cellular Telecommunications & Internet Association (www.ctia.org). Guidelines are available on the two websites that provide valuable information, such as opt-in and opt-out rights. Following best practices helps assure marketers that their promotions and ads are not only legal, but they reach the people who are most interested.[17]

Application

Describe some examples of text messages sent to you by businesses. How effective were those that were of an informational nature and those that were persuasive in their intent?

explores timely communication issues, often with a technology focus, and provide student feedback with a holistic grading scale.

Expanded Team Development Resources

As one of the strategic forces influencing business communication, team environment is an integral part of *16e*. Students learn about the importance of team skills and strategies for maximizing group effectiveness in Chapters 1 and 2. Strategic Forces feature boxes address team writing skills, technologies that support collaborative skills, team interviews, and more. A team training guide, *Building High-Performance Teams 4e*, packaged with each new copy of *16e*, offers groups a guided process for advancing through the various stages of team development and acquiring essential skills for a team-oriented workplace. New content on virtual teams is included, and each of five projects provides students an opportunity for exploring, applying, and reflecting on key team skills. Sample team documents in the handbook and online templates give students a head start for effective team development within student teams.

Abundance of Assessment Strategies

A cadre of assessment tools responds to the current surge in requirements for assessment from regional accreditation bodies, the AACSB, and other agencies.

- Course pretest and posttest demonstrate students' progress over the term.
- Online quizzes and chapter assessments are available at the companion website at www.cengage.com/bcomm/lehman and in your WebTutor product. Students can measure their progress and receive feedback for improvement.
- Text itself offers a variety of assessment tools:
    - Vast array of assessment items suited for your students appears at the end of each chapter. The application tabs are arranged for focus on the important skill areas of Reading, Thinking, Writing, Speaking, and Collaborating.

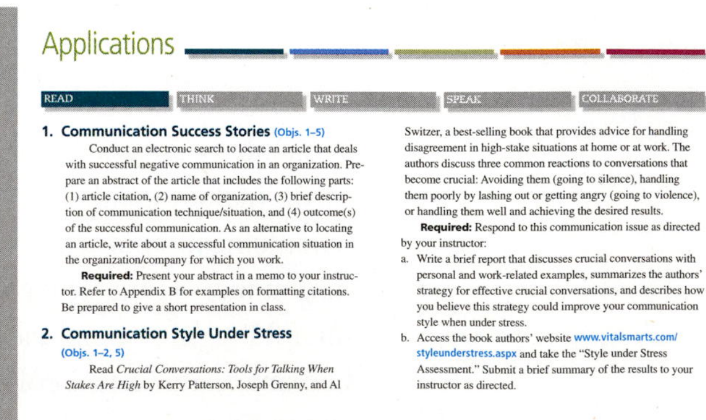

Applications

READ | THINK | WRITE | SPEAK | COLLABORATE

1. **Communication Success Stories** (Objs. 1–5)
Conduct an electronic search to locate an article that deals with successful negative communication in an organization. Prepare an abstract of the article that includes the following parts: (1) article citation, (2) name of organization, (3) brief description of communication technique/situation, and (4) outcome(s) of the successful communication. As an alternative to locating an article, write about a successful communication situation in the organization/company for which you work.
Required: Present your abstract in a memo to your instructor. Refer to Appendix B for examples on formatting citations. Be prepared to give a short presentation in class.

2. **Communication Style Under Stress** (Objs. 1–2, 5)
Read *Crucial Conversations: Tools for Talking When Stakes Are High* by Kerry Patterson, Joseph Grenny, and Al Switzer, a best-selling book that provides advice for handling disagreement in high-stake situations at home or at work. The authors discuss three common reactions to conversations that become crucial: Avoiding them (going to silence), handling them poorly by lashing out or getting angry (going to violence), or handling them well and achieving the desired results.
Required: Respond to this communication issue as directed by your instructor:
a. Write a brief report that discusses crucial conversations with personal and work-related examples, summarizes the authors' strategy for effective crucial conversations, and describes how you believe this strategy could improve your communication style when under stress.
b. Access the book authors' website www.vitalsmarts.com/styleunderstress.aspx and take the "Style under Stress Assessment." Submit a brief summary of the results to your instructor as directed.

-
    - Your Turn: Assessment feature in each chapter guides students in assessing a critical communication area. Students assess cultural awareness in Chapter 1, writing anxiety in Chapter 4, ethics in Chapter 8, plagiarism in Chapter 9, and others. At the end of the term, summary results of the 14 communication assessments can be assimilated as evidence of student learning in the course.

- Your Turn: Career Portfolio feature directs students in creating a representative set of documents they can use to showcase their communication skills for portfolio assessment or employment.

Your Turn 7-4
Career Portfolio

Saying "no" while maintaining goodwill is definitely challenging. Consider a situation in your career field in which you will have to say no to a request from a client or customer.

TAKE ACTION:

Compose a letter to a fictitious individual that conveys the "no" with tact and consideration. See Appendix A for appropriate letter format.

Your Turn 7-5
Assessment

Because hiring a new employee costs a firm considerable time and resources, the cost of bad hires can have a dramatic effect on the company's bottom line. Some companies use personality tests to assess human relations skills and provide management with insight concerning their employees and job applicants.[9]

TAKE ACTION:

- Take a "human resource department" test actually used by some businesses at www.personalitytest.net/funtest/index.htm, or go to your companion website, www.cengage.com/bcomm/lehman, for updated links.
- Prepare a short written summary of what you learned from taking the quiz and whether you think the test score was an accurate indicator of your human relations behaviors.

Flexible Design Offers Options to Fit Your Needs

With *Business Communication, 16e*, you can have it your way. Whether your course is online, hybrid, or face to face, *Business Communication, 16e* can be customized to meet the unique needs of your course and students.

The text is available in traditional print and digital formats. Your book can also be customized to include just the chapters you teach. Available supplements include:

- *Building High-Performance Teams* handbook, designed to guide students easily through the team process.
- Free companion website with enrichment content to supplement text coverage, interactive chapter quizzes and language tutorial, convenient download of PowerPoint slides and assignment templates, up-to-date links to web resources, additional model documents, holistic assessment writing tips, and much more.
- Several custom content modules can be added to your *16e*.
- WebTutor product with text-specific content created for this edition. Included are e-lectures, quizzes, and discussion questions, as well as games and puzzles to make the learning experience more enjoyable for students with various learning styles.
- Aplia, an online, interactive learning tool that enables your students to review language skills and reinforce concepts presented in *Business Communication, 16e*. Learn more about this product at www.aplia.com/cengage.

About the Author Team

Carol Lehman and Debbie DuFrene are professors in AACSB-accredited schools of business, each with more than 25 years' experience teaching business communication in traditional, hybrid, and distance classes. Actively engaged in research, they are frequent presenters at national and regional meetings of the Association for Business Communication, for which they sponsor the Meada Gibbs Outstanding Teacher Award. Their recent research on cognitive theory and technology-mediated learning reflects their commitment to identifying factors that affect the successful implementation of educational technology. This research has provided direction in designing a textbook and a technology-mediated learning package that is easy to use and directly related to course outcomes—instruction that is worthy of your and your students' time and money. You are encouraged to access the "Author Insights" link at the companion website for more detailed information about Carol and Debbie.

Leading the Way with Exceptional Instructor's Resources

A total package of instructional resources complements the *Business Communication, 16e*, to make your planning and presentation easier and more effective and to simplify and strengthen the study of business communication for your students. To provide you with relevant and timely resources, the authors are actively involved in the development of the supplemental elements and work daily with business communication educators who are carefully chosen to create various components.

Instructor's Resource CD

Provides convenient, one-stop access to the wide assortment of instructional resources supporting *16e*. Browse through the easy-to-navigate menu to view them all.

Instructor's Resource Guide

The *Instructor's Resource Guide* organizes each chapter by learning objectives and includes an arsenal of teaching suggestions conveniently integrated with handy thumbnails of the PowerPoint slides and answers to chapter activities. Practical advice is provided for employing the text's distinctive features, teaching business communication in various formats, and assessing learning.

Test Bank

The *Test Bank* contains more than 1,000 questions, 25 percent of which are new to *16e*. A blend of items of various levels of difficulty includes applications requiring students to practice critical-thinking skills as they apply chapter concepts. Each question is classified according to learning objective, type, and level of difficulty for easy selection. Items are also tagged according to AACSB key concepts for simplified assessment data tracking. A course pre-test and post-test further facilitates the documentation of student learning.

ExamView Testing Software

The entire *Test Bank* is available electronically via ExamView on the Instructor's Resource CD. Instructors can create custom exams by selecting questions, editing existing questions, and adding new questions. Instructors can also have exams created by calling Cengage Learning's Customer Service at 1-800-354-9706 (8:00 a.m. to 6 p.m. EST).

PowerPoint Lecture and Resource Slides

PowerPoint resource slides provide supplementary information, activities to reinforce key concepts, and solutions to end-of-chapter activities. Students can view the lecture slides on the Web and print copies for taking notes or listen to the narrated version available with the WebTutor product.

Instructor Website

This robust password-protected teaching/learning center provides innovative teaching suggestions for traditional and distance delivery, assessment guidelines, holistic assessment applications, supplementary case problems, and much more. Go to the companion website at www.cengage.com/bcomm/lehman for more details about these comprehensive classroom resources.

WebTutor

WebTutor includes text-specific content created for this edition. Included are e-lectures, quizzes, and discussion questions, as well as games and puzzles to make the learning experience more enjoyable for students with various learning styles.

Aplia

Aplia is an online, interactive tool that enables your students to review language skills and reinforce concepts presented in *Business Communication, 16e*. Aplia improves learning by increasing student effort and engagement. Visit www.aplia.com/cengage for more details.

Acknowledgments

Business Communication and its numerous support tools reflect the contributions of many talented people. These appreciated individuals include our faculty colleagues, our students at Mississippi State and Stephen F. Austin who have participated in our research studies and field tested our ideas, the publishing team at Cengage, and the many professional educators whose insightful reviews have been essential to the development of each edition of *Business Communication.* For their insights and suggestions, we extend sincere thanks to those who reviewed the previous edition and provided meaningful feedback and suggestions for *16e*:

Priscilla Berry, Jacksonville University
Shavawn M. Berry, Arizona State University
Kendra S. Boggess, Concord University
Jean L. Bush-Bacelis, Ph.D., Eastern Michigan University
Dr. Deborah V. Collins, Anne Arundel Community College
Mike Cryer, Arizona State University
Dale Cyphert, University of Northern Iowa
Dr. Cynthia W. Drexel, Western State College of Colorado
Linda Burak Gretton, Ph.D., Elon University
Bonnie Grossman, College of Charleston
Emile H. Hawkins, Sr., Oklahoma Wesleyan University
Marcia L. James, University of Wisconsin-Whitewater
Jeff Lewis, Ph.D., The Metropolitan State College of Denver
Dr. Jeré Littlejohn, University of Mississippi
Vershun L. McClain, Jackson State University
Dr. Minchella, Consulting Management Associates, LLC
Dawnita T. Moore, Wayne County Community College District
Chynette Nealy, University of Houston Downtown
Dr. Connie Roberts, Central Washington University
Cynthia Ryan, University of Alabama at Birmingham
Catherine Siskron, San Francisco State University
Leticia Slabaugh, Arizona State University-Tempe
Lynn M. Staley, Ph.D., University of Missouri – St. Louis
Shani Watkins, Central Washington University
Peter Wegner, Arizona State University
Juli White, Arizona State University
Charlotte Williams, Ph.D., Jones County Junior College
Lisa Gueldenzoph Snyder, North Carolina A&T State University
S. Ann Wilson, Stephen F. Austin State University
Dr. Paula R. Wood, Fayetteville State University
Diane K. Young, Glendale College

Gratitude is extended to the following committed and talented business communication educators who worked closely with us to plan and develop important components of the comprehensive *16e* package.

Judith Biss, Stephen F. Austin State University (selected assessment and *Instructor's Resource Guide* content)

Denise Cosper, Mississippi State University (*The Office* video cases and selected *Instructor's Resource Guide* content)

Deepest appreciation also goes to our devoted spouses who have supported us through this lengthy and demanding project, as well as to our young adult children who served as a convenient focus group for content issues and technology design.

16e

Business Communication

Part 1
Communication Foundations

Chapter 1
Establishing a Framework for Business Communication

"When anyone dies at an early age from a preventable cause, it's my fault."
CDC Director, Dr. Thomas Frieden

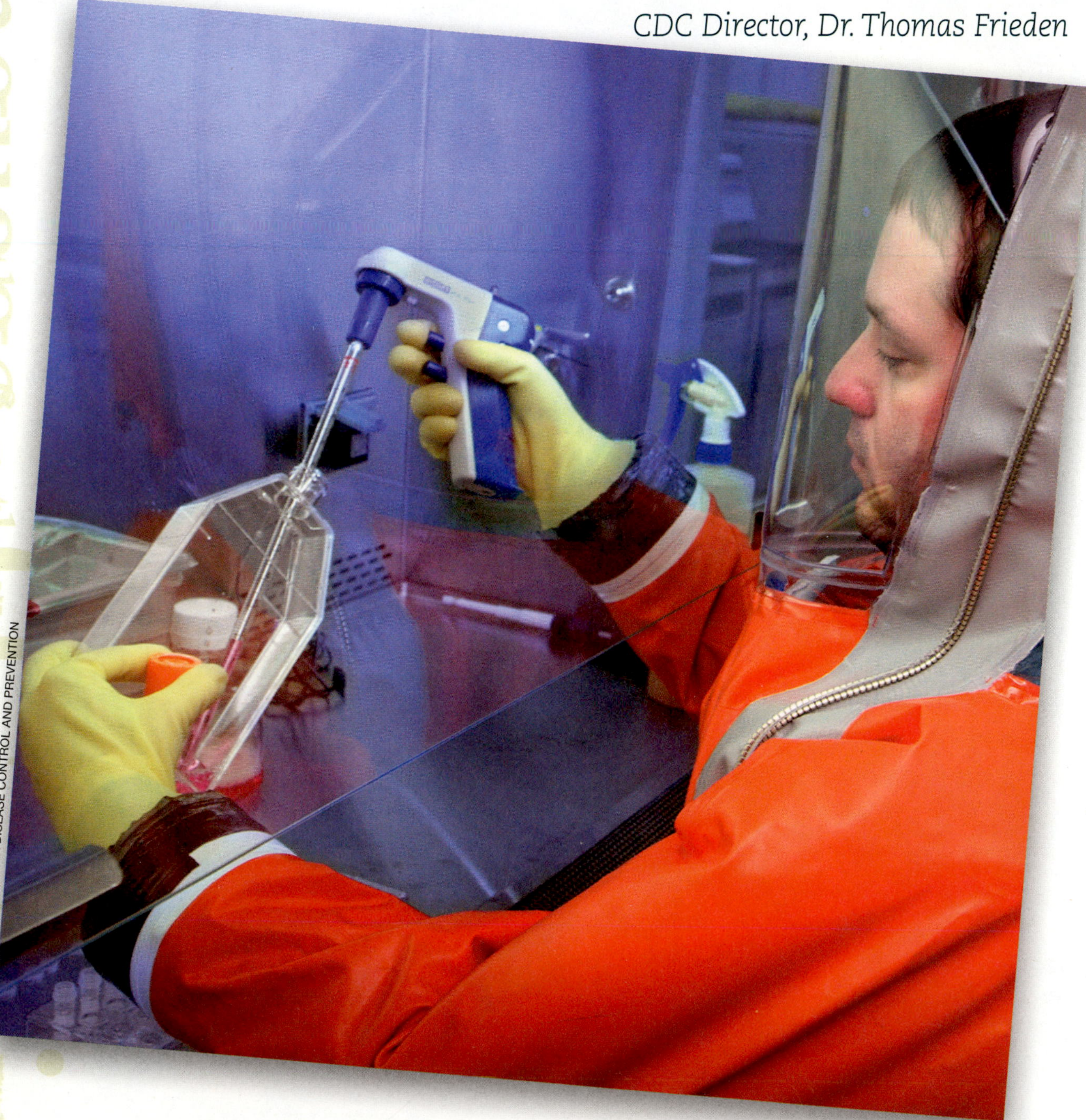

JAMES GATHANY, CENTERS FOR DISEASE CONTROL AND PREVENTION

Objectives When you have completed Chapter 1, you will be able to:

1. Define communication and describe the value for communication in business.
2. Explain the communication process model and the ultimate objective of the communication process.
3. Discuss how information flows in an organization (formally and informally; downward, upward, and horizontally, and through various levels).
4. Explain how legal and ethical constraints, diversity challenges, changing technology, and team environment act as strategic forces that influence the process of business communication.

SHOWCASE PART 1 

Communication Challenges at the CDC

The events of September 11, 2001, affected every American citizen as well as the nation's business community. One agency whose mission was changed forever was the Centers for Disease Control and Prevention (CDC). The Atlanta-based federal agency, which is responsible for protecting Americans against infectious diseases and other health hazards, was instantly required to retool to meet the looming threat of bioterrorism, including anthrax, smallpox, and other deadly disease agents.

The CDC is one of 11 federal agencies under the Department of Health and Human Services. The agency stores and controls the nation's stockpile of smallpox vaccine and leads 3,000 local public health departments in devising a plan for containing an outbreak or epidemic and administering the vaccine. It must also meld its work with national security agencies, such as the CIA, the FBI, and the Department of Homeland Security.[1]

The leadership of the CDC must balance the urgent goal of preparing for a bioterrorism emergency with the agency's fundamental mission of preventing and controlling infectious disease and other health hazards. AIDS, cigarette smoking, obesity, Type II diabetes, and asthma are among the real, long-term problems that are equally crucial to public health. In addition, new threats, such as the swine and avian flu, regularly present themselves. Research and evaluation of ongoing health communications programs have affirmed the value of using various communication strategies to promote health and prevent disease. Effective strategies combine approaches based in the behavioral sciences, communication, social marketing, and health education. Pamphlets, billboards, public service announcements, and educational programs are some of the ways the CDC spreads its messages about health and safety risks and educates the American people about how to respond appropriately.

Health communication can take many forms, depending on the audience and the urgency of the risk. With any health risk there is always the danger of overreacting; however, the CDC has the responsibility of letting people know what is happening and what to do about it. According to Dr. Thomas Frieden, director of the CDC, "when anyone dies at an early age from a preventable cause . . . , it's my fault.[2] He views his agency's key communication partners as the state and local health departments who monitor citizens' health, the people who run health plans and market preventive services, and the entire business community, which has a strong interest in promoting the health of its employees. He knows the importance of effective communication with a broad audience. Such a process identifies strengths and weaknesses in programs and helps make the CDC a more credible advocate when it asks for funding to address potential episodes of infectious disease, chronic health problems, and bioterrorism.

As at the CDC, the success of all businesses and organizations hinges to a large degree on the effectiveness of the communication that takes place. To be effective in any work setting, you will need to understand the process of communication, the challenges of reaching diverse audiences, and the dynamic environment in which communication occurs.

http://www.cdc.gov

SEE SHOWCASE, PART 2, ON PAGE 13
FOR SPOTLIGHT COMMUNICATOR THOMAS FRIEDEN, DIRECTOR OF THE CDC.

1 OBJECTIVE Value of Communication

We communicate to satisfy needs in both our work and private lives. Each of us wants to be heard, appreciated, and wanted. We also want to accomplish tasks and achieve goals. Obviously, then, a major value of communication is to help people feel good about themselves and about their friends, groups, and organizations. Generally people communicate for three basic purposes: to inform, to persuade, and to entertain.

What is communication? For our purposes, communication is the process of exchanging information and meaning between or among individuals through a common system of symbols, signs, and behavior. Other words used to describe the communication process include expressing feelings, conversing, speaking, corresponding, writing, listening, and exchanging. Studies indicate that managers typically spend 60 to 80 percent of their time involved in communication. In your career activities, you may communicate in a wide variety of ways, including

Does the importance of communication skills increase with the management level? Explain.

- attending meetings and writing reports related to strategic plans and company policy.
- presenting information to large and small groups in face to face and virtual environments.
- explaining and clarifying management procedures and work assignments.
- coordinating the work of various employees, departments, and other work groups.
- evaluating and counseling employees.
- promoting the company's products/services and image.

Whatever your chosen career field, communication skills will be an important requirement for you as a job applicant. Throughout this text, you will have the opportunity to develop and document your business communication skills through your Career Portfolio. This portfolio will provide evidence to you and future employers that you possess the essential knowledge and skills to be an effective communicator in today's workplace.

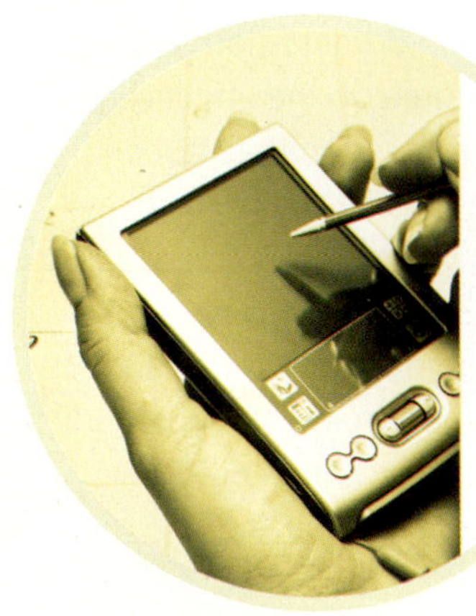

Your Turn 1-1
Career Portfolio

For eight years in a row, employers in a large national survey listed communication skills as a job seeker's most important qualities.[3] Regardless of your chosen career field, skills and ability in communication are necessary for workplace efficiency and healthy relationships.

TAKE ACTION:

- Conduct an online search related to communication in your chosen career field.
- Write a brief paper providing information such as (a) evidence of the value of communication in the profession, (b) major audiences with whom you will communicate, and (c) typical communication requirements.
- Be prepared to share your results with the class.

OBJECTIVE 2 The Communication Process

Effective business communication is essential to success in today's work environments. Recent surveys of executives document that abilities in writing and speaking are major determinants of career success in many fields.[4] Though essential to personal and professional success, effective business communication does not occur automatically. Your own experiences likely have taught you that a message is not interpreted correctly just because you transmitted it. An effective communicator anticipates possible breakdowns in the communication process—the unlimited ways the message can be misunderstood. This mind-set provides the concentration to design the initial message effectively and to be prepared to intervene at the appropriate time to ensure that the message received is on target—that is, as close as possible to what is intended.

Consider the communication process model presented in Figure 1-1. These seemingly simple steps actually represent a very complex process.

The Sender Encodes the Message

DIVERSITY CHALLENGES

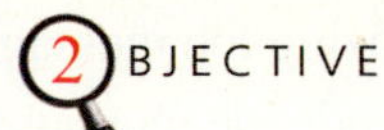

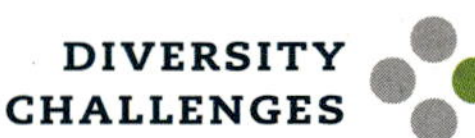

The sender carefully designs a message by selecting (1) words that clearly convey the message and (2) nonverbal signals (gestures, posture, facial expression, and so on) that

FIGURE 1-1

The Communication Process Model

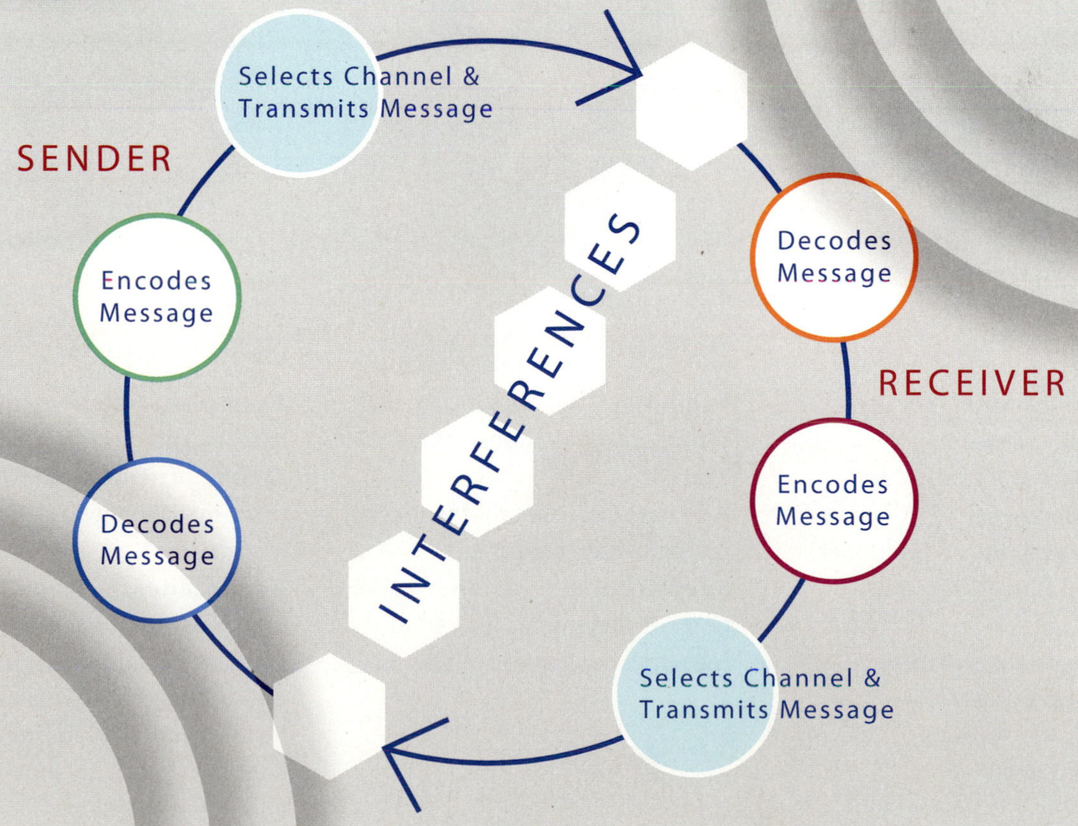

What breakdowns in the encoding process have you experienced?

reinforce the verbal message. The process of selecting and organizing the message is referred to as ***encoding***. The sender's primary objective is to encode the message in such a way that the message received is as close as possible to the message sent. Knowledge of the receiver's educational level, experience, viewpoints, and other information aids the sender in encoding the message. If information about the receiver is unavailable, the sender can use empathy for the receiver's position to gain fairly accurate insight for encoding the message. Chapter 2 will assist you in refining your nonverbal communication, and Chapters 3 and 4 will help you learn to use language effectively.

The Sender Selects an Appropriate Channel and Transmits the Message

To increase the likelihood that the receiver will understand the message, the sender carefully selects an appropriate channel for transmitting the message. Three typical communication channels are illustrated in Figure 1-2.

Selecting an inappropriate channel can cause the message to be misunderstood and can adversely affect human relations with the receiver. For example, for a complex subject, a sender might begin with a written document and follow up with a face-to-face, phone, or video conference discussion after the receiver has had an opportunity to study

FIGURE 1-2

Channels of Communication

© STEVE COLE/PHOTODISC RED/GETTY IMAGES

TWO-WAY, FACE-TO-FACE

Examples: Informal conversations, interviews, oral presentations, speeches, and videoconferences
Advantages: Instant feedback, nonverbal signals, personal connection
Special considerations: Usually appropriate for conveying sensitive or unpleasant news

© FLYING COLOURS LTD./DIGITAL VISION/GETTY IMAGES

TWO-WAY, NOT FACE-TO-FACE

Examples: Telephone conversations, text messages, online chats
Advantages: Instant feedback, real-time connection
Special considerations: Lacks nonverbal elements, so verbal message must be especially clear

© TRIANGLE IMAGES/DIGITAL VISION/GETTY IMAGES

ONE-WAY, NOT FACE-TO-FACE

Examples: Letters, memos, reports, and electronic communications including email, fax, voice mail, and web page information
Advantages: Message considered more permanent and official
Special considerations: Lacks both nonverbal elements and instant feedback, so possible confusion must be anticipated and prevented

the document. Written documents are required when legal matters are involved and written records must be retained.

The Receiver Decodes the Message

Give examples of nonverbal gestures that have different meanings among generations or cultures.

The receiver is the destination of the message. The receiver's task is to interpret the sender's message, both verbal and nonverbal, with as little distortion as possible. The process of interpreting the message is referred to as ***decoding***. Because words and nonverbal signals have different meanings to different people, countless problems can occur at this point in the communication process:

- The sender inadequately encodes the original message with words not present in the receiver's vocabulary; ambiguous, nonspecific ideas; or nonverbal signals that distract the receiver or contradict the verbal message.
- The receiver is intimidated by the position or authority of the sender, resulting in tension that prevents effective concentration on the message and failure to ask for needed clarification.

- The receiver prejudges the topic as too boring or difficult to understand and does not attempt to understand the message.
- The receiver is close-minded and unreceptive to new and different ideas.

With the infinite number of breakdowns possible at each stage of the communication process, it is indeed a miracle that effective communication ever occurs. The complexity of the communication process amplifies the importance of the next stage in the communication process—feedback to clarify misunderstandings.

The Receiver Encodes the Message to Clarify Any Misunderstandings

Both internal and external barriers make communication challenging. How?

When the receiver responds to the sender's message, the response is called ***feedback***. The feedback may prompt the sender to modify or adjust the original message to make it clearer to the receiver. Feedback may be verbal or nonverbal. A remark such as "Could you clarify . . ." or a perplexed facial expression provides clear feedback to the sender that the receiver does not yet understand the message. Conversely, a confident "Yes, I understand," and a nod of the head likely signal understanding or encouragement.

Interferences Hinder the Process

What factors contributed to a miscommunication you have experienced? What could have been done to ensure successful communication?

Senders and receivers must learn to deal with the numerous factors that hinder the communication process. These factors are referred to as ***interferences*** or ***barriers*** to effective communication. Previous examples have illustrated some of the interferences that may occur at various stages of the communication process. For example,

- differences in educational level, experience, culture, and other characteristics of the sender and the receiver increase the complexity of encoding and decoding a message.

- physical interferences occurring in the channel include a noisy environment, interruptions, and uncomfortable surroundings.
- mental distractions, such as preoccupation with other matters and developing a response rather than listening.

You can surely compile a list of other barriers that affect your ability to communicate with friends, instructors, coworkers, supervisors, and others. By being aware of them, you can concentrate on removing these interferences.

Your Turn 1-2
Miscue

The death of an 8-year-old school bus rider in Florida could have been prevented if the driver had received complete instructions about the child's drop-off point. As a dispatcher dictated route information, the substitute driver failed to note that the child should be dropped off on the west side of a specific intersection. The child was hit by traffic as she attempted to cross the intersection to the corner where she should have been dropped off.[5]

TAKE ACTION:

- Can you describe a similar communication misstep?
- What were the consequences?
- What steps could have been taken to have avoided this dilemma?

OBJECTIVE 3

Communicating Within Organizations

Organizational structure is the overall design of an organization, much like a blueprint developed to meet the company's specific needs and to enhance its ability to accomplish goals. A company's organizational structure is depicted graphically in an organization chart, as illustrated in Figure 1-3. An organizational chart helps define the scope of the organization and the division of specialized tasks among employees who work interdependently to accomplish common goals.

To be successful, organizations must create an environment that energizes and provides encouragement to employees to accomplish tasks by encouraging genuine openness and effective communication. ***Organizational communication*** is concerned with the movement of information within the company structure. Regardless of your career or level within an organization, your ability to communicate will affect not only the success of the organization but also your personal success and advancement within that organization.

Communication Flow in Organizations

Communication occurs in a variety of ways in an organization. Some communication flows are planned and structured; others are not. Some communication flows can be formally depicted, whereas some defy description.

FIGURE 1-3

Organization Chart of an Internet Company

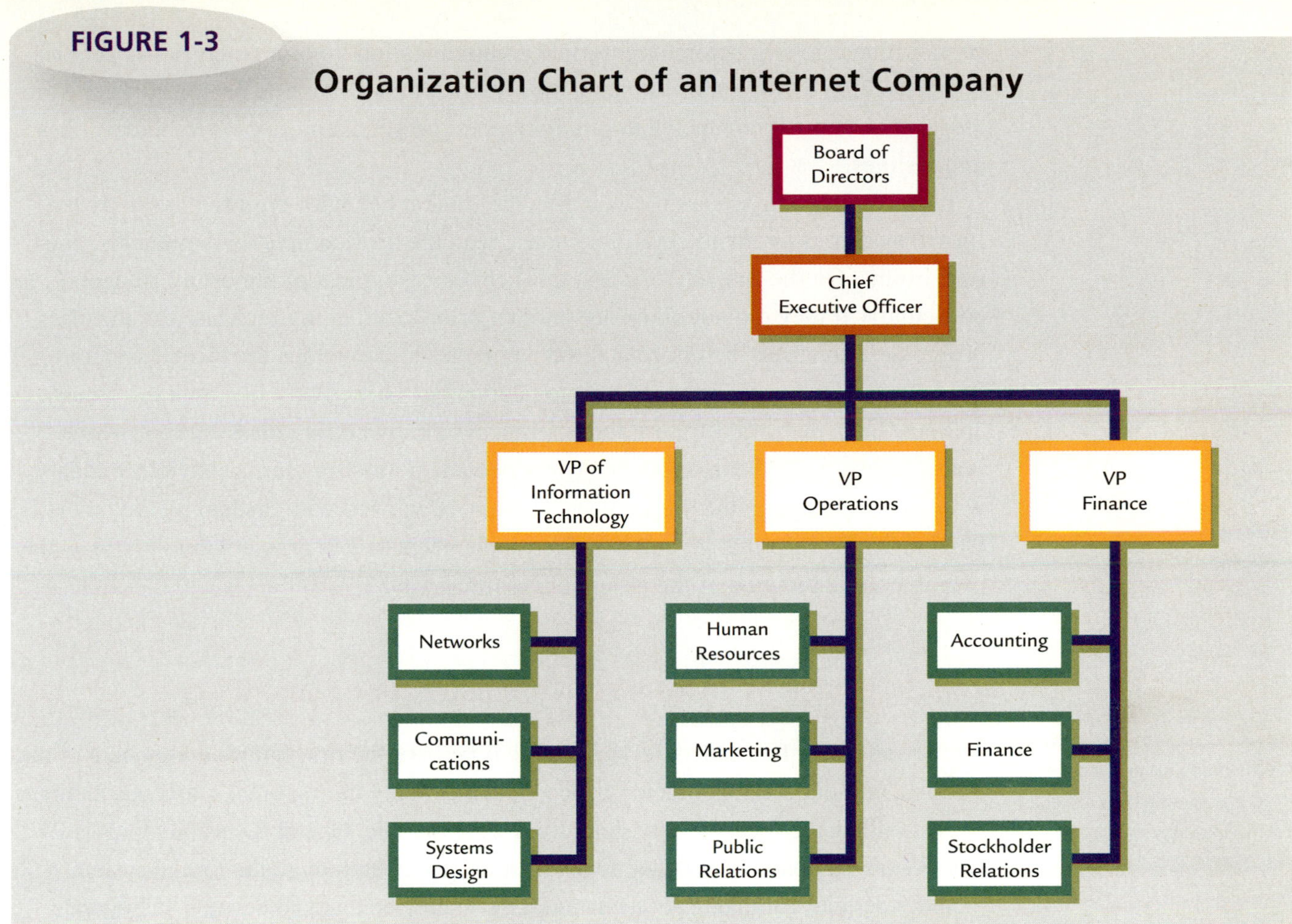

Formal and Informal Channels

The flow of communication within an organization follows both formal and informal channels.

- **Formal communication channel.** This channel is typified by the formal organization chart (see Figure 1-3), which is created by management to define individual and group relationships and to specify lines of responsibility. Essentially, the formal system is dictated by the technical, political, and economic environment of the organization. Within this system, people are required to behave in certain ways simply to get work done.
- **Informal communication channel.** This channel continuously develops as people interact within the formal system to accommodate their social and psychological needs. Because the informal channel undergoes continual changes, it cannot be depicted accurately by any graphic means.

Why do organizations tend to become more bureaucratic as they grow in size?

When employees rely almost entirely on the formal communication system as a guide to behavior, the system might be identified as a *bureaucracy*. Procedures manuals, job descriptions, organization charts, and other written materials dictate the required behavior. Communication channels are followed strictly, and red tape is abundant. Procedures are generally followed exactly; terms such as *rules* and *policies* serve as sufficient reasons for actions. Even the most formal organizations, however, cannot function long before an informal communication system emerges. As people operate within the organized system, they interact on a person-to-person basis and create an environment conducive to satisfying their personal emotions, prejudices, likes, and dislikes.

In the college classroom, for example, the student behavior required to satisfy the formal system is to attend class, take notes, read the text, complete assignments, and pass exams. On the first day of class, this behavior is typical of almost all students, particularly if they did not know one another prior to attending the class. As the class progresses, however, the informal system emerges and overlaps the formal system. Students become acquainted, sit next to people they particularly like, talk informally, and may even plan ways to beat the external system by cutting class and borrowing notes, for example. Soon, these behaviors become norms for class behavior. Students who do not engage in the informal system may be viewed with disdain by the others. Obviously, the informal system benefits people because it is efficient, and it affects the overall communication of the group in important ways.

The Grapevine as an Informal Communication System

Why do managers who ignore the grapevine have difficulty achieving organizational goals?

The ***grapevine***, often called the *rumor mill*, is perhaps the best-known component of the informal communication system. As people talk casually during breaks, text one another, or chat online, the focus usually shifts from topic to topic. One of the usual topics is work—job, company, supervisor, fellow employees. Even though the formal system includes definite communication channels, the grapevine tends to develop and operate within all organizations. Consider these points related to the accuracy and value of grapevine communication:

- As a communication channel, the grapevine has a reputation for being speedy but inaccurate. In the absence of alarms, the grapevine may be the most effective way to let occupants know that the building is on fire. It certainly beats sending an email.
- Although the grapevine often is thought of as a channel for inaccurate communication, in reality it is no more or less accurate than other channels. Even formal communication may become inaccurate and filtered as it passes from level to level in the organizational hierarchy.

Considering a "grapevine" communication you sent or received, how reliable was the message? How time efficient?

- The inaccuracy of the grapevine has more to do with the message input than with the output. For example, the grapevine is noted as a carrier of rumor, primarily because it carries informal messages. If the input is rumor, and nothing more, the output obviously will be inaccurate. But the output may be an accurate description of the original rumor.
- In a business office, news about promotions, personnel changes, company policy changes, and annual salary adjustments often is communicated by the grapevine long before being conveyed by formal channels. The process works similarly in colleges, where information about choice instructors typically is not officially published but is known by students from the grapevine. How best to prepare for examinations, instructor attitudes on attendance and homework, and even faculty personnel changes are messages that travel over the grapevine.

- A misconception about the grapevine is that the message passes from person to person until it finally reaches a person who can't pass it on—the end of the line. Actually, the grapevine works as a network channel. Typically, one person tells two or three others, who each tell two or three others, who each tell two or three others, and so on. Thus, the message may spread to a huge number of people in a short time especially now that the grapevine has gone hi-tech with social networking sites becoming "gossip central."
- The grapevine has no single, consistent source. Messages may originate anywhere and follow various routes.

Due at least in part to widespread downsizing and corporate scandals during the last few years, employees in many organizations are demanding to be better informed. Some companies have implemented new formal ways, such as newsletters and intranets, as well as informal ways, including blogs, and Twitter sites, for sharing information with their internal constituents. Company openness with employees about management decisions and financial issues means more information in the formal system rather than risking its miscommunication through informal channels. Zappos—named one of the best companies to work for in America—has become a model for nurturing employees by following core values of humility, fun and weirdness, and open and honest communication. Employees, who describe the culture as "flat-out fun," are free to be creative and enjoy free lunches and spending time with managers at numerous zany team gatherings.[6]

An informal communication system will emerge from even the most carefully designed formal system. Managers who ignore this fact are attempting to manage blindfolded. Instead of denying or condemning the grapevine, the effective manager will learn to *use* the informal communication network. The grapevine, for instance, can be useful in counteracting rumors and false information.

Directions for Communication Flow

The direction in which communication flows in an organization may be downward, upward, or horizontal, as shown in Figure 1-4. Because these three terms are used frequently in communication discussions, they deserve clarification. Although the concept of flow seems simple, direction has meaning for those participating in the communication process.

What would be an appropriate "rule of thumb" for a manager in deciding whether to send a written or spoken message to subordinates?

Downward Communication. ***Downward communication*** flows from supervisor to employee, from policy makers to operating personnel, or from top to bottom on the organization chart. A simple policy statement from the top of the organization may grow into a formal plan for operation at lower levels. Teaching people how to perform their specific tasks is an element of downward communication. Another element is orientation to a company's rules, practices, procedures, history, and goals. Employees learn about the quality of their job performance through downward communication.

Downward communication normally involves both written and spoken methods and makes use of the following guidelines:

- People high in the organization usually have greater knowledge of the organization and its goals than do people at lower levels.

FIGURE 1-4

Flow of Information Within an Organization

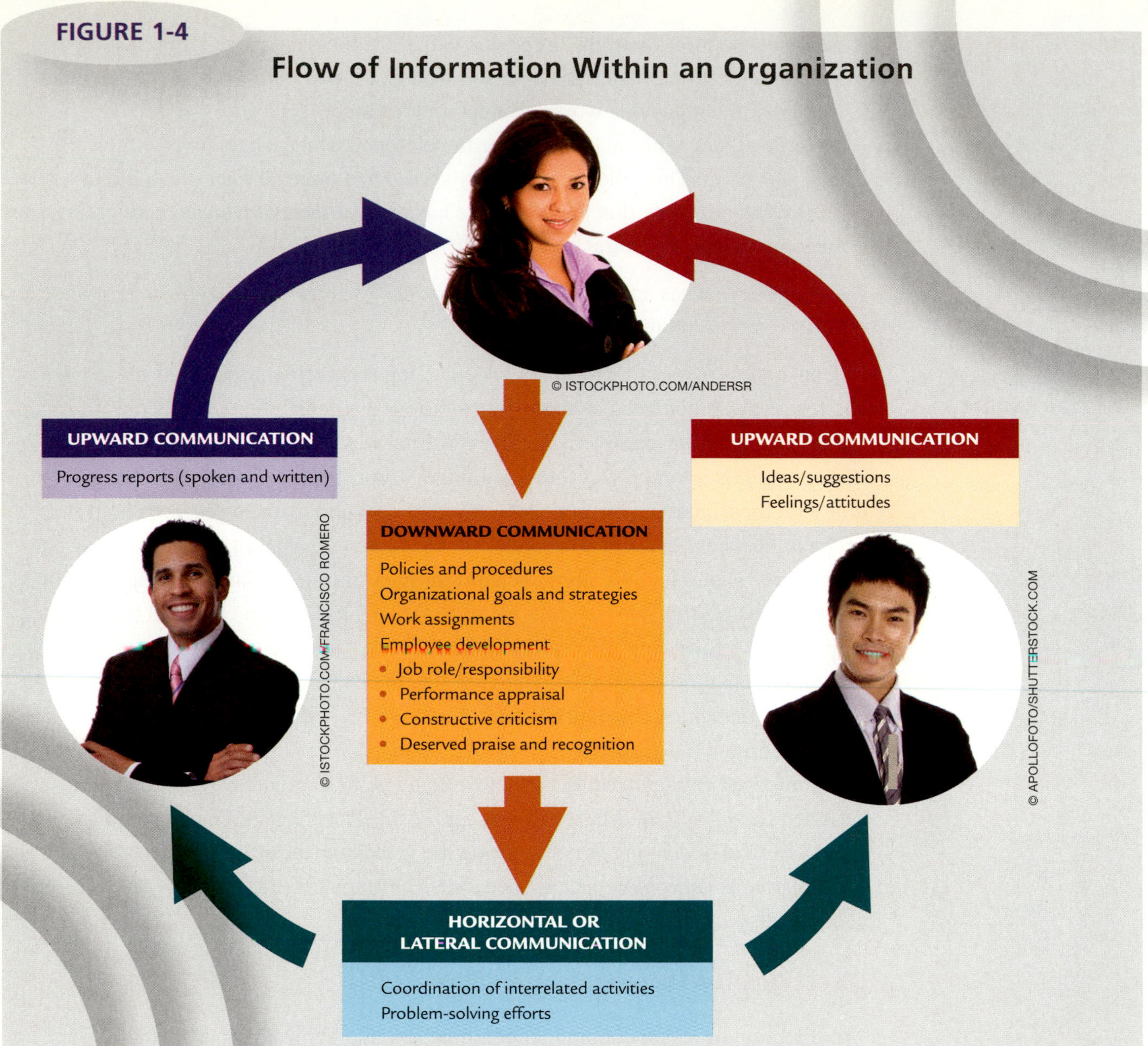

- Both spoken and written messages tend to become larger as they move downward through organizational levels. This expansion results from attempts to prevent distortion and is more noticeable in written messages.
- Spoken messages are subject to greater changes in meaning than are written messages.

When a supervisor sends a message to a subordinate employee who then asks a question or nods in agreement, the question and the nod are signs of feedback. Feedback may flow both downward and upward in organizational communication through traditional as well as informal channels.

How does the free flow of information on social networking sites affect organizational communication?

Upward Communication. ***Upward communication*** generally is feedback to downward communication. When management requests information from lower organizational levels, the resulting information becomes feedback to that request. Employees talk to supervisors about themselves, their fellow employees, their work and methods of doing it, and their perceptions of the organization. These comments are feedback to the downward flow transmitted in both spoken and written form by group meetings, procedures or operations manuals, company news releases, the company intranet, and the grapevine.

Although necessary and valuable, upward communication involves risks. The following factors are important to consider when upward communication flow is involved.

- Upward communication is primarily feedback to requests and actions of supervisors.
- Upward communication may be misleading because lower-level employees often tell the superior what they think the superior wants to hear. Therefore, their messages might contradict their true observations and perceptions.
- Upward communication frequently involves risk to an employee and is dependent on trust in the supervisor.
- Employees will reject superficial attempts by management to obtain feedback.

When effectively used, upward communication keeps management informed about the feelings of lower-level employees, taps the expertise of employees, helps management identify both difficult and potentially promotable employees, and paves the way for even more effective downward communication. Upward communication is key to keeping employees engaged and informed and is especially critical in tapping the power of younger employees who expect to collaborate rather than to be supervised.[7]

How can a manager maximize the effectiveness of horizontal communication among subordinates?

Horizontal Communication. Horizontal, or ***lateral, communication*** describes interactions between organizational units on the same hierarchical level. These interactions

SHOWCASE PART 2 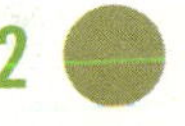 

Leadership for the Times

SPOTLIGHT COMMUNICATOR: THOMAS FRIEDEN DIRECTOR, CENTERS FOR DISEASE CONTROL

Dr. Thomas Frieden assumed the role of director of the Centers for Disease Control (CDC) shortly following the election of President Barack Obama and in the midst of the swine flu outbreak of 2009. At the age of only 48, Frieden arrived at a time of great opportunity and substantial challenge. Frieden is a visible spokesperson for the CDC, appearing before Congress, on television ads, and at public meetings, in addition to overseeing the nation's largest public health agency. Frieden successfully combines professional talent as an infectious disease physician with exemplary leadership and effective communication skills. Read more at your companion website (www.cengage.com/bcomm/lehman) about Frieden's controversial strategies for communicating messages about living more healthy.

SEE SHOWCASE, PART 3, ON PAGE 35
TO EXPAND YOUR KNOWLEDGE ABOUT COMMUNICATION AT THE CDC.

reveal one of the major shortcomings of organizational charts: They do not recognize the role of horizontal communication when they depict authority relationships by placing one box higher than another and define role functions by placing titles in those boxes. Yet management should realize that horizontal communication is the primary means of achieving coordination in a functional organizational structure:

- Informal, horizontal communication takes place when people are available to one another, either in person or electronically. Through horizontal communication units coordinate their activities to accomplish task goals just as adjacent workers in a production line coordinate their activities.
- In an organization divided into cross-functional teams, horizontal communication among the team members is extremely important to achieve individual and team goals.
- Total Quality Management (TQM) experts emphasize that honest, open communication is the single most important factor in successfully creating a TQM environment. According to one TQM author, "if people keep talking to one another, they can work through their problems, overcome barriers, and find encouragement and support from others involved in quality efforts."[8]

TEAM ENVIRONMENT

A Ford Foundation study found that productivity increased in companies that show concern for employees' personal lives and needs. Explain this finding.

Many companies realize that the traditional hierarchy organized around functional units is inadequate for competing in increasingly competitive global markets. They value work teams that integrate work-flow processes rather than specialists in a single function or product. Such work teams break down communication barriers between isolated functional departments, and communication patterns take on varying forms to accommodate team activities.

Levels of Communication

Communication can involve sending messages to both large and small audiences. ***Internal messages*** are intended for recipients within the organization. ***External messages*** are directed to recipients outside the organization. When considering the intended audience, communication can be described as taking place on five levels: intrapersonal, interpersonal, group, organizational, and public. Figure 1-5 depicts the five audience levels: intrapersonal, interpersonal, group, organizational, and public. Regardless of the communication level, effective communicators have a clearly defined purpose for each message and selected strategies for targeting their intended audience.

Strategic Forces Influencing Business Communication

As we have discussed, communication is often a complicated process. Furthermore, communication does not take place in a vacuum, but rather is influenced by a number of forces at work in the environment. The effective communicator carefully considers each of these influences and structures communication responsively. Four critical forces influence the communication process and help to determine and define the nature of the communication that occurs, as shown in Figure 1-6.

FIGURE 1-5

Levels of Communication

© IMAGE100/JUPITER IMAGES

© DIGITAL VISION/DIGITAL VISION/ GETTY IMAGES

© IT STOCK FREE/JUPITER IMAGES

INTRAPERSONAL

- Communication within oneself
- Not considered by some to be true communication as it does not involve a separate sender and receiver

Examples: Individual reminding himself of tasks to complete or daily schedule

INTERPERSONAL

- Communication between two people
- Goals are to (1) accomplish the task confronting them (task goal), and (2) feel better about themselves and each other because of their interaction (maintenance goal)

Examples: Supervisor and subordinate, two coworkers

GROUP

- Communication among more than two people
- Goal of achieving greater output than individual efforts could produce

Examples: Committee or college class

© COMSTOCK IMAGES/JUPITER IMAGES

© COLIN ANDERSON/BLEND IMAGES/ JUPITER IMAGES

ORGANIZATIONAL

- Groups combined in such a way that large tasks may be accomplished
- Goal of providing adequate structure for groups to achieve their purposes

Examples: Company or organization

PUBLIC

- The organization reaching out to its public to achieve its goals
- Goal of reaching many with the same message

Examples: Media advertisement, website communication

FIGURE 1-6

Strategic Forces Influencing Business Communication

DIVERSITY CHALLENGES

- Cultural Differences
- Language Barriers
- Gender Issues
- Education Levels
- Age Factors
- Nonverbal Differences

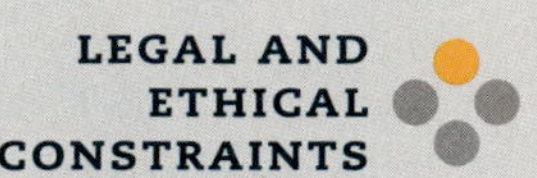

- International Laws
- Domestic Laws
- Code of Ethics
- Stakeholder Interests
- Ethical Frameworks
- Personal Values

BUSINESS COMMUNICATION

TEAM ENVIRONMENT

- Trust
- Team Roles
- Shared Goals and Expectations
- Synergy
- Group Reward
- Distributed Leadership

CHANGING TECHNOLOGY

- Accuracy and Security Issues
- Telecommunications
- Software Applications
- "High-touch" Issues
- Telecommuting
- Databases

Legal and Ethical Constraints as a Strategic Force Influencing Communication

How would you rank the four strategic forces in terms of magnitude of importance to business communication? Why?

Legal and ethical constraints act as a strategic force on communication in that they set boundaries in which communication rightfully occur. International, federal, state, and local laws affect the way that various business activities are conducted. For instance, laws specify that certain information must be stated in messages that reply to credit applications and those dealing with the collection of outstanding debts. Furthermore, one's own ethical standards will often influence what he or she is willing to say in a message. For example, a system of ethics built on honesty may require that the message provide full disclosure rather than a shrouding of the truth. Legal responsibilities, then, are the starting point for appropriate business communication. One's ethical belief system, or personal sense of right and wrong behavior, provides further boundaries for professional activity.

The press is full of examples of unethical conduct in business and government:

What recent events can you think of that have ethical themes?

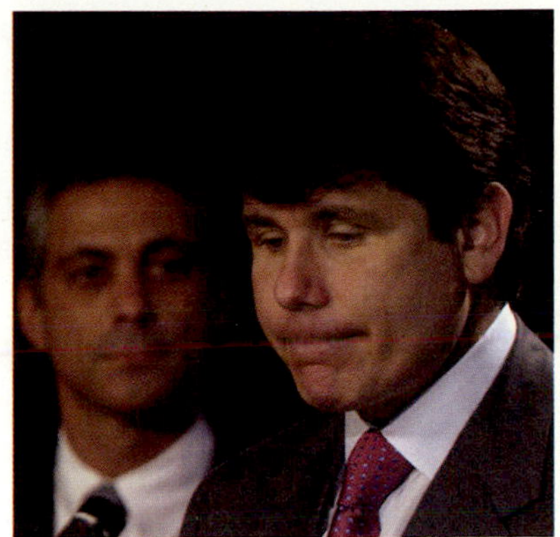
© AP IMAGES/M. SPENCER GREEN

- Federal corruption charges were filed against Illinois Governor Rod Blagojevich, including allegations that he conspired to sell or trade to the highest bidder the U.S. Senate seat left vacant by Barack Obama. Denying any wrongdoing, he refused to resign but was eventually impeached by the Illinois Congress.[9]
- AIG's payment of lucrative executive bonuses shortly after accepting a multi-billion dollar federal bailout resulted in public outrage and a Congressional hearing.[10]
- Federal employees working for the Minerals Management division of the Department of the Interior accepted gifts from the energy companies under their oversight, engaged in drug use and illicit sex with employees of energy firms, and steered contracts to favored clients.[11]
- Lapses in ethical behavior have occurred in businesses around the globe. For example, a recent scandal occurred at Satyam Computer Services, a leading Indian outsourcing company that services more than a third of the Fortune 500 companies. The chairman, who resigned after admitting he inflated his software company's profits by around $1 billion in recent quarterly results, was likened to India's version of Bernard Madoff, who cheated investors of billions in the largest Ponzi scheme in history.[12]

Incidents such as these have far-reaching consequences. Those affected by decisions, the ***stakeholders***, can include people inside and outside the organization. Employees and stockholders are obvious losers when a company fails. Competitors in the same industry also suffer, because their strategies are based on what they perceive about their competition. Beyond that, financial markets as a whole suffer due to erosion of public confidence. The sharp economic decline that began in 2008 and the sensational financial losses resulting from numerous Ponzi schemes caused many investors to abandon their stock market investments.

How are laws related to requirements for behavior linked to personal and societal ethics?

Business leaders, government officials, and citizens frequently express concern about the apparent erosion of ethical values in society. Even for those who want to do the right thing, matters of ethics are seldom clear-cut decisions of right versus wrong, and they often contain ambiguous elements. In addition, the pressure appears to be felt most strongly by lower-level managers, often recent business school graduates who are the least experienced at doing their jobs.

You can take steps now to prepare for dealing with pressure to compromise personal values:

- **Consider your personal value system.** Only if you have definite beliefs on a variety of issues and courage to practice them will you be able to make sound ethical judgments. Putting ethical business practices first will also benefit your employing firm as its reputation for fairness and good judgment retains long-term clients or customers and brings in new ones.

- **Learn to analyze ethical dilemmas.** Knowing how to analyze ethical dilemmas and identify the consequences of your actions will help you make decisions that conform to your own value system. Thus, unless you know what you stand for and how to analyze ethical issues, you become a puppet, controlled by the motives of others, too weak to make a decision on your own.

The Foundation for Legal and Ethical Behavior

Although ethics is a common point of discussion, many find defining ethics challenging. Most people immediately associate ethics with standards and rules of conduct, morals, right and wrong, values, and honesty. Dr. Albert Schweitzer defined *ethics* as "the name we give to our concern for good behavior. We feel an obligation to consider not only our own personal well-being, but also that of others and of human society as a whole."[13] In other words, ***ethics*** refers to the principles of right and wrong that guide you in making decisions that consider the impact of your actions on others as well as yourself.

What are the benefits to business organizations for making ethical decisions?

Though the recorded accounts of legal and ethical misconduct would seem to indicate that businesses are dishonest and unscrupulous, keep in mind that millions of business transactions are made daily on the basis of honesty and concern for others. Why should a business make ethical decisions? What difference will it make? James E. Perrella, executive vice president of Ingersoll-Rand Company, gave a powerful reply to these questions:[14]

> Our question of today should be, what's the right thing to do, the right way to behave, the right way to conduct business? Don't just ask, is it legal? Have you ever considered what business would be like if we all did it? If every businessman and businesswoman followed the Golden Rule? Many people, including many business leaders, would argue that such an application of ethics to business would adversely affect bottom-line performance. I say nay. . . . Good ethics, simply, is good business. Good ethics will attract investors. Good ethics will attract good employees. You can do what's right. Not because of conduct codes. Not because of rules or laws. But because you know what's right.

Identifying ethical issues in typical workplace situations may be difficult, and coworkers and superiors may apply pressure for seemingly logical reasons. To illustrate, examine each of the following workplace situations for a possible ethical dilemma:

- A mortgage lender approves loans to homebuyers without verifying their ability to repay the loans in order to achieve profit expectations of financial analysts.

What are the legal and ethical issues related to using others' wifi connections without their permission?

- Corporate officers deliberately withhold information concerning a planned spinoff to prevent an adverse effect on stock prices.
- To protect his job, a product engineer decides not to question a design flaw in a product that could lead to possible injuries and even deaths to consumers because the redesign would cause a delay in product introduction.

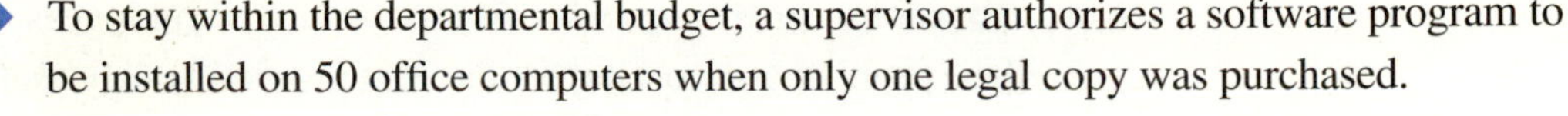

- To stay within the departmental budget, a supervisor authorizes a software program to be installed on 50 office computers when only one legal copy was purchased.

- Angry at a superior for an unfavorable performance appraisal, an employee leaks confidential information (e.g., trade secrets or marketing strategies) to an acquaintance who works for a competitor or posts highly derogative comments about the company on his or her social networking site.

Your fundamental morals and values provide the foundation for making ethical decisions. However, as the previous examples imply, even minor concessions in day-to-day decisions can gradually weaken an individual's ethical foundation.

Your Turn 1-3
You're the Professional

A senior executive in your company is running for the presidency of a professional organization. While assisting her in preparing a speech she will give to members of the organization, you read through the biographical information she provided to them. You note that some of the information does not match information in your company's files, as she seems to have claimed a fictitious degree and inflated other credentials. She tells you "It's nothing to worry about" when you meet with her and point out the discrepancies.[15] What do you do now?

TAKE ACTION:

Discuss which of the following actions would be most appropriate, explaining your reasoning:

a. Take her advice and not worry about it.

b. Contact the organization directly to correct the information without telling her about it.

c. Confront her, telling her you will have to report the incident if she does not correct the situation.

d. Bring the matter to the attention of senior management without saying anything more to the executive.

Causes of Illegal and Unethical Behavior

Understanding the major causes of illegal and unethical behavior in the workplace will help you become sensitive to signals of escalating pressure to compromise your values. Unethical corporate behavior can have a number of causes:

- **Excessive emphasis on profits.** Business managers are often judged and paid on their ability to increase business profits. This emphasis on profits may send a message that the end justifies the means. According to former Federal Reserve Chairman Alan Greenspan, "infectious greed" ultimately pushed companies such as Enron, Global Crossing, and WorldCom into bankruptcy.[16]
- **Misplaced corporate loyalty.** A misplaced sense of corporate loyalty may cause an employee to do what seems to be in the best interest of the company, even if the act is illegal or unethical.

- **Obsession with personal advancement.** Employees who wish to outperform their peers or are working for the next promotion may feel that they cannot afford to fail. They may do whatever it takes to achieve the objectives assigned to them.

Is ethical behavior more important for business people today than in the past? Explain.

- **Expectation of not getting caught.** Thinking that the end justifies the means, employees often believe illegal or unethical activity will never be discovered. Unfortunately, a great deal of improper behavior escapes detection in the business world. Believing no one will ever find out, employees are tempted to lie, steal, and perform other illegal acts.
- **Unethical tone set by top management.** If top managers are not perceived as highly ethical, lower-level managers may be less ethical as a result. Employees have little incentive to act legally and ethically if their superiors do not set an example and encourage and reward such behavior. "The speed of the leader is the speed of the pack" illustrates the importance of leading by example.
- **Uncertainty about whether an action is wrong.** Many times, company personnel are placed in situations in which the line between right and wrong is not clearly defined. When caught in this gray area, the perplexed employee asks, "How far is too far?"
- **Unwillingness to take a stand for what is right.** Often employees know what is right or wrong but are not willing to take the risk of challenging a wrong action. They may lack the confidence or skill needed to confront others with sensitive legal or ethical issues. They may remain silent and then justify their unwillingness to act.

Framework for Analyzing Ethical Dilemmas

Determining whether an action is ethical can be difficult. Learning to analyze a dilemma from both legal and ethical perspectives will help you find a solution that conforms to your own personal values. Figure 1-7 shows the four conclusions you might reach when considering the advisability of a particular behavior.

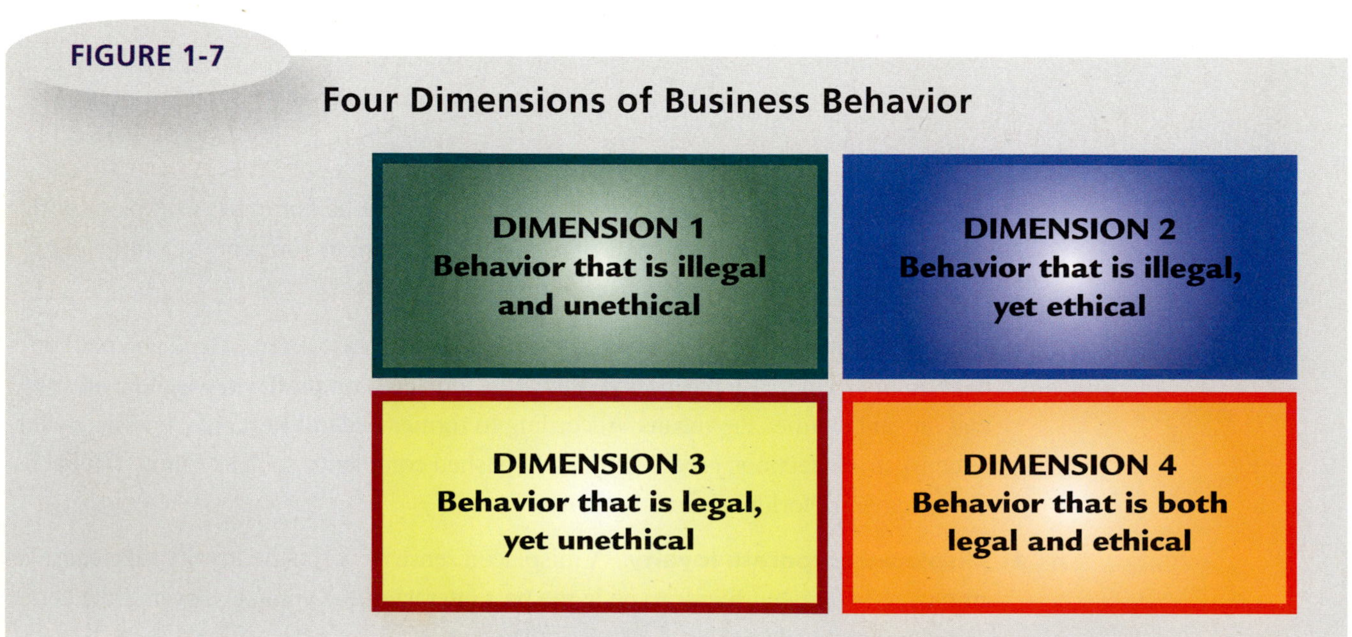

How can you keep up with the legal requirements in your field?

Dimension 1: Behavior that is illegal and unethical. When considering some actions, you will reach the conclusion that they are both illegal and unethical. The law specifically outlines the "black" area—those alternatives that are clearly wrong, and your employer will expect you to become an expert in the laws that affect your particular area. When you encounter an unfamiliar area, you must investigate any possible legal implications. Obviously, obeying the law is in the best interest of all concerned: you as an individual, your company, and society. Contractual agreements between two parties also offer guidance for legal decision making. Frequently, your own individual sense of right and wrong will also confirm that the illegal action is wrong for you personally. In such situations, decisions about appropriate behavior are obvious.

Dimension 2: Behavior that is illegal, yet ethical. Occasionally, a businessperson may decide that even though a specific action is illegal, there is a justifiable reason to break the law. A case in point is a law passed in Vermont that makes it illegal for a pharmaceutical company to give any gift valued at $25 or more to doctors or their personnel.[17] Those supporting the law charge that the giving of freebies drives up medical costs by encouraging doctors to prescribe new, more expensive brand-name drugs. The law's opponents contend that the gifts do not influence doctors and are merely educational tools for new products. Although a pharmaceutical firm and its employees may see nothing wrong with providing gifts worth in excess of $25, they would be well advised to consider the penalty of $10,000 per violation before acting on their personal ethics. A more advised course of action probably would be to act within the law while lobbying for a change in the law.

Dimension 3: Behavior that is legal, yet unethical. If you determine that a behavior is legal and complies with relevant contractual agreements and company policy, your next step is to consult your company's or profession's ***code of ethics***. This written document summarizes the company's or profession's standards of ethical conduct. Some companies refer to this document as a *credo* or *standards of ethical conduct*. If the behavior does not violate the code of ethics, then put it to the test of your own personal integrity. You may at times reject a legal action because it does not "feel right." Most Americans were appalled to learn that mortgage bankers' reckless abandonment of traditional lending standards led to the subprime mortgage meltdown. Although they may have acted legally, their profiting at the expense of company employees, stockholders, and the public hardly seemed ethical. You may be faced with situations in which you reject a behavior that is legal because you would not be proud of your family and community knowing that you engaged in it.

Dimension 4: Behavior that is both legal and ethical. Decisions in this dimension are easy to make. Such actions comply with the law, company policies, and your professional and personal codes of ethics.

The Pagano Model offers a straightforward method for determining whether a proposed action is advisable.[18] For this system to work, you must answer the following six questions honestly:

- Is the proposed action legal—the core starting point?
- What are the benefits and costs to the people involved?
- Would you want this action to be a universal standard, appropriate for everyone?

- Does the action pass the light-of-day test? That is, if your action appeared on television or others learned about it, would you be proud?
- Does the action pass the Golden Rule test? That is, would you want the same to happen to you?
- Does the action pass the ventilation test? Ask the opinion of a wise friend with no investment in the outcome. Does this friend believe the action is ethical?

© AP IMAGES/LOUIS LANZANO

Which of the ethical frameworks do you find most appropriate for you personally? Why?

Martha Stewart was found guilty of conspiracy, obstruction of justice, and making false statements regarding her sale of shares of ImClone stock just before the company's downturn. Some have defended her action as neither illegal nor immoral, while others have argued that cracking down on Stewart sent an important message about stock-market manipulation. "It's very important for us to protect integrity of this system," said David Kelley, the U.S. attorney in Manhattan, after the verdict. "Failure to do so results in a flood of corruption."[19] Visit your companion website www.cengage.com/bcomm/lehman to learn about other frameworks for examining the correctness of an action.

Diversity Challenges as a Strategic Force Influencing Communication

Diversity in the workplace is another strategic force influencing communication. Differences between the sender and the receiver in areas such as culture, age, gender, and education require sensitivity on the part of both parties so that the intended message is the one that is received.

Understanding how to communicate effectively with people from other cultures has become more integral to the work environment as many U.S. companies are increasingly conducting business with international companies or becoming multinational. Candy manufacturer Jelly Belly learned a great deal about cultural differences when the company opened business operations in Thailand. The Thai culture is very family oriented, and the employer is expected to provide transportation to and from work as well as free meals and a workout facility for its employees.[20]

When addressing cultural differences, successful communication must often span barriers of language and differing world views resulting from societal and religious beliefs and practices. When a person fails to consider these factors, communication suffers, and the result is often embarrassing and potentially costly. McDonald's is an example of a large U.S. company that has expanded its operations to include most major countries in the world. To be successful on an international scale, managers had to be aware of cultural differences and be willing to work to ensure that effective communication occurred despite these barriers.

What is the relationship between political barriers and communication barriers?

Occasionally, however, a whopper of an intercultural communication faux pas occurs. That is what happened when McDonald's began its promotional campaign in Great Britain for the World Cup soccer championship. It seemed like a clever (and harmless) idea to reproduce the flags of the 24 nations participating in the event and print them on packaging—two million Happy Meal bags, to be exact. What marketing personnel

How can a business person stay informed about cultural differences?

failed to consider was that words from the *Koran* are printed on the Saudi flag. The idea that sacred words from Islam's holy book were mass printed to sell a product with the knowledge that the packages would be thrown into the trash angered and offended many Muslims, who immediately complained. McDonald's apologized for the gaffe and agreed to cooperate with the Saudis in finding a solution to the problem.[21]

While NAFTA has created new business opportunities for U.S. and Mexican entities, unique problems have also occurred. After seven trips to Mexico and nine months of courtship, a U.S. firm faxed the final contract to the Mexican CEO. This was a big mistake since Mexican protocol calls for a more formal face-to-face meeting when finalizing transactions.[22]

These errors serve as examples of how much "homework" is involved in maintaining good relations with customers or clients from other cultures. The potential barrier of language is obvious; however, successful managers know that much more is involved in communicating with everyone—across cultures, genders, ages, abilities, and other differences.

Communication Opportunities and Challenges in Diversity

As world markets continue to expand, U.S. employees at home and abroad will be doing business with more people from other countries. You may find yourself working abroad for a large American company, an international company with a plant in the United States, or a company with an ethnically diverse workforce. Regardless of the workplace, your ***diversity skills***, that is, your ability to communicate effectively with both men and women of all ages and with people of other cultures or minority groups, will affect your success in today's culturally diverse, global economy.

- **International issues.** Worldwide telecommunications and intense international business competition have fueled the movement of many industries into world markets. During the past four decades, U.S. firms have established facilities in Europe, Central and South America, and Asia. For many U.S. corporations, such as Proctor and Gamble, more than 70 percent of total sales in recent years has come from international operations. Asians and Europeans have built plants in the United States, and many U.S. workers are now employed in facilities owned and operated by foreign interests. Understanding a person of another culture who may not speak your language well or understand your culturally based behaviors is a daily challenge faced by many. Specific guidelines for writing and speaking with an international audience are provided in later chapters.

How has diversity affected the development of the United States as a world leader?

- **Intercultural issues.** Changing demographics in the United States are requiring businesses to face ethnic diversity in the workplace. U.S. labor statistics reflect the declining proportion of white males in the labor force and growing proportions of minorities and women. The U.S. workforce is predicted to be smaller and increasingly more diverse over the next three decades.[23] Rather than being a melting pot for people from many countries, the United States offers an environment in which people of varying cultures can live and practice their cultural heritage. People with a common heritage often form their own neighborhoods and work at retaining their traditional customs and language, while still sharing in the common culture. Consequently, *mosaic* seems to be a more accurate term than *melting pot* to reflect U.S. cultural diversity. As in a tile mosaic, small, distinct groups combine to form the pattern or design of the U.S. population and workforce. People from different backgrounds invariably bring different values, attitudes, and perceptions to the workplace.

What is the "graying of America"? How does it impact workplace interactions?

- **Intergenerational issues.** While age diversity has always been present in the workplace, recent trends have made it a more important issue than ever. The so-called "graying of America" has changed the age distribution in the U.S. population. The older segment of the population is larger today than at any time previously. The maturing of the "baby boomer" generation (those born between 1946 and 1964), a relatively low birthrate, and increasing life spans have led to a higher average age in the population. Today's workforce reflects the advancing age of the general populace. By 2010, more than half of U.S. workers will be over 40.[24] Because of changes in laws affecting retirement benefits, financial considerations, and better overall health, many older workers will choose to continue longer in their professional activities than in past years. Because of the broadening of the age span in the workplace, businesses will be faced with new challenges related to differences in perceptions, values, and communication styles of the generations. Chapter 3 includes a Strategic Forces focus on generational differences and their impact on workplace communication.
- **Gender issues.** The flood of women entering the job market has substantially changed the American workforce. Old social patterns of behavior that defined the appropriate roles for men and women do not fit in a work environment free from discrimination. Civil rights laws prohibiting sex discrimination and pay equity requirements have been in place for more than 40 years, yet charges continue to be filed by individuals who feel that their rights have been violated. The number of sexual harassment cases has increased in recent years, resulting from a broader-based definition of what constitutes sexual harassment. Although a charge of sexual harassment may be based on actions with sexual overtones, the offense has also been interpreted to include comments, visual images, or other conditions that create a hostile working environment. One result of the increased focus on sexual harassment in the workplace is the reluctance of some to communicate with other workers for fear that their actions or words might be misconstrued. Both men and women confront workplace communication challenges.

What other aspects of diversity can influence communication?

Workplace diversity can lead to misunderstandings and miscommunications, but it also poses opportunities to improve both workers and organizations. Managers must be prepared to communicate effectively with workers of different nationalities, genders, races, ages, abilities, and so forth.

Managing a diverse workforce effectively will require you to communicate with *everyone* and to help all employees reach their fullest potential and contribute to the company's goals. When miscommunication occurs, both sides are frustrated and often angry. To avoid such problems, increasing numbers of companies have undertaken ***diversity initiatives*** and are providing diversity training seminars to help workers understand and appreciate gender and age differences and the cultures of coworkers. To prepare for these communication challenges, commit the time and energy to enhance your diversity skills while you are attending classes as well as after you enter the workplace.

Culture and Communication

What are some examples in your own community of culture-oriented activities?

Managers with the *desire* and the *skill* to conduct business in new international markets and to manage a diverse workforce effectively will confront problems created by cultural differences. The way messages are decoded and encoded is not just a function of the experiences, beliefs, and assumptions of the person sending or receiving those messages but also are shaped by the society in which he or she lives.

© JAMES CARMEN/BLEND IMAGES/ JUPITERIMAGES

People learn patterns of behavior from their ***culture***. The *culture* of a people is the product of their living experiences within their own society. Culture could be described as "the way of life" of a people and includes a vast array of behaviors and beliefs. These patterns affect how people perceive the world, what they value, and how they act. Differing patterns can also create barriers to communication. Visit your companion website www.cengage.com/bcomm/lehman to learn more about the characteristics of culture that shape communication.

Your Turn 1-4
Assessment

Our nation and economy will demand an expanded and educated workforce to replace the large number of retiring "baby boomers" who will vacate jobs crucial for the nation to maintain its preeminence especially in research, technology, science, and engineering. Many businesses recognize the significant advantage of integrating workers from culturally diverse backgrounds. To realize these benefits, workers must understand and embrace differences.

TAKE ACTION:

- Take the Cultural Awareness Quiz located at www.ethnoconnect.com/html/quiz.asp, or go to your companion website www.cengage.com/bcomm/lehman for updated links.
- Prepare a short written summary of what you learned from taking the quiz and how your future attitudes and actions might be impacted.

Barriers to Intercultural Communication

Because cultures give different definitions to such basics of interaction as values and norms, people raised in two different cultures may clash in various ways.

- **Ethnocentrism.** Problems occur between people of different cultures primarily because people tend to assume that their own cultural norms are the right way to do things. They wrongly believe that the specific patterns of behavior desired in their own cultures are universally valued. This belief, known as ***enthnocentrism***, is certainly natural; but learning about other cultures and developing sensitivity will help minimize ethnocentric reactions when dealing with other cultures.

Give several examples of stereotypes that prevail concerning certain cultural groups.

- **Stereotypes.** We often form a mental picture of the main characteristics of another group, creating preformed ideas of what people in this group are like. These pictures, called ***stereotypes***, influence the way we interact with members of the other group. When we observe a behavior that conforms to the stereotype, the validity of the preconceived notion is reinforced. We often view the other person as a representative of a class of people rather than as an individual. People of all cultures have stereotypes about other cultural groups they have encountered. These stereotypes can interfere with communication when people interact on the basis of the imagined representative and not the real individual.

What are some miscommunications that can occur due to differences in time perception?

- **Interpretation of time.** The study of how a culture perceives time and its use is called ***chronemics***. In the United States, we have a saying that "time is money." Canadians, like some northern Europeans who are also concerned about punctuality, make appointments, keep them, and do not waste time completing them. In some other cultures, time is the cheapest commodity and an inexhaustible resource; time represents a person's span on earth, which is only part of eternity. To these cultures, engaging in long, casual conversations prior to serious discussions or negotiations is time well spent in establishing and nurturing relationships. On the other hand, the time-efficient American businessperson is likely to fret about waste of precious time.
- **Personal space requirements.** Space operates as a language just as time does. The study of cultural space requirements is known as ***proxemics***. In all cultures, the distance between people functions in communication as "personal space" or "personal territory." In the United States, for example, for intimate conversations with close friends and relatives, individuals are willing to stay within about a foot and a half of each other; for casual conversations, up to two or three feet; for job interviews and personal business, four to twelve feet; and for public occasions, more than twelve feet. However, in many cultures outside the United States, closer personal contact is accepted, or greater distance may be the norm.
- **Body language.** The study of body language is known as ***kinesics***. Body language is not universal, but instead is learned from one's culture. Even the most basic gestures have varying cultural meanings—the familiar North American symbol for "okay" means zero in France, money in Japan, and an expression of vulgarity in Brazil. Similarly, eye contact, posture, and facial expressions carry different meanings throughout the world. Chapter 2 contains an expanded discussion of nonverbal communication.

What words and phrases have different meanings for speakers of British English than for speakers of American English?

- **Translation limitations.** Words in one language do not always have an equivalent meaning in other languages, and the concepts the words describe are often different as well. Translators can be helpful, but keep in mind that a translator is working with a second language and must listen to one language, mentally cast the words into another language, and then speak them. This process is difficult and opens the possibility that the translator will fall victim to one or more cultural barriers. The Holistic Assessment following Chapter 3 provides additional opportunity for you to explore translation issues.
- **Lack of language training.** The following is an anecdote that speaks to the need for language training:

  What do you call someone who speaks two languages? (Reply: bilingual)

  What do you call someone who speaks three languages? (Reply: trilingual)

  What do you call someone who speaks one language? (Reply: an American)

This tongue-in-cheek humor reinforces the language illiteracy of most U.S. citizens. Since familiarity with a second language improves your competitiveness as a job applicant, be sure to showcase that ability in your résumé. In some situations, learning a second language may not be feasible—you are completing a short-term assignment, you must leave immediately, or the language is extremely difficult to learn. Learning Japanese, for instance, involves understanding grammar, pronunciation, the writing system, and acquiring adequate vocabulary. While the sound system is simple to master compared with those of other languages, the challenging writing system requires learning 1,945 kanji characters.[25]

Even if you cannot speak or write another language fluently, people from other cultures will appreciate simple efforts to learn a few common phrases. Other suggestions for overcoming language differences are discussed in the accompanying Strategic Forces feature "Viva la Difference!"

Changing Technology as a Strategic Force Influencing Communication

Electronic tools have not eliminated the need for basic communication skills; they can, in fact, create new obstacles or barriers to communication that must be overcome. These tools, however, also create opportunities, which range from the kinds of communications that are possible to the quality of the messages themselves. Electronic tools, as shown in Figure 1-8, can help people in various ways, such as (1) collecting and analyzing data, (2) shaping messages to be clearer and more effective, and (3) communicating quickly and efficiently with others in geographically dispersed locations.

In your opinion, what communication technology has most changed the way business is conducted?

Using various communication technologies, individuals can often work in their homes or other remote locations and send and receive work from the company office electronically. ***Telecommuting*** (also referred to as **teleworking**) offers various advantages, including reduced travel time and increased work flexibility. Laptops and smartphones provide computing power and connectivity for professionals wherever they are. While the public Internet is accessible to everyone and offers a wide array of information, private databases provide specialized and advanced information on specific topics. Databases enable decision makers to obtain information quickly and accurately and offer these advantages:

- **Data organization**—the ability to organize large amounts of data.
- **Data integrity**—assurance that the data will be accurate and complete.
- **Data security**—assurance that the data are secure because access to a database is controlled through several built-in data security features.

Internal databases contain proprietary information that is pertinent to the particular business or organization and its employees. External databases (networks) allow users to access information from remote locations literally around the world and in an instant transfer that information to their own computers for further manipulation or storage. Information is available on general news, stocks, financial markets, sports, travel, weather, and a variety of publications.

Knowing how to "tunnel" through the vast amounts of irrelevant information available on the Internet to find what you want can be overwhelming. The experience can also

(continues on p. 31)

DIVERSITY CHALLENGES

STRATEGIC FORCES

Viva la Difference!

With so many barriers, communicating with people of other cultures can be difficult. Anyone who enters the business world today must be aware of potential trouble spots and of ways to avoid them. Application of some common sense guidelines can help to overcome intercultural barriers.

- **Learn about that person's culture.**

  Many sources of useful information are available, including university courses in international business communication and books that recount some of the subtle but important ways that people from other cultures communicate. Various Internet sites are dedicated to sharing information to help the intercultural communicator. Networking can generate the names of other businesspeople who have made successful contact with another culture. A telephone conversation or a lunch meeting may provide useful pointers on proper and improper behavior. Corporations with frequent and extensive dealings in other countries often establish workshops in which employees receive briefing and training before accepting overseas assignments. Learning the language is an invaluable way of becoming more familiar with another culture.

- **Have patience—with yourself and the other person.**

  Conversing with someone from another culture, when one of you is likely to be unfamiliar with the language being used, can be difficult and time consuming. By being patient with mistakes, making sure that all questions are answered, and not hurrying, you are more likely to make the outcome of the conversation positive. You must also learn to be patient and tolerant of ambiguity. Being able to react to new, different, and unpredictable situations with little visible discomfort or irritation will prove invaluable. The author Howard Schuman writes that "a sense of humor is indispensable for dealing with the cultural mistakes and faux pas you will certainly commit."[26]

© ISTOCKPHOTO.COM/JACOB WACKERHAUSEN

- **Get help when you need it.**

  If you are not sure what is being said—or why something is being said in a certain way—ask for clarification. If you feel uneasy about conversing with someone from another culture, bring along someone you trust who understands that culture. You will have a resource if you need help.

Instead of ignoring cultural factors, workers and employers can improve communication by recognizing them and by considering people as individuals rather than as members of stereotypical groups. Many companies view the implementation of a diversity initiative as a way to improve organizational communication. The goal of such a program is to increase awareness and appreciation for areas of differences among employees and to build stronger rapport by finding commonalities. Firms with successful diversity initiatives find that promoting common understanding among workers boosts morale, creativity, and productivity.

Application

Interview a person from a cultural group other than your own. Include the following questions:

1. What examples can you give of times when you experienced discrimination or isolation?
2. What information can you provide to aid other groups in understanding your cultural uniqueness?
3. What advice would you give for improving intercultural understanding?

FIGURE 1-8

Communication Technology Tools

TOOLS FOR DATA COLLECTION AND ANALYSIS

Knowing how to collect information from the Internet and communicate in a networked world is critical. Generally, electronic communication provides researchers with two distinct advantages:

- Electronic searches can be done in a fraction of the time required to conduct manual searches of printed sources.
- The vast amount of information available allows researchers to develop better solutions to problems.

© NICK KOUDIS/PHOTODISC GREEN/GETTY IMAGES

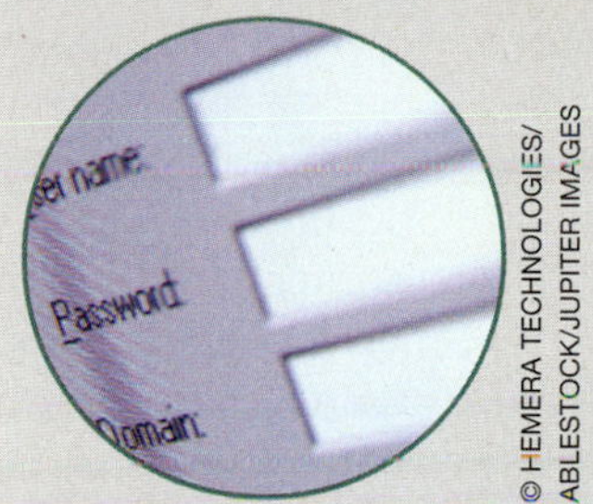

© HEMERA TECHNOLOGIES/ ABLESTOCK/JUPITER IMAGES

INTERNET

Vast "network of networks" links computers throughout the world in the form of text, images, audio, and video is quickly available and easily searchable.

INTRANETS

Password-protected resources available via the Internet allow companies to post information and resources for employees.

EXTRANETS

Protected information and resources on company site are made available to customers, partners, or others with need to know.

TOOLS FOR SHAPING MESSAGES TO BE CLEARER AND MORE EFFECTIVE

Documents that took days to produce during the b.c. (before computers) era can now be created in hours and with a wide array of creative elements.

© MANCHAN/PHOTODISC RED/ GETTY IMAGES

© COLIN ANDERSON/BRAND X PICTURES/JUPITER IMAGES

© COMSTOCK IMAGES/JUPITER IMAGES

© COLIN ANDERSON/BRAND X PICTURES/JUPITER IMAGES

DOCUMENT PRODUCTION SOFTWARE

- Production of documents is expedited by ability to save, retrieve, and edit.
- Quality of messages is improved through spell check, thesaurus, writing analysis software, and print features.

ELECTRONIC PRESENTATIONS

- Multimedia presentations combine visuals that combine text, images, animation, sound, and video.
- Quality royalty-free multimedia content is available from third-party sources.

WEB PUBLISHING TOOLS

- Pages can be created without need for extensive knowledge of hypertext markup language, or HTML.
- Hyperlinks to other documents and websites can be included in the design.

COLLABORATIVE SOFTWARE

- Groups can write collaboratively, with each author marking revisions and inserting document comments for distribution to all coauthors.

(continued on next page)

FIGURE 1-8

Communication Technology Tools (*Continued*)

- Reports preparation is simplified by built-in styles, automatic generation of contents page, indexes, and documentation references.
- Mail merge feature allows for personalization of form documents. Typography and design elements can be used to create persuasive, professional communications.

- Images can be scanned or captured with digital cameras and recorders or generated using specialized software.
- Interactive whiteboards give speakers direct control over computer applications from the board, facilitate interaction by annotating with electronic markers, and record annotated files for electronic distribution for later use.

- Formatted web pages may be viewed using a variety of web browsers.
- **Weblogs** (blogs), or wikis, are websites that are updated on a frequent basis with new information about a particular subject(s). Information can be written by the site owner, gleaned from other websites or other sources, or contributed by users.

- Some collaborative software programs allow multiple authors to work on documents at the same time.
- When placed on an **electronic whiteboard**, drawings or information written on its surface can be displayed simultaneously on team members' computer screens.

TOOLS FOR COMMUNICATING REMOTELY

Technology networks have placed the world at our fingertips. To exploit the possibilities, whole new channels for communication have emerged.

© AP IMAGES/PRNEWSFOTO/ MEZEO SOFTWARE CORPORATION

SMARTPHONES

- A smartphone combines the functionality of a cell phone with an operating system that supports productivity applications. Many specialized applications can be downloaded to meet individual needs.
- Powerful communication applications include email, text, and instant messaging; personal organizers, software to access and edit documents, data storage, web access, camera, music, global positioning services, etc.
- Unlike a cell phone, a smartphone can sync data from the phone to a computer and may include a QWERTY keyboard rather than a numeric keypad to increase efficiency.

© MARK WRAGG/IMAGESTATE/ JUPITER IMAGES

EMAIL & INSTANT MESSAGING

- Email messages and attached files are distributed at the sender's convenience to an electronic mailbox to be read at the receiver's convenience.
- Instant messaging is interactive email that allows a varying number of people to log on to a "chat room" and exchange text dialog that can be seen by all logged-in participants.
- Video chat allows participants to see and hear each other as they chat.

© ANDERSEN ROSS/BRAND X PICTURES/JUPITER IMAGES

ELECTRONIC CONFERENCES

- Teleconferencing and videoconferencing are cost-efficient alternatives to face-to-face meetings for people in different locations.
- Using collaborative software with web camera technology, users can see each other.
- Videoconferencing restores the nonverbal elements lost with telephone, email, and instant messaging.

be expensive in terms of human time spent and charges incurred for online time. Locating information from electronic sources requires that you know the search procedures and methods for constructing an effective search strategy. You will develop these skills when studying the research process in Chapter 9.

Effective use of various communication technologies helps ensure timely, targeted messages and responses and helps to build interpersonal relationships. This responsiveness leads to positive interactions with colleagues and strong customer commitment.

Your Turn 1-5
Electronic Café

INSTANT MESSAGING JOINS THE WORKFORCE

Instant messaging (IM) is not just for the younger set and their social conversations. Many firms are adopting instant messaging as a legitimate and valuable business tool, using it to complement or even replace existing media such as email and voice messages. Some corporate leaders, however, have expressed concerns over productivity and security that might be jeopardized when using IM.

TAKE ACTION:

- Read more about how instant messaging can be both an advantage and a disadvantage at work. Access your companion website www.cengage.com/bcomm/lehman to link to the readings.
- Participate in an online chat. Your instructor will give you directions about how and when to participate in an online chat on the following topic: *Instant messaging can be an effective business tool if . . .*

Legal and Ethical Implications of Technology

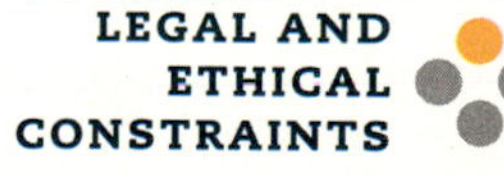

Have you personally been affected by a loss of privacy because of technology? If so, how?

In addition to its many benefits, technology poses some challenges for the business communicator. For instance, technology raises issues of ownership, as in the case of difficulties that arise in protecting the copyright of documents transmitted over the Internet. Technology poses dilemmas over access, that is, who has the right to certain stored information pertaining to an individual or a company.

Technology threatens our individual privacy, our right to be left alone, free from surveillance or interference from other individuals or organizations. Common invasions of privacy caused by technology include

- collecting excessive amounts of information for decision making and maintaining too many files.
- monitoring the exact time employees spend on a specific task and between tasks and the exact number and length of breaks, and supervisors' or coworkers' reading of another employee's electronic mail and computer files.
- integrating computer files containing information collected from more than one agency without permission.[27]

The privacy issue is explored further in the accompanying Strategic Forces feature "Is Anything Private Anymore?"

DIVERSITY CHALLENGES

STRATEGIC FORCES

Is Anything Private Anymore?

We all live in the Internet society, whether or not we spend time online. For most people the convenience of email, cell phones, and voice mail has proved irresistible, but many are experiencing the downside of cyber vulnerability. Expanding technology capabilities make it possible for information to be shared globally with little effort, with or without the information owner's knowledge. Passage of the USA Patriot Act following the attacks of September 11, 2001, initiated new federal safety measures that many feel further endanger constitutional privacy rights.

Despite the passage of federal legislation and additional state laws designed to enhance and strengthen electronic privacy, most Americans feel they have less privacy today than ever. According to a Harris poll, 69 percent of Americans believe they have lost all control over personal information.[28] Various privacy protection services have sprung up in recent years to provide individuals with some security. Workplace privacy has also become an area of concern, as computer monitoring and surveillance capabilities expand. According to a recent employer survey, 43 percent of companies monitor external and internal emails, and 50 percent monitor Internet connections. The data shows that more than one-quarter of employers surveyed have fired employees for misusing email, and almost one-third have fired employees for misusing the Internet.[29]

George Orwell, in his classic novel *1984*, described what many believe to be the ultimate in privacy-shattering totalitarianism as he offered a foreboding look at future society. In his fictitious account ". . . there was of course no way of knowing whether you were being watched at any given moment. . . . It was even conceivable that they watched everybody all the time. . . . You had to live—did live—from habit that became instinct in the assumption that every sound you made was overheard, and, except in darkness, every movement scrutinized."[30] We have now advanced technologically to the point that, if desired, such surveillance is easily possible, even in darkness.

COURTESY OF VERISIGN, INC.

An important aspect of technology is its seductive power: If a technology exists, it must be used. Experts in the area of individual privacy have suggested three key aspects in the ethical management of information and protection of privacy:[31]

- **Relevance**

  An inquiring party should have a clear and valid purpose for delving into an individual's information.

- **Consent**

  An individual should be given the right to withhold consent prior to any query that might violate privacy.

- **Methods**

  An inquiring party should distinguish between reasonable methods and those that are of questionable ethical grounding.

While technology offers tremendous advantages and endless possibilities for enhancing communication, it poses challenges for both individuals and organizations in the maintenance of a proper degree of privacy. Most of us are not ready for the all-seeing eye of Orwell's "Big Brother."

Application

Read a book review of George Orwell's *1984*. In a two-page written summary, cite instances in which Orwell described futuristic technological capabilities that have been realized in recent years. How has society's response to these capabilities differed from the fictional plot?

Team Environment as a Strategic Force Influencing Communication

As firms around the world face problems of decreasing productivity, faltering product quality, and worker dissatisfaction, work teams are seen as a way to help firms remain globally competitive. Decentralized decision making enables teams of people to communicate in a peer-to-peer fashion, rather than following traditional lines of authority, and new technologies give employees the ability to communicate easily and openly with one another and with those outside the firm.

Although worker involvement in the management process has long been the hallmark of Japanese business, many businesses in the U. S. and elsewhere are empowering self-directed work teams to accomplish various assignments.[32] The list of companies using self-directed work teams is diverse, including Hunt-Wesson, the Internal Revenue Service, and the San Diego Zoo, Hewlett-Packard, Southwest Airlines, Toyota, Motorola, General Electric, and Corning.

1 + 1 = 3. The concept of synergy is that the whole is greater than the sum of the parts. It occurs when team members function so well together that their output significantly exceeds what each could have achieved working alone. Synergy is promoted when participants have a common vision, share in leadership, and have mutual trust in one another. As productive discussions occur, creative ideas build upon one another so that outcomes often exceed expectations. Problems and mistakes are seen as opportunities to learn and improve. Open and honest communication among team members who respect one another enables the group to move to higher levels of productivity and enjoy a more satisfying work environment.

Work Team Defined

The terms *team, work team, group, work group, cross-functional team,* and *self-directed team* are often used interchangeably.[33] Whatever the title, a ***team*** is a small number of people with complementary skills who work together for a common purpose. Team members set their own goals, in cooperation with management, and plan how to achieve those goals and how their work is to be accomplished. The central organizing element of a team is that it has a common purpose and measurable goals for which the team can be held accountable, independent of its individual members. Employees in a self-directed work team handle a wide array of functions and work with a minimum of direct supervision.[34] Some major strengths of teams are as follows:[35]

- Teams make workers happier by causing them to feel that they are shaping their own jobs.
- Teams increase efficiency by eliminating layers of managers whose job was once to pass orders downward.
- Teams enable a company to draw on the skills and imagination of a whole workforce. A key element in team success is the concept of ***synergy***, defined as a situation in

which the whole is greater than the sum of the parts. Teams provide a depth of expertise that is unavailable at the individual level, as illustrated in the Ziggy cartoon. Teams open lines of communication that then lead to increased interaction among employees and between employees and management. The result is that teams help companies reach their goals of delivering higher-quality products and services faster and with more cost effectiveness.

Communication Differences in Work Teams

How can team functioning be deterred by emotional and cultural barriers?

In the past most businesses were operated in a hierarchical fashion, with most decisions made at the top and communication following a top-down/bottom-up pattern. Communication patterns are different in successful team environments as compared with traditional organizational structures:

- Trust building is the primary factor that changes the organization's communication patterns.
- Open meetings are an important method for enhancing communication, as they educate employees about the business while building bridges of understanding and trust.
- Shared leadership, which involves more direct and effective communication between management and its internal customers, is common.
- Listening, problem solving, conflict resolution, negotiation, and consensus become important factors in group communication.
- Information flows vertically up to management and down to workers, as well as horizontally among team members, other teams, and supervisors.

Communication is perhaps the single most important aspect of successful teamwork. Open lines of communication increase interaction between employees and management. All affected parties should be kept informed as projects progress.

Maximization of Work Team Effectiveness

Grouping employees into a team structure does not mean that they will automatically function as a team. A group must go through a developmental process to begin to function as a team. Members need training in such areas as problem solving, goal setting, and conflict resolution. Teams must be encouraged to establish the "three R's"—roles, rules, and relationships.[36]

What do you see as the three major challenges to the success of work teams?

The self-directed work team can become the basic organizational building block to best ensure success in dynamic global competition. Skills for successful participation in team environments are somewhat different from those necessary for success in old-style organizations:

- Ability to give and take constructive criticism, listen actively, clearly impart one's views to others, and provide meaningful feedback.
- Skills in breaking down emotional barriers, such as insecurity or condescension.
- Ability to promote team functioning by removing process barriers, such as rigid policies and procedures.

(continues on p. 36)

Communicating Internationally Looms as a CDC Challenge

The Centers for Disease Control (CDC) is charged with the responsibility of protecting the health and safety of people at home and abroad. The agency develops and provides disease control information and distributes it to enhance healthy decisions and behaviors. Communication with other health partners as well as the public is essential to ensuring the health of the people of the United States and elsewhere in the world.

Tom Frieden, director of the CDC, has acknowledged the challenge of balancing the urgent goal of preparing for a bioterrorism emergency with the agency's fundamental mission of preventing and controlling infectious diseases and other health hazards. "Frieden is an expert in preparedness and response to health emergencies, and has been at the forefront of the fight against heart disease, cancer, obesity, and infectious diseases such as tuberculosis and AIDS," says a White House spokesman.[39]

- Visit the CDC website at www.cdc.gov and read the organization's mission statement. What aspects of the CDC's mission focus on communication?
- Locate the following online article that describes efforts of the CDC to educate people about their HIV status:

  HIV prevention in America. (2009, April 16). *Avert.* Available at www.avert.org/hiv-prevention-america.htm

www.cdc.gov

Activities

- Refer to the Communication Process Model presented in Figure 1-1. In a class discussion, identify barriers that the CDC might experience in communicating its AIDS campaign to people in various subcultures.
- The CDC TV ads to get 9- to 13-year-olds off their duffs and into exercise focus on the value of a healthy lifestyle instead of the dangers of obesity. Read the following article that describes the positive advertising communication strategy:

  Many kids are aware of CDC obesity campaign. (2004, March 21). *Medical Letter on the CDC & FDA*, 59. Available at http://www.newsrx.com/newsletters/Medical-Letter-on-the-CDC-and-FDA/2004-03-21/0321200433362DC.html

Consider the information presented in this chapter about intergenerational communication issues. Prepare a three-column chart that shows reasons to avoid obesity that might appeal to persons ages 12, 25, and 50.

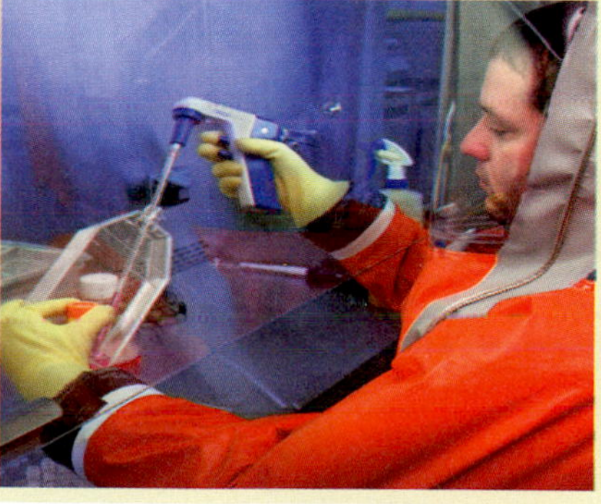
JAMES GATHANY, CENTERS FOR DISEASE CONTROL AND PREVENTION

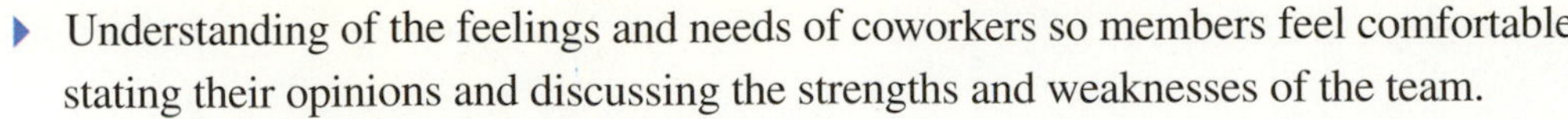

- Understanding of the feelings and needs of coworkers so members feel comfortable stating their opinions and discussing the strengths and weaknesses of the team.

- Skills in overcoming cultural barriers, such as stereotyped roles and responsibilities, that can separate workers from management.[37]
- Application of leadership skills that apply to a dynamic group setting and lead to team success. In dynamic team leadership, referred to as *distributed leadership*, the role of leader may alternate among members, and more than one leadership style may be active at any given time.[38]

To improve group communication, time needs to be set aside to assess the quality of interaction. Questions to pose about the group process might include the following:

- What are our common goals?
- What roles are members playing? For instance, is one person dominating while others contribute little or nothing?
- Is the group dealing with conflict in a positive way?
- What in the group process is going well?
- What about the group process could be improved?

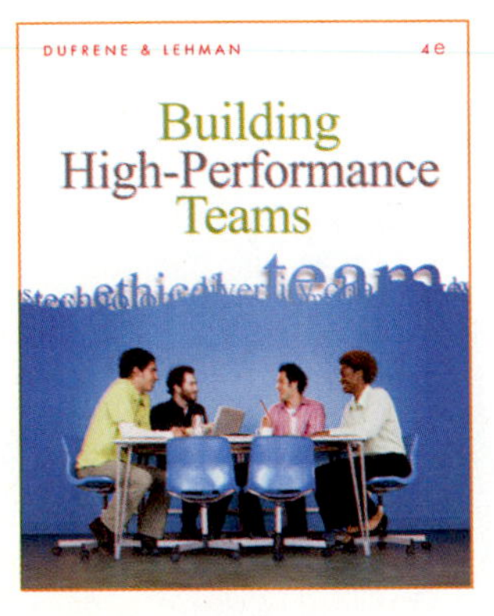

Gender, cultural, and age differences among members of a team can present barriers to team communication. Knowing what behaviors may limit the group process is imperative to maximizing results. Team members may need awareness training to assist in recognizing behaviors that may hinder team performance and in overcoming barriers that may limit the effectiveness of their communication. You can explore the team model versus reward for individual effort by completing the Holistic Assessment at the end of this chapter. *Building High-Performance Teams,* a handbook that accompanies this text, will guide you through the stages of team development and various collaborative processes as you pursue a team-based class project.

Summary

1. Define communication and describe the main purposes for communication in business.

Communication is the process of exchanging information and meaning between or among individuals through a common system of symbols, signs, and behavior. Managers spend most of their time in communication activities.

2. Explain the communication process model and the ultimate objective of the communication process.

People engaged in communication encode and decode messages while simultaneously serving as both senders and receivers. In the communication process, feedback helps people resolve possible misunderstandings and thus improve communication effectiveness. Feedback and the opportunity to observe nonverbal signs are always present in face-to-face communication, the most complete of the three communication levels.

3. Discuss how information flows within an organization (formally and informally; downward, upward, and horizontally; and through various levels).

Both formal and informal communication systems exist in every organization; the formal system exists to accomplish tasks, and the informal system serves a personal maintenance purpose that results in people feeling better about themselves and others. Communication flows upward, downward, and horizontally or laterally. These flows often defy formal graphic description, yet each is a necessary part of the overall communication activity of the organization. Communication takes place at five levels: intrapersonal (communication within one person), interpersonal (communication between two people), group (communication among more than two people), organizational (communication among combinations of groups), and public (communication from one entity to the greater public).

4. Explain how legal and ethical constraints, diversity challenges, changing technology, and team environment act as strategic forces that influence the process of business communication.

Communication occurs within an environment constrained by legal and ethical requirements, diversity challenges, changing technology, and team environment requirements.

- International, federal, state, and local laws impose legal boundaries for business activity, and ethical boundaries are determined by personal analysis that can be assisted by application of various frameworks for decision making.
- Communication is critically impacted by diversity in nationality, culture, age, gender, and other factors that offer tremendous opportunities to maximize talent, ideas, and productivity but pose significant challenges in interpretation of time, personal space requirements, body language, and language translation.
- Significant strides have occurred in the development of tools for data collection and analysis, creation of messages that are clearer and more effective, and quick and easy communication with audiences in remote locations. The use of technology, however, poses legal and ethical concerns in regard to ownership, access, and privacy.
- Team environment challenges arise because communication in teams differs from communication in traditional organizational structures. The result of effective teams is better decisions, more creative solutions to problems, and higher worker morale.

Chapter Review

1. What are the three purposes for which people communicate? What percentage of a manager's time is spent communicating? Give examples of the types of communication managers use. (Obj. 1)
2. Describe the five stages in the communication process using the following terms: (a) sender, (b) encode, (c) channel, (d) receiver, (e) decode, (f) feedback, and (g) interferences or barriers. (Obj. 2)
3. What is the difference between intrapersonal and interpersonal communication? (Obj. 3)
4. How is the formal flow of communication different from the informal flow of communication? (Obj. 3)
5. What are some common causes of unethical behavior in the workplace? (Obj. 4)
6. Describe several intercultural communication barriers and how they might be overcome. (Obj. 4)
7. Describe several ways that communication technology can assist individuals and organizations. (Obj. 4)
8. What legal and ethical concerns are raised over the use of technology? (Obj. 4)
9. How does communication in work teams differ from that of traditional organizations? (Obj. 4)
10. Why has communication been identified as perhaps the single most important aspect of teamwork? (Obj. 4)

Digging Deeper

1. What aspect of cultural diversity do you feel will impact you most in your career: international, intercultural, intergenerational, or gender? Explain your answer, including how you plan to deal with the challenge.
2. Lack of Internet access is causing some nations to be classified as information "have nots." What international communication problems could result?
3. Considering the four strategic forces discussed, how is business communication today different from that of 30 years ago? In what ways is it easier? In what ways is it more difficult?

Assessment

To check your understanding of the chapter, take the available online quizzes as directed by your instructor.

Activities

1. Shadowing a Manager's Communication Activities (Obj. 1)

Shadow a business manager for a day. Keep a log of his/her communication activities for the time period you are observing. Divide the communication activities into the following categories: (1) attending meetings, (2) presenting information to groups, (3) explaining procedures and work assignments, (4) coordinating the work of various employees and departments, (5) evaluating and counseling employees, (6) promoting the company's products/services and image, and (7) other activities. Calculate the percentage of time spent in each activity. Be prepared to share your results with the class.

2. Clocking Your Own Communication Activities (Obj. 1)

Prepare a record of your listening, speaking, reading, and writing activities and time spent in each during the hours of 8 a.m. to 5 p.m. for the next two days. You should attempt to record the time spent doing each activity for each one-hour time block in such a way that you obtain a total time for each activity. Be prepared to share your distribution with the class.

3. Communication Barriers (Obj. 2)

In groups of three, develop a list of 10 to 12 annoying habits of yours or of others that create barriers (verbal and nonverbal) to effective communication. Classify each according to the portion of the communication process it affects. For each, give at least one suggestion for improvement. Access a downloadable version of this activity from your companion website www.cengage.com/bcomm/lehman.

4. Organizational Communication Flows (Obj. 3)

Draw an organizational chart to depict the formal system of communication within an organization with which you are familiar. How is the informal system different from the organization chart? How are the five levels of communication achieved in the organization? Be prepared to discuss these points in class.

5. Identifying Ethical Dilemmas (Obj. 4)

Using an online index, locate a current newspaper or magazine article that describes an illegal or unethical act by a business organization or its employee(s). Choose an incident as closely related as possible to your intended profession. Be prepared to share details of the incident in an informal presentation to the class.

6. Diversity Challenges as a Strategic Force (Obj. 4)

Conduct an online search to locate examples of intercultural communication mistakes made by U.S. companies doing business in another country. How can an organization improve its diversity awareness to avoid such problems? Be prepared to share your ideas with the class.

7. Classroom Diversity Initiative (Obj. 4)

In your class, locate other students to form a "diverse" group; your diversity may include age (more than five years difference), gender, race, culture, geographic origin, etc. Discuss your areas of diversity; then identify three things the group members all have in common, excluding your school experience. Share your group experiences with the class.

8. Changing Technology as a Strategic Force (Objs. 2, 4)

Indicate which of the following communication mediums would be most appropriate for sending each of the following messages: email, fax, phone, or face-to-face communication. Justify your answers.

a. Seeking advice from a peer regarding a challenging task.
b. Notifying employees of dates and registration procedures for the annual sales meeting.
c. Informing employees that a decline in product demand will require a two-week plant shutdown.
d. Responding to a court subpoena, a medical clinic must submit electronic copies of a client's personal and medical records to a lawyer's office in an adjacent state.
e. Alerting a customer that an unexpected failure of production equipment will delay delivery of an order.
f. Exchanging workbook data files among employees collaborating on an annual budget.

Applications

READ | THINK | WRITE | SPEAK | COLLABORATE

1. Communication Challenges in the Future Workplace (Objs. 1–4)

Locate the following article about predicted communication trends:

Communication technology in the future. (2009). *Technology Awards*. Available at http://www.technologyawards.org/future_technology/Communication_Technology_in_the_Future.html

In small groups, discuss the following:

a. What communication trends are predicted in the workplace? Are any of these surprising? Why?
b. Which trends are likely to impact your chosen career field most significantly? In what ways?
c. How do the predicted trends relate to the four strategic forces presented in this chapter?

Select one of the communication means discussed in the article and prepare a brief presentation to be given to the class about trends in that aspect of communication.

2. Shifting Workplace Demographics (Obj. 4)

Locate the following article about changes in workplace demographics:

Demographic change and local government: Workplace issues. (2008, April 4). Municipal Research and Services Center of Washington. Available at www.mrsc.org/Subjects/Governance/demogWork.aspx

In an online discussion as directed by your instructor, post a message that describes what you perceive to be the three most important trends in workforce demographics and how workplace communication will be impacted.

READ | THINK | WRITE | SPEAK | COLLABORATE

3. Analyzing an Ethical Dilemma (Obj. 4)

Ethical dilemmas in a workplace situation are (subject is Ethical dilemmas) often difficult to identify. Locate the following article that poses such an ethical dilemma for your consideration:

Dubinsky, J. E. (2002, October). When an employee question presents an ethical dilemma. *Payroll Manager's Report, 1,* 12–15. Available from Business Source Complete database.

After reading the article, refer to your companion website www.cengage.com/bcomm/lehman for information on frameworks for reaching ethical decisions. Respond to the following questions in a written summary.

a. Who are the stakeholders in the case? What does each stand to gain or lose, depending on your decision?
b. How does the situation described in the case relate to the four-dimension model shown in Figure 1-7?
c. What factors might influence your decision as the manager in the case?
d. How would *you* respond to the employee in the case? Why?

4. Workplace Internet Use (Obj. 4)

While an increasing number of employees enjoy checking out their social networking site while at work, many employers have banned the practice and even blocked access to the sites. Locate the following articles that address this issue:

Anderberg, K. (2008, November 1). Block MySpace? *Communication News*, p. 4. Available from Communication & Mass Media Complete database.

Humphries, S. (2009, January 10). Grapevine goes hi-tech. *The Courier Mail* (Australia), p. 4. Available from LexisNexis Academic database.

After reading the articles, prepare a visual that illustrates the advantages and disadvantages associated with employees accessing social network and entertainment sites while on the job. Share your visual with your class.

READ | THINK | WRITE | SPEAK | COLLABORATE

5. Writing About Your Team Orientation (Obj. 4)

Effective teamwork is important to many career paths. Access the following link and learn more about how you can create a better team; then take the team player quiz to assess your potential: www.quintcareers.com/team_player_quiz.html

Write a brief paper about your team orientation and how being a team player may affect your career success.

6. Exploring Use of Teams in the Workplace (Obj. 4)

Using the Internet, locate an article that describes how a company or organization is using teams in its operation. Write a one-page abstract of the article.

READ | THINK | WRITE | SPEAK | COLLABORATE

7. Understanding Diversity Issues (Obj. 4)

Read the discussion of "Culture and Communication" at your companion website www.cengage.com/bcomm/lehman. In groups of three, interview an international student at your institution and generate a list of English words that have no equivalents in his or her language. Learn about nonverbal communication that may differ from that used in American culture. Share your findings in a short presentation to the class.

READ | THINK | WRITE | SPEAK | COLLABORATE

8. So Many Ways to Fail (Objs. 1, 2)

Locate the following article about communication failures:

Olsztynski, J. (2006). Failures to communicate: Why they happened; how to make sure they don't. *National Driller, 20(2),* 14–16. Available from Business Source Complete database.

In a small group, summarize briefly the five reasons for communication failures in the workplace described in this article and suggestions for correcting them. Discuss experiences where "communication failure" was blamed for problems that occurred in your work, academic, or personal interactions. From your discussions, generate three to five additional ways communication can fail with suggestions for correcting them. Present to the class in a short presentation.

9. Technology's Impact on Communication (Obj. 4)

In pairs, read and discuss an article from a current magazine or journal about how technology is impacting communication. Send your instructor a brief email message discussing the major theme of the article. Include a complete bibliographic entry so the instructor can locate the article (refer to Appendix B for examples of formatted references).

CASES

© GIL FORD PHOTOGRAPHY

1. Ethics Put to the Test

(Obj. 4)

How brave are you? Are you brave enough to stand up for what you know is right even when what is right is not what is popular? Cynthia Cooper never intended to go public about the drama that resulted in the collapse of a hometown company she loved. As vice president of internal audit at WorldCom in 2002, her curiosity changed to discomfort and then to suspicion based on accounting entries she and her team identified and the curious responses given by financial executives. No one wanted to believe the CFO was perpetuating a multi-billion-dollar fraud.

Cooper and her team of auditors worked together, at night and in secret, to investigate and unearth $3.8 billion in fraud at WorldCom. At the time, this was the largest incident of accounting fraud in U.S. history. Several company officers received prison sentences; and the company, once the United States' second-largest long distance phone company, went through bankruptcy and was eventually sold to Verizon in 2006. On a broader scale, Cooper's actions are also credited as a catalyst for passage of Section 404, an addition to the Sarbanes-Oxley Act that addresses assessment of internal controls.

Cooper was named one of three "People of the Year" by *Time* magazine in 2002. Speaking about the WorldCom scandal and other related cases, Cooper says, "Frauds typically start small and then they begin to grow. People rationalize their decisions." When asked how she found the fortitude to stand up to company executives, Cooper said she had to dig down and find courage, which isn't always easy. She remembered the deeply ingrained advice of her mother: "Don't ever allow yourself to be intimidated." Cooper's book about her experiences at WorldCom, *Extraordinary Circumstances: The Journey of a Corporate Whistleblower,* was published in 2008. Profits from the book were given to universities for ethics education.

Required: As directed by your instructor, read the story of Cynthia Cooper, WorldCom whistleblower:

Cooper, C. (2008). *Extraordinary circumstances: The journey of a corporate whistleblower.* Hoboken, NJ: John Wiley & Sons.

Katz, D. M., & Homer, J. (2008, February 1). WorldCom whistle-blower Cynthia Cooper. *CFO Magazine.* Available at www.cfo.com/article.cfm/10590507

Ripley, A. (2008, February 4). Q & A: Whistle-blower Cynthia Cooper. *Time.* Available at www.time.com/time/arts/article/0,8599,1709695,00.html

Write a two-page report summarizing the ethical struggles Cooper faced and her insights related to ethical leadership and responsibility.

© BBC LTD / COURTESY: EVERETT COLLECTION

2. Video Case: The Office: Office Humor and Layoffs: A Bad Combination

In this clip, Manager David succeeds in making Malcolm feel worse about his job security by discounting his concerns and making light of past and future layoffs. David's cheeriness appears in direct contrast to Malcolm's concern and the seriousness of the situation.

Complete the following activities as directed by your instructor after the class has viewed the video:

1. In small groups, discuss how the communication process between David and Malcolm breaks down. Where do the barriers begin and how could these barriers have been avoided?
2. In what type network flow are David and Malcolm participating?
3. How do David's gestures, tone of voice, facial expressions, and use of personal space impact the interaction? How should David change in these areas?
4. As a group, write a script for an alternate way to conduct this conversation with the appropriate characters included. Be prepared to present your script as a short skit to the class.

© DAWN HUDSON/ SHUTTERSTOCK.COM

3. Inside View: Corporate Diversity

Thanks to the General Motors minority dealer development program, Harlem celebrated the grand opening of its first auto dealership in 40 years. The 300,000 square-foot multilevel auto mall, expected to bring nearly 200 new jobs to Harlem, is boosting the local economy. This project is one example of how smart companies recognize the importance of serving the needs of their important minority customer base and the commitment to diverse markets. Diversity within a company also can pay off, as Henry Ford showed many years ago when he pioneered equal pay for black workers.

How can encouraging minority enterprise development benefit a company's diversity efforts? Companies that invest their resources in minorities are supporting a very important segment of the population and may realize tremendous sales potential from diverse markets.

View the video segment online at your companion website www.cengage.com/bcomm/lehman to learn more about this issue.

Reflect:

1. How is diversity good for a company?
2. How can diversity among employees within a company help that company do a better job in the marketplace?
3. What are some possible differences between an effective company diversity program and a company's public relations efforts related to diversity?
4. Why would more than 60 companies write to the Supreme Court supporting the right for a university to consider race as a factor for admission? How do you think businesses will benefit from minority college graduates in the long run?

React:

Locate the following article that contains an interview with former Kodak chairman Daniel A. Carp about the link between diversity in the workplace and universities. He believes, as do other CEOs, that higher education is doing a poor job producing students who are comfortable in the diverse settings of today's business environment:

D. A. Carp. (2006, January 26). A Kodak moment: Former chairman Daniel A. Carp makes the case for collegiate and corporate diversity. *Diverse Issues in Higher Education.* Available from Academic Search Premier database.

Identify ways that companies depend on universities for qualified minority employees. What difficulties occur when the pool of talented graduates is small and homogenous? Give a brief presentation on this article with your recommendations for solving the problem.

4. Can the United States Succeed Without Rewarding Rugged Individuality?

A basic element of the fabric of U.S. entrepreneurship is faith in the ingenuity of the individual person's ability to conceive, develop, and profit from a business endeavor. The frontier spirit and triumph of the individual over looming odds has been a predominant force in the development of the United States. Such individualism has historically been recognized by organizations, with rewards going to those who contribute winning ideas and efforts.

The recent shift in organizational structures toward team design has caused management to reassess reward systems that focus on individual recognition and to consider rewards that are based on team performance. Some fear that removing individual incentive will lead to mediocrity and a reduction in personal effort. They argue that while the team model might work in other cultures, it is inconsistent with the U.S. way of thinking and living. According to Madelyn Hoshstein, president of DYG Inc., a New York firm that researches corporate trends, America is moving away from the model of team building in which everyone is expected to do everything and toward focusing on employees who are the best at what they do. She describes this change as a shift toward social Darwinism and away from egalitarianism, in which everyone has equal economic, political, and social rights.[40]

Team advocates say that teams are here to stay and liken those who deny that reality to the proverbial ostrich with its head in the sand. They stress the need for newly structured incentive plans to reward group effort.

Visit your companion website www.cengage.com/bcomm/lehman to link to web resources related to this topic.

Respond to one or more of the following activities, as directed by your instructor:

1. How would you respond to those with concerns about loss of individual incentive? Argue for or against the increased emphasis on team reward, using either personal examples or examples from business.
2. Structure a reward system that would recognize both individual and team performance. You may use an organization of your choice to illustrate.
3. Select a specific corporation or nation that has implemented the team model. Describe the transition away from a hierarchical structure and the consequences that have resulted from the shift, both positive and negative.

Chapter 2
Focusing on Interpersonal and Group Communication

"Focusing on diversity helps us to better understand and meet the health care needs of the unique communities we serve—while actually becoming part of their cultural fabric."

CEO Angela Braly

Objectives When you have completed Chapter 2, you will be able to:

1. Explain how behavioral theories about human needs, trust and disclosure, and motivation relate to business communication.
2. Describe the role of nonverbal messages in communication.
3. Identify aspects of effective listening.
4. Identify factors affecting group and team communication.
5. Discuss aspects of effective meeting management.

SHOWCASE PART 1

WellPoint Embraces a Service Culture

As the nation's largest health benefits company, WellPoint provides health insurance to nearly 35 million members. One in nine Americans is covered by WellPoint's affiliate companies, operating as Blue Cross and Blue Shield plans in 14 states. As a member of the Fortune 50 and with average earnings increasing 55 percent a year since 2000, the company's 42,000 associates work to deliver consistent, quality service to members.[1]

WellPoint attributes much of its success to a strong commitment to core values that guide strategy and operations. Putting the customer first and conveying that philosophy through the products and services offered is the driving force. Integrity and personal accountability for excellence are emphasized, and associates are encouraged to take ownership for high performance achievement. The motto "one company, one team" reminds employees of the need to collaborate with others to achieve results.[2]

According to the WellPoint website, the company seeks to develop associates who are values-based, focused, achievement driven, and human. An incentive policy pays hospitals more when patients have fewer complications, and an employee bonus system pays associates more when the overall health of the 35 million subscribers improves.[3] While performance metrics provide motivation for peak performance, the company is not merely profit driven. Commitment to community is demonstrated through the WellPoint Foundation, a $30 million fund established to serve the health needs of the uninsured.

In 2008, *DiversityInc* magazine ranked WellPoint among the Top 50 Companies for Diversity. This distinction recognizes the company's ongoing commitment to advancing diversity, such as promotion of a supplier base that includes businesses owned by minorities, women, and disabled veterans. WellPoint also reaches out to diverse audiences, promoting effective communication through its Spanish websites as well as tools for seniors seeking conversations with younger family members about end-of-life care.

According to CEO Angela Braly, "Focusing on diversity helps us to better understand and meet the health care needs of the unique communities we serve—while actually becoming part of their cultural fabric."[4] As evidence of its impressive strides to promote diversity, WellPoint has also been recognized by additional publications, including *Profiles in Diversity Journal*, *Working Mother*, *Black EOE Journal*, *Careers & the disABLED, and Hispanic Network*.[5]

WellPoint was named in 2008 to the top five in the 100 Best Places to Work in Healthcare by *Modern Healthcare* magazine. The list recognizes companies that excel in leadership and planning, culture and communications, job role satisfaction, working environment, relationship with supervisor, training and development, pay and benefits, and overall associate satisfaction. WellPoint also received recognition for two years straight as one of America's Most Admired Companies by *Fortune* magazine.[6]

Understanding employee motivation and focusing on excellence has enabled WellPoint to become a leader in the health care industry. To be effective in the ever-changing environment of business, you will need to have an understanding of human behavior and motivation and its influences on organizational and external communication.

www.wellpoint.com

SEE SHOWCASE, PART 2, ON PAGE 58
FOR SPOTLIGHT COMMUNICATOR ANGELA BRALY, CEO OF WELLPOINT.

Behavioral Theories that Impact Communication

Interpersonal intelligence pertains to the ability to read, empathize, and understand others.[7] People with interpersonal intelligence are good with people and thrive in social interaction. Rather than being a quality that some are born with while others are not, interpersonal intelligence can be improved by broadening your understanding of human behavior and motivation and practicing certain behaviors when in interpersonal situations. Knowledge from the fields of sociology and psychology is helpful to understanding human needs and providing you with valuable insights about how to achieve effective communication in the workplace.

Recognizing Human Needs

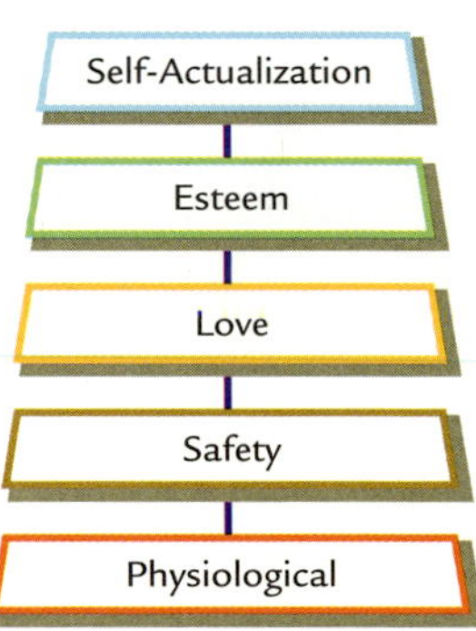

Psychologist Abraham Maslow developed the concept of a hierarchy of needs through which people progress. In our society, most people have reasonably satisfied their two lower-levels of needs: (1) physiological needs (food and basic provision) and (2) their security and safety needs (shelter and protection from the elements and physical danger). Beyond these two basic need levels, people progress to satisfy the three upper levels: (3) social needs for love, acceptance, and belonging; (4) ego or esteem needs to be heard, appreciated, and wanted; and (5) self-actualizing needs, including the need to achieve one's fullest potential through professional, philanthropic, political, educational, and artistic channels.

To which need level would each of the following apply: private office, years of service award, expanded retirement program, and alternative work schedules?

As people satisfy needs at one level, they move on to the next. The levels that have been satisfied still are present, but their importance diminishes. Effective communicators are able to identify and appeal to need levels in various individuals or groups. Advertising is designed to appeal to need levels. Luxury car and dream vacation ads appeal to ego needs, teeth whitening and anti-aging product messages appeal to social needs, and identity theft, health and fitness, and environmentally friendly commercials appeal to security and safety needs. Efforts to help employees satisfy their needs are essential, since a satisfied worker is generally more productive than a dissatisfied one. In communication activities, a sender's message is more likely to appeal to the receiver if the receiver's need is accurately identified.

Stroking

People engage in communication with others in the hope that the outcome may lead to mutual trust, mutual pleasure, and psychological well-being. The communication exchange is a means of sharing information about things, ideas, tasks, and selves.

Each communication interaction, whether casual or formal, provides an emotional **stroke** that may have either a positive or a negative effect on your feelings about yourself and others. Getting a pat on the back from the supervisor, receiving a congratulatory phone call or text message, and being listened to by another person are examples of everyday positive strokes. Negative strokes might include receiving a hurtful comment, being avoided or left out of conversation, and receiving a reprimand from a superior. By paying attention to the importance of strokes, managers can greatly improve communication and people's feelings about their work.

Exploring the Johari Window

Discuss the types of information you (1) share freely, (2) share only with close friends, and (3) keep hidden.

As relationships develop, the people involved continue to learn about each other and themselves, as shown by the Johari Window in Figure 2-1. Area I, the free or open area, represents what we know about ourselves and what others know about us. Area II, the blind area, designates those things others know about us but that we don't know about ourselves; for example, you are the only person who can't see your physical self as it really is. Things we know about ourselves but that others don't know about us occupy the hidden or secret area III. Area IV includes the unknown: things we don't know about ourselves and others don't know about us, such as our ability to handle emergency situations if we've never been faced with them.

Each of the window areas may vary in size according to the degree to which we learn about ourselves and are willing to disclose things about ourselves to others. Reciprocal sharing occurs when people develop *trust* in each other. When a confidant demonstrates that he or she can be trusted, trust is reinforced and leads to an expansion of the open area of the Johari Window. Usually we are willing to tell people about various things that aren't truly personal. But we share personal thoughts, ambitions, and inner feelings only with selected others—those whom we have learned to trust. The relationships existing between supervisor and employee, doctor and patient, and lawyer and client are those of trust, but only in specific areas. In more intimate relationships with significant others, siblings, and parents, deeper, personal feelings are entrusted to each other.

Trust is earned over time through consistent behaviors.

The idea that trust and openness lead to better communication between two people also applies to groups. Managers engaged in **organizational development** (OD) are

FIGURE 2-1

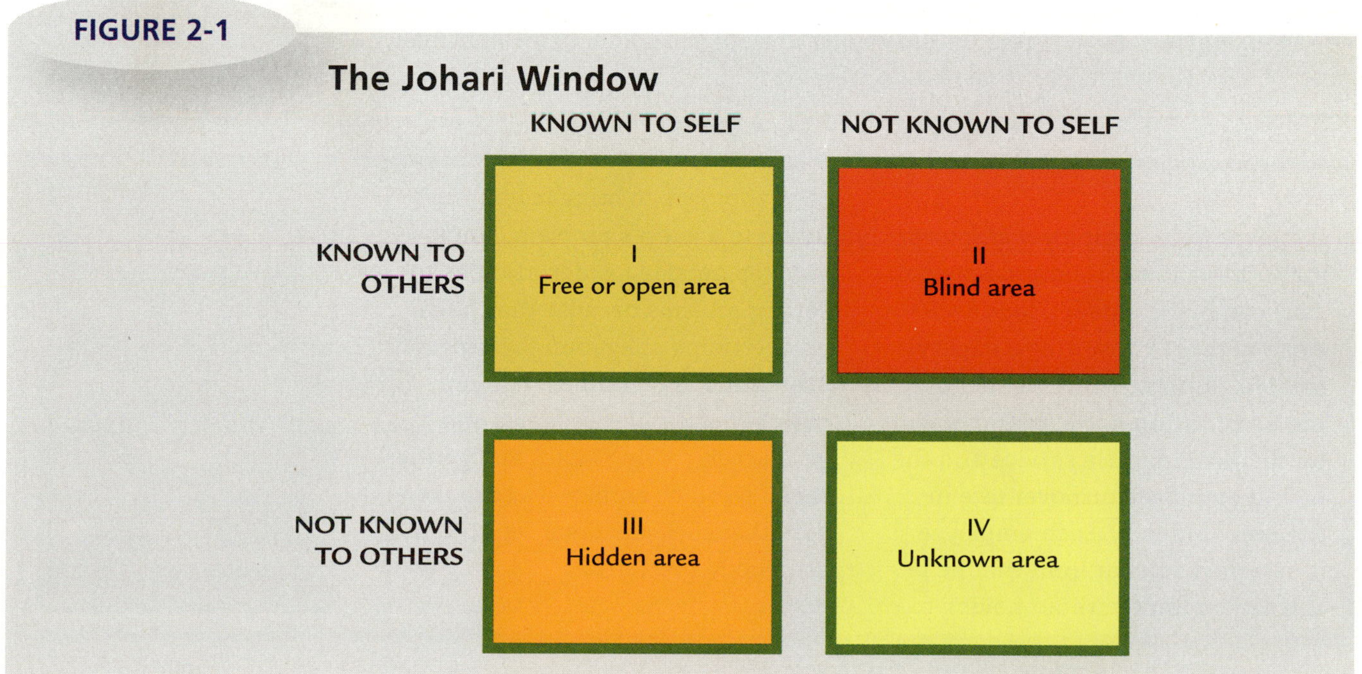

concerned with developing successful organizations by building effective small groups. They believe small group effectiveness evolves mostly from a high level of mutual trust among group members. The aim of OD is to open emotional as well as task-oriented communication. To accomplish this aim, groups often become involved in encounter sessions designed to enlarge the open areas of the Johari Window.[8]

Contrasting Management Styles

Douglas McGregor, a management theorist, attempted to distinguish between the older, traditional view that workers are concerned only about satisfying lower-level needs and the more contemporary view that productivity can be enhanced by assisting workers in satisfying higher-level needs. Under the older view, management exercised strong control, emphasized the job to the exclusion of concern for the individual, and sought to motivate solely through external incentives—a job and a paycheck. McGregor labeled this management style Theory X. Under the contemporary style, Theory Y, management strives to balance control and individual freedom. By treating the individual as a mature person, management lessens the need for external motivation; treated as adults, people will act as adults.

The situational leadership model developed by Paul Hersey and Kenneth Blanchard does not prescribe a single leadership style, but advocates that what is appropriate in each case depends on the follower (subordinate) and the task to be performed. ***Directive behavior*** is characterized by the leader's giving detailed rules and instructions and monitoring closely that they are followed. The leader decides what is to be done and how. In contrast, ***supportive behavior*** is characterized by the leader's listening, communicating, recognizing, and encouraging. Different degrees of directive and supportive behavior can be desirable, given the situation.[10] Combining the ideas of Maslow and McGregor with those of Hersey and Blanchard leads to the conclusion that "the right job for the person" is a better philosophy than "the right person for the job."

The ***Total Quality Management*** movement focuses on creating a more responsible role for the worker in an organization. In a Total Quality Management environment,

"My Pleasure" Reflects Employer Empowerment. Employer empowerment refers to ways nonmanagerial staff can make independent decisions without consulting a supervisor. The popular term originated with the Ritz-Carlton hotel chain known for its incomparable service and the lowest employee turnover rate in the hotel industry. Each employee is assigned a dollar limit that he or she can commit without having to seek approval, to bring instant resolution to a guest's problem. Employees step outside job descriptions to settle problems because they have an overriding obligation to surpass customers' expectations. The company's motto, "We are ladies and gentlemen serving ladies and gentlemen," reminds employees to make sure that each customer feels, "I'm somebody special."[9]

© AP PHOTO/JACQUELINE LARMA, FILES/AP IMAGES

decision-making power is distributed to the people closest to the problem, those who usually have the best information sources and solutions. Each employee, from the president to the custodian, is expected to solve problems, participate in team-building efforts, and expand the scope of his or her role in the organization. The goal of employee empowerment is to build a work environment in which all employees take pride in their work accomplishments and begin motivating themselves from within rather than through traditional extrinsic incentives.[11] Managers of many companies understand that empowering employees to initiate continuous improvements is critical for survival. Only companies producing quality products and services will survive in today's world market.

Your Turn 2-1
You're the Professional

You have just learned that you were selected to fill the position as department manager in a company with which you interviewed. Ms. Blake, the previous manager, was well liked; but productivity in the department was considerably below what your supervisor desires it to be. You plan to call a meeting with your staff on your first day at work. Which of the following will be the theme of your presentation?

TAKE ACTION:

Discuss the merit of each of the following choices, explaining your reasons:

a. I'm not Ms. Blake, so some things will be different around here.

b. We will get along fine if everyone does his/her work well.

c. This is a great department, and together we can make it better.

d. Productivity is a problem that together we must address.

OBJECTIVE 2

Nonverbal Communication

Managers use verbal and nonverbal messages to communicate an idea to a recipient. Verbal means "through the use of words," either written or spoken. Nonverbal means "without the use of words." Although major attention in communication study is given to verbal messages, studies show that nonverbal messages can account for over 90 percent of the total meaning.[12] Nonverbal communication includes *metacommunication* and *kinesic* messages.

Metacommunication

A ***metacommunication*** is a message that, although *not* expressed in words, accompanies a message that *is* expressed in words. For example, "Don't be late for work" communicates caution; yet the sentence may imply (but not express in words) such additional ideas as "You are frequently late, and I'm warning you," or "I doubt your dependability" (metacommunication). "Your solution is perfect" may also convey a metacommunication such as "You are efficient," or "I certainly like your work." Whether you are speaking or writing, you can be confident that those who receive your messages will be sensitive to the messages expressed in words and to the accompanying messages that are present but not expressed in words.

Kinesic Messages

What nonverbal messages might be conveyed by a job applicant? A customer? A salesperson?

People constantly send meaning through kinesic communication, an idea expressed through nonverbal behavior. In other words, receivers gain additional meaning from what they see and hear—the visual and the vocal:

- **Visual**—gestures, winks, smiles, frowns, sighs, attire, grooming, and all kinds of body movements.
- **Vocal**—intonation, projection, and resonance of the voice.

Some examples of kinesic messages and the meanings they may convey follow.

Action	Possible Kinesic Message
A wink or light chuckle follows a statement.	*"Don't believe what I just said."*
A manager is habitually late for staff meetings and with email replies.	*"My time is more important than yours. You can wait for me." Alternately, the action may be ordinary for a non-U.S. born manager.*
A group leader sits at a position other than at the head of the table.	*"I want to demonstrate my equality with other members."*
An employee wears clothing that reveals tattoos, which violates the company's dress code.	*"Rules are for other people; I can do what I want." Alternately, "I do not understand the expectations."*
A job applicant submits a résumé containing numerous errors.	*"My language skills are deficient." Alternately, "I didn't care to do my best."*

Understanding Nonverbal Messages

What nonverbal messages did you convey today through your attire, posture, gestures, etc.?

Metacommunications and kinesic messages have characteristics that all communicators should take into account.

- **Nonverbal messages cannot be avoided.** Both written and spoken words convey ideas in addition to the ideas contained in the words used. All actions—and even the lack of action—have meaning to those who observe them.
- **Nonverbal messages may have different meanings for different people.** If a team member smiles after making a statement, one member may conclude that the

Proper Attire for a Professional Image. Does the way you dress convey an image of professionalism to customers, employers, and colleagues? Of course, what is considered proper attire varies greatly from one organization to another. Casual, business casual, or business professional may be in order. Observe the clothing of those in positions you would like to hold; then select good quality items you can add to as your budget permits. No matter what type of clothing you choose, make sure it is not worn, stained, or wrinkled. Keep in mind when you dress for business you are not just dressing for yourself. You convey messages about your organization at all times.[13]

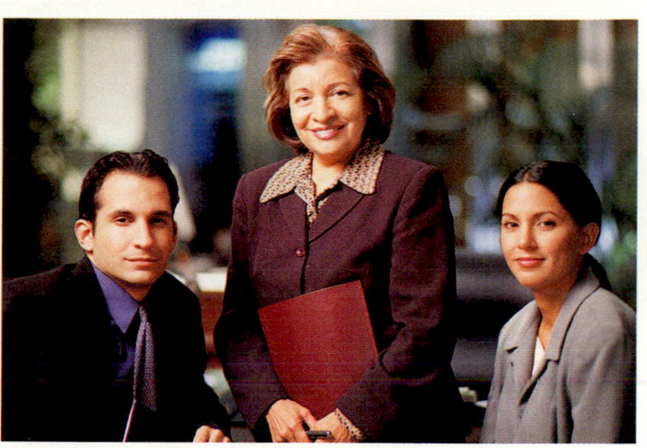

speaker was trying to be funny; another may conclude that the speaker was pleased about having made such a great contribution; another may see the smile as indicating friendliness.

DIVERSITY CHALLENGES

- **Nonverbal messages vary between and within cultures.** Not only do nonverbal messages have different meanings from culture to culture, but men and women from the same culture typically exhibit different body language. As a rule, U.S. men make less body contact with other men than do women with women. Acceptable male body language might include a handshake or a pat on the back, while women are afforded more flexibility in making body contact with each other. The accompanying Strategic Forces feature "Cultural Differences in Nonverbal Messages" provides more information on cultural differences in nonverbal communication.
- **Nonverbal messages may be intentional or unintentional.** "You are right about that" may be intended to mean "I agree with you" or "You are right on *this* issue, but you have been wrong on all others discussed."

Have you experienced a situation in which the verbal and nonverbal message did not agree? Describe it. Which message did you believe? Why?

- **Nonverbal messages can contradict the accompanying verbal message, and affect whether your message is understood or believed.** The adage "Actions speak louder than words" reveals much about how people perceive messages. Picture a person who says, "I'm happy to be here," but looks at the floor, talks in a weak and halting voice, and clasps his hands timidly in front of his body. Because his verbal and nonverbal messages are contradictory, his audience may not trust his words. Similarly, consider the negative effect of a sloppy personal appearance by a job candidate.
- **Nonverbal messages may receive more attention than verbal messages.** If a supervisor repeatedly glances at his cell phone for text messages or rhythmically taps a pen while making a statement, the words may not register in the employee's mind. An error in basic grammar may receive more attention than the idea that is being transmitted.

DIVERSITY CHALLENGES

STRATEGIC FORCES

Cultural Differences in Nonverbal Messages

International communication poses particular challenges for nonverbal communication. At the opening session of a parliament session in Bangladesh, legislators reacted with fury to a gesture by U.S. Shipping Minister A. S. M. Abdur Rob. "This is a dishonor not only to parliament but to the nation," said Dr. A. Q. M. Badruddoza Chowdhury, the Bangladesh Nationalist Party's deputy leader.

What Rob had done to provoke such anger was to give the thumbs up sign. In the United States, the gesture means "good going!" But in Bangladesh, it is a taunt; in other Islamic countries, it is an obscenity. This example illustrates the array of cross-cultural gaffes a naive U.S. businessperson could make on an overseas assignment.[14]

Becoming familiar with subtle and not-so-subtle differences in nonverbal communication in other cultures can avoid the barriers to effective communication. Some cultural examples of nonverbal behavior include the following:

- Many Japanese greet with a respectful bow rather than the western handshake. Middle Easterners may exchange kisses on the cheek when greeting.
- While North Americans believe that eye contact is an indicator of interest and trust, Japanese believe that lowering the eyes is a sign of respect. Asian females and many African Americans listen without direct eye contact. Extended facial gazing typified by the French and Brazilians is often seen by Americans as aggressive.
- Time-conscious North American can expect to be kept waiting for appointments in Central America, the Middle East, and other countries where the sentiment that "time is money" is not accepted.
- North Americans, who often slap each other on the back or put an arm around the other as a sign of friendship, receive disapproval from the Japanese, who avoid physical contact. Japanese shopkeepers place change on a plastic plate to avoid physical contact with customers.[15]

© JEREMY WOODHOUSE/BLEND IMAGES/ JUPITERIMAGES

Numerous research studies point out the importance of nonverbal communication in international negotiations. A study of negotiation styles in 17 cultures revealed that Japanese negotiators behaved least aggressively, typically using a polite conversation style with infrequent use of "no" and "you" as well as more silent periods. The style of French negotiators was most aggressive, including more threats and warnings, as well as interruptions, facial gazing, and frequent use of "no" and "you." Brazilians were similarly aggressive, with more physical touching of their negotiating partners. Germans, the British, and Americans fell somewhat in the middle.[16]

The negotiation process is the sum of factors including the number of parties, existence of external audiences, issues to be discussed, deadlines, laws, ethics, customs, and physical setting. Emphasis on nonverbal cues is often lost on North American negotiators who rely on the inherent advantage provided by their mastery of global languages. Cultural awareness includes both education and sensitivity concerning behaviors, expectations, and interpretations of persons with different backgrounds and experiences.[17]

Application

Interview a person from another culture or subculture to determine how his or her expectations for nonverbal behavior differ from your own. Chart three to five particular nonverbal actions and their meanings in each of the cultures.

- **Nonverbal messages provide clues about the sender's background and motives.** For example, excessive use of big words may suggest that a person reads widely or has an above-average education; it may also suggest a need for social recognition or insecurity about social background.
- **Nonverbal messages are influenced by the circumstances surrounding the communication.** Assume that two men, Ganesh and Jacob, are friends at work. When they are together on the job, Ganesh sometimes puts his hand on Jacob's shoulder. To Jacob, the act may mean nothing more than "We are close friends." But suppose Ganesh is a member of a committee that subsequently denies a promotion for Jacob. Afterward, the same act could mean "We are still friends," but it could also cause resentment. Because of the circumstances, the same act could now mean something like "Watch the hand that pats; it can also stab."
- **Nonverbal messages may be beneficial or harmful.** Words or actions can be accompanied by nonverbal messages that help or hurt the sender's purpose. Metacommunications and kinesic communications can convey something like "I am efficient in my business and considerate of others," or they can convey the opposite. They cannot be eliminated, but you can make them work for you instead of against you.

OBJECTIVE 3

Listening as a Communication Skill

Despite the fact that many professionals believe incorrectly that business communication is about presentation and not interaction, most managers spend a major part of their day listening and speaking with others. Listening to supervisors, employees, customers, and colleagues commonly consumes more of business employees' time than reading, writing, and speaking combined. Listening is an interpersonal skill as critical as the skill of speaking. Effective listening is essential at Dell Computers, a company that has built its reputation on providing customers with custom computers based on individual needs. CEO Brad Anderson of Best Buy explains that effective listening is central to the work culture of his young retail employees who have grown up in a digital age to expect a two-way conversation in a peer-to-peer fashion rather than a one-way lecture. Anderson emphasizes that being perceived as a poor listener would "shut him down as a CEO." [18]

DIVERSITY CHALLENGES

Effective listening habits pay off in several ways:

How will improved listening skills benefit you in your career advancement?

- Good listeners are liked by others because they satisfy the basic human needs of being heard and being wanted.
- People who listen well are able to separate fact from fiction, cope effectively with false persuasion, and avoid having others use them for personal gain.
- Effective listening leads to sensitivity and tolerance toward key individuals who are critical to the organization's success, such as employees, customers, and suppliers.
- Effective listeners are engaged and constantly learning—gaining knowledge and skills that lead to increased creativity, job performance, advancement, and satisfaction.
- Job satisfaction increases when people know what is going on, when they are heard, and when they participate in the mutual trust that develops from good communication.

Listening depends on your abilities to receive and decode both verbal and nonverbal messages. The best-devised messages and sophisticated communication systems will not work unless people on the receiving end of spoken messages actually listen. Senders of spoken messages must assume their receivers can and will listen, just as senders of written messages must assume their receivers can and will read.

Your Turn 2-2
Miscue

A nurse reported a severe reaction suffered by a patient due to a listening error. The patient's physician had given the nurse a verbal order via cell phone to "discontinue the I.V. for now." However, what the nurse heard was "just continue the I.V. for now." She even repeated the orders back to the doctor because the connection wasn't crystal clear; she then documented what she had heard in the patient's chart. The patient developed negative symptoms before the physician was able to see her and review her chart.[19]

TAKE ACTION:

Discuss the following issues with others in your class:

- How could this communication error have been prevented?
- If the patient sued for injury, who would be at fault?
- What are the implications of using cell phones for critical conversations?

Listening for a Specific Purpose

Individuals satisfy a variety of purposes through listening: (1) interacting socially, (2) receiving information, (3) solving problems, and (4) sharing feelings with others. Each activity may call for a different style of listening or for a combination of styles.

- **Casual listening.** Listening for pleasure, recreation, amusement, and relaxation is casual listening. Some people listen to music all day long to relax the brain and mask unwanted sounds during daily routines, work periods, and daily commutes. Aspects of casual listening are as follows:
  - It provides relaxing breaks from more serious tasks and supports our emotional health.
  - It illustrates that people are selective listeners. You listen to what you want to hear. In a crowded room in which everyone seems to be talking, you can block out all the noise and engage in the conversation you are having with someone.
  - It doesn't require much emotional or physical effort.

How have your class notes changed during your college career?

- **Listening for information.** Listening for information involves the search for data or material. In a lecture class, for example, the instructor usually has a strategy for guiding the class to desired goals. The instructor will probably stress several major points and use supporting evidence to prove or to reinforce them. When engaged in this type of listening, you could become so focused on recording every detail that you take copious notes with no organization. When listening for information:
  - Use an outlining process to help you capture main ideas and supporting subpoints in a logical way.

- ▷ Watch the speaker as well as listen to him or her, since most speakers exhibit a set of mannerisms composed of gestures and vocal inflections to indicate the degree of importance or seriousness that they attach to portions of their presentation.
- ▷ Separate fact from fiction, comedy from seriousness, and truth from untruth.

Intensive listening. When you listen to obtain information, solve problems, or persuade or dissuade (as in arguments), you are engaged in intensive listening. Intensive listening involves greater use of your analytical ability to proceed through problem-solving steps. When listening intensively:

- ▷ Gain an understanding of the problem, recognize whatever limitations are involved, and know the implications of possible solutions.
- ▷ Become a good summarizer.
- ▷ Trace the development of the discussion and then move from there to your own analysis.
- ▷ Feel free to "tailgate" on the ideas of others; creative ideas are generated in an open discussion.

How would you score yourself as an empathetic listener? How can you improve? How will empathetic listening be important in your career?

Empathetic listening. ***Empathy*** occurs when a person attempts to share another's feelings or emotions. Counselors attempt to use empathetic listening in dealing with their clients, and good friends listen empathetically to each other. Empathy is a valuable trait developed by people skilled in interpersonal relations. When you take the time to listen to another, the courtesy is usually returned. When listening empathetically:

- ▷ Avoid preoccupation with your own problems. Talking too much and giving strong nonverbal signals of disinterest destroy others' desire to talk.
- ▷ Remember that total empathy can never be achieved simply because no two people are exactly alike. The more similar our experiences, however, the better the opportunity to put ourselves in the other person's shoes. Listening with empathy involves some genuine tact along with other good listening habits.
- ▷ Whenever possible, listen in a one-to-one situation. Close friends who trust each other tend to engage in self-disclosure easily. Empathetic listening is enhanced when the participants exhibit trust and friendship.

Effective listening skills are essential to career success.

Can empathy be carried too far? Explain.

Many people in positions of authority have developed excellent listening skills that apply to gaining information and to problem solving. However, an equal number of people have failed to develop good listening practices that work effectively in listening for feelings. An "open door" policy does not necessarily indicate an "open ear." A supervisor's poor listening habits may interfere with problem solving and reduce employee morale.

Frequently you may have to combine listening intensively and listening for feelings. Performance appraisal interviews, disciplinary conferences, and other sensitive discussions between supervisors and employees require listening intensively for accurate understanding of the message and listening empathetically for feelings, preconceived points of view, and background. The interviewing process also may combine the two types of listening. Job interviewers must try to determine how someone's personality, as well as skill and knowledge, will affect job performance. Whatever the situation, good listeners stay focused on their intended purpose.

Give other examples of situations in which combined listening is required.

Bad Listening Habits

Physicians must first diagnose the nature of a person's medical problems before prescribing treatment. In the same way, you can't improve your listening unless you understand some of the nonphysical ailments of your own listening. Most of us have developed bad listening habits in one or more of the following areas:

- **Faking attention.** Have you ever left a class lecture and later realized that you had no idea what went on? Have you ever been introduced to someone only to realize 30 seconds later that you missed the name? If you had to answer "yes" to these questions, join the huge club of "fakers of attention." Isn't it amazing that we can look directly at a person, nod, smile, and pretend to be listening?

What is your own worst listening habit? What can you do to eliminate it?

- **Allowing disruptions.** Listening properly requires both physical and emotional effort. As a result, we welcome disruptions of almost any sort when we are engaged in somewhat difficult listening. The next time someone enters your classroom or meeting room, notice how almost everyone in the room turns away from the speaker and the topic to observe the latecomer.
- **Overlistening.** Overlistening occurs when listeners attempt to record in writing or in memory so many details that they miss the speaker's major points. Overlisteners "can't see the forest for the trees."

- **Stereotyping.** Most people use their prejudices and perceptions of others as a basis for developing stereotypes. As a result, we make spontaneous judgments about others based on their appearances, mannerisms, dress, speech delivery, and whatever other criteria play a role in our judgments. If a speaker doesn't meet our standards in any of these areas, we simply turn off our listening and assume the speaker can't have much to say.
- **Dismissing subjects as uninteresting.** People tend to use "uninteresting" as a rationale for not listening. Unfortunately, the decision is usually made before the topic is ever introduced. A good way to lose an instructor's respect when you have to miss class is to ask, "Are we going to do anything important in class today?"
- **Failing to observe nonverbal aids.** Good listening requires the use of eyes as well as ears. To listen effectively, you must observe the speaker. Facial expressions and

body motions always accompany speech and contribute much to messages. If you do not watch the speaker, you may miss the meaning.

Defend or reject this statement, giving reasons: The listener has an ethical responsibility to give full, unbiased attention to the speaker's verbal and nonverbal message.

In addition to recognizing bad listening habits and the variety of barriers to effective listening, you must recognize that listening isn't easy. Many bad listening habits develop simply because the speed of spoken messages is far slower than our ability to receive and process them. Normal speaking speeds are between 100 and 150 words a minute. The human ear can actually distinguish words in speech in excess of 500 words a minute, and many people read at speeds well beyond 500 words a minute. Finally, our minds process thoughts at thousands of words a minute.

Because individuals can't speak fast enough to challenge our ability to listen, listeners have a responsibility to make spoken communication effective. Good listening typically requires considerable mental and emotional effort.

Suggestions for Effective Listening

Because feedback and nonverbal signs are available, you can enhance the effectiveness of your face-to-face listening by following these suggestions:

- **Minimize environmental and mental distractions.** Take time to listen. Move to a quiet area where you are not distracted by noise or other conversation. Avoid becoming so preoccupied with thoughts of other projects or what you will say next that you fail to listen.

Analyze your listener response to your instructor. How can it be maximized?

- **Get in touch with the speaker.** Maintain an open mind while attempting to understand the speaker's background, prejudices, and points of view. Listen for emotionally charged words and watch for body language, gestures, facial expressions, and eye movements as clues to the speaker's underlying feelings.
- **Use your knowledge of speakers to your advantage.** Through experience, you will begin to recognize the unique speaking and organizing traits of particular individuals. Some people seem to run on and on with details before making the point. With this speaker, you will learn to anticipate the major point but not pay much attention to details. Other speakers give conclusions first and perhaps omit support for them. In this case, you will learn to ask questions to obtain further information.
- **Let the speaker know you are actively involved.** Show genuine interest by remaining physically and mentally involved; for example, avoid daydreaming, yawning, frequently breaking eye contact, looking at your cell phone or papers on your desk, whispering, or allowing numerous interruptions (phone calls, etc.). Encourage the speaker to continue by providing appropriate feedback either orally or nonverbally.
- **Do not interrupt the speaker.** Try to understand the speaker's full meaning, and wait patiently for an indication that you should enter the conversation.
- **Ask reflective questions that assess understanding.** Simply restate in your own words what you think the other person has said. This paraphrasing will reinforce what you have heard and allow the speaker to correct any misunderstanding or add clarification.

- **Use probing prompts to direct the speaker.** Use probing statements or questions to help the speaker define the issue more concretely and specifically.
- **Use lag time wisely.** Listening carefully should be your primary focus; however, you can think ahead at times as well. Thinking ahead can help you develop a sense of the speaker's logic, anticipate future points, and evaluate the validity of the speaker's ideas. Making written or mental notes allows you to provide useful feedback when the opportunity arises. If you cannot take notes during the conversation, record important points as soon as possible so you can summarize the speaker's key points.

You can learn more about developing effective listening skills by completing the Holistic Assessment at the end of this chapter.

Your Turn 2-3
Assessment

Good listening is not an inherited quality. It requires a great deal of effort and focus and a willingness to recognize weaknesses and work to overcome them. Complete the listening questionnaire located at www.queendom.com/tests/access_page/index.htm?idRegTest=703 or go to your companion website (www.cengage.com/bcomm/lehman) for updated links.

TAKE ACTION:

Send your instructor an email that summarizes your thoughts on the following:

- *How did you rate as a listener?*
- *What areas did you target for improvement in your listening skills?*

Group Communication

Although much of your spoken communication in business will occur in one-to-one relationships, another frequent spoken communication activity will likely occur when you participate in groups, primarily groups within the organizational work environment. The work of groups, committees, and teams has become crucial in most organizations.

Increasing Focus on Groups

Developments among U.S. businesses in recent years have shifted attention away from the employment of traditional organizational subunits as the only mechanisms for achieving organizational goals and toward the increased use of groups.

How does downsizing affect a company's organizational charts? The communication process?

- **Flat organizational structures.** Many businesses today are downsizing and eliminating layers of management. Companies implementing Total Quality Management programs are reorganizing to distribute the decision-making power throughout the organization. The trend is to eliminate functional or departmental boundaries. Instead, work is reorganized in cross-disciplinary teams that perform broad core processes (e.g., product development and sales generation) and not narrow tasks (e.g., forecasting market demand for a particular product).

In a flat organizational structure, communicating across the organization chart (among the cross-disciplinary teams) becomes more important than communicating up and down in a top-heavy hierarchy. An individual may take on an expanded ***role*** as important tasks are assumed. This role may involve power and authority that surpasses the individual's ***status***, or formal position in the organizational chart. Much of the communication involves face-to-face meetings with team members rather than numerous, time-consuming "handoffs" as the product moves methodically from one department to another.

The time needed to design a new card at Hallmark Cards decreased significantly when the company adopted a flat organizational structure. Team members representing the former functional areas (graphic artists, writers, marketers, and others) now work in a central area, communicating openly and frequently, solving problems and making decisions about the entire process as a card is being developed. For example, a writer struggling with a verse for a new card can solicit immediate input from the graphic artist working on the team rather than finalizing the verse and then "handing it off" to the art department.[20]

Motorola's new organizational structure divides IT staff into three basic teams: "Plan" composed of business analysts who interface with the rest of the business; "Build," the application developers; and "Run," the maintenance staff. An unexpected consequence of connecting the IT staff so tightly to business partners has been a significant increase in project activity.[21]

What place do competition and cooperation have in contemporary organizations?

Heightened Focus on Cooperation. Competition has been a characteristic way of life in U.S. companies, not only externally with other businesses, but also internally. Organizations and individuals compete for a greater share of scarce resources, for a limited number of positions at the top of organizations, and for esteem in their professions. Such competition is a healthy sign of the human desire to succeed, and, in terms of economic behavior, competition is fundamental to the private enterprise system. At the same time, when excessive competition replaces the cooperation necessary for success, communication may be diminished, if not eliminated.

Just as you want to look good in the eyes of your coworkers and supervisors, units within organizations want to look good to one another. This attitude may cause behavior to take the competitive form, a "win/lose" philosophy. When excessive competition has a negative influence on the performance of the organization, everyone loses.

Although competition is appropriate and desirable in many situations, many companies have taken steps through open communication and information and reward systems to reduce competition and to increase cooperation. Cooperation is more likely when the competitors (individuals or groups within an organization) have an understanding of and appreciation for others' importance and functions. This cooperative spirit is characterized as a *win/win philosophy*. One person's success is not achieved at the expense or exclusion of another. Groups identify a solution that everyone finds satisfactory and is committed to achieving. Reaching this mutual understanding requires a high degree of trust and effective interpersonal skills, particularly empathetic and intensive listening skills, and the willingness to communicate long enough to agree on an action plan acceptable to everyone.

SHOWCASE PART 2

© PRNEWSFOTO/WELLPOINT, INC./AP IMAGES

SPOTLIGHT COMMUNICATOR:
ANGELA BRALY,
CEO OF WELLPOINT

Making the Complex Simple

Angela Braly has been called a woman to watch and a rising star. As one of only 10 women CEOs of Fortune 500 companies and the only woman leading a Fortune 50 company, she manages more than 42,000 associates and oversees coordination of health benefits for 35 million Americans. There's no disputing that Braly has a tough job, yet she successfully leads the largest health care organization in America. "Effective communication takes the complex and makes it simple," says Braly.[22] Visit your companion website (www.cengage.com/bcomm/lehman) to learn more about Braly's management style.

www.wellpoint.com

SEE SHOWCASE, PART 3, ON PAGE 68
TO EXPAND YOUR KNOWLEDGE ABOUT COMMUNICATION AT WELLPOINT.

Characteristics of Effective Groups

TEAM ENVIRONMENT

Groups form for synergistic effects; that is, through pooling their efforts, group members can achieve more collectively than they could individually. At the same time, the social nature of groups contributes to the individual goals of members. Communication in small groups leads to group decisions that are generally superior to individual decisions. The group process can motivate members, improve thinking, and assist attitude development and change. The emphasis that a particular group places on task and maintenance activities is based on several factors.

Recall a group of which you were a member. Why was the group formed? How did you achieve your group goals?

As you consider the following factors of group communication, try to visualize their relationship to the groups to which you have belonged, such as in school, religious organizations, athletics, and social activities.

- **Common goals.** In effective groups, participants share a common goal, interest, or benefit. This focus on goals allows members to overcome individual differences of opinion and to negotiate acceptable solutions.
- **Role perception.** People who are invited to join groups have perceptions of how the group should operate and what it should achieve. In addition, each member has a self-concept that dictates how he or she will behave. Those known to be aggressive will attempt to be confrontational and forceful; those who like to be known as moderates will behave in moderate ways by settling arguments rather than initiating them. In successful groups, members play a variety of necessary roles and seek to eliminate nonproductive ones.
- **Longevity.** Groups formed for short-term tasks, such as arranging a dinner and program, will spend more time on the task than on maintenance. However, groups formed for long-term assignments, such as an audit of a major corporation by a

team from a public accounting firm, may devote much effort to maintenance goals. Maintenance includes division of duties, scheduling, record keeping, reporting, and assessing progress.

Why do many prefer groups with an odd number of members?

- **Size.** The smaller the group, the more its members have the opportunity to communicate with each other. Conversely, large groups often inhibit communication because the opportunity to speak and interact is limited. When broad input is desired, large groups may be good. When extensive interaction is the goal, smaller groups may be more effective. Interestingly, large groups generally divide into smaller groups for maintenance purposes, even when the large group is task oriented. Although much research has been conducted in the area of group size, no optimal number of members has been identified. Groups of five to seven members are thought to be best for decision-making and problem-solving tasks. An odd number of members is often preferred because decisions are possible without tie votes.
- **Status.** Some group members will appear to be better qualified than others. Consider a group in which the chief executive of the organization is a member. When the chief executive speaks, members agree. When members speak, they tend to direct their remarks to the one with high status—the chief executive. People are inclined to communicate with peers as their equals, but they tend to speak upward to their supervisor and downward to lower-level employees. In general, groups require balance in status and expertise.

How can a group achieve conformity without sacrificing individual expression?

- **Group norms.** A **norm** is a standard or average behavior. All groups possess norms. An instructor's behavior helps establish classroom norms. If an instructor is generally late for class, students will begin to arrive late. If the instructor permits talking during lectures, the norm will be for students to talk. People conform to norms because conformity is easy and nonconformity is difficult and uncomfortable. Conformity leads to acceptance by other group members and creates communication opportunities.
- **Leadership.** The performance of groups depends on several factors, but none is more important than leadership. Some hold the mistaken view that leaders are not necessary when an organization moves to a group concept. The role of leaders changes substantially, but they still have an important part to play. The ability of a group leader to work toward task goals while contributing to the development of group and individual goals is often critical to group success. Leadership activities may be shared among several participants, and leadership may also be rotated, formally or informally. The leader can establish norms, determine who can speak and when, encourage everyone to contribute, and provide the motivation for effective group activity.[23]

Group Roles

Groups are made up of members who play a variety of roles, both positive and negative. Negative roles detract from the group's purposes and include the following:

- **Isolate**—one who is physically present but fails to participate
- **Dominator**—one who speaks too often and too long

Which role do you view as being more destructive to group function?

- **Free rider**—one who does not do his or her fair share of the work
- **Detractor**—one who constantly criticizes and complains
- **Digresser**—one who deviates from the group's purpose
- **Airhead**—one who is never prepared
- **Socializer**—one who pursues only the social aspect of the group

Perhaps you recognize one or more of the negative roles, based on your personal group experiences. Or perhaps your group experiences have been positive as a result of members' playing positive group roles that promote the group's purposes:

- **Facilitator** (also known as ***gatekeeper***)—one who makes sure everyone gets to talk and be heard
- **Harmonizer**—one who keeps tensions low
- **Record keeper**—one who maintains records of events and activities and informs members
- **Reporter**—one who assumes responsibility for preparing materials for submission
- **Leader**—one who assumes a directive role

What group roles have you played? What were the results?

In healthy groups, members may fulfill multiple roles, which rotate as the need arises. Negative roles are extinguished as the group communicates openly about its goals, strategies, and expectations. The opinions and viewpoints of all members are encouraged and expected.

From Groups to Teams

While some use the terms *group* and *team* interchangeably, others distinguish between them. The major distinction between a group and a team is in members' attitudes and level of commitment. A team is typified by a clear identity and a high level of commitment on the part of members. A variety of strategies has been used for organizing workers into teams:

- A **task force** is generally given a single goal with a limited time to achieve it.
- A **quality assurance team**, or quality circle, focuses on product or service quality, and projects can be either short- or long-term.
- A **cross-functional team** brings together employees from various departments to solve a variety of problems, such as productivity issues, contract estimations and planning, and multidepartment difficulties.
- A **product development team** concentrates on innovation and the development cycle of new products, and is usually cross-functional in nature. Recall the organizational chart illustrated in Figure 1-3. Now consider the impact of team structures, as shown in Figure 2-2.

While chain of command is still at work in formal organizational relationships and responsibilities, team structures unite people from varying portions of the organization. Work teams are typically given the authority to act on their conclusions, although the

FIGURE 2-2

Organizational Chart with Hierarchical and Team Structures

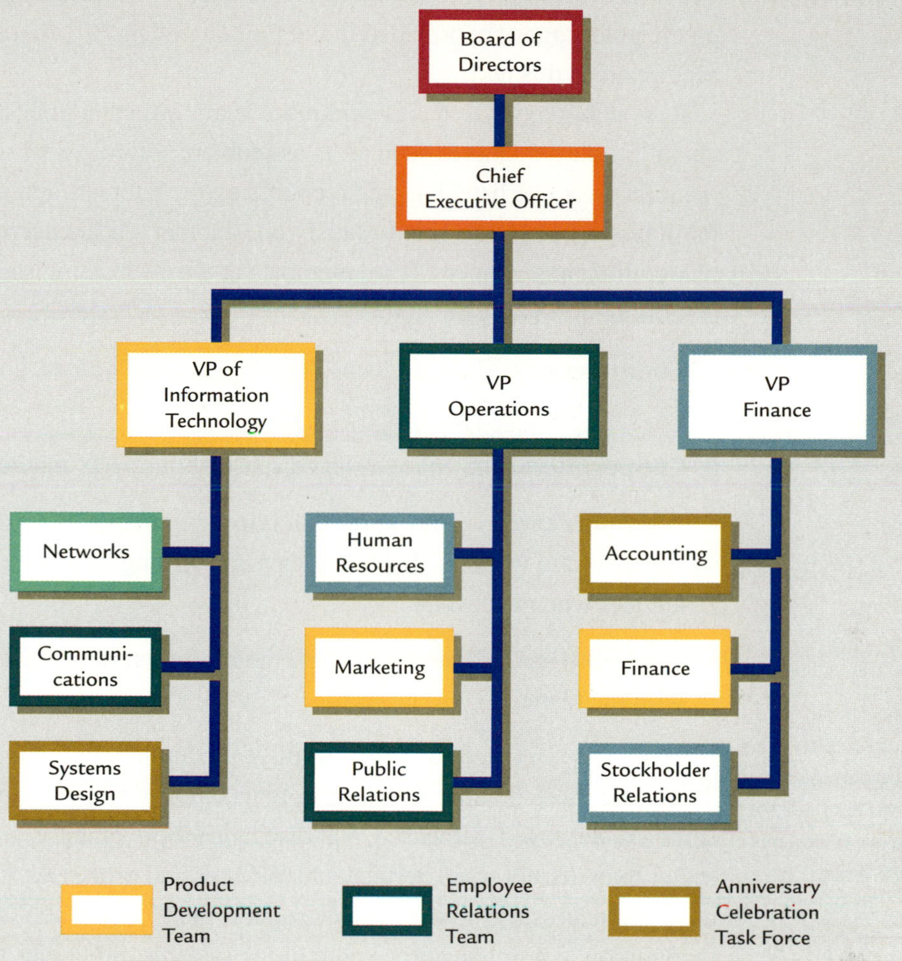

Board of Directors
Chief Executive Officer
VP of Information Technology
VP Operations
VP Finance
Networks
Communi-cations
Systems Design
Human Resources
Marketing
Public Relations
Accounting
Finance
Stockholder Relations
Product Development Team
Employee Relations Team
Anniversary Celebration Task Force

level of authority varies, depending on the organization and the purpose of the team. Typically, the group supervisor retains some responsibilities, some decisions are made completely by the team, and the rest are made jointly.

Merely placing workers into a group does not make them a functional team. A group must go through a developmental process to begin to function as a team. The four stages of team development include:

- **forming** (becoming acquainted with each other and the assigned task)
- **storming** (dealing with conflicting personalities, goals, and ideas)
- **norming** (developing strategies and activities that promote goal achievement)
- **performing** (reaching the optimal performance level).

Forming
Storming
Norming
Performing

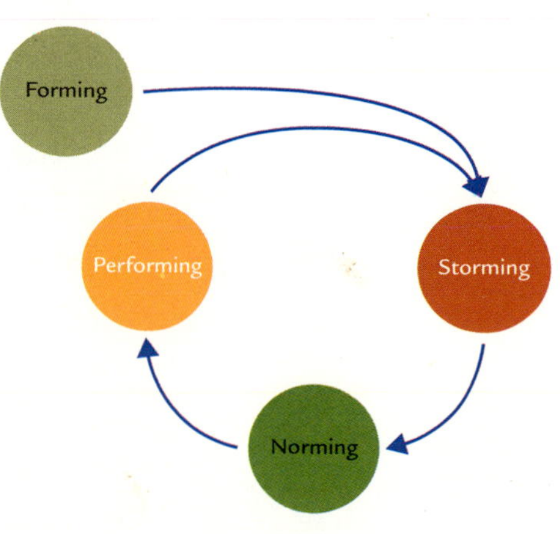

For a variety of reasons, teams are often unable to advance through all four stages of

Why might a team be unable to advance to the performing stage of team development?

development. Even long-term teams may never reach the optimal performing stage, settling instead for the acceptable performance of the norming stage.

Projects and activities to promote your team's successful movement through the predictable stages are provided in the *Building High-Performance Teams* handbook that accompanies this text.

Research into what makes workplace teams effective indicates that training is beneficial for participants in such areas as problem solving, goal setting, conflict resolution, risk taking, active listening, and recognizing the interests and achievement of others. Participants need to be able to satisfy one another's basic needs for belonging, personal recognition, and support. Team members at the performing stage of team development exhibit the following behaviors:[24]

- **Commitment.** They are focused on the mission, values, goals, and expectations of the team and the organization.
- **Cooperation.** They have a shared sense of purpose, mutual gain, and teamwork.
- **Communication.** They know that information must flow smoothly between top management and workers. Team members are willing to face confrontation and unpleasantness when necessary.
- **Contribution.** All members share their different backgrounds, skills, and abilities with the team.

Does position on the organizational chart indicate an employee's power in the organization? Why?

Teams have existed for hundreds of years throughout many countries and cultures. Teams are more flexible than larger organizational groupings because they can be assembled, deployed, refocused, and disbanded more quickly, usually in ways that enhance rather than disrupt more permanent structures and processes. Organizational changes are often necessary, however, since support must be in place for performance evaluation, recognition, communication, and training systems. Strategies for bringing about needed change might include arranging site visits to similar organizations that already have teams, bringing a successful team to speak to the organization, and bringing in consultants to discuss the team development process.

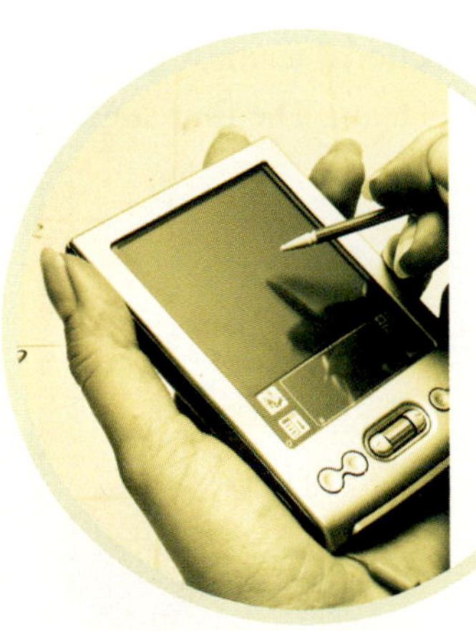

Your Turn 2-4
Career Portfolio

- Understanding your own communication style can help you identify ways to be more effective and to relate better with others. Take the Communications Style survey located at http://occonline.occ.cccd.edu/online/klee/CommunicationsStyleInventory.pdf, or go to your companion website www.cengage.com/bcomm/lehman for updated links.

TAKE ACTION:

- Print out the information about your dominant communication style(s).
- Write a short summary of what the survey results reveal to you in terms of your interactions with others.
- What are your apparent strengths?
- What are your areas for improvement?

Meeting Management

Meetings are essential for communication in organizations. They present opportunities to acquire and disseminate valuable information, develop skills, and make favorable impressions on colleagues, supervisors, and subordinates. U.S. businesses spend more money on conducting meetings than any other country in the world, and they also spend more time in meetings than do people of other countries.[26] International meetings are imperative for solid business reasons but are facing greater planning scrutiny with tightening travel budgets and a recovering global economy.

Workers frequently have a negative attitude toward meetings because they perceive they are a waste of time. Studies support this opinion, revealing that as much as one third of the time spent in meetings is unproductive. Negative attitudes toward meetings can be changed when meetings are conducted properly, giving attention to correct procedures and behavior. Successful meetings don't just happen; rather, they occur by design. Careful planning and attention to specific guidelines can help ensure the success of your meetings, whether they are conducted in a face-to-face format or electronically.

Face-to-Face Meetings

Face-to-face meetings continue to be the most-used meeting format in most organizations. They offer distinct advantages and are appropriate in the following situations:[27]

- When you need the richest nonverbal cues, including body, voice, proximity, and touch.
- When the issues are especially sensitive.

Technology Facilitates Electronic Meetings. Meeting productivity software helps guide participants through various meeting stages by assisting with preparation and follow-up as well as the meeting itself. Meeting goals, agenda items, and relevant files can be stored in an electronic workspace for each member to review prior to the meeting. During the meeting, the software can record ideas discussed and decisions that are made, creating a permanent record of the meeting's activities. A timer feature can help guide discussions, assuring that members stay on task and on schedule. Following the meeting, the software emails a meeting summary to each participant. By implementing an electronic meeting process, actual meeting time can be reduced by approximately 50 percent.[25]

© JON FEINGERSH/BLEND IMAGES/JUPITERIMAGES

- When the participants don't know one another.
- When establishing group rapport and relationships are crucial.
- When the participants can be in the same place at the same time.

Face-to-face meetings may be enhanced with the use of various media tools such as flipcharts, handouts, and electronic slide decks. While face-to-face meetings provide a rich nonverbal context and direct human contact, they also have certain limitations. In addition to the obvious logistical issues of schedules and distance, face-to-face meetings may be dominated by overly vocal, quick-to-speak, and high-status members. An additional potential obstacle to communication results from the differences in communication styles that men and women typically exhibit. The Strategic Forces feature "Communication Styles of Men and Women" describes how such problems can occur and what can be done to overcome possible difficulties in communicating.

Electronic Meetings

Electronic meetings allow companies to reduce travel budgets, save professional time, and minimize the environmental impact caused by travel. A variety of technologies is available to facilitate electronic meetings. Participants may communicate with one another through telephones, computers, or video broadcast equipment using groupware or meeting management software applications. Electronic meetings offer certain advantages. They facilitate geographically dispersed groups, because they provide the choice of meeting at different places/same time, different places/different times, same place/same time, or same place/different times. Electronic meetings also speed up meeting follow-up activities because decisions and action items may be recorded electronically.

Electronic meetings also have certain limitations:[29]

- They cannot replace face-to-face contact, especially when group efforts are just beginning and when groups are trying to build group values, trust, and emotional ties.
- They may make it harder to reach consensus, because more ideas are generated and because it may be harder to interpret the strength of other members' commitment to their proposals.
- The success of same-time meetings is dependent on all participants having excellent keyboarding skills to engage in rapid-fire, in-depth discussion. This limitation may be overcome as the use of voice input systems becomes more prevalent.

TEAM ENVIRONMENT

STRATEGIC FORCES

Communication Styles of Men and Women

Research on communication patterns in mixed-gender work groups shows that the traditional behaviors of men and women may restrict the richness of discussion and limit group productivity. The basic male approach to work tasks is confrontational and results oriented, while the female method of working is collaborative and oriented toward concern for individuals. The adversarial male style leads to respect, while the collaborative female style engenders rapport.

Differences in male and female behavior that accentuate gender differences are often so subtle that group members may not be aware of what is happening. Here is a partial listing of those differences:

- Men are more likely to control discussion through introducing topics, interrupting, and talking more than women.
- Women not only talk less, but often assume supportive rather than leadership roles in conversation and receive less attention for their ideas from the group.
- Both men and women may expect group members to follow gender-stereotyped roles that can limit each individual's contributions (for example, always selecting a man as leader or a woman as note taker).
- Either women or men may use exclusionary language that reinforces gender stereotypes or offends others in the group.
- Women may exhibit verbal characteristics of submissiveness (allowing sentence endings to trail off) or reinforcing stereotypes (using a shrill voice), while men communicate in ways that restrict and control a group (raising the voice or ignoring ideas generated by women).
- Men's nonverbal behavior (extended eye contact, a condescending touch, or overt gestures) may convey messages of dominance, while women's nonverbal behavior (smiling, hair-twirling, or primly crossed legs) may suggest a lack of self-confidence and power.
- Men and women may sit separately, thereby limiting cross-gender interaction.

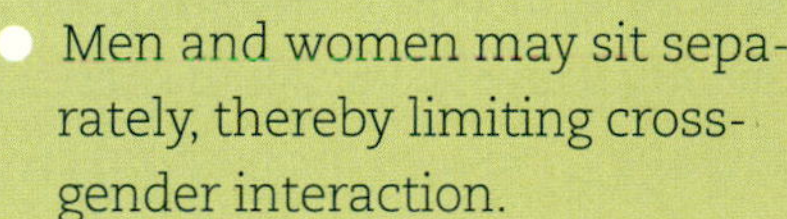

© IMAGESHOP/JUPITERIMAGES

Until recently, most research on the communication styles of men and women focused on face-to-face interactions. Current research has also addressed computer-mediated communication (CMC), such as email, instant messaging, and electronic meetings. Such studies validate gender differences in communication patterns. For example, women using CMC with other women develop more disclosure and sense of community, whereas men using CMC with other men seem to ignore the socioemotional aspects of group functioning and are more likely to use mild flaming (emotional language outbursts). Overall, men are less satisfied with CMC experiences and show lower levels of group development than do women.[28]

While caution is advised concerning stereotyping of men and women in communication situations, knowing what behaviors may limit the group process is imperative to maximizing results. Group members may need awareness training to assist in recognizing behaviors that hinder team performance and in overcoming barriers that limit communication effectiveness. Differences can also be used to productive advantage. You will explore age-related barriers to group communication in Chapter 3.

Application

Locate an article on cross-gender communication. Compose a list of suggestions for improving cross-gender communications in the work environment. Indicate those you feel would be most helpful to you in your professional activities and that you will commit to work on as part of your self-improvement.

Your Turn 2-5
Electronic Café

SECURE EMAIL PROTECTS CORPORATE INFORMATION

Organizations need secure control over incoming and outgoing email. Regulations may also require that certain types of information be transmitted through email only in an encrypted form. A number of vendors offer software solutions for managing secure messaging so that the receiver doesn't know anything is different. Various software firms offer products that help secure organizations' borders against unwanted intrusion into their email. The following electronic activities will allow you to explore the topic of secure email in more depth:

TAKE ACTION:

- Learn more about secure email systems and how email poses security threats including confidentiality breaches, legal liability, lost productivity, and damage to company reputation. An email usage policy is the first step a company should take to protect itself. The following website offers ideas about the content of an email policy: http://humanresources.about.com/od/policiesandsamples1/a/email_policy.htm
- Interview a business manager of your choice about email policies that are in place in the individual's company. Compare your findings with those of other students in your class.

Suggestions for Effective Meetings

Whether you engage in face-to-face or electronic meetings, observing the following guidelines may help to ensure that your meetings are productive:

- **Limit meeting length and frequency.** Any meeting held for longer than an hour or more frequently than once a month should be scrutinized. Ask yourself whether the meeting is necessary. Perhaps the purpose can be achieved in another way, such as email, instant messaging, or telephone.
- **Make satisfactory arrangements.** Select a date and time convenient for the majority of expected participants. For face-to-face meetings, plan the meeting site with consideration for appropriate seating for attendees, media equipment, temperature and lighting, and necessary supplies. For electronic meetings, check hardware and software and connectivity components.
- **Distribute the agenda well in advance.** The **agenda** is a meeting outline that includes important information: date, beginning and ending time, place, and topics to be discussed and responsibilities of those involved. Having the agenda prior to the meeting allows participants to know what is expected of them. A sample agenda is provided in the *Building High-Performance Teams* handbook.

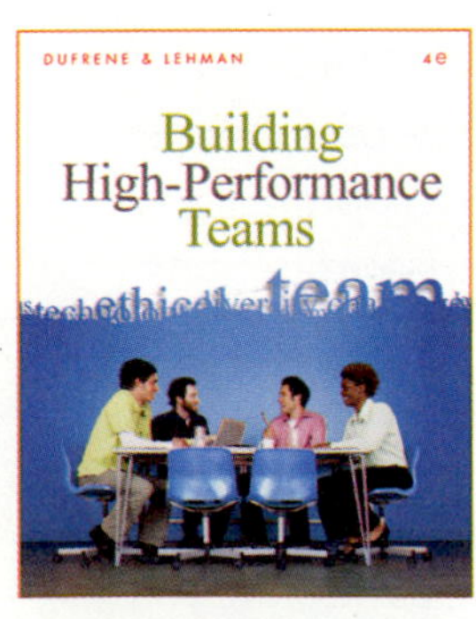

- **Encourage participation.** While it is certainly easier for one person to make decisions, the quality of the decision making is often improved by involving the team. Rational decision making may begin with **brainstorming**, the generation of many ideas from among team members. Brainstormed ideas can then be discussed and ranked, followed by some form of voting.
- **Maintain order.** An organized democratic process ensures that the will of the majority prevails, the minority is heard, and group goals are achieved as expeditiously as possible. Proper parliamentary procedure may be followed in formal meetings, as outlined in sources such as *Robert's Rules of Order* and *Jones' Parliamentary Procedure at a Glance*. For less formal meetings, a more relaxed approach may be taken to ensure that everyone has an opportunity to share in the decision making.
- **Manage conflict.** In an autocratic organization, conflict may be avoided because employees are conditioned to be submissive. Such an environment, however, leads to smoldering resentment. On the other hand, conflict is a normal part of any team effort and can lead to creative discussion and superior outcomes. Maintaining focus on issues and not personalities helps ensure that conflict is productive rather than destructive.

What is the relationship between conflict and consensus?

- **Seek consensus.** While unanimous agreement on decisions is an optimal outcome, total agreement cannot always be achieved. ***Consensus*** represents the collective opinion of the group, or the informal rule that all team members can live with at least 70 percent of what is agreed upon.
- **Prepare thorough minutes.** Minutes provide a concise record of meeting actions, ensure the tracking and follow-up of issues from previous meetings, and assist in the implementation of previously reached decisions. A format for meeting minutes is provided in the *Building High-Performance Teams* handbook.

Meetings are an important management tool and are useful for idea exchange. They also provide opportunities for you, as a meeting participant, to communicate impressions of power and status. Knowing how to present yourself and your ideas and exhibiting knowledge about correct meeting management will assist you in your career advancement.

CHANGING TECHNOLOGY

Employees working to establish virtual teams at Dow Chemical take courses in virtual team etiquette and online meeting management. You may also visit your text companion website www.cengage.com/dcomm/lehman to learn more about maximizing the effectiveness of ***virtual teams*** that have members in more than one location. The Electronic Café in Chapter 10 will provide additional experiences designed to make you a more effective meeting participant.

© AP IMAGES

SHOWCASE PART 3

WellPoint Gives Back

According to the WellPoint website, the company's mission is "to improve the lives of the people we serve and the health of our communities." Management and associates demonstrate commitment to their mission through notable community involvement. Recently, WellPoint Inc. associates generously pledged more than $15 million to more than 9,000 not-for-profit organizations, with the WellPoint Foundation matching at 50 percent. WellPoint's Community Service Day is another way employees give back through volunteering in a variety of ways, most of which involve community health, in 140 cities spanning 30 states. Contributions of time, talent, muscles, and money help address needs throughout local communities.[30]

www.wellpoint.com

© PRNEWSFOTO/WELLPOINT, INC./ AP IMAGES

Activities

- Visit the WellPoint website at www.wellpoint.com. Click on "Our Business" and choose the link to view the company mission, vision, and values.
- Locate the following article about WellPoint's community service. Then locate an article discussing the community service of another organization of your choice. Compare the level of involvement and overall impact of the two organizations' community efforts.

  Matthews, C. S. (2008, July/August). Community service day. *Profiles in Diversity Journal, 10*(4), 42. Available from Business Source Complete database.
- Post your findings to a discussion board, following your instructor's directions.

Summary

1. Explain how behavioral theories about human needs, trust and disclosure, and motivation relate to business communication.

Behavioral theories that address human needs, trust and disclosure, and motivation are essential aspects of interpersonal communication. The needs of all individuals to be heard, appreciated, wanted, and reinforced significantly affect their interpersonal communications.

2. Describe the role of nonverbal messages in communication.

Nonverbal communication conveys a significant portion of meaning and includes metacommunications, which are wordless messages that accompany words, and kinesic communications, which are expressed through body language. The meanings of nonverbal messages are culturally derived.

3. Identify aspects of effective listening.

Effective listening, which requires effort and discipline, is crucial to effective interpersonal communication and leads to career success. Various types of listening require different strategies.

4. Identify factors affecting group and team communication.

Organizations are increasingly using group structures to achieve goals. Effective group communication results from shared purpose, constructive activity and behaviors, and positive role fulfillment among members. A team is a special type of group that is typified by strong commitment among members; this commitment results in behaviors that produce synergy.

5. Discuss aspects of effective meeting management.

Face-to-face meetings and electronic meetings each offer certain advantages and disadvantages. Effective meeting management techniques and behaviors can enhance the success of meetings.

Chapter Review

1. What is meant by stroking? How does it affect interpersonal communication in the workplace? (Obj. 1)
2. When a manager says to an employee, "May I see you in my office," what are some of the possible metacommunications? (Obj. 2)
3. What roles do culture and gender play in nonverbal communication? (Obj. 2)
4. How is the activity of listening impacted by the particular situation? (Obj. 3)
5. Discuss six bad listening habits. Which do you think is the biggest challenge for you personally? (Obj. 3)
6. What is a possible cause of most conflict between or among groups? (Obj. 4)
7. How are a group and a team different? (Obj. 4)
8. Discuss how a flat organizational structure affects communication. (Obj. 4)
9. What are some factors to consider in deciding whether to hold a face-to-face meeting or an electronic meeting? (Obj. 5)
10. Why are records such as agendas and minutes important to group success? (Obj. 5)

Digging Deeper

1. How can managers use Maslow's need levels, the Johari Window, and the management theories of McGregor and Hersey and Blanchard to improve communication with employees?
2. How do effective conversation and listening impact a business' overall success?
3. Why do some teams never reach the highest stage of team development? What can be done to overcome the obstacles to peak team performance?

Assessment

To check your understanding of the chapter, take the available online quizzes as directed by your instructor.

Activities

1. Applying Behavioral Theories to Communication Situations (Obj. 1)

Considering Maslow's hierarchy of needs, the Johari Window, McGregor's Theory X and Y, and Hersey and Blanchard's situational leadership theory, select one of the theories and relate it to a personal communication experience you have had. How was communication enhanced or worsened by the events and behaviors that occurred? What were the ethical implications of the situation? Prepare a brief written summary of your analysis.

2. Understanding the Importance of Nonverbal Messages (Obj. 2)

In small groups, compose a list of nonverbal messages (gestures, facial expressions, etc.) that might be used by a businessperson, along with their meanings. What are some possible ways that each might be misinterpreted?

3. Identifying Appropriate Listening Styles (Obj. 3)

Identify a situation you have experienced that would be appropriate for each of the following listening styles: casual listening, listening for information, intensive listening, and empathetic listening. Describe how you could maximize your listening experience in each case.

4. Identifying Deterrents to Group Success (Obj. 4)

In small groups, discuss negative group situations in which you have participated. These groups could be related to school, organizations, sports teams, performing groups, etc. Referring to the chapter information, identify reasons for each group's lack of success. Make a list of the most common problems identified in the team. Compare your list with that of other small groups in the class.

5. Analyzing a Meeting for Effective Behaviors (Obj. 5)

Attend a meeting of an organization of your choice. Compare the activities of the attended meeting with the "Suggestions for Effective Meetings" presented in the chapter. Email your instructor, describing the meeting attended and summarizing how well the meeting reflected the chapter suggestions and how it might have been more effective.

6. Assessing the Professional Value of Interpersonal and Group Communication Skills (Objs. 1–5)

Considering your career goal, select the three concepts presented in the chapter that you feel will be most important to your professional success. Write a one-page summary, justifying and explaining your selections.

Applications

READ | THINK | WRITE | SPEAK | COLLABORATE

1. Boosting Team Effectiveness: Trend in Corporate America (Objs. 1, 4)

Locate the following article that describes the importance of team development activities:

Linley, A. (2008, January 29). Our top ten team building exercises. *Ezine*. Available at http://ezinearticles.com/?Our-Top-Ten-Team-Building-Exercises&id5955336

In a small groups, discuss the shift in corporate team building over the past 25 years and the value gained from various types of team-building activities. Brainstorm ways you believe these approaches could be used to boost the effectiveness of teams in an academic setting and the projected results. Share your ideas with the class in a short presentation.

2. Gaining Insights from Nonverbal Communication (Obj. 2)

Locate the following article that gives useful suggestions for ensuring that nonverbal behavior communicates the intended message:

Shephard, L. C. (2007, May 1). Reading body language can offer insight to HR pros. *Employee Benefit News*. Available from Business Source Complete database.

Expand the list of recommended and nonverbal messages and their interpretations. Share your list with the class, complete with demonstrations, in an informal presentation.

READ | THINK | WRITE | SPEAK | COLLABORATE

3. Analyzing Limitations of Electronic Communications (Objs. 2, 3, 5)

Consider a distance learning conference or course in which you have participated. How were nonverbal communication, listening, and other factors different from what you have experienced in traditional class settings? How do your experiences relate to the conducting of electronic meetings?

READ | THINK | WRITE | SPEAK | COLLABORATE

4. Recognizing Events that Involve Metacommunication (Obj. 2)

Keep a journal over the next two to five days that records events that involve metacommunication. Describe how each incident influences the understanding of the verbal message involved. Go to your companion website www.cengage.com/dcomm/lehman for a downloadable version of this activity.

5. Maximizing the Effectiveness of Virtual Teams (Objs. 4, 5)

Visit your companion website to read about how to maximize the effectiveness of a virtual team. Consider the significance of this statement that appears in the posting: "Certain personality types are more likely to thrive in the virtual team experience." Develop a list of personality attributes that would enable a person to work effectively as part of a virtual team. In a short written or oral report, share your list, justifying your selections with facts and references.

6. Documenting Meeting Activities (Obj. 5)

Consult *Building High-Performance Teams* (your separate team handbook) for guidelines for preparing agendas and minutes. Attend a meeting of an organization of your choice. Obtain a copy of the agenda, and prepare minutes of the meeting. Submit your meeting documentation to your instructor.

READ | THINK | WRITE | SPEAK | COLLABORATE

7. Locating Information on Nonverbal Communication in Other Cultures (Obj. 2)

Locate one or more articles from a database or the Internet that discuss nonverbal communication in various cultures. Compile a list of body language and behaviors that have different meanings among cultures. Discuss how ignorance of these differences might affect interpersonal communication.

8. Discussing the Impact of Flat Organizational Structure on Communication (Obj. 4)

Using an online database, locate an article about a company that has adopted a flat organizational structure. Write a brief summary emphasizing the effect this change in organizational structure has had on the communication process.

9. Analyzing Group and Team Experiences (Obj. 4)

As a team, visit the website of the Institute for Performance Culture at http://teaming-up.com/. From the Free Resources menu tab, click on "Your Team's Performance Blind Spots?" and together take the survey. Some of the items may not relate to your short-term project team but will provide you with ideas of issues faced in real-world work teams. Discuss the evaluation report produced from your survey. Send your instructor an email message, summarizing what your team survey revealed and how you will use the information to improve your team performance.

10. Using Instant Messaging to Communicate (Objs. 3, 4)

Following directions from your instructor, participate in an online chat with your class about one of the following topics: (a) how to overcome listening barriers, or (b) guidelines for effective group communication.

CASES

COURTESY OF NETAPP

1. Boosting Employee Morale in Uncertain Economic Times

How does a company keep employee morale high, even in a depressed economic environment? In an economy fraught with business closures and employee downsizing, just having a job gives many workers a reason to be happy. Fear of layoffs and budget cuts, however, make their impact on employee morale. This situation was prevalent in early 2009. Not every organization, however, was experiencing doom and gloom. Companies named to Fortune's "100 Best Companies to Work For" reveal some effective strategies that may also help other companies motivate their employees in tough economic times.

When NetApp, a data storage company, received the number one spot in early 2009 in Fortune's rating, management attributed its success to its egalitarian culture, salary, unique benefits, and a down-to-earth management style.[31] According to NetApp's CEO DanWarmenhoven, "Our employees are the heart of our company and the strength of our global culture. That company values teamwork, productivity, leadership, and innovation."[32] In addition to receiving wide recognition for its work climate, NetApp, which employs 8,000 people worldwide, was still hiring at the beginning of 2009, a time when many other companies were cutting positions. Market share was growing, and the company had cash on hand to weather the financial slump.[33]

Application:

1. Find out more about the selection of the "100 Best Companies" and why NetApp achieved the number one spot at www.greatplacetowork.com.
2. Read more about the strategies used by NetApp to motivate employees: NetApp: 100 Best Companies to Work For. (2009). Money.cnn.com. Available at http://money.cnn.com/magazines/fortune/bestcompanies/2009/snapshots/1.html
3. Study the various employee benefits and perks offered by NetApp. Devise a checklist that includes NetApp's employee benefits, and arrange an interview with an employee of a company with which you are familiar. Have that employee indicate on the checklist the benefits offered by his or her particular company. Ask questions about the current morale in the company and the impact the employee feels the unchecked benefits from the checklist might have on the level of morale. Summarize your interview, ending with recommendations to the organization for how to improve employee morale. Submit your checklist and written interview summary to your instructor.

© BBC LTD./COURTESY: EVERETT COLLECTION

2. Video Case: The Office: Gestures: Do They Say What You Mean?

In this clip, Gareth communicates with his coworker with gestures and three words. His lack of words, his tone, and the specificity of his gestures communicate more than the words themselves.

Complete the following activities as directed by your instructor after the class has viewed the video:

1. In small groups, discuss what meanings could be attributed to Gareth's body language. What should Gareth do to be a more effective communicator in this situation?
2. As Gareth, compose a short email to your coworker apologizing for your earlier impatience and explaining the need to continue working for a moment.

3. Using High-Tech and High-Touch Methods to Enhance Collaboration

Various technologies are available to assist in the collaboration of people in organizations. Some of the more popular ones include email, voice mail, shared calendars, electronic meeting systems, and videoconferencing systems. While technology offers many possibilities for business people to connect and communicate, the available capabilities are often underutilized or not used at all. According to a recent survey of IT executives, the biggest obstacles to successful integration of collaboration tools into companies are a resistant corporate culture and insufficient support. Few senior executives surveyed use collaboration tools other than email, telephone, and shared calendars. The lack of technology usage by upper management tends to have a dampening effect on corporate culture and on support for technology. Senior managers who want to increase collaboration across the organization should embrace technology tools that enable it.

While research supports that younger employees are quick to adopt collaborative technologies, older workers typically embrace technologies that prove themselves valuable. The foreign-based workforce can also often be a source of new ideas for using collaborative technologies.[34]

Application

1. Read the article that summarizes the results of the study on collaboration tools:
   Alter, A. (2008, March 6). Collaboration: Unlocking the power of teams. *CIO Insight*. Available at www.cioinsight.com/c/a/Research/Collaboration-Unlocking-the-Power-of-Teams/
2. Locate the following corporate news release that discusses "low-tech" methods used by one company to build a collaborative culture: Inside Enerplus: Corporate culture based on collaboration and respect. (2008). Available at www.enerplus.com/news_releases/documents/Corporateculture.pdf
3. Write a two-page paper that describes the place of both "high-tech" and "high-touch" in building a collaborative corporate culture. Incorporate other business examples of companies that have been successful in establishing a culture of collaboration.

4. Is Anyone Listening?

The ability to listen effectively is consistently rated as one of the most important skills necessary for success in the workplace. A survey of North American executives reveals that 80 percent believe that listening is one of the most important skills needed in the corporate environment. The same survey participants, however, also rated the skill as one of the most lacking. Effective listening is crucial to providing quality service, facilitating groups, training staff, improving teamwork, and supervising and managing for improved performance. In times of stress and change, effective listening is the cornerstone of workplace harmony, since it furthers interpersonal and intercultural understanding. Listening is more than just hearing. It is an interactive process that takes concentration and commitment.

Although listening is critical to our daily lives, it is taught and studied far less than the other three basic communication skills: reading, writing, and speaking. Overreliance on television and computers also contributes to our listening problems. Much of the trouble we have communicating with others is because of poor listening skills. Studies show that we spend about 80 percent of our waking hours communicating, and at least 45 percent of that time listening. Most people can benefit from improving their listening skills. You can arrive at a fairly accurate assessment of your listening skills by thinking about your relationships with the people in your life—your boss, colleagues, best friends, family. If asked, what would they say about how well you listen? Do you often misunderstand assignments, or only vaguely remember what people have said to you? If so, you may need to improve your listening skills. These suggestions may assist you in your listening improvement:

- Become aware of biases and filters that keep you from listening effectively.
- Identify the aspects of listening that you need to improve upon.
- Get comfortable with silence.
- Monitor your body language, facial expressions, and other nonverbal signals that might appear negative.
- Listen between words for feelings.
- Give signals that you are listening.
- Take notes.
- Hear people out before cutting in with your reply.
- Don't begin answers with "I."
- Learn to ask nonaggressive questions.
- Understand that listening does not mean agreeing.

Listening skills can have a dramatic effect on your personal and professional success. By becoming an effective listener, you're likely to gain the trust of those with whom you communicate.[35] The resulting relationships will lead to better workplace environments, better customer relations, and better community relationships.[36]

Visit your companion website www.cengage.com/bcomm/lehman to link to web resources related to this topic. Respond to one or more of the following activities, as directed by your instructor.

1. Tell why you are either a good or poor listener. Support your conclusion with reasons and/or evidence of one or more situations in which your listening was put to the test.
2. One of the sites you visited identified a plan for improving the listening skills of a negotiator. Prepare a similar plan for a position in your chosen career field (human resources manager, auditor, salesperson, etc.), adapting the points to fit the activities and expectations of the position.
3. Outline and implement a plan for improving your own listening skills. Your plan should include the following: (1) identification of your major listening weaknesses; (2) one or more strategies for overcoming each of the stated weaknesses; (3) activities or occasions in which you applied the corrective strategies, with dates and times; and (4) outcomes of your corrective strategies. Implement your plan for one week, or some other time period as specified by your instructor. Summarize in writing the results of your self-improvement project.

Part 2
Communication Analysis

Chapter 3 Planning Spoken and Written Messages

"We're not filling all the needs that people have when it comes to their relationships, but we have their 'permission' and opportunities to do so."

Hallmark CEO Donald J. Hall, Jr.

Objectives When you have completed Chapter 3, you will be able to:

1. Identify the purpose of the message and the appropriate channel.
2. Develop clear perceptions of the audience to enhance the impact of the communication and human relations.
3. Apply techniques for adapting messages to the audience, including strategies for communicating ethically and responsibly.
4. Recognize the importance of organizing a message before writing the first draft.
5. Select the appropriate message pattern (deductive or inductive) for developing messages to achieve the desired response.

SHOWCASE PART 1  

Hallmark Crafts Messages for Changing Consumer Market

Nationwide, American consumers spend about $7.5 billion a year on greeting cards.[1] Greeting cards can be a meaningful communication tool for customers, coworkers, and important business contacts and can provide a memorable, cost-effective way to build loyalty and increase customer retention. Hallmark Cards, Inc., located in Kansas City, Missouri, has been helping people say the right things at the right time for 100 years, and the continued success of its cards is directly tied to effective analysis of an ever-changing audience.

As American society has become increasingly heterogeneous, Hallmark product offerings have also become more diverse. Realizing that Hispanics currently account for 15 percent of the U.S. population, the company has extended the appeal of its cards to Hispanics through its Sinceramente Hallmark line, which includes more than 2,500 Spanish-language cards. Hallmark targets its African American consumers with its Mahogany line. The Tree of Life series, meanwhile, is aimed at Jewish customers, and in 2003, Hallmark began carrying Diwali and Eid al-Fitr cards to appeal to its Muslim clientele. Expansion into international markets has shown Hallmark that message appeal is largely influenced by cultural values. The Dutch audience, for instance, tends to be more direct than Americans, while British consumers are more reserved and less direct.

Shifting cultural demographics is only one challenge faced by Hallmark. Referring to recent internal research, Hallmark's CEO Donald J. Hall, Jr. says, "We're not filling all the needs that people have when it comes to their relationships, but we have their 'permission' and opportunities to do so."[2] Generational changes, such as the tendency of baby boomers to purchase fewer cards than their parents, and the current popularity of e-cards and m-cards designed for delivery to mobile devices have given rise to the design of new products to entice consumers to card shop more often. Because women buy 80 percent of all greeting cards, Hallmark works to attract today's women, particularly those older than 45 who no longer have children at home. The Shoebox and Fresh Ink lines are designed to provide offbeat and entertaining options for those who prefer an alternative to traditional sentiments. "Green" cards made with recycled paper, musical greeting cards, and recordable voice cards are all recent additions to the card line up that appeal to various subsets of the card market.[3]

Hallmark knows that building good communication with friends and family, as well as customers and business partners, means that it must design text and visual messages that effectively convey intended meanings and emotions. The company must accurately visualize its ever-changing audience in order to design appealing greeting cards.

You, too, will need skills in audience analysis to communicate effectively in your profession. In this chapter you will learn various skills for developing effective spoken and written messages that achieve your desired purpose—whomever the particular audience might be.

www.hallmark.com

SEE SHOWCASE PART 2, ON PAGE 86
FOR SPOTLIGHT COMMUNICATOR DEAN RODENBOUGH, DIRECTOR OF CORPORATE COMMUNICATIONS AT HALLMARK CARDS.

In a report titled "Writing: A Ticket to Work . . . or a Ticket Out," the National Commission on Writing reported that two thirds of salaried employees in large companies have some writing responsibilities, and getting hired and promoted in many industries requires strong writing abilities. While writing is important in most managerial level jobs, the Commission also concluded that one third of employees in corporate America write poorly. Knowing that effective communication is tied to the corporate bottom line and many employees can't write well, businesses are investing $3.1 billion annually to train employees to write.[4] Remedies are needed to prevent confusion, waste, errors, lost productivity, and damaged corporate image—all caused by employees and customers and clients muddling their way through unreadable messages.

It has been said that all business messages have some persuasive intent. Do you agree or disagree?

As a capable communicator, you can immediately add value to your organization and set yourself apart from your peers who are struggling to articulate ideas in writing and presentations. Communication that commands attention and can be understood easily is essential for survival in today's information explosion. On the job, you will be expected to process volumes of available information and shape useful messages that respond to the needs of customers or clients, coworkers and supervisors, and other key business partners. Additionally, increased use of electronic communication (email, text, and instant messages; blogs, videoconferences, etc.) will require you to be technologically savvy and capable of adapting the rules of good communication to the demands of emerging technology.

How can you learn to plan and prepare powerful business messages? The systematic analysis process as outlined in Figure 3-1 will help you develop messages that save

FIGURE 3-1

Process for Planning and Preparing Spoken and Written Messages

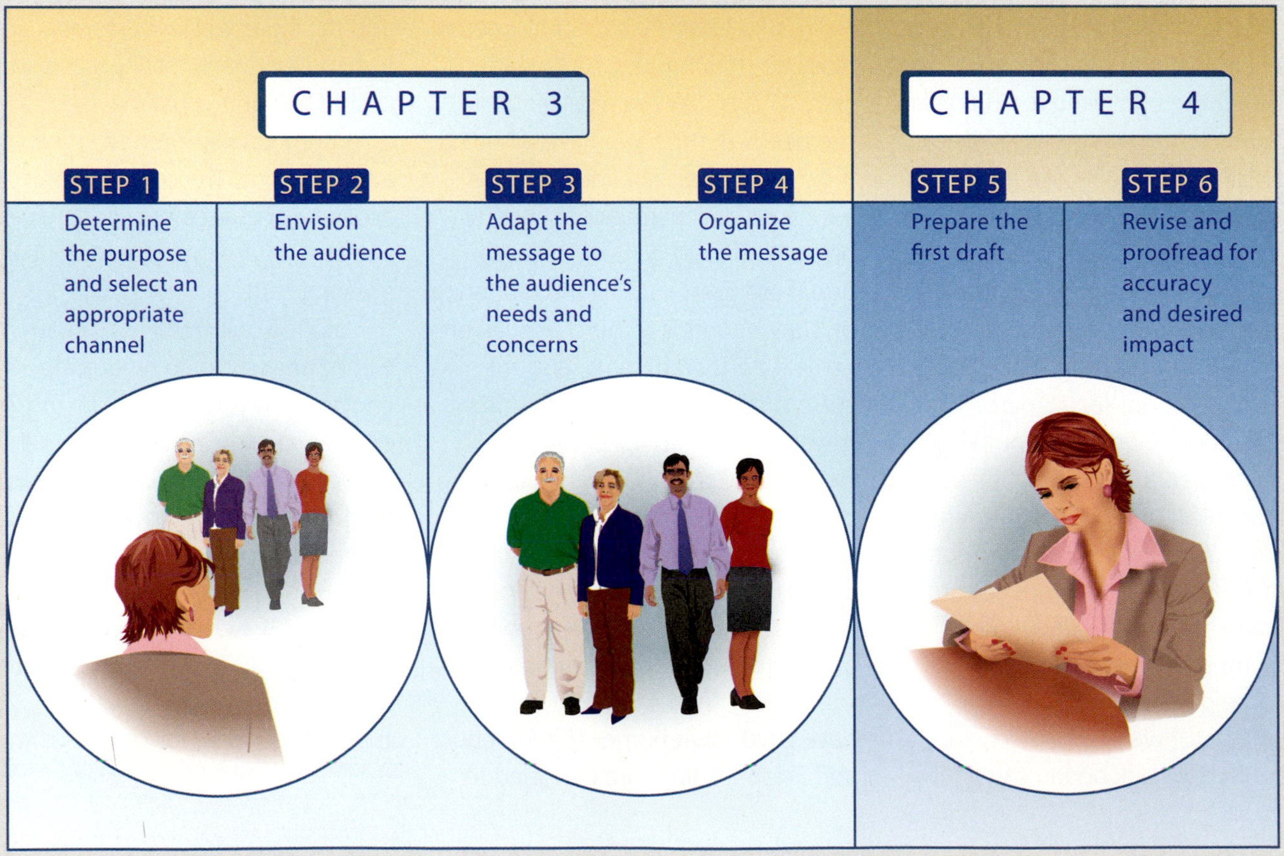

CHAPTER 3				CHAPTER 4	
STEP 1	STEP 2	STEP 3	STEP 4	STEP 5	STEP 6
Determine the purpose and select an appropriate channel	Envision the audience	Adapt the message to the audience's needs and concerns	Organize the message	Prepare the first draft	Revise and proofread for accuracy and desired impact

you and your organization valuable time and resources and portray you as a capable, energetic professional. A thorough analysis of the audience and your specific communication assignment will empower you to write a first draft efficiently and to revise and proofread your message for accuracy, conciseness, and appropriate tone. You will focus on the planning process in this chapter, and then learn to prepare the message in Chapter 4.

1 OBJECTIVE

Step 1: Determining the Purpose and Channel

If you are to speak or write effectively, you first must think through what you are trying to say and understand it thoroughly before you begin. Ask yourself why you are preparing the message and what you hope to accomplish. Is the purpose to get information, to answer a question, to accept an offer, to deny a request, to seek support for a product or idea? Condense the answers into a brief sentence that is the purpose for writing or the central idea of your message. You will use the central idea to organize your message to achieve the results you desire.

The major purpose of many business messages is to have the receiver understand logical information. Informative messages are used to convey the vast amounts of information needed to complete the day-to-day operations of the business—explain instructions to employees, announce meetings and procedures, acknowledge orders, accept contracts for services, and so forth. Some messages are intended to persuade—to influence or change the attitudes or actions of the receiver. These messages include promoting a product or service and seeking support for ideas and worthy causes presented to supervisors, employees, stockholders, customers/clients, and others. You will learn to prepare messages for each of these purposes.

Identify the appropriate channel for (a) telling a customer a damaged product will be replaced, (b) notifying a worker of a layout, or (c) informing employees of a new policy.

With your purpose in mind, you can now select an appropriate channel that will increase the likelihood that the receiver will understand and accept your message. Recall the varying degree of efficiency and effectiveness of each of the typical communication channels discussed in Chapter 1. Follow the guidelines in Figure 3-2 for selecting a communication channel that is most appropriate depending on the nature and location of the audience, formality and content of the message, and the need for feedback, written record, or privacy.

2 OBJECTIVE

Step 2: Envisioning the Audience

Perception is the part of the communication process that involves how we look at others and the world around us. It's a natural tendency to perceive situations from our own limited viewpoint. We use the context of the situation and our five senses to absorb and interpret the information bombarding us in unique ways.

What is your favorite visual illusion? Why?

Individual differences in perception account for the varied and sometimes conflicting reports given by eyewitnesses to the same accident. A popular television series focuses on Adrian Monk, the "defective" detective who can see things that scores of trained

FIGURE 3-2

Selecting an Appropriate Communication Channel

CHANNEL	RECOMMENDED USE
TWO-WAY, FACE-TO-FACE	
In-person	Communicate an unpleasant or highly emotional message that may be subject to misinterpretation, a persuasive message, follow-up to a complex written message, or a personal message.
Traditional group meeting	Provide an optimal communication environment for discussing and reaching consensus on critical issues.
Video or teleconference	Provide an optimal communication environment for discussing and reaching a consensus on critical issues when members are geographically dispersed.
TWO-WAY, NOT FACE-TO-FACE	
Phone call	Deliver or obtain pleasant or routine information instantly.
Voice mail message	Leave message the receiver can reply to when convenient, eliminating telephone tag.
Text messaging	Give immediate access to short, important messages that can be retrieved discreetly between events or detailed information that can be sent accurately and easily.
ONE-WAY, NOT FACE-TO-FACE	
Letter or memorandum	Deliver written record of information, procedures, or policy, internally or externally.
Report or proposal	Communicate complex or lengthy information.
Electronic mail or instant messaging	Deliver message to a colleague or a large, dispersed audience; inappropriate for personal, confidential, or highly sensitive messages because of privacy issues.
Web page, blog, or wiki	Engage in a free-flowing dialog that ensures timely distribution and capture of knowledge about a topic of interest.

police workers cannot see although they've all been looking at the same crime scene. Illusions can help us understand how our senses can be tricked when there is a difference in what we expect and what really is happening. Search the Internet for optical illusions. How does your perception affect your ability to interpret the image accurately or completely?

Perception of reality is also limited by previous experiences and our attitudes toward the sender of the message. We filter messages through our own frames of reference and tend to see only the things that we want to see. We support ideas that are in line with our own and decide whether to focus on the positive or the negative of a situation. We may simply refuse to hear a message that doesn't fit into our view of the world.

Much of the confusion in communication is caused by differences in the sender's and receiver's perceptions. For example, team members may clash when some members perceive the task to be of greater importance than do other people involved in the work. A manager's brief email requesting a status report on a task may come across as curt to the co-worker. Perceptions vary between individuals with similar backgrounds, and even more so when people from different cultures, generations, and genders communicate. You'll explore these communication challenges in later Strategic Forces features.

Overcoming perceptual barriers is difficult but essential if you are to craft messages that meet the needs and concerns of your audience. To help you envision the audience, first focus on relevant information you know about the receiver. The more familiar you are with the receiver, the easier this task will be. When communicating with an individual, you immediately recall a clear picture of the receiver—his or her physical appearance, background (education, occupation, religion, culture), values, opinions, preferences, and so on. Most importantly, your knowledge of the receiver's reaction in similar, previous experiences will aid you in anticipating how this receiver is likely to react in the current situation. Consider the following audience characteristics:

- **Age.** A message answering an elementary-school student's request for information from your company would not be worded the same as a message answering a similar request from an adult.
- **Economic level.** A solicitation for a business donation for a charity project written to a small business owner would likely differ from one written to a representative of a major corporation.
- **Educational/occupational background.** The technical jargon and acronyms used in a financial proposal sent to bank loan officers may be inappropriate in a proposal sent to a group of private investors.
- **Needs and concerns of the receiver.** Just as successful sales personnel begin by identifying the needs of the prospective buyer, an effective manager attempts to understand the receiver's frame of reference as a basis for organizing the message and developing the content.

What other information about your receiver might help to shape your message?

- **Culture.** The vast cultural differences between people (language, expressions, customs, values, religions) increase the complexity of the communication process. An email containing typical American expressions (e.g., "The frustration should *cool down* soon," "the company is *in too deep* to *pull out now*," and "*the competition is backed to the wall*") would likely confuse a manager from a different culture.

Differences in values influence communication styles and message patterns. For example, Japanese readers value the beauty and flow of words and prefer an indirect writing approach, unlike Americans who prefer clarity and conciseness.[5] This chapter's Electronic Café and the Holistic Assessment Case allow you to explore one of the greatest challenges related to international commerce—the ability to prepare clear, accurate translations into numerous languages.

- **Rapport.** A sensitive message prepared for a long-time client may differ significantly from a message prepared for a newly acquired client. Emails discussing expectations for completing an assignment may be briefer and more direct when sent to an employee with whom you share a strong business relationship built on mutual trust. The rapport created by previous dealings with the recipient aids understanding in a current situation.
- **Expectations.** Because accountants, lawyers, and other professionals are expected to meet high standards, a message from one of them containing errors in grammar or spelling would likely cause a receiver to question the credibility of the source.

In communicating with someone of another culture, how can we effectively focus on similarities while being aware of differences?

You may find that envisioning an audience you know well is often such a conscious action that you may not even recognize that you are doing it. On the other hand, envisioning those you do not know well requires additional effort. In these cases, simply assume an empathetic attitude toward the receiver to assist you in identifying his or her frame of reference (knowledge, feelings, and emotions). In other words, project mentally how you believe you would feel or react in a similar situation and use that information to communicate understanding back to the person.

Consider the use (or lack) of empathy in the following workplace examples:

SAMPLE MESSAGE	PROBLEM ANALYSIS
Example 1: A U.S. manager's instructions to a new employee from an Asian culture: Trying to manufacture a product with a zero failure rate would be a train wreck. We have to strike the right balance between customer safety and cost efficiency. We cannot be held hostage by threats of class action lawsuits. Do you understand?	• The use of acronyms and expressions peculiar to U.S. environment confuse and intimidate. • Open-ended question disregards importance of saving face to a person of Asian culture. Cultural influences may prevent employee from asking questions that might indicate lack of understanding.

SAMPLE MESSAGE	PROBLEM ANALYSIS
Example 2: An excerpt from a message sent to Mr. Sandy Everret:	
Ms. Everett: The wireless iPod kit that you expressed an interest in is now available in at your local car dealer. This innovative Bluetooth technology can be demonstrated at your convience. Please call you local sales representative to schedule a appointment.	• Misspelling receiver's name, misinterpreting gender, and overlooking mechanical errors imply incompetence or carelessness and disrespect for receiver. • Omission of contact information reduces writer's credibility and shows lack of genuine concern for sender's needs.

Taking the time and effort to obtain a strong mental picture of your audience through firsthand knowledge or your empathetic attitude *before* you write will enhance your message in the following ways:

1. **Establishes rapport and credibility needed to build long-lasting personal and business relationships.** Your receivers will appreciate your attempt to connect and understand their feelings. A likely outcome is mutual trust, which can greatly improve communication and people's feelings about you, your ideas, and themselves (as shown in the discussion of the Johari Window in Chapter 2).
2. **Permits you to address the receiver's needs and concerns.** Such knowledge allows you to select relevant content and to communicate in a suitable style.

A Soft Answer Turns Away Wrath. Contestants on the American Idol television show must accept the judges' pointed criticism gracefully, even when it is seemingly malicious. Various business organizations have found that an effective response to criticism can sometimes be a positively focused reply rather than a forceful rebuttal. Responding to a stock analyst's negative comments about CEC Entertainment's stock price, Chuck E. Cheese, the company's large rodent icon, crafted a lighthearted response focusing on the company's fun-loving slogan, "Where a Kid Can Be a Kid!" Read Chuck E.'s letter available at your companion website, www.cengage.com/bcomm/lehman, and consider how the tone of the letter affected the overall impact of the message and the company's public relations efforts.

© AP IMAGES/PRNEWSFOTO/CEC ENTERTAINMENT INC.

3. **Simplifies the task of organizing your message.** From your knowledge of yourself and from your experiences with others, you can reasonably predict receivers' reactions to various types of messages. To illustrate, ask yourself these questions:

   - Would I react favorably to a message saying my request is being granted or that a new client is genuinely pleased with a job I'd just completed?
   - Would I experience a feeling of disappointment when I learn that my request has been refused or that my promised pay raise is being postponed?
   - Would I need compelling arguments to convince me to purchase a new product or support a new company policy or an employer's latest suggestion for improvement?

Now, reread the questions as though you were the message recipient. Because you know *your* answers, you can predict *others*' answers with some degree of accuracy. Such predictions are possible because of commonality in human behavior.

DIVERSITY CHALLENGES

Your commitment to identifying the needs and concerns of your audience before you communicate is invaluable in today's workplace. Organizations must focus on providing quality customer service and developing work environments supportive of talented, diverse workers. Alienating valuable customers and talented employees as a result of poor audience analysis is not an option in today's competitive environment. Empathy is also central to handling the challenges of communicating across the generations, as you'll learn in the accompanying Strategic Forces feature "Becoming Generationally Savvy."

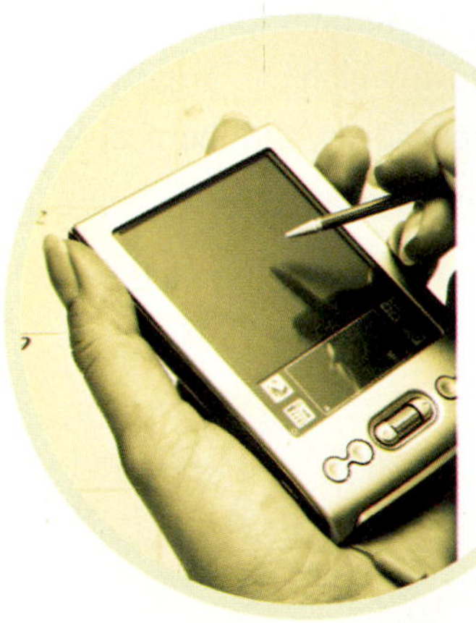

Your Turn 3-1
Electronic Café

TRANSLATION CHALLENGES

When traveling abroad, Americans expect—and in fact depend on—the people in the countries they visit to speak English. Often much gets mangled in the translations. In Budapest, Hungary, for example, a sign outside a hotel elevator reports: "The lift is being fixed for the next day. During that time we regret that you will be unbearable." A Bangkok, Thailand, dry cleaning establishment urges customers to "drop your trousers here for best results."[8] While humorous, such butchered translations illustrate a serious problem: The United States remains dependent on others to know the English language. We are linguistically underdeveloped when compared with other nations.

TAKE ACTION:

- *Read about the need for over-the-phone interpreters.* Read about how insurance companies meet the translation needs of their diverse clientele. Search for the following article:

  Chordas, L. (2005, February). *Ending the global disconnect: Over-the-phone interpreters help insurers bridge the gap.* Best's Review. Available from Business Source Complete database.

STRATEGIC FORCES

Becoming Generationally Savvy

Age diversity is a reality in the workforce, and the span increases as younger workers enter the workplace and older workers choose to work longer or re-enter the job market due to good health and dwindling retirement savings. Nearly three out of five U.S. workers age 50 or older plan to work elsewhere after retiring from their current job. Losing their seniority when they retire, these workers will be in direct competition with candidates their children's ages.[6] Companies committed to innovative team-based systems face the challenge of fostering teamwork between four generations whose ages span more than 60 years.

© ISTOCKPHOTO.COM/CARMEN MARTINEZ BANUS

- **Matures or seniors.** Americans over 65 years of age make up about 10% of the workforce. Their survival of hard times caused them to value hard work, sacrifice, and a strong sense of right and wrong. Many plan to re-enter the job market after retirement or stay there for the long haul.
- **Baby boomers.** Boomers account for about 45% of the workforce and are referred to as the "Me" generation because they grew up in boom times following World War II, indulged and encouraged by their parents to believe their opportunities were limitless. They will work longer than their parents because of greater financial strain and a limited retirement budget.
- **Generation Xers.** Born in the 1960s and '70s, the "latchkey" kids are fiercely independent, self-directed, and resourceful. As a whole, they are skeptical of authority and institutions because they entered the workforce in a time of downsizing and cutbacks.
- **Millennials (also called Generation Yers).** The children and grandchildren of the boomers are the "young folks" of the workforce. Millennials are technologically savvy, active, and visually oriented due to their lifetime experience in a high-tech world. They perceive work as a chance to develop their personal skills portfolios. Publicized corporate scandals have taught them to be more concerned about themselves than their employer.[7]

Studies indicate that concerns over generational conflict are often unfounded. For instance, boomer resistance to Generation X might be based on an assumption that the casual attitude of Gen Xers indicates that they are slackers. Experience, however, has revealed the group's positive characteristics. When properly managed, companies with a strong mix of older and younger workers have a distinct competitive edge. Younger workers bring new ideas, a broad range of technology skills, and an eagerness to adopt new ideas; older workers bring a strong work ethic, experience, and institutional memory. Getting these workers to work together requires effective communication, an appreciation for the value of diversity, and patience in learning new ways of interacting with vastly talented, yet differing generations. Visit your companion website, www.cengage.com/bcomm/lehman, to learn about ways to gain generational competence critical for career success in today's age-diverse workplace.

Application

1. **Interview a person from a generation other than your own. Assist him/her in identifying the generation to which he/she belongs. Include the following questions in your interview:**
   - Considering your own experiences with supervisors and coworkers, what type of management styles and communication patterns do you find to be most effective?
   - What guidelines can you offer to managers of older (or younger) generations for communicating successfully with persons of your generation?
2. **Based on interviews and your own reading, develop a list of organizational guidelines for communicating most effectively with persons from the interviewee's generation.**

Write a 100-word abstract of the article, reflecting the important ideas presented.

- *Practice your language translation.* Go to your companion website, www.cengage.com/bcomm/lehman, for the Chapter 3 Electronic Café that provides more information and activities related to translating from English to other languages.

Step 3: Adapting the Message to the Audience

After you have envisioned your audience, you are ready to adapt your message to fit the specific needs of your audience. Adaptations include focusing on the receiver's point of view; communicating ethically and responsibly; building and protecting goodwill; using simple, contemporary language; writing concisely; and projecting a positive, tactful tone.

Focus on the Receiver's Point of View

Ideas are more interesting and appealing if they are expressed from the receiver's viewpoint. Developing a "you attitude" rather than a "me attitude" involves thinking in terms of the other person's interests and trying to see a problem from the other's point of view. A letter, memo, email, or phone call reflecting a "you attitude" sends a direct signal of sincere concern for the receiver's needs and interest.

The use of the word *you* (appropriately used) conveys to receivers a feeling that messages are specifically for them. However, if the first-person pronoun *I* is used frequently, especially as the subject, the sender may impress others as being self-centered—always talking about self. Compare the following examples of sender-centered and receiver-centered statements:

"I"- OR SENDER-CENTERED	"YOU"- OR RECEIVER-CENTERED
I want to take this opportunity to offer my congratulations on your recent promotion to regional manager	• Congratulations on your recent promotion to regional manager.
We charge customers a 12 percent annual finance charge on past due invoices.	• Customers pay a 12 percent annual finance charge only on past due invoices. (*You* could be the subject in a message to a customer.)

Compliments (words of deserved praise) are another effective way of increasing a receiver's receptiveness to ideas that follow. Give sincere compliments judiciously as they can do more harm than good if paid at the wrong time, in the wrong setting, in the presence of the wrong people, or for the wrong reasons. Likewise, avoid flattery (words of undeserved praise). Although the recipient may accept your flattery as a sincere compliment, chances are the recipient will interpret your undeserved praise as an attempt to seek to gain favor or special attention. Suspicion of your motive makes effective communication less likely.

To cultivate a "you attitude," concentrate on the following questions:

- Does the message address the receiver's major needs and concerns?
- Would the receiver feel this message is receiver-centered? Is the receiver kept clearly in the picture?
- Will the receiver perceive the ideas to be fair, logical, and ethical?
- Are ideas expressed clearly and concisely (to avoid lost time, money, and possible embarrassment caused when messages are misunderstood)?
- Does the message promote positive business relationships—even when the message is negative? For example, are *please*, *thank you*, and other courtesies used when appropriate? Are ideas stated tactfully and positively and in a manner that preserves the receiver's self-worth and cultivates future business?
- Is the message sent promptly and through the preferred channel to indicate courtesy?
- Does the message reflect the high standards of a business professional: accurate and appealing document design, quality printing, and absence of misspellings and grammatical errors?

Concentrating on these points will boost the receiver's confidence in the sender's competence and will communicate nonverbally that the receiver is valued enough to merit your best effort. For people who practice courtesy and consideration, the "you attitude" is easy to incorporate into written and spoken messages.

Communicate Ethically and Responsibly

The familiar directive "with power comes responsibility" applies especially to your use of communication skills. Because business communication affects the lives of many, you must accept responsibility for using it to uphold your own personal values and your company's standards of ethical conduct. Before speaking or writing, use the following guidelines to help you communicate ethically and responsibly.

- **Is the information stated as truthfully, honestly, and fairly as possible?** Good communicators recognize that ensuring a free flow of essential information is in the interest of the public and the organization. The Spotlight Communicator from Hallmark shares the positive effect open, timely internal communication has had on the company's financial performance and its relationship with employees. On the other hand, Merck, the manufacturer of the prescription pain reliever Vioxx, was sued by thousands of patients and patients' families for withholding information about known heart risks associated with taking the drug.[9] Similarly, failure to report the nature of his investment practices led to the arrest of the accountant of Bernard Madoff, the man who admittedly cheated thousands of investors out of billions of dollars in an illegal scheme. The SEC has accused Madoff's accountant, David Friehling, of lying to the American Institute of Certified Public Accountants rather than subject his audit work to peer review.[10] Your honor, honesty, and credibility will build strong, long-lasting relationships and lead to the long-term success of your

© AP PHOTO/LOUIS LANZANO

SPOTLIGHT COMMUNICATOR: DEAN RODENBOUGH, DIRECTOR OF CORPORATE COMMUNICATIONS, HALLMARK CARDS

Openness a "Hallmark" at Hallmark Cards, Inc.

Hallmark's private ownership and a highly competitive retail and intellectual property environment had led to a culture in which senior management had traditionally shared little with employees in terms of company finances, business plans, and market challenges. Management's guarded approach to communication had resulted in declining trust levels among employees. Director of Corporate Communications, Dean Rodenbough, directed an extensive communications audit that led to the establishment of a much more open atmosphere for the exchange of ideas and information throughout the company. Read more at your companion website www.cengage.com/bcomm/lehman, about what Hallmark learned from the communication audit and how internal communication was improved.

www.hallmark.com

company. Sending complete, accurate, and timely information regardless of whether it supports your interests will help you build credibility.

Were you ever the recipient of an unethical business practice? Describe the incident, your feelings, and the outcome.

- **Does the message embellish or exaggerate the facts?** Legal guidelines related to advertising provide clear guidance for avoiding *fraud*, the misrepresentation of products or services; however, overzealous sales representatives or imaginative writers can use language skillfully to create less-than-accurate perceptions in the minds of receivers. Businesses have learned the hard way that overstating the capabilities of a product or service (promising more than can be delivered) is not good for business in the long run. Researchers are at times tempted to overstate their findings to ensure continued funding or greater publicity. Eric T. Peohlman, a medical researcher, acknowledged that while at the University of Vermont he fabricated data in 17 applications for federal grants to make his work seem more promising. Under a plea agreement, he was barred for life from receiving federal funding and had to pay back $180,000, as well as asking scientific journals to retract and correct 10 articles he had authored.[11]

In small groups, discuss the ethics of inflating a résumé to increase the chances of getting a job interview.

While surveys indicate many job seekers believe companies expect résumé padding, companies repeatedly report that this perception is not true. Marilee Jones, dean of admissions at Massachusetts Institute of Technology, and David Edmonson, the former CEO of Radio Shack, resigned high-profile jobs for misstating their academic records. George O'Leary stepped down five days after been named head football coach at Notre Dame, admitting he lied about receiving a master's degree and playing college football.[12]

Skill in communicating persuasively will be important throughout your profession. The techniques you will read about in this text, such as those related to writing a winning résumé and application message, will be helpful as you begin your career; however, these techniques should *not* be used if your motive is to exploit the receiver.

- **Are the ideas expressed clearly and understandably?** If a message is to be seen as honest, you must be reasonably confident that the receiver can understand it. Ethical communicators select words that convey the exact meaning intended and that are within the reader's vocabulary. Consider a plumber's frustration with the following message from the Bureau of Standards: "The effect of HCL is incompatible with the metallic piping" and "We cannot assume responsibility for the production of toxic and noxious residues with HCL." Finally the Bureau sent a message the plumber could understand: "Don't use HCL. It eats the heck out of pipes!"[13] To protect consumers, some states have passed "Plain English" laws that require certain businesses and agencies to write policies, warranties, and contracts in language an average reader can understand. You can learn more about the importance of Plain English laws by completing the Holistic Assessment Case in Chapter 4.

How bound is a business professional to "tell the truth, the whole truth, and nothing but the truth"?

- **Is your viewpoint supported with objective facts?** Are facts accurately documented to allow the reader to judge the credibility of the source and to give credit where credit is due? Can opinions be clearly distinguished from facts? Have you evaluated honestly any real or perceived conflict of interest that could prevent you from preparing an unbiased message? You will learn to develop objective, well-documented written reports and presentations in Chapters 9–12.

- **Are ideas stated with tact and consideration that preserves the receiver's self-worth?** The metaphor, "An arrow, once it is shot, cannot be recalled," describes the irrevocable damage caused by cruel or unkind words.[14] Ego-destroying criticism, excessive anger, sarcasm, hurtful nicknames, betrayed secrets, rumors, and malicious goss[illegible]e serious ethical problems in the workplace because they can ruin reputat[illegible]iliate, and damage a person's self-worth. Serious legal issues arise when n[illegible]atements are false, constituting defamation. Written defamatory remark[illegible]red to as ***libel***, and similar spoken remarks are referred to as ***slander***. If you c[illegible]make negative statements about a person, be sure the facts in question are supp[illegible]ditionally, you'll hone your abilities to convey negative information and to h[illegible]sitive situations in a constructive, timely manner rather than ignoring them un[illegible]t out of control. For considerate, fair, and civilized use of words, follow this [illegible]e: Communicate with and about others with the same kindness and fairness t[illegible]ish others to use when communicating with and about you.

- **Are graphics carefully designed to avoid distorting facts and relationships?** Communicating ethically involves reporting data as clearly and accurately as possible. Misleading graphics result either from the developers' deliberate attempt to confuse the audience or from their lack of expertise in constructing ethical graphics. You will study the principles of creating graphics that show information accurately and honestly in a Strategic Forces feature in Chapter 10.

Build and Protect Goodwill

Goodwill arises when a business is worth more than its tangible assets. Things such as a good name and reputation, a desirable location, a unique product, and excellent customer service, can assure earnings, and so the business has more value than simply its tangible assets. Businesses go to great lengths to build and protect goodwill and thus their future. It is no surprise that effective communication is a key strategy.

Insensitive messages—whether directed to customers, employees, or business partners—can offend and alienate and will diminish a company's goodwill. Most of us don't intend to be insensitive but simply may not think carefully about the impact the tone of our words may have on others. ***Tone*** is the way a statement sounds and conveys the writer's or speaker's attitude toward the message and the receiver. To build and protect your company's goodwill, eliminate words that are overly euphemistic, condescending, demeaning, and biased.

Use Euphemisms Cautiously

In groups, identify two more euphemisms you have heard recently. Do you believe their use is acceptable?

A ***euphemism*** is a kind word substituted for one that may offend or suggest something unpleasant. For example, the idea of picking up neighborhood garbage does not sound especially inviting. Someone who does such work is often referred to as a *sanitation worker*. This term has a more pleasant connotation than *garbage collector*.

Choose the euphemistic terms rather than the negative terms shown in the following examples:

NEGATIVE TONE	EUPHEMISTIC TONE
aged or elderly	senior citizen
dying	fading away/near the end
used or secondhand	pre-owned
prison	correctional facility
disabled/handicapped	physically challenged/differently abled
patient management	care coordination/supportive services

Effective communicators use clear, jargon-free language that can be easily understood by non-native readers and can be easily translated.

Using euphemisms that ridicule or mislead the recipient can undermine your trust and credibility.

Generally, you can recognize such expressions for what they are—unpleasant ideas presented with a little sugar coating. Knowing the sender was simply trying to be polite and positive, you are more likely to react favorably. You should avoid, however, euphemisms that excessively sugarcoat and those that suggest subtle sarcasm. For example, to refer to a janitor as a *maintenance engineer* is to risk conveying a negative metacommunication, such as "This person does not hold a very respectable position, but I did the best I could to make it sound good." To the receiver (and to the janitor), just plain *janitor* would sound better.

LEGAL AND ETHICAL CONSTRAINTS

You will also want to avoid ***doublespeak***, also known as doubletalk or ***corporate speak***. Such terms refer to euphemisms that deliberately mislead, hide, or evade the truth. This distortion of the truth is often found in military, political, and corporate language. A loss of credibility and respect results when a police officer refers to "nontraditional organized crime" rather than gang activity or a military spokesperson or politician talks of "enhanced interrogation technique" rather than "torture," or "collateral damage" or "friendly fire" rather than civilians killed accidentally by the military's own weapons. Companies use doublespeak when they make "workforce reductions" or offer workers a "career opportunity adjustment" or "voluntary termination." One company called the permanent shutdown of a steel plant an "indefinite idling" in an attempt to avoid paying severance or pension benefits to the displaced workers.[15]

Despite your training in writing, you may fall in the trap of mirroring the writing of people above you on the career ladder who prefer writing in doublespeak. They choose doublespeak over clear, concise writing because of the misguided belief that doublespeak makes them sound informed and professional. Such vagueness protects them when they're unsure how their messages will be received and makes writing easy once they

© ANDRE JENNY/IMAGESTATE/JUPITERIMAGES

Doublespeak Has a High Price. **Doublespeak**, or **doubletalk**, is language that disguises or distorts actual meaning. Doublespeak can result in partial understanding or confusion. At times intentional, it may take the form of euphemisms (e.g., "downsizing" for layoffs) or deliberate ambiguity intended to mislead. In other instances it is an unintentional result of poor communication. A sobering example of business doublespeak occurred in a paragraph-long memo that was thrown aside because the standard buzzwords filling the memo led the manager to believe it was unimportant. The memo, sent to the engineering operating staff at the nuclear power plant at Three Mile Island two weeks before a major accident occurred, warned of exactly the things that went wrong. The cost of doublespeak in internal communication is estimated at $3 billion annually.[16]

learn the code. Instead of falling into doublespeak, learn to develop clear, concise messages that clarify ideas and provide direction to recipients regardless of their culture while enhancing your credibility as an honest communicator. A CEO of a writing training company has another interesting angle on clear writing. He contends that "articulation of thought is an element of intelligence, and you can increase your intelligence through writing." Working to articulate ideas clearly and logically through writing makes people smarter![17] That is a motivating reason for perfecting writing (and speaking) skills in our professional and personal lives.

Your Turn 3-2
You're the Professional

Doublespeak usage occurs in all professional groups. Provide straightforward translations for the following doublespeak words and phrases:

- aerial ordinance
- detainee
- ethnic cleansing
- person of interest
- regime change
- rightsize
- take down
- vertically deployed anti-personnel devices

TAKE ACTION:

Check your translations of the listed doublespeak terms and read other examples of doublespeak at the following website: www.sourcewatch.org/wiki.phtml?title=Doublespeak. You may link to this URL or other updated sites from your companion website, www.cengage.com/bcomm/lehman.

Avoid Condescending or Demeaning Expressions

Condescending words seem to imply that the communicator is temporarily coming down from a level of superiority to join the receiver on a level of inferiority; such words damage efforts to build and protect goodwill. Note how the reminders of inequality in the following examples hamper communication:

Ineffective Example 

Since I took a leadership role in this project, the team's performance has improved.
You were not selected, as we are looking for a candidate with exceptional skills.

A demeaning expression (sometimes called a *dysphemism*) makes an idea seem negative or disrespectful. Avoid demeaning expressions because they divert attention from the real message to emotional issues that have little to do with the message.

Many examples can be taken as contempt for an occupation or a specific job/position ("bean counters" for accountants, "ambulance chasers" for lawyers, "spin doctors" for politicians or public relations directors, and "shrinks" for psychiatrists). Like words that attack races or nationalities, words that ridicule occupations work against a communicator's purpose.

Many demeaning expressions are common across regions, ages, and perhaps even cultures. Some demeaning expressions belong to a particular company; for example, "turtles" was coined in one firm to mock first-year employees for their slow work pace. President Obama quickly recognized and apologized for his late-night talk show quip that equated his bowling skills to those of athletes with disabilities. Seeing the president's gaffe as a "teachable moment" for the country, Special Olympics Chairman Tim Shriver emphasized that "words hurt and words do matter and these words that in some respect can be seen as humiliating . . . do cause pain."[18] Effective communicators choose respectful expressions that build and protect goodwill.

DIVERSITY CHALLENGES

© AP PHOTO/GERALD HERBERT

Use Connotative Tone Cautiously

Human relations can suffer when connotative words are inadvertently or intentionally used instead of denotative words. The ***denotative meaning*** of a word is the literal

Positive Words, Negative Words. A **dysphemism** is a harsh word or demeaning expression used instead of a neutral or polite term. Dysphemisms are rough opposites of euphemisms. A dysphemism may be blatantly offensive or humorously negative. Examples of dysphemisms include "a bald-faced lie" for an inaccurate statement and "dead tree edition" for the paper version of an online magazine. In pitching a robust software program, a sales representative mistakenly referred to his product as "no Mickey Mouse" system. The cost to him was one very large account—Walt Disney Studios. Oddly, some humorous expressions can be either euphemistic or dysphemic, depending on context, because some dysphemic terms also can be affectionate. For example, *pushing up daisies* can be taken as either softer or harsher than *died*. Such variance also can be cultural; for instance, to Americans "twit" is a dysphemism for "idiot," but in British English it is nearly always a humorous or affectionate term.[19]

© AP PHOTO/DISNEY, KENT PHILLIPS

meaning that most people assign to it. The ***connotative meaning*** is the literal meaning plus an extra message that reveals the speaker's or writer's qualitative judgment, as shown in this example:

CONNOTATIVE MEANING WITH NEGATIVE IMPLICATION	DENOTATIVE MEANING (PREFERRED)
The production manager harped on the new quality assurance regulations for nearly an hour.	The production manager discussed the new quality assurance regulations for nearly an hour.

What connotative messages are conveyed by the terms "chick flick" and "drama queen"? What terms would convey the denotative meaning?

The connotative meaning of "harped on" carries an additional message that the writer has a bias against quality assurance regulations. The connotation may needlessly introduce thoughts about whether regulations are beneficial and distract the receiver from paying sufficient attention to statements that follow. Connotations, like metacommunications discussed in Chapter 2, involve messages that are implied. In the preceding example, the connotation seems to be more harmful than helpful.

At times, however, connotations can be helpful, as seen in the following examples:

CONNOTATIVE MEANING WITH POSITIVE MEANING (PREFERRED)	DENOTATIVE MEANING
Our corporate think tank has developed an outstanding production process.	Research and Development has developed an outstanding production process.
Julia's likable personality makes her a miracle worker at contract negotiation.	Julia's likable personality is beneficial in contract negotiation.

In crafting business messages, rely mainly on denotative or connotative words that will be interpreted in a positive manner. To be sure that your connotative words are understood and will generate goodwill, consider your audience, the context, and the timing of the message.

- **Connotative words may be more easily misinterpreted than denotative words.** Because of differences in peoples' perceptions based on their life experiences, words that are perceived positively by one person may be perceived negatively by another. In some cases, receivers may simply not understand the connotative words. Damaged human relations occur when managers repeatedly convey connotative messages without considering whether employees can interpret the meanings as they are intended.
- **The appropriateness of connotations varies with the audience to which they are addressed and the context in which they appear.** For example, referring

to a car as a "foreign job" or "sweet" might be received differently by teenagers than by senior citizens. Such expressions are less appropriate in a research report than in a blog or popular magazine.

Use Specific Language Appropriately

To help the receiver understand your message easily, select words that paint intense, colorful word pictures. Creating clear mental images adds energy and imagination to your message, thus increasing its overall impact.

GENERAL	SPECIFIC (PREFERRED)
Congratulations on your <u>recent honor</u>.	Congratulations on being named <u>employee of the month</u>.
Complete the report <u>as soon as possible</u>.	Complete the report <u>by May 2</u>.
The stock price <u>plummeted</u> after management's announcement.	The stock price <u>fell 10 percent</u> after management's announcement.

Sometimes, using general statements can be useful in building and protecting goodwill. General words keep negative ideas from receiving more emphasis than they deserve. In addition, senders who don't have specific information or for some reason don't want to divulge it use general words.

GENERAL (PREFERRED)	SPECIFIC
Thank you for the explanation of your <u>financial status</u>.	Thank you for informing me of your <u>problems with your creditors and the possibility of filing bankruptcy</u>.
Greg told me about <u>what happened last week</u>.	Greg told me about the <u>tragedy in your family</u>.

Use Bias-Free Language

Being responsive to individual differences requires you to make a conscious effort to use bias-free (nondiscriminatory) language. Using language that does not exclude, stereotype, or offend others permits them to focus on your message rather than to question your

How can a sensitive communicator assure the use of bias-free language?

sensitivity. Goodwill can be damaged when biased statements are made related to gender, race or ethnicity, religion, age, or disability.

Avoid Gender Bias. The following guidelines will help you avoid gender bias:

1. **Avoid referring to men and women in stereotyped roles and occupations.** The use of *he* to refer to anyone in a group was once standard and accepted; however, this usage is considered insensitive and, to some, offensive. Therefore, do not use the pronoun *he* when referring to a person in a group that may include women or the pronoun *she* to refer to a group that may include men; otherwise you may unintentionally communicate an insensitive message that only women or only men can perform certain tasks or serve in certain professions. Follow these four approaches to avoid gender bias:

GUIDELINE	GENDER-BIASED	IMPROVED
Avoid using a pronoun:	Each employee must complete <u>his</u> online health assessment.	Employees must complete an online health assessment.
Repeat the noun:	the courtesy of your guide. Ask <u>him</u> to . . .	the courtesy of your <u>guide</u>. Ask the <u>guide</u> to . . .
Use a plural noun:	A nurse must complete <u>her</u> in-service training to update <u>her</u> certification.	Nurses must complete in service training to update <u>their</u> certification.
Use pronouns from both genders (when necessary, but not repeatedly):	Just call the manager. <u>He</u> will in turn . . .	Just call the manager. <u>He or she</u> will in turn . . .

Revise to avoid gender bias: "Managers and their wives are invited to this event."

2. **Use occupational titles that reflect genuine sensitivity to gender.** Note the gender-free titles that can be easily substituted to avoid bias:

GENDER-BIASED	GENDER-FREE
foreman	supervisor
working mother	working parent

3. **Avoid designating an occupation by gender.** For example, omit "woman" in "A woman doctor has initiated this research." The doctor's profession, not the gender, is the point of the message. Similarly, avoid using the *-ess* ending to differentiate genders in an occupation:

GENDER-BIASED	GENDER-FREE
waiter or waitress	server
hostess	host

4. **Avoid using expressions that may be perceived to be gender-biased.** Avoid commonly used expressions in which "man" represents all humanity, such as "To go where no man has gone before," and stereotypical characteristics, such as "man hours," "man-made goods," and "work of four strong men." Note the improvements made in the following examples by eliminating the potentially offensive words.

GENDER-BIASED	IMPROVED
Preparing the proposal was a <u>man-sized</u> task.	Preparing the proposal was an <u>enormous</u> task.
Luke is the best <u>man</u> for the job.	Luke is the best <u>person</u> for the job.

What actions are companies taking to raise employee awareness of diversity issues?

5. **Avoid Racial or Ethnic Bias.** Include racial or ethnic identification only when relevant and avoid referring to these groups in stereotypical ways.

RACIALLY OR ETHNICALLY BIASED	IMPROVED
Assign the task to Alfonso Perez, the <u>Japanese</u> clerk in Payroll.	Assign the task to Alfonso Perez, the clerk in Payroll.
Dan's <u>Irish</u> temper flared today.	Dan's temper flared today.
The articulate <u>African American</u> engineer overseeing the product redesign plans suggested . . .	The engineer overseeing the product redesign plans suggested . . .

6. **Avoid Age Bias.** Include age only when relevant and avoid demeaning expressions related to age.

AGE-BIASED	IMPROVED
Bryan Paxton, the 55-year-old president of Glyn Bank, has resigned.	Bryan Paxton, president of Glyn Bank, has resigned.

Give examples of words and phrases that can be used to avoid race, ethnicity, or disability bias.

7. **Avoid Disability Bias.** When communicating about people with disabilities, use people-first language. That is, refer to the person first and the disability second so that focus is appropriately placed on the person's ability rather than on the disability. Also avoid words with negative or judgmental connotations, such as *handicap*, *unfortunate*, *afflicted*, and *victim*. When describing people without disabilities, use the word *typical* rather than *normal*; otherwise you may inadvertently imply that people with disabilities are abnormal. Consider these more sensitive revisions:

INSENSITIVE	SENSITIVE (PEOPLE-FIRST)
Blind employees receive . . .	Employees with vision impairments receive . . .
The elevator is for the exclusive use of handicapped employees and should not be used by normal employees.	The elevator is for the exclusive use of employees with disabilities.

Use Contemporary Language

Business messages should reflect correct, standard English and contemporary language used in a professional business setting. Outdated expressions, dull clichés, and profanity reduce the effectiveness of a message and the credibility of a communicator.

Eliminate Outdated Expressions

Using outdated expressions will give your message a dull, stuffy, unnatural tone. Instead, substitute fresh, original expressions that reflect today's language patterns.

OUTDATED EXPRESSIONS	IMPROVEMENT
Pursuant to your request, the physical inventory has been scheduled for May 3.	As you requested, the physical inventory has been scheduled for May 3.
Enclosed please find a copy of my transcript.	The enclosed transcript should answer your questions.
Very truly yours (used as the complimentary close in a letter)	Sincerely

The accompanying Strategic Forces feature "E-Cards Offer Greeting Alternatives" explores yet another challenge for contemporary communication, the effective use of e-cards as alternatives for traditional greetings.

Eliminate Clichés

At what point does a word become a cliché? Substitute original wording for "We were dealt a bad hand."

Clichés, overused expressions, are common in our everyday conversations and in business messages. These handy verbal shortcuts are convenient, quick, easy to use, and often include simple metaphors and analogies that effectively communicate the most basic idea or emotion or the most complex business concept. However, writers and speakers who routinely use stale clichés may be perceived as unoriginal, unimaginative, lazy, and perhaps even disrespectful. Less frequently used words capture the receiver's attention because they are original, fresh, and interesting.

CLICHÉ	IMPROVEMENT
Pushed (or stretched) the envelope	Took a risk or considered a new option
Skin in the game	Committed to the project
Cover all the bases	Get agreement/input from everyone
That sucks!	That's unacceptable/needs improvement

What clichés do your friends, instructors, or coworkers use? How do you feel when these expressions are used frequently?

Clichés present another serious problem. Consider the scenario of shoppers standing in line at a discount store with the cashier saying to each, *Thanks for shopping with us today; please come again*. Because the last shopper has heard the words several times already, he or she may not consider the statement genuine. The cashier has used an expression that can be stated without thinking and possibly without meaning. A worn expression can convey messages such as "You are not special" or "For you, I won't bother to think; the phrases I use in talking with others are surely good enough for you." Original expressions convey sincerity and build strong human relations.

STRATEGIC FORCES

E-Cards Offer Greeting Alternatives

They are fun and clever, and better yet, they arrive instantly. Electronic greeting cards are widely available on the Internet, many for free, and can be sent easily to individuals or groups.

Blue Mountain is the largest electronic greeting card site on the Web and has plenty of cards to choose from. Beginning as a free site, Blue Mountain now offers a free trial subscription with access to an extensive assortment of greetings. You can add music and pick from greetings that range from sentimental to businesslike or customize your message. Another feature is the ability to send cards in several languages—a real plus in a world that is becoming ever smaller.

© AP IMAGES/PRNEWSFOTO/SMILEBOX, INC.

Many card sites allow the sender to "attach" gifts; the Hallmark website allows customers to send free e-cards and include a gift certificate to one of nearly 300 merchants. Distinctiveness has led to the growing popularity of Regards.com. As with some other sites, you can use your own photos and images to create an original design or select one of its uniquely animated cards, some of which are so elaborate that they are like sending tiny cartoons.

Another site called My Fun Cards allows you to create a card in a simple, step-by-step process. You pick out illustrations, headlines, and colors, with the result being a card that you created yourself.[20]

Perfect Greetings is able to offer free card service because it is sustained by its business sponsors. To send a card, customers must click on one of three randomly generated ads and read about a business offering while their card processing is completed.

Of course, if you're really international, you should check out the Digital Postcard. A wide array of languages is available, including Arabic and Turkish, and cards can be customized from a database of more than 1,000 photos. You can also include a link to a web page with your card, as well as upload a music or voice file.

In response to worries about the network bandwidth that electronic greeting cards might consume, some sites sell compressed cards that load faster and take up fewer computer resources. Managers, however, are typically more concerned with lost worker productivity that may result as more workers access to the Internet for this purpose. Companies that offer digital greeting cards, however, maintain that these products have a place in business. For example, they can be used to inform clients of an office move or thank clients in a less costly, faster manner than with the traditional alternative of addressing and mailing company cards.

Application

Visit the following greeting card sites:

www.bluemountain.com

www.regards.com

www.myfuncards.com

www.perfectgreetings.com

www.hallmark.com

Rate the sites according to their suitability for sending business greetings. What considerations should be made when deciding whether to send an electronic greeting card rather than a traditional card or short typed message to a client or business associate?

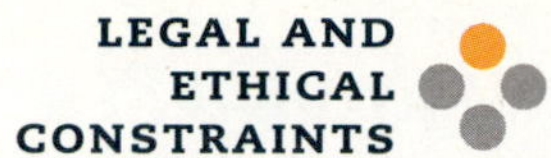

Curb Profanity

Increasing tolerance of profanity is an issue of concern to society as a whole and also for employers and employees as they communicate at work. You must consider the potential business liabilities and legal implications resulting from the use of profanity that may offend others or create a hostile work environment. Recognize that minimizing or eliminating profanity is another important way you must adapt your language for communicating effectively and fostering human relations in a professional setting.

Your Turn 3-3
Miscue

The use of profanity in the workplace can be seen not only as insensitive and offensive; it can also be interpreted as creating a hostile work environment, a legal offense, and eroding the civility of society. New York City reporter Arthur Chi'en was fired from his job as a WCBS-TV reporter for shouting profanities at hecklers. Thinking he was off the air following the completion of his report, he used strong language while the camera was still rolling. Although he apologized for his action, the station terminated him, citing the recent crackdown on obscenity by the Federal Communications Commission.[21]

TAKE ACTION:

In groups, discuss the answers to the following questions:

- What constitutes profanity?
- How have societal ideas changed concerning the use of profanity?
- How would your workplace likely respond to the use of profanity?

Use Simple, Informal Words

Business writers prefer simple, informal words that are readily understood and less distracting than more difficult, formal words. If a receiver questions the sender's motive for using formal words, the impact of the message may be diminished. Likewise, the impact would be diminished if the receiver questioned a sender's use of simple, informal words. That distraction is unlikely, however, if the message contains good ideas that are well organized and well supported. Under these conditions, simple words enable a receiver to understand the message clearly and quickly.

Simplify the message: "Management has become cognizant of the necessity of the elimination of undesirable vegetation surrounding the periphery of our facility."[23]

To illustrate, consider the unnecessary complexity of a notice that appeared on a corporate bulletin board: "Employees impacted by the strike are encouraged to utilize the hot line number to arrange for alternative transportation to work. Should you encounter difficulties in arranging for alternative transportation to work, please contact your immediate supervisor." A simple, easy-to-read revision would be, "If you can't get to work, call the hot line or your supervisor."[22] For further illustration, note the added clarity of the following words:

FORMAL WORDS	INFORMAL WORDS
terminate	end
procure	get
remunerate	pay
corroborate	support

DIVERSITY CHALLENGES

Using words that have more than two or three syllables when they are appropriate is acceptable. However, you should avoid regular use of a long, infrequently used word when a simpler, more common word conveys the same idea. Professionals in some fields often use specialized terminology, referred to as ***jargon***, when communicating with colleagues in the same field. In this case, the audience is likely to understand the words, and using the jargon saves time. However, when communicating with people outside the field, professionals should select simple, common words to convey messages. Using clear, jargon-free language that can be readily understood by non-native recipients and easily translated is especially important in international communication.

You should build your vocabulary so that you can use just the right word for expressing an idea and can understand what others have said. Just remember the purpose of business messages is not to advertise a knowledge of infrequently used words but to transmit a clear and tactful message. For the informal communication practiced in business, use simple words instead of more complicated words that have the same meaning.

Your Turn 3-4
Assessment

Having an extensive vocabulary at your disposal will aid you in choosing precise words for particular situations. Visit the College Board Vocabulary quizzing website at http://iteslj.org/v/e/jb-college.html. You may link to this URL or other updated sites from your companion website at www.cengage.com/bcomm/lehman

TAKE ACTION:

- Quiz yourself on the first 25 terms that are generated at the website. Write down the words for which you chose an incorrect definition.
- Provide email feedback to your instructor as to your percentage of correct responses and the words that gave you trouble.
- Continue to quiz on this website for the remainder of the course term, if directed by your instructor.

Communicate Concisely

What is the difference between conciseness and brevity?

Concise communication includes all relevant details in the fewest possible words. Abraham Lincoln's two-minute Gettysburg Address is a premier example of concise communication. Mark Twain alluded to the skill needed to write concisely when he said, "I would have written a shorter book if I had had time."

In groups, generate a list of wordy phrases you have heard. Describe ways to simplify ideas in writing and speaking.

Some executives have reported that they read memos that are two paragraphs long but may only skim or discard longer ones. Yet it's clear that this survival technique can lead to a vital message being discarded or misread. Concise writing is essential for information workers struggling to handle an avalanche of information that often is read on the run on a Blackberry or iPhone. Concise messages save time and money for both the sender and the receiver, as the receiver's attention is directed toward the important details and is not distracted by excessive words and details.

The following techniques will produce concise messages:

- **Eliminate redundancies.** A **redundancy** is a phrase in which one word unnecessarily repeats an idea contained in an accompanying word. "Absolutely necessary" and "negative misfortune" are redundant because both words have the same meaning; only "necessary" and "misfortune" are needed. A few of the many redundancies in business writing are shown in the following list. Be conscious of redundancies in your speech and writing patterns.

REDUNDANCIES TO AVOID

Needless repetition:	advance forward, it goes without saying, best ever, cash money, important essentials, each and every, dollar amount, pick and choose, past experience
Unneeded modifiers:	new innovations, personal friend, actual experience, brief summary, complete stop, collaborate together, disappear from sight, honest truth, trickle down, month of May, personal opinion, red in color, severe crisis, currently available
Repeated acronyms:	ATM machine, PIN number, SAT tests, SIC code

How can the effective communicator restate without being redundant?

Redundancy is not to be confused with repetition used for emphasis. In a sentence or paragraph, you may need to use a certain word again. When repetition serves a specific purpose, it is not an error. Redundancy serves no purpose and *is* an error.

- **Use active voice to reduce the number of words.** Passive voice typically adds unnecessary words, such as prepositional phrases. Compare the sentence length in each of these examples:

PASSIVE VOICE	ACTIVE VOICE
The documentation was prepared by the systems analyst.	The systems analyst prepared the documentation.
The loan approval procedures were revised by the loan officer.	The loan officer revised the loan approval procedures.

- **Review the main purpose of your writing and identify relevant details needed for the receiver to understand and take necessary action.** More information is not necessarily better information. You may be so involved and perhaps so enthusiastic about your message that you believe the receiver needs to know everything that you know. Or perhaps you just need to devote more time to audience analysis and empathy.
- **Eliminate clichés that are often wordy and not necessary to understand the message.** For example, "Thank you for your letter," "I am writing to," "May I take this opportunity," "It has come to my attention," and "We wish to inform you" only delay the major purpose of the message.

Nonconcise letters sometimes begin with an "empty acknowledgment." Give some examples of such openings.

- **Do not restate ideas that are sufficiently implied.** Notice how the following sentences are improved when ideas are implied. The revised sentences are concise, yet the meaning is not affected.

WORDY	CONCISE
She took the Internet marketing course and passed it.	She passed the Internet marketing course.
The editor checked the advertisement and found three glaring errors.	The editor found three glaring errors in the advertisement.

Attention to careful revision of the first draft will eliminate most wordiness.

- **Shorten sentences by using suffixes or prefixes, making changes in word form, or substituting precise words for phrases.** In the following examples, the expressions in the right column provide useful techniques for saving space and being concise. However, the examples in the left column are not grammatically incorrect. Sometimes their use provides just the right *emphasis*.

WORDY	CONCISE
She was a manager who was courteous to others.	She was a courteous manager.
He waited in an impatient manner.	He waited impatiently.
The production manager disregards methods considered to be of no use.	The production manager disregards useless methods.
Sales staff with high energy levels . . .	Energetic sales staff . . .
. . . arranged in chronological order.	. . . arranged chronologically . . .

- **Use a compound adjective.** By using the compound adjective, you can reduce the number of words required to express your ideas and thus save the reader a little time.

WORDY	CONCISE
The document requires language that is gender-neutral . . .	The document requires gender-neutral language.
B. J. Dahl, who holds the highest rank at Medder Enterprises, is . . .	B. J. Dahl, the highest-ranking official at Medder Enterprises, is . . .
The café will begin serving breakfast all day on July 1.	The café's all-day breakfast begins on July 1.

Project a Positive, Tactful Tone

Being adept at communicating negative information will give you the confidence you need to handle sensitive situations in a positive, constructive manner. The following suggestions reduce the sting of an unpleasant thought:

- **State ideas using positive language.** Rely mainly on positive words—words that speak of what can be done instead of what cannot be done, of the pleasant instead of the unpleasant. In each of the following pairs, both sentences are sufficiently clear, but the positive words in the improved sentences make the message more diplomatic and promote positive human relations.

  Positive words are normally preferred, but sometimes negative words are more effective in achieving the dual goals of *clarity* and positive *human relations*. For example, addition of negative words can sharpen a contrast (and thus increase clarity):

> Use an oil-based paint for this purpose; do not use latex.
>
> Original copies are to be submitted to the certification board; photocopies will not be accepted.

Word choice is vital!

NEGATIVE TONE	POSITIVE TONE
<u>Don't forget</u> to submit your time and expense report.	Remember to submit your time and expense report.
We <u>cannot</u> ship your order until you send us full specifications.	You will receive your order as soon as you send full specifications.
You <u>neglected</u> to indicate the product specifications.	Please send the product specifications so your order can be processed.

Think of examples of negative language you have heard (or used) that could easily be stated using positive words.

When pleasant, positive words have not brought desired results, negative words may be justified. For example, a supervisor may have used positive words to instruct an accounts payable clerk to verify that the unit price on the invoice matches the unit price on the purchase order. Discovering later that the clerk is not completing the task correctly, the supervisor may use negative words such as "*No,* that's the *wrong way*" to demonstrate once more, and explain. If the clerk's error continues, the supervisor may feel justified in using even stronger negative words. The clerk may need the emotional jolt that negative words can provide.

- **Avoid using second person when stating negative ideas.** Avoid second person for presenting unpleasant ideas, but use second person for presenting pleasant ideas. Note the following examples:

Pleasant idea (second person preferred)	*You* substantiated your argument sufficiently.	*The person will appreciate the emphasis placed on his or her excellent performance.*
Unpleasant idea (third person preferred)	This report contains numerous mistakes.	*"You made numerous mistakes on this page" directs undiplomatic attention to the person who made the mistakes.*

However, use of second person with negative ideas is an acceptable technique on the rare occasions when the purpose is to jolt the receiver by emphasizing a negative.

What advice would you give a businessperson for balancing tact and assertiveness?

- **Use passive voice to convey negative ideas.** Presenting an unpleasant thought emphatically (as active verbs do) makes human relations difficult. Compare the tone of the following negative thoughts written in active and passive voices:

ACTIVE VOICE	PASSIVE VOICE PREFERRED FOR NEGATIVE IDEAS
Melissa did not proofread the bid proposal carefully.	The bid proposal lacked careful proofreading.
Melissa completed the bid two weeks behind schedule.	The bid was completed two weeks behind schedule.

Because the subject of each active sentence is the doer, the sentences are emphatic. Since the idea is negative, Melissa probably would appreciate being taken out of the picture. The passive voice sentences place more emphasis on the job than on who failed to complete it; they retain the essential ideas, but the ideas seem less irritating. For negative ideas, use passive voice. Just as emphasis on negatives hinders human relations, emphasis on positives promotes human relations. Which sentence makes the positive idea more vivid?

PASSIVE VOICE	ACTIVE VOICE PREFERRED FOR POSITIVE IDEAS
The bid was completed ahead of time.	Melissa completed the bid ahead of schedule.

Because "Melissa" is the subject of the active voice sentence, the receiver can easily envision the action. Pleasant thoughts deserve emphasis. For presenting positive ideas, use active voice. Active and passive voice are discussed in greater detail in the "Write Powerful Sentences" section in Chapter 4.

Compose another sentence that uses subjunctive mood to de-emphasize a negative idea.

- **Use the subjunctive mood.** Sometimes the tone of a message can be improved by switching to the subjunctive mood. ***Subjunctive sentences*** speak of a wish, necessity, doubt, or condition contrary to fact and use such conditional expressions as *I wish, as if, could, would, might,* and *wish.* In the following examples, the sentence in the right column conveys a negative idea in positive language, which is more diplomatic than negative language.

NEGATIVE TONE	SUBJUNCTIVE MOOD CONVEYS POSITIVE TONE
I cannot approve your transfer to our overseas operation.	If positions were available in our overseas operation, I would approve your transfer.
I am unable to accept your invitation to speak.	I could accept your invitation to speak only if our scheduled speaker were to cancel.
I cannot accept the consultant's recommendation.	I wish I could accept the consultant's recommendation.

Sentences in subjunctive mood often include a reason that makes the negative idea seems less objectionable, and thus improves the tone. Tone is important, but clarity is even more important. The revised sentence in each of the preceding pairs sufficiently *implies* the unpleasant idea without stating it directly. If for any reason a writer or speaker suspects the implication is not sufficiently strong, a direct statement in negative terms is preferable.

- **Include a pleasant statement in the same sentence.** A pleasant idea is included in the following examples to improve the tone:

NEGATIVE TONE	POSITIVE TONE
Your personnel rating for communication ability was satisfactory.	While your personnel rating for communication ability was satisfactory, your rating for technical competence was excellent.
Because of increased taxes and insurance, you are obligated to increase your monthly payments.	Because of increased taxes and insurance, your monthly payments will increase to $50; however, your home has increased in value at the monthly rate of $150.

Step 4: Organizing the Message

After you have identified the specific ways you must adapt the message to your specific audience, you are ready to organize your message. In a discussion of communication, the word *organize* means "the act of dividing a topic into parts and arranging them in an appropriate sequence." Before undertaking this process, you must be convinced that the message is the right message—that it is complete, accurate, fair, reasonable, ethical, and logical. If it doesn't meet these standards, it should not be sent. Good organization and good writing or speaking cannot be expected to compensate for a bad decision.

If you organize and write simultaneously, the task seems hopelessly complicated. Writing is much easier if questions about the organization of the message are answered first: What is the purpose of the message, what is the receiver's likely reaction, and should the message begin with the main point? Once these decisions have been made, you can concentrate on expressing ideas effectively.

Outline to Benefit the Sender and the Receiver

When a topic is divided into parts, some parts will be recognized as central ideas and the others as minor ideas (details). The process of identifying these ideas and arranging them in the right sequence is known as ***outlining***. Outlining *before* communicating provides numerous benefits:

- **Encourages accuracy and brevity.** Outlining reduces the chance of leaving out an essential idea or including an unessential idea.
- **Permits concentration on one phase at a time.** Having focused separately on (a) the ideas that need to be included, (b) the distinction between major and minor ideas, and (c) the sequence of ideas, total concentration can now be focused on the next challenge—expressing.
- **Saves time in structuring ideas.** With questions about which ideas to include and their proper sequence already answered, little time is lost in moving from one point to the next.

How can the business communicator make sure the message outline is a time saver and not a time waster?

- **Provides a psychological lift.** The feeling of success gained in preparing the outline increases confidence that the next step—writing or speaking—will be successful, too.
- **Facilitates emphasis and de-emphasis.** Although each sentence makes its contribution to the message, some sentences need to stand out more vividly in the receiver's mind than others. An effective outline ensures that important points will appear in emphatic positions.

The preceding benefits derived from outlining are sender oriented. Because a message has been well outlined, receivers benefit, too:

- The message is more concise and accurate.
- Relationships between ideas are easier to distinguish and remember.
- Reaction to the message and its sender is more likely to be positive.

A receiver's reaction to a message is strongly influenced by the sequence in which ideas are presented. A beginning sentence or an ending sentence is in an emphatic position. (Other emphasis techniques are explained later in this chapter.) Throughout this text, you will see that outlining (organizing) is important.

Sequence Ideas to Achieve Desired Goals

When planning your communication, you should strive for an outline that will serve you in much the same way a blueprint serves a builder or an itinerary serves a traveler. Organizing your message first will ensure that your ideas are presented clearly and logically and all vital components are included. To facilitate your determining an appropriate sequence for a business document or presentation, follow the three-step process illustrated in Figure 3-3. This process involves answering the following questions in this order:

1. **What is the central idea of the message?** Think about the *reason* you are writing or speaking—the first step in the communication process. What is your purpose—to extend a job offer, decline an invitation, or seek support for an innovative project? The purpose is the central idea of your message. You might think of it as a message condensed in one brief statement.

FIGURE 3-3

Process of Selecting an Outline for a Spoken or Written Business Message

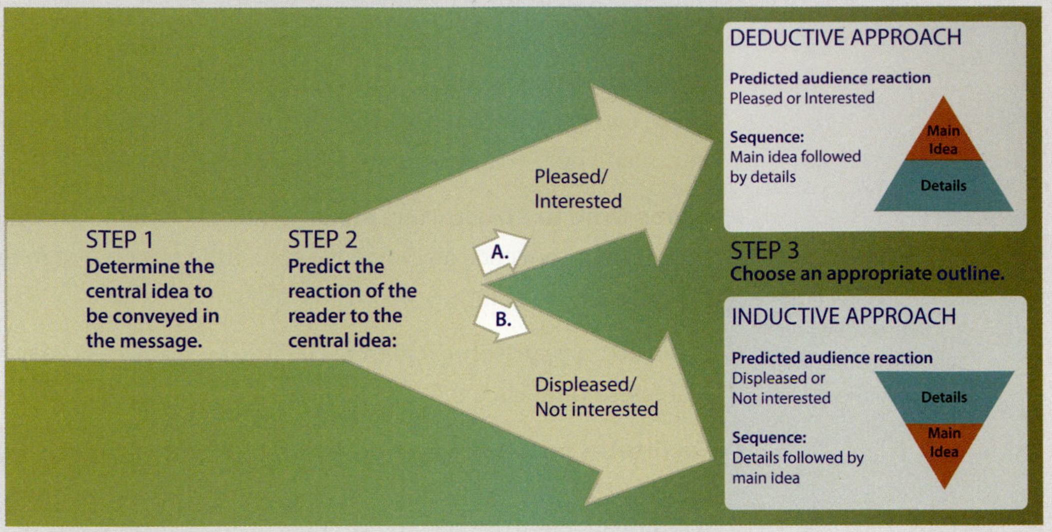

What organizational sequence is appropriate for accepting a speaking invitation and denying credit to a customer?

2. **What is the most likely receiver reaction to the message?** Ask, "If I were the one receiving the message I am preparing to send, what would *my* reaction be?" Because you would react with pleasure to good news and displeasure to bad news, you can reasonably assume a receiver's reaction would be similar. By considering anticipated receiver reaction, you build goodwill with the receiver. Almost every message will fit into one of four categories of anticipated receiver reaction: (1) pleasure, (2) displeasure, (3) interest but neither pleasure nor displeasure, or (4) no interest, as shown in Figure 3-3.

3. **In view of the predicted receiver reaction, should the central idea be listed first in the outline or should it be listed as one of the last items?** When a message begins with the major idea, the sequence of ideas is called ***deductive***. When a message withholds the major idea until accompanying details and explanations have been presented, the sequence is called ***inductive***.

Consider the receiver to determine whether to use the inductive or deductive sequence. If a receiver might be antagonized by the main idea in a deductive message, lead up to the main idea by making the message inductive. If a sender wants to encourage receiver involvement (to generate a little concern about where the details are leading), the inductive approach is recommended. Inductive organization can be especially effective if the main idea confirms the conclusion the receiver has drawn from the preceding details—a cause is worthy of support, a job applicant should be interviewed, a product/service should be selected, and so on. As you learn in later chapters about writing letters, memos, and email messages and about planning spoken communications, you will comprehend the benefits of using the appropriate outline for each receiver reaction:

DEDUCTIVE ORDER (MAIN IDEA FIRST)	INDUCTIVE ORDER (DETAILS FIRST)
When the message will *please* the receiver	When the message will *displease* the receiver
When the message is *routine* (will not please nor displease)	When the receiver *may not be interested* (will need to be persuaded)

For determining the sequence of minor ideas that accompany the major idea, the following bases for idea sequence are common:

- **Time.** When writing a report or email message about a series of events or a process, paragraphs proceed from the first step through the last step.
- **Space.** If a report is about geographic areas, ideas can proceed from one area to the next until all areas have been discussed.
- **Familiarity.** If a topic is complicated, the presentation can begin with a known or easy-to-understand point and proceed to progressively more difficult points.
- **Importance.** In analytical reports in which major decision-making factors are presented, the factors can be presented in order of most important to least important, or vice versa.
- **Value.** If a presentation involves major factors with monetary values, paragraphs can proceed from those with greatest values to those with least values, or vice versa.

The same organizational patterns are recommended for written and spoken communication. These patterns are applicable in email messages, blogs, letters, memos, and reports.

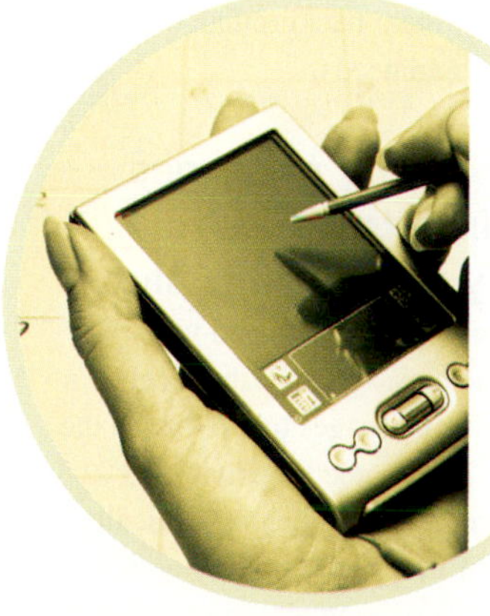

Your Turn 3-5
Career Portfolio

Assume you are to give a presentation on wireless digital cameras, cameras with the ability to off-load pictures to a PC or website via Wi-Fi. Read the following article:

Sullivan, T. (2005, December 27). Digital cameras go wireless. *PC Magazine,* 24(23), 46–47. Available from Business Source Complete database.

TAKE ACTION:

- After reading the article, decide which one you think is the superior product and develop your presentation to persuasively convince your audience of the better choice.
- Develop two versions of your presentation outline, one in inductive and one in deductive order. You may want to refer to Chapter 12 for more information on preparing outlines.

SHOWCASE PART 3

Hallmark Tips for Writing Business Greetings

Hallmark has been helping people say the right thing at the right time for nearly 100 years. Getting and sending greeting cards make people feel good. But the "warm fuzzy" responses that make greeting cards so effective can also make some professional types a little nervous, especially if you are used to keeping in touch through phone calls, email, memos, and other less personal types of communication. If you are uneasy about using cards to stay in touch, relax—Hallmark has some helpful suggestions to help you personalize your messages and say just the right thing.

- Visit the Hallmark website section designed for people to submit their own card ideas. Read the writing tips for greeting card messages.
- What advantages are offered by sending a greeting card rather than crafting your own original message?

www.hallmark.com

Activities

Referring to the chapter, read the Strategic Forces feature on e-cards. In a class discussion, compare the roles of traditional greeting cards and e-cards in conveying business messages. Does audience impact differ? If so, how?

Summary

1. Identify the purpose of the message and the appropriate channel.

Writing is a systematic process that begins by determining the purpose of the message (central idea) and identifying how the central idea will affect the receiver. In view of its effect on the receiver, you can determine the appropriate channel for sending a particular message (e.g., face-to-face, phone call/text, letter/memo, email, instant message, blog, voice mail, or fax).

2. Develop clear perceptions of the audience to enhance the impact of the communication and human relations.

Before you compose the first draft, commit to overcoming perceptual barriers that will limit your ability to see an issue from multiple perspectives and thus plan an effective message. Then, consider all you know about the receiver, including age, economic level, educational/occupational background, culture, existing relationship, expectations, and needs.

3. Apply techniques for adapting messages to the audience, including strategies for communicating ethically and responsibly.

The insights you gain from seeking to understand your receiver will allow you to adapt the message to fit the receiver's needs. Developing concise, sensitive messages that focus on the receiver's point of view will build and protect goodwill and demand the attention of the receiver. Communicating ethically and responsibly involves stating information truthfully and tactfully, eliminating embellishments or exaggerations, supporting viewpoints with objective facts from credible sources, and designing honest graphics.

4. **Recognize the importance of organizing a message before writing the first draft.**

Outlining involves identifying the appropriate sequence of pertinent ideas. Outlining encourages brevity and accuracy, permits concentration on one phase at a time, saves writing time, increases confidence to complete the task, and facilitates appropriate emphasis of ideas. From a receiver's point of view, well-organized messages are easier to understand and promote a more positive attitude toward the sender.

5. **Select the appropriate message pattern (deductive or inductive) for developing messages to achieve the desired response.**

An essential part of the planning process is deciding whether the message should be deductive (main idea first) or inductive (explanations and details first). The main idea is presented first and details follow when the receiver is expected to be pleased by the message and the message is routine and not likely to produce a feeling of pleasure or displeasure. When the receiver can be expected to be displeased or not initially interested, explanations and details precede the main idea.

Chapter Review

1. Why is selecting an appropriate communication channel important to the overall effectiveness of the message? Provide two examples. (Obj. 1)
2. How does perception and audience analysis affect the communication process? What factors about the audience should you consider? (Obj. 2)
3. What differences in the ideals of the older and younger generations may explain communication clashes between these groups in the workplace? (Objs. 2, 3)
4. What value is gained from cultivating a "you attitude" in spoken and written messages? Give an example of a writer- and a reader-centered message to make your point. (Obj. 3)
5. Discuss five writing techniques that enable communicators to build and protect goodwill. (Obj. 3)
6. When is the use of a euphemism appropriate? When is it detrimental? Under what conditions are connotative words acceptable? Why are specific words generally preferred in business writing and speaking? In what situations would general words be preferred? (Obj. 3)
7. Provide five guidelines for projecting a positive, tactful tone. (Obj. 3)
8. Why is conciseness valued in business communication? Provide at least three suggestions for reducing word count without sacrificing content. (Obj. 3)
9. What primary benefits does the writer gain from outlining before writing or speaking? How does the receiver benefit? (Obj. 4)
10. What three questions assist a communicator in the decision to organize a message deductively or inductively? (Obj. 5)

Digging Deeper

1. What is empathy and how does it affect business communication? How are empathy and sympathy different?
2. Explain what is meant by writing to *express* and not to *impress*.
3. How can you ensure quality in a collaboratively written document? Perhaps someone on your team makes unnecessary additions or questionable edits such as revising to make the document "sound more professional" while sacrificing clarity. What would you do?

Assessment

To check your understanding of the chapter, take the available online quizzes as directed by your instructor.

Activities

1. Empathetic Attitude (Obj. 2)

In small groups, identify possible communication problems created from a manager's lack of empathy when communicating to employees. Select a spokesperson to share your group's ideas.

a. An audit manager for a U.S. firm, who has been transferred to the company's office in Japan, provides the following message:

"We are backed into a corner here. The SEC reporting deadline is set in concrete, so let's put the pedal to the metal to get this audit completed. Keep me in the loop, but don't waste my minutes. Everybody got it?"

b. After months of uncertainty at Downs, Inc., a corporate official visits a regional office and gives the following response to mostly lower-wage technical and support staff regarding layoffs and office closures:

"We are realigning our resources companywide to be more competitive in the marketplace and to maximize wealth creation for our stockholders. Our stock has been declining at an unprecedented rate, but we are confident that these initiatives will ensure future market viability. Furthermore, we pledge to remain completely transparent during this restructuring process. Corporate is aware of your concerns and will continue these discussions to provide a forum for dialogue."

c. After several trips to Mexico and nearly a year of negotiation to set up a joint venture, a U.S. partner faxed the final contract to the Mexican chief executive officer. The document included a request that the CEO personally guarantee the loan, a stipulation that had not been discussed previously.

Check Your Communication
Guidelines for Planning a Spoken or Written Message

FOCUS ON THE RECEIVER'S POINT OF VIEW

- ☐ Present ideas from the receiver's point of view, conveying the tone the message is specifically for the receiver.
- ☐ Give sincere compliments.

COMMUNICATE ETHICALLY AND RESPONSIBLY

- ☐ Present information truthfully, honestly, and fairly.
- ☐ Include all information relevant to the receiver.
- ☐ Avoid exaggerating or embellishing facts.
- ☐ Use objective facts to support ideas.
- ☐ Design graphics that avoid distorting facts and relationships.
- ☐ Express ideas clearly and understandably.
- ☐ State ideas tactfully and positively to build future relationships.

BUILD AND PROTECT GOODWILL

- ☐ Use euphemisms to present unpleasant thoughts politely and positively. Use dysphemisms only when they will be viewed humorously. Avoid using euphemisms as well as dysphemisms when they will be taken as excessive, sarcastic, or cruel.
- ☐ Avoid doublespeak or corporate speak that confuses or misleads the receiver.
- ☐ Avoid using condescending or demeaning expressions.
- ☐ Rely mainly on denotative words. Use connotative words that will elicit a favorable reaction, are easily understood, and are appropriate for the setting.
- ☐ Choose vivid words that add clarity and interest to your message.
- ☐ Use bias-free language:
  - Do not use the pronoun *he* when referring to a group of people that may include women or *she* when a group may include men.
  - Avoid referring to men and women in stereotyped roles and occupations, using gender-biased occupational titles, or differentiating genders in an occupation.
  - Avoid referring to groups (based on gender, race and ethnicity, age, religion, and disability) in stereotypical and insensitive ways.
  - Do not emphasize race and ethnicity, age, religion, or disability when these factors are not relevant.

CONVEY A POSITIVE, TACTFUL TONE

- ☐ Rely mainly on positive words that speak of what can be done instead of what cannot be done, of the pleasant instead of the unpleasant. Use negative words when the purpose is to sharpen contrast or when positive words have not evoked the desired reaction.
- ☐ Use second person and active voice to emphasize pleasant ideas. Avoid using second person for presenting negative ideas; instead, use third person and passive voice to de-emphasize the unpleasant.
- ☐ Consider stating an unpleasant thought in the subjunctive mood.

USE SIMPLE, CONTEMPORARY LANGUAGE

- ☐ Avoid clichés and outdated expressions that make your language seem unnatural and unoriginal.
- ☐ Use simple words for informal business messages instead of using more complicated words that have the same meaning.

WRITE CONCISELY

- ☐ Do not use redundancies—unnecessary repetition of an idea.
- ☐ Use active voice to shorten sentences.
- ☐ Avoid unnecessary details; omit ideas that can be implied.
- ☐ Shorten wordy sentences by using suffixes or prefixes, making changes in word form, or substituting precise words for phrases.

d. Your unit manager, Mark, accused Joshua, a highly talented member of your design team, of being permanently attached to his Blackberry, laptop, and other technology fads that are timewasters and believes Joshua's work ethic is right up there with his flip-flops, faded jeans, and baggy sweaters. Joshua is frustrated at Mark's insistence on frequent progress reports, criticism when the team isn't willing to work past five o'clock to get a job done, and general disinterest in expanding his technology skills.

2. Appropriate Outline and Channel (Objs. 1, 2, 5)

Complete the following analysis to determine whether a deductive or an inductive outline is appropriate for the following situations. Identify the channel you believe would be most appropriate for conveying this message; be prepared to justify your answer. Use the format shown in the following example. Access a downloadable version of this activity from your companion website, www.cengage.com/bcomm/lehman.

Situation	Recommended channel	Central idea	Likely receiver reaction
The annual merit raise has increased to 5 percent.	Mailed memo or email message; pleasant information that should reach all employees in a timely manner.	Inform employees of an increase in annual merit raise.	Deductive

a. Seller to customer: An e-commerce site is promoting an extended warranty to customers who recently purchased a plasma television.
b. Quality manager to production manager: Discontinue production until a flaw just discovered in the production process has been corrected.
c. Seller to customer: We cannot provide a free cellular phone upgrade until the service contract is renewed.
d. U.S. CEO to Canadian business partner: Delivery of promised shipment will be delayed due to inability to obtain raw products from a war-torn country.
e. Management to employees: A meeting to announce upcoming professional development opportunities.
f. Seller to customer: Refunds are being issued to customers who purchased a specific production run of Model DX cell phone because the glass is overly susceptible to scratching.
g. Seller to customer: An increase in the company's share of health care insurance premiums, costs will require a price increase effective June 1.
h. Assistant to manager: The assistant has been asked by his manager to research an issue and respond immediately while the manager is still on the phone with the customer.
i. Management to employees: A new policy prohibiting visible body art.
j. Technology department to customer: A solution is made available to all current and prospective customers for a common problem users are encountering while upgrading software versions.

3. Audience Analysis (Obj. 2)

Write a brief analysis of the audience for each of the situations presented in Activity 2.

4. Receiver-Centered Messages (Obj. 3)

Revise the following sentences to emphasize the reader's viewpoint and the "you" attitude. Access a downloadable version of this activity from your companion website, www.cengage.com/bcomm/lehman.

a. We're encouraging all employees to take advantage of the annual wellness benefits provided by our health insurance carrier.
b. Human Resources requires all employees who work with dangerous goods or hazardous materials to have a complete physical annually.

5. Statements that Build and Protect Goodwill (Obj. 3)

Revise the following sentences to eliminate a tone that will damage human relations. Identify the specific weakness in each sentence. Access a downloadable version of this activity from your companion website, www.cengage.com/bcomm/lehman.

a. Management expresses appreciation for all the environmental health officers.
b. Our call center has exhibited substantial signs of workflow inefficiencies over the past budgetary period which has triggered potential irreparable damage to the customer fulfillment and branding initiatives instigated in conjunction with the operationalization of the board's strategic plan.
c. As expected, the spin doctors fired a quick response to the complaints of the consumer advocacy group.
d. As anyone must surely know, the average employee is concerned about his retirement savings.
e. Did you hear that Hunter was crowned the top sales rep at last week's meeting?
f. Several patient satisfaction surveys have included negative comments about Jim Koch, a male ER nurse.
g. Our quadriplegic first-shift supervisor moves around the plant in a motorized wheelchair.
h. Meanwhile back at the reservation, quality control is working to design a more green packaging solution.
i. Brad Hankins was recognized for his efforts.

6. Positive, Tactful Tone (Obj. 3)

Revise the following sentences to reduce the negative tone. Access a downloadable version of this activity from your companion website, www.cengage.com/bcomm/lehman.

a. The taxpayer's failure to make quarterly estimated tax payments resulted in penalties and interest.
b. You cannot receive benefits until you have been with our company for three months.
c. You neglected to inform these potential buyers of the 10-day cancellation period.

7. Conversational Language (Obj. 3)

Substitute fresh, original expressions for each cliché or outdated expression. Access a downloadable version of this activity from your companion website, www.cengage.com/bcomm/lehman.

a. That 3 on 3 basketball game during my lunch break was a reality check!
b. Give me a minute here; I'm drinking from a fire hose.
c. We are in receipt of your letter of July 15.

8. Simple Words (Obj. 3)

Revise the following sentences using shorter, simpler words. Access a downloadable version of this activity from your companion website, www.cengage.com/bcomm/lehman.

a. The ethics committee has abrogated its oversight responsibilities to the human resources department.
b. Jan's dubious disappearance yesterday instigated a police investigation.
c. The attendees of the convocation concurred that it should terminate at the appointed hour.

9. Conciseness (Obj. 3)

Revise the following sentences to eliminate redundancies and other wordy construction. Access a downloadable version of this activity from your companion website, www.cengage.com/bcomm/lehman.

a. Although some damage to the building was visible to the eye, we were directed by our attorneys not to repair or change anything until the adjuster made a damage assessment.
b. Mia's past work history includes working as a sales clerk, waiting tables in a restaurant, and stocking shelves in a bookstore.
c. Jacob was given instructions to make note of any strange and unusual transactions completed in the recent past.

10. Adapting the Message to the Audience (Objs. 1–3)

Revise the following sentences by adapting the message to meet the audience's needs. Identify the specific weaknesses in each sentence. Access a downloadable version of this activity from your companion website, www.cengage.com/bcomm/lehman.

a. We want our employees to begin using Twitter as a way of identifying customer complaints and humanizing the people behind our products.
b. An effective presenter is never surprised by the reaction of his audience.
c. She thought she was flying under the radar, but Marie has been called on the carpet for spending so much time on Facebook at work.
d. Please be advised that the company's new smoke-free policy is effective on January 1.
e. Since I took a leadership role on this project, the team's performance has improved.
f. I know he is good at diagnosing computer problems, but he's such a dork.
g. You failed to read the disclaimer on our website that clearly indicates that the transmitter you ordered does not work with older generation MP3 players. Unfortunately, we cannot honor your request for a refund.
h. Through strategic alliances and by internal expansion of programs, Lox Enterprises is seeking to develop a substantial market presence as the leading provider of management consulting services in Illinois and its neighboring states.
i. The best computers available for lease through corporate channels are horribly outdated.
j. The supervisor asked Quan to go back and make revisions to the final draft of the report so the data will be completely accurate.

Applications

READ | THINK | WRITE | SPEAK | COLLABORATE

1. Diversity Awareness Strategies in Real Companies (Objs. 2, 3)

Conduct an online search to identify strategies companies have adopted to raise their employees' awareness of diversity in the workplace. In chart form, summarize the indexes you used to locate your articles, the companies you read about, and the successful strategies they have used to promote diversity.

2. Application of Empathy in Company Strategies (Objs. 2, 3)

Visit the website of a company in which you are interested to explore evidence of the company's empathy for its employees and customers/clients. Alternately, you may choose a company from Fortune's Best 100 Companies to Work For or Fortune's Most Admired Companies. In a short oral report, explain the role of empathy in the strategies you identified.

3. A Culture of Candor (Obj. 3)

Locate the following article:

O'Toole, J., & Bennis, W. (2009). What's needed next: A culture of candor. *Harvard Business Review, 87*(6), 54–61. Available from Business Source Complete database.

After reading the article, respond to the following questions:

a. What does the author mean by a culture of candor?
b. How does candor improve corporate performance?
c. What part does communication play in creating transparency both internally and with the public?

READ | THINK | WRITE | SPEAK | COLLABORATE

4. Choosing Communication Channels Wisely (Obj. 1)

Locate the following article:

Seckler, S., & Toomey, R. (2005, December 18). Commentary: E-mail: Career opportunities and pitfalls in workplace communication. *The Daily Record (Kansas City, MO)*. Available from Lexis-Nexis database.

After reading the article, compile a list of the advantages and recommended use for email, as well as the precautions in its use.

5. Building a Strong Vocabulary (Obj. 3)

Successful people have powerful vocabularies that equip them with the precise word to use when needed to reach their audience. To build your vocabulary, complete these activities as directed by your instructor:

1. Review the useful vocabulary building suggestions at **http://grammar.ccc.commnet.edu/GRAMMAR/vocabulary.htm** and choose one or more technique that you believe will be beneficial.
2. Go to **www.visualthesaurus.com** and subscribe to the 14-day trial of Visual Thesaurus, an interactive tool that allows you to search for connections between words in a visually captivating display. Read the "How It Works" section to learn how to create your own word lists for later use. After your trial expires, email your instructor your analysis of the usefulness of this writing tool.

6. Building Strong Interpersonal Skills (Objs. 1–3)

The guidelines presented in this chapter for adapting your message to convey sensitivity for the receiver are an excellent means for building the relationships and strong interpersonal skills needed in today's highly competitive global market and in diverse work teams. Identify a specific situation in your work or educational experience, or school or community organizations, that illustrates the negative effects of an individual who did not consider the impact of his/her message on the receiver. Send your example to your instructor as an attachment to an email message. Be prepared to discuss your idea with the class or in small groups.

READ | THINK | WRITE | SPEAK | COLLABORATE

7. Business Writing Can Be Just Plain Awful (Objs. 1–3)

Businesses with better communication standards can communicate more effectively. Yet a staggering number of employees in the corporate world are considered poor writers. Remedies are needed for a multitude of bad writing practices, including millions of vague emails that clog business computers daily, setting off emails asking for clarification that also can't be understood. Review the good writing practices presented in this chapter and locate one or more articles from an online database that addresses writing strategies for business communicators. Begin your research by locating the following articles:

Craig, T. (2008, August 19). How to write with impact. *Personnel Today,* 9. Available from Business Source Complete database.

Korkki, P. (2007, August 26). Young workers: U Nd 2 improve ur writing skills. *The New York Times,* p. 2. Available from Academic Search Premier database.

Complete the following activities designed to raise communication standards as directed by your instructor:

1. Compile a list of mistakes employees make regularly in business writing and speaking. Which do you feel are more damaging, errors in print or in speech? Explain. Discuss how failure to correct these problems might affect the business and employees' career potential.
2. Prepare a two- to three-minute presentation that uses a memorable metaphor to describe what you consider to be the three most damaging writing problems. For example, apply the lessons of music, theatrics, or a sport to business communication. Be prepared to deliver the presentation in small groups or to the class.
3. Write a "Blog Question of the Day" discussing your biggest grammar pet peeve. Review the postings at **http://grammargirl.com** for suggestions, if necessary. Post your contribution to the class discussion board or wiki; monitor postings to learn what errors irritate your classmates.

8. Tweet Your Way to Success (Objs. 1, 2)

What was once a way for friends to tell friends that they were on the way to the gym has become a hypergrapevine news source for exchanging messages about topics of personal interest and consumer "rants and raves." Social networking services, such as Twitter, keep people updated on what they are doing at any given moment of the day via cell phone, instant messenger, or the Web. The service is even credited with breaking news about fires and other natural disasters. Conduct an online search to learn more about this new communication media. Begin by reading the following article:

Graham, J. (2008, July 21). Twitter took off from simple to "tweet" success. *USA Today.* Available from Lexis-Nexis Academic database.

After conducting your research, complete the following activities as directed by your instructor:

1. Compile a list of advantages and disadvantages of this communication medium, including examples of how two businesses have used this social networking service.
2. Register at Twitter and exchange messages with a small group of students in the class. Prepare an engaging flier describing efficient use of Twitter that will be distributed to staff as an electronic attachment to an email.

9. Prohibition on Profanity (Obj. 3)

The use of profanity in the workplace can create various problems related to productivity, morale, and image, but not everyone considers swear words offensive. Locate the following article that looks at the issue from social and cultural perspectives:

Wild, S. (2009, May 23). Profanity for morale: Experts swear by it. *Business Day* (South Africa). Available from General Businessfile database.

Search the Web for additional advice and examples for developing a policy that prohibits the use of profanity in the workplace. Draft a policy that clearly states the prohibition on profanity and includes penalties for violations.

READ | THINK | WRITE | SPEAK | COLLABORATE

10. Cultural Barriers to Communication (Objs. 2, 3)

Generate a list of phrases and nonverbal expressions peculiar to your culture that a person from another culture might not understand. Share your ideas with the class in a short presentation.

11. Sensitive Language (Objs. 2, 3)

Interview a person with a disability to find out ways to communicate acceptably using bias-free language. Share your findings with the class in a short presentation.

12. Trickery of Illusions (Obj. 2)

In small groups, select an illusion from the links provided at your companion website, www.cengage.com/bcomm/lehman, or use one provided by your instructor. Allow each member to view the illusion independently and then share his or her individual interpretation with the team. Relate this experience with the concept of perception and its effect on the communication process. Be prepared to share your ideas with the class.

13. Contemporary Language for the Workplace (Objs. 2, 3)

In small groups generate a list of phrases peculiar to your generation that could be confusing and inappropriate for workplace communication. Refer to Merriam-Webster's list of new words for ideas. For each phrase, substitute an expression that would be acceptable for use in a professional setting. Prepare a visual to aid you in presenting your list to the class.

14. Blogging to Promote Business and Your Own Ideas (Objs. 1, 2)

Businesses are experienced at writing formal business documents, such as press releases, advertising, and financial reports; however, creating an online brand or authentic voice through an online blog provides a new challenge for business communicators. To learn more, locate the following articles:

Cardis, P. (2008, October). Blogging for business. *Professional Builder.* Available from Lexis-Nexis database.

Get caught in the net. (2007, May 31). *Financial Advisor.* Available from Lexis-Nexis database.

How to write a better blog. (July 2007). *Business World* (Weekender). Available from Lexis-Nexis database.

Brown, M. (2007). From the boardroom to the break room to the blog. *Performance Magazine.* Available from Business Source Complete database.

- After reading the articles, prepare an engaging flier describing efficient blog communication that will be distributed to staff as an attachment to an email message.
- Respond to a blog posting your instructor has made concerning clear communication. Read the posting of other students and be prepared to comment on the knowledge gained from the experience.

CASES

1. Tackling the Challenge of Age Diversity at FedEx

FedEx is made up of more than 290,000 team members from various walks of life. "We strive to create an environment where people can contribute and grow, and where the values of diversity are woven through our organization," says the company on its website. More than 40 percent of the company's U.S. workforce and 27 percent of the management team are minorities. Additionally, FedEx has been honored by *Pink* magazine as a great place for women to work.

FedEx also maintains a Corporate Diversity Council that focuses on a global culture of diversity and inclusiveness. The Council works to ensure greater employee awareness and positive perception of FedEx's diversity commitment, and supports multicultural programs within the company and in its various communities. FedEx treats the boomer-millennial generational challenge as part of its overall diversity commitment to corporate diversity. The company has instituted a mentoring program for its Information Technology division to help mature pros and newcomer twenty-somethings work together effectively. Veterans gain valuable insight into millennials' socially driven work habits, and younger workers benefit from knowledge of long-term technology solutions.

Mentoring has traditionally been seen as a means of furthering knowledge and enculturation of an organization's newcomers, by matching them with supportive, experienced workers. The FedEx mentoring model encourages mutual benefit for both the pro and the novice, blurring the lines between the mentor and the mentee, or protégé. The term "reverse mentoring" has been used to describe a mentoring arrangement in which the experienced worker gains as much or more from the arrangement than does the new worker.

Read the following articles that will provide more information:

Corporate responses to age diversity challenges:

Waxer, C. (2009, February 16). Clash of the generations: IT vets and fresh talent scramble for the same jobs. *Computerworld.* Available at www.computerworld.com/action/article.do?command=viewArticleBasic&articleId=333298

Reverse mentoring:

Biss, J. L., & DuFrene, D. D. (2006). An examination of reverse mentoring in the workplace. *Business Education Digest*, 15, 30–41. Available from Business Source Complete database.

FedEx website: www.fedex.com (See Corporate Diversity)

Application:

- Design a brochure for FedEx that promotes the values of the IT mentoring program to both experienced personnel and new hires. Use your knowledge of the program at FedEx and in similar programs at other companies to communicate the purpose, activities, and benefits.
- Craft a short piece for posting to the FedEx website that describes the mentoring initiative as an effective way to respond to the challenges of age diversity in the organization.

© BBC LTD./COURTESY: EVERETT COLLECTION

2. Video Case: The Office: Conflict Resolution: Do Offices Need a Manual for Interpersonal Communication?

In this clip, Gareth needs information from Tim, who is sitting right outside Gareth's cubicle. Tim refuses to communicate directly with Gareth, taking personal conflict into the workplace and hindering everyday activities.

Complete the following activities as directed by your instructor after the class has viewed the video:

1. In small groups, discuss what you observed about Tim and Gareth's relationship based on this interaction. Do they work well together? Explain.
2. In small group, discuss how Tim and Gareth's communication breaks down. In what kinds of conflict do they engage? How might a team leader or supervisor manage their conflict?
3. Based on the problems seen in this interaction, outline a presentation for employees that discusses appropriate interpersonal communication in the workplace. Be prepared to discuss the presentation in your online course discussion tool or deliver the presentation to your class as directed by your instructor.

3. It's All in the Translation

Businesspeople frequently communicate by exchanging documents, either printed on paper or transmitted electronically. Those with overseas clients, customers, and contacts can improve their communications dramatically by using software to translate these documents. Such software is used by organizations to produce documents ranging from international correspondence and invoices to complex financial and legal documents. Growth in the use of the Internet has boosted demand for language translation as users around the world struggle to understand pages in languages other than their own.

Multilingual translators allow companies to open up their websites to everyone around the globe. The software determines the country of origin of the viewer, displays the site in the appropriate language, and provides a menu for selecting an alternate language if preferred. Translation packages are typically based on two types of bilingual dictionaries, one for word-for-word translations and another for semantic and idiomatic phrases. Speed of translation is about 20,000 words per hour, with a 90 percent or higher degree of accuracy. Various web-based translation systems are available. Arguably the best known online translation system is Babel Fish, which is a web-based application on Yahoo! that machine translates text or web pages from one of several languages to another. Babel Fish was originally developed by Alta Vista and relies on Systran software. The service makes no claim to produce a perfect translation.[24] Language translation software that includes interfaces for text and speech is also available for handheld computers. Users enter words as text and can have the translation returned as text or speech.[25]

Translation systems work best when they are customized for a particular subject area; this involves analyzing typical documents and adding common words and technical terms to the system's dictionary. Using the software to translate Internet pages, which can be about anything at all, often produces dismal results. To make matters worse, most translation systems were designed for use with high-quality documents, whereas many web pages, chat rooms, and email messages involve slang, colloquial language, and ungrammatical constructions. Internet users, however, typically want speed of translation, rather than quality, and are more likely to accept poor results.

It is also possible to use commercial computer-based translation facilities via the telephone, using modems and fax. Messages can be translated using a message translation service for a per-word fee. Although such services may appear costly, imagine the benefit that an organization may derive from conveying an appropriately translated message to a potential client or customer.

In a technological environment that greatly simplifies language translation, some challenges still exist. Often the problem is not to translate the words, but to convey ideas across cultures. A writer from the audience's culture may be employed to take translated material and write the ideas in the local language. Experienced practitioners understand the need to consider cultural as well as linguistic differences.

Visit your companion website, www.cengage.com/bcomm/lehman, to link to web resources related to this topic.

Respond to one or more of the following activities as directed by your instructor.

1. Write a one-page summary explaining the factors that have led to the need for more translation services.
2. Write a one-page summary explaining the difference between word translation and culture translation. Give

examples of interpretation problems that result when word translation alone is used. Provide instances when word translation would be beneficial to a company.

3. Download a free online translator and translate a sample document such as your personal web page into a target language of your choice. Ask a person who speaks the target language (preferably a native speaker) to evaluate the effectiveness of the translation. Write a one-page summary explaining the quality of the translation. Work in groups if directed by your instructor.
4. Assume you work for a company that has just entered the Japanese market. Your company wishes to translate correspondence, promotional materials, and invoices into the Japanese language. Using the sites previously listed as starting points, visit four sites of organizations that offer translation and interpretation services. Prepare a two-page written report that (1) compares the services offered by each organization and the accompanying costs, and (2) recommends the one your company should use for its translation services.
5. Research the two software translation programs mentioned in this case. Prepare a chart that summarizes the capabilities and features available with each. Write a recommendation for the superior product.

Chapter 4
Preparing Spoken and Written Messages

"The overall idea behind requiring plain language is to try to make prospectuses less intimidating for the average reader."

SEC spokesperson

© ALEX WONG/GETTY IMAGES

Objectives When you have completed Chapter 4, you will be able to:

1. Apply techniques for developing effective sentences and unified and coherent paragraphs.
2. Identify factors affecting readability and revise messages to improve readability.
3. Prepare visually appealing documents that grab the receiver's attention and increase comprehension.
4. Revise and proofread a message for content, organization, and style; mechanics; and format and layout.

SHOWCASE PART 1  

Securities and Exchange Commission Promotes Reader-Friendly Disclosures

When deciding how to invest one's money, being able to accurately interpret information in a company's financial prospectus is critical. This task has not always been easy, since the concepts discussed can be complex and the language complicated. In 1998, the Securities and Exchange Commission (SEC) took a giant step toward assuring readability of the all-important financial prospectus.

The SEC requirements specify the use of reader-friendly plain English, also known as plain language, in companies' investment prospectuses. An issuing company is directed to write with the uninformed shareholder in mind. Guidelines include the use of shorter sentences and paragraphs; concrete, everyday language; active voice with strong verbs; and tabular presentation of complicated information whenever possible. Bullet lists are recommended when information is embedded in paragraphs, and concise summaries with explanatory sentences are encouraged. The guidelines also specify the avoidance of obscure business jargon and multiple negatives. Risk factors must be presented concretely and concisely and provide enough information to allow an investor to assess the degree of risk. Wider margins are specified to aid in visual appeal.

Mastering the simplification of technical documents can present a significant learning curve. *A Plain English Handbook* published by the SEC (www.sec.gov/pdf/handbook.pdf) was written to aid writers of SEC disclosure documents. In a quote from the preface, writers are encouraged to "Write with a specific person in mind."[1] Picturing a sibling or parent who, though highly intelligent, is not an expert in accounting or finance will make the task of explanation much easier. While the SEC's plain language requirements initially caused delays for some companies, subsequent filings have typically gone more smoothly. The general consumer response has been favorable.

Prudential Insurance Company of America distinguished itself as one of the first companies to comply with the SEC requirements for plain English. In addition to simplifying its prospectuses, Prudential makes liberal use of graphics, colors, summaries, large type, an index, and captions. Metropolitan Life Insurance Company's overhauled report features characters from the "Peanuts" comic strip to illustrate key points. Boldface type, charts, and sidebars help make the prospectus more interesting and easier for customers to understand.[2]

A spokesperson for the SEC emphasized that writing in plain English doesn't mean writing with less substance. The Commission's intent is not for issuers to "dumb down" their prospectuses. "The overall idea behind requiring plain language is to try to make prospectuses less intimidating for the average reader, with the hope that individuals making investments will be more likely to read and study shorter, more readable documents."[3]

Regardless of the types of messages you prepare in your professional life, you will always need to focus on audience needs and expectations. In this chapter, you will learn to apply specific techniques for writing reader-friendly documents for various situations.

www.sec.gov

SEE SHOWCASE PART 2, ON PAGE 130
FOR SPOTLIGHT COMMUNICATOR MARY SCHAPIRO, SEC CHAIR.

OBJECTIVE 1

In Chapter 3, you learned about the importance of following a systematic process to develop business messages. The applications in Chapter 3 guided you in developing a clear, logical plan for your message that focuses on the needs of the receiver (Steps 1–4). Effectively capturing your ideas for various business communication situations involves skillful use of language and careful attention to accuracy and readability issues—the remaining two steps in this important process are shown in Figure 4-1.

FIGURE 4-1

Process for Planning and Preparing Spoken and Written Messages

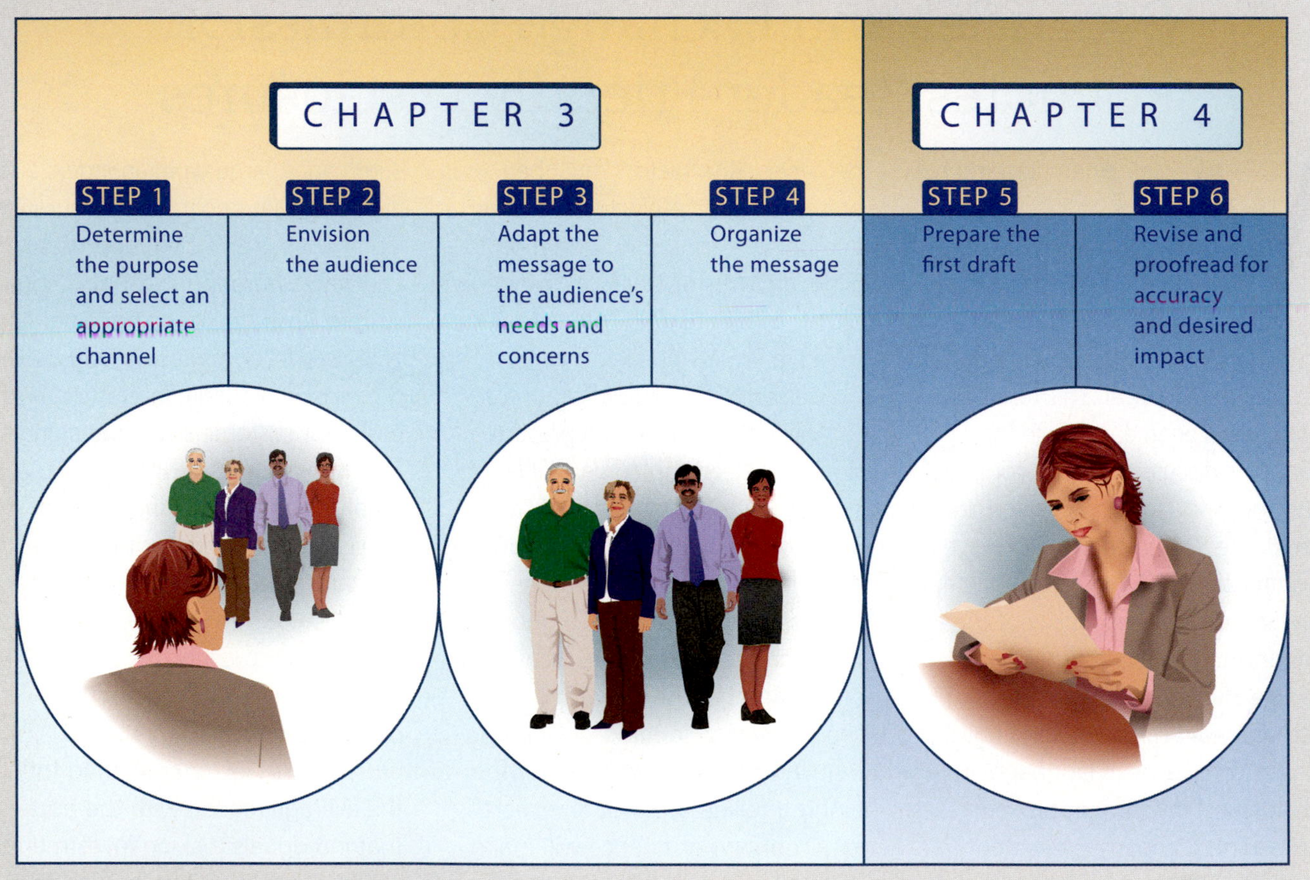

CHAPTER 3
CHAPTER 4
STEP 1
Determine the purpose and select an appropriate channel
STEP 2
Envision the audience
STEP 3
Adapt the message to the audience's needs and concerns
STEP 4
Organize the message
STEP 5
Prepare the first draft
STEP 6
Revise and proofread for accuracy and desired impact

Prepare the First Draft

Once you have determined whether the message should be presented deductively (main idea first) or inductively (explanation and details first) and have planned the logical sequence of minor points, you are ready to begin composing the message.

Normally, writing rapidly (with intent to rewrite certain portions, if necessary) is better than slow, deliberate writing (with intent to avoid any need for

What writing methods work well for you? What habits hinder your success or enjoyment of writing? How can you overcome them?

rewriting portions). The latter approach can be frustrating and can reduce the quality of the finished work. Time is wasted in thinking of one way to express an idea, discarding it either before or after it is written, waiting for new inspiration, and rereading preceding sentences.

Concentrating on getting your ideas down as quickly as you can is an efficient approach to writing. During this process, remember that you are preparing a draft and not the final copy. If you are composing at the computer, you can quickly and easily revise your draft throughout the composition process. This seamless approach to writing allows you to continue to improve your "working draft" until the moment you are ready to submit the final copy. Numerous electronic writing tools are available, and technology will continue to unfold to enhance the writing process. The accompanying Strategic Forces feature, "Improving Your Writing with the Computer," will aid you in maximizing the power of these electronic tools to write effectively and efficiently.

CHANGING TECHNOLOGY

Automated speech recognition software has been promoted as a vehicle for improving the cost effectiveness of business writing with predictions that writers in the future would use the keyboard only for revising text and not for primary input. Many users have been disappointed with the time and energy required to "train" the product to recognize their voices and the software's poor accuracy rates (e.g., garbled words and the absence of end punctuation).[4] However, improvements in voice activation and speech processing powering are leading to a much wider range of reliable speech-enabled applications, many of which are embedded within smartphones. With the convenience and safety of hands-free operation and no training time, communicators can record and hear email messages, receive updates about scheduled appointments; and access many types of information from current bank balances to real-time traffic, stock, and weather updates. You will learn more in Chapter 5 about these emerging technologies that enhance workers' ability to access and disseminate information quickly and efficiently.

Do you think keyboards will disappear from computers? Explain.

Mea Culpa. Words are carefully analyzed and scrutinized when they are part of an apology. Olympic gold-medalist Michael Phelps found that true when he apologized for newspaper photos that showed him inhaling from a marijuana pipe. Describing his behavior as "regrettable" and referring to his "bad judgment," Phelps' apology was convincing enough for the International Olympic Committee, whose issued statement said "He apologized . . . we have no reason to doubt his sincerity and his commitment to continue to act as a role model."[5] Phelps fared far better following his publicized indiscretion than did Alex Rodriguez after being caught lying about taking performance-enhancing drugs while playing professional baseball. Rodriguez's apology was viewed by many as clumsy, vague, and parsed to avoid taking blame.[6]

Your Turn 4-1
Assessment

A blank computer screen can be so intimidating! Writing anxiety afflicts everyone at one time or another, but it can be dealt with. Following your instructor's directions, contribute your thoughts to a blog related to writing anxiety and success strategies.

TAKE ACTION:

Discuss your answers to the following questions:

- Does writing intimidate you? Why or why not?
- What strategies have helped you cope with or overcome writing anxiety?

Powerful Sentences

© BANANASTOCK/JUPITER IMAGES

Well-developed sentences help the receiver understand the message clearly and react favorably to the writer or speaker. In this section, you will learn about predominant use of active voice and emphasis of important points that affect the clarity and human relations of your message. Visit your companion website at www.cengage.com/bcomm/lehman to learn other strategies for using correct sentence structure and crafting powerful messages.

Rely on Active Voice

Business communicators normally use active voice more heavily than passive voice because active voice conveys ideas more vividly. In sentences in which the subject is the *doer* of action, the verbs are called ***active***. In sentences in which the subject is the *receiver* of action, the verbs are called ***passive***. Review the differences in the impact of passive and active voice:

PASSIVE VOICE	ACTIVE VOICE
Reports are transferred electronically from remote locations to the corporate office.	Our sales reps transfer reports electronically from remote locations to the corporate office.

How does using active voice suggest to the receiver that you are action oriented and decisive?

The active sentence invites the receiver to see the sales reps using a computer to complete a report. The passive sentence draws attention to a report. Using active voice makes the subject the actor, which makes the idea easier to understand. Sentences written using passive voice give receivers a less-distinct picture. In the passive sentence, the receiver becomes aware that something was done to the reports, but it does not reveal who did it.

Even when a passive sentence contains additional words to reveal the doer, the imagery is less distinct than it would be if the sentence were active: *Reports compiled by our sales representatives are transferred electronically from remote locations to the home office.*

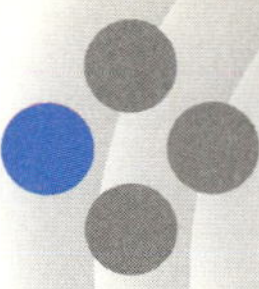

CHANGING TECHNOLOGY

STRATEGIC FORCES

Improving Your Writing with the Computer

Computer tools are a tremendous aid in the writing process. Good writers recognize the strengths and limitations of software.

1. **Hone your computer skills to spend more time writing and less time formatting.**
   - Draft in a font style and size easily read on screen; postpone formatting until the revision is done.
   - Use the *find* and *go to* commands to search and make changes.
   - Learn time-saving keyboard shortcuts for frequently used commands such as *copy* and *cut*. Customize software so that you can access these commands easily.
   - Use automatic numbering to arrange numerical or alphabetical lists and to ensure accuracy.
   - Save time by using built-in styles: cover pages, headers/footers, list and table formats, text boxes, and graphical effects.
   - Save frequently used text such as a letterhead or your signature line so you can select with a single click.
   - Use the citations and bibliography command to format references and the document styles feature to automatically generate a content page and index.
2. **Use formatting features to create an organized and polished appearance.**
   - Add spacing between lines and paragraphs and use crisp, open fonts such as Calibri for a contemporary look that is easy to read on-screen.
   - Apply color-infused document themes and built-in styles to reflect a consistent brand identity.
   - Create high-impact graphics using SmartArt and WordArt features.
3. **Integrate the thinking and writing processes.**
   - Identify key points, issues these points address, supporting evidence, and sources you intend to use.
   - Input and compile ideas as you think, and then develop these ideas using an appropriate approach.
   - Scroll through the document, looking for improvements in the content and transitions among ideas affected by adding, cutting, or moving text.
4. **Use proofing features to locate errors.**
   - Use spell-check frequently as you draft and revise. Be aware that spell-check will not identify miskeyings (*than* for *then*), commonly misused words, homophones (*principle, principal*), omitted words, missing or out-of-order enumerations, and content errors.
   - Use grammar check to provide feedback on usage, reading level, comprehension factors, and other errors and weaknesses that cannot be detected electronically.
   - Use thesaurus only when you can recognize the precise meaning needed.

© KHARIDEHAL ABHIRAMA ASHWIN/ SHUTTERSTOCK.COM

5. **Proofread the document on-screen.**
   - Input revisions, and run spell-check again.
   - Use print preview to check for placement, visual appeal, and appropriate use of headers, footers, and page numbering.

Application

- Identify word processing features that would help you write more effectively and commit to using them.
- Following guidelines provided by your instructor, use the computer to write a message. Be prepared to discuss perceived changes in the quality of your writing and the efficiency with which you completed the message.

Write several sentences in both active and passive voice; note the difference in the vividness of the sentences.

"Reports" gets the most attention because it is the subject. The sentence seems to let a receiver know the *result* of action before revealing the doer; therefore, the sentence is less emphatic.

Although active voice conveys ideas more vividly, passive voice is useful

- In concealing the doer. ("The reports have been compiled.")
- In placing more emphasis on *what* was done and who or what it was *done to* than on who *did* it. ("The reports have been compiled by our sales representatives.")
- In subordinating an unpleasant thought. ("The Shipping Department has not been notified of this delay" rather than "You have not notified the Shipping Department of this delay.") Review the previous discussion of using passive voice to de-emphasize negative ideas in the "Project a Positive, Tactful Tone" section of Chapter 3.

When is use of passive voice recommended?

Emphasize Important Ideas

A landscape artist wants some features in a picture to stand out boldly and others to get little attention. A musician sounds some notes loudly and others softly. Likewise, a writer or speaker wants some ideas to be *emphasized* and others to be *de-emphasized*. Normally, pleasant and important ideas should be emphasized; unpleasant and insignificant ideas should be de-emphasized. Emphasis techniques include sentence structure, repetition, words that label, position, and space and format.

Sentence Structure

For emphasis, place an idea in a simple sentence. The simple sentence in the following example has one independent clause. Because no other idea competes with it for attention, this idea is emphasized.

SIMPLE SENTENCE IS MORE EMPHATIC	COMPOUND SENTENCE IS LESS EMPHATIC
Nicole accepted a position in insurance.	Nicole accepted a position in insurance, but she really preferred a job in accounting.

Should a significant idea be placed in the dependent or independent clause? Why?

For emphasis, place an idea in an independent clause; for de-emphasis, place an idea in a dependent clause. In the following compound sentence the idea of taking a job is in an independent clause. Because an independent clause makes sense if the rest of the sentence is omitted, an independent clause is more emphatic than a dependent clause. In the complex sentence, the idea of taking a job is in a dependent clause. By itself, the clause would not make complete sense. Compared with the independent clause that follows ("Nicole really preferred . . ."), the idea in the dependent clause is de-emphasized.

COMPOUND SENTENCE IS MORE EMPHATIC	COMPLEX SENTENCE IS LESS EMPHATIC
Nicole accepted a position in insurance, but she really preferred a position in accounting.	Although she accepted a position in insurance, Nicole really preferred a position in accounting.

How can an effective communicator restate without being redundant?

Repetition

To emphasize a word, let it appear more than once in a sentence. For example, a clever advertisement by OfficeMax used the word *stuff* repeatedly to describe generically several types of office needs ranging from paper clips to color copies, and then ended succinctly with "OfficeMax . . . for your office stuff." Likewise, in the following example, "success" receives more emphasis when the word is repeated.

LESS EMPHATIC	MORE EMPHATIC
The project was successful because of . . .	The project was successful; this success is attributed to . . .

Words that Label

For emphasis or de-emphasis, use words that label ideas as significant or insignificant. Note the labeling words used in the following examples to emphasize or de-emphasize an idea:

But most important of all . . .
A less significant aspect was . . .

Position

To emphasize a word or an idea, position it first or last in a sentence, clause, paragraph, or presentation. Note the additional emphasis placed on the words *success* and *failure* in the examples in the right column because these words appear as the *first* or the *last* words in their clauses.

LESS EMPHATIC	MORE EMPHATIC
Your efforts contributed to the success of the project; otherwise, failure would have been the result.	Success resulted from your efforts; failure would have resulted without them.
The project was successful because of your efforts; without them, failure would have been the result.	The project was a success; without your efforts, it would have been a failure.

What hidden meaning (metacommunication) is communicated by a message in which most paragraphs begin with *I*?

In paragraphs, the first and last words are in particularly emphatic positions. An idea that deserves emphasis can be placed in either position, but an idea that does not deserve emphasis can be placed in the middle of a long paragraph. The word *I*, which is frequently overused in messages, is especially noticeable if it appears as the first word. *I* is more noticeable if it appears as the first word in *every* paragraph. *However* is to be avoided as the first word in a paragraph if the preceding paragraph is neutral or positive. These words imply that the next idea will be negative. Unless the purpose is to place emphasis on negatives, such words as *denied*, *rejected*, and *disappointed*, should not appear as the last words in a paragraph.

Likewise, the central idea of a written or spoken report appears in the introduction (the beginning) and the conclusion (the end). Good transition sentences synthesize ideas at the end of each major division.

Space and Format

The various divisions of a report or spoken presentation are not expected to be of equal length, but an extraordinary amount of space devoted to a topic attaches special significance to that topic. Similarly, a topic that receives an exceedingly small amount of space is de-emphasized. The manner in which information is physically arranged affects the emphasis it receives and consequently the overall impact of the document.

Develop Coherent Paragraphs

A deductive paragraph begins with the main idea followed by the details. How does an inductive paragraph differ?

Well-constructed sentences are combined into paragraphs that discuss a portion of the topic being discussed. To write effective paragraphs, you must learn to (a) develop deductive or inductive paragraphs consistently, (b) link ideas to achieve coherence, (c) keep paragraphs unified, and (d) vary sentence and paragraph length.

Position the Topic Sentence Appropriately

Typically, paragraphs contain one sentence that identifies the portion of the topic being discussed and presents the central idea. That sentence is commonly called a ***topic sentence***. For example, consider operating instructions prepared for company-owned GPS navigation systems. The overall topic is how to get satisfactory performance from the device. One portion of that topic is setup; another portion (paragraph) discusses operation; and so forth. Within each paragraph, one sentence serves a special function. Sentences that list the steps can appear as one paragraph, perhaps with steps numbered as follows:

To set up the system, take the following steps:

1. Connect . . .
2. Go to menu settings to . . .

In this illustration, the paragraphs are ***deductive***; that is, the topic sentence *precedes* details. When topic sentences *follow* details, the paragraphs are ***inductive***. As discussed previously, the receiver's likely reaction to the main idea (pleased, displeased, interested, not interested) aids in selecting the appropriate sequence.

When the subject matter is complicated and the details are numerous, paragraphs sometimes begin with a main idea, follow with details, and end with a summarizing sentence.

But the main idea may not be in the first sentence; the idea may need a preliminary statement. Receivers appreciate consistency in the placement of topic sentences. Once they catch on to the writer or speaker's pattern, they know where to look for main ideas.

These suggestions seldom apply to the first and last sentences of letters, memos, and email messages. Such sentences frequently appear as single-sentence paragraphs. But for reports and long paragraphs of letters, strive for paragraphs that are consistently deductive or inductive. Regardless of which is selected, topic sentences are clearly linked with details that precede or follow.

Link Ideas to Achieve Coherence

Careful writers use coherence techniques to keep receivers from experiencing abrupt changes in thought. Although the word ***coherence*** is used sometimes to mean "clarity" or "understandability," it is used throughout this text to mean "cohesion." If writing or speaking is coherent, the sentences stick together; each sentence is in some way linked to the preceding sentences. Avoid abrupt changes in thought, and link each sentence to a preceding sentence.

The following techniques for linking sentences are common:

1. **Repeat a word that was used in the preceding sentence.** The second sentence in the following example is an obvious continuation of the idea presented in the preceding sentence.

   . . . to take responsibility for the decision. This responsibility can be shared . . .

2. **Use a pronoun that represents a noun used in the preceding sentence.** Because "it" means "responsibility," the second sentence is linked directly with the first.

   . . . to take this responsibility. It can be shared . . .

3. **Use connecting words.** Examples include *however, therefore, yet, nevertheless, consequently, also,* and *in addition*. "However" implies "We're continuing with the same topic, just moving into a different phase." Remember, though, that good techniques can be overused. Unnecessary connectors are space consuming and distracting. Usually they can be spotted (and crossed out) in proofreading.

   . . . to take this responsibility. However, few are willing to . . .

What techniques can you use to provide cohesion in your writing?

Just as sentences within a paragraph must link, paragraphs within a document must also link. Unless a writer or speaker is careful, the move from one major topic to the next will seem abrupt. A good transition sentence can bridge the gap between the two topics by summing up the preceding topic and leading a receiver to expect the next topic:

Cost factors, then, seemed prohibitive until efficiency factors were investigated.

This sentence could serve as a transition between the "Cost" and "Efficiency" division headings. Because a transition sentence comes at the end of one segment and before the next, it emphasizes the central idea of the preceding segment and confirms the relationship of the two segments. While transition sentences are helpful if properly used, they can be overused. For most reports, transition sentences before major headings are sufficient. Normally, transition sentences before subheadings are unnecessary.

SHOWCASE PART 2

© JOSE M. OSORIO/MCT/LANDOV

SPOTLIGHT COMMUNICATOR
MARY SCHAPIRO,
SEC CHAIRPERSON

Simplicity in Words and Numbers

In 2009, Mary Schapiro became the 29th chairperson and the first woman to head the Securities and Exchange Commission (SEC). In her previous role as CEO of National Association of Securities Dealers (NASD), she led the effort to dissect and rewrite the rules of the NASD and the New York Stock Exchange into a single rulebook. Currently at the SEC, Schapiro seeks to restore sagging consumer confidence in the financial market through her commitment to investor protection, transparency, and accountability.[7] Visit your companion website at www.cengage.com/bcomm/lehman to learn more about the development of global accounting standards and the interactive data reporting requirement.

www.sec.gov

SEE SHOWCASE PART 3, ON PAGE 144
TO LEARN ABOUT THE EFFORTS OF HEALTH CARE PROVIDERS TO DISCLOSE PATIENT'S RIGHTS USING PLAIN ENGLISH.

Keep Paragraphs Unified

How are unity and coherence related concepts?

Receivers expect the first paragraph of a message to introduce a topic, additional paragraphs to discuss it, and a final paragraph to tie them together. The in-between paragraphs should be arranged in a systematic sequence, and the end must be linked easily to some word or idea presented in the beginning. The effect of a message that is *not* unified is like that of an incomplete circle or a picture with one element obviously missing.

- An email message, letter, memo, or report with unity covers its topic adequately but will not include extraneous material. The document will have a beginning sentence appropriate for the expected receiver reaction, paragraphs that present the bulk of the message, and an ending sentence that is an appropriate closing for the message presented.
- A report or presentation with unity begins with an introduction that identifies the topic, reveals the thesis, and previews upcoming points. The introduction may also include some background, sources of information, and the method of treating data. Between the beginning and the ending, a unified report will have paragraphs arranged in a systematic sequence. A summary or conclusion brings all major points together.

Vary Sentence and Paragraph Length

Sentences of short or average length are easy to read and preferred for communicating clearly. However, keeping *all* sentences short is undesirable because the message may sound monotonous, unrealistic, or elementary. A two-word sentence is acceptable; so is a 60-word sentence—if it is clear. Just as sentences should vary in length, they should also vary in structure. Some complex or compound sentences should be included with simple sentences.

Variety is just as desirable in paragraph length as it is in sentence length. A paragraph can be from one line in length to a dozen lines or more. However, just as with sentence length, average paragraph length also should be kept short, as appropriate to the document type:

- Paragraphs in letters, memos, and email messages are typically shorter than paragraphs in business reports.
- First and last paragraphs are normally short (one to four lines), and other paragraphs are normally no longer than *six lines*. A short first paragraph is more inviting to read than a long first paragraph, and a short last paragraph enables a writer to emphasize parting thoughts.
- The space between paragraphs is a welcome resting spot. Long paragraphs are difficult to read and make a message appear uninviting. Paragraph length will vary depending on the complexity of the subject matter. However, as a general rule paragraphs should be no longer than *eight to ten lines*. This length usually allows enough space to include a topic sentence and three or four supporting statements. If the topic cannot be discussed in this space, divide the topic into additional paragraphs.

Why are paragraphs in a business message typically shorter than those in a literary essay?

To observe the effect large sections of unbroken text have on the overall appeal of a document, examine the memos in Figure 4-2 that contain identical information. Without question, the memo with the short, easy-to-read paragraphs is more inviting to read than the memo with one bulky paragraph.

Although variety is a desirable quality, it should not be achieved at the expense of consistency. Using *I* in one part of a message and then without explanation switching to *we* is inadvisable. Using the past tense in one sentence and the present tense in another sentence creates variety at the expense of consistency—unless the shift is required to indicate actual changes in time. Unnecessary changes from active to passive voice and from third to first person are also discouraged.

Refer to the "Check Your Communication" checklist at the end of the chapter to review the guidelines for writing a first draft of the message that can be easily understood and received positively.

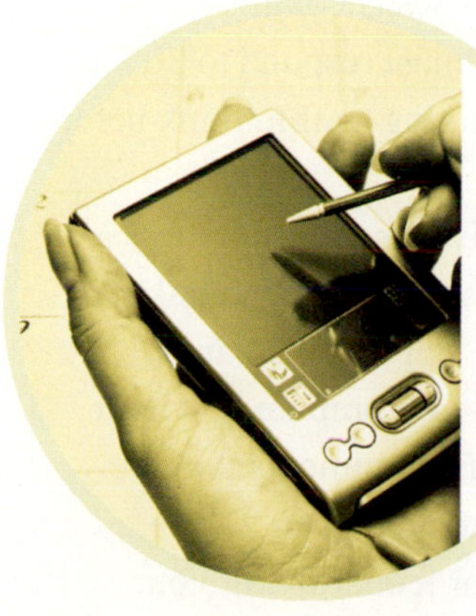

Your Turn 4-2
Career Portfolio

The ability to communicate clearly is a valuable skill appreciated across career fields. Assume you are the director of corporate communication and have been asked to write a 500-word news article for posting on your company's intranet that emphasizes to employees the importance of clear written communication.

TAKE ACTION:

Compose your article, including an effective title. Submit it according to your instructor's directions.

FIGURE 4-2

Contrast the Readability and Appeal of Bulky (left) vs. Broken (right) Text

To:	All employees
From:	Mary Kendall Welch, HR Manager
Subject:	Training Available through Podcasts

Everyone,

Can you imagine the convenience of upgrading your management skills as you make the daily commute to your office? It's possible with podcast training set to begin next week that includes an intriguing segment on leadership communication. All required training seminars, previously available via streaming video over the company intranet, are now available to be downloaded to your iPod. To encourage you to take advantage of this innovative learning method, you can purchase the latest generation iPod for $100—a substantial discount to the retail price. Simply order directly from the vendor's website and input LC413 for the discount code. Call technology support should you need assistance in downloading your first podcast. When you're not advancing your management skills to the next level, use your iPod to enjoy your favorite tunes and movies.

To:	All employees
From:	Mary Kendall Welch, HR Manager
Subject:	Training Available through Podcasts

Everyone,

Can you imagine the convenience of upgrading your management skills as you make the daily commute to your office? It's possible with podcast training set to begin next week that includes an intriguing segment on leadership communication.

All required training seminars, previously available via streaming video over the company intranet, are now available to be downloaded to your iPod. To encourage you to take advantage of this innovative learning method, you can purchase the latest generation iPod for $100—a substantial discount to the retail price. Simply order directly from the vendor's website and input LC413 for the discount code.

Call technology support should you need assistance in downloading your first podcast. When you're not advancing your management skills to the next level, use your iPod to enjoy your favorite tunes and movies.

Revise and Proofread

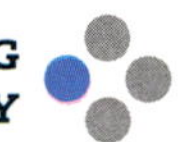

The speed and convenience of today's electronic communication have caused many communicators to confuse informality with sloppiness. Sloppy messages contain misspellings, grammatical errors, unappealing and incorrect formats, and confusing content—all of which create a negative impression of the writer and the company and affect the receiver's ability to understand the message. Some experts believe the increased use of email is leading to bosses becoming ruder. To combat against the harsh tone that often sets in when managers must respond to 300 to 500 emails weekly, Unilever is providing writing training and urging staff to think before they press the send button.[8]

As the sender, you are responsible for evaluating the effectiveness of each message you prepare. You must not use informality as an excuse to be sloppy. Instead, take one consultant's advice: "You can still be informal and not be sloppy. You can be informal and correct."[9] Take a good hard look at the messages you prepare. Commit to adjusting your message to the audience, designing appealing documents that are easily read, and following a systematic proofreading process to ensure error-free messages. This effort may save you from being embarrassed or jeopardizing your credibility.

How do you draw the line between informal and sloppy?

Your Turn 4-3
You're the Professional

As part of your managerial responsibilities, you are reviewing the performance of an employee you hired six months ago who is now completing his probationary period. While the individual has good work habits and strong interpersonal skills, his writing skills are very weak. You have in front of you two memos he wrote to departmental personnel, each with numerous grammatical errors, missing punctuation, and inappropriate word choices that apparently resulted from ineffective thesaurus usage. Additionally, the employee regularly sends out email messages to company employees with similar errors, and you have even been copied on several sloppy messages that went out to customers. How will you respond?

TAKE ACTION:

Discuss which of the following actions would be most appropriate, explaining your reasoning:

a. Talk to the employee about the need for better written communication skills.

b. Move the employee to a position that will require less writing.

c. Let the employee go, explaining that the job requires strong communication skills, which he lacks.

d. Let the employee remain with the company, with the stipulation that he enroll in a writing course at the local college.

Improve Readability

Although sentences are arranged in a logical sequence and are written coherently, the receiver may find reading the sentences difficult. Several indexes have been developed to measure the reading difficulty of your writing. Electronic tools aid you in making computations and identifying changes that will improve readability.

Understand Readability Measures

The grammar and style checker feature of leading word processing software calculates readability measures to aid you in writing for quick, easy reading and listening. The Fog index, a popular readability index developed by Robert Gunning, as well as the Flesch-Kincaid Grade Level available in Microsoft Word, consider the length of sentences and the difficulty of words to produce the approximate grade level a person would need to understand the material. For example, a grade level of 10 indicates a person needs to be able to read at the tenth-grade level to understand the material. Fortunately, you won't have to calculate readability manually, but understanding the manual calculation of the Fog index will illustrate clearly how

© ISTOCKPHOTO.COM/WILLIE B. THOMAS

What factors affect the readability of a message?

sentence length and difficulty of words affect readability calculations and guide you in adapting messages. Review the Fog index calculations for a sample business document at your companion website at www.cengage.com/bcomm/lehman.

Trying to write at the exact grade level of the receiver is not advised. You may not know the exact grade level, and even those who have earned advanced degrees appreciate writing they can read and understand quickly and easily. Also, writing a passage with a readability index appropriate for the audience does not guarantee the message will be understood. Despite simple language and short sentences, the message can be distorted by imprecise words, biased language, jargon, and translations that ignore cultural interpretations, to name just a few. The value of calculating a readability measure lies in the feedback you gain about average length of sentences and the difficulty of the words. Revise and recalculate the readability index and continue revising until you feel the reading level is appropriate for the intended audience.

How can writing analysis software improve your writing?

The grammar and style feature in word processing programs also locates grammatical errors, including misspellings and common usage errors, such as the use of fragments, run-on sentences, subject-verb disagreement, passive voice, double words, and split infinitives. Because it can only guess at the structure of a sentence and then apply a rigid set of rules, a grammar and style checker, like spell-check, must be used cautiously. It is not a reliable substitute for a human editor who has an effective writing style and is familiar with the rules the software displays. Allow the software to flag misspellings and writing errors as you write, accept or reject the suggested changes based on your knowledge of effective writing, and use the readability measures to adjust your writing levels appropriately as shown in Figure 4-3. For further support of writing, you may consider other technology tools such as *Bullfighter*, a program that helps business writers reduce jargon, corporate speak, and wordiness. Developed by the authors of *Why Business People Speak Like Idiots*, this free download is available at http:fightthebull.com and works as a convenient add-in to Microsoft Word and PowerPoint.

FIGURE 4-3

Improving Readability through Cautious Use of a Grammar and Style Checker

Step 1:
Evaluate and respond to advice given for grammar and style errors detected.

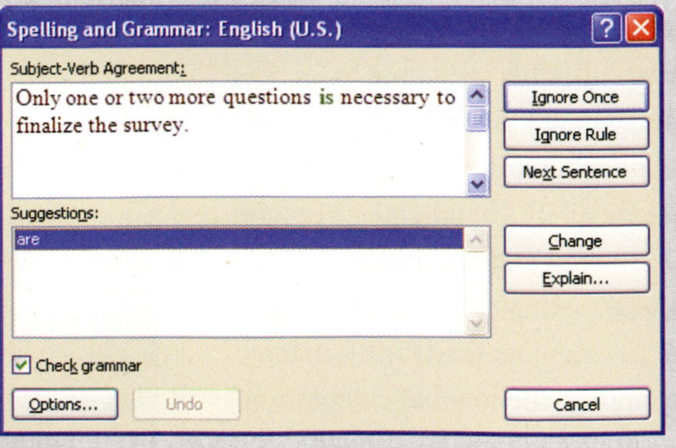

Step 2:
Use counts, averages, and readability indexes as guides for adjusting writing level appropriately.

Readability Statistics

Counts	
Words	309
Characters	1572
Paragraphs	4
Sentences	12
Averages	
Sentences per Paragraph	3.0
Words per Sentence	25.7
Characters per Word	4.9
Readability	
Passive Sentences	8%
Flesch Reading Ease	43.2
Flesch-Kincaid Grade Level	13.6

OK

Apply Visual Enhancements to Improve Readability

What visual enhancements can make your document easy to read and understand?

The vast amount of information created in today's competitive global market poses a challenge to you as a business writer. You must learn to create visually appealing documents that entice a receiver to read rather than discard your message. Additionally, an effective design will enable you to highlight important information for maximum attention and to transition a receiver smoothly through sections of a long, complex document. These design techniques can be applied easily using word processing software. However, add visual enhancements only when they aid in comprehension. Overuse will cause your document to appear cluttered and will defeat your purpose of creating an appealing, easy-to-read document.

Enumerations

To emphasize units in a series, place a number, letter, or bullet before each element. Words preceded by numbers, bullets, or letters attract the receiver's special attention and are easier to locate when the page is reviewed.

ORIGINAL	HIGHLIGHTED
The human resources problems have been narrowed into three categories: absenteeism, tardiness, and pilferage.	The human resources problems have been narrowed into three categories: (1) absenteeism, (2) tardiness, and (3) pilferage.

Enumerated or Bulleted Lists

Many times writers want to save space; however, cluttered text is unappealing and difficult to read. *Chunking*—a desktop publishing term—is an answer to the problem. Chunking involves breaking down information into easily digestible pieces. It's the communication equivalent of Butterfinger® BBs, rather than the whole candy bar. The added white space divides the information into blocks, makes the page look more organized, and increases retention by 50 percent.[10]

Enumerated or bulleted lists can be used to chunk and add even greater visual impact to items in a series. Items appear on separate lines with numerals, letters, or various types of bullets (•, ◆, ❑, ✓, and so on) at the beginning. Multiple line items often are separated by a blank line. This design creates more white space that isolates the items from other text and demands attention. Bullets are typically preferred over numerals unless the sequence of the items in the series is critical (e.g., steps in a procedure that must be completed in the correct order). In the following excerpt from a long analytical report, the four supporting reasons for a conclusion are highlighted in a bulleted list:

ORIGINAL	HIGHLIGHTED
For our needs, then, the most appropriate in-service training method is web-based instruction. This training is least expensive, allows employees to remain at their own workstations while improving their skills, affords constant awareness of progress, and lets employees progress at their own rates.	Web-based instruction is the most appropriate in-service training method because it • is least expensive. • allows employees to remain at their own workstations while improving their skills. • affords constant awareness of progress. • lets employees progress at their own rates.

Headings

Headings are signposts that direct the receiver from one section of the document to another. Studies have shown that readers find documents with headings easier to grasp; readers also report they are more motivated to pay attention to the text, even in a short document such as a half-page warranty.[11] You'll find that organizing the content of various types of documents will be more readable and appealing when you add logical, well-written headings. Follow these general guidelines for writing effective headings:

What is a "talk" heading?

- Compose brief headings that make a connection with the receiver, giving clear cues as to the usefulness of the information. (How Do I Apply?) Consider using questions rather than noun phrases to let readers know they are reading the information they need (Choose "Who Is Eligible to Apply?" rather than "Eligible Loan Participants.")[12] Consider talking headings that reveal the conclusions reached in the following discussion rather than general topic headings. For example, "Costs Are Prohibitive" is more emphatic than "Cost Factors."
- Strive for parallel structure of readings within a section. For example, mixing descriptive phrases with questions requires additional mental effort and distracts readers who expect parallel writing.
- Follow a hierarchy, with major headings receiving more attention than minor headings or paragraph headings. To draw more attention to a major heading, center it and use a heavier, larger typestyle or brighter text color. Note the position and spacing of three levels of headings shown in Appendix A and the sample reports in Chapter 11.

Tables and Graphs

Tables and graphs are used to simplify and clarify information and to add an appealing variety to long sections of dense text. The clearly labeled rows and columns in a table organize large amounts of specific numeric data and facilitate analysis. Graphics such as pie, line, and bar charts visually depict relationships within the data; they provide quick estimates rather than specific information. In Chapter 10, you will gain proficiency in selecting an appropriate graphic format for data and in designing effective and accurate tables and graphs.

Lines and Borders

Horizontal and vertical lines can be added to partition text or to focus attention on a specific line(s). For example, a thin line followed by a thick line effectively separates the identification section of a résumé from the qualifications. Placing a border around a paragraph or section of text sets that information apart; adding shading inside the box adds greater impact. For example, a pull-quote format might spotlight a testimonial from a satisfied customer in a sales letter, important dates to remember in a memorandum, or a section of a document that must be completed and returned. Current word processing software provides a variety of appealing built-in formats for enhancing a document with one quick keystroke.

Relevant Images

A variety of interesting shapes can be used to highlight information and add appeal. Examples include creating a rectangular callout box highlighting a key idea with an arrow pointing to a specific number in a table, surrounding a title with a shaded oval for added impact, and using built-in designs to illustrate a process, relationship, cycle, hierarchy, and more. Clip art or photos can also be added to reinforce an idea and add visual appeal. The following example from the Plain English website shows how visual communication can convey important safety information more effectively than words.

Before

This is a multipurpose passenger vehicle which will handle and maneuver differently from an ordinary passenger car, in driving conditions which may occur on streets and highways and off road. As with other vehicles of this type, if you make sharp turns or abrupt maneuvers, the vehicle may roll over or may go out of control and crash. You should read driving guidelines and instructions in the Owner's Manual, and WEAR YOUR SEAT BELTS AT ALL TIMES.

After

WARNING: HIGHER ROLLOVER RISK

Avoid Abrupt Maneuvers and Excessive Speed.

Always Buckle Up.

See Owner's Manual For Further Information.

COURTESY OF NATIONAL HIGHWAY TRAFFIC SAFETY ADMINISTRATION

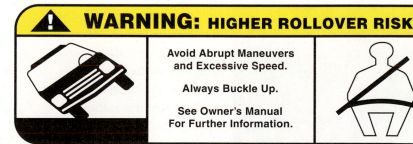

Battling to manage an avalanche of information, the recipients of your messages will appreciate your extra effort to create an easy-to-read, appealing document. These fundamental techniques will be invaluable as you enhance printed documents such as letters, memos, reports, agendas, handouts, and minutes for meetings. You'll also build on this foundation as you learn to design effective web documents and high-impact presentation visuals in later chapters.

Your Turn 4-4
Electronic Café

INTRANETS EXPAND INTERNAL COMMUNICATIONS

The emergence of the global marketplace has led many organizations to view an intranet as providing a single, unified structure to help meet their internal communication needs.

TAKE ACTION:

a. Locate the following online article that offers tips on intranet design:

Ten tips for building an effective intranet. (2009). *All Business.* Available at www.allbusiness.com/technology/computer-networking/638-1.html

b. Give an example or situation that illustrates the application of each of the 10 tips.

c. Go to your text companion website at www.cengage.com/bcomm/lehman for more information on how to make an intranet work for you.

Use Systematic Procedures for Revising and Proofreading

What are other examples of negative effects of spelling errors made by companies or organizations?

Errors in writing and mechanics may seem isolated, but the truth is, proofreading *is* important. You don't have to look too far to see silly typos or obvious instances of writers relying only on the computer spell-check. The classifieds in a small-town newspaper advertised "fully fascinated and spade damnation puppies." The advertisement was for fully vaccinated and spayed Dalmatian puppies. These errors clearly illustrate how spell-check can fail, but goofs like that are not limited to small-town newspapers.

It was not a spelling error but a simple transposition in a telephone number that created an unbelievably embarrassing situation for a telecommunications giant. AT&T customers calling to redeem points earned in a True Rewards program were connected to pay-by-the-minute erotic phone entertainment.[13] Mistakes ranging from printing ordinary typos to running entirely erroneous ads forced newspapers to refund $10.6 million to dissatisfied

© AP IMAGES/PRNEWSFOTO/AT&T CORPORATION

© AP IMAGE/CHRIS PIZZELLO

Spelling Matters. If you're going to impersonate Rachael Ray, be sure you can spell her name. In a Yahoo! blog post allegedly written by media celebrity and cookbook author Rachael Ray, the author misspelled Ms. Ray's first name as Rachel a dozen times.[16]

In a related snafu, Robert Whitney could probably die of embarrassment. A recurring spelling error led police to connect him to holdup notes used in a string of bank robberies in Florida. A note used in one robbery read: "If a die [dye] pack blows, so do you." Finding the same mistake in two other holdup notes, investigators collected forensic evidence linking Mr. Whitney to the crimes.[17] Spelling matters and should be an absolute priority for business writing.

advertisers and to print $10.5 million in free, make-good ads.[14] The University of California at San Diego inadvertently sent an acceptance email message to all 28,000 students it had rejected, raising their hopes only to dash them when the mistake was discovered and corrected.[15] Each of these actual mistakes illustrates that inattention to proofreading can be potentially embarrassing and incredibly expensive.

Using spell-check is only the first step in locating errors. What types of errors can spell-check not help to locate?

Following systematic revision procedures will help you produce error-free documents that reflect positively on the company and you. Using the procedures that follow, you will see that effective proofreading must be done several times, each time for a specific purpose.

Follow these simple procedures to produce a finished product that is free of errors in (1) content, organization, and style; (2) mechanics; and (3) format and layout:

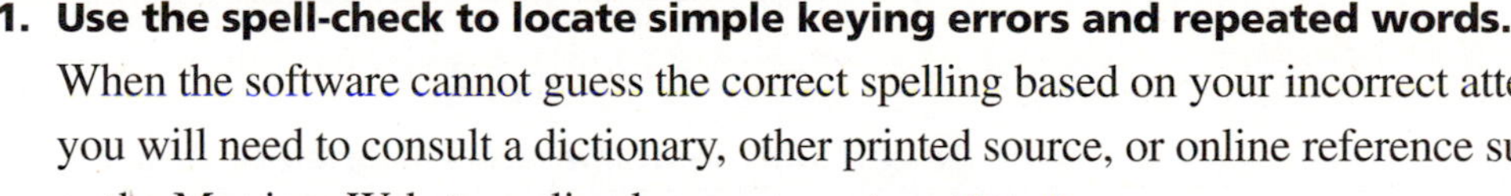

1. **Use the spell-check to locate simple keying errors and repeated words.** When the software cannot guess the correct spelling based on your incorrect attempt, you will need to consult a dictionary, other printed source, or online reference such as the Merriam-Webster online language center at http://m-w.com.

2. **Proofread the document onscreen, concentrating first on errors in content, organization, and style.** To locate errors, ask the following questions:

   Content: Is the information complete? Have I included all the details the receiver needs to understand the message and to take necessary action? Is the information accurate? Have I checked the accuracy of any calculations, dates, names, addresses, and numbers? Have words been omitted?

   Organization: Is the main idea presented appropriately, based on the receiver's likely reaction (deductive or inductive organization)? Are supporting ideas presented in a logical order?

   Style: Is the message clear? Will the receiver interpret the information correctly? Is the message concise and written at an appropriate level for the receiver? Does the message reflect a considerate, caring attitude and focus primarily on the receiver's needs? Does the message treat the receiver honestly and ethically?

How much proofreading is enough?

3. **Proofread a second time concentrating on mechanical errors.** You are searching for potentially damaging errors that a spell-check cannot detect. These problem areas include

   - **Grammar, capitalization, punctuation, number usage, abbreviations.** Review the grammatical principles presented in Appendix C and other available online resources, if necessary.
   - **Word substitutions.** Check the proper use of words such as *your* and *you* and words that sound alike (*there, they're*, or *their; affect* or *effect*).
   - **Parts of the document other than the body.** Proofread the entire document. Errors often appear in the opening and closing sections of documents because writers typically begin proofreading at the first paragraph.

4. **Display the document in print preview mode and edit for format and layout.** Follow these steps to be certain the document adheres to appropriate business formats and is visually appealing:

- **Format according to a conventional format.** Compare your document to the conventional business formats shown in Appendix A and make any revisions. Are all standard parts of the document included and presented in an acceptable format? Are all necessary special parts (e.g., attention line, enclosure) included? Does the message begin on the correct line? Should the right margin be justified or jagged?
- **Be sure numbered items are in the correct order.** Inserting and deleting text may have changed the order of these items.
- **Evaluate the visual impact of the document.** Could you increase the readability of long, uninterrupted blocks of texts by using enumerated or indented lists, headings, or graphic borders or lines? Would adding images or varying print styles add visual appeal? View web documents on several different browsers to assure readability and appeal.
- **Be certain the document is signed or initialed (depending on the document). Ensure that email messages are addressed to the appropriate person(s).**

5. **Print a draft copy and proofread a third time if the document is nonroutine and complex.** Read from *right to left* to reduce your reading speed, allowing you to concentrate deliberately on each word. If a document is extremely important, you may read the document aloud, spelling names and noting capitalization and punctuation, while another person verifies the copy.
6. **Print written documents on high-quality paper.** Refer to Appendix A for paper specifications and other information related to the overall appearance of a document on the page.

The message in Figure 4-4 has been revised for (1) content, organization, and style; (2) mechanics; and (3) format and layout. Study the revisions made using the track-changes feature in word processing software. The commentary makes it easy to see how revising this draft improved the document's quality. Standard proofreading marks are used to mark revisions on printed documents. A handy list of proofreading marks is available at your companion website at www.cengage.com/bcomm/lehman.

Your Turn 4-5
Miscue

Poor communication was blamed for the crash of a commuter plane, killing all 14 aboard, because a horizontal stabilizer's leading edge came off in flight. A maintenance crew had started removing both leading edges of the plane the night prior to the accident. When their task had not been completed at the time of the shift change, the shift change document was written up as "Removed top edge screws." Two mechanics coming on duty read the message, unaware that the left side screws had also been removed. Had the write-up said, "Removed top edge screws on stabilizer left and right leading edge," people might still be alive. Specific language is needed, especially when communicating technical information.[18]

TAKE ACTION:

a. How could careful proofreading have prevented the interpretation error?

b. Give an example of technical information you may be required to share in your career field. Why will accuracy of interpretation be important?

FIGURE 4-4

Rough Draft of a Letter (excerpt)

January 14, 2011

FAX TRANSMISSION

Mr. Thomas Johnston, Manager
Worldwide Enterprises, Inc.
5097 Mill Street
Richmond, ~~Virginia~~ VA 22318-5097

Dear Mr. Johnston:

With your proven ability to produce high quality electronic parts, our entrance into the touchscreen technologies market is certain to~~o~~ be successful. We're excited about other ways our companies can benefit through sharing our expertise.

An objective of our recent merger is to increase your competitiveness by updating your information systems. The first step of this process is to form a steering committee. The committee's primary function ~~whose rudimentary function~~ is to direct ~~the development of the~~ new system development and ~~to~~ ensure ~~that it~~ the system ~~at it~~responds to both ~~incorporates the information needs of the~~ user and ~~the~~ organization needs. To accomplish this goal, the committee membership must

- Include representation from inventory control, shipping, purchasing, accounting, and marketing. ~~Further, the group must~~
- Reflect ~~consist of members from~~ a variety of organizational levels. ~~and members must~~
- Encompass~~possess~~ varying degrees of computer proficiency.

Mr. Johnston, because of your knowledge of company operations, your input is essential. Your serving on this committee will be clear, tangible evidence of management's commitment to significant change. Please ~~advise~~ let me know by February 1 that ~~whether or not~~ you will serve on the Information Systems Steering Committee. A meeting will be scheduled as soon as all ~~members'~~ members have been selected.

Adds mailing notation.

Uses 2-letter state abbreviation.

Corrects spelling of name.

Adds a smooth transition to next paragraph.

Replaces with simple word for clarity.

Divides into two sentences for easy reading and revises for conciseness and clarity.

Bullets list for emphasis and conciseness.

Inserts comma to separate multiple adjectives.

Eliminates cliché and includes specific action.

Corrects grammatical error.

Errors Undetectable by Spell Check

- Verify spelling of receiver's name, "Johnston."
- Correct word substitutions "to" for "too" and "your" for "you."

Cultivate a Frame of Mind for Effective Revising and Proofreading

The following suggestions will guide your efforts to develop business documents that achieve the purpose for which they are intended.

- **Attempt to see things from your audience's perspective rather than from your own.** Being empathetic with your audience isn't as simple as it seems, particularly when dealing with today's diverse workforce. Erase the mind-set, "I know what *I* need to say and how *I* want to say it." Instead, ask, "How would my audience react to this message? Is this message worded so that my audience can easily understand it? Does it convey a tone that will build goodwill?"

- **Revise your documents until you cannot see any additional ways to improve them.** Resist the temptation to think of your first draft as your last draft. Instead, look for ways to improve and be willing to incorporate valid suggestions once you have completed a draft. Experienced writers believe that there is no such thing as good writing, but there is such a thing as good rewriting. Author Dorothy Parker, writer for *Vanity Fair* and *Esquire*, once said, "I can't write five words but that I change seven."[19] Skilled speech writers might rewrite a script 15 or 20 times. Writers in public relations firms revise brochures and advertising copy until perhaps only a comma in the final draft is recognizable from the first draft. Even simple email messages require revision for clarity and mechanical errors with extra passes needed depending on the number of people receiving the email and the context of the message. Regardless of the message type, your careful revising will aid you in producing accurate, readable documents that produce results.

Why are your own errors more difficult to detect than the errors of others?

- **Be willing to allow others to make suggestions for improving your writing.** Because most of us consider our writing personal, we may feel reluctant to share it with others and may be easily offended if they suggest changes. This syndrome, called *writer's pride of ownership*, can prevent us from seeking needed assistance from experienced writers—a proven method of improving communication skills. On the job, especially in today's electronic workplace, your writing will be showcased to your supervisor, clients/customers, members of a collaborative writing team, and more. You have nothing to lose but much to gain by allowing others to critique your writing. This commitment is especially important considering the mistake hardest to detect is your own. However, as the "Blondie" cartoon illustrates, you have the ultimate responsibility for your document; don't simply trust that someone else will catch and correct your errors.

The ability you've gained in following a systematic process for developing effective business messages will prove valuable as you direct your energies to developing effective messages as a member of a team. The accompanying Strategic Forces feature, "Using Collaborative Technologies to Support Work Teams," will showcase exciting technologies that facilitate productive collaboration with others regardless of physical location. Refer to the "Check Your Communication" checklist at the end of this chapter to review the guidelines for preparing and proofreading a rough draft.

Seemingly small proofreading oversights can cause big problems.

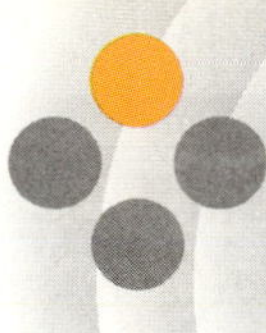

LEGAL AND ETHICAL CONSTRAINTS

STRATEGIC FORCES

Using Collaborative Technologies to Support Work Teams

Workgroup systems and software bring team members together and allow them to share data quickly no matter where they are located. Teams are able to reach better and faster decisions because they have necessary information and the forum to participate in discussion and idea exchange. Work-group computing or collaborative computing are terms used to describe this cooperative environment.

Leading groupware products include Lotus Notes and Domino software from IBM's Lotus Software Group and Microsoft Exchange Titanium. Groupware facilitates effective communication, collaboration, and coordination. Productivity enhancements result from the following advantages:[20]

- **Shared work area for teams to keep track of projects.** Up-to-date information can be accessed quickly and securely by everyone simultaneously. This "knowledge base" enables quick response to new market opportunities.
- **Bulletin boards for discussing ideas, sharing and editing documents, and obtaining team member approval.** Comments and questions are posted, stored, routed, and organized by topic so they can be accessed and reviewed quickly when a decision must be made. Rather than call a hurried meeting to ask a question or make an important announcement, teams can access and respond to a posted message and spend the saved time completing critical tasks.
- **Advanced real-time communication.** Participants are linked together to read and respond to posted information, participate in brainstorming sessions, and vote on issues anonymously. Users in different locations can work simultaneously on the same documents and hold face-to-face meetings. if videoconferencing technology is available.
- **Group calendar and scheduling.** The software identifies a convenient time for a team meeting and detects scheduling conflicts. Success is dependent on the team's commitment to maintaining a complete and accurate calendar and concern for privacy.
- **Workflow monitoring.** Groupware helps track the status of documents—who has them, who is behind schedule, and who gets the document next.

© JOSE LUIS PELAEZ INC./BLEND IMAGES/JUPITERIMAGES

To achieve optimal results from collaborative software, employees need training in the technology and how to work collaboratively. They need a clear understanding of their roles and responsibilities so members can reach agreement and support others. Employees must also be committed to sharing information, files, and resources freely, with respect for confidentiality when appropriate—a concept in direct opposition to the traditional view that "knowledge is power." Visit your companion website at www.cengage.com/bcomm/lehman to learn more about ways for developing people to work with collaborative technologies.

Application

Complete the following activities as directed by your instructor:

- Identify an organization that uses workgroup software for authoring and editing documents.
- Interview a collaborative team member within the organization for the following information: (1) software used for collaborative writing, (2) number and expertise of colleagues who typically collaborate on a single document, and (3) advantages and disadvantages of collaborative software.
- Present the results of your interview in written or spoken form, as directed by your instructor.

SHOWCASE PART 3

Plain English Requirements for Patient Privacy Disclosures

Health care providers are required by law to provide privacy notices that inform patients about how their personal information is used and how they can control their medical records. The problem, however, has been how to convey this information without using confusing legal and medical jargon.

Providers are required to provide the privacy notice in plain English to patients on their first doctor visit or when signing up for health insurance. Many health care professionals worked cooperatively to develop a simplified, yet informative document. Following the lead of food labels, the idea was to design the document so patients can easily spot the topics of interest to them.[21]

www.sec.gov

Activities

- Visit the HIPA Advisory website at www.hipaadvisory.com/action/privacy/Plain.htm to read about how to effectively use plain language in the privacy notice.
- Compare the plain language issues faced by health care providers in writing privacy disclosures with those faced by the SEC in promoting clear financial disclosures. Prepare a short report about the challenges involved in developing clear disclosures, whether a health care professional or a company.

© ALEX WONG/GETTY IMAGES

Summary

1. Apply techniques for developing effective sentences and unified and coherent paragraphs.

Well-written sentences and unified and coherent paragraphs will help the receiver understand the message clearly and respond favorably. To craft powerful sentences, rely on active voice and emphasize important points. To write effective paragraphs, develop deductive or inductive paragraphs consistently, link ideas to achieve coherence, keep paragraphs unified, and vary sentence and paragraph length.

2. Identify factors affecting readability and revise sentences to improve readability.

The readability of a message is affected by the length of the sentences and the difficulty of the words. For quick, easy reading, use simple words and short sentences. A readability index (grade level necessary for reader to understand the material) in the eighth-to-eleventh grade range is appropriate for most business writing. Writing a message with a readability index appropriate for an audience does not guarantee understanding but does provide feedback on the average length of the sentences and the difficulty of the words.

3. Prepare visually appealing documents that grab the receiver's attention and increase comprehension.

Visually appealing documents entice the reader to read the document, focus attention on important ideas, and move the reader smoothly through the organization of the document without adding clutter. Techniques for preparing appealing, easy-to-read documents include enumerations, enumerated or bulleted lists, headings, tables and graphs, lines and borders, and drawing tools and clip art.

4. **Revise and proofread a message for content, organization, and style; mechanics, format, and layout.**

Be willing to revise a document as many times as necessary to be certain that it conveys the message effectively and is error free. Use the spell-check to locate keying errors; then follow systematic procedures for proofreading an onscreen and/or printed copy of the document. Proofread systematically for content, organization, and style; and then for mechanics, format, and layout.

Chapter Review

1. Is writing rapidly with intent to revise or writing slowly and deliberately more effective? Explain. (Obj. 1)
2. How has automated speech recognition software affected the preparation of business messages? What changes are predicted in the near future? (Obj. 1)
3. When is active voice preferred? When is passive voice preferred? (Obj. 1)
4. Discuss several strategies that will enhance the quality and efficiency of writing with a computer. (Obj. 1)
5. Explain the benefits collaborative technology provides to work teams. Include several examples of the capability this technology provides. (Obj. 1)
6. What value does knowing the readability level of a document serve? What two factors should be evaluated for possible revision in an effort to reduce the readability index of a report? (Obj. 2)
7. What are the benefits and limitations of electronic spell-check and writing-analysis software? (Objs. 3, 4)
8. Explain the importance of creating a visually appealing document, and provide four guidelines for accomplishing this objective. (Obj. 3)
9. How has instantaneous communication made possible by technology affected the proofreading stage of the writing process? (Obj. 4)
10. What are the seven steps for proofreading a document systematically to locate all errors? (Obj. 4)

Digging Deeper

1. What habits hinder your success or enjoyment of writing? Identify ways to overcome them.
2. How does online writing challenge a writer's effort to develop a seamless, coherent document?
3. Why do some writers rush through the proofreading phase of message development?

Assessment

To check your understanding of the chapter, take the available online quizzes as directed by your instructor.

Activities

1. Active and Passive Voice (Obj. 1)

Revise the following sentences using active and passive voice appropriately. Justify your decisions. Access a downloadable version of this activity from your companion website at www.cengage.com/bcomm/lehman.

a. The funding for the European expansion was generated from the IPO.
b. The recommendation to implement a fraud management program came from J. D. Reese.
c. Elizabeth polled only the clients in the Southeast, thereby producing an inaccurate marketing report.
d. Adoption of a few financial strategies will increase the likelihood that financial goals will be achieved.

2. Emphasis Techniques (Obj. 1)

Choose the preferred sentence from each pair and justify your choice.

a. (1) Lindsay's request to telecommute was denied, but she will begin a flextime schedule.
   (2) Although her request to telecommute was denied, Lindsay will begin a flextime schedule.
b. (1) A microblogging site on Twitter will go online next week, thanks to Genni's efforts.
   (2) Genni deserves the credit for designing the microblogging site on Twitter that will go online next week.
c. (1) Thank you for donating time to work with the United Way campaign this year.
   (2) Congratulations on your outstanding work as the coordinator for the Making a Difference campaign. Our company goal was easily exceeded thanks to your exceptional leadership abilities.
d. (1) We appreciate your sharing your concerns.
   (2) We appreciate your letting us know about the long wait time, irritating music, and language differences that prevented you from understanding the instructions provided by our call center representatives.
e. (1) Your warranty does not cover these auto repair charges.
   (2) Had you completed all scheduled maintenance, your warranty would have covered these auto repair charges.

Check Your Communication
Preparing and Proofreading a Rough Draft

POWERFUL SENTENCES

- ☐ Use correct structure when writing simple, compound, complex, and compound-complex sentences. Avoid run-on sentences and comma splices.
- ☐ Use active voice to present important points or pleasant ideas. Use passive verbs to present less significant points or unpleasant ideas.
- ☐ Emphasize important ideas:
  - Place an idea in a simple sentence.
  - Place an idea in an independent clause; for de-emphasis, place an idea in a dependent clause.
  - Use an important word more than once in a sentence.
  - Place an important idea first or last in a sentence, paragraph, or document.
  - Use words that label ideas as significant or insignificant.
  - Use headings, graphics, and additional space to emphasize important ideas.

COHERENT PARAGRAPHS

- ☐ Write deductively if a message will likely please or at least not displease. Write inductively if a message will likely displease or if understanding of major idea is dependent on prior explanations.
- ☐ Make sure the message forms a unit with an obvious beginning, middle, and ending and that in-between paragraphs are arranged in a systematic sequence, either deductively or inductively, as needed.
- ☐ Avoid abrupt changes in thought, and link each sentence to a preceding sentence. Place transition sentences before major headings.
- ☐ Vary sentence and paragraph length to emphasize important ideas.
- ☐ Limit paragraphs in letters, memos, email messages, and web pages to six lines and paragraphs in reports to eight to ten lines to maximize comprehension.

READABILITY

- ☐ Use simple words and short sentences for quick, easy reading (and listening).
- ☐ Strive for short paragraphs but vary their lengths.
- ☐ Create appealing, easy-to-read documents by
  - Preceding each unit in a series by a number, a letter, or a bullet. For stronger emphasis, use an enumerated or bulleted list.
  - Using headings, tables and graphs, lines and borders, and images to focus attention on important information.

SYSTEMATIC PROOFREADING

- ☐ Use spell-check to locate simple keying errors.
- ☐ Proofread once concentrating on content, organization, and style and a second time on mechanics, format, and layout.

3. Emphasis and Ordering Techniques (Objs. 1–3)

Revise the following sentences, adding emphasis to the lists.

a. Access a downloadable version of this activity from your companion website at www.cengage.com/bcomm/lehman. Employees should follow these basic tips for a more healthful lifestyle. Adding physical activity to your day will help you manage your weight and make you feel like you have more energy. Try 5-10 minutes a day spread throughout the day. Adequate water is needed to quench your thirst and hydrate your body. Your diet should include less fat and more nutritious fruits and vegetables. Having healthy choices cut up and ready to eat will entice you to choose them rather than something else. Also, it's important that you start your day with breakfast as eating breakfast fuels your body to start the day and makes you less likely to overeat later. Reducing stress is easier said than done, but is important to a healthy lifestyle. Recommended techniques are keeping a positive outlook on life, spending 30 minutes a day doing something you enjoy, and counting to ten to avoid losing your temper, etc. Making sure you get enough sleep each night will recharge and refresh your body.

b. Employees should be allowed a choice between overtime pay or compensatory time off. Many of our employees are parents and would appreciate having more time to spend with their children. Others are more interested in earning extra money. Therefore, offering a choice would improve morale and reduce employee absenteeism, leading to a more efficient, committed workforce.

c. The company should modify its management incentive plan. Congress is expected to pass legislation that will increase the tax rate on year-end bonuses. As a result of the current economic environment, the investing public perceives incentive bonuses to be exorbitant and unjustified. The company risks having significant institutional investors exert influence by placing a representative on the board of directors. In short, the company's ability to continue providing incentive-based compensation to managers will be in danger if changes are not made.

4. Coherence Techniques (Obj. 1)

Link each sentence to the preceding sentence to improve coherence (avoid abrupt changes in thought). Access a downloadable version of this activity from your companion website at www.cengage.com/bcomm/lehman.

a. The marketing department reviews television ratings every month. They use these ratings to adjust the advertising spent with the various networks. These changes ensure that our advertising reaches our target demographics. It also allows us to maximize the return on our advertising expenditures.

b. Customers have not been swayed by the new buyer incentives. They don't trust that the company will be able to meet the expanded warranty. Traditional incentive plans, such as zero percent financing, continue to be more effective.

c. Diversity awareness training seems important to some employees. It is very effective in improving communication and understanding. Employees should participate in this training.

d. Our company has initiated a new work scheduling plan. Employees can choose between flexible scheduling or four 10-hour days. This could improve morale and productivity.

e. New computer software is being loaded onto our local area network (LAN). Personnel will be able to generate expense statements from their workstations. This will make the old paper forms obsolete.

5. Improving Readability (Obj. 2)

Improve readability by dividing each of the following sentences into shorter sentences. Access a downloadable version of this activity from your companion website at www.cengage.com/bcomm/lehman.

a. Top management received approval for sending employees weekly emails during this time of financial instability in order to keep them up-to-date and to reassure them the company is healthy.

b. Several members of our firm will be touring the manufacturing plant in Tokyo during the week of May 16, 2011, and upon return to the United States will present a slide show documenting the trip, followed by a question-and-answer session, both to be held in the banquet hall of the Ashton Hotel in Denver on Friday, May 27.

c. The accountant will be arriving on Thursday to perform the audit, and will be using the 2nd floor break room as a work area, meaning that employees should take morning and afternoon breaks in either the courtyard or the 3rd floor lounge, and employees who use the 2nd floor break room for lunch should report to the cafeteria at that time.

d. People from such different backgrounds as today's workers invariably bring different values, attitudes, and perceptions to the workplace, which can lead to misunderstandings, miscommunications, and missed opportunities to improve both the workers and the organizations.

Now suggest short, simple words in the following sentences to replace difficult words that raise the readability index.

e. The derisive tone of his email can only be perceived as an insidious act designed to undermine employee confidence in current management.

f. The new concentration of the agency reflects a ubiquitous necessity for clean energy.

g. The supervisor's deprecatory remarks demoralized the employees.

h. After a meticulous search, the committee has concurred on an epitome location for the convention.

6. Proofreading Application (Obj. 4)

Use proofreaders' marks to correct errors in spelling, grammar, punctuation, numbers, and abbreviations in the following message sent to Berch Enterprises. Do not revise a sentence and state its idea in an entirely different way. Access a downloadable version of this activity from your companion website at www.cengage.com/bcomm/lehman.

Congratulations! Your application too participate in our international management exchange program has been approved. Your 9-month assignment in our London office will provide you with a greater appreciation for the needs and concerns of our international partners, making you a better manager upon your return. The following five traveling tips compiled by previous London participants will assist you in preparing for you two week orientation trip scheduled for Febuary 3-12:

1. Begin the process of obtaining or updating your passport immediately.
2. Register your trip with the U.S. Department of State at http://travel.state.gov and review the State Departments website carefully for travel advisories and other conditions that may effect your safety and security while abroad.
3. Link to the "International Management Exchange Program on the company intranet to access extensive information about the program and your assignment. You'll learn about the country's geography, climate, and customs, the most convenient way to get around in the city, top tourist attractions, important security travel tips, and much more.
4. Check current exchange rates and obtain an appropriate level of local currency for you stay.
4. Purchase a London Travelcard to be delivered to you prior to your arrival in Paris. The card will allow you to begin using the public transport system (the London Tube and buses) as soon as you arrive.
5. Notify the fraud divisions of your credit card companies to ensure that charges in the U.K. will not be rejected as suspicious transactions.

Joshua, you have an enriching experience ahead of you with much to learn and to share with others at Birch Enterprises. While your on assignment, you can conveniently share your valuable experiences and photographs by posting to your international travel blog already set up for you on the intranet. Bon Vogue!

Applications

READ | THINK | WRITE | SPEAK | COLLABORATE

1. Effective Professionals Must Communicate Technical Information Clearly (Objs. 1–4)

Locate the following article that offers tips on writing powerful business messages:

Jolley, D. A. (2009). Clear and compelling messages–The foundation for effective communication. *Public Relations Tactics*. Available from Business Source Complete database.

After reading the article, respond to the following questions:

a. What are the "Master P's"?
b. Explain what the writer means by a "memorable quote." Could you foresee exceptions to the use of this approach for all business messages? Provide examples.
c. What is the role of rehearsing in assuring clear and compelling messages?

2. Crafting Powerful Communication (Obj. 1)

Go to your companion website at www.cengage.com/bcomm/lehman to explore other strategies for crafting powerful messages. Complete the activities that appear at the end of the document and email to your instructor.

READ | THINK | WRITE | SPEAK | COLLABORATE

3. Identifying Common Business Usage Errors (Objs. 1-4)

Complete the business usage quiz at http://businesswriting.com/tests/commonusage.html

Assess your understanding of 26 common business writing problems. Review the feedback provided for each question and compile a list of areas in which improvement is needed. Email your score to your instructor, along with your plan for improvement.

4. Visual Enhancements (Obj. 3)

Access the Plain Language website at www.plainlanguage.gov/examples/index.cfm, a website designed to improve communication from the federal government to the public. View a variety of documents revised for easy reading following Plain English principles. Choose the "Before and After Comparisons" link and review carefully the examples posted under the "Using Visual Explanations to Convey Information More Clearly" section. Complete the following activities as directed by your instructor:

a. Prepare a brief paper explaining how applying plain English principles improved the readability of these documents. Suggest revisions you believe would improve the documents further.
b. Using a document that you have received or one that your instructor provides, develop a new example that could be added to this website as a "before and after comparison." Place your two documents on a slide and be prepared to summarize your changes and explain how they improved the impact of the document.

5. Tackling Typical Professional Writing Problems (Objs. 1-4)

Some companies, facing the reality that poor writing is costly, are initiating training programs for effective writing. You can develop your own self-improvement program by completing these activities:

a. Download the training podcast at http://ewh.ieee.org/soc/pcs/index.php?q=audio that provides tips for avoiding several grammar or usage problems that occur frequently in email and when professionals are communicating in a hurry.
b. Review the content at the following websites and others that you locate. Then, write a brief description of at least five communication topics you will commit to study over the course of the course term. Be prepared to share your "course of study" and progress reports in the format requested by your instructor. As you prepare these assignments, bookmark useful websites for future professional development.
   www.mapnp.org/library/commskls/cmm_writ.htm
   www.the-writestuff.co.uk
   www.plainlanguage.gov/howto/quickreference/index.cfm
   www.quintcareers.com/writing_skills_on_job.html
   owl.english.purdue.edu

READ | THINK | WRITE | SPEAK | COLLABORATE

6. The Emergence of Speech Technology (Obj. 1)

Conduct an online search related to recent developments in speech (voice-recognition) technology. Prepare a brief written report providing information such as (a) current status of speech technology as a viable business application, including challenges that have hampered past developments; (b) examples of leading speech technology applications with related results; and (c) projections for future development of this technology. Be prepared to share your ideas with the class.

7. Improving Readability (Obj. 2)

Create a substitution list of easier words for 10 to 15 difficult words. Be prepared to share your list with the class.

READ THINK WRITE **SPEAK** COLLABORATE

8. Corporate Speak Limits Executives' Effectiveness. (Objs. 1–2, 4)

Jon Warshawsky, coauthor of *Why Business People Speak Like Idiots,* was interviewed by Martha Barnette, who is host of *A Way with Words*, a program that airs on National Public Radio. Listen to the interview at www.fightthebull.com/jwarshawskyinterview1.asp.

In the interview, Jon says that many executives might feel "it's dangerous to have an original thought," which may lead to the use of a series of words they think they have to use to be seen as smart. Martha refers to this tendency as *corporate speak*. Complete the following activities:

a. Conduct an interview in person, by phone, or online, with an executive in your chosen career field. Ask him or her if corporate speak is a noticeable problem in the work environment and, if so, to identify common examples of corporate speak. Ask the executive for advice related to communicating effectively in your career field.

b. Make a short presentation to your class about how to avoid corporate speak and communicate effectively in your career field. Alternately, you may video record your presentation and post it electronically for class access.

9. The Price Companies Pay for Human Errors (Obj. 4)

Using an online database or the Internet, locate an example of an error in a printed document made by an actual company. Errors might be caused by overreliance on spell-check or poor proofreading for mechanical, content, or style errors. Prepare a brief presentation describing the error, specific consequences experienced as a result of the error, and actions taken to overcome negative effects.

READ THINK WRITE SPEAK **COLLABORATE**

10. FAQ: How Can Communication Skills Boost Career Skills? (Objs. 1–4)

You are certain that your ability to write and speak well has been a career boost to you. You've earned favorable ratings on your written and spoken communication component of your performance appraisal and received more than your share of sincere compliments from your supervisor and coworkers for well-written documents and presentations that led to new business for the company. Your supervisor has assigned you to a companywide work team to design an intranet site for business communication training. Complete the following activities as directed by your instructor

a. Before the first meeting, you are assigned to develop a list of suggestions that you believe would help an employee prepare a clear, understandable business message. Use the websites in Application 5 to generate ideas.

b. Interview a person you perceive to be an effective communicator and write a 100-word spotlight on this person's success and advice for others wanting to become a better communicator.

c. In small groups, compile your suggestions into a short list of frequently asked questions that will appear in a FAQ section of the website. Phrase your questions so that employees recognize the content as something they need to read. Each member of the team will write a brief answer to assigned questions and provide useful websites for learning more.

d. Using the information you've gained from preparing the FAQs, write a 200- to 300-word article encouraging employees to improve writing skills and showcasing the contents of your website. The article will be featured on the opening page of the intranet site. Have one person design the web page (including the article, FAQs, and graphics), one person write the opening article, and two members write the spotlights on two effective communicators, including photographs.

11. Document for Analysis: Readability Assessment (Objs. 1–4)

In teams, complete the following tasks as assigned by your instructor. Access a downloadable version of this activity from your companion website at www.cengage.com/bcomm/lehman.

a. Key the following document into your word processing program.

SPL Family is preparing to initiate a program whereby employees may participate in a telework program. We anticipate that implementation of the program will begin sometime next quarter. To qualify for this program, an employee must secure the approval of his superior and also meet specific criteria. It has been learned that companies can realize substantial savings through the implementation of telework, such as savings from reduced use of energy and other office resources, reduced need for office space and employees have less absenteeism and higher productivity. In order to qualify for the telework program, employees must meet the following criteria: must own a computer with all company-installed licensed application, communication, and security software and secured wireless Internet connectivity, must agree to work in the office a minimum of one day per week, must submit time and expense reports online daily instead of weekly, and personnel must be within a job classification approved for teleworking. Please see your supervisor if you are interested in this program. He will assist you in assessing whether telecommuting is a good option for you. SPL Family Enterprises is pleased to offer this new program to it's employees who qualify and will continue to be supportive of a flexible innovative work environment.

b. Complete a readability analysis using a grammar and style checker. Download the free download of *Bullfighter* at http://fightthebull.com for additional advice.

c. Revise the document using the track changes feature to mark revisions. Incorporate relevant suggestions provided by the grammar checker for accuracy and improved readability.
d. Complete a readability analysis for your revision and compare with the original readability analysis.

Send your instructor an email message with the revised document attached and a brief summary that notes the areas where improvements were made.

CASES

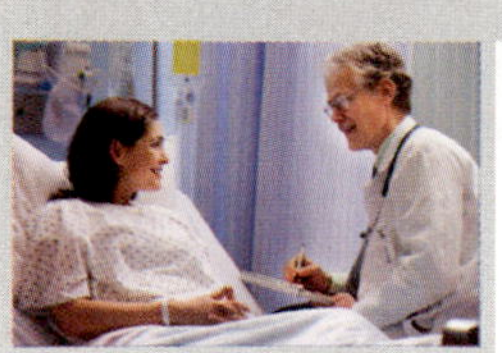

© BLEND IMAGES/JUPITERIMAGES

1. Misunderstandings Can Be Costly

Nearly half of the U.S. adult population lacks the reading and numeracy skills required to process, understand, and act appropriately on health information. Individuals with low literacy skills may be at a particular risk for misunderstanding information on drug labels and thus incorrectly dosing themselves or their loved one. A recent study indicated that more than a quarter of emergency room visits are drug related, with another two thirds of those preventable with better understanding.[22]

Various factors can complicate understanding of dosing instructions, including multiple step instructions, reading level of material, choice of icons, use of color, and message clarity. Confused patients might miss medication doses, take doses that are too large, or improperly ingest the medication—such as chewing rather than swallowing whole. As health care delivery continues to shift from in-hospital to out-patient services, the burden of medication dosing falls more and more on the patient rather than on the health care provider. The U.S. Food and Drug Administration and health care providers continue to seek effective ways to communicate effectively with patients concerning their medication dosing.

Read the following article that provides more information about the cost of medication errors:

Medication errors injure 1.5 million people and cost billions of dollars annually. (2006, September 25). NaturalNews.com. Available at www.naturalnews.com/z020515.html

Following directions provided by your instructor, complete one or more of the following activities.

1. Visit the following website with information about a commonly prescribed prescription drug called Zithromax Z-pack: http://www.drugs.com/mtm/zithromax-z-pak.html. Develop the wording for a dosage label with clear instructions for using the oral suspension.
2. Using the information on the website, develop a one-page information sheet explaining the correct use of the Z-pack and possible side effects. Your intended audience is the U.S. adult population. You may use a combination of words and images to convey your message.
3. Develop an electronic slide show designed to educate physicians and physicians' assistants about how to convey dosing information to patients who may lack literacy skills to be able to read written instructions about their medication.

© BBC LTD./COURTESY: EVERETT COLLECTION

2. Video Case: The Office: Professionalism: Not Just for the Boardroom

In this clip, manager Tim is discussing his night out with Dawn, his employee. After telling her how much he drank the night before, he confronts HER about her lack of professionalism.

Complete the following activities as directed by your instructor after viewing the video:

1. In a small group, discuss David's idea of professionalism. Is his behavior appropriate for a supervisor-employee interaction? Should information about social activities be discussed in the workplace? Explain.
2. Does Dawn behave appropriately in this interaction? Explain.
3. As Dawn's colleague, assume she has come to you for advice about this interaction that she perceives to be inappropriate. Compose an email to Dawn offering empathy and suggestions for dealing with future uncomfortable situations with David.

3. Understanding the Plain English Campaign

Effective communication is a major part of a manager's job. Yet many managers continue to bury what they want to say in pompous jargon or polysyllabic babble. Such communication fails miserably because the people to whom it is aimed either do not understand it or regard it as garbage and ignore it. A Plain English movement is gaining momentum in Great Britain and the United States. The Plain English Campaign, founded in 1979, is an independent U.K.-based organization that fights to stamp out all forms of gobbledygook, a term that includes legalese, small print, and bureaucratic language. The organization is funded by its professional services, which include editing, writing, design, and training in Plain English for a variety of companies as well as government and local authorities. The Plain English Campaign-USA, a subsidiary of the England-based campaign, is based in Miami, Florida.

Documents that achieve a good standard of clarity may qualify for endorsement with the Campaign's Crystal Mark, a widely recognized and respected symbol of clarity. The Crystal Mark can be found on over 7,000 documents around the world, and more than 1,000 organizations worldwide have received the Crystal Mark for at least one document. It is a powerful marketing tool because customers can see the Crystal Mark on documents and know they can be confident that the information is clear. The Plain English Campaign also recognizes outstanding offenders of Plain English with its Golden Bull awards; criteria for selection include worst examples of gobbledygook and the negative impact of the documents on the lives of ordinary people.

Misconceptions exist concerning Plain English writing. Writing in Plain English does not mean deleting complex information to make the document easier to understand. Using Plain English assures the orderly and clear presentation of complex information so that the audience has the best possible chance of understanding; it presents information to meet its audience's needs. A Plain English document uses words economically and at a level the audience can understand. Its sentence structure is tight. Its tone is approachable and direct, and its design is visually appealing. A Plain English document is easy to read and looks as if it is meant to be read.[23]

Visit your companion website at www.cengage.com/bcomm/lehman to link to web resources related to this topic. As directed by your instructor, respond to one or more of the following:

1. Compile a chart that lists companies, agencies, and other organizations that have benefited from Plain English assistance and the stated results that have been realized. Arrange a telephone interview with a person representing one of the organizations to obtain firsthand information about the impact of Plain English in that organization.
2. Using links provided in the web resources for this case, familiarize yourself with a recent news story that points out the need for Plain English. Summarize the reported incident in a one-page abstract that includes the following parts: (1) bibliographic citation, (2) brief overview of the article, (3) discussion of the major points covered in the article, and (4) application section that tells who might benefit from reading the article and why.
3. Select an organization of your choice that could benefit from Plain English assistance; you may consult the "List of Shame" organizations or identify one on your own. Recommend a plan for implementing Plain English that includes the following: (1) reasons for implementing Plain English, (2) training courses that are available, (3) other services that can be accessed through the Plain English Campaign, and (4) the advantages of corporate membership in the Plain English Campaign.

© DAWN HUDSON/ SHUTTERSTOCK.COM

4. Inside View: *Seinfeld:* Language and Meaning

As sitcoms go, *Seinfeld*, which began airing on NBC in 1989, was one of the longest running and best received shows in television history. This "show about nothing" brought new words and phrases into the daily lives of millions of Americans. And from "double dipping" to the famous "yada, yada, yada," Seinfeldisms still live on in popular culture. *Seinfeld* characters' use of language filtered into both mainstream English and slang. How has this language affected societal uses today?

View the "Seinfeld: Language and Meaning" video segment at the companion website at www.cengage.com/bcomm/lehman to learn more about how the language used in this sitcom influenced American conversation and vocabulary and the power of language in a global workplace.

Reflect:

1. Analyze an episode of your favorite television sitcom and generate a list of catch phrases that you or others have incorporated into your own speech.
2. The Kramer character from the show is known for reinforcing his language with distinctive gestures and mannerisms. Discuss another movie or TV character that is known for his or her body language and be prepared to share with the class how those mannerisms set the character apart.
3. Select a commonly used word or phrase with multiple meanings. Discuss the possibility of misunderstanding, inappropriate uses, etc.

React:

Visit http://wikipedia.org, the online encyclopedia anyone can edit, and locate the entry on *Seinfeld*. Based on the wide variety of information in the article, write a short summary of the show's impact on American communication.

Part 3

Communication Through Voice, Electronic, and Written Messages

Chapter 5
Communicating Electronically

"A big key to our growth and success over the years is that we've always treated our owners like family."

President and CEO Franz Hanning

© NEWSCOM

Objectives When you have completed Chapter 5, you will be able to:

1. Discuss the effective use of email, instant messaging, and text messaging in business communication.
2. Explain principles for writing effectively for the Web.
3. Discuss the effective use of voice and wireless technologies in business communication.
4. Identify legal and ethical implications associated with the use of communication technology.

SHOWCASE PART 1  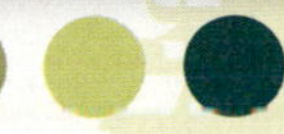

Wyndham Vacation Ownership Utilizes Web to Provide Owner Satisfaction

From its beginnings in the late 1960s, vacation ownership has become the fastest growing segment of the U.S. travel and tourism industry. Today more than three million households have bought into vacation ownership, an industry that produces more than $7 billion a year in sales.

Timeshare resorts are found across the globe in popular vacation areas near beaches, rivers and lakes, mountains, and even major cities. Resort development is strong with significant growth in mixed-use properties that include timeshare and luxury hotel units often integrated with retail and entertainment space. By locking in the purchase price of accommodations, vacation ownership helps assure consistent pricing for future vacations. And through vacation exchange programs, timeshare owners have the flexibility to travel to popular destinations around the world.[1]

Wyndham Vacation Ownership, Inc., (WVO) the world's largest timeshare company and the first to use a flexible point system successfully, owns more than 145 resorts with more under development under two primary brands: Fairfield Resorts and Trendwest Resorts. The company's point system enables more than 800,000 owners to purchase an allotment of points rather than a specific timeframe at a particular location.[2] The points can then be used as an exchange value like currency. Members have the freedom to choose the resort locations, dates, unit sizes, and lengths of stay of their annual vacations. "According to Franz Hanning, WVO president and CEO, "a big key to our growth and success over the years is that we've always treated our owners like family."[3]

Wyndham's flexible points-based system allows owners to spend their points on vacation expenses such as air fare and rental cars. Owners can even use their points to stay in an increasing number of Wyndham luxury hotels. When they cannot get away for a vacation, owners are allowed to bank their points for future use or to send family or friends on a dream vacation.

Prior to the introduction of web-based vacation planning sites, vacation arrangements were typically made by telephone, necessitating several lengthy calls to obtain information and confirm options. WVO members have enjoyed greater communication power since the advent of the company's comprehensive web-based vacation planning site. Full-service travel planning capabilities allow site visitors to

- use the site's search function to select resorts by destination, features, and amenities.
- access photos, maps, directions, resort activity calendars, local attractions, and even virtual tours of affiliated resorts.
- look up point requirements to stay at any of the WVO resorts and affiliates.
- reserve units by location, date, length of stay, and unit size and view online confirmations.
- make airline, hotel, and car rental reservations.
- take advantage of special cruise and package deals.
- obtain door-to-door directions and current weather reports for all WVO resorts.

The ability to share information effectively is a primary advantage of electronic communications. As you will see in the chapter, the primary communication challenge of technology is mastery of online dynamics.

www.wyndhamworldwide.com

SEE SHOWCASE PART 2, ON PAGE 168
FOR SPOTLIGHT COMMUNICATOR FRANZ HANNING, PRESIDENT AND CEO, WYNDHAM VACATION OWNERSHIP, INC.

1 OBJECTIVE

Electronic Mail Communication

As you read in Chapter 1, the continuous evolution of technology has expanded communication options. Email, instant messaging, web communications, and voice and wireless technologies are important tools for accomplishing company goals. A 2007 study indicated that email has overtaken the telephone in terms of the most common workplace communication tool.[4] The ability to use email communications effectively is essential to success in virtually every career.

Advantages of Email

Electronic mail, or email, offers numerous advantages. Its ready availability, convenience, and ease of use have resulted in its skyrocketing popularity. The advantages of email are numerous:

- **It facilitates the fast, convenient flow of information among users at various locations and time zones.** Mail service is often too slow for communicating timely information, and the telephone system is inconvenient and costly when communicating with people located in several locations and time zones. For these reasons, email is especially effective when sending a single message to several recipients and when needing to communicate 24 hours a day, 365 days a year.

What are some negative aspects of using email?

- **It increases efficiency.** Email reduces "telephone tag" and unnecessary telephone interruptions caused when delivering messages that are unlikely to require a verbal response.
- **It reduces costs.** Sending email messages represents a substantial savings to companies in long-distance telephone costs and postal mail-outs.
- **It reduces paper waste.** Often an electronic message can be read and immediately discarded without the need for a printed copy.

Hello; I'm sflander@acme.com. Your career success will depend largely on your ability to exchange ideas effectively with others via email. Nearly 90 percent of U.S. workers who use the Internet at work access business email.[6] You'll likely email your boss, colleagues, clients, and prospective employers. Since some business contacts will know you only through your email communication, the tone you convey in your online messages should be respectful, friendly, and approachable. Make sure every message reflects positively on you. Because email is often saved and forwarded numerous times, the messages you convey can survive for years and be resurrected at the most unlikely occasion.

© RUBBERBALL/JUPITERIMAGES

Your Turn 5-1
Electronic Café

PAPERLESS INFORMATION EXCHANGE

In 1970, the futurist Alvin Toffler proclaimed the paperless society to be just around the corner. If he's like the rest of us, he's probably surrounded by more paper than ever before. While numerous technologies have emerged to help eliminate the need for paper, they tend to shift the role of paper to drafts and back up copies rather than replacing it. The following activities will allow you to explore the advantages and limitations of paperless information exchange.

TAKE ACTION:

- Read two articles on paperless exchange, one that defends the use of paper and one that supports the move to paperless. Both articles can be found at your companion site, www.cengage.com/bcomm/lehman.
- Deliver a paperless assignment to your online course on the following topic or one that your instructor assigns. Write a one-page summary of how technological developments of the last 20 years have revolutionized business communication.

Guidelines for Preparing Email Messages

The principles of style and organization that you learned about in Chapters 3 and 4 are applicable to email messages, while other techniques are specific to email. Following these guidelines will enable you to use email efficiently and effectively when communicating with both valued coworkers and outside parties:

- **Send to single or multiple addressees.** The same message can be sent to one or many recipients simultaneously. Sending an email message to multiple recipients simply involves keying the email address of each recipient into a distribution list and selecting the distribution list as the recipient.

Write an effective subject line for a memo announcing software training classes for the upcoming month.

- **Provide a useful subject line.** A descriptive subject line assists the receiver's current understanding of the message and serves as a reference point for future reference to it. Additionally, a well-written subject line in an email message will help the receiver sort through an overloaded mailbox and read messages in priority order. When writing a subject line, think of the five W's—Who, What, When, Where, and Why—to give you some clues for wording. For instance, "Budget Committee Meeting on Thursday" is a more meaningful subject line than "Meeting."
- **Restate the subject in the body of the message.** The body of the message should be a complete thought and should not rely on the subject line for elaboration. A good opening sentence might be a repetition of most of the subject line. Even if the reader skipped the subject line, the message would still be clear, logical, and complete.
- **Focus on a single topic directed toward the receiver's needs.** An email message is generally limited to one idea rather than addressing several issues. If you address more than one topic in a single email message, chances are the recipient will forget to respond to all points discussed. Discussing one topic allows you to write a descriptive subject line, and the receiver can file the single subject message in a separate mailbox if desired. If you must send a lengthy message, divide it into logical sections for easy comprehension.

What place does inductive and deductive ordering have in the composition of email?

- **Sequence your ideas based on anticipated reader reaction.** As you learned previously, ideas should be organized deductively when a message contains good news or neutral information; inductive organization is recommended when the message contains bad news or is intended to persuade. Email messages may be organized according to the sequence of ideas, for example, time order, order of importance, or geography. As a general rule, present the information in the order it is likely to be needed. For example, describe the nature and purpose of an upcoming meeting before giving the specifics (date, place, time). You will learn more about message strategies in Chapters 6, 7, and 8.

- **Make careful use of jargon, technical words, and shortened terms.** The use of jargon and technical terms is more common in email messages than in business letters. Such shortcuts save time with audiences who will understand the intent. In practicing empathy, however, consider whether the receiver will likely understand the terms used.
- **Use graphic highlighting to add emphasis.** Enumerated or bulleted lists, tables, graphs, pictures, or other images may be either integrated into the content of the email or attached as supporting material.
- **Revise your email before clicking to send.** Even the average email requires at least one pass to ensure that the intended message is clear, concise, and error-free. The number of passes increases depending on the number of people receiving the email and the complexity of the issue. Revising for brevity and conciseness is a primary goal for messages read often on the run and on mobile devices. Keep to one screen, eliminate redundancies, and tighten wording as you've already learned, but also avoid off-topic material that detracts from the email's single subject as well as clever or amusing statements that are funny only to the writer.[6] Direct, concise messages may at times sound impersonal and curt if not revised for goodwill. Question whether a phone call would be more appropriate for the message being sent as a businesslike, yet conversational tone may sound less aggressive or demanding. Revise emails to achieve a similar tone.[7] Use the email spell check and then proofread onscreen for content and grammatical errors.

Effective Use of Email

The email message in Figure 5-1 illustrates guidelines for using professional email. The recipient's financial advisor begins his email message to his client by suggesting the need for a change in her investment strategy. The paragraphs that follow include timely information and a specific request for action to be taken. Details for formatting an email message in accordance with acceptable protocol are included in Appendix A.

While email offers various advantages in speed and convenience, problems arise when it is managed inappropriately. Learning fundamental ***netiquette***, the buzzword for proper behavior on the Internet, will assure your online success. The following guidelines will assist you in using email effectively:

- **Check mail promptly.** Generally, a response to email is expected within 24 hours. Ignoring messages from coworkers can erode efforts to create an open, honest, and cooperative work environment. On the other hand, responding every second may indicate that you are paying more attention to your email than your job.

FIGURE 5-1

Good Example of an Email Message

To:	Mary Blette
From:	J. Lawrence Tillman
Subject:	Changing Mutual Fund Allocations

Provides subject line that is meaningful to reader and writer.

Includes salutation and closing to personalize message.

Conveys short, concise message limited to one idea and one screen.

Mary,

For the past three years we have heavily weighted your 401(k) contribution toward international mutual funds to take advantage of the declining dollar. Because the current economic crisis has spread around the globe, it is time for us to reconsider that strategy.

Our firm believes that the dollar has stabilized and will rise as signs of a recovery appear. Switching your investment strategy to mutual funds focused on domestic large-cap stocks should enable you to take advantage of the expected rise in the dollar. Although you may feel reluctant to make a change, our firm believes that the "buy and hold" strategy that has worked so well for decades may no longer optimize your investment income in today's dynamic global economy.

Let's schedule a conference within the next two weeks to discuss transferring some of your international funds to domestic mutual funds.

Regards,

Larry

Which of these tips will be most helpful in managing your email use?

- **Do not contribute to email overload.** To avoid clogging the system with unnecessary messages, follow these simple guidelines:
  - Be certain individuals need a copy of the email, and forward an email from another person only with the original writer's permission.
  - Never address an email requesting general action to more than one person if you want to receive individual response. Sharing responsibility will lead to no one taking responsibility.
  - Avoid sending formatted documents. Messages with varying fonts, special print features (e.g., bold, italics, etc.), and images take longer to download, require more storage space, and may be unreadable on some computers. In addition, enhancing routine email messages does not support the goals of competitive organizations, and employees and clients/customers may resent such frivolous use of time.
  - Edit the original message when you reply to email if the entire body of the original message is not needed for context. Instead, you can cut and paste pertinent sections within a reply that you believe will help the recipient understand your reply. You can also key brief comments in all caps below the original section.
  - Follow company policy for personal use of email, and obtain a private email account if you are job hunting or sending many private messages to friends and relatives.

What legal responsibilities does an organization have for abusive or harassing messages generated on the company system?

Hostile and insulting online interaction, known as *flaming*, can be an attempt to assert authority or establish a position of superiority over other users.

- **Use email selectively.** Send short, direct messages for routine matters that need not be handled immediately (scheduling meetings, giving your supervisor quick updates, or addressing other uncomplicated issues).
- **Do not send messages when you are angry.** Email containing sensitive, highly emotional messages may be easily misinterpreted because of the absence of nonverbal communication (facial expressions, voice tone, and body language). Sending a ***flame***, the online term used to describe a heated, sarcastic, sometimes abusive message or posting, may prompt a receiver to send a retaliatory response. Email messages written in anger and filled with emotion and sarcasm may result in embarrassment or even end up as evidence in litigation. Because of the potential damage to relationships and legal liability, read email messages carefully before clicking "Send." Unless a response is urgent, store a heated message for an hour until you have cooled off and thought about the issue clearly and rationally. When you *must* respond immediately, you might acknowledge that your response is emotional and has not been thoroughly considered. Give this warning by using words such as "I need to vent my frustration for a few paragraphs" or "flame on—I'm writing in anger."[8]

LEGAL AND ETHICAL CONSTRAINTS

- **Exercise caution against email viruses and hoaxes.** An ounce of prevention can avert the problems caused by deadly **viruses** that destroy data files or annoying messages that simply waste your time while they are executing. Install an **antivirus software program** that will scan your hard drive each time you start the computer or access external devices, and keep backups of important files. Be suspicious of email messages that contain attachments if they are from people you don't know. Email text is usually safe to open, but the attachment may contain an executable file that can affect your computer's operations. **Social networking sites** such as Facebook and MySpace are also common sources of viruses and spyware.

What computer hoaxes have you received through email?

Additionally, be wary of **computer hoaxes**—email messages that incite panic typically related to risks of computer viruses or deadly threats and urge you to forward them to as many people as possible. Forwarding a hoax can be embarrassing and causes inefficiency by overloading email boxes and flooding computer security personnel with inquiries from alarmed recipients of your message. Investigate the possible hoax by visiting websites such as the following that post virus alerts and hoax information and provide tips for identifying a potential hoax:

- **U.S. Department of Energy CIAC Internet hoaxes page:** hoaxbusters.ciac.org/
- **Urban legends:** www.urbanlegends.com

- **Snopes:** www.snopes.com
- **Truth or Fiction:** www.truthorfiction.com

If a bogus message is forwarded to you, reply to the person politely that the message is a hoax. This action allows you to help stop the spread of the malicious message and will educate one more person about the evils of hoaxes.

- **Develop an effective system for handling email.** Some simple organization will allow you to make better use of your email capability:
  - Set up separate accounts for receiving messages that require your direct attention.
  - Keep your email inbox clean by reading an email and taking action immediately. Delete messages you are not using and those not likely to be considered relevant for legal purposes.
  - Move saved messages into a limited number of email folders for quick retrieval. The email search feature is also useful for identifying saved messages quickly. If you receive many messages, consider purchasing an email handler to sort and prioritize messages, send form letters as replies to messages received with a particular subject line, automatically forward specified email, and sound an alarm when you receive a message from a particular person.

Your Turn 5-2
Assessment

New terminology has emerged to describe what we do with technology. Consider the following terms and whether they describe you:

- **Netizen:** A positive term used to describe an Internet user who is aware of the culture and rules governing Internet usage.
- **Newbie:** A somewhat derogatory term used to describe an inexperienced, obnoxious Internet user. The terms refers to those who are ignorant of the Internet's traditions, takes little time to learn them, and acts rudely.

TAKE ACTION:

- Take the netiquette quiz concerning email use at www.albion.com/netiquette/netiquiz.html. You may also go to your companion website, www.cengage.com/bcomm/lehman, for updated links.
- Send an email message to your instructor in which you explain the area(s) of email netiquette that you find most challenging or difficult. Your message should exhibit proper rules and netiquette for using email.

Source: Test your email etiquette knowledge! (2008). *NetManners.com.* Retrieved from http://www.netmanners.com/email-etiquette-quiz.html

Instant Messaging

Instant messaging (IM), or chat, represents a blending of email with conversation. This real-time email technology allows you to maintain a list of people with whom you want to interact. You can send messages to any or all of the people on your list as long as the people are online. Sending a message opens up a window in which you and your contact can key messages that you both can see immediately. The Electronic Café in Chapter 1 provides opportunities for exploring the features and uses of instant messaging. Figure 5-2 illustrates a sample IM conversation that occurred as a follow-up to a previous email from a legal services director to a software compliance officer.

What are some business uses of instant messaging and texting?

Business use of instant messaging has experienced phenomenal growth. Analysts estimate that in 90 percent of companies, some employees use IM, whether to close a sale, collaborate with a colleague, or just trade pleasantries with a colleague.[9] The best known IM programs are free and require no special hardware and little training. With some programs, users can exchange graphics and audio and video clips. Many of the guidelines that apply to the use of email for business purposes apply also to instant messaging. With IM, however, spelling and grammar matter less when trading messages at high speed. IM users often use shorthand for common words and phrases. IM and telephone communication also share common challenges: being sure that the sender is who he or she claims to be and that the conversation is free from eavesdropping.

Some managers worry that employees will spend too much work time using IM to chat with buddies inside and outside the company. They also emphasize that IM is not the right tool for every business purpose; employees should still rely on email when they need a record and use the telephone for the personal touch.

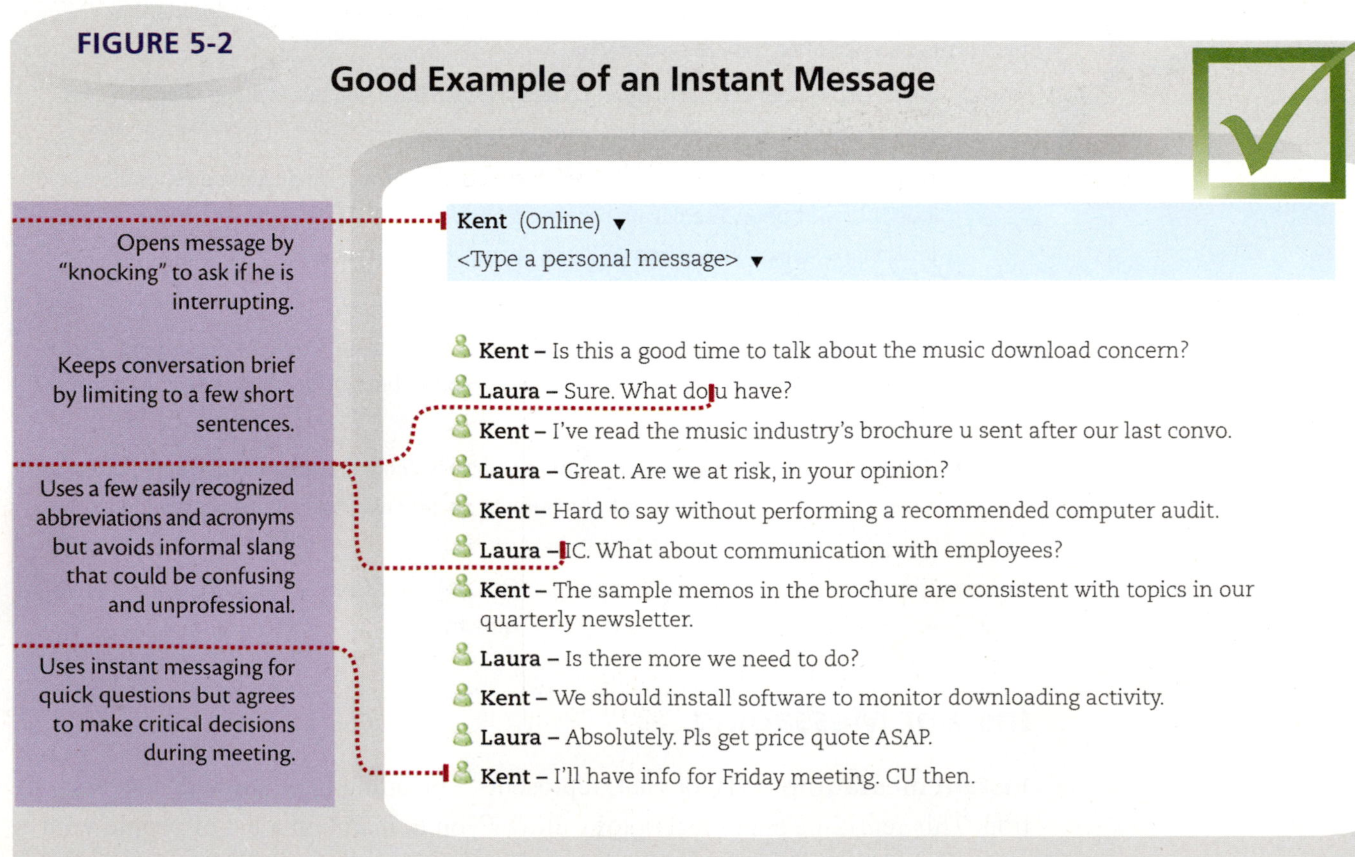

FIGURE 5-2
Good Example of an Instant Message
Opens message by "knocking" to ask if he is interrupting.
Keeps conversation brief by limiting to a few short sentences.
Uses a few easily recognized abbreviations and acronyms but avoids informal slang that could be confusing and unprofessional.
Uses instant messaging for quick questions but agrees to make critical decisions during meeting.
Kent (Online)
<Type a personal message>
Kent – Is this a good time to talk about the music download concern?
Laura – Sure. What do u have?
Kent – I've read the music industry's brochure u sent after our last convo.
Laura – Great. Are we at risk, in your opinion?
Kent – Hard to say without performing a recommended computer audit.
Laura – IC. What about communication with employees?
Kent – The sample memos in the brochure are consistent with topics in our quarterly newsletter.
Laura – Is there more we need to do?
Kent – We should install software to monitor downloading activity.
Laura – Absolutely. Pls get price quote ASAP.
Kent – I'll have info for Friday meeting. CU then.

Text Messaging

Text messaging has grown in popularity as cell phones and other handheld devices with text capability have proliferated. Messages can be sent from one cell phone to another, a cell phone to a computer, or computer to computer. **Text messaging** on a cell phone or personal digital assistant is a refinement of computer instant messaging. But because the typical cell phone screen can accommodate no more than 160 characters, and because the keypad is far less versatile, text messaging puts an even greater premium on conciseness. An entire code book of acronyms and abbreviations has emerged, ranging from CWOT (complete waste of time) to DLTBBB (don't let the bed bugs bite). The use of emoticons has also advanced far beyond the traditional smiley face and includes drooling (:-) . . .) and secrecy (:X). Inventive and young users frequently insert their own style, substituting "z" for "s," or "d" for "th." Shortened lingo or "txt" has emerged that gets right to the point. For instance, a sender might send the following message that can be easily deciphered by most: Pk u up @730. Cell phone programs are also available to assist in efficiency when texting. T9 (text on nine keys) and similar programs uses predictive text to finish words after the first few characters are keyed. T9 can be "trained" to recognize new vocabulary.[10]

Texting is a viable alternative to phone calls for those with hearing impairments. Economic and cultural factors have also driven the advancement of text messaging in some parts of the world where voice conversations are more expensive than texting and short conversations are considered impolite. Some of the most avid text messagers are clustered in Southeast Asia. The Chinese language is particularly well-suited to text messaging, because in Mandarin the names of the numbers are also close to the sounds of certain words.[11] Japanese commuters use their cell phones to text silently, as talking on the phones on the train would be impolite. In the United States, teenagers have popularized texting and carry the habit into places of work. Both abroad and at home, text messaging can be used as an avoidance mechanism that preserves the feeling of communication without the burden for actual intimacy or substance. Most text messages are superficial greetings and are often sent when the two parties are within speaking distance of each other. Like a wave or nod, they are meant to merely establish connection without getting specific.

While text messaging is generally a social communication tool, it does have some applications for business. Text messages can be sent or retrieved in situations, such as meetings, when a ringing phone would be inappropriate. With research showing that many more text messages are opened than are email messages, advertisers are using text messages to send their marketing messages.[12] Refer to Figure 5-3, which compares the completeness and relative formality of the email message to the informal nature of the instant message and the abbreviated style of the text message. Each medium requires its own appropriate writing style to maximize effectiveness and social expectations.

Electronic Messages and the Law

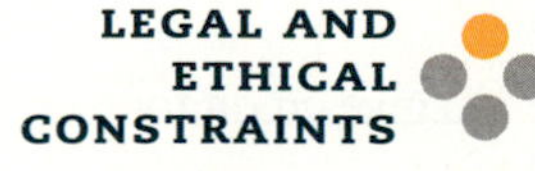

U.S. courts have established the right of companies to monitor the electronic mail of an employee because they own the facilities and intend them to be used for job-related communication only. On the other hand, employees typically expect that their email messages should be kept private. To protect themselves against liability imposed by the

FIGURE 5-3

Levels of Formality Required by Various Technology

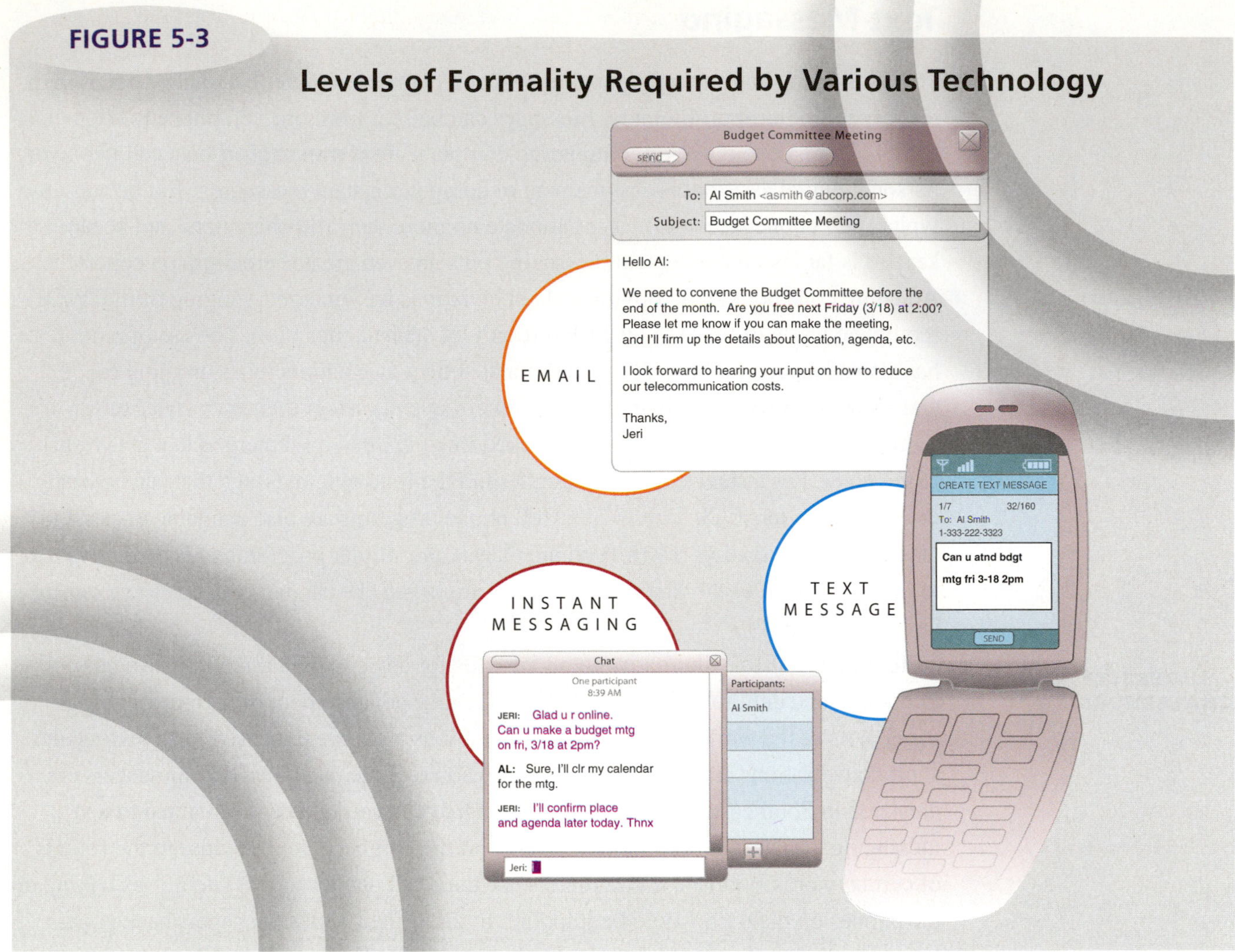

What pending legislation are you aware of that would address privacy issues?

Electronic Communications Privacy Act (ECPA), employers simply provide a legitimate business reason for the monitoring (preventing computer crime, retrieving lost messages, regulating employee morale) and obtain written consent to intercept email or at least notify employees. Employees who use the system after the notification may have given implied consent to the monitoring.[13]

The legal status of text messaging has been murkier. A 2008 court ruling made a distinction between electronic communications employers store on their servers and communication that is contracted out to third parties. Employers must have either a warrant or the employee's permission to view messages stored by someone other than the employer. Employers who intend to monitor must be specific in their written employee policy statements that they intend to access text messages sent with company-issued devices.[14]

Remember that you are responsible for the content of any electronic message you send. Because electronic messages move so quickly between people and often become very informal and conversational, individuals may not realize (or may forget) their responsibility. If a person denies commitments made via an electronic message, someone involved may produce a copy of the message as verification.

Electronic communicators must abide by copyright laws. Be certain to give credit for quoted material and seek permission to use copyrighted text or graphics from printed or

What guidelines do you suggest for posting electronic message?

electronic sources. Unless you inform the reader that editing has occurred, do not alter a message you are forwarding or re-posting, and be sure to ask permission before forwarding it.

Federal and state bills related to employee privacy are frequently introduced for legislative consideration. Although litigation related to present privacy issues is underway, the development of law is lagging far behind technology; nevertheless, employers can expect changes in the laws as technology continues to develop. The Strategic Forces feature "Legal and Ethical Implications of Technology" explores laws that affect other aspects of privacy as related to technology.

Electronic messages have often become the prosecutor's star witness, the corporate equivalent of DNA evidence, as it and other forms of electronic communication are subject to subpoena in litigation. Referring to this issue, Former New York attorney general Eliot Spitzer had this to say: "Never write when you can talk. Never talk when you can nod. And never put anything in an email [that you don't want on the front page of the newspaper]."[15] Several perils of "e-vidence" mail that companies must address are illustrated in these cases:

- Including inappropriate content can humiliate and lead to indictment. Detroit Mayor Kwame Kilpatrick and his chief of staff were charged in a 12-count indictment including perjury and obstruction of justice when text messages exchanged between the two were revealed. The pair's secret love affair played out in the messages was also disclosed to a shocked public.[16] The press dubbed the resulting disastrous professional result as "death by Blackberry."
- Failing to preserve or destroying email messages in violation of securities rules is a sure path to destruction. Arthur Andersen's destruction of Enron-related messages led to a criminal conviction and eventually to Enron's implosion.
- Using inability to locate emails and other relevant documents demanded by the courts (negligence) is unacceptable to the courts. Penalties have included monetary fines, assessment of court costs or attorney's fees, and dismissal of the case in favor of the opposing side.[17]

On the other hand, e-vidence mail can protect a company from lawsuits. A company being sued by a female employee because a male executive had allegedly sexually abused her retrieved a trail of emails with lurid attachments sent by the female employee to the male executive named in the case.[18]

To avoid the legal perils of electronic communications, employees must be taught not to write loose, potentially rude, and overly casual messages; to avoid carelessly deleting messages; and to take the time to identify and organize relevant messages for quick retrieval.

Your Turn 5-3

You're the Professional

In your work for an accounting firm, you rely heavily on email for both internal and external communication. Today as you were checking your email, you came upon a message that was apparently sent to your email address by mistake. (Your email address is only one character different from the company CEO's address.) The message indicated that your good friend and coworker Nancy is scheduled to be "laid off" as a part of a workforce reduction next week. You happen to know that Nancy is pregnant but that she hasn't told her supervisor yet *because she really needs to continue working for a few months to save money before the new baby arrives.*[19]

TAKE ACTION:

a. *What should you do? Whose privacy and right to know should be respected?*

b. *How would your actions differ if the message indicated that*
   - *two employees were planning to steal a computer?*
   - *two employees were having an affair?*
   - *the company was to be closed?*

Web Page Communication

The World Wide Web is truly a universal communication medium, reaching a broad audience in diverse locations. The familiar web platform also may be used for offering a company **intranet** to distribute various types of information to employees at numerous locations.

© NETPICS/ALAMY

Business partners such as vendors, suppliers, and customers can utilize the Web to access a company's **extranet**. Both intranets and extranets restrict access to those visitors with authorization such as a password. An organization can also establish a **public web presence** to extend its reach significantly and provide potential customers or clients with an always-available source of information and contact.

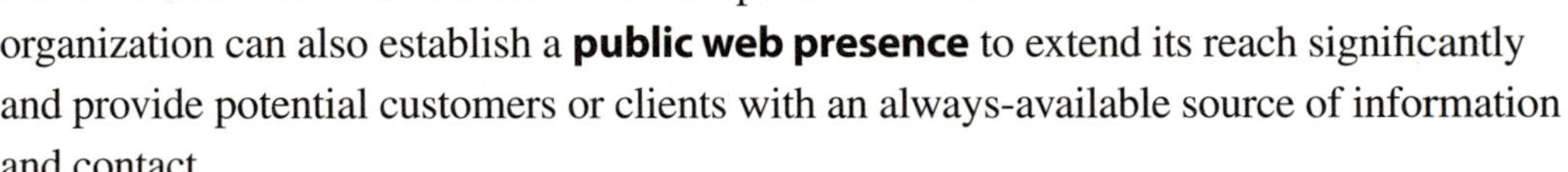

While effective web page development is a highly specialized activity, understanding of the process will be useful to any business communicator. Organizations can use the Web not only to communicate with customers and clients but to interact with business partners. The Strategic Forces feature "Web Assists Interorganizational Teams" describes the role of the Web in promoting team effectiveness.

Designing web pages that are accessible by the millions of people with permanent or temporary disabilities is good for business, especially with the aging population that increases the number of people with disabilities, including visual impairments.[22] Research by the 2004 Disability Rights Commission has found that the most accessible websites for users with disabilities were also easier for people without disabilities to operate, with some online tasks performed 35 percent faster when using the more accessible sites.[23] U.S. businesses have legal requirements for online content to be available to everyone under equal opportunity and anti-discrimination laws. The National Federation of the Blind filed a class action suit against Target Corporation because the online store offered values that could not be accessed by screen reader software.[24] The Web Content Accessibility Guidelines provided by The World Wide Web Consortiums (W3C) at www.w3.org are helpful resources for assuring web accessibility. The same group has also developed Mobile Web Accessibility Guidelines for making websites usable from mobile devices.

TEAM ENVIRONMENT

STRATEGIC FORCES

Web Assists Interorganizational Teams

Maintaining efficient communication is crucial in business today, especially now that more companies are working with outside vendors, rather than doing everything themselves. In product design and building projects, a project team is typically composed of various company personnel and a variety of outside parties that provide goods and services necessary for project completion. Completion is often delayed unnecessarily by misunderstandings and faulty coordination between various vendors and company personnel. Compounding the problem are the differences in computer systems, terminology, and processes that can result in incompatibilities. Fortunately, the Web can now provide a neutral environment to bridge those gaps and help teams get more work done correctly and on time.

Web-based project software applications allow information to be viewed from any computer with Internet access, as long as the user has the proper security clearance and passwords. This means you don't necessarily have to own the same kind of system as the people with whom you are sharing data. Comfort with the familiar Internet platform means that users can be trained in a matter of minutes. The Web-based software provides a quick, convenient, and controlled way to share information with colleagues and vendors. Project team members have easy access regardless of their technical ability, location, application, or computer platform.[37]

A successful example of web-based project software is the Centric Apparel Suite, a comprehensive application that encompasses all phases of fashion product development. The suite designed for the apparel industry offers a set of applications to manage the entire fashion process from design line planning to product introduction. The integrated system uses the web as a communication mechanism to enable a team of people in various locations and with diverse contributions to work together on the fashion project. They don't need a shared system or shared software applications to exchange information, react to each other's work contributions, and contribute collaboratively to the project.[38]

© DREAMPICTURES/BLEND IMAGES/ JUPITERIMAGES

The Centric software suite offers support for fashion collection and line planning, as well as product specification and product sourcing. The web application helps assure on-time delivery since project team members can view critical deadlines and provide their information and responses at appropriate times throughout the project's development. Bringing new collections to market in response to rapidly changing seasons is a major industry challenge to remaining competitive. The dedicated planning and analytical tools that Centric offers enable up-to-the-minute collaboration from companies' global teams. The result is that companies can effectively coordinate their development efforts and release more fashion collections each year.[39] Improved efficiency in the development process leads to broader market success and higher profits for the various organizations that participate in the development of the fashion collections.

Application

In small groups, discuss the following issues:

- How would the efforts of fashion designers, suppliers, manufacturers, and distributors be enhanced through the use of web-based team software?
- How would cost, employee resources, communication, and time be impacted?
- What other types of business problems might be solved effectively using Web-based team software?

SHOWCASE PART 2

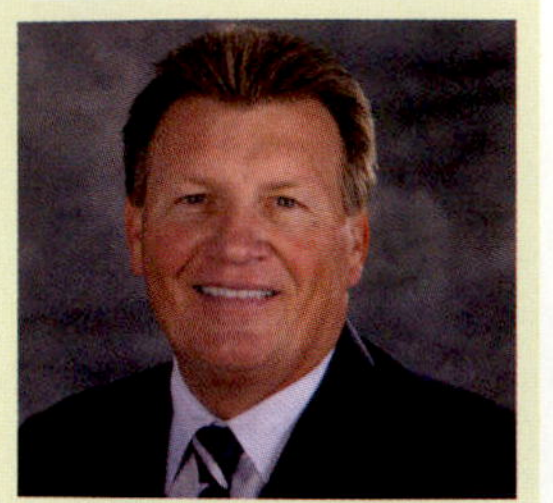

© PHIL MCCARTEN/LANDOV

SPOTLIGHT COMMUNICATOR:
FRANZ S. HANNING
PRESIDENT AND CEO,
WYNDHAM VACATION
OWNERSHIP, INC.

Vacation Planning Website Appeals to Today's Techno-Savvy Members

When Franz Hanning took over as president and CEO of Fairfield Resorts, which became Wyndham Vacation Ownership, he already had two decades of management experience with the growing company and had been instrumental in the creation of timeshare points program. Since the 2000 launch of the company's comprehensive web-based vacation planning site, members have convenient access to information as well as planning flexibility. Hanning sees the Vacation Planning website as extending the firm's commitment to offering diverse marketing channels and reaching new consumers with more product choices. Visit your companion website, **www.cengage.com/bcomm/lehman**, to learn more about Franz Hanning's vision for communication through Wyndham's website.

www.wyndhamworldwide.com

REFER TO SHOWCASE PART 3, ON PAGE 177
TO LEARN HOW WYNDHAM VACATION OWNERSHIP, INC., REACHES OUT TO VARIOUS CONSTITUENTS.

Writing for a Website

How can knowing your web audience help you structure effective messages for your website?

Many standard rules for writing apply whether for the Web or print. However, some important differences exist between readers of paper material and web users:[25]

- Web users do not want to read. They skim, browse, and hop from one highlighted area to another trying to zero in on the word or phrase that relates to their search.
- English-speaking readers typically start scanning at the top left side of the main content area. They move top to bottom, left to right. Given this pattern, placing frequently accessed items close to the top of the content area is important. Information should follow the pyramid style of writing common in newspaper writing: The main idea or conclusion is presented first, and subsequent sections and pages expand upon it.
- Users can more quickly scan items in columns rather than rows, especially if they are categorized, grouped, and have headings. You can have more lists on the Web than in a typical print document.
- Users refer infrequently to directions. It is unlikely they will read little notes, sidebars, and help files, so directions must appear in simple, numbered steps.

In recognition of these web user characteristics, writers should tailor their styles accordingly. The following tips will help you compose appropriate web content:[26]

- **Be brief.** A rule of thumb is to reduce the wording of any print document by 50 percent when you put it on the Web.
- **Keep it simple.** Use short words that allow for fast reading by people of various educational backgrounds. Use mixed case, since all capitals are slower to read.

- **Consider appropriate jargon.** If all your site users share a common professional language, use it. Otherwise, keep to concise yet effective word choices.
- **Use eye-catching headlines.** They may catch interest, ask a question, present the unusual, or pose a conflict.
- **Break longer documents into smaller chunks.** Provide ways to easily move through the document and return to the beginning.
- **Use attention-getting devices judiciously.** Bold, font changes, color, and graphics do attract attention but can be overdone, causing important ideas to be lost.
- **Avoid placing critical information in graphic form only.** Many users are averse to slow-loading graphics and skip over them.

Effective web writing involves moving beyond the paper mode into the web mode of thinking. Understanding the distinctive expectations of web readers will allow you to structure your ideas effectively and efficiently.

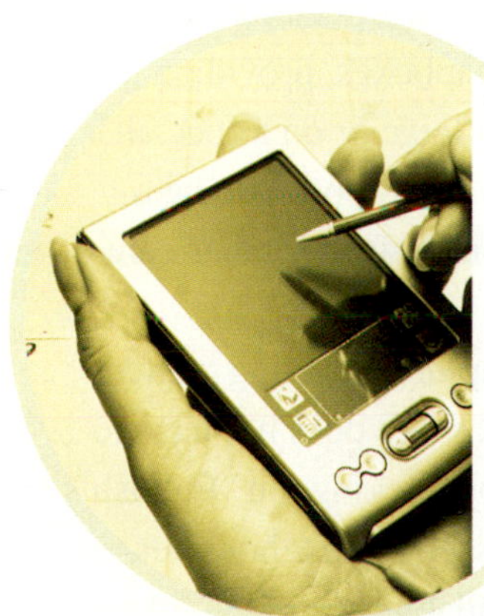

Your Turn 5-4
Career Portfolio

- Create your own web page using WebSpawner or another program as directed by your instructor. WebSpawner is a free software application and can be accessed from http://www.webspawner.com. You may go to your companion website, www.cengage.com/bcomm/lehman, for updated links.

TAKE ACTION:

- Design your web page to serve as an employment tool, including the following elements:
  - your career goal
  - a summary of your most important professional qualifications/qualities
  - a link to your résumé document
  - a link to a communication document you have created
  - weblinks to your university and organizations to which you belong
  - other items that demonstrate your professional abilities.
- Provide your instructor with information for accessing your web page.

Writing Wikis

While a traditional website's content is usually controlled by the sponsoring individual or agency, a wiki is a collaborative website that hosts the collective work of many authors.

Similar to a blog in structure and logic, a wiki allows anyone to edit, delete, or modify content, even the work of previous authors. While allowing everyday users to create and edit a website encourages cooperative use of electronic information, the content posted at such sites should not be considered authoritative. When wiki writing, avoid the first-person blogging style and conform to the tone and flow of the existing article. Wikis are not typically the place for personal opinion and analysis. Instead, present factual information in clear, concise, and neutral language.[27]

Many businesses make use of wikis to encourage free flow of ideas within the organization. Content in a wiki can be updated in real time, without any real administrative effort, and without the need for deliberate distribution. Contributors simply visit and update a common website. Wikis facilitate the exchange of information within and between teams. They allow maintenance of a series of unique documents with evolving content. Placing a document in a wiki does not necessarily make it editable by everyone with access to the wiki. For example, the marketing department can make a PowerPoint slide deck available to the sales team or the company at large without letting them change or overwrite it. Most companies implement their wikis behind a firewall to limit participation to their internal user base.[28]

Writing for Weblogs

In contrast to a wiki, a **weblog,** or **blog,** is a type of online journal typically authored by an individual and does not allow visitors to change the original posted material, but to only add comments. Some of the millions of blogs now populating the Web are online scrapbooks for pasting links, information, and quotes. Some resemble personal diaries, often illustrated with digital snapshots; others serve as digital soapboxes, providing a platform for airing opinions and commentary about the world at large or on a specialist topic of interest. Users (known as bloggers) add entries (referred to as posts) using a simple online form in their browsers, while the weblog publishing software takes care of formatting the page layout and creating archive pages.[29]

Blogs differ from websites in that blogs are dynamic, with rapidly changing content that does not require authorization to post. The creator of the message does not have to be familiar with special coding and uploads a message simply by clicking the "Publish" button.[30] Blogging allows average citizens to become publishers. Bloggers, however, should write each post with the realization that it is publicly available.

How do you explain the enormous popularity of Twitter?

Blog formats have been adapted for business uses, including commercial publishing, marketing, and as a knowledge management tool. Blogs can store knowledge in searchable archives for future use. This function can be helpful, for example, for service teams as they search past communications to troubleshoot current problems. Many companies, such as Microsoft, Sun Microsystems, and General Motors, encourage blogging among employees.[31] An effective corporate blog begins with a clear goal, such as winning business or building customer loyalty, and then provides relevant, frequently updated information for the target audience to return to regularly. Like other effective web communications, blogs must be promoted creatively to attract avid readers.[32] Companies such as Dell and Southwest Airlines employ "communities and conversation teams" or a "social media team" who track comments posted on sites such Twitter, YouTube, Flickr, and Facebook, verify facts, and respond quickly to any customer complaint appearing in cyberspace. In addition to being an early warning system, these online conversations are sources of feedback on customer needs and pain points that lead to innovation in products and services.[33]

Your Turn 5-5
Miscue

Matthew Brown, a Starbucks employee, was terminated from his job because of profanity-laced remarks he made about a manager and the company on his blog. Brown said he didn't use his real name and gave the blog address to a select group of people, so he doesn't know how the diary ended up in Starbucks' hands. While the blog was not easy to find, postings are permanently archived on the Internet. The derogatory posting violated the contract Starbucks employees sign agreeing not to make negative comments about the company.[34]

TAKE ACTION:

- *Do you know of a similar faux pas related to blogging? What were the consequences?*
- *Speak briefly about the advice you would give to a coworker who plans to start a blog.*

Internal blogs can be established that are not published to anyone outside the company. They present similar legal issues to those surrounding email and instant messaging. One of the most important considerations is whether posts are truly anonymous. The potential for anonymous speech creates an atmosphere that can encourage irresponsible behavior, such as harassment, defamation, and gossip. To reduce this problem, IT professionals can configure internal blogs so that all users can be identified, at least by the company.[35]

Voice and Wireless Communication

Not so long ago voice communication referred to telephone usage, and using the telephone effectively is still an important skill in any profession. You can visit your companion website at www.cengage.com/bcomm/lehman for telephone etiquette tips. While the traditional telephone still plays an important role in business activity, voice communication extends to voice mail systems and cell phone usage. Both voice and data can be transmitted now using wireless communication systems.

Voice Mail Communication

© TETRA IMAGES/JUPITERIMAGES

Voice mail technology allows flexibility in staying in touch without the aid of a computer and reduces telephone tag. Just as email communication can be enhanced by adhering to some basic principles, voice mail communication can be more effective by following recommended guidelines:[40]

- Update your greeting often to reflect your schedule and leave special announcements.
- Leave your email address, fax number, or mailing address on your greeting if this information might be helpful to your callers.

Weblogs Serve the Public and Organizations. Blogs are easy to use, flexible, and cost effective. In the aftermath of Hurricane Katrina, the *Times Picayune* New Orleans newspaper was forced to suspend all of its print news for several days. Having to rely on its website for news reporting, the newspaper set up a Hurricane Katrina weblog that was visited by 20 to 30 million people daily. The blog proved valuable in connecting people with missing relatives and friends and giving updates on conditions. Many businesses use weblogs as a marketing tool to open dialogue with the public and internally to discuss problems and keep track of their solutions.[36]

- Encourage callers to leave detailed messages. If you need certain standard information from callers, use your greeting to prompt them for it. Such information may eliminate the need to call back.
- Instruct callers on how to review their message or be transferred to an operator.
- Check your voice mail regularly, and return all voice messages within 24 hours.

  When leaving a message, you can improve your communication by following these tips:[41]

  - Speak slowly and clearly, and repeat your name and phone number at the beginning and end of the message.
  - Spell your name for the recipient who may need the correct spelling.
  - Leave a detailed message, not just your name and number, to avoid prolonged phone tag.
  - Keep your message brief, typically 60 seconds or less.
  - Ensure that your message will be understandable. Don't call from places with distracting background noise; or an inadequate signal connection.

The sound of your voice makes a lasting impression on the many people who listen to your greeting or the messages you leave. To ensure that the impression you leave is a professional one, review your voice greeting before you save it. Rerecord to eliminate verbal viruses (um, uh, stumbles), flat or monotone voice, and garbled or rushed messages that are difficult to understand. Consider scripting the message to avoid long, rambling messages. As you are recording, stand, smile, and visualize the person receiving the message; you'll hear the added energy, enthusiasm, and warmth in your voice.[42]

LEGAL AND ETHICAL CONSTRAINTS

Remember that the voice mail message you leave should be seen as permanent. In some systems the digital files are backed up and stored for possible retrieval by managers or other company personnel. A voice mail message can also be used as evidence in a lawsuit or other legal proceeding.[43]

Cell Phone Communication

How have cell phones redefined interpersonal communication?

Mobile telephones, once a rarity, are now a standard accessory for many people throughout the world. In the United States, cell phones are as commonplace as landline phones, and the number continues to rise.

The increasing functionality and ease of use of cell phones have outstripped the development of rules for proper cell phone etiquette. According to a recent poll, almost 7 out of 10 Americans say they observe poor cell etiquette at least once every day.[44] Cell phone abuse in the workplace causes much annoyance and intrusion that leads to ineffectiveness and may endanger employee safety. Your attention to a few commonsense guidelines will help assure that you are not seen as a rude phone user.[45]

- **Observe wireless-free quiet zones.** This obviously includes theaters, performances, and religious services, but may also include meetings, restaurants, hospitals, and other public places. Exercise judgment about silencing your ringer, switching to vibrate mode, or turning off your phone. To increase the effectiveness of meetings, cell phone policies in place in some businesses ask that employees leave their cell phones at their desk; vibrating mode is acceptable for an anticipated emergency. To encourage proper cell phone etiquette, one business requires managers to deposit a designated amount of money in a jar should their cell phones ring during a meeting; monies collected are donated to a charity.

- **Respect others in crowded places.** Speak in low conversational tones, and consider the content of your conversation.
- **Think safety.** Some states and municipalities have banned the use of cell phones while driving. Others allow the use of hands-free devices only. Even if not illegal, cell phone usage increases the risk of accident by distracting the driver. Cell phone policies that prohibit operators of company-owned vehicles from using cell phones or other communication devices while driving are being implemented by many companies to minimize risks to their employees and liability resulting from accidents.

Cell phone users should remember that the technology is not secure. Perhaps you have overheard another party's phone conversation when using your cell phone. The radio frequencies that transmit the voice signals can be picked up by other equipment. For this reason, information that is confidential or sensitive should be shared using an alternate communication channel.

Wireless Communication and the Future

With the many communication innovations that have occurred in the last 20 years, one can only wonder what the next 20 years will hold. Whatever the breakthroughs, wireless technology will figure strongly in the changes. Wireless communication has freed us from the necessity of being literally plugged in while enabling us to communicate voice and high-speed data transmission virtually any time, anywhere.

Describe a typical computer in the year 2020.

Wireless technology drives many of the significant changes that are affecting today's business. Smartphones offer advanced capabilities beyond a typical mobile phone, with PC-like functionality. Applications include email access, data processing, and entertainment. Other functionality might include an additional interface such as a miniature

QWERTY keyboard, touch screen or D-pad, built-in camera, contact management, navigation hardware and software, media software for playing music, browsing and viewing capability for photos and video clips, and Internet browsers. Phone data can be synchronized with a computer and other communication devices for easy information access and manipulation. The future promises increased use of smartphones, especially touchscreens, by both consumers and professionals and the development of many innovative **phone apps** (shorthand for phone applications) that customize smartphone capabilities to fit users' needs. Security will continue to be a challenging consideration as workers use their phones to hold and transmit confidential information.[46]

The impact of wireless communication will be even more significant as voice-to-text and text-to-voice technology continues to develop. Voice input and output technology offers the ability to communicate with a computer system without a keyboard. While such technology has been around for more than two decades, newer systems have more powerful processors, are more miniaturized, and better tolerate variances in speakers' accents and inflections without sacrificing speed and accuracy.

Wireless capability will increase the timeliness of key business decisions, resulting in greater revenues and profitability. However, just being able to make decisions quickly does not ensure that they are the right decisions. As in the past, workers will need to have correct and timely information for making decisions. An additional challenge for the wireless era will be balancing electronic communication capabilities with the need for human interaction.

Appropriate Use of Technology

While technology offers numerous advantages, a technological channel is not always the communication method of choice. In fact, companies such as Intel and US Cellular, are experimenting with policies designed to restrict email usage. Despite the strong initial resistance, policies such as email-free Fridays or weekends are helping employees overcome email addiction. The intent of the policies are to increase face-to-face and phone contact with customers and coworkers, raise productivity, and give employees reprieve from the stress of flooded mailboxes. One employee admitted that while it has taken three years, his supervisor's insistence on face-to-face communication has helped him curb his email usage by about 20 percent. A ban on nonessential email on weekends at Deloitte & Touché allows managers to work productively on weekends without feeling chained to incoming email.[47]

Before sending a message, be certain the selected channel of communication is appropriate by considering the message's purpose, confidentiality issues, and human relations factors.

Determine the Purpose of the Message

If a message is straightforward and informative, chances are a technological option might be appropriate. While the use of instantaneous and efficient communication methods is quite compelling, keep in mind that written communication, printed or online, cannot replace the personal interaction so essential in today's team-based work environments. While employees floors apart or in different offices or time zones benefit from email and web communications, two people sitting side by side or on the same floor shouldn't have to communicate solely by electronic means.

A second question when selecting among communication options concerns whether a permanent record of the message is needed or if a more temporary form such as a phone call or instant message would suffice.

Determine Whether the Information Is Personal or Confidential

As a general guideline, keep personal correspondence off-line if you don't want it to come back and haunt you. The content of an email message could have embarrassing consequences since such documents often become a part of public records and wireless communications might be unexpectedly intercepted. Your company technically "owns" your electronic communications and thus can monitor them to determine legitimate business use or potential abuse. Undeliverable email messages are delivered to a mail administrator, and many networks routinely store backups of all email messages that pass through them.

Even deleted messages can be "resurrected" with little effort, as several public figures discovered when investigators retrieved archived email as evidence in court cases. For sensitive situations, a face-to-face encounter may be preferred. Legal and ethical considerations may also impact your choices when considering technology, as described in the accompanying Strategic Forces feature "Legal and Ethical Implications of Technology."

Decide Whether Positive Human Relations are Sacrificed

Be wary of using an electronic communication tool as an avoidance mechanism. Remember, too, that some people may not regularly check their email or voice mail, and some have unreliable systems that are slow or prone to lose messages. Some news will be received better in person than through an electronic format that might be interpreted as cold and impersonal.

Additionally, some people, especially those of certain cultures, may prefer a personal meeting even if you perceive that an electronic exchange of information would be a more efficient use of everyone's time. Choose the communication channel carefully to fit both your purpose and the preference of the receiver.

Before composing electronic messages, study carefully the overall suggestions presented in Chapters 3 and 4. Then, study the specific suggestions in the "Check Your Communication" checklist at the end of this chapter. Compare your work with this checklist after you have written a rough draft, making any needed corrections.

STRATEGIC FORCES

Legal and Ethical Implications of Technology

Technology threatens our privacy, our right to be left alone, free from surveillance or interference from other individuals or organizations. Common invasions of privacy caused by technology include collecting excessive amounts of information for decision making and maintaining too many files, monitoring the exact time employees spend on a specific task and between tasks and the exact number and length of employee breaks, and supervisors' or coworkers' reading another employee's electronic mail and computer files. Additionally, integrating computer files containing information collected from more than one agency without permission is a major threat to privacy. Although an

© FEDERAL TRADE COMMISSION—WWW.FTC.GOV

individual may have authorized the collection of the individual information, merging the information may reveal things the individual may want to remain private.[20]

Our right to privacy is protected primarily by the First Amendment (which guarantees freedom of speech and association), and the Fourth Amendment (which protects against unreasonable search and seizure of one's person, documents, or home, and assures due process). However, the Fair Information Practices (FIP) forms the basis of 13 federal statutes that ensure the security and integrity of personal information collected by governmental and private agencies. Set forth in the FIP are conditions for handling information about individuals in such areas as credit reporting, education, financial records, newspaper records, cable communications, electronic communications, and video rentals. The FIP also holds managers responsible and liable for the reliability and security of company information systems.[21]

Government response to terrorism and other security threats has resulted in further erosion of privacy for Americans. In the present climate of controversy over privacy and ownership of information, the following ethical practices are appropriate for the collection and access of information:

- Collect only information needed as opposed to what you would like to know.
- Develop (and use) safeguards for the security of information and instill in data handlers the values of privacy and confidentiality.
- Require employees to use passwords to gain access to the system and enforce routine changes of passwords on a periodic basis.
- Require users to "sign off" or "log out" of email when they leave their computers.
- Assign user identification passwords and levels of access that limit information a person can observe and change.
- Consider the use of encryption facilities if you are sending extremely confidential information.
- Develop a clear privacy policy that complies with the law and does not unnecessarily compromise the interests of employees or employers.

Application

Stage a classroom debate with two teams of four; one team represents the right of the employer to monitor computer activities and the other team represents the right of the employee to maintain privacy in communication. Each team will study the issue and prepare its arguments. During the debate, each team will have five minutes to present its side of the issue, followed by a two-minute cross-examination by the opposing team. Class members who are not participating on the debate teams will act as judges to determine which team presents the stronger case.

Wyndham Vacation Ownership, Inc., Reaches Out to Various Constituents

The Web provides an organization with a highly interactive medium for communicating with its various stakeholders, including customers, employees, business partners, investors, and the general public. Not only can various types of company information be presented, but the site can open the door to participation and discussion.

Current news releases, expanded services, and corporate philosophy and values can all be communicated via the company website. Comments and inquiries are also easily posted for efficient company response.

www.wyndhamworldwide.com/

Activities

- Access the following article that provides further elaboration on how organizations can avoid common website problems to use their sites as positive communication tools:

  Roeder, L. (2006, August 3). 7 problems with your web site. *About.com*. Available at http://personalweb.about.com/od/customizeyourwebdesign/a/407usability.htm
- Visit the Wyndham Vacation Ownership website at www.wyndhamworldwide.com. Review the site options and available information.
- Compose a brief report to your instructor that describes how WVO is using its web page to communicate with owners, potential owners, and employees. Submit to your instructor as an email attachment.

© NEWSCOM

Summary

1. Discuss the effective use of email, instant messaging, and text messaging in business communication.

Email may be sent to receivers both inside and outside the organization. Email provides a fast, convenient way to communicate by reducing telephone tag and telephone interruptions, facilitating the transmission of a single message to multiple recipients, reducing telephone bills, eliminating time barriers, and fostering open communication among users in various locations. While general writing principles apply, email formats are less formal than business letter formats. Real-time email, known as instant messaging, allows two or more people to converse online. Text messaging occurs primarily between users of portable devices. Abbreviations and online "shorthand" help to speed these means of rapid communication.

2. Explain principles for writing effectively for the Web.

Web pages facilitate an organization's continual communication with a wide audience. HTML and a web browser turn ordinary text into a web page. Writing for web pages should be concise, jargon-free, and chunked to allow for scanning of content. Weblogs serve important needs in capturing information for further use but should be considered public and not confidential.

3. Discuss the effective use of voice and wireless technologies in business communication.

Voice recordings and messages should be clear and complete and considered as permanent records. While offering convenience, cell phones should be used with consideration for the receiver and the public. Cell phone communications should not be viewed as secure communications. Text messaging offers a limited avenue for exchanging quick, quiet messages. Applications and equipment to accommodate wireless communications continue to expand and offer flexibility for transmitting voice and data. Business decisions can be improved through the appropriate use of voice and wireless technologies.

4. **Identify legal and ethical implications associated with the use of communication technology.**

Legal and ethical considerations should be taken into account when communicating through technology: (a) Be certain that information technology does not violate basic rights of individuals and that you abide by all laws related to the use of technology; (b) understand that email is not private and can be monitored by a company; (c) develop and use procedures that protect the security of information; and (d) develop a clear and fair privacy policy.

Chapter Review

1. What can you do to limit the excessive amount of email that lowers productivity? (Obj. 1)
2. What practices should be followed to avoid sending a "flame"? (Obj. 1)
3. How does communication differ when emailing, instant messaging, and texting? (Objs. 1, 3)
4. Describe the legal issues related to the use of email. (Obj. 1)
5. How does writing for a weblog or a wiki differ from writing for a website? What precautions should be followed? (Obj. 2)
6. How are interorganizational project teams using the Web to achieve goals? (Obj. 2)
7. What guidelines apply to recording an effective voice message? to leaving an effective voice message on another's phone? (Obj. 3)
8. Describe the courteous use of a cell phone. (Obj. 3)
9. Which communication channels are preferred when sending a message that is personal or confidential? Why? (Obj. 4)
10. How is the use of technology impacted by legal limitations and requirements? (Obj. 4)

Digging Deeper

1. Describe three business communication situations in which a technology channel would be inappropriate for exchanging information. Explain your choices.
2. How does a communicator balance the equally important goals of communicating efficiently and building team camaraderie?
3. How is web communication different from other forms of business communication? How is it similar?

Assessment

To check your understanding of the chapter, take available online quizzes as directed by your instructor.

Activities

1. Useful Subject Lines (Obj. 1)

Write effective email subject lines for the following situations:

a. Accept an invitation to judge a business case competition at an area college.
b. Encourage employees to participate in a program for contributing money-saving ideas.
c. Direct public relations manager to handle announcement of plant closure.
d. Explain that customary employee bonuses will not be paid because of sales decline.
e. Send a follow-up message with attached résumé to a career fair recruiter you talked with on your campus.
f. Alert subscribers to your online newsletter of an upcoming web seminar on workplace bullying.

2. Document for Analysis: Email Message (Obj. 1)

Analyze the following email message for content, tone, formatting, and email practices. Revise the email message if directed by your instructor. Access a downloadable version of this activity at your companion website, www.cengage.com/bcomm/lehman.

Email from Sarah Howard-Berry sent 12/2/2011 at 1:45 p.m.

To: MS. HALEY LAND, MANAGER, CUSTOMER SERVICE CENTER
Subject: GOAL FINALLY ACHIEVED
Cc: Jason Carson, Anna Bryant, Ellen Son

DEAR HALEY

AS YOU KNOW, WE HIRE AN INDEPENDENT CUSTOMER QUALITY ASSURANCE FIRM TO LISTEN TO THE PHONE RECORDINGS OF OUR CUSTOMER SERVICE REPRESENTATIVES. OVER THE PAST YEAR THAT FIRM HAS REPORTED THAT THE QUALITY AND EFFICIENCY OF OUR REPRESENTATIVES HAS FAILED TO IMPROVE.

HOWEVER, LAST MONTH THE FIRM FINALLY REPORTED THAT YOUR SALES REPRESENTATIVES ACHIEVED OUR ESTABLISHED GOALS. WE COMMEND YOU ON THIS ACHIEVEMENT. THANK YOU FOR ENSURING THAT "THE CUSTOMER IS KING" IS NOT JUST AN EMPTY ADVERTISING SLOGAN.

BCNU,

HALEY

3. Not All Electronic Writing Is the Same (Obj. 1)

Develop a professional email communicating the same message as the following text message:

bob ok'd rept. :) Cud u pruf
and ruff out sldes b4 mtg on Mon.
fone me asap if prblm. TY

Send the email message to your instructor. Be prepared to explain the differences in the writing style, formality, and format of these forms of electronic communication.

4. Instant Messaging and Texting Shortcuts (Objs. 1, 3)

In small groups, make a list of "shorthand"—expressions that make online chatting and text messaging faster and more efficient.

5. Text Messaging Etiquette (Objs. 1, 3)

Listen to the following advice from business etiquette coach, Phyllis Davis, on the etiquette of instant messaging and texting: www.videojug.com/interview/text-messaging-business-etiquette#what-is-the-etiquette-for-instant-messaging-and-texting-in-business.

In small groups, summarize the advice given and add additional suggestions of your own.

6. Writing for the Web (Obj. 2)

Consider the following passage, which is also available in a downloadable version from your companion site, www.cengage.com/bcomm/lehman. Revise the material for posting to the home page for Green Leaf, a lawn maintenance business.

> Some companies use a cookie cutter approach to lawn care. We think you deserve more than that. We know what works in another neighborhood may not be right for you. We will provide you with a service program tailored to your lawn's needs, and we include extras like our double overlap application technique to ensure even growth and thickening without unsightly streaking or spotting of your lawn. You don't have to be home during our visits. You can count on us for timely service. We will provide you with information through newsletters, notes left at the time of service, and progress reports on your lawn condition. Our website address is http://www.greenleafco.com where you can get other information on yard care tips, seasonal planting, lawn disease control, lawn insect control, tree maintenance, weed control, and landscaping. You can also request a free quotation.

7. Blog Posting and Twittering (Obj. 2)

Prepare the text of a blog post providing anonymous feedback to management on a new company policy prohibiting use of email on Fridays. Condense your post to 140 words assuming it will be posted at a social media site such as Twitter. Read the following article to learn more about the rationale for the policy and potential objections:

Wakefield, J. (2007, October 7). Turn off the email and do some work. *BBC News.* Available from http://news.bbc.co.uk/2/hi/technology/7049275.stm

8. Voice Mail Recording (Obj. 3)

Compose scripts for the following voice mail recordings:

a. You will be away from your job as loan counselor at Hometown Bank for three days while you attend a professional conference. Fellow loan counselor, James Lumas, will be handling your calls while you are away. Compose a script of the voice mail recording you will leave on your phone prior to departing for your conference.

b. As owner and operator of Sis's Florist Shop, you close your shop on Sundays. You do, however, accept orders via your home telephone for flowers and plants to be picked up or delivered on Monday or later. Compose a message to be left on your phone when you close the shop on Saturday evenings, informing customers who call in as to how to reach you for ordering.

c. You are the office administrator for Medical Associates, a physicians' clinic. Compose a voice mail message that will be heard by patients and other parties who call after hours. You will need to explain how to reach the voice mail box for the appointment desk, each physician, the insurance office, and the laboratory.

9. Preparing Voice Mail Messages (Obj. 3)

Compose scripts for the following situations for which you would leave a voice mail message:

a. Upon returning from a meeting, you have a message on your phone from your real estate agent that says your bid on a house you wish to buy was rejected by the seller. When you call your agent to tell her you want to raise your initial offer by $2,000, you get her voice mail. What will you say in your voice mail message to her?

b. As human resources manager, you call a job applicant to tell her she has been selected to fill a job position as sales associate. You get a voice mail message saying that she is not at home right now. What will you say in your voice mail message?

c. Your voice mail contains an offer for an office interview with Keller Corporation, a potential employer in Atlanta. The message includes instructions for making hotel and airline reservations and an invitation to dinner the night before the interview. Glancing at your calendar, you realize you will already be in Atlanta interviewing with Patman Industries and have scheduled dinner with Patman on the same evening Keller is requesting dinner. How will you respond in your voice mail message to this firm?

d. You've listened to a customer's voice message six times and still cannot understand how many tickets she wants to order. The phone system recorded the phone number, but you are also not sure of the pronunciation of her name. What will you say in your voice message that will enable you to confirm the order?

10. Choosing an Appropriate Channel (Obj. 4)

Indicate one or more appropriate message channels for each of the following situations. A downloadable version of this activity is available at your companion website, www.cengage.com/bcomm/lehman. Be prepared to discuss your choices in a class discussion.

a. Laying off an employee
b. Contacting a customer concerning late payment
c. Sending an RSVP for a dinner party invitation
d. Sending a customer-requested price quote on an order
e. Contacting a reference for a job applicant
f. Notifying staff of a change in work procedures
g. Recommending an action to upper management
h. Sending selected employees' test results performed by an outside laboratory to human resources
i Alerting a coworker who is video recording a city council meeting that he is needed for a family emergency.
j. Responding to a weblog posting made by a customer venting about a negative experience with one of your customer service representatives. Your responsibility is to monitor the Web for customer dissatisfaction issues such as these.

Check Your Communication
Electronic Communication

Email Messages

ORGANIZATION, CONTENT, STYLE, AND MECHANICS

- ☐ Provide a subject line that is meaningful to the recipient.
- ☐ Include only one main message idea related to the receiver's needs.
- ☐ Show empathy and logic to determine idea sequence.
- ☐ Use jargon, technical words, and shortened terms carefully.
- ☐ Use bulleted lists, tables, graphs, or images as needed.
- ☐ Avoid flaming and use of overly emotional language.

FORMAT

- ☐ Include an appropriate salutation, ending, and signature file (your name, address, phone, etc.)
- ☐ When possible, limit message width and length to one screen. Use attachments for longer messages.
- ☐ Single-space lines with a blank space between unindented paragraphs.
- ☐ Use mixed-case letters unless emphasis is needed with capital letters or quotation marks.
- ☐ Use emoticons and abbreviations in moderation only if the receiver understands them and content is informal.

Instant Messages

ORGANIZATION, CONTENT, STYLE, AND MECHANICS

- ☐ Consider previously listed email guidelines.
- ☐ Choose your message participants appropriately.
- ☐ Be aware of unwanted eavesdropping.

FORMAT

- ☐ Use understandable shorthand and abbreviations for frequent words and phrases.
- ☐ Focus more on efficiency and less on spelling and grammar.

TEXT MESSAGES

- ☐ Choose for exchanging quick, quiet messages.
- ☐ Avoid using text messaging as a substitute for richer communication mediums.

Web Communications

WRITING FOR WEBSITES

- ☐ Create brief, simple documents for easy reading. Break longer documents into smaller chunks.
- ☐ Use eye-catching headlines and techniques.
- ☐ Use jargon and technical terms cautiously.
- ☐ Avoid placing critical information only in graphic form that may be skipped by users of slow systems.

WRITING FOR WIKIS

- ☐ Avoid first-person language and conform to tone and flow of existing article.
- ☐ Present factual information in clear, concise, and neutral language.

WRITING FOR BLOGS

- ☐ Consider previously listed email guidelines.
- ☐ Communicate responsibly and ethically when writing anonymously.
- ☐ Develop a clear goal that leads to relevant content for the target audience. Revise and update regularly and promote actively to attract and retain readers.

Voice and Wireless Communications

VOICE RECORDINGS

- ☐ Leave your email address, fax number, or mailing address on your greeting if helpful to callers.
- ☐ Encourage callers to leave detailed messages.
- ☐ Instruct callers in how to review their messages or be transferred to an operator.
- ☐ Check voice mail regularly, replying within 24 hours.

VOICE MESSAGES

- ☐ Speak slowly and clearly.
- ☐ Repeat your name and phone number at the beginning and end, spelling your name if helpful.
- ☐ Leave a detailed, specific message.
- ☐ Keep your message brief, typically 60 seconds or less.
- ☐ Ensure your message is understood; avoid calling from noisy environments and weak signal areas.

VOICE AND WIRELESS ETIQUETTE

- ☐ Use judgment about silencing or turning off your phone.
- ☐ Respect others around you by speaking in low conversational tones and monitoring your content.
- ☐ Practice safety when using wireless communication devices while driving.

Applications

READ | THINK | WRITE | SPEAK | COLLABORATE

1. Communication Technology Success Stories (Objs. 1–4)

Conduct an electronic search to locate an article that deals with the successful use of electronic communication in a company or organization. Prepare an abstract of the article that includes the following parts: (1) article citation, (2) name of organization/company, (3) brief description of communication technique/situation, and (4) outcome(s) of the successful communication. As an alternative to locating an article, write about a successful communication situation in the organization/company for which you work.

Required: Present your abstracts as an email attachment to your instructor. Refer to Appendix B for information about formatting citations. Be prepared to give a short class presentation.

2. Email Emerges as "Evidence Mail" (Objs. 1, 4)

Electronic communication, like any other written communication, is subject to subpoena in court proceedings. Because of its extensive use, email provides an ongoing record of many business activities and transactions. Even deleted emails frequently are not really gone, as they may still exist in backup files. Email has become the corporate equivalent of DNA evidence, the single hair at the crime scene that turns the entire case. Locate the following article that explains more about email as "evidence mail":

O'Donnel, B., & Lincoln, T. A. (2007, August 3). Authenticating email discovery as evidence. *The Legal Intelligencer*. Available at www.law.com/jsp/legaltechnology/pubArticleLT.jsp?id51186736525985

Required: Outline a plan to help an organization ensure that its email communications are not used as negative legal evidence.

3. Using Wikis in Business: Wikitorial Web Goes Down in Flames (Objs. 2, 4)

The Los Angeles Times once featured a "Wikitorial Web," an interactive editorial site where readers could add their supporting and opposing viewpoints along with hyperlinks. According to newspaper officials, the result would be a "constantly evolving collaboration among readers in a communal search for the truth." Inappropriate posts to the first interactive editorial outweighed the collaboration, and the feature was pulled after only 72 hours. You can view the original wikitorial site with the removal message, at www.latimes.com/news/opinion/editorials/la-wiki-splash,0,1349109.htmlstory

Read the following articles that specifically discuss the *Los Angeles Times* and how its "Wikitorial Web" did not work as editors expected:

Behr, R. (2005, June 26). Internet's new wave proves hard to catch: The press wants to get bloggers on its side, but a U.S. experiment shows it may not be easy. *The Observer*. Available from Business and Company Resource Center database.

Gentile, G. (2005, June 20). L.A. Times suspends its experiment with letting readers rewrite the paper's editorials. *The America's Intelligence Wire*. Available from the Business Index ASAP database.

Required:

1. Access an available library database and read two or more articles concerning wikis and their possible uses in business communication. After completing your research, make a short presentation to the class about wikis and their value to organizations.
2. Based on your reading, analyze what the *Times* could have done differently in managing their Wikitorial Web. Post your comments to a class discussion board as directed by your instructor.

READ | THINK | WRITE | SPEAK | COLLABORATE

4. Critique of Email Messages Produced by Real Companies (Obj. 1)

Locate a company example of both a well-written and a poorly written email message. Analyze the strengths and weaknesses of each document. Be prepared to discuss your analysis in class.

5. Electronic Medical Records: Are Your Records Really Private? (Objs. 1–2, 4)

In 2004, the U.S. Department of Health and Human Services unveiled a 10-year plan to create a nationwide network with electronic medical records for all Americans where doctors can access all of a patient's records with a few clicks of the mouse. At the same time, Kaiser Permanente, the largest nonprofit health plan in the United States that serves more than 8 million members began automating the medical records of all its plan participants. The nationwide group set up its automated system to

- eliminate the inefficiencies and errors often found in traditional paper medical records.
- provide immediate access to complete, up-to-the-minute information on tests, medicines, etc.
- allow patient members to schedule appointments conveniently, request medication refills, and ask for referrals.

Consumers, however, remain leery of the prospect of their medical records being available to the prying eyes of hackers and computer savvy medical office personnel. A 2005 national survey by Massachusetts-based Forrester Research found that consumers, while aware of the enhancements available with electronic records, still worry about the misuse of information and do not know their rights concerning their records.

For more information on Kaiser Permanente, visit the company's media relations website at http://newsmedia.kaiserpermanente.org/. For additional information on electronic medical records in general and on privacy issues specifically, read the following articles:

Kornblum, J. (2008, June 12). Online medical records offer convenience, may limit privacy. *USA Today*. Available at www.usatoday.com/news/health/2008-06-11-online-medical-records_N.htm

Consumers Union of U.S., Inc. (2006, March). The new threat to your medical privacy. *Consumer Reports, 71*(3), 39–42. Available from LexisNexis Academic database.

Required:

1. Based on your reading, analyze what Kaiser Permanente could have done differently in rolling out its automated records system. Post your comments to a class discussion board or give a short presentation to the class as directed by your instructor.
2. As corporate communication specialist for Kaisar Permanente, compose a message that can be posted to the company website that explains the privacy policy associated with the automated system and the measures the company takes to ensure that consumer privacy is protected.

READ | THINK | WRITE | SPEAK | COLLABORATE

6. Assessing the Effectiveness of Web Communication (Obj. 2)

Read the enrichment content, "Developing a Web Page" at your companion website, www.cengage.com/bcomm/lehman. Visit the *Web Pages that Suck* website, designed to help you "learn good web design by looking at bad web design," at www.webpagesthatsuck.com.

Required:

1. Study the suggestions offered on the site and examine the poor websites that are linked. Using your analysis and the information in the chapter, develop a checklist of factors that contribute to a successful web page and design a form that could be used for evaluation of sites.
2. Select five organizations' websites to examine, or visit sites selected by your instructor. Select all five of your organizations from *one* of the following categories: service organizations, retail operations, educational institutions, manufacturing companies, or recreational entities. Using the evaluation form, critique each of the selected sites, placing them in rank order of effectiveness. Use a computer projection system to demonstrate the best site to the class, explaining its exemplary features.

7. Ensuring Accessibility to the Web (Obj. 2)

For a website to be a truly universal communication medium, it must be able to reach all audiences, including those with disabilities. Locate the following article that discusses strategies for making web information accessible to those who cannot access information in various ways:

Tierney, J. (2007, April). Ignore universal web design at your own peril. *Multichannel Merchant,* p. 8. Available at http://multichannelmerchant.com/ecommerce/ignore_universal_web/

Required: Visit a corporate website of your choice. Evaluate the accessibility of information on that site by viewers who are physically challenged. Assuming that you are an employee of that organization, send an email message to your instructor with recommendations for making the information in the site more accessible.

READ | THINK | WRITE | SPEAK | COLLABORATE

8. Enhancing Telephone Etiquette (Obj. 3)

In today's world, most initial contact with a person is via the telephone, so those important first impressions are dependent on practicing proper telephone etiquette. Visit your companion website at www.cengage.com/bcomm/lehman to explore strategies for increasing levels of telephone courtesy as an image and trust builder.

Required: Prepare a brief presentation providing suggestions for placing calls, answering calls, and taking telephone messages.

9. Coping with Email Addiction (Obj. 1-2)

A growing number of employers are imposing "no email" Fridays or weekends as a means of addressing a phenomenon being called "email addiction" and "crack berry addiction." While bans typically halt only the routine internal email and not client communication or responses to urgent matters, many companies have faced rebellion of their employees.

Required: Access a campus library database and read two or more articles to learn more about "no email" policies and the rationale for implementation. After completing your research, make a short presentation to the class including the value of such policies and suggestions to companies considering the implementation of a no-email policy that you believe will increase employee acceptance.

10. Electronic Communication Usage Policy (Objs. 1, 4)

As with other electronic communication channels, technology often advances faster than the organization's ability to develop adequate procedures for using it. Using your group members' work experience and information obtained from an online search, develop a company policy that applies to acceptable use of email, instant messaging, text messaging, wikis, and weblogs. Address such issues as message security, company monitoring of messages, appropriate message content, etc. Provide a detailed explanation of acceptable electronic messaging usage that employees can follow consistently.

Required: Send your policy as an attachment to an email message to your instructor; or, if directed, bring a copy of the policy to class for discussion.

11. Etiquette Assessment (Obj. 3)

In small groups, discuss incidents of inappropriate cell phone behavior you have experienced in a school, work, or public setting. Explain how each incident affected the individuals involved. Discuss etiquette rules you believe are critical for courteous, productive cell phone use. Are some netiquette rules appropriate for business calls but not for personal calls or vice versa?

Required: Prepare a brief presentation on the Dos and Don'ts of Cell Phone Usage. If directed by your instructor, prepare a cell phone policy appropriate for the workplace.

CASES

© AP IMAGES

1. Podcasting to Employees: Kraft Re-invents the Nutrition Wheel

As society becomes more weight-conscious and more concerned about obesity in children, food manufacturers are experimenting with new products that offer fewer calories, lower fat content, and less sodium while still maintaining good taste. In response to this obesity crisis, Kraft Foods has committed to reducing portion size, developing healthier products, and changing the products it markets to children. According to the corporate website, Kraft's goal is "to offer a broad range of product choices across the many different types of food we sell." In response to criticism of the company's products and marketing policies, Kraft developed new product labels and smaller portions, healthier versions of current products, and new products to meet the demand for health-conscious convenience foods. Health-related initiatives include:

- **The Sensible Solution program**—a marketing tool in product packaging to point out "better-for-you" nutrition criteria.
- **Healthy Living Principles**—information on the company's website designed to express Kraft's beliefs about nutrition and fitness and their role in a healthy lifestyle.
- **South Beach Diet products**—products designed to meet the new diet craze's criteria for healthy food, balancing the right carbs, the right fats, and lean sources of protein.
- **More nutritious Lunchables for kids**—new products and revamped classics (41 products total) that have cut calories by 10 percent, fat by 24 percent, and sodium by 20 percent.

For more information about Kraft's new products and programs, visit the company's website www.kraft.com or read these articles:

Voight, J. (2007, August 7). Fit to be tried. Adweek, 48(29), 22. Available from Business Source Complete database.

Thompson, S. (2005.) Kraft query: Is good for kids °bad for business? Cuts calories on some Lunchables, but critics say it hasn't gone far enough. Advertising Age, 76(38), 4. Available from Business Source Complete database

Required. In groups of three, respond to this communication as directed by your instructor.

1. As employee management director for Kraft Foods, Inc., you have received more than 100 requests from Kraft employees requesting information about Kraft's new Healthy Living Principles and an overview of products the company plans to launch to fight the obesity crisis. You've arranged a 15-minute interview with Kraft CEO Roger Deromedi and vice president for global technology Charles W. Davis so that they can highlight the new programs and products for employees. The interview will be available as a podcast via the Kraft employee intranet. Compose interview questions and answers to make up this 15-minute podcast.
2. Record the podcast, with each group member assuming the role of one of the three Kraft employees outlined in Requirement 1.
3. With the podcast information, complete a 500-word article for the front page of your company newsletter. Have one person design the front page of the newsletter (including the article and photos), one person write the article, and one person take three creative photos to use with the article.

© BBC LTD./COURTESY: EVERETT COLLECTION

2. Video Case: The Office: The Office and Email: Are Sexy Emails Funny or Offensive?

In this clip, David discovers an email message that includes a risqué picture of himself.

Complete the following activities as directed by your instructor after the class has viewed the video:

1. Does email have ethical and legal ramifications for the sender, the receiver, and the company? What might those be in this situation?
2. In small groups, discuss the manner in which David handles the issue of a sexually explicit email message. How could he have handled the interaction differently?
3. As David, a supervisor, compose an email to all employees outlining the company's policies for email and Internet use in the workplace. Your discussion of the policy should focus on personal use of the Internet while at work; email use for forwarding jokes, rumors, etc.; personal email usage on company time; and email use for specific types of work-related projects.

3. Using the Internet to Bridge the Cultural Gap

The Internet has the potential to help people of the world understand each other and view citizens of other cultures as real individuals living similar lives, while in different ways. Exploring the cultures of the world via the Internet is one step toward tolerance and acceptance of all people, regardless of race, ethnicity, religion, or national heritage.

Additionally, the Internet is a one-stop reference for information about a country you may visit for business or pleasure. A helpful site is the Central Intelligence Agency's online World Factbook, which contains vast information on every country in the world, as collected by the agency. Chat sites, such as the Yahoo! Culture Site, provide less formal cultural information. When planning travel outside the country, you might want to consult the U.S. State Department site's area for "Crisis Abroad." The site also includes the latest travel warnings, consular information, entry requirements, crime information, and embassy locations for the country you will visit.

If you need to know at least a little of the language of the culture you plan to visit, be sure to check the Foreign Language for Travelers site. Here you can select from among more than 80 different languages for translating. The site not only displays the words, but actually recites them for you via short audio files. And of course you will want to know what your U.S. dollars will convert to in your visited country. The Currency Converter site lets you input the number of dollars and obtain the exchanged amount for another currency.

Armed with accurate information about a given country, you are able to understand and appreciate cultural variety. As globalization of business results in a world that grows progressively smaller, it becomes imperative for professionals to possess broad-based cultural awareness.

Visit your companion website, www.cengage.com/bcomm/lehman, to link to web resources related to this topic. As directed by your instructor, respond to one or more of the following:

1. Select a country for study. Collect the following information from the web resources: the country's location and size, official language(s), religion(s), customs, currency, major products, and crime statistics. Learn three phrases in the predominant language of the country. Share your information in a short oral report.
2. Locate other websites that provide information about your selected country. Prepare a list of dos and don'ts for the traveler visiting that country.
3. Prepare a one-page essay that uses the metaphor of a bridge to describe the role of the Internet in linking cultures.

Chapter 6
Delivering Good- and Neutral-News Messages

*"Customer service isn't just a department—
it is the entire company."*
CEO Tony Hsieh

Objectives When you have completed Chapter 6, you will be able to:

1. Describe the deductive outline for good and neutral news and its adaptations for specific situations and for international audiences.
2. Prepare messages that convey good news, including thank-you and appreciation messages.
3. Write messages presenting routine claims and requests and favorable responses to them.
4. Write messages acknowledging customer orders, providing credit information, and extending credit.
5. Prepare procedural messages that ensure clear and consistent application.

SHOWCASE PART 1

Zappos: Customer Service at the Heart of Attitudes and Actions

"You just can't get decent service these days. Companies don't care about their customers." Such cynical observations are widely held today because far too many companies do, in fact, treat customers as though they were an afterthought. This is not the case, however, at Zappos.

The name is loosely derived from *zapatos*, the Spanish word for shoes. The company began in 1999 as the brainchild of Nick Swinmurn whose vision was to create a website offering the best selection in shoes in terms of brands, styles, colors, sizes, and widths. The Las Vegas company has doubled its sales every year since and now boasts one fifth of the $3 billion online footwear market. While shoes are Zappos' foundation, the company is regularly expanding their product line, which now includes clothing, handbags, and accessories.

Superior customer service has been a major reason for Zappos' amazing success. While the company was not the first dot.com business to offer free shipping, CEO Tony Hsieh's idea was to also offer free return shipping. Customers wishing to make a return are given a link to print out a prepaid return shipping label. The free shipping policy is a long-term retention strategy that seems to be working; on a given day, 75 percent of Zappos shoppers are repeat customers.[1]

The Zappos website is simple and clean. Keeping the site relatively stripped down has made it extremely fast, even for dial-up customers. The company's toll-free number is displayed prominently on every page of their website, which also displays in various places that shipping is free. The Zappos website also allows customers to search by shoe size, style, or brand.

To assure a speedy delivery after purchase, Zappos warehouses everything it sells and will not make an item available on its website unless it is physically present in the warehouse. Zappos knows that simply stocking a full line of products does not assure customer satisfaction; it's the service that builds customer loyalty.

Every new employee is required to undergo four weeks of Customer Loyalty training before starting work in any department. "Customer service isn't just a department—it is the entire company," according to the Zappos website.[2] The company's customer service philosophy appears to be paying off; in a recent customer service survey conducted by the National Retail Federation, Zappos beat out competitors Amazon, Land's End, and Nordstrom for customer satisfaction.[3]

Perhaps you will want to pass the Zappos success story along whenever you hear someone say "You can't get decent service these days. Companies don't care about their customers." Skillfully communicating good news and neutral information to customers is one way to express appreciation and demonstrate a service attitude. Effective communication—whether directed to customers, employees, or business partners—reaches the intended audience, is organized to achieve the desired effect, and demonstrates an impeccable command of the language.

www.zappos.com

SEE SHOWCASE PART 2, ON PAGE 197, FOR SPOTLIGHT COMMUNICATOR TONY HSIEH, CEO OF ZAPPOS.

Deductive Organizational Pattern

You can organize business messages either deductively or inductively depending on your prediction of the receiver's reaction to your main idea. Learning to organize business messages according to the appropriate outline will improve your chances of preparing a document that elicits the response or action you desire.

In this chapter, you will learn to compose messages that convey ideas that a receiver likely will find either *pleasing* or *neutral*. Messages that convey pleasant information are referred to as ***good-news messages***. Messages that are of interest to the receiver but are not likely to generate an emotional reaction are referred to as ***neutral*** messages. The strategies discussed for structuring good-news and neutral-news messages generally can be applied to North American audiences. Because message expectations and social conventions differ from culture to culture, the effective writer will adapt as necessary when writing for various audiences. Refer to the Strategic Forces feature "Basic Cultural Values Influence Communication Styles" that discusses international message adaptations.

People in organizations use a number of channels to communicate with internal and external audiences. When sending a message that is positive or neutral, you have numerous choices, as shown in Figure 6-1. Depending on the message, the recipient, and constraints of time and location, the best channel might be spoken or electronic. In addition to the electronic and verbal tools presented in Chapter 5 (email, instant messaging, web communications, and phone), companies also use written documents such as memorandums and letters to communicate information.

The principles for preparing memorandums (commonly referred to as *memos*) are similar to those you've already applied when composing email messages as both are chan-

Adapting Culture to Culture. The Internet provides a wealth of up-to-date information about the world's cultures. A businessperson going abroad would benefit from the World Factbook, a helpful site provided by the Central Intelligence Agency: https://www.cia.gov/library/publications/the-world-factbook/. Clicking on a country displays a map and links to important topics such as people, geography, government, transnational issues, and more. Knowledge of a particular culture aids in adapting a message to meet the expectations and social conventions of that culture. To ensure clarity, many companies require that a professional staff member proficient in both English and the particular foreign language review correspondence sent to an international recipient.

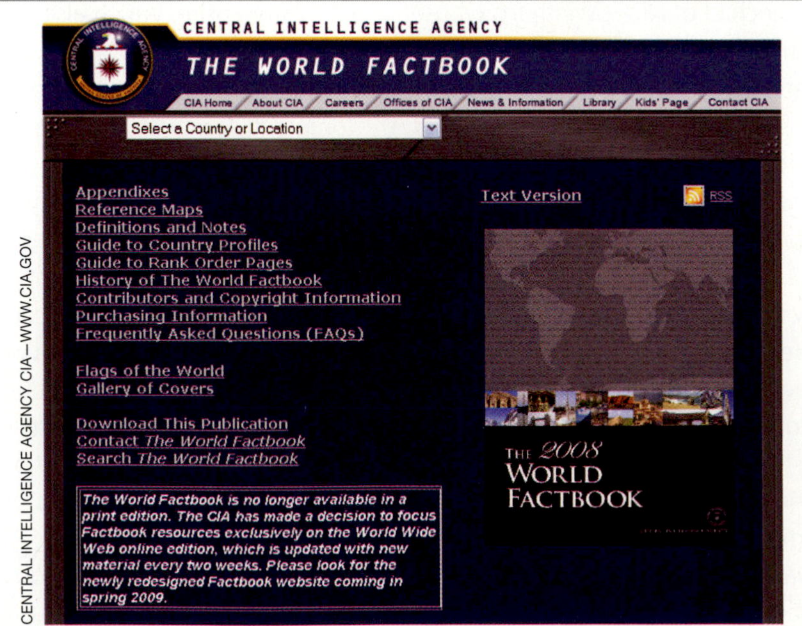

CENTRAL INTELLIGENCE AGENCY CIA—WWW.CIA.GOV

FIGURE 6-1

Direct Outline Used in Good- and Neutral News Messages Sent in Written, Electronic, or Spoken Form

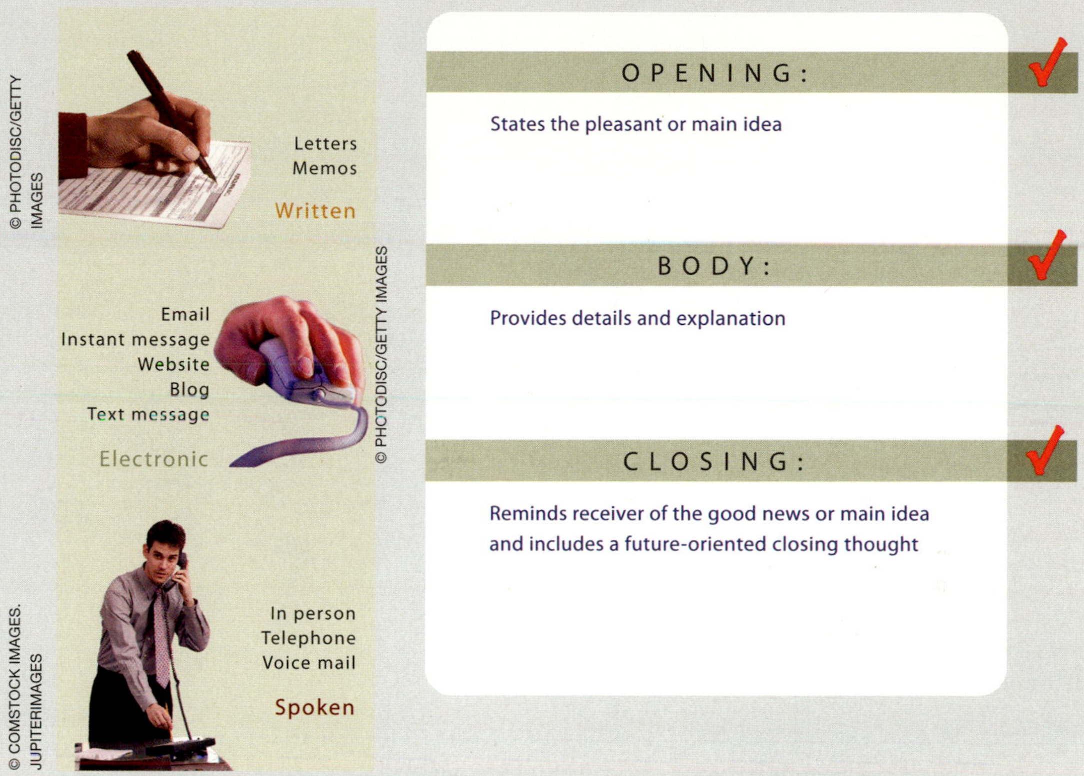

Letters
Memos
Written

Email
Instant message
Website
Blog
Text message
Electronic

In person
Telephone
Voice mail
Spoken

OPENING:
States the pleasant or main idea

BODY:
Provides details and explanation

CLOSING:
Reminds receiver of the good news or main idea and includes a future-oriented closing thought

nels for sharing information of a somewhat informal nature. Memos provide a tangible means of sharing information with people inside an organization. Letters are more formal, because they are used to convey information to external audiences such as customers, clients, business partners, or suppliers. Regardless of whether the audience is an internal or external one, communication should be carefully structured to achieve the desired purpose.

What other words can be substituted for deductive and inductive?

Good-news or neutral messages follow a ***deductive*** or ***direct sequence***—the message begins with the main idea. To present good news and neutral information deductively, begin with the major idea, followed by supporting details as depicted in Figure 6-1. In both outlines, the third point (closing thought) may be omitted without seriously impairing effectiveness; however, including it unifies the message and avoids abruptness.

The deductive pattern has several advantages:

- The first sentence is easy to write. After it is written, the details follow easily.
- The first sentence gets the attention it deserves in this emphatic position.
- Encountering good news in the first sentence puts receivers in a pleasant frame of mind, and they are receptive to the details that follow.
- The arrangement may save receivers some time. Once they understand the important idea, they can move rapidly through the supporting details.

Will all deductive messages have at least three paragraphs? Explain.

DIVERSITY CHALLENGES

STRATEGIC FORCES

Basic Cultural Values Influence Communication Styles

Message patterns vary from culture to culture and are largely the product of the values held by each society. Differences in societal values influence social behavior, etiquette, communication styles, and business transactions. U.S. businesspeople are typically aware of basic differences in the business behaviors and practices of popular trade partners, but they may fail to recognize and understand the underlying values that shape behavior. For instance, values accepted in Japanese culture that differ from those held in U.S. culture include the following:

- U.S. corporations value independence in the workplace, whereas Japanese corporations value dependence.
- U.S. corporations value honesty in business practices; if someone says he or she can do something, it means just that. Japanese corporations, on the other hand, value "saving face," and to admit they can't produce what you are asking for is an embarrassment. The Japanese would sooner tell you they can do something while knowing they cannot than bear the shame of admitting they can't do it.[4]
- The Japanese value building business partnerships for life, whereas Americans often focus on short-term transactions. The Japanese prefer to develop a business relationship through a business courtship—typically beginning the alliance by placing a small trial order, to see "how things go." If the customer is satisfied, more orders follow and continue to grow with the relationship.[5]
- In negotiating situations, the Japanese are likely more comfortable when in the buyer position than the seller position, since buyers have higher status than do sellers in the Japanese culture.
- The fact that Japanese businesspeople tend to make decisions much more slowly than their U.S. counterparts has at least two explanations that stem from culture. Time is valued differently in Japan than in the United States; and group decisions, which are not known for their expediency, are valued over individual decisions that can be made more quickly.

Understanding such value differences can aid in understanding variations in message patterns. When writing for intercultural audiences, keep these suggestions in mind:

- *Write naturally but avoid abbreviations, slang, acronyms, technical jargon, sports and military analogies, and other devices.* Such expressions help clarify an idea and personalize messages; however, they may be confusing to those unfamiliar with North American usage. Those speaking English as a second language learned it from a textbook; therefore, they may have difficulty understanding "ASAP" (as soon as possible) or "OTC" (over the counter). They may be mystified when you reject bid proposals that are "below par," instruct employees to "drill down" for better results, and refer to problems as "pain points" and the main point of a presentation as a "take away."
- *Avoid words that trigger emotional responses such as anger, fear, or suspicion.* Such words are often referred to as *red flag* words because they elicit the same response as a red flag waved in front of a raging bull. Using *hot buttons*—terms that make political judgments, show condescension, or make cultural judgments, for example—is a sure way to shut a reader's mind to your message.
- *Use simple terms but attempt to be specific as well.* Some of the simplest words must be interpreted

within the context of each situation in which they are used (e.g., *fast* has several meanings). Likewise, avoid the use of superlatives such as *fantastic* and *terrific* because they may be misinterpreted as overly dramatic or insincere. Also avoid overly formal and difficult words and expressions that may be confusing or considered pompous; for example, *pursuant to your request*, *ostentatious*, or *nebulous*.

- *Consider the subtle differences in the ways specific cultures organize messages.* Asians, for example, typically use indirect patterns of writing, even when writing about good news; they avoid negative messages or camouflage them so expertly that the reader might not recognize them. On the other hand, Germans tend to be more direct than North Americans, even with bad news.
- *Use graphics, visual aids, and forms whenever possible because they simplify the message.* When language barriers can be minimized through visual means, the opportunity for confusion is reduced.
- *Use figures for expressing numbers to avoid confusion with an international audience.* Be aware, however, of differences in the way numbers and dates are written. As a general rule, use figures for numbers, and keep in mind that most people in the world use the metric system. Note the following examples:

United States	***Other Countries***
$2,400.00	2400,00
January 29, 2011	29 January 2011

- *Write out the name of the month in international correspondence to avoid misunderstandings.* When using a number to represent the month, many countries state the day before the month as shown in the following examples:

United States	Other Countries
2/10/11	10.2 2011 or 10.2.11
March 26, 2011	26th of March 2011

- Become familiar with the traditional format of letters in the country of the person to whom you are writing and adapt your format as much as possible. Note differences in the formality of the salutation and complimentary close. The Germans, who prefer a formal salutation such as "Very Honored Mr. Professor Whelan," might be offended by your choice of an informal "Dear Jason," a salutation you believed was appropriate because you had met and done prior business with Professor Whelan. You will also want to check the position of various letter parts such as the letter address and the writer's name and title. For example, in German letters the company name follows the complimentary close and the typed signature block is omitted, leaving the reader responsible for deciphering the writer's signature.[6]

Application

While the Japanese tend to write in a more indirect manner, even when conveying good news, Germans tend to prefer the direct message pattern for both positive and negative messages. Research the German culture to determine value differences that might account for the directness in communication. Write a one-page summary of your explanation.

As you study sample deductive messages in this chapter, note the *ineffective example* notation that clearly marks the examples of poor writing. Detailed comments highlight important writing strategies that have been applied or violated. While gaining experience in developing effective messages, you will also learn to recognize standard business formats. Fully formatted messages are shown as printed documents (letters on company letterhead or paper memos) or as electronic formats (email messages or online input screens). Details about formatting letters, memos, and email messages are included in Appendix A.

Your Turn 6-1
Career Portfolio

The ability to deliver effective messages and help others do so will likely be necessary skills to your career ladder climb. As a manager in your career field, you have the responsibility of helping your staff improve their customer/client relations.

TAKE ACTION:

Referring to Appendix A for proper memo format, prepare a memo to the staff that summarizes when to use a deductive (direct) approach and when to use an inductive (indirect) approach. Include examples of situations that would fit each pattern.

Good-News Messages

Messages delivering good news are organized using a direct approach as illustrated in Figure 6-1. For illustration, you'll study examples of messages that convey positive news as well as thank-you and appreciation messages that generate goodwill.

Positive News

The memo sent to all employees in Figure 6-2 begins directly with the main idea, the approval of a business casual dress policy. The discussion that follows includes a brief review of the policy and ends positively by encouraging employees to seek additional information from the company website or contact the writer.

Thank-You and Appreciation Messages

What other ways can businesspeople build lasting relationships with customers or clients?

Empathetic managers take advantage of occasions to write goodwill messages that build strong, lasting relationships among employees, clients, customers, and various other groups. People usually are not reluctant to say, "Thank you," "What a great performance," "You have certainly helped me," and so on. Despite good intentions, however, often people don't get around to sending thank you messages and appreciations. Because of their rarity, written appreciation messages are especially meaningful—even treasured.

Thank-You Messages

After receiving a gift, being a guest, attending an interview, or benefiting in various other ways, a thoughtful person will take the time to send a written thank-you message. A simple handwritten or electronically sent note is sufficient for some social situations. However, when written from a professional office to respond to a business situation, the message may be printed on company letterhead. Your message should be written deductively and reflect your sincere feelings of gratitude. The following thank-you messages (a) identify the circumstances for which the writer is grateful and (b) provide specific reasons the action is appreciated.

FIGURE 6-2

Good Example of a Good-News Message

INTEROFFICE MEMORANDUM

TO: All Employees
FROM: Gloria Martinello, Human Resources Manager *GM*
DATE: May 15, 2011
SUBJECT: Casual Dress Policy Takes Effect July 1

Starts with main idea—announcement of new policy.

A casual dress policy has been approved for First National Bank and will be effective July 1. As most of us agree, casual attire in the banking industry generally means "dressy casual," since virtually all of us interact with our clientele regularly throughout the day.

Provides clear explanation to ensure policy is understood. Formats as table for quick, easy reference to specific details.

To maintain our traditional professional image while enjoying more relaxed attire, please follow these guidelines:

Men	Women
Sport or polo shirt, with collars	Pant suit
Khakis or corduroys	Sweater or blouse with pants or skirt
Loafers with socks	Loafers with socks
	Low heels with hosiery

Continues with additional discussion of policy.

Tennis shoes, open-toed shoes, sandals, jogging suits, shorts, jeans, sweatpants, and sweatshirts are inappropriate. Formal business attire should be worn when meeting with clients outside the office.

Encourages readers to ask questions or view additional information on company intranet.

Please visit the HR website for the complete casual attire policy and illustrations of appropriate casual attire. If you have questions as you begin making changes in your wardrobe, please call me at ext. 59.

Format Pointers

- Uses template with standard memo headings for efficient production. Review other formatting guidelines in Figure A-4 in Appendix A.
- Includes writer's initials after printed name and title.

TO EXPRESS THANKS FOR A GIFT

After conducting your strategic planning seminar, I was pleasantly surprised to receive a certificate to your online music site. Downloading music added some "jazz" to my day while giving me more insight into your business model. Thanks for your kindness and for this useful gift.

TO EXTEND THANKS FOR HOSPITALITY

Matthew and I thoroughly enjoyed the weekend excursion you hosted at Lake Jaspar for our work team. Since we moved here from Destin, sailing has become a rare pleasure. You were kind to invite us. Thanks for a delightful time.

Appreciation Messages

You will write appreciation messages to recognize, reward, and encourage the receiver; however, you will also gain happiness from commending a deserving person. Such positive thinking can be a favorable influence on your own attitude and performance. In appropriate situations you may wish to address an appreciation message to an individual's supervisor and send a copy of the document to the individual to share the positive comments. In any case, an appreciation message should be sent to commend deserving people and not for possible self-gain.

For full potential value, follow these guidelines for appreciation messages:

How effective is email for sending appreciation messages?

- **Send in a timely manner.** Sending an appreciation message within a few days of the circumstance will emphasize your genuineness. The receiver may question the sincerity of appreciation messages that are sent long overdue.
- **Avoid exaggerated language that is hardly believable.** You may believe the exaggerated statements to be true, but the recipient may find them unbelievable and insincere. Strong language with unsupported statements raises questions about your motive for the message.
- **Make specific comments about outstanding qualities or performance.** The following cold, mechanical message may have only minimal value to a speaker who has worked hard and has not been paid. While the sender cared enough to say thank you, the message could have been given to any speaker, even if the sender had slept through the entire speech. Similarly, a note merely closed with *sincerely* does not necessarily make the ideas seem sincere. Including specific remarks about understanding and applying the speaker's main points makes the message meaningful and sincere.

Original: Your speech to the Lincoln Jaycees was very much appreciated. You are an excellent speaker, and you have good ideas. Thank you.

Improved: This past week I have found myself applying the principles you discussed last week at your presentation to the Lincoln Jaycees.

When I completed the time analysis you suggested, I easily identified a number of areas for better management. Taking time to prioritize my daily tasks will be a challenge, but I now see its importance for accomplishing critical goals. Thank you for an informative and useful presentation.

The appreciation in Figure 6-3 sent from a manager to the facilitator of a ropes course that employees recently completed conveys a warmer, more sincere compliment than a generic, exaggerated message. The net effects of this message are positive: The sender feels good for having passed on a deserved compliment and the facilitator is encouraged by the client's satisfaction with her team development program.

FIGURE 6-3

Good Example of an Appreciation Message

To:	Ren Nagano <rnagano@ch.com>
From:	Nolan Sherrod <nsherrod@gemco.com
Subject:	Appreciation for Outstanding Work

Ren,

Completing the ropes course at Camp Horizon was a memorable and life-changing experience for every member of our office staff.

Extends appreciation for company's providing quality opportunities for team growth.

Your facilitators were masterful in allowing our teams to take risks while ensuring their safety. The course provided a diverse series of activities that enabled each staff member to participate, regardless of our physical limitations. Identifying the real leaders in our office was extremely interesting.

Provides specific examples without exaggerating or using overly strong language or insincere statements.

In the words of one colleague, "The ropes course has shown me I can do more than I have come to expect of myself." Thank you for helping us see our potential.

Assures reader of tangible benefits gained.

Best wishes,

Nolan Sherrod

Nolan Sherrod
Human Resources Director
Gemco, Inc.
901-555-1616, Fax 901-555-1302
nsherrod@gemco.com

Format Pointers

- Uses short lines, mixed case; omits special formatting such as emoticons and email abbreviations for improved readability.
- Includes .sig file for complete reference; reflects other format considerations covered in Appendix A.

An apology is written much like an appreciation message. A sincere written apology is needed to preserve relationships when regrettable situations occur. While often difficult to prepare, the recipient will usually respond favorably to a well-written apology. Visit your companion website at www.cengage.com/bcomm/lehman for tips for handling apologies.

© RICHARD B. LEVINE/NEWSCOM

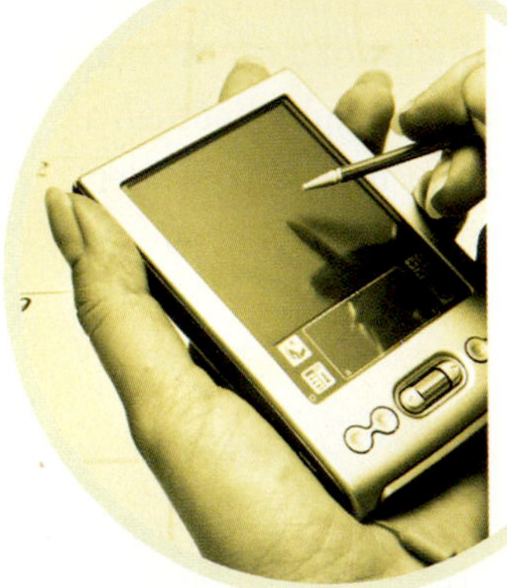

Your Turn 6-2
You're the Professional

You are the administrator of a public health facility that has recently undergone its reaccreditation process. This work involved preparing an extensive written report documenting your activities and accomplishments as well as a two-day visit from accreditation inspectors. Today you received a letter stating that your organization has been successful in receiving reaccreditation from its governing body. You appreciate all the hard work from your staff and want to express that to them.

TAKE ACTION:

How will you announce the good news and express thanks? Explain your choice.

a. Call a meeting for all staff members at 8 tomorrow morning.

b. Send an email immediately to all staff.

c. Prepare a memo for distribution to all staff members.

d. Post an announcement to the company intranet.

Routine Claims

A *claim* is a request for an adjustment. When business communicators ask for something to which they think they are entitled (such as a refund, replacement, exchange, or payment for damages), the message is called a *claim message*.

Claim Message

What situations have you encountered that would be classified as routine claims? What distinguished them from persuasive claims?

Requests for adjustments can be divided into two groups: ***routine claims*** and ***persuasive claims***. Persuasive claims, which are discussed in Chapter 8, assume that a request will be granted only after explanations and persuasive arguments have been presented. Routine claims (possibly because of guarantees, warranties, or other contractual conditions) assume that a request will be granted quickly and willingly, without persuasion. Because you expect routine claims to be granted willingly, a forceful, accusatory tone is inappropriate.

When the claim is routine, the direct approach shown in Figure 6-1 is appropriate. Let's consider the situation referred to in Figures 6-4 and 6-5. Surely the software company intended the new release to be free of bugs. Because the existence of the bugs

FIGURE 6-4

Poor Example of a Routine Claim

Reader Response

Reader Response	
	Ms. Sansing,
Yes, we know about your purchase. So, what's the problem?	Our company recently purchased the upgrade of your Audit Partner 7.0 software. We have used the 6.2 release in the past and were interested in the new features promoted in your advertisements. Unfortunately, your new software version does not work.
Oh, really?	When our computer technology advisory group tested the new version, we discovered several bugs, especially in the reporting modules. The attached logs and error messages prove, and your technical support staff agree, that these problems were caused by the software.
Why so hostile?	We are not willing to distribute the upgrade to our audit staff unless these errors are corrected.
We want to do things right, but you could be a bit nicer about the whole situation. . . .	Please modify the program or refund our money.

appears to be obvious, the software company can be expected to correct the problem without persuasion. Thus, the technology specialist can ask for the adjustment *before* providing an explanation, as shown in Figure 6-5. Beginning with the request for an adjustment gives it the emphasis it deserves. Note, however, that the message in Figure 6-4 is written inappropriately using an indirect approach—the details are presented before the main idea, and the tone is unnecessarily forceful.

SHOWCASE PART 2  

Customer Relations Key to Success

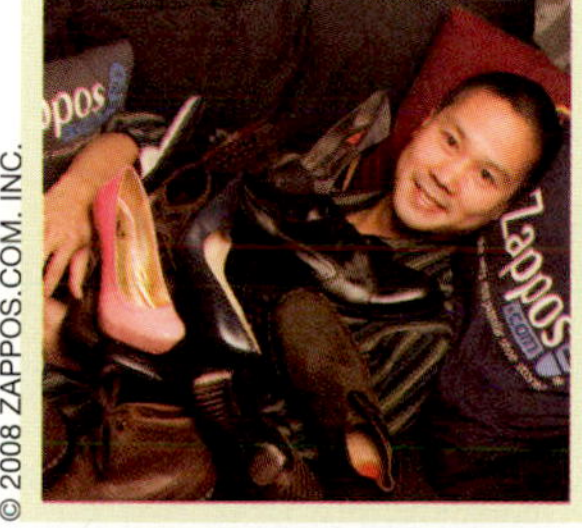

SPOTLIGHT COMMUNICATOR: TONY HSIEH, CEO, ZAPPOS

"Powered by service"—that's Zappos CEO Tony Hsieh's philosophy for leading the remarkably successful company in its second decade of existence. Hsieh says Zappos' goal with every interaction is for the customer to walk away saying "Wow, that was the best experience I ever had." It's why the company provides free shipping and free return shipping and offers a 365-day return policy. At Zappos, it's okay if an employee spends an hour on the phone with a customer that does not result in a sale. The bottom line is that the company went above and beyond for the customer. Visit your companion website, **www.cengage.com/bcomm/lehman,** to learn more about Tony Hsieh's corporate vision and customer-centered leadership style.

www.zappos.com

REFER TO SHOWCASE PART 3, ON PAGE 214
TO LEARN HOW ZAPPOS USES ITS WEBSITE TO SIMPLIFY THE HANDLING OF ROUTINE CLAIMS.

FIGURE 6-5

Good Example of a Routine Claim

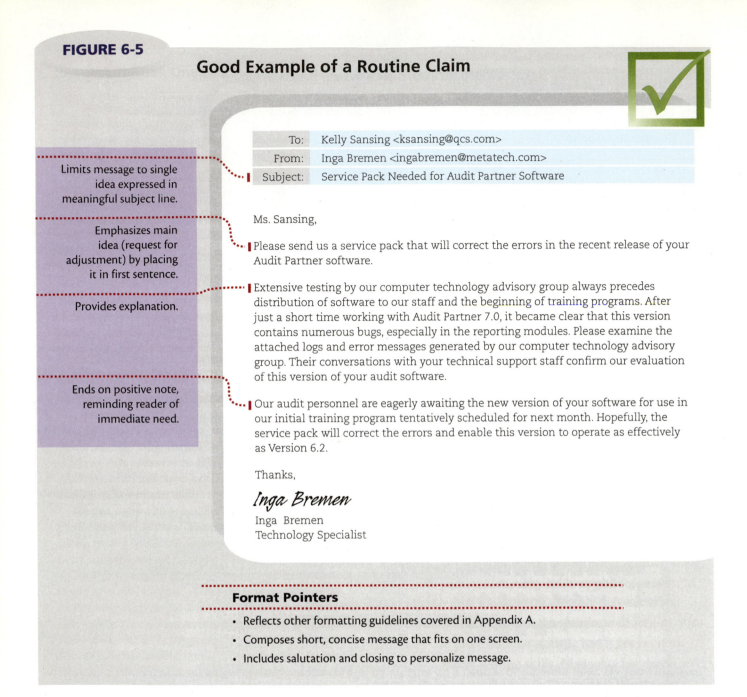

To:	Kelly Sansing <ksansing@qcs.com>
From:	Inga Bremen <ingabremen@metatech.com>
Subject:	Service Pack Needed for Audit Partner Software

Limits message to single idea expressed in meaningful subject line.

Ms. Sansing,

Emphasizes main idea (request for adjustment) by placing it in first sentence.

Please send us a service pack that will correct the errors in the recent release of your Audit Partner software.

Provides explanation.

Extensive testing by our computer technology advisory group always precedes distribution of software to our staff and the beginning of training programs. After just a short time working with Audit Partner 7.0, it became clear that this version contains numerous bugs, especially in the reporting modules. Please examine the attached logs and error messages generated by our computer technology advisory group. Their conversations with your technical support staff confirm our evaluation of this version of your audit software.

Ends on positive note, reminding reader of immediate need.

Our audit personnel are eagerly awaiting the new version of your software for use in our initial training program tentatively scheduled for next month. Hopefully, the service pack will correct the errors and enable this version to operate as effectively as Version 6.2.

Thanks,

Inga Bremen

Inga Bremen
Technology Specialist

Format Pointers

- Reflects other formatting guidelines covered in Appendix A.
- Composes short, concise message that fits on one screen.
- Includes salutation and closing to personalize message.

Favorable Response to a Claim Message

Businesses *want* their customers to communicate when merchandise or service is not satisfactory. They want to learn of ways in which goods and services can be improved, and they want their customers to receive value for the money they spend. With considerable confidence, they can assume that writers of claim messages think their claims are valid. By responding fairly to legitimate requests in **adjustment messages**, businesses can gain a reputation for standing behind their goods and services. A loyal customer is likely to become even more loyal after a business has demonstrated its integrity.

Ordinarily, a response to a written message is also a written message. Sometimes people communicate to confirm ideas they have already discussed on the phone. When the response to a claim is favorable, present ideas in the direct sequence. Although the word *grant* is acceptable when talking about claims, its use in adjustment messages is discouraged. An expression such as "Your claim is being granted" unnecessarily implies that you are in a position of power.

What is meant by resale and sales promotional material? How are they different from sales messages?

Because the subject of an adjustment is related to the goods or services provided, the message can include a brief sales idea. With only a little extra space, the message can include resale or sales promotional material. ***Resale*** refers to a discussion of goods or services already bought. It reminds customers and clients that they made a good choice in selecting a company with which to do business, or it reminds them of the good qualities of their purchase. ***Sales promotional material*** refers to statements made about related merchandise or service. For example, a message about a company's recently purchased office furniture might also mention available office equipment. Mentioning the office equipment is using sales promotional material. Subtle sales messages that are included in adjustments have a good chance of being read, while direct sales messages may not be read at all.

Consider the ineffective response in Figure 6-6 to Inga Bremen's claim letter and the message it sends about the company's commitment. Now notice the deductive outline and the explanation in the revision in Figure 6-7. Because the writer knows that Inga will be pleased the service pack will be sent with only a brief delay, the good news appears in the first sentence. The details and closing sentence follow naturally and show a desire to correct the problem.

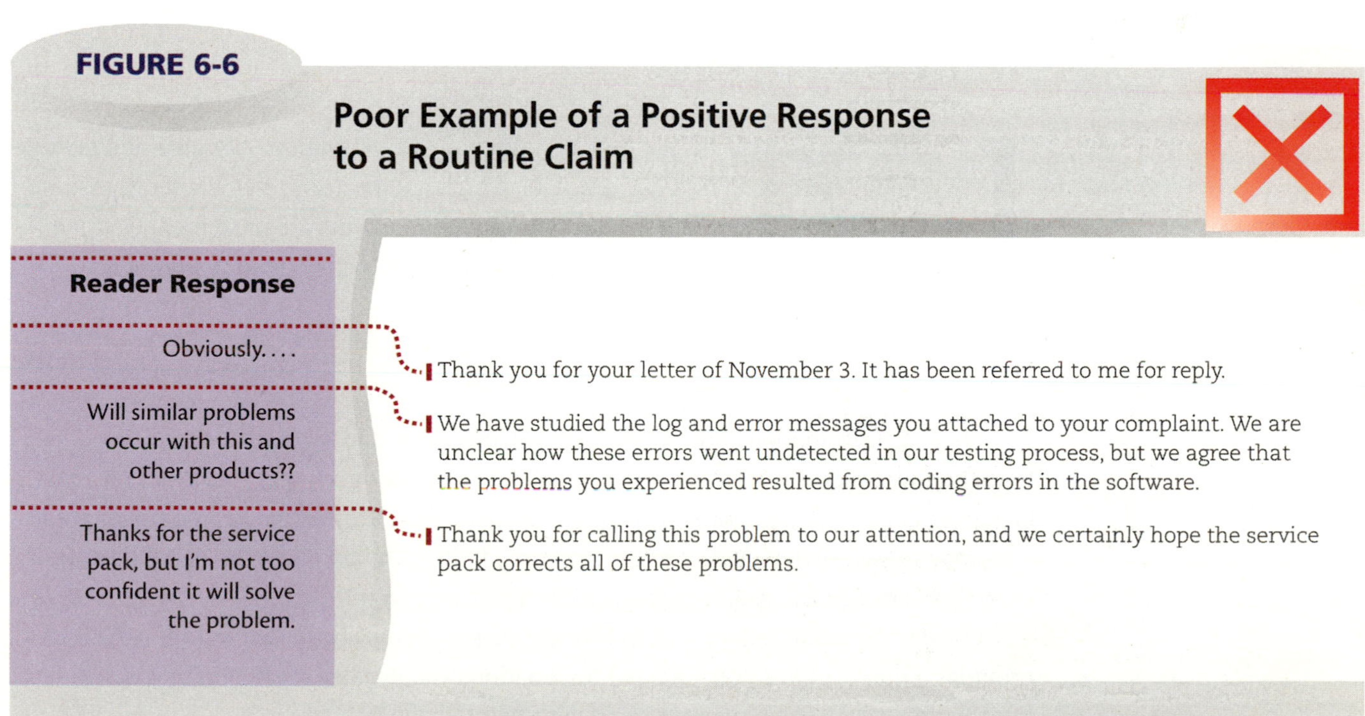
FIGURE 6-6

Poor Example of a Positive Response to a Routine Claim

Reader Response
Obviously. . . .
Thank you for your letter of November 3. It has been referred to me for reply.
Will similar problems occur with this and other products??
We have studied the log and error messages you attached to your complaint. We are unclear how these errors went undetected in our testing process, but we agree that the problems you experienced resulted from coding errors in the software.
Thanks for the service pack, but I'm not too confident it will solve the problem.
Thank you for calling this problem to our attention, and we certainly hope the service pack corrects all of these problems.

FIGURE 6-7

Good Example of a Positive Response to a Routine Claim

To:	Inga Bremen <inga.bremen@metatech.com>
From:	Kelly Sansing <ksansing@qcs.com>
Subject:	Service Pack Underway

Ms. Bremen,

The service pack for Audit Partner 7.0 will be shipped to you within three weeks.

Thank you for bringing this situation to our attention so quickly while we are still in the early stages of distributing this software. Although the software was subjected to our normal quality control review, our sample data sets did not trigger the errors you experienced using realistic data.

Our developers are proud of the new functionality added to Version 7.0. Please call us at 555-0800 if our control review team can assist your technology advisory group in testing the software after installing the service pack.

Thanks,

Kelly Sansing
Kelly Sansing
Sales Manager

Begins with good news (main idea) with assurance of desired action.

Expresses appreciation for being informed about problems.

Presents explanation and assurance of a process for quality control.

Attempts to regain possible lost goodwill by offering personalized assistance.

Routine Requests

Like claims, requests are divided into two groups: ***routine requests*** and ***persuasive requests***. Persuasive requests, which are discussed in Chapter 8, assume that action will be taken after persuasive arguments are presented. Routine requests and favorable responses to them follow the deductive sequence.

Routine Request

Requests for information about people, prices, products, and services are common. Because these requests from customers and clients are door openers for future business, businesses accept them optimistically. At the same time, they arrive at an opinion about the sender based on the quality of the message. Follow the points in the deductive outline for preparing effective requests you are confident will be fulfilled.

What can you do to make sure your routine requests don't seem just "routine"?

Consider the email link on Central Reservations' web page shown in Figure 6-8. It provides a quick, convenient channel for a national sales manager to obtain specific information essential for planning an event. Because the email message is vague, the sales manager is unlikely to receive information that will prove useful.

FIGURE 6-8

Poor Example of a Routine Request

Reader Response

Reader Response	
The subject line could be more informational.	Subject: Need Information
Why are you writing?	I have been searching for a unique location for my company's national sales meeting to be held in late January of next year. From looking at your website, it appears that Jackson Hole meets almost all our criteria. However, I have been unable to identify a hotel with meeting and banquet rooms to accommodate 400 people.
I think I know what you are requesting. . . .	We want to offer our sales reps and their spouses the opportunity to learn to ski but are concerned whether the ski school could handle all of us. Our experienced skiers are interested in knowing the difficulty level of the resort. As you may know, the difficulty of "blue slopes" can vary greatly between ski resorts. What activity would you recommend for those who don't want to ski?
What a canned closing! I'll get to this when I have the chance. . . .	I look forward to receiving your reply as quickly as possible.

Note that the revision in Figure 6-9 starts with a direct request for specific information. Then as much detail as necessary is presented to enable the receiver to answer specifically. The revision ends confidently with appreciation for the action requested. The message is short, but because it conveys enough information and has a tone of politeness, it is effective.

Favorable Response to a Routine Request

The message in Figure 6-10 responds favorably, but with little enthusiasm to an online request for detailed information related to conference accommodations in a Wyoming mountain resort. With a little planning and consideration for the executive planning a major event, the message in Figure 6-11 could have been written just as quickly. Note the specific answers to the manager's questions prepared in the convenient Q&A format and the helpful, sincere tone.

Positive Response to a Favor Request

What type favors may you be asked to provide in your chosen career field?

Occasionally, as a business professional, you will be asked for special favors. You may receive invitations to speak at various civic or education groups, spearhead fund-raising and other service projects, or offer your expertise in other ways. If you say "Yes," you might as well say it enthusiastically. Sending an unplanned, stereotyped acceptance suggests that the contribution will be similar.

If you find yourself responding to invitations frequently, you can draft a form message that you'll revise for each invitation you receive. Go to your companion website at www.cengage.com/bcomm/lehman to view a TV production manager's gracious acceptance of an

FIGURE 6-9

Good Example of a Routine Request

To:	Reservation Center <info@jacksonhole.com>
From:	Hunter Barksdale <hbarksdale@hutton.com>
Subject:	Information Needed for Planning Large Conference in Jackson Hole

Attn Reservation Center:

States request clearly.

The excellent information on your website describing the breathtaking winter scenery and legendary slopes suggests that Jackson Hole could be an ideal location for Hutton Enterprises' five-day national sales meeting. To assist us in selecting a site for this event scheduled for late January 2011, please provide the following information:

Asks specific questions with necessary explanation; uses list for emphasis.

- Do any of the hotel(s) provide a convention center with space for a general session and meal functions for 400 attendees and a minimum of 10 concurrent breakout sessions? Can this conference hotel provide a block of 400 rooms, preferably at a conference rate? If not please recommend several suitable hotels near the conference hotel.
- Do your ski schools at SnowKing and Teton Village have the capacity to handle as many as 200 beginning skiers or snowboarders on a single day? To minimize time employees spend away from the conference, could you arrange all equipment rentals prior to our arrival and secure a private clubhouse for an on-site hospitality center?
- What are the ratings for each level of skiing (green/blue/black) for both resorts? We must be confident that the slopes will challenge our most experienced skiers, while providing a comfortable place for our beginners to learn.
- What unique indoor activity can you recommend as an alternative to downhill skiing or snowboarding?

Expresses appreciation and alludes to benefits for quick action.

Opens door for a personal dialogue by providing telephone number.

The information you provide could likely confirm our expectation that Jackson Hole can meet our conference needs. At that point, you will be contacted to assist us in making the many necessary reservations. Should you wish to talk with me directly, please call (630) 555-3910, Ext. 132.

Thanks,

Hunter Barksdale

Hunter Barksdale
National Sales Manager
Hutton Enterprises
307-555-2800, Fax 307-555-2427
hbarksdale@hutton.com

Format Pointers

- Provides salutation appropriate for company.
- Includes needed .sig file identification below writer's name for complete reference.

FIGURE 6-10

Poor Example of a Positive Response to a Routine Request

Reader Response

The subject line could be more informational. I almost deleted the message without reading.

Sorry to trouble you. . . .

Well, that's interesting. But what about the answers to my questions?

This doesn't sound like a very business-like operation.

You've not convinced me you will be of much help.

RE: Information Needed

Mr. Barksdale,

I read your request and hopefully my hurried response will provide the information you need.

The Jackson Hole Convention Center can serve your needs with several hotels nearby for your employees. The ski schools at both slopes are exceptional. Just show up early to beat the crowds. You're right, Jackson Hole does have a reputation for being a brutal beast. The difficulty of the terrain, the vertical drops, and the constantly changing snow conditions help us attract the best skiers around. In fact, we're the training site for Olympic athletes from many countries. You should see them. Wow!

On-site hospitality—that's a new one on me—can't help you there. Sounds cool! There are lots of things to do here besides skiing; it's all on our website. Just take a look and see what looks interesting to you.

We are happy you're considering Jackson Hole for your sales conference. We can make reservations for the hotels and anything you want to do. Just let us know how we can help.

invitation to emcee an awards program for a civic group. This well-written acceptance illustrates how form messages can be effectively individualized to enable businesses to communicate quickly and efficiently.

Form Messages for Routine Responses

Form messages are a fast and efficient way of transmitting frequently recurring messages to which receiver reaction is likely favorable or neutral. Inputting the customer's name and address and other variables (information that differs for each receiver) personalizes each message to meet the needs of its receiver. Companies may use form paragraphs that have been saved as template documents. When composing a document, you would select the appropriate paragraph according to your receiver's request. After assembling the selected files on the computer screen, you would input the particular information for the situation (e.g., name and address) and print a copy of the personalized message on letterhead to send to the receiver. View an example of a form letter that has been personalized at your companion website, www.cengage.com/bcomm/lehman. Select the enrichment content, "Using the Mail Merge Feature to Produce Personalized Form Letters."

FIGURE 6-11

Good Example of a Positive Response to a Routine Request

Revises subject line after clicking "reply" to communicate enthusiasm for providing exceptional personalized service.

Shows sincere interest in request and person.

Highlights specific answers to recipient's questions using an articulate, concise writing style.

Encourages direct call and provides more useful information that communicates genuine interest in person and event.

To:	Hunter Barksdale <hbarksdale@hutton.com>
From:	Kira Lenoir <infojacksonhole.com>
Subject:	Assistance for Planning Exciting Conference in Jackson Hole

Mr. Barksdale:

Jackson Hole is the ideal location for Hutton Enterprise's national sales meeting. At Central Reservations, we can assist you with all your lodging and entertainment reservations.

Q: Do any of the hotel(s) provide a convention center with space for a general session and meal functions for 400 attendees and a minimum of 10 concurrent breakout sessions?

A: The new Jackson Hole Convention Center and its two adjoining hotels can easily meet your needs. The Teton Mountains ballroom can accommodate a formal dinner for 600 people, and the 12 conference rooms surrounding the ballroom seat 50 people in a presentation arrangement. The Waverly and Majestic hotels have over 500 rooms with covered walkways to the convention center.

Q: Do your ski schools have the capacity to handle as many as 200 beginning skiers or snowboarders on a single day? To minimize time away from the conference, could you arrange equipment rentals prior to our arrival and secure a private clubhouse for an on-site hospitality center?

A: With two weeks advanced reservations, the ski schools can easily provide for 200 beginners daily. The ski schools provide fast, convenient equipment rentals slope side. Although a private clubhouse is unavailable, the spacious Elk Lounge provides a relaxing break from the slopes.

Q: What are the ratings for each level of skiing for both resorts?

A: Despite our reputation for high challenge, about 25% of our trails provide safe environments for first-time skiers and provide a modest challenge to skiers preparing to advance to intermediate (blue) slopes.

Please call my direct line (307) 555-6180 for more advice on organizing a dynamic event in the natural beauty of the Teton Mountains. You can also register at our website to receive snow reports, current activities, and more.

Thanks,

Kira Lenoir

Kira Lenoir, Hospitality Agent
Central Reservations

Format Pointer

- Uses Q&A format to enhance readability of response to series of detailed questions.

Why do form letters have such a bad image? How can the weaknesses of a form letter be overcome?

Form letters have earned a negative connotation because of their tendency to be impersonal. Many people simply refuse to read such letters for that reason. Personalizing a form letter can circumvent this problem. To make a form letter more personal,

- add more variables to the standard text to tailor the message to the individual.
- use personalized envelopes instead of mass-produced mailing labels.
- be sure to spell names correctly.
- produce a higher-quality document by using a good grade of paper and high-quality printer.

Your Turn 6-3
Electronic Café
EXPRESSING YOURSELF THROUGH A PERSONAL WEB PAGE

As the number of people with Internet access increases exponentially, so does the number of personal web pages. Using personal web pages, individuals have access to powerful tools for sharing information for leisure and professional purposes. But not every personal web page achieves its desired purpose. What makes a good web page? The following electronic activities will assist you in learning more about the development of an effective personal web page.

TAKE ACTION:

- Read more about the design of effective web pages. Access your companion website at www.cengage.com/bcomm/lehman to link to these readings.
- Develop your own home page. Log on to your online course and follow the directions of your instructor for developing your own personal web page.

Routine Messages About Orders and Credit

Routine messages, such as customer order acknowledgments, are written deductively. Normally, credit information is requested and transmitted electronically from the national credit reporting agencies to companies requesting credit references. However, when companies choose to request information directly from other businesses, individual credit requests and responses must be written.

CHANGING TECHNOLOGY

STRATEGIC FORCES

Making Voice Mail Messages Work for You

Voice mail has both simplified and complicated our ability to communicate. While it provides another option for exchanging information, it can also result in partial or broken communication. You can do several things to ensure that voice messaging is effective.

When preparing a voice message to leave on your phone system:[8]

- Keep menu choices to a minimum to avoid confusion and annoyance.
- Make sure callers are able to get through to a human party by pressing a button or waiting briefly.
- Keep your messages up-to-date and change them regularly.
- Check the quality of your voice system by pretending you don't know your direct line or extension number and placing a call to yourself. How many menus did you have to go through? How long were you on hold? What kind of music or messages were you forced to listen through?
- Set aside time each day to return calls. If you do not wish to talk extensively to a person, time your call when the party is away and leave your return message on voice mail. If you are not interested in what the person has to offer, leave a message saying so and that you wish to be removed from the call list.

Chances are greater that you will be leaving a message rather than talking to someone on most business phone calls. When leaving a voice message for another person:[9]

- Prepare for your call. Write out key points before you call to organize your thoughts for the message you will leave or for the conversation with a live person.
- If you suffer a mental block at the sound of the tone, hang up, organize your thoughts, and call back. This action is preferable to leaving a rambling, incoherent message.
- Start your message by greeting the person. Then identify yourself by name, affiliation, and phone number.
- Write the phone number as you state it to slow yourself down to the pace of the listener's writing speed. If the party does not know you, write each letter of your name as you speak it.
- State the purpose of your call candidly and concisely. Provide enough information for the person to meet your request by leaving a message on your phone if necessary.
- Do not leave personal information or emotionally charged verbiage in your message, as it could be an embarrassment if played back on speakerphone or forwarded to someone else.
- Close your message with directions on how to respond and times when you will be available.

© BANANASTOCK/JUPITER IMAGES

Voice mail can simplify the process of giving and receiving information. Paying close attention to your messaging techniques can promote your image as an effective communicator.

Application

Assume you have moved to a new town and desire to open a bank checking account. To aid you in obtaining comparison information from local banks, outline what you will ask in a phone conversation or leave as a message if you are transferred to the new accounts voice mail system.

COURTESY OF TWITTER, INC.

Twittering the Internet. Email links, chat rooms, and bulletin boards on corporate websites foster dialogue that leads to strong relationships. In addition to hosting various information exchange methods on corporate websites, an increasing number of business people are participating in social exchange networking and blogging services such as the award-winning Twitter (www.twitter .com). Businesses such as Apple, Dell, CNN, JetBlue, and, Zappos use Twitter to provide updates to customers. "Tweet" postings must be brief, as messages cannot exceed 140 characters.[7] Such forced brevity may be one reason for the service's popularity. If customers are invited to talk, companies must be prepared to respond with timely, effective—even if brief—messages.

Acknowledging Customer Orders

How can a company encourage future orders by sending customer order acknowledgments?

When customers place orders for merchandise, they expect to get exactly what they ordered as quickly as possible. Most orders can be acknowledged by shipping the order; no message is necessary. For an initial order and for an order that cannot be filled quickly and precisely, companies typically send an ***acknowledgment message***, a document that indicates the order has been received and is being processed. Typically, acknowledgment messages are preprinted letters or copies of the sales order. An immediate email message acknowledges an order placed online and confirms the expected date of shipment as shown in Figure 6-12. Individualized letters are not cost effective and will not reach the customer in a timely manner. Although the form message is impersonal, customers appreciate the order acknowledgment and information as to when the order will arrive.

Nonroutine orders, such as initial orders, custom orders, and delayed orders, require individualized acknowledgment messages. When well-written, these messages not only acknowledge the order but also create customer goodwill and encourage the customer to place additional orders. Because saying "Yes" is easy, some writers develop the habit of using clichés and words that make messages sound cold and mechanical. The acknowledgment letter available at your companion website, www.cengage.com/bcomm/lehman, confirms shipment of goods in the first sentence, includes concrete resale on the product and company, and is sincere and original. When communication with the customer has occurred electronically, an acknowledgment by email is often appropriate.

Providing Credit Information

Replies to requests for credit information usually are simple—just fill in the blanks and return the document. If the request does not include a form, follow a deductive plan in writing the reply: the major idea first, followed by supporting details.

What are the legal implications of credit information messages?

When providing credit information, you have an ethical and legal obligation to yourself, the credit applicant, and the business from whom credit is requested. You must be able to document any statement you make to defend yourself against a defamation charge. Thus, good advice is to stick with facts; omit any opinions. "I'm sure he will pay promptly" is an opinion that should be omitted, but include the documentable fact that

FIGURE 6-12

Good Example of an Online Order Confirmation

Provides warm, personal subject line.

Welcomes new customer and acknowledges receipt of online order.

Assures quality service by encouraging open communication to make process easy.

Provides phone number and email address to reinforce commitment to customer service.

To:	Jack Lynch
From:	Sheila Tobin-Joyce <stobin@4imprint.com>
Subject:	4imprint welcomes Jack as a valued customer

Jack,

Welcome to 4imprint! I'm excited to see you placed your first order with us yesterday.

Your personal Customer Service Representative, Tricia Finley, is a promotional products expert and will take great care of you throughout the ordering process. She has been specially trained to help you find products that fit your needs and will see to it that your order arrives on time and looking great.

As the Customer Service Manager responsible for your order, it's my job to be sure that you get off to a great start with 4imprint and that we do everything possible to make sure that you'll come back to us in the future.

I have complete confidence in the care you'll receive from Tricia, but if for any reason you aren't completely satisfied, or if you have any questions or suggestions for improvement, please let me know right away.

You can reach me at 212-555-2942, extension 8200, or you can e-mail me anytime at stobin@4imprint.com.

Thank you again for ordering from us!

Best regards,

Sheila Tobin-Joyce
Sheila Tobin-Joyce
Customer Service Manager
4imprint

P.S. Be sure to watch your mailbox for our exclusive Blue Boxes. They're loaded with free samples and ideas to help you market your organization. And they're only available to 4imprint customers.

"His payments are always prompt." Can you safely say a customer is a good credit risk when all you know is that he/she had a good credit record when he/she purchased from you?

Extending Credit

A timely response is preferable for any business document, but it is especially important when communicating about credit. The Equal Credit Opportunity Act (ECOA) requires that a credit applicant be notified of the credit decision within 30 days of receipt of the request or application. The party granting the credit must also disclose the terms of the credit agreement, such as the address for sending or making payments, due dates for payments, and the interest rate charged. You will learn more about other legal implications related to credit when you study credit denials in Chapter 7.

DEPARTMENT OF JUSTICE

When extending credit, follow these guidelines as you write deductively:

1. **Open by extending credit and acknowledging shipment of an order.** Because of its importance, the credit aspect is emphasized more than the acknowledgment of the order. In other cases (in which the order is for cash or the credit terms are already clearly understood), the primary purpose of writing may be to acknowledge an order.

What legal requirements apply to letters extending credit?

2. **Indicate the basis for the decision to extend credit and explain the credit terms.** Indicating that you are extending credit on the basis of an applicant's prompt-paying habits with present creditors may encourage this new customer to continue these habits with you.

3. **Present credit policies.** Explain policies (e.g., credit terms, authorized discounts, payment dates). Include any legally required disclosure documents.

4. **Communicate a genuine desire to build a strong business relationship.** Include resale, sales promotional material, and comments that remind the customer of the benefits of doing business with you and encourage additional orders.

The letter in Figure 6-13 was written to a retailer; however, the same principles apply when writing to a consumer. Each message should be addressed in terms of individual interests. Dealers are concerned about markup, marketability, and display; consumers are concerned about price, appearance, and durability. Individual consumers may require a more detailed explanation of credit terms.

Companies receive so many requests for credit that the costs of individualized letters are prohibitive; therefore, most favorable replies to credit requests are form letters. To personalize the letter, however, the writer should merge the customer's name, address, amount of loan, and terms into the computer file containing the form letter information. Typically, form messages read something like this:

> Dear [TITLE] [LAST NAME]
> Worldwide Industries is pleased to extend credit privileges to you. Initially, you may purchase up to [CREDIT LIMIT] worth of merchandise. Our credit terms are [TERMS]. We welcome you as a credit customer at Worldwide Industries and look forward to serving your needs for fine imported goods from around the world.

Although such form messages are effective for informing the customer that credit is being extended, they do little to build goodwill and promote future sales. Managers can personalize form messages that recipients do not perceive as canned responses.

FIGURE 6-13

Good Example of a Letter Extending Credit

CENTURY IMAGES
985 Hunter Avenue
Boston, MA 02194-0965
614-555-6790

July 20, 2011

Lincoln Technologies
Order Department
461 Beech Street
Fort Lauderdale, FL 33310-0461

Ladies and Gentlemen:

Welcome to the most contemporary library of photographs available on the Internet. Our expert photographers are continually touring every region of the world, supplying the library with over 400 new photographs every day.

Because of your favorable current credit rating, we are pleased to provide you with a $25,000 credit line subject to our standard 2/10, n/30 terms. By paying your invoice within ten days, you can save 2 percent on your photograph purchases.

You can access our exclusive PhotoSearch system using the login name NelsonPublishing and the password JU12x34V. Use PhotoSearch to search our extensive photograph library by topic and date. After making your selections, digital files will be made available to you at a secure website. To ensure your photographs will not appear in any other publication, your selections are removed from the library.

The best photographs for your publications are available to you right now, and they are just a click away.

Sincerely,

Craig Wynne

Craig Wynne
Credit Manager

Acknowledges customer's electronic access to product and implies credit extension.

Recognizes dealer for earning credit privilege and gives reason for credit extension.

Includes credit terms and encourages taking advantage of discount.

Presents resale as reminder of product benefits and to encourage future business.

Includes sales promotion; assumes satisfaction with initial order and looks confidently for future business.

Legal and Ethical Constraints Issue

- Provides answer to request for credit within required time frame (30 days from receipt of request) and mentions terms of credit that will be provided, as required by law.
- Uses letter channel rather than email to communicate a contractual message.

Your Turn 6-4
Assessment

Do you communicate as well as you think you do? A recent study reported by the Society for Human Resource Management found that more than nine in ten managers rate themselves as good or excellent communicators, but only seven in ten employees agree with them.[10]

TAKE ACTION:

- Take the quiz at the following site to assess your own interpersonal communication skills: http://discoveryhealth.queendom.com/communication_short_access.html. You may also go to your companion website at www.cengage.com/bcomm/lehman for updated links.
- Print the page with your resulting score. Email your instructor to report your score and what it says about your communication abilities.

Procedural Messages

Memos or email messages are the most frequently used methods of communicating standard operating procedures and other instructions, changes related to personnel or the organization, and other internal matters for which a written record is needed. Visit your companion website, www.cengage.com/bcomm/lehman, to explore strategies for preparing confirmation memos or "to file" memos written to confirm spoken decisions or discussions.

What types of procedural messages will you write in your career field?

Instructions to employees must be conveyed clearly and accurately to facilitate the day-to-day operations of business and to prevent negative feelings that occur when mistakes are made and work must be redone. Managers must take special care in writing standard operating procedures to ensure that all employees complete the procedures accurately and consistently.

Before writing instructions, walk through each step to understand it and to locate potential trouble spots. Then attempt to determine how much employees already know about the process and to anticipate any questions or problems. Then, as you write instructions that require more than a few simple steps, follow these guidelines:

1. **Begin each step with an action statement to create a vivid picture of the employee completing the task.** Using an action verb and the understood subject *you* is more vivid than a sentence written in passive voice. For example, a loan officer attempting to learn new procedures for evaluating new venture loans can more easily understand "*identify* assets available to collateralize the loan" than "assets available to collateralize the loan should be identified."

2. **Itemize each step on a separate line to add emphasis and to simplify reading.** Number each step to indicate that the procedures should be completed in a particular order. If the order of steps is not important, use bullets rather than numbers.

3. **Consider preparing a flow chart depicting the procedures.** The cost and effort involved in creating a sophisticated flow chart may be merited for extremely important and complex procedures. For example, take a look at the flow chart in

Figure 10-8, which simplifies the steps involved in processing a telephone order in an effort to minimize errors.

4. **Complete the procedure by following your instructions step-by-step.** Correct any errors you locate.
5. **Ask a colleague or employee to walk through the procedures.** This walk-through will allow you to identify ambiguous statements, omissions of relevant information, and other sources of potential problems.

Consider the seemingly simple task of reporting a computer problem. The help-desk manager might quickly respond, "No need for written instructions; just report your problem any way you wish." Ambiguous verbal instructions (reported in haste) could lead to inefficient technology service and suspicion about the equity of the process. The clear, consistent procedures in Figure 6-14 were prepared after the manager anticipated potential employee issues in reporting computer problems. The policy is sent as an email attachment and posted to the company intranet for easy reference.

Your Turn 6-5
Miscue

An arrest affidavit for an alleged rapist in Arapahoe County, Colorado, sat unsigned for more than a month because of communication problems. By the time a judge signed the warrant, the accused no longer lived at the known address. Reportedly, the district attorney's office sent emails to the lead investigator for his signature, but the Aurora police officer didn't have an email account. As no alert indicated the message was not delivered, the D.A.'s office assumed it had been received. Follow-up phone calls to the police department in the ensuing weeks revealed the problem, and the document was finally hand delivered for the required signature. The suspect was finally arrested, nearly two months after the preparation of the arrest affidavit, but not until he had allegedly committed additional sex crimes for which he has been charged.[11]

TAKE ACTION:

- How could the problem with the undelivered email have been prevented?
- How could the procedure for gaining needed signatures be improved?

Before writing a pleasant or routine message, study carefully the overall suggestions in the "General Writing Guidelines" available at your companion website, www.cengage.com/bcomm/lehman. After you have written a rough draft, compare your work with the "Check Your Communication" checklist at the end of this chapter and make any revisions.

FIGURE 6-14

Good Example of a Procedural Email with an Attachment

To:	All Employees
From:	Emily Carter <ecarter@lincolnco.com>
Subject:	New Procedures for Requesting Computer Service
Attachment:	Computer_Service_Request_Procedures.docx

Includes attached file of document requiring involved formatting.

Everyone,

Introduces main idea.

The number of computer service requests has increased proportionately to the recent dramatic growth of the company. To continue to provide you with timely and effective service, additional technicians have been hired and a new service reporting system is in place beginning July 1.

Explains new procedures outlined in attached file.

To report a computer problem or request software installation, follow the procedures outlined in the attached file and posted to the company intranet under Technology Services. If your computer or email system is inoperative, complete these procedures at any computer.

Thanks,

Emily Carter

Emily Carter
Help Desk Manager

Provides descriptive title that clearly identifies procedures.

Procedures for Requesting Computer Service

Enumerates to direct attention to each step and emphasizes need for sequence.

Begins each item with action verb to help employees visualize completing procedures.

1. Access http://www.drmc.com/it/index.html, and click the Service option.
2. Provide the information requested. Be certain to complete the required items denoted with asterisks.
3. Check your email for a service order confirmation, typically within 24 hours.
4. Complete normal shutdown procedures when leaving your computer station. Although the service work will be performed after hours, technicians will start your computer using their personal login procedures.
5. Check your email for a service completion notice, and message us if the work was not completed to your satisfaction.

Includes date of last revision to ensure currency.

Revised 6/20/2011

SHOWCASE PART 3

Zappos Simplifies Routine Claims

At Zappos, customer service is an investment, not an expense. Grossing more than $1 billion in merchandise sales each year, the company has built its solid reputation on outstanding customer service. Free shipping on orders and returns, plus a 365-day return policy have differentiated Zappos from competing brick and mortar stores as well as from other online businesses. Customers can handle their returns online and print out a return request form and free shipping label for either UPS or the United States Postal Service. A toll free number facilitates easy product exchange and other types of customer assistance. Many consumer questions that previously would have necessitated a telephone call to the company are anticipated and answered through the frequently asked questions (FAQs) section of the website. Zappos uses the Web to save time for customers and employees, assuring that each customer interaction is a "wow" experience.

www.zappos.com

Activities

- Visit the Zappos website and find out more about its FAQs.
- Compare the FAQ method for obtaining product information to the traditional text format.

Write a short, informative paper that compares the overall effect to the customer and the company that is achieved by the two approaches.

Summary

1. Describe the deductive outline for good and neutral news and its adaptations for specific situations and for international audiences.

When the receiver can be expected to be *pleased* by the message, the main idea is presented first and details follow. Likewise, when the message is *routine* and not likely to arouse a feeling of pleasure or displeasure, the main idea is presented first. The deductive approach is appropriate for positive news and thank-you and appreciation messages, routine claims, routine requests and responses to routine requests, routine messages, and responses about credit and orders. Cultural differences of international audiences may necessitate adjustments in writing style and to the typical deductive pattern for good-news and neutral messages.

2. Prepare messages that convey good news, including thank-you and appreciation messages.

Use the deductive approach for letters, memos, and email messages that contain positive news as the central idea. Thank-you messages express appreciation for a kindness or special assistance and should reflect sincere feelings of gratitude. Appreciation messages highlight exceptional performance and should avoid exaggerations and strong, unsupported statements that the receiver may not believe.

3. Write messages presenting routine claims and requests and favorable responses to them.

A routine claim requests the adjustment in the first sentence because you assume the company will make the adjustment without persuasion. It continues with an explanation of the problem to support the request and an expression of appreciation for taking the action. An adjustment extends the adjustment in the first sentence and explains the circumstances related to correcting the problem. The closing may include sales promotional material or other futuristic comments indicating your confidence that the customer will continue doing business with a company that has a reputation for fairness. A routine request begins with the major request, includes details that will clarify the request, and alludes to the receiver's response. A response to a routine request provides the information requested, provides necessary details, and closes with a personal, courteous ending.

4. Write messages acknowledging customer orders, providing credit information, and extending credit.

Form or computer-generated acknowledgment messages or email messages assure customers that orders will be filled quickly. With individualized acknowledgments that confirm shipment and include product resale, the company generates goodwill and future business.

When providing credit information, provide only verifiable facts to avoid possible litigation. A message extending credit begins with an approval of credit, indicates the basis for the decision, and explains credit terms. The closing may include sales promotional material or other futuristic comments. Credit extension messages must adhere to legal guidelines.

5. Prepare procedural messages that ensure clear and consistent application.

When preparing instructions, highlight the steps in a bulleted or numbered list or a flow chart and begin each step with an action statement. Check the accuracy and completeness of the document and incorporate changes identified by following the instructions to complete the task and asking another person to do likewise.

Chapter Review

1. List the steps in the deductive outline recommended for good- and neutral-news messages. (Obj. 1)
2. Discuss guidelines for communicating with an international audience. (Obj. 1)
3. What suggestions will contribute to a warm, genuine tone in a thank-you or appreciation message? (Obj. 2)
4. Explain how claim messages and responses to requests both use the deductive message pattern. (Obj. 3)
5. What is the difference between resale and sales promotional material? Provide an example of each. Why should resale and sales promotional material be included in an adjustment letter? (Obj. 3)
6. Distinguish between the two major types of request messages, and specify the outline preferable for each type. (Obj. 3)
7. Describe the procedure typically used by companies to acknowledge orders. Provide three situations when sending an individualized order acknowledgment would be appropriate and explain why. (Obj. 4)
8. Provide suggestions for writing a legally defensible credit information letter. (Obj. 4)
9. What information should be included in a letter extending credit? (Obj. 4).
10. Provide guidelines for writing instructions that can be understood and followed consistently. (Obj. 5)

Digging Deeper

1. What criteria should be used in determining whether a good- or neutral-news message would best be communicated on paper, electronically, or verbally?
2. What considerations should be given to a message recipient's culture when planning a good-news or neutral-news message?
3. What role does goodwill play in composing effective deductive messages?

Assessment

To check your understanding of the chapter, take the available online quizzes as directed by your instructor.

Activities

1. Deductive Openings (Objs. 1–5)

Revise the following openings so that they are deductive.

a. In last week's budget meeting, the controller underscored that budgets are lean this quarter. However, she has approved your request for computer upgrades for your staff.
b. The Marion Club is a service organization that has always been held in high esteem within the telecommunications industry. Our membership is honored to extend an invitation for you to join us as we help the industry move forward.
c. It is rare that we receive a claim regarding a defect in our self-service photo kiosks. However, because of our belief in our product, a sales representative will deliver a replacement.

2. Perfecting Opening Statements (Objs. 1, 2)

Decide which opening statement is preferable for a positive response message and describe why the others are less effective.

Version 1

Your employee-of-the-month award proposal reflects value for the company and our employees. So that we can consider the feasibility of the idea, please provide a few more details.

Version 2

I have read your proposal for the employee-of-the-month award and think it is a great idea. However, before it can be submitted to the board, I need to have a few more details.

Check Your Communication

Good- and Neutral-News Messages

CONTENT

- ☐ Clearly identify the principal idea (pleasant or routine idea).
- ☐ Present sufficient supporting detail in logical sequence.
- ☐ Ensure accuracy of facts or figures.
- ☐ Structure the message to meet legal requirements and ethical dimensions.

ORGANIZATION

- ☐ Place the major idea in the first sentence.
- ☐ Present supporting details in logical sequence.
- ☐ Include a final idea that is courteous and indicates a continuing relationship with the receiver; it may include sales promotional material.

STYLE

- ☐ Ensure that the message is clear and concise (e.g., words will be readily understood).
- ☐ Use active voice predominantly and first person sparingly.
- ☐ Make ideas cohere by avoiding abrupt changes in thought.
- ☐ Use contemporary language; avoid doublespeak and clichés.
- ☐ Use relatively short sentences that vary in length and structure.
- ☐ Emphasize significant thoughts (e.g., position and sentence structure).
- ☐ Keep paragraphs relatively short.
- ☐ Adjust formality and writing style to the particular medium of delivery (letter, memo, email, text message, etc.).

MECHANICS

- ☐ Ensure that keyboarding, spelling, grammar, and punctuation are perfect.

FORMAT

- ☐ Use a correct message format.
- ☐ Ensure that the message is appropriately positioned.
- ☐ Include standard message parts in appropriate position and special parts as needed (subject line, enclosure, copy, etc.).

CULTURAL ADAPTATIONS

- ☐ Avoid abbreviations, slang, acronyms, technical jargon, sports and military analogies, and other devices peculiar to your own culture.
- ☐ Avoid words that trigger emotional responses.
- ☐ Use simple terms but attempt to be specific.
- ☐ Consider the communication style of the culture when selecting an organizational pattern.
- ☐ Use graphics, visual aids, and forms when possible to simplify the message.
- ☐ Use figures for expressing numbers to avoid confusion.
- ☐ Be aware of differences in the way numbers and dates are written, and write out the name of the month to avoid confusion.
- ☐ Adapt the document format for expectations of the recipient's country.

Version 3

Enclosed please find my comments regarding your employee-of-the-month award proposal. The idea appears to be a win-win situation for the company and our employees.

3. Perfecting Closing Statements (Objs. 1, 3)

Decide which closing statement is preferable for a positive response message and describe why the others are less effective.

Version 1

I am pleased that you submitted this proposal and I look forward to submitting the revised version to the board of directors at their next meeting.

Version 2

Thank you for providing a proposal that may enable our company to provide a much-deserved reward to our employees. Completing your revision by this Friday will ensure the proposal will be addressed at the upcoming board of directors meeting.

Version 3

Please submit a more detailed analysis of your proposal as soon as possible. Thank you in advance.

4. Form Letter: Need for Personalization (Objs. 1,3)

The U.S. Army had to apologize to thousands of families who received letters in late 2008 beginning "Dear John Doe" after losing a soldier in Afghanistan. The letters that contained information on services for surviving families were printed by a contracting company and also had improper information in place of the recipient name and address. In trying to rectify the error, the army chief of staff sent a personal letter to each family.[12]

Required: Discuss the impact of receiving an unpersonalized or improperly addressed form letter. What are some of the results to an organization that sends such communications?

5. Document for Analysis: Thank You (Objs. 1, 2)

Analyze the following letter. Pinpoint its strengths and weaknesses, and then revise the letter as directed by your instructor. Access a downloadable version of this activity from your companion website at www.cengage.com/bcomm/lehman.

Dear Mary Kendall:

We never expected to ever have to implement the disaster contingency plan we established with you a few years ago. The strange twists of fate that caused the levy to fail plunged our company into potential chaos. I am pleased to see that your company effectively implemented the recovery plan as promised.

I would like to thank you and your company for your assistance in getting our office relocated after the break in the levy flooded our building. We appreciate you and your team arriving so quickly and working "around the clock" to obtain new furniture and restore our computer systems. Please communicate our appreciation to your team for their efforts.

6. Document for Analysis: Claim Request (Objs. 1, 3)

Analyze the following letter. Pinpoint its strengths and weaknesses, and then revise the letter as directed by your instructor. Access a downloadable version of this activity from your companion website at www.cengage.com/bcomm/lehman.

Dear Mr. Berkin:

When I ordered my Zeratus notebook last month, you assured me that it provided state-of the-art-security. After viewing the specifications, I believed in your product and your company and soon placed my order. I received the notebook on January 12.

After watching the instructional demo, I was able to set up the fingerprint and password security. However, I often have to reboot the computer several times before I can get the notebook to recognize my fingerprint and allow me access to my files.

I have read and followed all the instructions, and even rescanned my fingerprint several times; but each time the notebook rarely recognizes me on the first attempt.

I would like this problem solved, either through a new computer being sent to me free of charge, or a refund after I return this one.

Please contact me at 706-555-3800 and advise me how I should resolve this problem.

7. Document for Analysis: Routine Request (Obj. 3)

Analyze the following letter. Pinpoint its strengths and weaknesses, and then revise the letter as directed by your instructor. Access a downloadable version of this activity from your companion website at www.cengage.com/bcomm/lehman.

Dear Ms. Fondren:

I am the Vice President of Operations for Sherman Corporation, a manufacturer of golf ball components. We have operated plants across the Midwest for thirty years, and we are contemplating opening a facility in the South within the next two years.

As we evaluate our operational needs and requirements, we are collecting data from various locations we think may provide a site that will generate the maximum benefit for both Sherman and the locale under consideration. Therefore, I would appreciate it if you could send me some information about Knoxville and its surrounding area, including information on population demographics and major employers, as well as a geographic description of the area. I'd also like to know about the weather, education, and cultural opportunities in the area, and, of course, the cost of living.

Thank you for your assistance, and I look forward to your response.

8. Document for Analysis: Procedural Message (Objs. 1, 5)

Analyze the following section of a procedures memo intended to communicate procedures for completing a certification exam. Pinpoint its strengths and weaknesses, and then revise the memo as directed by your instructor. Access a downloadable version of this activity from your companion website at www.cengage.com/bcomm/lehman.

Email from Ladonna Sicilia, sent 1/3/2011 at 1:45 p.m.

TO: Professional Staff

SUBJECT: Certification Preparation

We encourage you to complete the certified interrogator examination before the end of the fiscal year. Order the review course from the CI Association. Allow approximately two weeks for delivery. Install the software on your computer and begin taking the 12 interactive sessions. A minimum score of 80 percent is required to advance to the next session. While you are completing the course, submit your application to the CI Association. Once you have completed the course and your application has been accepted, you can apply to take the course at a local testing center. For your information, it took about 8 weeks for me to complete this process.

9. Thank-You Message: Thanks for a Favor (Objs. 1, 2)

A number of individuals have been especially helpful as you have pursued your degree, and you want to express your appreciation. Your choices might include writing to an instructor who served as a job reference or advised you to complete an internship program that has led to a full-time position, a cooperative education supervisor who provided an exceptional experience, or a speaker in a class or student organization meeting who has become your mentor.

Required: Compose an email message or letter expressing thanks to one of these individuals. Alternately, your instructor may direct you to prepare an outline of a telephone conversation or the script of a voice mail message conveying your appreciation.

Applications

READ | THINK | WRITE | SPEAK | COLLABORATE

1. Communication Success Stories (Objs. 1–5)

Conduct an electronic search to locate an article that deals with successful communication in a company or organization. Prepare an abstract of the article that includes the following parts: (1) article citation, (2) name of organization/company, (3) brief description of communication technique/situation, (4) and outcome(s) of the successful communication. As an alternative to locating an article, write about a successful communication situation in the organization or company for which you work.

Required: Present your abstract in a memo. Refer to Appendix B for information about formatting citations. Be prepared to give a short presentation in class.

2. Real-World Example: Handling Apologies (Objs. 1, 2)

Professional apologies are inevitable for companies if they wish to prevent unfortunate situations from undermining even the strongest relationships with customers, clients, and employees. Visit your companion website, www.cengage.com/bcomm/lehman, to explore strategies for handling apologies effectively. Then use an online database to locate the following articles that provide additional information and examples of apologies made by companies or individuals. Consider how each apology was handled and improvements you would recommend.

Duncan, R. D. (2008). Good apology. *Personal Excellence, 13*(6), 15. Available from Business Source Complete database.

Weinsten, B. (2007, June 22). The ethics of apologies. *Business Week Online*. Available online at: www.businessweek.com/careers/content/jun2007/ca20070621_930786.htm?campaign_id=rss_daily

Required: In teams of three or four, prepare a presentation on the topic of business apologies. If directed by your instructor, prepare a sample written apology a team member might send for missing an important team meeting.

READ | THINK | WRITE | SPEAK | COLLABORATE

3. Critique of Good- and Neutral-News Messages Produced by Real Companies (Objs. 1–5)

Find an example of both a well-written and a poorly written good-news or routine memo, email message, or letter. Analyze the strengths and weaknesses of each document. Be prepared to discuss them in class.

4. Routine Response: Guest Speaker Concerns (Objs. 1, 3)

As a member of your company's annual meeting planning committee, you have received a message from the committee chair with a recommendation for the dinner speaker. The proposed speaker gained a national reputation for his role in one of the nation's most costly financial frauds. After having served several years in federal prison for his crime, he now speaks to companies and government agencies about his experience, encouraging them to enhance their internal controls and crisis intervention training for managers.

Required: Determine whether you support a convicted felon as a speaker choice and prepare your response in an email to the committee chair. Be prepared to present your argument in a debate format in class if directed by your instructor.

5. Reply to Routine Request: Approval to Investigate Employee Suggestion (Objs. 1, 3)

Marc Son, a college intern working in the human resources department, sent the following email to the firm's suggestion box:

> I've been maintaining a log of my work with the company during my internship. After a month it is clear to me that I spend too much of my time answering emails. Although the sender does receive a quick reply, I feel that these continual interruptions negatively impact my productivity. Just as I feel I am in a rhythm working on a project, I find myself distracted by another email alert. Many companies are introducing the concept of "no email Fridays" in an effort to increase productivity and personal interaction. I would encourage our company to consider implementing this concept on a trial basis.

Required: As the chief executive officer, write a memo or email message to Marc Son indicating interest in his idea and asking him to provide you with additional information that would help in making your decision.

6. Procedural Message: American Red Cross: Committed to Preventing Fraud (Objs. 1, 5)

Outlays of the American Red Cross for Hurricane Katrina relief efforts exceeded $2 billion, with funds being used to meet survivors' needs for food and shelter, emergency financial assistance, and physical and mental health services. Red Cross workers usually meet individually with victims of disaster to determine how much money will be needed to get through the first few days. Because so many of the 1.2 million evacuees fled their homes with little more than the clothes on their backs, the organization had to use less traditional processes to help the hurricane victims.

To meet the overwhelming need quickly, the Red Cross set up call centers nationwide and contracted out the labor needed to answer the phones. Some call centers managed some 16,000 calls per day, and workers had to switch among three or four hard-to-use databases to determine eligibility. Evacuees had to provide name, address, and birth date to show eligibility, but the setup made cheating the system too easy by not cross-checking for multiple claims. As a result, nearly 50 people from the Bakersfield, California, call center were indicted for submitting false claims that cheated the Red Cross of $400,000.

For more information on the Red Cross and its response to fraud in general and specifically after Hurricane Katrina, read the following articles or visit the Red Cross website at www.redcross.org.

More than 600 accused of Hurricane Katrina fraud. (2007, Monday, April 2). *Foxnews.com.* Available at www.foxnews.com/story/0,2933,263206,00.html

Las Vegas man charged with presenting false claim for Hurricane Katrina benefits. (2006, April 26). U.S. Department of Justice. Available at www.usdoj.gov/katrina/Katrina_Fraud/pr/press_releases/2006/apr/04-26-06hawkindict.pdf

Required: Respond to this communication as directed by your instructor.

1. Look at other charities and see what policies they have in place to curb fraudulent applications and payments. As an interested citizen, compose an email to the Red Cross that includes a list of possible strategies and policies that the organization could use to prevent future fraudulent claims and payments.
2. Prepare a procedural document that Red Cross workers could use to guide their decisions to grant relief services to applicants.

7. Thank-You Message: Thanks for a Favor (Objs. 1, 2)

People who have accumulated large amounts of credit card debt are often bombarded by advertisements offering seemingly quick, easy fixes to their problems. As a financial consultant with a debt resolution agency, you know that painless solutions do not exist. Nancy Maey recently worked with you to restructure her $13,500 of credit card debt and began attending your weekly financial counseling sessions.

Required: Send Nancy a letter congratulating her for selecting your agency to address her debt problems. Knowing the magnitude of her decision and the difficulty of her recovery, you want to provide encouragement that she has taken the correct path toward correcting her negative financial situation.

READ | THINK | WRITE | SPEAK | COLLABORATE

8. Positive News: Personal Employment Information a Click Away (Objs. 1, 2)

Byrne & Company is scheduled to launch a personal information website for employees on May 15 with all access-related problems being handled by the Technology Help Desk. This website will provide employees their payroll history such as past pay stubs including deductions for benefits and withholdings, personal leave information, detailed benefit information such as insurance coverage and retirement plans, etc. Access will be provided through a pre-assigned user identification number and a password that must be changed by May 30.

Required: As human resources director, prepare a memo informing employees of the availability of the personal information website. Describe the benefits employees can gain from the availability of this online system, location on the company's intranet, and secure procedures for accessing information.

9. Claim Letter: Parking Issue Affects Company Interns (Objs. 1, 3)

Watkins Industries owns several condominiums used to house its interns during their short-term assignments. In your position as a human resources manager, you received the following email from one of the interns:

> Could you please assist us with a problem we are having at the condominium. The condominium next to us is being rented by four college students, each with his own car. They are constantly parking in the two parking spots assigned to our unit. Due to limited visitor spots, we often must park in the shopping center across the 4-lane highway. We have repeatedly asked the complex manager to address the problem. Her response has been that she can't control the number of cars renters have. Because the company owns the condominium, I am hoping you are in a stronger position to resolve the issue.

Required: As the human resources manager, write an email message to Nina Valdez, apartment complex manager, requesting a solution to the parking problem. Alternately, your instructor may direct you to prepare a voice script of a telephone conversation with Nina.

10. Routine Request: Arrangement of Facilities (Objs. 1, 3)

Your consulting firm, Kessler & Associates, recently developed a code of professional conduct. To ensure that all employees understand the code and its importance to the firm, the managing partner has directed you to organize a retreat at an out-of-town resort to be held within the next three to six months. The retreat is to begin on Thursday afternoon with a golf scramble followed by a private dinner and social time. Friday will consist of a series of interactive sessions designed to enable employees to experience ethical dilemmas and correctly apply the new code of professional conduct. The Friday luncheon will be highlighted by a national speaker discussing legal and privacy issues. Employees will depart after an informal breakfast on Saturday.

Required:

1. Prepare a script of a voice mail message you will leave for the sales manager at the resort where you hope to schedule the retreat. The message should inquire whether the resort has the facilities and availability for holding the retreat. Use the Web or advertisements to identify a potential location.
2. Prepare an email message you will send to your managing partner, informing him of the plans you have made with the retreat resort.

11. Credit Approval and Customer Order Acknowledgment: New Golf Course Tees Off (Objs. 1, 4)

As the marketing manager for Pacific Golf Supply Co. (PGS), you have just approved a credit account for Highland Lake Golf Club, a new golf course in northern California. Send Jordan Martin, the golf pro, a letter stating that you have approved his club for a $25,000 initial credit line. PGS offers its customers 2/10, n/30 payment terms and charges interest at an 18 percent annual rate on overdue accounts. Each quarter PGS reviews its outstanding accounts and offers an increase in the credit line to any customer having a current account. The letter should confirm that the initial order of golf balls, clubs, and accessories has been shipped via UPS ground (expected delivery time, 10 days). Encourage Kevin to use his remaining $12,400 credit line to invest in quality display units. Explain that experience demonstrates that sales increase by 25 percent when the product is displayed using your display units.

Required: Write the credit approval/order acknowledgment letter to Jordan at 2500 Country Club Drive, Klamath, CA 95548-1200.

12. Procedural Message: Earning a Recruitment Bonus (Objs. 1, 5)

The rapid growth at Southern Communications has strained its ability to attract an adequate supply of qualified accounting, computer, and communication professionals. In response, management has adopted a policy rewarding employees for recruiting and outlined specific procedures for implementing this policy. An employee who recruits an individual to fill a position listed on the company's "Most Wanted" list receives a $2,500 cash bonus. To earn the bonus, the employee must have completed a Recruitment Bonus Request before any communication occurs between the recruit and the company. The form identifies important information, such as the recruit's name, current position, and qualifications. After being signed by the employee, the recruit, and the recruiting director, the completed form is submitted to the human resources department. The recruiting director updates the "Most Wanted" list on a weekly basis.

Required: Prepare a memo or email message to announce the policy to the employees and to identify the procedures to be followed to earn a bonus.

13. Informational Message: Book-Buying in the Digital Age (Objs. 1, 2)

Amazon.com burst onto the Internet scene in 1995 as "Earth's Biggest Bookstore." Amazon's newest offering to book-buying customers is "Amazon Pages," which allows online access to pages, sections, or chapters of a book. Customers can unbundle the needed pages and purchase them at a reduced rate. Although publishers set the rates for individual books, Amazon CEO Jeff Bezos says pages will cost a few cents each. Some industry analysts compare this breakthrough offering from Amazon to what Apple's iTunes did for the music world. According to Bezos, university faculty might benefit from this program by being able to assemble a course kit from three or four chapters from different textbooks and requiring the students to purchase the specific chapters. For more information on Amazon Pages, read these articles:

Chillingsworth, M. (2005, December). Amazon to carve up book delivery. *Information World Review,* 219. Available from Business Source Complete database.

Ouchi, M. S. (2005, November 4). A new chapter for Amazon: Selling online access to books. *The Seattle Times,* p. NA. Available from http://seattletimes.nwsource.com/html/businesstechnology/2002602993_amazon04.html

Required: Respond to this communication as directed by your instructor.

1. As marketing coordinator for the digital content at Amazon.com, design a creative email message to send to past digital content customers announcing the new service available with Amazon Pages. Use creativity in design and wording to show these current customers how the new service can work for them.
2. As web support specialist, write the script of the text that will appear on the Amazon.com website that describes how the pay-per-page service works. Use reader focus and highlight the benefits to be gained by this new book-buying model.

READ | THINK | WRITE | SPEAK | COLLABORATE

14. Analyzing International Business Messages (Objs. 1–5)

Obtain a copy of a business letter written by someone from another culture. Identify the major differences between this letter and a traditional U.S. letter. Include information about cultural differences that might be reflected in the message style. Create a visual of your message and share your analysis with the class as directed by your instructor.

15. Information Message: Conveying Change (Objs. 1, 2)

Dr. Tom Gladen, DDS, has purchased a pediatric dental practice that had seen few changes in its office procedures over the past 20 years. One of Dr. Gladen's first changes was to install a touch screen where patients log in on their arrival, learn about the procedure to be performed, and see other important announcements (such as the arrival of a new video game in the "Sparkles" room).

Required: Prepare the following two client messages:

1. Design a creative postcard or clever e-card to be sent to young patients, introducing the dentist and announcing the opening of the "Sparkles" room, a place where children can play video games while waiting for their appointments. Refer to the Strategic Forces Feature on e-cards in Chapter 3 to learn more about the use of e-cards for business messages and a list of greeting card websites.
2. Write a letter or email to parents introducing the new dentist and other changes in the office, including an automated email reminder system for upcoming appointments.

Place your messages on a visual and share with the class. Be prepared to discuss the adaptations that were necessary based on the audience.

16. Ford Motor Company: Telling Product Development What Customers Want

(Objs. 1, 3)

When Ford products are still in the design stage, Ford asks potential buyers to identify features they might include if they designed their "dream" vehicle. The "Build Your Ford" web interface at www.fordvehicles.com collects information about customer demands that product developers use to determine available features that might be added to the final design.

Your job as marketing director for Ford's Concept Division requires you to oversee the website where this information is collected. When reviewing the data for the Ford Edge CUV, you notice that 40 percent of customers who built an Edge during its concept phase chose to add Sirius Satellite Radio to their options. Your data also show that 65 percent of males aged 18–35 want to add satellite radio. You must meet with the product development team to share this knowledge before they finalize the available options list next week.

Required: Respond to this communication as directed by your instructor.

1. Compose a voice mail message to leave for Derrick Kuzak, group vice president for product development, explaining your immediate need to meet with him, and provide him a list of days and times that you are available.
2. In pairs, meet in your course chat room and assume the two of you are the marketing director and the head of product development. Using your research into the Edge, role play what might happen when these two discuss the issue of adding satellite radio to the available options.

READ | THINK | WRITE | SPEAK | COLLABORATE

17. Form Letters: How Well Do They Work?

(Objs. 1–5)

Many companies naively rely on a file of form letters composed to fit almost any conceivable situation in order to protect against potentially poor writing and to get messages out as quickly as possible. While these form letters may form the basis for routine communication, they often miss the mark.

Required:

1. Read and discuss the following article about a form letter Apple sent to would-be iPhone application developers: www.theregister.co.uk/2008/03/15/apple_iphone_developer_form_letter/
2. In groups of three or four serving as a company's product development team, compose a form letter to send to customers who asked for changes in your product or service. Use your team's experiences and available consumer research to identify and support an innovative change of your choice (e.g., new feature such as unique ring tones, added features, or new phone design). Consider including an incentive to try the new product/service.

18. Appreciation Message: Amara Creekside Resort Caters to Travelers (Objs. 1, 2)

The Amara Creekside Resort in Sedona, Arizona, received the "Connoisseur's Choice"award from *Resort & Great Hotels*, which praised the resort's exceptional commitment to quality, service, and overall guest experience. The resort includes 100 guest rooms, each with either red rock or creek views and with amenities to suit the needs of both business and leisure travelers. The resort's restaurant, the Gallery on Oak Creek, showcases original art in changing exhibits where diners can purchase their favorites for their at-home walls. The resort features an on-site spa, which provides massages, facials, and body treatments for an extra fee. Amara also has meeting space for up to 80 people and social space for up to 100 guests. For more information on the resort, visit www.amararesort.com.

Required: Working in pairs, respond to this communication as directed by your instructor.

1. As co-owners of the Amara Creekside Resort, you annually write to your best customers, thanking them for their visits and encouraging them to return in the upcoming year. Martha Byrne, who played the character Lily Snyder on the daytime drama "As the World Turns," visited your resort the first time after she received a gift certificate from a charity group. She liked your service and amenities so much that she has returned with her family at least twice a year in the last three years. Write a letter to her (and her family) thanking her for her business and inviting her back. (You might consider offering her a discount for booking by a certain date.) Learn more about Martha Byrne by visiting Wikipedia, the free encyclopedia that anyone can edit.
2. Design a creative e-vite to send to community leaders, suppliers, and vendors, inviting them to a celebration of the resort's recent recognition as a "Connoisseur's Choice" property. The celebration will be held May 10 at 7 p.m. and the dress is semi-formal. Develop a theme for the evening that can also be used on the e-card.

19. Information Message: Internet Usage Policy Announced (Objs. 1, 2)

Concerns have been raised over the increasing number of employees listening to Internet radio on the job. Current company policy prohibits listening to the radio while on the job, as Internet radio is distracting workers in adjacent cubicles and affecting overall productivity. Related Internet usage problems include employee time spent managing investment portfolios, shopping, keeping up with favorite sports teams, blogging, and visiting questionable sites. New procedures are necessary to address these new technology capabilities. As director of human resources, you have been authorized to develop an appropriate company Internet usage policy that will go into effect on September 1. Using your group members' own work experience and information obtained from an online search, develop a policy that applies to acceptable Internet usage. Provide a detailed explanation of acceptable behavior that employees can follow consistently.

Required: Send your policy as an attachment to an email message to your instructor or, if directed, bring a copy of the policy to class for discussion.

20. Reply to Routine Request: Feedback from Blog Requires Action (Objs. 1, 3)

You are employed by Everything Electronics, a company that sells and services computer and audio equipment. You were just alerted to a recurring topic being discussed at the social networking sites your company monitors. There appears to be a great deal of confusion over the need to properly eject flash drives, especially by individuals who have lost access to their data. Now that you are aware of the problem, develop a message to customers reminding them of the proper ejection procedures for flash drives.

Required: In small groups, develop a creative message communicating the company's response to this valuable customer feedback. You may choose to post a new question to your frequently asked questions (FAQ) page on the website; design a creative flyer to be mailed to customers; write a letter, email message, or blog post as directed by your instructor.

CASES

© JOSHUA KRISTAL/ALAMY

1. Customer Communication: Kindle Propels Popularity of Ebooks (Objs. 1, 3, 5)

Though ebooks have been around for more than a decade, consumers largely ignored electronic book reader devices, which were often cumbersome and hard to read. The Kindle, introduced in 2007 by Amazon.com, changed that trend. The Kindle is about the size of a paperback book and initially retailed for $359, though more streamlined and less expensive models have followed. Electronic books can be purchased online, downloaded onto the Kindle, and read from the screen. The Kindle holds about 200 books, and users can also subscribe to newspapers and blogs. During the first nine months after its introduction, Kindle sales produced $100 million in revenue for Amazon. Adopters during this initial period were primarily early adopters and avid readers who traveled extensively. The device appeared to be equally attractive to both men and women, and was most popular among 55- to-64-year-olds.

While competing products appeared on the market, the Kindle received a big boost in October 2008, when Oprah Winfrey endorsed the product on her show. Available supplies could not keep up with demand during the Christmas 2008 season, and Amazon was forced for several weeks to show the item as out of stock and take reservations for order fulfillment.

You can read more about the Kindle at the Amazon website (www.amazon.com/Kindle-Amazons-Wireless-Reading-Device/dp/B000FI73MA) and by accessing the following articles:

Ricadela, A. (2008, August 28). Amazon beefs up Kindle franchise. *Business Week Online*, p. 12. Available from Business Source Complete database.

Stone, B., & Rich, M. (2008, December 23). Turning page, e-books start to take hold. *The New York Times*. Available at www.nytimes.com/2008/12/24/technology/24kindle.html?em

Required: Respond to the following communication situations as directed by your instructor.

1. As customer service manager, you receive frequently asked questions from customers interested in purchasing a Kindle. Compose a series of FAQs about the Kindle, along with answers, that can be placed on the Amazon website.
2. Compose an email message that can be sent to customers on the wait list who have reserved a Kindle.

© BBC LTD. COURTESY: EVERETT COLLECTION

2. Video Case: The Office: Delivering Good News the Rock Star Way??

In this clip, David gathers his employees to inform them about the future of their positions.

Complete the following activities as directed by your instructor after viewing the video:

1. In small groups, discuss David's entrance at the beginning of the video. How does the "rock star" quality of the entrance add to or detract from the news he is delivering?
2. What mistakes does David make in the way he delivers his news once he takes the microphone?
3. As David, compose an email message to employees explaining that they are keeping their jobs and that you are staying on as manager. Attach to your message a creative electronic invitation asking them to join you in a celebration of the company and the part they play in making the company a success.

3. Snoop Proof Your PC

Protecting the security of data files and computer activities is high priority for individuals and businesses alike. However, your PC is ready and able to reveal not only your data but what you've been doing with your computer. Within a few hours, a snoop can determine and find the incoming and outgoing mail you deleted, websites you visited, data you've entered on web forms, and even phrases you deleted from documents. Fortunately, you can take steps to protect yourself.

Using effective password protection is a simple first step. Lock important files by using carefully chosen passwords. The best passwords aren't real words or dates; they use a combination of letters, numbers, and punctuation. Knowing how to truly rid your computer of deleted and trashed files is another important security step. Regularly clearing temporary menus and files, as well as history listings, will assure that your recent file activities are not recorded for the would-be snoop to peruse.

An obvious way to protect your information is to encrypt sensitive information. Good encryption and locking solutions are increasingly user friendly and inexpensive. Numerous products are available, with the most effective tools encrypting both file contents and passwords used to access them. Encryption usually defeats casual efforts at intrusion and complicates even advanced snooping attempts.

Cookies can also provide information from your computer to remote third parties. *Cookies* are short pieces of data used by web servers to help identify the user and possibly to track a user's browsing habits. Cookies can tell a web server that you have been there before and can pass short bits of information from your computer to the server. If you are concerned about being identified or about having your activities traced, set your browser to not accept cookies or use one of the new cookie blocking packages. Remember, though, that blocking all cookies prevents some online services from working.

Another potential PC leak that is often overlooked is the discarded hard drive. About 150,000 hard drives are retired each year, but many find their way back onto the market. Stories occasionally surface about personal and corporate information turning up on used hard drives, raising concerns about privacy and danger of identity theft. A Nevada woman bought a used computer and discovered it contained prescription records on 2,000 customers of an Arizona pharmacy.[13] In most operating systems, simply deleting a file and even emptying it from the trash folder does not necessarily make the information irretrievable. The information can live on until it is overwritten by new files. Even reformatting a drive may not eradicate all data.

The most common breaches of computer privacy are committed by those who have the most opportunity: coworkers, friends, and family members. But nameless, faceless hackers can also invade your computer via your Internet connection. Installing a firewall can help protect you from unauthorized access, possible file damage, and even identity theft.

Visit your companion website, www.cengage.com/bcomm/lehman, for links to several articles that provide helpful information about how to snoop proof your computer. As directed by your instructor, complete one or more of the following:

1. Locate other articles that discuss ways to protect your computer files and activities. Prepare an oral presentation about your findings.
2. Mark Twain once said, "There is no security in life—only opportunity." How does this philosophy relate to the use of computers in an environment of inherent security risks? Prepare a one-page essay that explains your reasoning.
3. Make a chart that summarizes the major snoop risks on your PC and actions that can be taken to minimize each risk.

© DAVID R. FRAZIER PHOTOLIBRARY, INC./ALAMY

4. Informative Presentation: AMBER Alert Portal Uses Real-Time Information (Objs. 1, 3)

Created in 1996, The AMBER Alert System is a missing child response program named for 9-year-old Amber Hagerman, who was kidnapped from Arlington, Texas, and brutally murdered. The program, which means America's Missing: Broadcast Emergency Response, uses the resources of law enforcement and the media to notify the public when a suspected predator kidnaps a child. The system is used in all 50 states and has assisted in the rescue of more than 200 children.

In July 2004, the AMBER Alert System aided in the launch of the AMBER Alert Portal. The seamless, national portal is a private/public partnership between state governments, law enforcement agencies, broadcasters, organizations, and private corporations. The portal has reduced the time to issue an alert by 90 percent, which greatly increased the chances of recovering kidnapped children. Through the portal, law enforcement can input information into one web portal where software reconfigures the information for different types of broadcast, including radio, road signs, cell phone, email, and wireless devices.

You can learn more about the Amber Alert at http://www.amberalert911.com/faq.php and by reading the article following article:below linked from the AMBER Alert website at

Morris, B. R. (2004, July 29). How it works: Using the Web to sound an alarm on missing children. *New York Times*. Available at http://www.nytimes.com/2004/07/29/technology/how-it-works-using-the-web-to-sound-an-alarm-on-missing-children.html

Required: Respond to the following communication situations as directed by your instructor.

1. You are the executive assistant for the Director of the Mississippi Highway Patrol, Colonel Marvin Curtis. He has asked you to research the AMBER Alert Portal Consortium because he believes Mississippi, which currently participates in the AMBER Alert program, should take steps necessary to access and use the portal for state law enforcement. You must provide a list of talking points for his presentation to the Mississippi Department of Public Safety Commissioner, George Phillips, next week. Complete an outline for a 10–15-minute presentation for Colonel Curtis that discusses the AMBER Alert Portal and Consortium, the processes for joining the consortium, and how using the portal could benefit law enforcement in Mississippi.
2. Design an electronic presentation (including speaker's notes) for Col. Curtis to use to support his presentation.

© CHRIS HONDROS/ GETTY IMAGES

5. Routine Request: ASPCA Members Can Help Animals Affected by Hurricane Katrina (Objs. 1, 3)

In September 2005, the American Society for the Prevention of Cruelty to Animals set up two web-based databases to help recover animals affected by Hurricane Katrina, a category 5 hurricane that affected Louisiana, Mississippi, and Alabama in September 2005. One database solicited volunteers for help in affected areas while the other provided a place to register lost pets and view photos of pets found. You may learn more about the ASPCA by visiting its website at www.aspca.org. You also may learn more about its programs to help animals affected by Hurricane Katrina by reading the following article:

Sullivan, J. (2005, September 3). ASPCA sets up database for lost pets and volunteer opportunities. *PR Newswire*, NA. Available at http://cats.about.com/od/disaster/a/katrinaASPCA.htm

Required: Respond to the following communication situations as directed by your instructor.

1. As membership director of your local ASPCA chapter, send an email message to all of your members announcing the databases and emphasizing how your members can help. You might highlight volunteer opportunities at affected shelters, monetary donation opportunities, or temporary animal adoption opportunities. While members need specific information about how they can help, you can safely assume they are interested in the health and well-being of animals and want to help. Persuasive techniques are not necessary because this message can be considered routine.
2. As a group, complete a public service announcement to run on your local public radio station. The purpose of the PSA is to provide information about the plight of animals following a natural disaster and give information about how the average person can help. Be sure to provide contact information for your local ASPCA chapter. Be creative in how you provide this information; consider using a skit or imaginative concept that will fit the radio medium.

Chapter 7
Delivering Bad-News Messages

"Once they found out that we thought they were alive, they really should have come out and told the families that was incorrect information."

Nephew of a deceased miner

© CHIP SOMODEVILLA/GETTY IMAGES

Objectives When you have completed Chapter 7, you will be able to:

1. Explain the steps in the inductive outline and understand its use for specific situations.
2. Discuss strategies for developing the five components of a bad-news message.
3. Prepare messages refusing requests and claims.
4. Prepare messages handling problems with customers' orders and denying credit.
5. Prepare messages providing constructive criticism, communicating negative organizational news, and responding to crises.

SHOWCASE PART 1  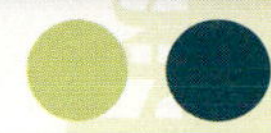

Sago Mine Tragedy Illustrates Difficulties in Sharing Bad News

Miracle in the mines! Alive! One of the most widespread cases of misinformation occurred on January 4, 2006. Headlines in *USA Today*, *The New York Times*, the *Minneapolis Star Tribune*, and *The Washington Post*, along with more than half of all the newspapers in the country, erroneously reported in front-page stories that 12 trapped miners in West Virginia had been found alive.[1] In reality, only one miner had survived.

How did such a grave inaccuracy become so widely publicized? Many believe that reporters and editors got carried away by what seemed to be miraculous news. Newspapers were also under deadline pressure, as many were finalizing the next day's edition as the story broke. Rather than print the story as unconfirmed, almost all reported without qualification that the miners were safe.

After receiving word that their loved ones were alive, relatives were asked to gather in a local church where they informally celebrated the miracle. Three long hours later, however, joy gave way to grief when mine officials broke the terrible news that only one miner had survived. International Coal Group president, Ben Hatfield, said the company knew within 20 minutes that initial reports that all the men had survived were incorrect but were unsure as to how many had survived. Attempting to explain the confusion, Hatfield said that stray cell phone conversations from the rescue team underground to the command center were picked up by various people and spread like wildfire. Another company spokesperson explained that the misunderstanding resulted because the mine rescuers treating the lone survivor were wearing muffling, full-face oxygen masks when they used radios to report their findings to the fresh-air base, who then contacted command center personnel.

Hatfield said the company tried to send word through state police to the church that they didn't know whether others survived. That word apparently never got through, and company personnel did not go to the church themselves to communicate their doubts. "We got the high and then they waited too long to really tell us," said the nephew of one of the deceased miners. "Once they found out that we thought they were alive, they really should have come out and told the families that was incorrect information."[2]

"We fully recognize the criticism the company has received," said Hatfield. "Rightly or wrongly, we believe it was important to make factual statements to the families and we believed word had been sent to the church that additional reports may not have been accurate. . . . They needed good information, and we were trying to get them good information."[3]

Disappointing news is never welcomed, but the timing and manner of delivery can certainly impact a receiver's reaction. You'll certainly have to share bad news from time to time. In this chapter, you will learn how to present negative news tactfully and in the least offensive manner.

www.msha.gov/sagomine/sagomine.asp

SEE SHOWCASE PART 2, ON PAGE 255
FOR SPOTLIGHT COMMUNICATOR JOE MANCHIN, WEST VIRGINIA GOVERNOR, AND HIS ROLE IN COMMUNICATING WITH THE FAMILIES AFFECTED BY THE MINING TRAGEDY.

Choosing an Appropriate Channel and Organizational Pattern

How does empathy assist in conveying bad news?

The Sago mine disaster illustrates vividly that perceptions of employees, local citizens, and the public at large are closely tied to an organization's ability to handle difficult situations with tact and empathy. As a skilled communicator, you will attempt to deliver bad news in such a way that the recipient supports the decision and is willing to continue a positive relationship. To accomplish these goals, allow empathy for the receiver to direct your choice of an appropriate channel and an outline for presenting a logical discussion of the facts and the unpleasant idea. Use tactful and effective language to aid you in developing a clear, yet sensitive, message.

Channel Choice and Commitment to Tact

Personal delivery of bad news has been the preferred medium for delivering bad news because it signals the importance of the news and shows empathy for the recipient. Face-to-face delivery also provides the benefit of nonverbal communication and immediate feedback, which minimizes the misinterpretation of these highly sensitive messages. Personal delivery, however, carries a level of discomfort and the potential for escalation of emotion. A voice on the telephone triggers the same discomfort as a face-to-face meeting, and the increased difficulty of interpreting the intensity of nonverbal cues over the telephone only adds to the natural discomfort associated with delivering negative information.

The widespread use of electronic media for organizational communication and studies related to the interaction dynamics of various communication media may challenge the current practice of delivering bad news in person. A study by the Institute for Operations Research concluded that negative messages delivered by email rather than personally or by telephone are more honest and accurate and cause less discomfort for the sender. While inappropriate for extremely personal or potentially legal situations, such as firing an employee, email can be a viable communication channel for facilitating the delivery of bad news when face-to-face interaction is not possible due to geographic

© CREATAS IMAGES/JUPITER IMAGES

How Do You Like Your Bad News Served? While face-to-face sharing of bad news has its advantages, increasing dependence on electronic communication has led to the cautious use of email for delivering some negative messages. Email provides quick, same-time delivery to employees who are geographically dispersed and can make the job of sharing bad news easier for those who become overly emotional in difficult situations. Honest, candid electronic communication delivered on a regular basis is more effective than occasional dire pronouncements made when disaster hits. A commitment to open internal communications builds a sense of community and trust that prepares employees for bad news when it must be delivered.

separation. Furthermore, the straight talk fostered by email may also improve upward communication and thus the performance of the company as reluctant employees may feel more comfortable relaying unpopular news to their superiors.[4]

Recall an incident when you had either a positive or a negative feeling for a person or company who gave you unpleasant news. What approach was used in sharing the news?

You must be cautious when you deliver bad news electronically, whether by email or electronic postings. While you may feel more comfortable avoiding the discomfort of facing the recipient, the impersonal nature of the computer may lead to careless writing that is tactless and unempathetic, and perhaps even defamatory. Stay focused and follow the same communication strategies you would apply if you were speaking face to face or writing a more formal message. Regardless of the medium, your objective is to help the audience understand and accept your message, and this requires empathy and tact.

"You're fired" became a familiar phrase immortalized by Donald Trump on the hit show *The Apprentice*. Though such bluntness may work on television, it is rarely recommended in actual work situations. Tactlessness can be serious when your personal response fails to soothe negative feelings and ensure a harmonious relationship with a customer, client, or employee. You may find it difficult to show tact when you doubt the legitimacy of a request or simply don't have the time to prepare an effective bad-news message. When this conflict exists, you must remember that your message delivered on behalf of the company is a direct reflection on the company's image.

ALI GOLDSTEIN/© NBC/COURTESY EVERETT COLLECTION

Your Turn 7-1
Miscue

University of Washington quarterback Casey Paus learned for the first time at a press conference that he would no longer be his team's starting quarterback. Coach Keith Gilbertson said after revealing the news to the media that he assumed Paus had been previously informed by the offensive coordinator and quarterbacks' coach. Responding to charges of poor communication among his coaching staff, Gilbertson said, "I want to make sure that any characterization that I am not first and foremost sincere about my players' welfare or their treatment or how we talk to them or how we feel is (wrong). I'm very careful to let those people know that we have their best interest at heart."[5]

TAKE ACTION:

- Discuss how Gilbertson could have better demonstrated his commitment to his player's best interest.
- List examples of other situations of which you are aware of bad news being shared in an inappropriate manner or location.

Use of the Inductive Approach to Build Goodwill

Just as good news is accompanied with details, bad news is accompanied with supporting reasons and explanations. If the bad news is presented in the first sentence, the reaction is likely to be negative: "They never gave me a fair chance"; "That's unfair"; "This just can't be." Having made a value judgment on reading the first sentence, receivers are naturally reluctant to change their minds before the last sentence—even though the intervening sentences present a valid basis for doing so. Once disappointed by the idea contained in the first sentence, receivers are tempted to concentrate on *refuting* (instead of *understanding*) supporting details.

From the communicator's point of view, details that support a refusal are very important. If the supporting details are understood and believed, the message may be readily accepted and good business relationships preserved. Because the reasons behind the bad news are so important, the communicator needs to organize the message in such a way as to emphasize the reasons.

What are the consequences if bad news is shared too early? Too late?

The chances of getting the receiver to understand the reasons are much better *before* the bad news is presented than *after* the bad news is presented. If the bad news precedes the reasons, (1) the message might be discarded before this important portion is even read, or (2) the disappointment experienced when reading the bad news might interfere with the receiver's ability to comprehend or accept the supporting explanation.

The five-step outline shown in Figure 7-1 simplifies the process of organizing bad-news messages. These five steps are applied in messages illustrated in this chapter.

Although the outline has five points, a bad-news message may or may not have five paragraphs. More than one paragraph may be necessary for conveying supporting reasons. In the illustrations in this chapter (as well as examples in Appendix A), note that the first and final paragraphs are seldom longer than two sentences. In fact, one-sentence paragraphs at the message's beginning look inviting to read.

The inductive sequence of ideas has the following advantages:

- Sufficient identification of the subject of the message without first turning off the receiver.
- Presentation of the reasons *before* the refusal, where they are more likely to be understood and will receive appropriate emphasis.
- Avoidance of a negative reaction. By the time the reasons are read, they seem sensible, and the refusal is foreseen. Because it is expected, the statement of refusal does not come as a shock.
- De-emphasis of the refusal by closing on a neutral or pleasant note. By showing a willingness to cooperate in some way, the sender conveys a desire to be helpful.

When would a deductive approach be appropriate for presenting bad news?

You might speculate that receivers may become impatient when a message is inductive. Concise, well-written explanations are not likely to make a receiver impatient. They relate to the receiver's problem, present information not already known, and help the receiver understand. However, if a receiver becomes impatient while reading a well-written explanation, that impatience is less damaging to understanding than would be the anger or disgust that often results from encountering bad news in the first sentence.

Exceptions to the Inductive Approach

Normally, the writer's purpose is to convey a clear message and retain the recipient's goodwill; thus, the inductive outline is appropriate. In the rare circumstances in

FIGURE 7-1

Indirect Outline Used in Bad-News Messages Sent in Written, Electronic, or Spoken Form

© PHOTODISC/GETTY IMAGES

Letters
Memos
Written

Email
Instant message
Website
Blog
Text message
Electronic

© PHOTODISC/GETTY IMAGES

In person
Telephone
Voice mail
Spoken

© COMSTOCK IMAGES/ JUPITERIMAGES

OPENING:

Begins with neutral idea that leads to refusal or bad news

BODY:

1. Presents facts, analysis, and reasons for refusal or bad news
2. States bad news using positive tone and de-emphasis techniques
3. Includes counterproposal or "silver lining" idea

CLOSING:

Closes with ideas that shift focus away from refusal or bad news and indicates continuing relationship with receiver.

which a choice must be made between the two, clarity is the better choice. When the deductive approach will serve a communicator's purpose better, it should be used. For example, if you submit a clear and tactful refusal and the receiver submits a second request, a deductive presentation may be justified in the second refusal. Apparently, the refusal needs the emphasis provided by a deductive outline. Placing a refusal in the first sentence can be justified when one or more of the following circumstances exists:

- The message is the second response to a repeated request.
- A very small, insignificant matter is involved.
- The request is obviously ridiculous, immoral, unethical, illegal, or dangerous.
- The sender's intent is to "shake" the receiver.
- The sender–recipient relationship is so close and longstanding that satisfactory human relations can be taken for granted.
- The sender *wants* to demonstrate authority.

In most situations, the preceding circumstances do not exist. When they do, a sender's goals may be accomplished by stating bad news in the first sentence.

Your Turn 7-2
Electronic Café

DISCUSSION BOARDS ACCOMMODATE ONLINE BRAINSTORMING

When Diane Watkins, State Farm senior marketing specialist, posted her 10 best sales tips on the company's intranet discussion board, what happened next was a sales manager's dream come true. Over 40 agents nationwide added their own tips, and hundreds read the postings.[6] Online brainstorming through discussion boards, also known as electronic bulletin boards, is one of the most important success stories of the digital economy.

TAKE ACTION:

- Read more about the value of discussion boards and how to use them effectively. Access your companion website at www.cengage.com/bcomm/lehman to link to the readings.
- Participate in a discussion board. Your instructor will give you directions about how to access the discussion board in your online course and post your thoughts on the following: Discussion board communication fills a niche not addressed by other forms of communication because . . .

Developing a Bad-News Message

Developing a bad-news message following the inductive outline is challenging. The following suggestions will aid you in writing the (a) introductory paragraph, (b) explanation, (c) bad-news statement, (d) offering a counterproposal or silver lining idea, and (e) closing paragraph.

Writing the Introductory Paragraph

Consider bad news you might have to share. How would you word your introductory "buffer" paragraph?

The introductory paragraph in the bad-news message should accomplish the following objectives: (1) provide a buffer to cushion the bad news that will follow, (2) let the receiver know what the message is about without stating the obvious, and (3) serve as a transition into the discussion of reasons without revealing the bad news or leading the receiver to expect good news. If these objectives can be accomplished in one sentence,

It's Not Just What You Say, But How You Say It. Effective communication strategies vary with the needs and expectations of the audience. While U.S. businesspeople typically prefer the indirect style for delivering bad news, the Dutch and Germans tend to prefer the direct pattern for positive and negative messages. Asians and Latinos may avoid saying "no" or give a qualified "no" in order to save face. As compared with younger Americans, baby boomers typically prefer more formal communication channels and respond to appeals to fairness to all rather than to achievement of personal goals. Understanding value differences can aid in interpreting messages from people of different cultures and generations.[7]

that sentence can be the first paragraph. Avoid the following weaknesses when writing the introductory paragraph:

- **Avoid empty acknowledgments of the obvious.** *"I am writing in response to your letter requesting . . ."* or *"Your message of the 14th has been given to me for reply"* wastes space to present points of no value. Beginning with *I* signals the message may be writer centered.
- **Avoid tipping off the bad news too early.** *"Although the refund requested in your letter of May 1 cannot be approved, . . ."* may cause an immediate emotional reaction resulting in the message being discarded or interfering with understanding the explanations that follow. The neutral statement *"Your request for an adjustment has been considered. However, . . ."* does not reveal whether the answer is "Yes" or "No," but the use of "however" signals that the answer is "No" before the reasons are presented. Such a beginning has about the same effect as an outright "No."
- **Avoid starting too positively so as to build false hopes.** Empathetic statements such as *"I can understand how you felt when you were asked to pay an extra $54"* may lead the receiver to expect good news. When a preceding statement has implied that an affirmative decision will follow, a negative decision is all the more disappointing.

Study the following examples that use transition statements to achieve a coherent opening:

Your application was reviewed separately by two loan officers.	Reveals the topic as a reply to a recipient's loan application.
Each officer considered . . .	Uses "officer" to transition from first to second paragraph. Discusses officers' reviews introduced in first sentence.

Following your request for permission to pick up food left over from the buffets served in our conference center, we reviewed our experiences of recent years.	Reveals subject of message as reply to humanitarian organization's request.
Last year, two incidents . . .	Uses "year" to tie second paragraph to first and transitions into discussion of "experiences" mentioned in first paragraph.

Here are several ideas that can be incorporated into effective beginning paragraphs:

Can you think of other ideas for effective opening paragraphs?

- **Compliment.** A message denying a customer's request could begin by recognizing the customer's promptness in making payments.
- **Point of agreement.** A sentence that reveals agreement with a statement made in the message could get the message off to a positive discussion of other points.

- **Good news.** When a message contains a request that must be refused and another that is being answered favorably, beginning with the favorable answer can be effective.
- **Resale.** A claim refusal could begin with some favorable statement about the product.
- **Review.** Refusal of a current request could be introduced by referring to the initial transaction or by reviewing certain circumstances that preceded the transaction.
- **Gratitude.** In spite of the unjustified request, the receiver may have done or said something for which you are grateful. An expression of gratitude could be used as a positive beginning.

Presenting the Facts, Analysis, and Reasons

What would be a good reason for a price increase from the customer's point of view?

The reasons section of the bad-news message is extremely important because people who are refused want to know why. When people say "No" they usually do so because they think "No" is the better answer for all concerned. They can see how recipients will ultimately benefit from the refusal. If a message is based on a sound decision, and if it has been well written, recipients will understand and accept the reasons and the forthcoming refusal statement as valid.

To accomplish this goal, begin with a well-written first paragraph that transitions the receiver smoothly into the reasons section. Then, develop the reasons section following these guidelines:

- **Provide a smooth transition from the opening paragraph to the explanation.** The buffer should help set the stage for a logical movement into the discussion of the reasons.
- **Include a concise discussion of one or more reasons that are logical to the receiver.** Read the section aloud to identify flaws in logic or the need for additional explanation.
- **Show receiver benefit and/or consideration.** Emphasize how the receiver will benefit from the decision. Avoid insincere, empty statements such as "To improve our service to you, . . ."
- **Avoid using "company policy" as the reason.** Disclose the reason behind the policy, which likely will include benefits to the receiver. For example, a customer is more likely to understand and accept a 15 percent restocking fee if the policy is not presented as the "reason" for the refusal. Note the letter in Figure 7-7 on page 246 presents specific benefits to the receiver for the company's restocking policy.

The principles for developing the reasons section are illustrated in Figure 7-2, a letter written by an accounting firm refusing to accept a financial audit engagement.

What is the value of balancing negative feedback with a few positives when evaluating performance on the job or in class?

Writing the Bad-News Statement

In a sense, a paragraph that presents the reasoning behind a refusal at least partially conveys the refusal before it is stated directly or indirectly. Yet one sentence needs to convey (directly or by implication) the conclusion to which the preceding details have been leading. A refusal (bad news) needs to be clear; however, you can subordinate the refusal so that the reasons get the deserved emphasis. The following techniques will help you achieve this goal.

- **Position the bad-news statement strategically.** Using the inductive outline positions the bad-news statement in a less important position—sandwiched between an opening buffer statement and a positive closing. Additionally, the refusal statement should be included in the same paragraph as the reasons, since placing it in a paragraph by itself would give too much emphasis to the bad news. When the preceding explanation is tactful and relevant, resentment over the bad news is minimized. Positioning the bad-news statement in the dependent clause of a complex sentence will also cushion the bad news. This technique places the bad news in a less visible, less emphatic position. In the sentence, *"Although current economic conditions prevent us from being a corporate sponsor this year, we do want to support your worthy project in the future,"* the emphasis is directed toward a promise of help at another time.
- **Use passive voice, general terms, and abstract nouns.** Review the *emphasis techniques* that you studied in Chapter 3 as you consider methods for presenting bad news with human relations in mind.

What other words could you add to the following lists of negative and positive words?

- **Use positive language to accentuate the positive.** Simply focus on the good instead of the bad, the pleasant instead of the unpleasant, what can be done instead of what cannot be done. Compared with a negative idea presented in negative terms, a negative idea presented in positive terms is more likely to be accepted. When you are tempted to use the following terms, search instead for words or ideas that sound more positive:

Ineffective Example

complaint	incompetent	misled	regrettable
error	inexcusable	mistake	unfortunate
failure	lied	neglect	wrong

To businesspeople who conscientiously practice empathy, such terms may not even come to mind when communicating the unpleasant. Words in the preceding list evoke negative feelings that contrast sharply with the positive feelings evoked by words such as:

Effective Example

accurate	concise	enthusiasm	productive
approval	durable	generous	recommendation
assist	energetic	gratitude	respect

To increase the number of pleasant-sounding words in your messages, practice thinking positively. Strive to see the good in situations and in others.

Compose a sentence that implies management's refusal to adopt a company sponsored volunteer program. Contrast that sentence to a direct statement of refusal.

Imply the refusal when the receiver can understand the message without a definite statement of the bad news. By *implying* the "No" answer, the response achieves several purposes: (1) uses positive language, (2) conveys reasons or at least a positive attitude, and (3) seems more respectful. For example, during the noon hour one employee says to another, "Will you go with me to see this afternoon's baseball game?" "No, I won't" communicates a negative response, but it seems unnecessarily direct and harsh. The same message (invitation is rejected) can be clearly stated in an *indirect* way (by implication) by saying "I must get my work done," or even, "I'm a football fan." Note the positive tone of the following implied refusals:

IMPLIED REFUSAL	UNDERLYING MESSAGE
I wish I could.	• Other responsibilities prohibit, but recipient would like to accept.
Had you selected the variable mortgage rate, you could have taken advantage of the recent drop in interest rates.	• States a condition under which answer would have been "Yes" instead of "No." Note use of subjunctive words "if" and "would."
By accepting the arrangement, Akers Industries would have tripled its insurance costs.	• States the obviously unacceptable results of complying with request.

Can you identify which of the suggested techniques were used to cushion the bad-news statement in the following example?

Although the Denley Road property was selected as the building site, nearness to the railroad was considered a plus for the Nicholson property.

1. States what was done rather than what was *not* done.
2. Includes a positive idea (*nearness to the railroad*) to accentuate a positive aspect and thus cushion the bad news.
3. Uses passive voice (*property was selected*) to depersonalize the message.
4. Places the bad news in the dependent clause of a complex sentence ("although the Denley property was selected"). The positive idea in the independent clause (*nearness* to the *railroad*) will receive more attention.

These de-emphasis techniques are illustrated in the messages that follow. The Strategic Forces feature, "Assessing Template Documents Available with Word Processing Software," addresses the advisability of using template documents available with major word processing software, especially those that convey bad news.

CHANGING TECHNOLOGY

STRATEGIC FORCES

Assessing Template Documents Available with Word Processing Software

Template letters and documents are a common feature of leading word processing programs. In Microsoft Word, for example, template documents are available as free downloads from Microsoft Office Online. Template documents are also available for download from various websites, some for a fee. To use such standard templates, you select a type of document from an extensive menu, including letters, memos, newsletters, brochures, flyers, minutes, and so on. Next, you select from a gallery of template documents classified by categories. The "Letters" category might include choices such as business, community, employment, personal, etc. By selecting, "Letters," and "Personal," you open a form letter for service complaint situations, for instance, that can be modified to fit the situation at hand.

The accompanying illustrated dispute over credit card charge template letter can be quickly modified for various situations. The template feature appears, at first, to be a great time saver for the busy writer. Unfortunately, however, such template examples frequently do not reflect the elements needed for effective inductive, deductive, or persuasive messages and may illustrate a document format that is not appropriate for a particular audience or purpose. Additionally, following a template too closely can result in a document that sounds "canned" and unoriginal to a customer, business associate, or future employer. The effective writer recognizes both the obvious advantages and the inherent disadvantages of templates and will make cautious use of such "instant" documents.

Application

Select a word processing program that includes template documents.

- Select a document type that should reflect the deductive (good-news or neutral-news) pattern. Using the checklist at the end of Chapter 6, evaluate how well the template document follows the recommended development pattern for deductive messages. Note in what areas the template deviates from the recommendations.
- Select a template document type that should reflect the inductive (bad-news) pattern. Using the checklist at the end of this chapter, evaluate how well the template document follows the recommended development pattern for inductive messages. Note how the template deviates from recommendations.

[Your Name]
[Street Address]
[City, ST ZIP Code]
July 9, 2011

[Recipient Name]
[Title]
[Company Name]
[Street Address]
[City, ST ZIP Code]

Dear **[Recipient Name]**:

On **[date]**, I notified you by telephone that the credit card issued to me by your company, **[credit card number]** expiration date **[expiration date]**, had been lost or stolen. My most recent statement shows unauthorized transactions charged to my card after I reported it missing.

I have enclosed a copy of the credit card statement with the unauthorized charges highlighted. I have also enclosed a copy of the credit card agreement, which states that I am not liable for any unauthorized charges occurring after I have reported my card missing.

Please remove these unauthorized charges from my statement. Thank you for your prompt attention to this matter.

Offering a Counterproposal or "Silver Lining" Idea

Following negative news with an alternative action, referred to as a *counterproposal*, will assist in preserving a relationship with the receiver. Because it states what you can do, including a counterproposal may eliminate the need to state the refusal directly. The counterproposal can follow a refusal stated in a tactful, sensitive manner. When global Internet services and media company AOL was faced with laying off 2000 workers, the silver lining offered was a generous severance package and aid in transitioning to other job opportunities.[8]

What counterproposal could you offer in a "No, thank you" letter to a job applicant?

While the counterproposal may represent a tangible benefit, at times it is more intangible in nature. For instance, in a letter that informs a job applicant that he or she was not selected to fill the position, the counterproposal might be an offer to reconsider the applicant's résumé when other appropriate positions become available. Any counterproposal must, of course, be reasonable. For instance, when informing a customer of an inability to meet a promised delivery deadline, an unreasonable counterproposal would be to offer the merchandise at no charge. A reasonable counterproposal might be to include some additional items at no charge or to offer a discount certificate good on the customer's next order.

When no reasonable counterproposal is apparent, the sender may be able to offer a "silver lining" thought that turns the discussion back into the positive direction. For instance, a statement to tenants announcing an increase in rent might be followed by a description of improved lighting that will be installed in the parking lot of the apartment complex. When offering a counterproposal or silver lining statement, care must be taken to assure that the idea does not seem superficial or minimize the recipient's situation.

Closing Positively

After presenting valid reasons and a tactful refusal followed with a counterproposal or silver lining, a closing paragraph should demonstrate empathy without further reference to the bad news. A pleasant closing paragraph should close with an empathetic tone and achieve the following goals:

Why should a reference to the refusal be avoided in the final paragraph?

- **De-emphasize the unpleasant part of the message.** End on a positive note that takes the emphasis away from the bad news previously presented. A statement of refusal (or bad news) in the last sentence or paragraph would place too much emphasis on it. Preferably, *reasons* (instead of bad news) should remain uppermost in the receiver's mind. Placing bad news last would make the ending seem cold and abrupt.
- **Add a unifying quality to the message.** Make your final sentence an *appropriate* closing that brings a unifying quality to the whole message. Repetition of a word or reference to some positive idea that appears early in the message serves this purpose well. Avoid restatement of the refusal or direct reference to it. This paragraph is usually shorter than the preceding explanatory paragraphs, often one or two sentences.

What feeling do you hope to create for your reader as you end your communication?

- **Include a positive, forward-looking idea.** This idea might include a reference to some pleasant aspect of the preceding discussion or a future aspect of the business relationship, resale or sales promotion, or an offer to help in some way. Consider the following closures that apply these suggestions:

  Reference to some pleasant aspect of the preceding discussion:

  "Your addition of the home mortgage rider to your policy last year was certainly a wise decision." Home mortgage and other provisions had been mentioned in the early part of a letter to a client who was refused a double-indemnity settlement.

  Use of resale or sales promotional material:

  "According to a recent survey, an advanced resolution 24-bit DVD produces sound qualities that are far superior; it was an ideal choice." A reminder that the DVD has a superior feature will assist in regaining goodwill after a customer's request for free repair has been refused.

  An expression of willingness to assist in some *other* way:

  Specifically, you may offer an alternative solution to the receiver's problem or useful information that could not be presented logically with the bad news.

  "Our representative will show you some samples during next week's sales call." The samples are being proposed as a possible solution to the receiver's problem.

  Avoid including the following types of statements in the closing paragraph:

Recall an incident in which you received a disappointing message. How could the messages have been improved?

- **Trite statements that may seem shallow and superficial.** The well-worn statement, *"Thank you for your interest,"* is often used thoughtlessly. It may seem shallow and superficial. *"When we can be of further help, please do not hesitate to call or write"* is also well worn and negative. *Further* help may seem especially inappropriate to someone who has just read a denial.
- **Statements that could undermine the validity of your refusal.** The statement *"We trust this explanation is satisfactory"* or *"We hope you will understand our position"* could be taken as a confession of doubt about the validity of the decision. Use of *position* seems to heighten controversy; positions are expected to be defended. Saying *"We are sorry to disappoint you"* risks a negative reply: "If it made you feel so bad, why did you do it?" It can also be interpreted as an apology for the action taken. If a decision merits an apology, its validity may be questionable.
- **Statements that encourage future controversy.** Statements such as *"If you have questions, please do not hesitate to let us know"* could also be perceived as doubt and possibly communicate a willingness to change the decision. If the decision is firm, including this type closing could result in your having to communicate the negative message a second time.

Note the closing paragraph in Figure 7-2 is a positive, forward-looking statement that includes sales promotion of other services the accounting firm can offer.

FIGURE 7-2

Developing the Components of a Bad-News Message

Annotation	Message
Begins with statement with which both can agree. Sets stage for reasons by presenting importance of quality audit.	Audited financial statements will improve your ability to negotiate contracts with suppliers, banks, and customers, as well as provide your stockholders with confidence
Reveals subject of message and transitions into reasons.	regarding their investment. For these reasons, the auditor you select must be capable of providing quality audit services.
Supports refusal with applicable rule from authoritative literature.	To eliminate the appearance of a conflict of interest, Rule 101 of the AICPA Code of Professional Conduct requires auditors to be independent of their clients. One of our audit partners, Ryan Bass, is a significant stockholder in the First National Bank, which currently has loaned a large amount of money to your company.
States refusal positively and clearly using complex sentence and positive language.	Because of this indirect financial interest, we recommend that you seek another firm to perform the 2010 financial statement audit.
Includes counterproposal as alternative.	Since the independence rule applies only to audits of financial statements, we are available to provide other professional services. Our tax accountants are ready to
Closes with focus on continuing business relationship.	assist you in finding methods to reduce your income tax liability. Please call me at 501-555-1245 to discuss these services.

Your Turn 7-3
You're the Professional

As payroll manager, you have received the names of company employees who will be laid off over the next two weeks due to downsizing. Stacy Simms, a member of the sales team, lives in your neighborhood and occasionally socializes with you and your spouse. She has emailed you to find out if she is on the layoff list, as she is considering buying a new home.

TAKE ACTION:

Discuss the following:

a. What are the ethical issues involved in this situation?

b. What will you tell Stacy?

c. Would your answer be different, depending on whether she is on the layoff list?

Refusing a Request

To minimize disappointment and to maintain a positive relationship, it's a good idea to use the inductive approach (reasons before refusal) for refusing requests for a favor, an action, or even a donation. Present clear, understandable reasons in a way that minimizes the receiver's disappointment.

You can examine a company's refusal to provide an executive to work for a community organization in Figure 7-3. This *response* to prior correspondence uses the

FIGURE 7-3

Good Example of a Refusal for a Favor

2700 Ridgeway • Cambridge, MA 02139-2700 • Phone 617 555-8700 • 617 555-7961

March 18, 2011

Mr. Jon Koch, President
Naperville Historical Society
375 Devon Building
Richmond, VA 23261-9835

Dear Jon

You are to be commended for your commitment to restore Naperville's historical downtown shopping district. In this age of megamalls and Internet shopping, the culture of a traditional main street lined with home-owned and operated shops needs to be preserved.

The success of this project depends on a good project director. The organizational, leadership, and public relations activities you described demand an individual with upper-level managerial experience. During the last year, Hilstrom has decentralized its organization, reducing the number of upper-level managers to the minimal level needed. Although our current personnel shortage prevents us from lending you an executive, we do want to support your worthy project.

Kevin Denny in our senior executive corps has a keen interest in historical preservation, having served on the board of a similar organization while living in Vermont. If you can benefit from his services, call him at 555-8700, extension 65.

Sincerely

Russ

Russ Cooper
Director

Introduces subject without revealing whether answer will be "Yes" or "No."

Gives reasons that will seem logical to reader.

Subordinates refusal by placing it in dependent clause of complex sentence. Alludes to help in another form.

Closes positively with counterproposal. Conveys genuineness by summarizing executive's responsibilities and providing telephone number.

Format Pointer

- Signs first name only because writer knows receiver well.

FIGURE 7-4

Poor Example of a Refusal to an Employee's Request

Reader Response

So the answer is no—why read further?

I should have known he wouldn't listen, even though the company "wants" us to share ideas.

He must not have read the article I sent about research showing that a few minutes playing online games can increase productivity.

Thanks, but that's not what I had in mind.

Subject: No Employee Video/Computer Lounge This Year

Josie,

How can you even consider asking for our company to fund a video game/computer lounge for employees?! Our employees are here to work, not to play.

Allowing our employees time with video games and unmonitored computer use goes against every management principle I've ever learned. Employees should conduct their personal computer business on personal time and use their spare time at home to play video or computer games. An office is for work, not play. Besides, the cost of installing a separate area for these video breaks would be exorbitant. Our vice president would never agree to spend money on this right now.

I will try to convince management to allow a fifteen-minute timeframe every day for personal Internet use within certain parameters, but you should not get your hopes up.

same principles of sequence and style that are recommended for messages that *initiate* communication about unpleasant topics. The same principles apply whether the communication is a spoken message, letter, memo, or email message.

Recall a time when you lost goodwill for a company or organization. What caused your reaction? Was your goodwill ever restored?

Companies have learned that building employee relationships is just as important as developing customer goodwill. Refusing employees' requests requires sensitivity and complete honest explanations, qualities not included in the poor email in Figure 7-4. The manager's hasty and vague response to a valued employee's request to create an employee video lounge uses a direct, blunt approach. In the revision illustrated in Figure 7-5, the manager takes the time to prepare a response that reflects detailed explanation supporting the refusal and genuine respect for the employee.

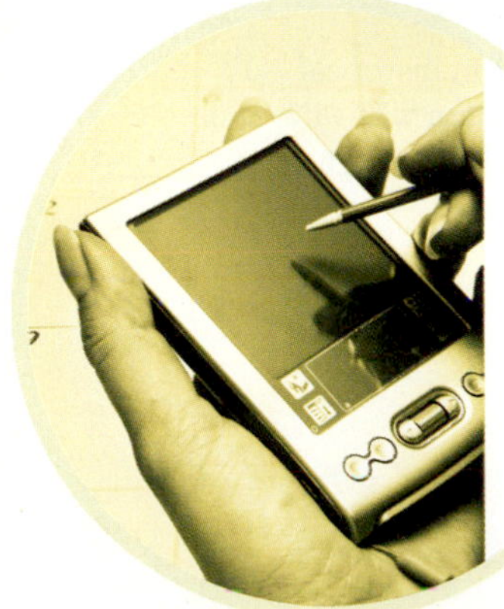

Your Turn 7-4
Career Portfolio

Saying "no" while maintaining goodwill is definitely challenging. Consider a situation in your career field in which you will have to say no to a request from a client or customer.

TAKE ACTION:

Compose a letter to a fictitious individual that conveys the "no" with tact and consideration. See Appendix A for appropriate letter format.

FIGURE 7-5

Good Example of a Refusal to an Employee's Request

To:	Josie Hill
From:	Cadmon Volnecki
Subject:	Request for Employee Video Game/Computer Lounge

Cushions bad news with sincere compliment for suggestion.

Transitions to reasons and provides complete explanation for refusal.

Restates reason to justify refusal.

Includes logical alternative and closes with positive look toward future expansion.

Josie,

Because we want you to work at the highest level possible, your suggestion to create an employee video game/computer lounge has been carefully considered. Taking a break from work for personal Internet use or playing a short game of Solitaire or Minesweeper can be a good way to keep the mind fresh and provide a short break from challenging projects.

Creating an employee computer lounge would be a complex and expensive project because of a lack of available space and funding for additional computers. To provide adequate access for all employees, we would need at least 20 new computers with desk space for each. The cost would start at $20,000, without considering finding space for the lounge.

In response to your idea, I have submitted a request to management that we consider adding an "e-break" to our company Internet policy that will allow employees to use the traditional 15-minute coffee break time to conduct personal business on their computers or play short games. The article you sent me last month provided some good research to support this idea.

Josie, let's see how the e-break goes and revisit the employee video game/computer lounge idea in the future.

Later,

Cadmon

Cadmon Volnecki
Operations Manager
ICUP Enterprises
Oakland, CA 90053
213-555-7634, Ext. 45, Fax 213-555-9900
cvolnecki@ICUP.com

Format Pointers

- Sends message by email—medium preferred by recipient.
- Includes .sig file to identify writer and provide contact information.

Denying a Claim

How do you justify "the customer is always right" philosophy in a situation in which the customer is clearly wrong?

Companies face a challenging task of refusing claims from customers while maintaining goodwill and building customer loyalty. Claim refusals are necessary when a warranty does not apply or has expired or a customer has misused the product. Companies must also write refusals when customers ask for something that a company simply can't do. For example, many retailers charge customers a \$25–\$40 fee on returned checks. A retailer who receives a customer's request to waive the charge must refuse because the claim is inconsistent with the retailer's policies and objectives.

The inductive approach is helpful in communicating this disappointing news to customers. Presenting the explanation for the refusal first leads customers through the reasoning behind the decision and helps them *understand* the claim is unjustified by the time the refusal is presented. Tone is especially important when denying claims. Present the reasons objectively and positively without casting blame or judgment on the customer for the problem. Avoid lecturing a customer on the actions he or she should have taken to have avoided the problem. Finally, close the message with resale or sales promotional material that indicates you expect future business. Although disappointed with your decision, customers continue doing business with companies who make fair, objective decisions and communicate the *reasons* for those decisions in a positive, respectful manner.

What reasons for denying a claim will likely be acceptable from the recipient's perspective?

Assume a manufacturer of ski equipment receives the following email from a customer.

> Please issue a credit to my account for \$365.25. Although you accepted \$2,435 of skis I returned, you only credited my account for \$2,069.75. Because I could find no explanation for the discrepancy, I assume an error has been made.

The company's return policy allows customers to return unsold merchandise at the end of the winter ski season, subject to a 15 percent restocking charge. The return policy is printed clearly on the inside cover of its catalog and in bold print at the bottom of both the printed and Internet order forms. Telephone operators explain the restocking charge to customers placing orders via the company's toll-free number.

The customer's inquiry shows a lack of understanding of the return policy. Although a frustrated company representative may question why the customer can't read the return policy, the response must be more tactful than that illustrated in Figure 7-6. The revision in Figure 7-7 on p. 246 reveals the subject of the message in the first sentence and leads into a discussion of the reasons. Reasons for the restocking fee, including benefits to the customer, precede the refusal. The tone is positive and respectful. The refusal statement uses several de-emphasis techniques to cushion its impact, and the final sentence turns the discussion away from the refusal with reference to future business with the customer.

Companies are also challenged when they must refuse an order for a variety of reasons yet still maintain goodwill and develop customer loyalty. Refer to your companion website at www.cengage.com/bcomm/lehman to explore strategies for handling this potentially damaging situation.

FIGURE 7-6

Poor Example of a Claim Denial

Reader Response	
Obviously!	Your message questioning your statement has been received.
You must not be too sorry, or you would say "yes."	I am sorry but we cannot adjust your account as you requested. Clearly, the statement is correct.
	Each of the order forms you have completed states that returns are subject to a 15 percent restocking charge.
How rude!	Surely you saw this information printed in **bold** print on the order forms, and our telephone operators also explain our return policy thoroughly when customers place orders.
What about MY cost and effort?	I am sure you can appreciate the cost and effort we incur to restock merchandise after the winter ski season is over.
If you want my business, you'll take care of this. You better believe I'll be calling....	Thank you for doing business with us. If you have any further questions, please do not hesitate to call or message us.

Denying Credit

Once you have evaluated a request for credit and have decided "No" is the better answer, your primary writing challenge is to refuse credit so tactfully that you keep the business relationship on a cash basis. When requests for credit are accompanied with an order, your credit refusals may serve as order acknowledgments. Of course, every business message is directly or indirectly a sales message. Prospective customers will be disappointed when they cannot buy on a credit basis. However, if you keep them sold on your goods and services, they may prefer to buy from you on a cash basis instead of seeking credit privileges elsewhere.

What motivation does a business have for maintaining goodwill when writing a credit refusal?

When the credit investigation shows that applicants are poor credit risks, too many credit writers no longer regard them as possible customers. They write to them in a cold, matter-of-fact manner. They do not consider that such applicants may still be interested in doing business on a cash basis and may qualify for credit later.

In credit denials, as in other types of refusals, the major portion of the message should be an explanation for the denial. You cannot expect your receiver to agree that your "No" answer is the right answer unless you give the reasons behind it.

Both writers and readers benefit from the explanation of the reasons behind the denial. For writers, the explanation helps to establish fair-mindedness; it shows that the decision was not arbitrary. For receivers, the explanation not only presents the truth to which they are entitled, it also has guidance value. From it they learn to adjust habits and, as a result, qualify for credit purchases later.

FIGURE 7-7

Good Example of a Claim Denial

NEWPORT LEISURE INDUSTRIES

860 MONMOUTH STREET
NEWPORT, KY 41071-6218

TELEPHONE: 800-424-6000
FAX: 800-424-0583

June 14, 2011

Snowcap Limited
Attention Lindsey Tucker
1905 Southhaven Street
Santa Fe, NM 87501-7313

Avoids corrective language that might insult, belittle, or offend.

Ladies and Gentlemen:

Uses subject line that identifies subject without revealing refusal.

Restocking of Returned Merchandise

Uses resale to cushion bad news and lead into explanation.

The HighFly skis you stocked this past season are skillfully crafted and made from the most innovative materials available. Maintaining a wide selection of quality skiing products is an excellent strategy for developing customer loyalty and maximizing your sales.

Presents clear explanation of reasons behind policy with emphasis on ways reader benefits.

Implies refusal by stating amount of enclosed check.

Our refund policies provide you the opportunity to keep a fully stocked inventory at the lowest possible cost. You receive full refunds for merchandise returned within 10 days of receipt. For unsold merchandise returned after the primary selling season, a modest 15 percent restocking fee is charged to cover our costs of holding this merchandise until next season. The enclosed check for $2,069.76 covers merchandise you returned at the end of February.

Shifts emphasis away from refusal by presenting silver lining sales promotion for next season's merchandise.

While relaxing from another great skiing season, take a look at our new HighFly skis and other items available in the enclosed catalog for the 2012 season. You can save 10 percent by ordering premium ski products before May 10.

Sincerely,

Galen Fondren

Galen Fondren
Credit Manager

Specifies enclosure to emphasize importance of exact items.

Enclosures: Check and catalog

LEGAL AND ETHICAL CONSTRAINTS

Because of the legal implications involved in denying credit, legal counsel should review your credit denial messages to ensure that they comply with laws related to fair credit practices. For example, the Equal Credit Opportunity Act (ECOA) requires that the credit applicant be notified of the credit decision within 30 calendar days following application. Applicants who are denied credit must be informed of the reasons for the refusal. If the decision was based on information obtained from a consumer reporting agency (as opposed to financial statements or other information provided by the applicant), the credit denial must include the name, address, and telephone number of the agency. It must also remind applicants that the Fair Credit Reporting Act provides them the right to know the nature of the information in their credit file. In addition, credit denials must include a standard statement that the ECOA prohibits creditors from discriminating against credit applicants on the basis of a number of protected characteristics (race, color, religion, national origin, sex, marital status, age). Additional information related to this legislation is included in the accompanying Strategic Forces feature, "The Fair Credit Reporting Act."

What is a good counter-proposal in a credit denial message?

To avoid litigation, some companies choose to omit the explanation from the credit denial letter and invite the applicant to call or come in to discuss the reasons. Alternately, they may suggest that the receiver obtain further information from the credit reporting agency whose name, address, and telephone number are provided. Visit your companion website at www.cengage.com/bcomm/lehman to view an example of a credit denial message.

Delivering Constructive Criticism

A person who has had a bad experience as a result of another person's conduct may be reluctant to write or speak about that experience. However, because one person took the time to communicate, many could benefit. Although not always easy or pleasant, communicating about negatives can be thought of as a social responsibility. For example, a person who returns from a long stay at a major hotel might, upon returning home, write a letter or email message to the management commending certain employees. If the stay had not been pleasant and weaknesses in hotel operation had been detected, a tactful message pointing out the negatives would probably be appreciated. Future guests could benefit from the effort of that one person.

What are the risks of delivering a message that points out another person's mistakes?

Before communicating about the problem, an individual should recognize the following risks: being stereotyped as a complainer, being associated with negative thoughts and perceived in negative terms, and appearing to challenge management's decisions concerning hotel operations. Yet such risks may be worth taking because of the benefits:

- The communicator gets a feeling of having exercised a responsibility.
- Management learns of changes that need to be made.
- The hotel staff about whom the message is written modifies techniques and is thus more successful.
- Other guests will have more enjoyable stays in the hotel.

In the decision to communicate about negatives, the primary consideration is intent. If the intent is to hurt or to get even, the message should not be sent. Including false information would be *unethical* and *illegal*. To avoid litigation charges and to respond ethically, include only specific facts you can verify and avoid evaluative words that present opinions about the person's character or ability. For example, instead of presenting facts, the message in Figure 7-8 judges the staff member sent to

LEGAL AND ETHICAL CONSTRAINTS

STRATEGIC FORCES
The Fair Credit Reporting Act

If you have ever applied for a charge account, a personal loan, insurance, or a job, someone is probably keeping a file on you. Your credit report contains information on how you pay your bills, and whether you have been sued, arrested, or have filed for bankruptcy in the past seven years. Also included in your report are your Social Security number, date of birth, current and previous addresses, telephone numbers, and employment information.

The companies that gather and sell this information are called credit reporting agencies, of which the most common type is the credit bureau. The three main credit bureaus, Equifax, Experian (formerly TRW), and TransUnion, sell information to employers, insurers, and other businesses in the form of consumer credit reports. Anyone with a "legitimate business need" can gain access to your credit history, including lenders, landlords, insurance companies, prospective employers to whom you have given consent, and state child support enforcement agencies.

In 1970, Congress passed the Fair Credit Reporting Act (FCRA) to give consumers specific rights in dealing with credit reporting agencies. The act was significantly overhauled in 1996, and various amendments have been enacted since then. The FCRA gives consumers specific protections when they apply for and are denied credit:

- When credit or employment is denied based on information in a credit report, the credit grantor must tell the consumer the name and address of the credit bureau used to secure the information.
- The credit bureau must supply the consumer with a free copy of his or her credit report if the consumer asks for it within 30 days of being denied credit. (Credit bureaus voluntarily extend this time to within 60 days of applying for credit.)
- If the consumer believes that information on the credit report is inaccurate, the credit bureau must investigate the item within a "reasonable time," generally defined as 30 days, and remove the item if it is inaccurate or cannot be verified as accurate.
- Consumers may request that the credit bureau not distribute their names and contact information for unsolicited credit and insurance offers.
- Complaints against credit reporting agencies may be filed with the Federal Trade Commission, Washington, DC.

Responsible consumers should check their credit reports periodically, since information in them could affect their ability to get jobs, mortgages, loans, credit cards, or insurance. A *Consumer Reports* study reported that more than 50 percent of credit reports checked contained errors. An individual may request a free copy of his or her credit report once every 12 months by contacting each of the credit reporting agencies or at www.annualcreditreport.com.

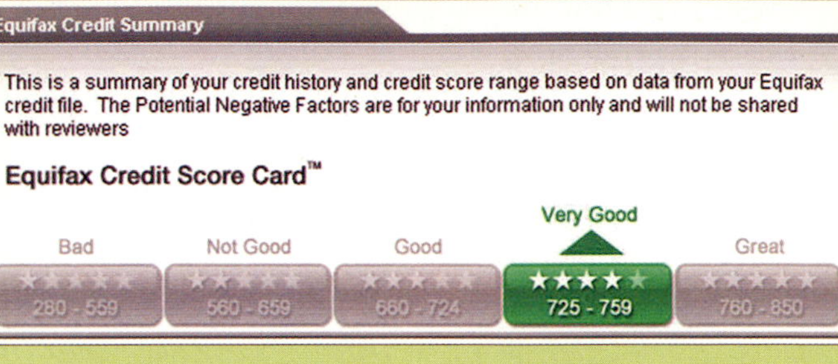
Equifax Credit Summary
This is a summary of your credit history and credit score range based on data from your Equifax credit file. The Potential Negative Factors are for your information only and will not be shared with reviewers
Equifax Credit Score Card™
Very Good
Bad
Not Good
Good
Great
280 - 559
560 - 659
660 - 724
725 - 759
760 - 850

Application

Visit the following websites to obtain further information about the Fair Credit Reporting Act, credit bureaus, and abuses in credit reporting:

http://what-credit-report-scores-mean.com

www.privacyrights.org/fs/fs6-crdt.htm

After reviewing the information, enumerate other specific consumer safeguards provided by the laws regarding credit reporting and some precautionary measures consumers can take to protect themselves against abuse.

FIGURE 7-8

Poor Example of a Constructive Criticism

Reader Response	
Wow—can it be that bad?	Samantha Davis, an IT specialist in your firm, is not working out well on our project. She is constantly accepting text messages, even while in meetings with our employees. While she doesn't interfere with conversation with her texting, the constant distraction of her reading messages has our employees complaining that she is preoccupied with personal matters. She has even made our managers repeat statements made as she received a message.
Have you given her a fair chance?	
Can you provide some support for your claim?	Although extensive knowledge of computer security is important, Davis's lack of respect for others far outweighs her technical expertise. I seriously hope Davis is able to take steps to correct the situation.
So what steps do you want her to take?	

perform a technology audit at a client's office. Overall, the message is short, general, and negative. By comparison, the revision in Figure 7-9 has positive intent, is factual, uses positive language, and leaves judgment to the recipient.

Visit your companion website at www.cengage.com/bcomm/lehman to learn strategies for providing constructive criticism during an employee performance review.

© FRANK MICELOTTA/GETTY IMAGES

Your Turn 7-5
Assessment

Because hiring a new employee costs a firm considerable time and resources, the cost of bad hires can have a dramatic effect on the company's bottom line. Some companies use personality tests to assess human relations skills and provide management with insight concerning their employees and job applicants.[9]

TAKE ACTION:

- Take a "human resource department" test actually used by some businesses at www.personalitytest.net/funtest/index.htm, or go to your companion website, www.cengage.com/bcomm/lehman, for updated links.
- Prepare a short written summary of what you learned from taking the quiz and whether you think the test score was an accurate indicator of your human relations behaviors.

FIGURE 7-9

Good Example of a Constructive Criticism

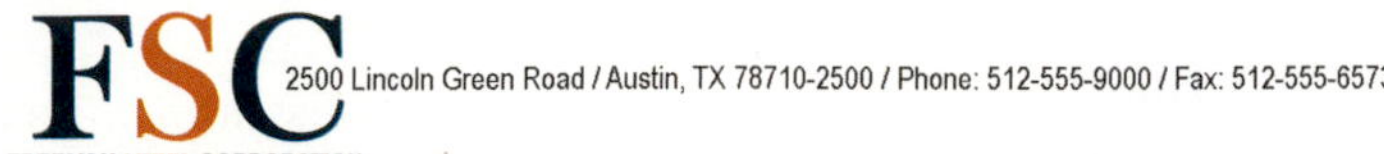

FSC
2500 Lincoln Green Road / Austin, TX 78710-2500 / Phone: 512-555-9000 / Fax: 512-555-6573
FREEMAN STEEL CORPORATION

December 6, 2011

Mr. Daniel Bailey
N. R. Larsen & Co.
7447 North Forest Street
Austin, TX 78710-8640

Dear Daniel:

Your IT team has been working with us on-site for about three weeks with excellent results. Early in its investigations, Samantha Davis, your IT specialist, identified several key security weaknesses that our systems implementation team had overlooked.

While working with our staff, Samantha's attention is constantly diverted from the conversation by her receipt of text messages. Although she rarely stops the conversation to key a response, the constant distraction of her reading the messages has caused some of our employees to comment that she is preoccupied with personal matters. Our managers cited several occasions where Samantha had to ask them to repeat a statement made just before receiving a message.

Samantha is obviously quite good at her job; her passion for technology explains why she is so proficient in evaluating computer security. Please convey my concerns to Samantha confidentially so that the rest of her time in our office will go more smoothly for her and for us.

Sincerely,

Nathan Bridges

Nathan Bridges
Controller

Introduces discussion of audit work underway.

Conveys fair-mindedness and establishes credibility by acknowledging good as well as bad points.

Presents verifiable statements without labeling them in negative, judgmental terms.

Ends on pleasant note that seeks to add credibility to preceding negatives.

Legal and Ethical Constraints Issues

- Conveys positive intent to help—not to hurt or get even.
- Avoids potential litigation charges by including specific, verifiable facts and avoiding evaluative, judgmental statements.
- Uses "confidential" as safeguard; information is intended for professional use only, not designed to hurt or be thought of as gossip.

Format Pointer

- Uses letter channel rather than email to communicate a sensitive message.

Communicating Negative Organizational News

Being able to initiate messages that convey bad news is as important as responding "No" to messages from customers/clients and others outside the company. Employees and the public are seeking, and expecting, *honest* answers from management about situations adversely affecting the company—slumping profits, massive layoffs, bankruptcy, a variety of major changes in the organization, and negative publicity that affects the overall health of the business and retirement plans, to name a few.

Managers who can communicate negative information in a sensitive, honest, and timely way can calm fears and doubts and build positive employee and public relations. Effective managers recognize that employee morale as well as public goodwill, is fragile—easily damaged and difficult to repair. If handled well, these bad-news messages related to the organization can be opportunities to treat employees, customers, and the general public with respect, thus building unity and trust.

How does the phrase "knowledge is power" fit in situations when bad news is shared with employees?

Strong internal communication is a key to involving employees in corporate strategies and building an important sense of community. Transparency can have a positive effect on an organization's culture. According to a recent workplace survey, open, honest communication between corporate leaders and employees can lead to a more productive and ethical workplace. According to Deloitte Chairman Sharon Allen, motivating communication patterns are "increasingly critical to retaining talent and preserving the health of today's organizations.[10]

Obviously, business and competitive reasons prevent a company from always being completely transparent with its staff, but every attempt should be made to do so when possible. The best companies use a variety of communication tools that promote an open exchange of honest, candid communication and welcome input from employees. Newsletters, email updates, town hall or focus meetings, videoconferencing, phone calls, and discussion boards drive home relevant messages and allow employees to pose questions to management. This quality two-way communication involves employees in corporate strategies; employees who are aware of company goals and potential problems feel connected and accountable. Informed employees are also better prepared for bad news when it must be shared.

Breaking Bad News

Assuming this long-term commitment to keep employees informed, the following suggestions provide guidance in breaking bad news to employees and the public: [11]

- **Convey the bad news as soon as possible.** Timeliness will minimize damage caused by rumors and will give employees the concern and respect they deserve. Nestlé Purina and others in the pet food industry acted early and effectively to recall potentially deadly pet food tainted with wheat gluten from China and to assure pet owners that steps were in place to ensure healthy ingredients.[12]
- **Give a complete, rational explanation of the problem.** Be candid about what is happening, why, and its effect on employees, customers, and the public. Provide

enough detail to establish your credibility and provide context so your audience can understand the situation. Stressing positive aspects will provide needed balance and avoid sugarcoating or minimizing the severity of the news to the point that the message is misunderstood. Bridgestone, makers of Firestone tires, was criticized as botching its recovery efforts from claims of accidents being caused by faulty tires when it initially attempted to blame Ford for the problems instead of taking responsibility and seeking corrective actions.[13]

- **Show empathy.** There is really no good way to break bad news to employees such as the announcement of layoffs or closures. The economic downturn and job insecurity has resulted in increased stress for many employees, which raises the potential for workplace aggression. However, methods that reflect respect and proper timing reduce the likelihood of an emotional boil over.[14]
- **Respond to the feelings.** Allow people adequate time to react to the bad news. Listen attentively for understanding and then address the concerns, issues, and potential problems presented.
- **Follow up.** Let people know what will happen next—what is expected of employees or customers, and what the company will do and when. Plan to repeat your explanations and assurances that you are available to respond to concerns in several communications that extend over a given time.

Consider the company president who emailed employees about a relocation of the company's manufacturing facility in Figure 7-10. The president should not be surprised

FIGURE 7-10

Poor Example of a Message Announcing Negative Organizational News

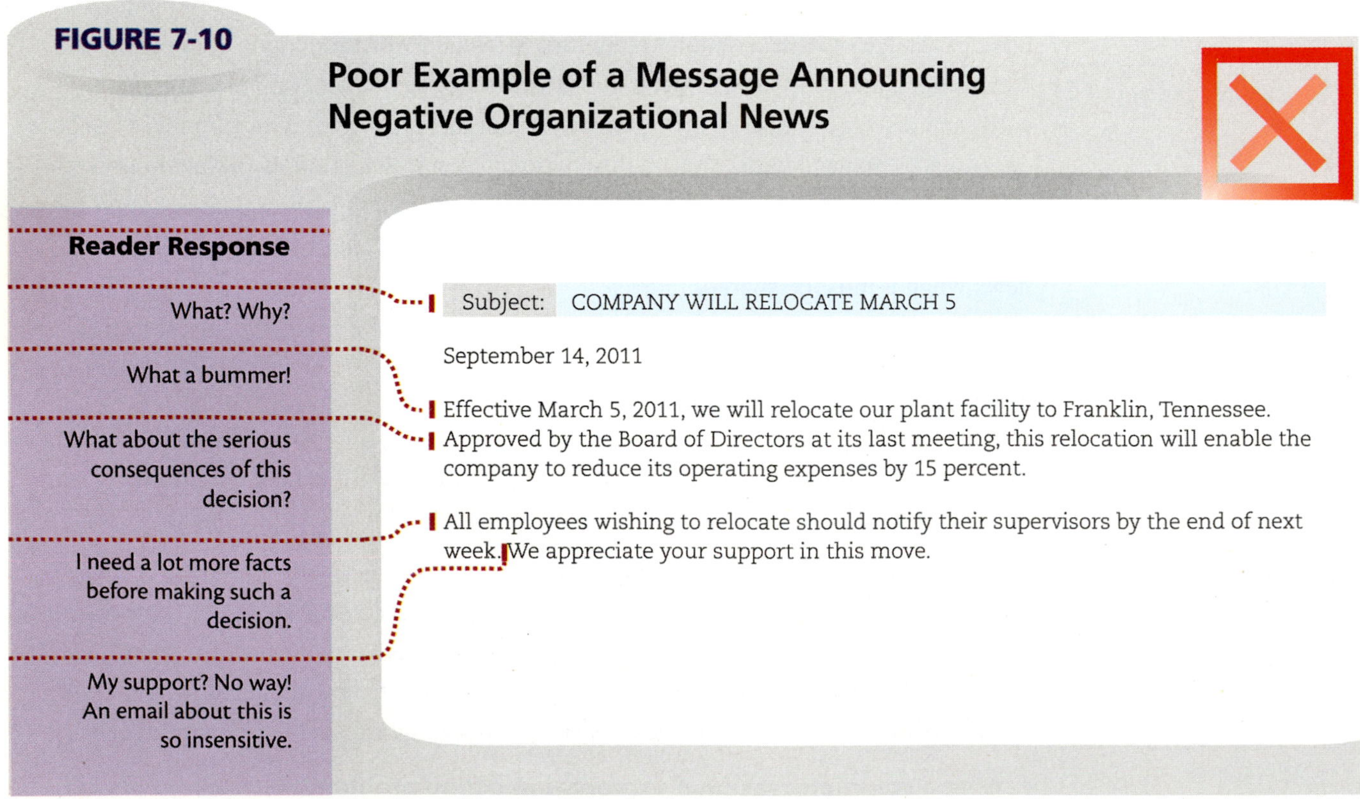

Reader Response
What? Why?
What a bummer!
What about the serious consequences of this decision?
I need a lot more facts before making such a decision.
My support? No way! An email about this is so insensitive.
Subject: COMPANY WILL RELOCATE MARCH 5
September 14, 2011
Effective March 5, 2011, we will relocate our plant facility to Franklin, Tennessee. Approved by the Board of Directors at its last meeting, this relocation will enable the company to reduce its operating expenses by 15 percent.
All employees wishing to relocate should notify their supervisors by the end of next week. We appreciate your support in this move.

to learn that employees are resisting the relocation; some perceive the company to be an enemy uprooting families from their homes simply for financial gain. The president's revision, Figure 7-11, anticipates the employees' natural resistance to this stunning announcement and crafts a sensitive message.

FIGURE 7-11

Good Example of a Message Announcing Negative Organizational News

Uses subject line to introduce topic but does not reveal bad news.

Uses buffer to introduce topic familiar to employees through previous communication and lead into reasons.

Provides rational explanation including benefits.

Presents bad news while reminding receiver of benefits.

Follows up assuring continued exchange of timely information through discussions and web pages.

Ends with positive appeal for unity.

INTEROFFICE MEMORANDUM

TO: All Employees
FROM: Bart Gustavsen, President *BG*
DATE: September 14, 2011
SUBJECT: Proposed Plan for Managing Future Growth

Our company has thrived by taking advantage of international business opportunities. Outsourcing our service call center to India 10 years ago helped to control our operating costs through a period of significant growth.

The dynamics of the economy in India have changed, and we can now justify relocating our call center within the United States. We believe that having all of our support personnel, from accounting to sales to engineering, under one roof will provide us the flexibility to meet the business challenges of the next decade. Our present facility in New York City is not capable of achieving this objective.

High property taxes and transportation cost increases each year are additional reasons to consider alternative sites. Likewise, attracting new talent into this high-cost metro area has become more difficult each year. In fact, both of our newly hired unit supervisors are commuting over one hour just to obtain affordable housing.

While relocating could provide a long-term economic benefit to the company, moving out of New York City could enhance the quality of life for us all. In a suburban city, we could enjoy day-to-day living in a relaxed, small-town environment with all the benefits of a large city only a short drive away. These factors have convinced us that moving the corporate offices to Franklin, Tennessee, a thriving suburb located approximately 18 miles south of Nashville, would benefit the company and our employees.

Your supervisor will explain the logistics of the relocation at your unit's next meeting. In the meantime, visit the Franklin link on the company intranet to read more about what Tennessee can offer us and our families. Check back often for updates on the FAQ page designed to respond to your concerns. Now let us all work together for a smooth transition to Franklin.

Legal and Ethical Constraints Issue

- Uses memo channel rather than email for conveying sensitive message.

A printed memo is a more effective channel for communicating this sensitive and official information than the efficient, yet informal, email message. The revision indicates that the company's internal communications (newsletters and intranet) have been used to prepare the employees for this negative announcement. Thus, the official memo is no surprise; nor is the company's commitment to listen to the employees' concerns and to provide up-to-date information as it develops.

Responding to Crisis Situations

Crises can occur in any organization, disrupting business activity and posing significant political, legal, financial, or governmental impacts. Crisis situations can result from various events, including accidents, weather-related disasters, equipment failures, procedural errors, and deliberate maliciousness. When crises occur, the communication that is offered can either help ease situations or worsen them. Rather than waiting for a crisis to occur, an organization should examine its state of preparedness and have a carefully considered plan of action that includes the following steps:

© PAUL SAKUMA/AP IMAGES

- Anticipate potential crisis in terms of areas of vulnerability and what could happen.
- Establish emergency procedures, including an alternate command center and chain of command. Assure that more than one employee is media trained and able to respond appropriately if needed.
- Identify who will need to be contacted and plan for multiple means of disseminating information. Reports that a finger was found in a bowl of Wendy's chili spread across the country, and the fast-food chain lost millions in revenue before the hoax was uncovered. Because cell phones, Blackberries, Internet blogs, and 24/7 news channels spread bad news faster, farther, and louder than did earlier media channels, companies must respond to crises quickly. While cell phones and text messaging have proved themselves valuable when other contact means may not work, telecommunication circuits can be overloaded in mass disaster situations, necessitating multiple means for sharing news.
- Assure current contact information is available for employees, media, and other pertinent parties.
- Maintain an up-to-date fact sheet about the company, its products/services, locations, and operations.

What are other examples of company responses to crisis situations? Were they effective? Why?

Miscommunication Worse than Silence in Bad-News Situations

Joe Manchin faced challenges of the Sago mine tragedy only a few months into his term as governor of West Virginia. He understood the agony of uncertainty experienced by families of the trapped miners as those on the ground waited for any word from recovery personnel. Having personally lost family members and friends in other mine disasters, Manchin's request of Sago managers and inspectors was to "please share all the factual information, good or bad." Visit your companion website at www.cengage.com/bcomm/lehman to learn more about Joe Manchin's response to families, media, and the public during and following the mine tragedy.

www.msha.gov/sagomine/sagomine.asp

© HARAZ N. GHANBARI/AP IMAGES

SPOTLIGHT COMMUNICATOR: JOE MANCHIN, GOVERNOR OF WEST VIRGINIA

SEE SHOWCASE PART 3, ON PAGE 256
TO LEARN MORE ABOUT THE RESPONSE TO THE CRISIS AT THE SAGO MINE.

In responding to a crisis, the message conveyed is extremely important in reassuring employees and business partners and in shaping public opinion. These guidelines can help assure an effective message:

- Determine what your message is and prepare a checklist of what it should contain before writing.
- Keep the message simple, and arrange it in logical sections.
- Include verbiage that demonstrates your concern, compassion, and control.
- Prepare separate messages for internal and external audiences, including the appropriate level of detail.

While crises can seldom be predicted, an organization can position itself to respond to them appropriately when they do occur. Having a well-prepared plan of action for dealing with emergencies can make the difference in an organization's survival and collapse.

Before developing a bad-news message, study the overall suggestions in the "General Writing Guidelines" at your companion website, www.cengage.com/bcomm/lehman, and the specific suggestions in this chapter's "Check Your Communication" checklist. Compare your work with this checklist again after you have prepared a rough draft, and make any revisions.

SHOWCASE PART 3

Communication Lessons Learned from Crisis Situations

In the aftermath of the Sago mine tragedy, International Coal Group's CEO Ben Hatfield had the ominous responsibility of serving as company spokesperson before the media and the American people. "This has been the most tragic period of my life," said Hatfield. "We will redouble our efforts to make sure that a tragedy like this never occurs again.[15] Critics charged that the company was responsible for two tragedies: the loss of human lives due to the accident and the bungled miscommunication that caused further mental and emotional anguish for families and friends. Three major tenants of an effective crisis communication plan were apparently broken: (1) control the flow of information from the command center, (2) designate one official spokesperson, and (3) post an immediate response on the corporate website.[16]

www.msha.gov/sagomine/sagomine.asp

Activities

- Visit the International Coal Group (ICG) website at www.intlcoal.com to read the company's response that was eventually posted concerning the Sago tragedy.
- Locate the following article that discusses how an organization can survive the unthinkable through crisis planning: http://management.about.com/cs/communication/a/PlaceBlame1000.htm
- Compose a list of elements that should be included in an organization's crisis communication plan, explaining the need or purpose for each.

© CHIP SOMODEVILLA/GETTY IMAGES

Summary

1. Explain the steps in the inductive outline and understand its use for specific situations.

Because the receiver can be expected to be displeased by the message, the inductive approach is appropriate for messages denying an adjustment, refusing an order for merchandise, refusing credit, sending constructive criticism, or conveying negative organizational messages.

The steps in the inductive outline include (1) introducing the topic with a neutral idea that sets the stage for the explanation; (2) presenting a concise, logical explanation for the refusal; (3) implying or stating the refusal using positive language; (4) offering a counterproposal or silver lining statement that shifts focus toward the positive; and (5) closing with a positive, courteous ending that shifts the focus away from the bad news. While bad-news messages are typically expressed using paper documents or face-to-face means, electronic channels may be appropriate under certain circumstances.

The deductive approach can be used to communicate bad news when (a) the message is the second response to a repeated request; (b) a very small, insignificant matter is involved; (c) a request is obviously ridiculous, immoral, unethical, illegal, or dangerous; (d) a writer's intent is to "shake" the receiver; or (e) a writer–reader relationship is so close and long-standing that satisfactory human relations can be taken for granted.

2. Discuss strategies for developing the five components of a bad-news message.

Follow these guidelines when developing the five components of a bad-news message.

Introductory Paragraph. The first sentence of a bad news message should (a) buffer the bad news that will follow, (b) identify the subject of the message without stating the obvious, and (c) serve as a transition into the explanation. Avoid empty acknowledgments of the obvious, tipping off the bad news too early, and starting too positively so as to build false hopes. Effective beginning paragraphs might include a compliment, a point of agreement, good news, resale, a review of the circumstances related to the message, or an expression of gratitude.

Facts, Analysis, and Reasons. This important section includes a concise, logical discussion of the reasons for the refusal that a receiver can understand and thus be prepared to accept the refusal statement as valid. The reasons section should (a) provide a smooth transition from the opening paragraph to the explanation, (b) present one or more reasons that are logical to the reader, (c) show reader benefit and/or consideration, and (d) avoid using "company policy" as the reason.

Bad-News Statement. When writing the bad-news sentence, position the bad news strategically by (a) using the inductive approach to sandwich the bad news between a logical explanation and a positive closing, (b) avoiding the placement of the refusal statement in a paragraph by itself where it would be highlighted, and (c) placing the negative message in the dependent clause of a complex sentence to de-emphasize the negative. Avoid overly negative words and statements that automatically set up barriers to your message. Instead, use positive techniques such as stating what you can do rather than what you cannot do or including a positive fact in the same sentence with the negative idea. Use the subjunctive mood or imply the bad news if you believe the reader will understand your refusal clearly. If you must state the bad news directly, avoid using a simple sentence for the refusal unless your intention is to emphasize the "No."

Counterproposal or Silver Lining Statement. Follow the bad news with a tangible or intangible counterproposal representing another outcome or course of action or with a silver lining statement that points to some positive aspect of the situation. This technique provides the shift away from the negative and provides a logical progression into the empathetic message of the closing paragraph.

Closing Paragraph. The closing paragraph should demonstrate empathy and should not include statements that may cause the reader to question the fairness of your decision. Do not mention the refusal in the final paragraph. Instead, end with an idea that

Check Your Communication
Bad-News Messages

CONTENT

- ☐ Be sure the principal idea (the unpleasant idea or the refusal) is sufficiently clear.
- ☐ Use sufficient supporting details, and present them in a logical sequence.
- ☐ Verify accuracy of facts or figures.
- ☐ Structure the message to meet ethical and legal requirements.
- ☐ Make appropriate cultural adaptations (e.g., organizational pattern, format, language usage).

ORGANIZATION

- ☐ Structure the first sentence to introduce the general subject
  - without stating the bad news.
  - without leading a receiver to expect good news.
  - without including obvious statements (e.g., "I am replying to your letter").
- ☐ Precede the main idea (bad news) with meaningful discussion.
- ☐ Follow up the bad news with a counterproposal or silver lining statement that moves discussion in a positive direction.
- ☐ Use a closing sentence that is positive (an alternative, resale, or sales promotion).

STYLE

- ☐ Write clearly and concisely (e.g., words are easily understood).
- ☐ Use techniques of subordination to keep the bad news from emerging with unnecessary vividness. For example, bad news may
  - appear in a dependent clause.
  - be stated in passive voice.
  - be revealed through indirect statement.
  - be revealed through the use of subjunctive mood.
- ☐ Use first person sparingly or not at all.
- ☐ Make ideas cohere by avoiding abrupt changes in thought.
- ☐ Keep sentences and paragraphs relatively short, and vary length and structure.
- ☐ Use original expression (sentences are not copied directly from the definition of the problem or from sample documents in the text); omit clichés.

MECHANICS

- ☐ Ensure that keyboarding, spelling, grammar, and punctuation are perfect.

FORMAT

- ☐ Use a correct document format.
- ☐ Ensure that the document is appropriately positioned.
- ☐ Include standard document parts in appropriate position.
- ☐ Include special parts if necessary (subject line, enclosure, copy, etc.).

brings a positive, unifying quality to the message, for example, referring to a pleasant idea mentioned earlier in the message or using resale, sales promotion, or a counterproposal.

3. Prepare messages refusing requests and claims.

A message refusing a request begins with a neutral idea and presents the reasons before the refusal. The close may offer a counterproposal—an alternative to the action requested.

A message denying a claim begins with a neutral or factual sentence that leads to the reason for the refusal. In the opening sentence you might include resale to reaffirm the reader's confidence in the merchandise or services. Next, present the explanation for the refusal and then the refusal in a positive, nonemphatic manner. Close with a positive thought such as sales promotion that indicates you expect to do business with the customer again.

4. Prepare messages handling problems with customers' orders and denying credit.

A message refusing an order implies receipt of the order and uses resale to reaffirm the customer's confidence in the merchandise or service. Continue with reasons for your procedures or actions and benefits to the customer. Close with information needed for the customer to reorder or anticipate later delivery.

Credit refusal messages must comply with laws related to fair credit practices and should be reviewed carefully by legal counsel. Begin the message by implying receipt of an order and using resale that could convince the applicant to buy your merchandise on a cash basis when he or she learns later that credit has been denied. You must provide an explanation for the refusal (in writing or verbally) and may encourage the customer to apply for credit later or offer a discount on cash purchases. Your legal counsel may advise that you omit the explanation and invite the applicant to call or come in to discuss the reasons or to obtain more information from the credit reporting agency whose name, address, and telephone number you provide in the message.

5. Prepare messages providing constructive criticism, communicating negative organizational news, and responding to crises.

Because of the importance of maintaining goodwill with employees and outside parties, convey constructive criticism and negative organizational news in a sensitive, honest, and timely manner; use the inductive approach. The motive for delivering constructive criticism should be to help, not to get even. The message includes verifiable facts and omits evaluative words, allowing the recipient to make logical judgments based on facts. Negative information about an organization should be timely, honest, empathetic, and helpful. Crisis communication should be well planned and organized and should demonstrate concern, compassion, and control.

Chapter Review

1. Explain the typical appropriate channels and outline for a message that conveys bad news. Under what conditions would a sender be justified in choosing an alternate outline or channel? (Obj. 1)
2. What three functions does the first paragraph of a bad-news message serve? Does "I am responding to your email" accomplish all of these functions? Explain. (Obj. 2)
3. Discuss how a counterproposal and implication can be used to de-emphasize the bad-news statement and assist a communicator in achieving the human relations goal of business communication. (Obj. 2)
4. What objectives should the final paragraph accomplish? Should the closing sentence apologize for action taken? Should it refer to the statement of refusal to achieve unity? Explain. (Obj. 2)
5. In which part of a refusal message would resale and sales promotional material be most appropriate? Explain. (Objs. 2, 3)
6. Are form letters recommended when handling problems related to orders? Explain. (Obj. 4)
7. What advice would you give regarding use of template documents available with word processing software? (Objs. 1–5)
8. Discuss the legal implications involved in writing credit refusals. (Obj. 4)
9. What elements make criticism "constructive"? (Obj. 5)
10. Why is the effective handling of negative or crisis information of such importance to a company? (Obj. 5)

Digging Deeper

1. *Saying "no" is not difficult; the challenge is to do so while protecting goodwill.* Explain the rationale and significance of this statement.
2. Frequent channels for delivering business messages include written, electronic, and face-to-face means. What criteria would you use in selecting the appropriate channel for delivering bad news?
3. How might standard practices for internal and external communication change when a company is facing uncertain times (e.g., an economic recession, bankruptcy proceedings, and so on)?

Assessment

To check your understanding of the chapter, take the available online quizzes as directed by your instructor.

Activities

1. Appropriateness of the Inductive Outline (Objs. 1, 2)

In pairs, describe either a personal or business-related situation you faced in which you had to share bad news with someone. How did you structure your message? What channel did you use for sharing the news? Was your strategy effective?

2. Determining Appropriate Sequence of Ideas: Deductive or Inductive (Objs. 1, 2)

Identify whether each of the following messages should be written deductively or inductively based on the receiver's likely reaction to the message. Explain your reasoning.

a. A message refusing an office complex tenant's request for a 30-day lease extension.
b. A message from a land developer informing building contractors that completion of utilities to a new subdivision will be delayed.
c. A message from an appliance manufacturer authorizing the replacement of a glass cook top that was broken in transit to the customer.
d. A message from a customer service manager saying "no" to a customer's third request for a refund that was previously denied.
e. A message from a company president to reject a contract proposal offered by an international business partner whose cultural style is direct and forthright.
f. A message refusing an employee's request that the human resources manager "fudge" to a lender about the employee's reported income to help him qualify for a home loan.
g. A message from a manager apologizing to an employee for unintentional gender biased language.
h. A message extending appreciation for the outstanding work of a consulting firm that spearheaded your successful effort to gain Sarbanes Oxley compliance.
i. A message notifying shareholders of a reduction in quarterly dividends.

3. Choosing an Effective Channel (Obj. 1)

For each of the situations in Activity 2, decide which communication channel would be most appropriate. Explain your reasoning.

4. Perfecting Buffer Statements (Obj. 3)

Decide which buffer statement is preferable and describe why the others are less effective.

Version 1

I am pleased and honored to have been asked to serve as treasurer of the United Way campaign for the coming year.

Version 2

Regrettably, I will not be able to accept your invitation to serve as treasurer of the United Way campaign in the coming years.

Version 3

All of us who feel proud of our community agree that the United Way is adding significant value to the lives of thousands of citizens. It has given shelter, health care, money, and hope to many with critical needs.

5. Perfecting the Refusal Statement (Obj. 3)

Decide which refusal statement is preferable and explain why the others are less effective.

Version 1

Under no circumstances can we grant the request you have made.

Version 2

Legal requirements prevent us from disclosing the information you have requested.

Version 3

Unfortunately, we are not able to release the requested information due to privacy laws that prohibit disclosure.

6. Revising for Positive Tone (Obj. 2)

Revise the following refusal sentences to ensure positive tone.

a. You cannot receive full tuition reimbursement for the Fraud Examination class you just completed since you earned a C and not an A.
b. Employees are forbidden from downloading copyright music from company computers.
c. I am sorry, but we cannot be responsible for the repairs on your car; the damage obviously occurred at the dealership, not at our factory.
d. Because your portable GPS system did not malfunction until three months after the warranty expired, we cannot honor your claim.
e. We received many applications for this position but decided to hire an internal candidate.
f. Company policy does not permit approval of the proposed transaction. Therefore, your request is denied.

7. Effective Opening and Closing Paragraphs (Objs. 1–5)

In pairs, choose one of the situations in Activity 2 and draft an opening and closing paragraph. Consider various approaches to begin and end the document in a positive way as illustrated in the chapter examples. Share your document with another team and revise based on the feedback you receive.

8. Document for Analysis: Denying an Employee's Request (Obj. 3)

Analyze the following email. Pinpoint its strengths and weaknesses and then revise the email as directed by your instructor. Access a downloadable version of this activity from your companion website at www.cengage.com/bcomm/lehman.

GPS Out of the Question

We can't afford to install an in-dash global positioning system (GPS) in our current fleet of company vehicles.

I would really like to afford you the luxury of having GPS navigate your trips. Unfortunately, the cost of installing GPS in our current trucks is excessive at over $500 per truck, and then there is the monthly service fee. Management would never agree to spend that much money at this time.

I'll do what I can to convince management to include GPS in the specifications of future company vehicles.

9. Document for Analysis: Denying a Claim (Obj. 3)

Analyze the following message. Pinpoint its strengths and weaknesses and then revise as directed by your instructor. Access a downloadable version of this activity from your companion website at www.cengage.com/bcomm/lehman.

I am sorry you were dissatisfied with the sports celebrity we subbed for your dedication ceremony. Although you obviously feel your claim has merit, refusing to pay us is just not going to work for us. Michelle Aker's injury and hospitalization was out of our control—just not our fault. We felt sure you would be overjoyed we came through with someone at the last minute. Our contract states specifically that we would provide you a substitute; we did our part and we expect you to do your part and pay us for our services.

We appreciate your business and hope that you will consider us the next time you need a sports celebrity for a function.

10. Document for Analysis: Constructive Criticism (Obj. 5)

Analyze the following email. Pinpoint its strengths and weaknesses and then revise the email to the training director of the Advanced Technology Center as directed by your instructor. Access a downloadable version of this activity from your companion website at www.cengage.com/bcomm/lehman.

The quality of the instruction provided by your computer training center did not live up to its billing. You promised a maximum class size of twenty students with three instructors, one to lead the class and two circulating to assist participants with individual problems. For much of the class time, the two instructors sat at available computers checking their email and oblivious to how the students were doing.

To their credit, when specifically asked a question, the instructors did respond quickly and provided good support. Due to instructor inattentiveness, however, we do not feel that the seven employees we enrolled received the level of training you promised. I doubt we will be sending any employees to your center for training in the future.

Applications

READ | THINK | WRITE | SPEAK | COLLABORATE

1. Communication Success Stories (Objs. 1–5)

Conduct an electronic search to locate an article that deals with successful negative communication in an organization. Prepare an abstract of the article that includes the following parts: (1) article citation, (2) name of organization, (3) brief description of communication technique/situation, and (4) outcome(s) of the successful communication. As an alternative to locating an article, write about a successful communication situation in the organization/company for which you work.

Required: Present your abstract in a memo to your instructor. Refer to Appendix B for information about formatting citations. Be prepared to give a short presentation in class.

2. Communication Style Under Stress (Objs. 1–2, 5)

Read *Crucial Conversations: Tools for Talking When Stakes Are High* by Kerry Patterson, Joseph Grenny, and Al Switzer, a best-selling book that provides advice for handling disagreement in high-stake situations at home or at work. The authors discuss three common reactions to conversations that become crucial: Avoiding them (going to silence), handling them poorly by lashing out or getting angry (going to violence), or handling them well and achieving the desired results.

Required: Respond to this communication issue as directed by your instructor:

a. Write a brief report that discusses crucial conversations with personal and work-related examples, summarizes the authors' strategy for effective crucial conversations, and describes how you believe this strategy could improve your communication style when under stress.
b. Access the book authors' website www.vitalsmarts.com/styleunderstress.aspx and take the "Style under Stress Assessment." Submit a brief summary of the results to your instructor as directed.

3. Making Criticism Pay Off (Obj. 5)

Visit your companion website at www.cengage.com/bcomm/lehman and read the enrichment content, "Tips for Conducting an Effective Employee Performance Review." Then read the following articles:

Thompson, S. (2007, March 15.) How to handle criticism at work. *Associated Content.* Available at www.associatedcontent.com/article/169549/how_to_handle_criticism_at_work.html?cat=31

Goldsmith, B. (2005, August). Ten tips for delivering (constructive) criticism. *Successful Meetings, 54*(9), 26–27. Available from Business Source Complete database.

Required: Recall an experience where you received or gave constructive criticism in an academic or work situation. What was your perception of the sender's motive? What outcome(s) was achieved by the confrontation? Using the advice from your text and the readings, summarize the techniques that you believe kept the criticism on target. What advice would you give for delivering the criticism that would have led to more positive results? Be prepared to present your ideas in a brief presentation to the class.

READ | THINK | WRITE | SPEAK | COLLABORATE

4. Bad-News Speeches (Objs. 1–2, 5)

Refer to a recent political or business event in which bad news was shared. Prepare a written critique that includes (1) your assessment of the effectiveness of the message and the manner in which it was delivered, (2) an analysis of the results, and (3) a summary of what you learned from your analysis. Be prepared to share with the class in a brief presentation.

5. Constructive Criticism: Training for Employee Sensitivity: A Priority at Wilson Street Grill (Objs. 1–2, 5)

The Wilson Street Grill in Madison, Wisconsin, is one of many restaurants that have successfully hired employees with mental disabilities. The federal Americans with Disabilities Act (ADA) prohibits employers with 15 or more employees from discriminating against disabled job applicants and employees. Many hotels and restaurants have found that employees with disabilities are often hard-working and committed, and the turnover rate for such workers is often lower than among high school and college students employed at these same restaurants.

At the Wilson Street Grill, more than one third of its employees have a disability. All new employees receive orientation about discrimination issues and ADA laws, and employees are trained and mentored to work effectively with those with disabilities. As manager of the Wilson Street Grill, you recently hired Jonathan, who completed his orientation a month ago. He regularly works with Sue, a mentally disabled employee with Down syndrome who has been an excellent employee for two years. Jonathan appears to be patient with the other employees who have disabilities but seems easily frustrated with Sue. Jonathan has refrained from speaking rudely to her in public, but his general behavior communicates a very negative attitude. You recently observed a negative communication exchange between the two. Jonathan often responds to Sue's questions by ignoring her or giving her terse answers. He has rudely interrupted her conversations with fellow employees on numerous occasions. Often when Sue begins a routine task, he takes over and does it for her, and he refuses her efforts to help him learn certain tasks. Sue has not complained to you, but she has talked to other employees about the problems with Jonathan. As the manager of Wilson Street Grill, you need to warn Jonathan about his unacceptable behavior and provide constructive criticism.

Required: Respond to this communication issue as directed by your instructor:

1. Write a memo to Jonathan that will be placed in his personnel file. The memo should adequately warn Jonathan about the consequences of his behavior and should contain relevant facts to explain the law. Access a database to complete additional research on the Americans with Disabilities Act so that you understand how this law impacts management.
2. Develop a voice script that could be used by the manager for delivering this warning and constructive criticism to Jonathan. Your instructor may ask you to role play your conversation with another student in the class.
3. In a small group, produce a short video presentation that could be shown to new hires at The Wilson Street Grill on working with those with disabilities.

6. Employee Bad News: Discontinue Downloading Audio Files (Objs. 1–2, 5)

Opened during the late 1990s in southern California, Aspire Consulting has allowed its office employees the freedom of personal expression. At the extreme, some employees bring their pets to work, rollerblade to meetings, and play guitars to relieve stress. However, most employees simply enjoy playing music on their personal computers. As the director of computer security, you are aware that the music industry prosecutes and seeks substantial fines against companies that allow employees to download copyrighted music files over the Web.

Required: Write a memo to your employees instructing them to immediately delete and discontinue downloading music files. Identify the legal methods currently available that will enable them to continue listening to music and, therefore, preserve corporate culture.

7. Request Refusal: One Size Doesn't Fit All (Objs. 1–3)

Belmont Financing Corporation provides its regional managers with a car for travel among the retail locations within their regions. The corporate office purchases these cars from a single dealer and has purchased the same model and color for the past nine years. In your position as corporate controller, you have received a request from one manager who wants authorization to purchase a different model and color. The manager maintains that the car does not fit his personality and does not comfortably fit his 6' 6" frame. After consulting with the legal department, you have decided to refuse his request to choose a color other than the "corporate color" but will allow him to select a larger car so long as it has a 5-star crash rating and portrays a professional, yet modest image.

Required: Compose an email message to the manager, Josh Hundley, communicating your decision and requiring him to obtain your approval of the model selected.

8. Adjustment Refusal: No Sympathy for Bank Customer with "Bounced Checks" (Objs. 1–3)

Banks that are located near universities frequently compete with each other to attract college students as customers. These banks may offer many services that are attractive to students. These services tailored to the college student market include free checking, debit cards, lower required account balances, convenient campus ATM locations, student loans, credit cards, and so on.

Rachel, a new college freshman living away from home for the first time, has opened a checking account with Regions Bank. During the first two months of the semester, she wrote checks for many purchases and used her debit card for cash withdrawals; she accurately recorded all these transactions in her checkbook. Once she became busy with classes and college activities, she became more careless, and didn't take time to record withdrawals or to balance her checking account. When making a deposit, she received a record of her balance to date which showed that she had money in her account. During the next few days, she used her debit card for several meals out with friends and wrote checks to pay for various items. She then received notice that 10 of these transactions had "bounced." The fee for each insufficient funds notice was $27. She has gone to the bank requesting that the fee be waived. The "balance to date" did not include several outstanding checks that were credited to her account the following day.

Required:

1. As the customer service manager, compose a letter to Rachel denying her request to waive this fee for checks with insufficient funds. Conduct research necessary to recommend a plan for protecting against future insufficient fund fees.
2. Develop a voice script of a conversation explaining the bank policy and offering Rachel assistance in managing her account.

9. Adjustment Refusal: Airline Passenger Struggles with Online Ticketing (Objs. 1–4)

Many airline passengers who travel frequently book their flights online using one of the many available websites, such as Orbitz.com, Travelocity.com, and Expedia.com. These websites provide access to detailed flight information, including costs. Customers conveniently make an airline reservation, pay for it, and receive a boarding pass prior to departure. The sites are user-friendly and relatively easy to navigate; users follow the step-by-step directions carefully and submit the appropriate information for the transaction to be completed. People who use these sites quickly become familiar with how they work; however, problems can occur for travelers who are not computer literate, who fly infrequently, or who are booking flights online for the first time.

You are a reservation agent for U.S. Airways and frequently handle calls from novice users of online sites. Today you receive a call from a customer who is frantic and complains that she cannot print a boarding pass for the flight she has "booked" using Travelocity.com. The flight is scheduled to depart for Florida, a popular winter destination, within 24 hours. By making airline reservations six weeks ahead of scheduled departure, the cost was less than $300. The customer is unable to recall if she received an email from Travelocity.com with the confirmation number of her reservation. After checking the reservation system, you discover no reservation for this person. Apparently, she did not complete the online reservation and properly submit the information, as she cannot find any charges for the ticket on her recent credit card bill.

Required:

1. Develop a voice script of how you should explain this problem to the customer and provide assistance for a new reservation that will cost 30 percent more. Your instructor may ask you to role-play your conversation with another student in the class.
2. Write an email to this customer explaining the problem and solution.

For further information, access the following article:

Air passenger complaints double as plane companies struggle with new computer systems. (2008, June 5). *Mail Online*. Available at: www.dailymail.co.uk/news/article-1024311/Air-passenger-complaints-double-plane-companies-struggle-new-systems.html

10. Adjustment Refusal: Extended Warranty Claims Must Be Preauthorized (Objs. 1–3)

In your new position as manager of the customer service department at Precision Warranty, you are concerned over the increasing number of customers cashing out of their extended warranties long before they expire. You are convinced that some customer dissatisfaction could be resulting from the following poorly written claim denial that you've seen for the first time today. This form letter is sent to customers who submit claims for auto repairs completed without your company's preauthorization. It's simple; claims are denied if the customer does not call your office for approval.

How can you revise this message to help the customer understand the importance and simplicity of the preauthorization process? You're just asking the auto repair department to call your 800 number to verify that the repairs are covered under the warranty contract and to record your authorization number on the customer's copy of the auto repair invoice, which the customer will mail directly to you at Precision Warranty.

Re: Contract # 793810; Date of claim, 2/8/11

Dear Sir/Madam:

We have reviewed your invoice for reimbursement of the above claim. Based upon this review, we are denying the claim due to the following reason(s):

THE TERMS OF YOUR CONTRACT STATE THAT PRIOR AUTHORIZATION FROM THE ADMINISTRATOR IS REQUIRED FOR ANY REPAIR. THIS PROCEDURE WAS NOT FOLLOWED.

Please review your service contract on procedures for filing a claim.

Required: As the customer service manager, revise the form letter to deny the claim while clarifying the policy and maintaining confidence in your extended warranty.

11. Refusing an Order: Online Shoppers Hit a Snag (Announcing Negative Organizational News) (Objs. 1–2, 5)

Online shopping for computers, smartphones, and other technological devices is a booming business. These products are available online for prices that are often unmatched by stores such as Best Buy and Radio Shack. Most buyers of these devices research product reviews, blogs, and informative websites in order to select a model. Because they know the exact product specifications, they frequently purchase online rather than at a traditional store that handles these products.

MPsuperstore.com is one of hundreds of online companies that sell a wide variety of communication technology devices. You handle customer service calls for the online orders. Recently, you have received numerous orders for the Hewlett Packard IPAQ, Model 2410. The company's order policy states that products will be shipped in 7 to 10 business days. Unfortunately, the product is on back order, but management has told you to tell customers placing orders that "it will ship in a few days." Some impatient customers have called daily, and their orders are now more than three weeks old. Management now informs you that this item will be discontinued by MPsuperstore.com. Fortunately, customers paying by credit card have not yet been charged for this item.

Required:

1. Compose an email message to all customers who have placed an order for the HP IPAQ Model 2410 explaining that this product is no longer carried by MPsuperstore.com. Address a sample document to Sam Carter, Order #30814.
2. Write a memo, email, or instant message to MPsuperstore.com customer service representatives announcing that your company will no longer be offering the HP IPAQ model 2410.

12. Order Refusal: Sound Enhancements Needed to Ensure Customer Satisfaction (Objs. 1–2, 4)

HGA Electronics is replacing its fleet of 100 automobiles used by its field representatives. As the regional corporate sales representative for the automobile manufacturer, you notice that HGA Electronics has not ordered sound system upgrades to accommodate mp3 players and smartphones that will enhance the employees' driving experience.

Required:

1. Research the Internet to identify other options that you believe employers should consider for company vehicles.
2. Write an email to Joanne Gayle, the buyer at HGA Electronics, suggesting that she add these options to these automobiles she's ordered.

13. Employee Bad News: Restricted Internet Access (Objs. 1–2, 5)

Concerned over the loss of productivity from employees' nonbusiness use of the Internet, VPX Corporation installed software to monitor and log Internet activity. Employees were notified of this change designed to reduce the level of nonbusiness Internet traffic (e.g., Internet radio, auction sites, electronic gaming, social networking sites, and so on). Unfortunately, after a brief drop in traffic, the number of hits to popular Internet sites has increased steadily. As a result, the company has decided to block the most popular Internet sites.

Required: As the chief information systems officer, write a memo to the employees announcing a change in Internet usage policy. Each month a list of the most popular sites will be distributed. Employees will have 10 days to document a legitimate business purpose for retaining access to the site.

14. Employee Bad News: Employees to Pay for Fitness Center (Objs. 1–2, 5)

For several years, GTW Corporation has provided its employees and their families with free memberships to the Fitness Club, a local health facility. The facility has recently undergone a significant expansion, including an indoor pool, climbing wall, and racquetball courts, and has notified its members of a rate increase effective next month. GTW's board of directors has rejected management's request to pay the incremental fees. Management must inform employees that they must now pay a portion of their membership fees. Specifically, each employee will be required to pay $10 per month and an additional $5 for each family member.

Required: As the director of human resources for GTW, write a memo announcing the rate increase. Your memo should request that employees complete a form authorizing an automatic withdrawal from their paychecks.

15. Critique of Bad-News Messages Produced by Real Companies (Objs. 1–5)

Locate an example of both a well-written and a poorly written bad-news message. Analyze the strengths and weaknesses of each document.

Required: Prepare a visual of each message and present your critique to the class.

READ | THINK | WRITE | SPEAK | COLLABORATE

16. Breaking Bad News (Obj. 3)

Security Software, Inc. (SSI) is hosting its first users conference. Security managers from more than 300 current and prospective client firms have paid the $500 registration fee for the two-day conference. As a sales specialist for SSI, you are responsible for organizing and monitoring the conference meals, breaks, and special evening events. At the first breakfast, you notice a long waiting line forming at the buffet. You soon learn that the conference hotel has run out of the contracted food items, even though only 180 tickets have been collected from attendees.

Required:

1. Develop a plan for communicating this problem to your supervisor, Jim, who you are sure will be displeased with your report. Should you send Jim an email or instant message hoping he's near his computer? Or send a text message for quick response? Or try to run him down in one of the meeting rooms? Whatever medium you choose, key your message and submit to your instructor with a rationale for the communication channel selected.
2. Assume Jim has asked you to talk with the hotel's conference planner about today's breakfast fiasco. Although the highest priority is to ensure this problem does not occur during future meals and events, you also believe your company is due a partial or full refund of the breakfast charges. You must consider the impact on SSI's image with conference attendees.
3. In small groups, identify situations you've encountered in an academic or work situation that required you to break bad news. Discuss the appropriateness of the channel you used to deliver the message, the approach (inductive or deductive) and your overall tone. What steps did you take to cushion the bad news and build goodwill? What changes would you make in your message that you believe would have led to positive results?

17. Request Refusal: Must Be Conveyed in Person (Obj. 3)

Gulf South Communications Corporation has purchased a significant number of season tickets to the Riverside Community Theatre since its inaugural season in 1979. Gulf South distributes the tickets to special customers, vendors, and employees to foster goodwill and promote the company. Because of the financial crisis in the telecommunications industry, Gulf South's management has regrettably been forced to eliminate all noncritical expenditures. As a supervisor in the human resources department, you have been asked by management to inform Steve Cafferty, the business manager of the theatre, that Gulf South will not purchase season tickets this year. Because the loss of your long-time support will be a hard blow to the theatre, you decide to break the news to Steve over lunch at his favorite restaurant.

Required: Develop a script of the conversation you will have with Steve conveying the company's disappointing decision. Your instructor may ask you to role-play your conversation with another student in the class.

18. Telephone Response: Order Problem Tests Customer Loyalty (Objs. 1–2, 4)

As an account manager of Patriot, a manufacturer of limited-edition furniture, you recently shipped six highback distressed-wood chairs to Nina Hughes, an interior designer and one of your premier accounts. Because these chairs were a special order, Nina's customer had waited for over a year for delivery. You received a voice mail message from Nina explaining that the chairs will not stay together. The customer has tried gluing them, but the supports still come apart. You reported the problem to product development, who uncovered a flaw in the design of this chair; the supports are too short for the chair. Because you want to answer Nina's question as quickly as possible, you prepare to phone her with an explanation and a promise to rush delivery of replacement chairs produced with the modified design, along with a $300 credit for the inconvenience caused.

Required: Develop a script explaining how you intend to deliver this negative news with your long-standing customer (you're replacing the chairs but the remanufacture will require approximately three months for delivery).

READ | THINK | WRITE | SPEAK | COLLABORATE

19. Breaking Up Is Hard to Do (Objs. 1–5)

Delivering bad news is a dreaded situation that is common in one's personal and professional life. From ending relationships to informing employees of major changes in their jobs, being the bearer of bad news is painful and often bungled or avoided. Go to your companion website at www.cengage.com/bcomm/lehman to review the advice Dana Bristol-Smith, a communications expert, provides in the YouTube video and a related article.

Required: In small groups, compare the expert's "quick band-aid removal" model to the guidelines presented in your text. Discuss how this four-step model could be applied to deliver a bad-news situation for a personal or professional situation that your group selects or your instructor assigns. Role-play the resulting conversation in your small groups and be prepared to present your exchange to the class.

20. Electronic Message Boards: The Good and the Bad (Objs. 1–5)

The "Your Turn: Electronic Café" for this chapter explores the powerful use of discussion boards to gather and share information on a topic and provides tips for effective participation in an online discussion. Despite the benefits of online brainstorming, waves are being generated as companies and individuals become victims of negative postings. The widespread electronic distribution of these unflattering and possibly slanderous comments, often posted anonymously, is a major concern to many. You may also examine the pros and cons of anonymity presented in this chapter's case, "Anonymity in Cyberspace."

Required: Respond to the following as directed by your instructor:

1. Learn more about the negative effects of being "zapped in cyberspace" as described in the following articles:

   Valiquette, L. (2006). The dangerous myth of online invulnerability, *Ottawa Business Journal, 11*(23), p. 6. Available from Business Source Complete database.

   Sneve, J. (2008, March 12). Professor rating websites entertaining, but not entirely accurate. *The Volante Online.* Available at www.volanteonline.com/home/index.cfm?event5displayArticle&ustory_id58bca1b50-f6cb-47ae-865a-0a5f12f575a3
2. Prepare a presentation that (a) summarizes the advantages and disadvantages of online discussions and (b) provides a checklist for writing an effective reply to an online posting calling for constructive criticism of a company or individual.
3. Visit the electronic bulletin board that allows students at your college/university to post faculty evaluations and select three to five postings for a professor(s) of your choice. Using your evaluation checklist, critique the postings, placing them in rank order of effectiveness. Make a brief team presentation to the class about your analysis that includes a visual illustrating an example of a poorly written and well-written posting. Be sure to omit all identification.

CASES

© YOSHIKAZU TSUNO/AFP/GETTY IMAGES

1. Damage Control at Mattel (Obj. 5)

Mattel, maker of Barbie, Fisher Price, and Hot Wheels, is the world's largest toy company. In 2007 and 2008, the company was rocked by discoveries of lead paint in toys and the use of small magnets in some toys that could separate and cause health concerns in children if swallowed. Millions of toys were recalled; and in 2009, Mattel and its Fisher-Price subsidiary agreed to pay a $2.3 million civil penalty in an agreement with the Consumer Product Safety Commission for selling toys with hazardous levels of lead and dangerous design. After the recalls by Mattel and other companies, the U.S. Congress overhauled consumer regulations, effectively banning lead in toys.

Locate the following articles that provide information about the company's response to the crises or at www.directorship.com/mattel-s-blues:

Mattel to pay $2.3 million penalty for lead in toys. (2009, June 6, 2009). *New York Times*, p. B2.

Warner, J. (2007/2008). Mattel's blues. *Directorship, 33*(6), 30–34, at http://www.directorship.com/mattel-s-blues

Garrahan, M. (2008, February 6). Mattel looking for a brighter future after weathering storm. *The Financial Times*, p. 27. Available from LexisNexis database.

After reading the articles, go to your companion website at www.cengage.com/bcomm/lehman to listen to the television interview with Mattel CEO Robert Eckert.

In small groups, discuss the following questions:

1. What responsibility did Mattel have in the toy manufacturing problems?
2. What measures did Mattel take to restore consumer confidence? How effective were those measures, and what could the company have done differently or in addition?

Required:

1. Develop the script of a television commercial for Mattel that could be aired in the preholiday season to assure consumers of the safety of Mattel products.
2. Prepare a memo report directed to your instructor that critiques the effectiveness of the television interview delivered by Mattel CEO Robert Eckert.
3. Prepare a report that reviews the crisis communication strategies used by Mattel and analyzes the effectiveness and overall impact on the company's success. Support your analysis with performance data for the time period following the product manufacturing crisis.

© BBC LTD./COURTESY: EVERETT COLLECTION

2. Video Case: The Office: Downsizing Employees: Midgets or Elves?

In this clip, David dismisses an employee while two other employees participate in the interaction.

Complete the following activities as directed by your instructor after viewing the video:

1. In small groups, discuss the effectiveness of David's delivery of bad news. Compile a list of suggestions for improvement.
2. In small groups, compose a script of a conversation between David and his supervisor in which the supervisor

outlines for David appropriate means for delivering bad news about employee layoffs. Be prepared to act out your script in small groups or to the class.

3. Anonymity in Cyberspace (Objs. 1–5)

Do you have a right to anonymity in cyberspace? Should you have this right? Two current views prevail about the right of anonymity. One view sees it as limiting the free flow of information; by having a wealth of information available, people can communicate, shop, and conduct business with ease. Access to information allows you to find a friend's email address that you had forgotten or to track down an old friend in another city. The opposing view sees the right to anonymity as a protection of individual privacy; without anonymity, unidentified parties can track where you go in cyberspace, how often you go there, and with whom you communicate. At the present time, you are typically required to reveal your identity when engaging in a wide range of activities. Every time you use a credit card, email a friend, or subscribe to an online magazine, an identifiable record of each transaction is created and linked to you. But must this always be the case? Are there situations where transactions may be conducted anonymously, yet securely? Several methods currently exist for surfers to protect their anonymity in cyberspace:[17]

- **Anonymous remailers:** A completely anonymous remailer, or chain remailer, sends mail through remailing locations. Each location takes the header information off the mail and sends it to the next location. When the mail gets to its final destination, the recipient has no idea where the mail originated. What makes the system truly anonymous is that the remailing locations that the message goes through typically keep no records of the mail that comes in or goes out. This procedure makes the mail impossible to track.
- **Pseudo-anonymous remailers:** These single remailers work similarly to the chain remailer. The mail is sent to a remailing location, the header information is stripped at this site, and the mail is forwarded to its final destination. As with the chain remailer, the recipient has no idea where the mail originated. What makes the single remailer pseudo-anonymous is the fact that single remailers typically keep records of the mail that comes into and goes out of their systems. This procedure makes the mail traceable.
- **Pseudonymity:** This process consists of sending mail through cyberspace under a false name. Like the single remailer, the recipient will not immediately know who the mail came from, but the mail is completely traceable.
- **Anonymizer website:** By visiting www.anonymizer.com, you can learn how to stop any specified website from gathering information on you. When you use the anonymizer software to access a particular website, the anonymizer goes to that website for you, grabs the information, and sends you the information from the site. As far as the website knows, it has been contacted only by the anonymizer website. This secures your transactions and keeps "nosy" websites from gathering information on you.

In spite of consumer interest in protecting anonymity, the federal government opposes total anonymity due to legitimate interests that are at stake. If total anonymity existed, the government would be unable to track down people who use cyberspace to violate the laws of libel, defamation, and copyrights.

Required:

Visit your companion website at www.cengage.com/bcomm/lehman to link to web resources related to this topic. As directed by your instructor, respond to one or more of the following activities:

1. Locate an additional article on the issue of online anonymity. Print the article and prepare a two-page abstract that includes the following sections: (1) reference citation, (2) overview, (3) major point, and (4) application.
2. Prepare a chart that summarizes the advantages and the disadvantages of online anonymity.
3. Take a position on the anonymity issue, either to support the right to anonymity or to defend the need for identification. In writing, present a defense of your position, giving reasons and/or evidence.

© NEWSCOM

4. Constructive Criticism: Food Critic Gives Restaurant Thumbs Down

(Objs. 1–2, 5)

One of the Downtown Disney restaurants in Orlando, Florida, is Bongos Cuban Café created by Gloria Estefan and her husband Emilio. Like many Disney restaurants, Bongos Cuban Café (www.bongoscubancafe.com) hires international college students as part of the Disney College Program at the Walt Disney World Resort. Food and beverage servers in these restaurants must have the ability to work in a fast-paced environment and prior experience in the restaurant industry. Similar to servers in most restaurants, these international students take menu orders, refill beverages, carry food and drink, bus tables, and handle payment.

Angelica is a new server from Brazil who has worked for a month at the Disney location of Bongos Cuban Café. Although Angelica seems to communicate well with customers, the manager of the restaurant has received several verbal complaints from customers about her service. Most recently, an irate customer sent a letter complaining about the bad service at the restaurant. Although Angelica was the server for this customer, not all of the problems mentioned in the letter were her fault. The customer was served on New Year's Eve when several servers called in sick; therefore, service was very slow. The restaurant ran out of iced tea during lunchtime, and the customer could not get any refills. The customer ordered a menu item that was not available, and orders were served to the wrong party at the table. The customer requested a credit on the bill for the iced tea, which the management approved, but the final bill was incorrect.

In the letter, the customer demands a credit for the cost of the total bill, which is about $120 for the party of four. Most important, the customer is a food critic for a travel magazine and has enclosed a copy of the negative review he wrote for your restaurant. Since the restaurant is on Disney Resort property, customers' satisfaction with their dining experience is especially important. The restaurant is expensive; and because of the location and the cost, people expect great food and excellent service. As the restaurant manager, your job involves ensuring that your staff provides this quality. You need to discuss with Angelica the problems that have been identified by customers who have complained about her service. You also need to decide how to respond to the customer complaint.

Required:

1. Develop a full-sentence outline of the conversation between you and this employee. Your instructor may ask you to role-play your conversation with a fellow student.
2. Write a memo for Angelica's employment file as a written record of this conversation.
3. Write a letter responding to the dissatisfied customer. How can you explain the problems that occurred? What alternatives can you offer besides a credit for the total cost of the bill?

For more information on Walt Disney World Resort internships, refer to:

Disney college program-roles onstage/backstage. (2006). Disney College Program. Retrieved January 17, 2006, from www.wdwcollege program.com/sap/its/mimes/zh_wdwcp/students/role_descr/onstage.html

Chapter 8
Delivering Persuasive Messages

"Give families in need shelter, self-respect, and the hope of a better life. Our ministry puts faith into action through empowerment and hard work."

Habitat for Humanity corporate website

Objectives When you have completed Chapter 8, you will be able to:

1. Develop effective outlines and appeals for messages that persuade.
2. Write effective sales messages
3. Write effective persuasive requests (claim, favor, and information requests, and persuasion within an organization)

SHOWCASE PART 1  

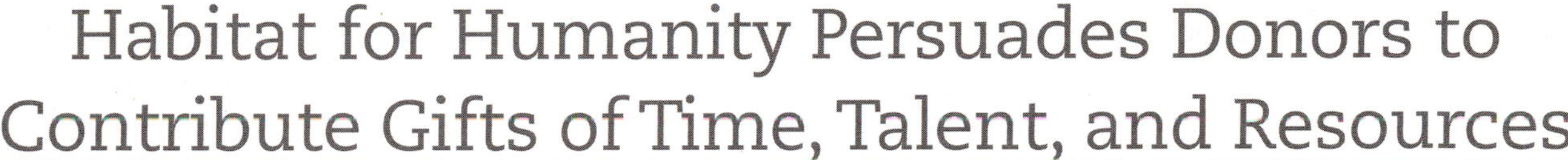

Habitat for Humanity Persuades Donors to Contribute Gifts of Time, Talent, and Resources

Providing low-income families with safe, decent, affordable housing is the mission of Habitat for Humanity International, headquartered in Americus, Georgia. Founded in 1976 by Millard and Linda Fuller, the home-building organization is made up of more than 2,300 local affiliates in nearly 100 countries. A Habitat home is completed somewhere in the world every 24 minutes.[1]

According to CEO Jonathan Reckford, Habitat for Humanity takes a "roll up your sleeves approach to putting faith into action."[2] Habitat invites people of all backgrounds, races, and religions to build houses together in partnership with families in need, who also provide sweat equity. The organization relies on gifts of materials, time, talent, and money. One reason donors are drawn to Habitat is that they can get their hands dirty and swing hammers rather than just mailing checks. Ranking among America's twenty largest charities, the faith-based organization relies on the idea that resources will come from shared gifts by those who feel they have more than they need and from working capital donated by supporters and those who will benefit from better housing.[3]

"With your help, more deserving families can have decent places to call home. Give families in need shelter, self-respect, and the hope of a better life. Our ministry puts faith into action through empowerment and hard work."[4] These words on Habitat's website challenge individual donors to make a one-time gift, contribute in honor or memory of a loved one, or join the monthly gift program. Individuals and groups are also invited to respond via email to opportunities to volunteer time and labor in various domestic and global projects. Potential donors receive direct mailings from Habitat to increase contributions. In addition to the contributions of individuals, church congregations, and civic groups, Habitat also seeks corporate sponsorships from companies such as Home Depot and Lowe's.

Habitat is one of a relatively few organizations that consider contributed time as important as donated dollars. Former U.S. president Jimmy Carter helped raise public awareness of the work of Habitat through his ongoing involvement. Working people from all walks of life, retirees, and college students work side by side to make the dream of ownership a reality for deserving families. Students who donate their spring break vacations to volunteer report that working alongside partner families is an unforgettable and rewarding life experience. Habitat strives to assure that those donating their time are not "hit over the head" with donation solicitations.[5]

Effective persuasion has enabled Habit for Humanity to raise in excess of $1 billion annually to support its goals. Your understanding of human motivation and skillful use of persuasive strategies will contribute to your success in influencing people and achieving organizational objectives.

www.habitat.org

SEE SHOWCASE PART 2, ON PAGE 293
FOR SPOTLIGHT COMMUNICATOR JONATHAN ROCKFORD, CEO OF HABITAT FOR HUMANITY INTERNATIONAL.

Persuasion Strategies

Business people regularly seek to persuade others. Persuasion is the ability to influence others to accept your point of view. It is not an attempt to trap someone into taking action favorable to the communicator. Instead, it is an honest, organized presentation of information on which a person may choose to act. Professionals in all fields benefit from well-prepared communications that persuade others to accept their ideas or buy their products, services, or ideas.

How do you learn to persuade others through spoken and written communication? Have you ever made a persuasive request, written employment documents or an essay for college entry or a scholarship, or given a campaign speech? If so, you already have experience with this type of communication. While the persuasive concepts discussed in this chapter are directed primarily at written communication, they can also be applied in many spoken communication situations.

What is the difference between motivation and manipulation?

For persuasion to be effective, you must understand your product, service, or idea; know your audience; anticipate the arguments that may come from the audience; and have a rational and logical response to those arguments. Remember, persuasion need not be a hard sell; it can simply be a way of getting a client or your supervisor to say, "Yes." Although much of this chapter concentrates on selling *products and services*, similar principles apply to selling an *idea*, *your organization*, and *your own abilities*.

Plan Before You Write

Success in writing is directly related to success in preliminary thinking. If the right questions have been asked and answered, the composing will be easier and the message will be more persuasive. Specifically, you need information about (1) your product, service, or idea; (2) your audience; and (3) the desired action.

© ANDREW SARNECKI/BRAND X PICTURES/JUPITERIMAGES

I Know What You Mean. Empathizing with customers involves treating them as you would want to be treated if you were a customer. A key ingredient of empathy is the ability to truly listen to customers to learn what is important to them. Organizations use various means to educate employees about the fine art of empathy. Gateway went to extremes to develop empathy in its employees by scheduling surfing clinics to essentially "scare" staffers into understanding first-time customers' fear of technology. One enthusiastic employee now shares with technophobic customers, "Hey, I went surfing—and I barely know how to swim. The important thing is to try."[1]

Know the Product, Service, or Idea

You cannot be satisfied with knowing the product, service, or idea in a general way; you need details. Get your information by (1) reading available literature; (2) using the product and watching others use it; (3) comparing the product, service, or idea with others; (4) conducting tests and experiments; and (5) soliciting reports from users.

What is the major difference that makes a product you currently use distinct from competing brands?

Before you write, you need concrete answers to such questions as these:

- What will the product, service, or idea do for the receiver(s)?
- What are its superior features (e.g., design and workmanship or receiver benefit)?
- How is the product or service different from its competition? How is the proposed idea superior to other viable alternatives?
- What is the cost to the receiver?

Similar questions must be answered about other viable alternatives or competing products. Of particular importance is the question, "What is the major difference?" People are inclined to choose an item (or alternative) that has some distinct advantage. For example, some people may choose a particular car model because of its style and available options; still others may choose the model because of its safety record.

Know the Receiver

Who are the people to whom the persuasive message is directed? What are their wants and needs? Is a persuasive message to be written and addressed to an individual or to a group? If it is addressed to a group, what characteristics do the members have in common? What are their common goals, their occupational levels, and their educational status? To what extent have their needs and wants been satisfied? How might cultural differences affect your message?

How can you determine receiver needs?

Recall the discussion of Maslow's need hierarchy in Chapter 2. Some people may respond favorably to appeals to physiological, security, and safety needs (to save time and money, to be comfortable, to be healthy, or to avoid danger). People with such needs would be impressed with a discussion of the benefits of convenience, durability, efficiency, or serviceability. Others may respond favorably to appeals to their social, ego, and self-actualizing needs (to be loved, entertained, remembered, popular, praised, appreciated, or respected). Consider the varying appeals used in a memo to employees and to supervisors seeking support of teleworking. The memo to employees would appeal to the need for greater flexibility and reduced stress. Appeals directed at supervisors would focus on increased productivity and morale, reduced costs for office space, and compliance with the Clean Air Act, a federal law requiring companies to reduce air pollution and traffic congestion.

Identify the Desired Action

What do you want the receiver to do? Complete an online order and make payment? Receive a demonstration version for trial examination? Return a card requesting a representative to call? Email for more information? Approve a request? Accept a significant change in service, style, and procedures? Whatever the desired action, you need to have a clear definition of it before composing your message.

Your Turn 8-1
Miscue

Sales message writers, take a lesson from the Ottawa furniture store that sent out a Mother's Day flyer advertising "Soft Stools for Mom." A New York firm noted that it only shipped within the "Untied States." In each case, the message received was not the intended one. With the pervasive presence of computers, professionals are writing more now than at any other point in history. Unfortunately, many of them do not do so proficiently.

TAKE ACTION:

- Recall or use the Web to find other advertising blunders.
- How can you ensure that your persuasive messages are accurately perceived by your audience?

Use the Inductive Approach

Does the AIDA strategy apply to persuasion through television advertisements? Explain.

Over 100 years ago, Sherwin Cody summarized the persuasive process into four basic steps called AIDA.[7] The steps have been varied somewhat and have had different labels, but the fundamentals remain relatively unchanged. The persuasive approach illustrated in Figure 8-1 on page 273 is inductive. The main idea, which is the request for action, appears in the *last* paragraph after presenting the details—convincing reasons for the receiver to comply with the request.

Each step is essential, but the steps do not necessarily require equal amounts of space. Good persuasive messages do not require separate sentences and paragraphs for each phase of the outline. The message *could* gain the receiver's attention and interest in the same sentence, and creating desire *could* require many paragraphs.

Apply Sound Writing Principles

The principles of unity, coherence, and emphasis are just as important in persuasive messages as in other messages. In addition, some other principles seem to be especially helpful in preparing persuasive messages:

- **Keep paragraphs short.** The spaces between paragraphs show the dividing place between ideas, improve appearance, and provide convenient resting places for the eyes. Hold the first and last paragraph to three or fewer lines; a one-line paragraph (even a very short line) is acceptable. You even can use paragraphs less than one sentence long by putting four or five words on the first line and completing the sentence in a new paragraph. Be careful to include key attention-getting words that either introduce the product, service, or idea or lead to its introduction.
- **Use concrete nouns and active verbs.** Concrete nouns and active verbs help receivers see the product, service, or idea and its benefits more vividly than do abstract nouns and passive verbs.
- **Use specific language.** General words won't mean much unless they are well supported with specifics. Specific language is space consuming (saying that something is

"great" is less space consuming than telling what makes it so); therefore, persuasive messages are usually longer than other messages. Still, persuasive messages need to be concise; they should say what needs to be said without wasting words.

- **Let receivers have the spotlight.** If receivers are made the subject of some of the sentences, if they can visualize themselves with the product in their hands, if they can get the feel of using it for enjoyment or to solve problems, the chances of creating a desire are increased.

Brainstorm possible central selling points for a particular DVD rental subscription service. With what audience would each selling point be most appropriate?

- **Stress a central selling point or appeal.** A thorough analysis ordinarily will reveal some feature that is unique or some benefit that is not provided by other viable alternatives. This point of difference can be developed into a theme that is woven throughout the entire message. Or, instead of using a point of difference as a central selling point, a writer may choose to stress a major satisfaction to be gained from using the item or doing as asked. A central selling point (*theme*) should be introduced early and reinforced throughout the remainder of the message.

You will apply sound writing principles and blend the steps in the four-step outline presented in Figure 8-1 to prepare effective persuasive messages.

FIGURE 8-1

Inductive Outline Used in Persuasive Messages Sent in Written, Electronic, or Spoken Form

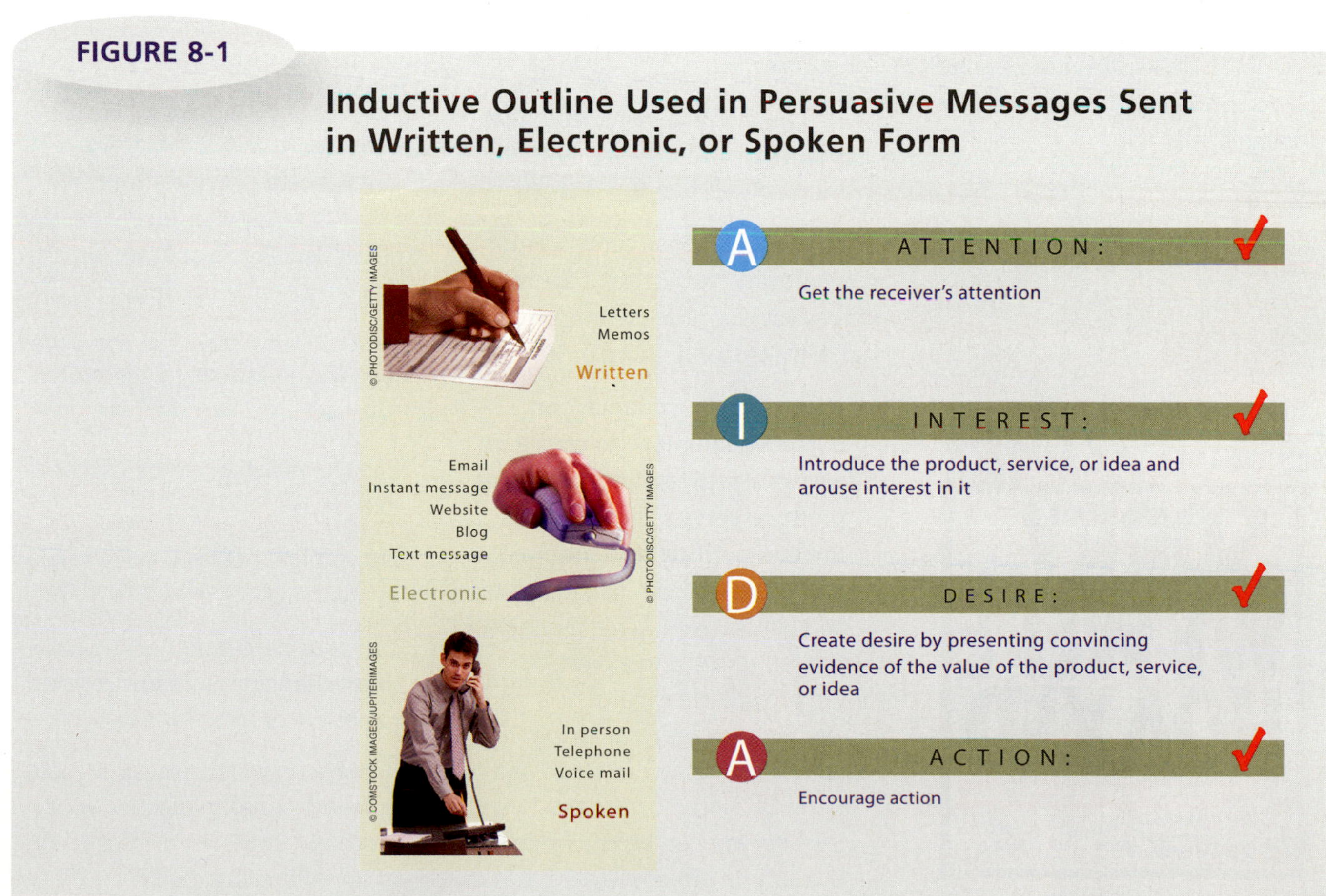
© PHOTODISC/GETTY IMAGES
Letters
Memos
Written
Email
Instant message
Website
Blog
Text message
Electronic
© PHOTODISC/GETTY IMAGES
© COMSTOCK IMAGES/JUPITERIMAGES
In person
Telephone
Voice mail
Spoken
A ATTENTION:
Get the receiver's attention
I INTEREST:
Introduce the product, service, or idea and arouse interest in it
D DESIRE:
Create desire by presenting convincing evidence of the value of the product, service, or idea
A ACTION:
Encourage action

LEGAL AND ETHICAL CONSTRAINTS

STRATEGIC FORCES

Ethical Persuasion Is Good Business

Businesses have learned that unethical behavior, such as overstating the capabilities of a product or service, is not beneficial in the long run. Developing effective persuasion skills will be important throughout your profession as you apply for a job, seek promotion, or persuade your supervisor to adopt your ideas. Use effective persuasion techniques to present your argument ethically, not to exploit the receiver. Ethical persuasion should include these elements:[8]

- **Clear definition.** Persuaders should not present products and their characteristics without clear explanation. Although the Federal Trade Commission and Food and Drug Administration may legally allow some "puffery," unsubstantiated claims may confuse or mislead.
- **Scientific evidence.** Claims of superior performance or quality of a product imply that objective data exist to support the statements. Whenever possible, the persuader should provide the source and nature of the evidence. Failure to do so may lead to lawsuits, loss of credibility, and harm to both consumers and the company.
- **Context for comparison.** Better, faster, cleaner, easier, and similar terms imply a comparison. Better than what? Better than it once was? Better than the competition? Or better than using nothing at all?
- **Audience sensitivity.** The multicultural and mixed-gender nature of most mass media audiences makes some messages objectionable. The persuader should consider those who might be offended.

DAILY Mirror

Saturday May 15 2004

NEWSPAPER OF THE YEAR 45p

SORRY.. WE WERE HOAXED

VOICE OF THE Mirror

Iraqi PoW abuse pictures handed to us WERE fake

© SCOTT BARBOUR/GETTY IMAGES

With these responsibilities in mind, the following two rules of thumb will assist you in presenting facts honestly, truthfully, and objectively:

- **Use concrete evidence and objective language to create an accurate representation of your product, service, or idea (and the competition if mentioned).** Be certain you can substantiate all claims made. Legal guidelines related to truth in advertising provide clear guidance for avoiding misrepresentation. If you exaggerate or mislead in a letter delivered by the U.S. Postal Service, you can be charged with the federal offense of mail fraud and incur significant fines or even imprisonment.
- **Do not deliberately omit, distort, or hide important information that does not support your argument so that the receiver completely misses it.** Consider the truthfulness of disclosing the financial benefits of a plant closing but omitting the fact that 3,000 employees were laid off in a town where the plant is the primary employer. The investor may realize the impact of the omission and lose faith in the CEO's credibility.

Application

Consider a written message or advertisement that promotes a product or service you have used or experienced (e.g., a cool technology gadget or a new restaurant).

- How accurate was the message's representation of the product or service?
- Did the message embellish or exaggerate?
- Do you feel that you were misled in any way?
- Did your perception of the company change as a result of your experience?
- Write a memo to your instructor or be prepared to discuss your firsthand experience in class or in an online discussion.

Your Turn 8-2
Assessment

Some career fields seem to have a negative public image. Lawyers, politicians, and reporters are often held in low esteem, but used car salespeople typically top the list of least trusted. They're often viewed as overly enthusiastic people who scream their way through annoying TV commercials. Even worse, they are often perceived as unscrupulous or even dishonest. Being trusted as an ethical person with good intentions is essential to effective persuasion. You can assess your own work ethics by completing the ethics quiz located at: http://encarta.msn.com/encnet/departments/elearning/?page=BizEthicsQuiz&Quizid=188>1=7004 You may link to this URL or other updated sites from your companion website at www.cengage.com/bcomm/lehman.

TAKE ACTION:

- Email your instructor, explaining what you learned from the quiz and how ethical persuasion will be important in your career activities.

OBJECTIVE 2

Sales Messages

Why are unsolicited sales letters often referred to as "junk mail"? What can the writer do to dispel this attitude?

The four-point persuasive outline is appropriate for an ***unsolicited sales message***—a letter, memo, or email message written to someone who has not requested it. A ***solicited sales message*** has been requested by a potential buyer or supporter; that is, the message is prepared to answer this interested person's questions. With the use of persuasive email on the rise, potential customers can also indicate willingness to receive electronic communication about products and services. Visit your companion website at www.cengage.com/bcomm/lehman to learn more about permission (opt-in) email communication.

© COMSTOCK IMAGES/ JUPITERIMAGES

A person requesting sales information has given some attention to the product, service, or idea already; therefore, an attention-getting sentence is hardly essential. However, such a sentence is needed when the receiver is not known to have expressed an interest previously. The very first sentence, then, is deliberately designed to make a receiver put aside other thoughts and concentrate on the rest of the message.

Kill the Popup Ads! Do we really need more research to prove that intrusive advertisements annoy consumers? A recent survey revealed that nearly three quarters of Internet users report leaving a favorite website due to "intrusive ads" that pop up and cover desired content. Features that consumers most disdain include popups that are hard to close, crash the computer, or have annoying sound or distasteful content. The 25- to 34-year-old crowd are the least tolerant, while all age groups show an increasing disdain for intrusive ads. Research suggests that marketers should carefully evaluate their online advertising strategies. Instead of being favorably impressed, users can be annoyed and made less likely to purchase.[9]

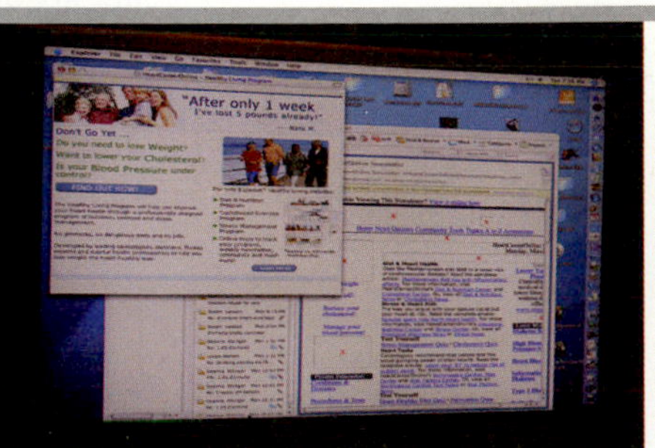

© SUSAN VAN ETTEN/PHOTOEDIT

Gaining Attention

Various techniques have been successful in convincing receivers to consider an unsolicited sales message. Some commonly used attention-getting devices include:

- **A personal experience:** When a doctor gives you instructions, how often have you thought, "I wish you had time to explain" or "I wish I knew more about medical matters"?
- **A solution to a problem (outstanding feature/benefit):** Imagine creating a customized multimedia presentation that. . . .
- **A startling announcement:** More teens die as a result of suicide each month than die in auto accidents in the same time period.
- **A what-if opening:** What if I told you there is a savings plan that will enable you to retire three years earlier?
- **A question:** Why should you invest in a company that has lost money for six straight years?
- **A story:** Here's a typical day in the life of a manager who uses a Blackberry.
- **A proverb or quote from a famous person:** Vince Lombardi, one of the most successful coaches in the history of football, once said, "If winning isn't everything, why do they keep score?" At Winning Edge, we specialize in making you the winner you were born to be.

Visit a quotation website and locate a quote that might be used to promote a product or service of your choice.

- **A split sentence:** Sandy beaches, turquoise water, and warm breezes . . . it's all awaiting you on your Mesa cruise.
- **An analogy:** Like a good neighbor, State Farm is there.

Other attention-getters include a gift, an offer or a bargain, or a comment on an enclosed product sample. Regardless of the technique used, the attention-getter should achieve several important objectives:

- **Introduce a relationship between the receiver and the product, service, or idea.** Remaining sentences grow naturally from this beginning sentence. If receivers do not see the relationship between the first sentence and the sales appeal, they may react negatively to the whole message—they may think they have been tricked into reading. For example, consider the following poor attention-getter:

Ineffective Example 

Would you like to be the chief executive officer of one of America's largest companies? As CEO of Graham Enterprises, you can launch new products, invest in third-world countries, or arrange billion-dollar buyouts. Graham Enterprises is one of several companies at your command in the new computer software game developed by Creative Diversions Software.

How can your opening sentence backfire and not achieve the desired result?

The beginning sentence of the preceding ineffective example is emphatic because it is a short question. However, it suggests the message will be about obtaining a top management position, which it is not. All three sentences combined suggest high-pressure. The computer software game has relevant virtues, and one of them could have been emphasized by placing it in the first sentence.

- **Focus on a central selling feature.** Almost every product, service, or idea will in some respects be superior to its competition. If not, such factors as favorable price, fast delivery, or superior service may be used as the primary appeal. This central selling point must be emphasized, and one of the most effective ways to emphasize a point is by position in the message. An outstanding feature mentioned in the middle of a message may go unnoticed, but it will stand out if mentioned in the first sentence. Note how the following opening sentence introduces the central selling feature and leads naturally into the sentences that follow:

  One of Soviet Georgia's senior citizens thought Dannon was an excellent yogurt. She ought to know. She's been eating yogurt for 137 years.

  Dannon Yogurt is a part of a healthy nutrition plan that can add years to your life, too. It's high in important nutrients including calcium, protein, vitamin B12, potassium, phosphorus, and riboflavin, as well as being a great way to reduce fat and calories from your meals.

What would be a creative attention-getter for a product or service of your choice?

- **Use an original approach.** To get the reader's attention and interest, you must offer something new and fresh. Thus, choose an anecdote likely unfamiliar to your receiver or use a unique combination of words to describe how a product, service, or idea can solve the receiver's problem:

  The nine-year old boy rushes to the store's toy department, unaware that his parents are far behind him in housewares. Surrounded by the latest action figures, electronic games, and cartoon DVDs, he hardly knows where to start in his search for the perfect gifts to include on his holiday wish list. For the next hour, his parents indulge his enthusiasm as he tries out every displayed product.

  In many ways, Adobe Photoshop Elements is like that toy department. The new Photoshop offers a plethora of powerful, useful features that will hold your attention for hours on end.

Introducing the Product, Service, or Idea

A persuasive message is certainly off to a good start if the first sentences cause the receiver to think, "Here's a solution to one of my problems," "Here's something I need," or "Here's something I want." You may lead the receiver to such a thought by introducing the product, service, or idea in the very first sentence. If you do, you can succeed in both getting attention and creating interest in one sentence. An effective introduction of the product, service, or idea is cohesive and action centered, and continues to stress a central selling point.

- **Be cohesive.** If the attention-getter does not introduce the product, service, or idea, it should lead naturally to the introduction. Note the abrupt change in thought and the unrelatedness of the attention-getter to the second paragraph in the following example:

Ineffective Example ☒

Employees appreciate a company that provides a safe work environment.

The Adcock Human Resources Association has been conducting a survey for the last six months. Their primary aim is to improve the safety of office work environments.

The last words of the first sentence, "safe work environment," are related to "safety of office work environments"—the last words of the last sentence. No word or phrase in the first sentence connects the words of the second sentence, which creates an abrupt, confusing change in thought. In the following revision, the second sentence is tied to the first by the word "that's." "Safety" in the second sentence refers to "protection" in the third. The LogicTech low-radiation monitor is introduced as a means of providing a safe work environment. Additionally, notice that the attention-getter leads smoothly to the discussion of the survey results.

> Employees appreciate a company that provides a safe work environment. That's one thing the Tucker Human Resources Association learned from its six-month survey of the safety of the office work environment. For added protection from radiation emissions, more companies are purchasing LogicTech's low-radiation computer monitors. . . .

In Figures 8-3 and 8-4, is the sender, the receiver, or the product or service the subject of the most sentences?

- **Be action oriented.** To introduce your offering in an interesting way, you must place the product, service, or idea in your receivers' hands and talk about their using it or benefiting from accepting your idea. They will get a clearer picture when reading about something happening than when reading a product description. Also, the picture becomes all the more vivid when the receiver is in the spotlight. In a sense, you do not sell products, services, or ideas; instead, you sell the pleasure people derive from their use. Logically, then, you have to focus more on that use than about the offering itself. If you put receivers to work using your product, service, or idea to solve problems, they will be the subject of most of your sentences.

Some product description is necessary and natural. In the following example, the writer focuses on the product and creates an uninteresting, still picture:

> ***The Body Solid Endurance treadmill has an oversized running surface. It has a shock-absorbent deck for added comfort.***

In the revision, a person is the subject of the message and is enjoying the benefits of the treadmill.

© BANANASTOCK/JUPITERIMAGES

When you step on to the Body Solid Endurance 8K Treadmill, the oversized 21" × 53" running surface will inspire you to go for an all out marathon session. Go ahead, that's what the 8K was made for. The shock-absorbent deck will keep you comfortable and your run smooth. The powerful 2.5 HP continuous duty (7.5 HP peak duty) motor will keep your pace fluid and consistent whether you are a beginner or a professional athlete.[10]

- **Stress a central selling point.** If the attention-getter does not introduce a distinctive feature, it should lead to it. Note how the attention-getter introduces the distinctive selling feature (convenience) and how the following sentences keep the receivers' eyes focused on that feature:

Where should the central selling point be mentioned in a persuasive message?

You can easily hold on-the-fly or scheduled presentations, perform live demos and collaborate on documents in real time. Clients and coworkers don't need your application to view your files. Even files created with specialized applications, such as CAD drawings, are viewable. Just use the GoToMeeting icon in your system tray, an email or an instant message. There are no complicated logins or setups. It takes just two minutes to set up and a few seconds to start a meeting. That's it! Meet as often as you want, for as long as you want— for one low rate. Try GoToMeeting for FREE and experience the simplest and most cost-effective online meeting solution on the market today.[11]

By stressing one main point, you do not limit the message to that point. For example, while convenience is being stressed, other features are also mentioned.

Providing Convincing Evidence

After you have made an interesting introduction to your product, service, or idea, present enough supporting evidence to satisfy your receivers' needs. Keep one or two main features uppermost in the receivers' minds, and include evidence that supports these features. For example, using fuel economy as an outstanding selling feature of hybrid cars while presenting abundant evidence about performance would be inconsistent.

Present and Interpret Factual Evidence

Few people will believe general statements without having supporting factual evidence. Saying a certain method is efficient is not enough. You must say *how* it is efficient and present some data to illustrate *how* efficient. Saying a piece of furniture is durable is not enough. Durability exists in varying degrees. You must present information that shows what makes it durable and also define *how* durable. Durability can be established, for example, by presenting information about the manufacturing process, the quality of the raw materials, or the skill of the workers:

If you're looking for plush comfort, then look no further than Ashley's DuraPella® upholstery collection. DuraPella® is a high-tech fabric that is a breakthrough in comfort and durability. DuraPella® consists of 100% MicroDenier Polyester Suede, which gives you the subtle look and elegant feel of suede, yet is durable and stain-resistant . . . the best of both worlds!

> Everyday spills like coffee, wine, and even ballpoint pen are cleaned easily and effectively with a mixture of low PH balance liquid soap and water. You can enjoy luxury in everyday living with DuraPella®.

How can the writer establish credibility in the receiver's mind?

Presenting research evidence (hard facts and figures) to support your statements is another way to increase your chances of convincing your audience. Presenting results of a research study takes space but makes the message much more convincing than general remarks about superior durability and appearance.

Evidence must not only *be* authentic; it must *sound* authentic, too. Talking about pages treated with special protectants to retard aging and machine-sewn construction suggests the sender is well informed, which increases receiver confidence. Facts and figures are even more impressive if they reflect comparative advantage, as illustrated in the following example:

> The Honda Accord sedan has a 255 horsepower engine, versus the 240 horsepower of the gasoline V-6. Boasting excellent fuel economy, it's rated at 38 miles per gallon on the highway and 32 in town. The cylinder shutoff feature allows the Accord to run on just three of its six cylinders to save even more fuel, with the electric motor kicking in when additional power is needed.

What concepts in your career field might need interpretation?

Naturally, your receivers will be less familiar with the product, service, or idea and its uses than you will be. Not only do you have an obligation to give information, you should interpret it if necessary and point out how the information will benefit the receiver. Notice how the following example clearly interprets *why* induction is superior to electric or gas cooktops. The interpretation makes the evidence understandable and thus convincing.

COLD STATEMENT WITHOUT INTERPRETATION	SPECIFIC, INTERPRETED FACT
Cooking with an induction cooktop is the latest in technology for a restaurant environment or for just the average household.	Induction cooking is an entirely new way of cooking. Forget about red hot electric coils or open gas flames. An induction cooktop converts your cookware into the heating element by using a magnetic field to energize the atoms in the cookware. Your food cooks faster, using less energy, while providing you with instantaneous temperature control.

The previous example uses a valuable interpretative technique—the comparison. You can often make a point more convincing by comparing something unfamiliar with something familiar. Most people are familiar with electric coils and gas flames, so they can now visualize how the cookware becomes the heating element. Comparison can also be used to interpret prices. Advertisers frequently compare the cost of sponsoring a child in a third-world country to the price of a fast-food lunch. An insurance representative might write this sentence: *The monthly premium for $300,000 of term life insurance is $18, the mere cost of two movie tickets.*

Do not go overboard and bore or frustrate your receivers with an abundance of facts or technical data. Never make your receivers feel ignorant by trying to impress them with facts and figures they may not understand.

Be Objective

Use language people will believe. Specific, concrete language makes your message sound authentic. Excessive superlatives, exaggerations, flowery statements, unsupported claims, and incomplete comparisons all make your message sound like high-pressure sales talk. Just one such sentence can destroy confidence in the whole message. Examine the following statements to see whether they give convincing evidence. Would they make a receiver want to buy? Or do they merely remind the receiver of someone's desire to sell? *This antibiotic is the best on the market today. It represents the very latest in biochemical research.*

Identifying the best-selling antibiotic requires gathering information about all antibiotics marketed and then choosing the one with superior characteristics. You know the sender is likely to have a bias in favor of the particular drug being sold. However, you do not know whether the sender actually spent time researching other antibiotics or whether he or she would know how to evaluate this information. You certainly do not know whether the sender knows enough about biochemical research to say truthfully what the very best and latest is.

What are some ways that the reader can be misled unethically?

Similarly, avoid preposterous statements *(Gardeners are turning handsprings in their excitement over our new weed killer!)* or subjective claims *(Stretch out on one of our memory foam mattresses. It's like floating on a gentle dream cloud on a warm, sunny afternoon. Ah, what soothing relaxation!).* Even though some people may be persuaded by such writing, many will see it as absurd.

Note the incomplete comparison in the following example: *SunBlock provides you better protection from the sun's dangerous ultraviolet rays.* Is SunBlock being compared with *all* other sunscreens, *most* other sunscreens, *one* unnamed brand, or others? Unless an additional sentence identifies the other elements in the comparison, you do not know. Too often, the writer of such a sentence hopes the receiver will assume the comparison is with *all* others. Written with that intent, the incomplete comparison is *unethical*. Likewise, statements of certainty are often inaccurate or misleading.

Your Turn 8-3

You're the Professional

As a professional in your selected career field, one of your subordinates has asked you for advice on making an effective persuasive appeal to clients/customers of your organization.

TAKE ACTION:

Which of the following best describes your response to your subordinate and why?

You reply that the focus of a good persuasive presentation should be on

a. the reputation of the sales firm.

b. the quality of the product offered for sale.

c. the customer's needs.

d. the monetary savings the product will introduce.

e. discounts and special offers.

Include Testimonials, Guarantees, and Enclosures

One way to convince prospective customers that they will like your product, service, or idea is to give them concrete evidence that other people like it. Tell what others have said (with permission, of course) about the usefulness of your offering. Guarantees and free trials convey both negative and positive connotations. By revealing willingness to refund money or exchange an unsatisfactory unit, a writer confesses a negative: The purchase could be regretted or refused. However, the positive connotations are stronger than the negatives: The seller has a definite plan for ensuring that buyers get value for money spent. In addition, the seller conveys willingness for the buyer to check a product, service, or idea personally and compare it with others. The seller also implies confidence that a free trial will result in a purchase and that the product will meet standards set in the guarantee. A long or complex guarantee can be included in an enclosure or attachment.

A message should persuade the receiver to read an enclosure, attachment, or file link that includes more detailed information. Thus, refer to the added material late in the message after the major portion of the evidence has been given. An enclosure or link is best referred to in a sentence that is not a cliché ("Enclosed you will find," or "We have enclosed a brochure") and says something else:

> The enclosed annual report will help you understand the types of information provided to small- and medium-sized companies by Lincoln Business Data, Inc.
>
> Click here to view the huge assortment of clearance-priced items and other end-of-season specials.

Subordinate the Price

What does the buyer hope to pay for a product? What does the seller hope to charge?

Logically, price should be introduced late in the message—after most of the advantages have been discussed. Use the following techniques to overcome people's natural resistance to price:

- **Introduce price only after creating a desire for the product, service, or idea and its virtues.** Let receivers see the relationship of features and benefits to the price.
- **Use figures to illustrate that the price is reasonable or that the receiver can save money.** Example: Purigard saves the average pool owner about $50 in chemicals each month; thus, the $200 unit pays for itself in a single swim season.
- **State price in terms of small units.** Thirty dollars a month seems like less than $360 a year.
- **Invite comparison of like products, services, or ideas with similar features.**
- **Consider mentioning price in a complex or compound sentence that relates or summarizes the virtues of the product, service, or idea.** Example: For a $99 yearly subscription fee, Medisearch brings you a monthly digest of recent medical research that is written in nontechnical language.

Motivating Action

How can the sender overcome receivers' potential objections so they will take the desired action?

For proper clarity and emphasis, the last paragraph should be relatively short. Yet it must accomplish three important tasks: specify the specific action wanted and present it as easy to take, encourage quick action, and ask confidently.

- **Make the action clear and simple to complete.** Define the desired action in specific terms that are easy to complete. For example, you might ask the receiver to complete an order blank and return it with payment, place a phone call, or order online. General instructions such as "Let us hear from you," "Take action on the matter," and "Make a response" are ineffective. Make action simple to encourage receivers to act immediately. Instead of asking receivers to fill in their names and addresses on order forms or return cards and envelopes, do that work for them. Otherwise, they may see the task as difficult or time consuming and decide to procrastinate.
- **Restate the reward for taking action (central selling point).** The central selling point should be introduced early in the message, interwoven throughout the evidence section, and included in the last paragraph as an emphatic, final reminder of the reason for taking action.
- **Provide an incentive for quick action.** If the receiver waits to take action on your proposal, the persuasive evidence will be harder to remember, and the receiver will be less likely to act. Therefore, you prefer the receiver to act quickly. Reference to the central selling point (assuming it has been well received) helps to stimulate action. Commonly used appeals for getting quick action are to encourage customers to buy while prices are in effect, while supplies last, when a rebate is being offered, when it is a particular holiday, or when they will receive benefits.

Why is reader procrastination such a common reaction to a persuasive appeal? What are some ways to reduce the likelihood of it?

- **Ask confidently for action.** If you have a good product, service, or idea and have presented evidence effectively, you have a right to feel confident. Demonstrate your confidence when requesting action: "To save time in organizing appointments and tasks, complete and return. . . ." Avoid statements suggesting lack of confidence, such as "If you want to save time in organizing appointments and tasks, complete and return. . . .," "If you agree. . . .," and "I *hope* you will. . . ." Observe how the following closing paragraph accomplishes the four important tasks: (1) refers to the central selling point, (2) makes a specific action easy, (3) provides an incentive for quick action, and (4) asks confidently for action.

> Simply dial 1-800-555-8341. Then input the five-digit number printed in the top right corner of the attached card. Your name and address will be entered automatically into our system, a speedy way to get your productivity software to you within five working days along with a bill for payment. When you order by August 12, you will also receive a free subscription to *Time Resource Magazine*. TMC's new productivity software is as easy to use as it is to order!

Figures 8-2 and 8-3 illustrate poor and good *unsolicited sales messages* for a product. Figure 8-4 presents an unsolicited sales message promoting a service. The same principles apply in writing a *solicited sales message*, with one exception: Because the solicited sales message is a response to a request for information, an attention-getter is not essential. Typically, sales messages are longer than messages that present routine information or convey good news. Specific details (essential in getting action) require space.

More and more organizations are using email as a means to persuade existing and potential customers to buy their products. While email marketing is a relatively new field, marketers are learning how to use email effectively with various audiences.

(continues on p. 287)

FIGURE 8-2

Poor Example of a Sales Message Promoting a Product

Reader Response	
	Dear Jessica:
That sounds expensive!	Buy a $399 JamPhone from comPear, and we will let you surf the web, manage your contacts and calendar, access your email, and play your favorite music, all on one device and all for just $20 more a month.
Are they stuck on themselves or what?	Our new JamPhone features are great!!!! And we are adding new features all the time. The software for the JamPhone can be navigated easily, and our PearMusic Store is chock full of music and apps we like. The quality is good and the music is better. We give you access to a wide variety of artists, and we also give you free 30-second previews of each song and a description of even the most expensive apps.
Is this a reputable company. I'm not sure....	Our phone uses the new HSDPA network, and you will love what it does for you! Our apps are great because we let anyone design for us and then we approve only the best. We make the deals.
So I would have to buy their device to play the music?	At $20 more per month for our data package, you will spend about the same amount as using someone else's web service. You can take your JH&H phone back to your local store and buy your JamPhone. And you can download as many apps and you want.
I don't think I need to make this expensive purchase.	You can use the enclosed authorization number to save $50 on the rather expensive JamPhone. You have to go to our website, comPear.com/JamPhone to use it. You can do it whenever you feel like it.

FIGURE 8-3

Good Example of a Sales Message Promoting a Product

comPear.com
Music downloads the right way (a division of ComPear Computers)
6223 North Frontgate Road ♪ Fort Wayne, IN 46485 ♪ 219-555-4877

May 20, 2011

Ms. Mary Kendall Hinson
891 Logan Street
Oxford, MS 38655-0891

Dear Ms. Hinson

Do you want to access the Internet you love no matter where you are? . . .want to manage your contacts, your calendar, and your email with one device? . . . want to listen to your music at the same time? . . . want fun applications to pass the time and to make you more productive while waiting for meetings? Then you want the JamPhone from comPear.com and JH&H phone service so you can take your office on the road.

Uses a series of phrases rather than complete sentences to gain attention. Introduces experiences familiar to receiver and presents "all in one" device as central selling point.

With comPear's fast, new 4G network and the features of the JamPhone, you can do all of the following, all on one slim, sleek device:

Presents "everything in one place" device as solution to problem and reinforces central selling point.

- ♪ Call anyone by tapping a name or send a text message with the built-in touch keyboard.
- ♪ Snap photos for storing and sharing.
- ♪ Listen to music or shop PearMusic with one finger.
- ♪ Surf the Web, get full email, or find anything with built-in mapping.
- ♪ Watch the latest YouTube videos to keep track of what's hot and what's not.
- ♪ Search your full contacts and manage your customer info by syncing with your computer's email software.
- ♪ Check out the APP Store for time-saving and time-wasting applications to make your work more efficient and your distractions more enjoyable.

Uses easy-to-read bulleted list to present evidence that reflects understanding receiver's desired flexibility.

Visit www.comPear.com/JamPhone today and check out the collection that is growing daily. Use the enclosed authorization number to save $50 on your purchase of a JamPhone (regular price $399) so that you can take your office wherever you go. Just key the authorization number into the "special offer" box on the checkout screen. The $50 savings offer expires July 31, so get your JamPhone today and keep your office on the road with compear.com.

Keeps focus on receiver by use of second person, active-voice sentences.

States specific action with reward. Makes action easy and provides incentive for quick response.

Sincerely

Carola Prysocia

Carola Prysocia
Sales Manager

Enclosure

FIGURE 8-4

Good Example of a Sales Message Promoting a Service

Sends customized email message to patients considered potential candidates for procedure.

To:	Inga Meincke imeincke@hotmail.com
From:	Jace Woodall <jwoodall@genesis.com>
Subject:	End Lifetime of Reliance on Glasses or Contacts

Gains attention by introducing familiar annoyances; presents freedom from corrective lenses as central selling point.

Introduces surgery as potential solution to reader's vision problem. Reduces resistance by indicating no pain is involved.

Builds interest by explaining process and providing easy access to detailed information.

Requests specific action and associated it with central selling point.

Inga,

Do you ever imagine being able to see the alarm clock when you wake each morning? No more hassle of daily contact maintenance? Perhaps you may have imagined playing your favorite sport with complete peripheral vision—no fogging or slipping glasses. Millions of people across the world have chosen LASIK, a laser vision correction procedure, as an alternative to glasses and contact lenses. They now are enjoying the freedom that you may have only imagined.

The Genesis Optical Center is eager to inform patients who are potential candidates for laser vision correction of the benefits of this remarkable new procedure. Take a moment to visit our website at www.genesis/optical.com to see skilled surgeons use an excimer laser to correct the shape of the cornea with absolutely no pain to the patient. Many of your questions will be answered by reading about the vision improvements you can realistically expect, testimonials of our many satisfied patients, and the experience of our five resident surgeons.

You are also invited to attend a special laser seminar held at our clinic on February 18 at 7 p.m. that will feature a live laser vision correction procedure followed by a question/answer period led by our laser correction experts. You'll have an opportunity to enter your name in a drawing for a free laser vision correction procedure to be presented at the close of the seminar.

Would you like to join the millions of people who have chosen LASIK vision correction and end a lifetime of reliance on glasses and contacts in a blink of an eye? Get started today by calling our clinic to register for the laser seminar or to schedule a personal consultation to determine whether you are a candidate for this life-changing procedure. Learn for yourself whether LASIK vision correction could do for you what it has done for so many.

Cordially,

Jace Woodall

Jace Woodall, Office Manager

Legal and Ethical Constraints Issue

- Abides by advertisement requirements under Federal Trade Commission Act, including guidance provided specifically for LASIK promotions (www.ftc.gov).

To gain desired attention from customers, email messages must be carefully timed to arrive when they will gain the most attention. Over-messaging can be annoying, while under-messaging may cause the company to miss potential sales opportunities. The subject line is of utmost importance, as it must catch the attention of the reader and create a desire to learn more. Other guidelines for using email to communicate sales messages can be found at your companion website at www.cengage.com/bcomm/lehman. The Strategic Forces feature addresses "Persuasive Communication via Text Messaging."

© COMSTOCK IMAGES/ JUPITERIMAGES

Persuasive Requests

The preceding discussion of sales messages assumed the product, service, or cause was sufficiently worthy to reward the receiver for taking action. The discussion of persuasive requests assumes requests are reasonable—that compliance is justified when the request is for an adjustment and that compliance will (in some way) be rewarded when the request is for a favor.

Common types of persuasive requests are claim requests and messages that ask for special favors and information. Although their purpose is to get favorable action, the messages invite action only after attempting to create a desire to take action and providing a logical argument to overcome any anticipated resistance.

Making a Claim

What is the difference between a persuasive claim and the routine claim message discussed in Chapter 6? When is each appropriate?

Claim messages are often routine because the basis for the claim is a guarantee or some other assurance that an adjustment will be made without need of persuasion. However, when an immediate remedy is doubtful, persuasion is necessary. In a typical large business, customer service representatives handle claims.

Often, any reasonable claim will be adjusted to the customer's satisfaction. Therefore, venting strong displeasure in the claim message will likely alienate the claims adjuster—the one person whose cooperation is needed. Remember, adjusters may have had little or nothing to do with the manufacture and sale of the product or direct delivery of the service. They did not create the need for the claim.

Companies should welcome claims. Only a small percentage of claims are from unethical individuals; the great bulk is from people who believe they have a legitimate complaint. Research indicates that only four percent of customers complain, so for every complaint received, many more customers have been dissatisfied. Complaints help companies identify problem areas and correct them. Another advantage that companies derive from the claim process is that when complaints are handled appropriately, complainers can become very loyal customers.[18] Thus, the way a complaint is handled determines, to a large extent, the goodwill toward the company.

Like sales messages, persuasive claims should use an inductive sequence. Unlike routine claim messages, persuasive claims do not begin by asking for an adjustment.

CHANGING TECHNOLOGY

STRATEGIC FORCES

Persuasive Communication via Text Messaging

A line from Disney's *Little Mermaid* sums up the technology scene today: "I've got gadgets and gizmos aplenty."[12] With cell phones, laptops, and smartphones, many people stay perpetually connected electronically. In 2007, more than 363 billion text messages were sent annually, but only 1 percent of all advertisements were sent via text message.[13] Tremendous growth is expected in the use of text messaging for marketing messages.

The United States Air Force uses mobile communication to help potential recruits make their decision to enlist. The Air Force invites contacts to download wallpaper, ringtones, and custom content to their mobile phones. Attendees at recruiting fairs who have special software on their phones can snap a picture of a bar code that provides direct access to promotional material. The Air Force hopes to not only share its informational message, but to convince tech savvy 18-year-olds that it is the high-tech branch of service where the sharpest technology minds belong.[14]

© CHRISTINA LICHTI/ALAMY

A growing number of people use their mobile devices to purchase and pay for items. In the first quarter of 2008, nine million mobile subscribers say they used their mobile devices to pay for goods or services.[15] Papa John's Pizza accepts text message ordering at its more than 2,700 stores. After first registering on Papa John's website with their payment and delivery preferences, customers can use their cell phones to text message orders. The store then text messages back requesting order confirmation.[16] Messages offering coupons and specials can be sent quickly to a vast audience who will likely see the message nearly instantly. The cost to send text messages is fractional as compared to the cost of a flyer or direct mailing.

Security remains a primary concern of mobile device users who do not participate in online transactions. They want proof that their mobile transactions will be a safe, affordable, and efficient complement to other shopping options. The Telephone Consumer Protection Act restricts unsolicited text messages, as well as phone calls. Various state laws also limit mobile advertising.

In addition to federal and state statutes, industry organizations have developed their own best-practice guidelines to aid consumers and advertisers alike. Two prominent sets of standards were developed by the Mobile Marketing Association (www.mmaglobal.com) and the Cellular Telecommunications & Internet Association (www.ctia.org). Guidelines are available on the two websites that provide valuable information, such as opt-in and opt-out rights. Following best practices helps assure marketers that their promotions and ads are not only legal, but they reach the people who are most interested.[17]

Application

Consider some examples of text messages sent to you by businesses.

- How effective were those that were of an informational nature and those that were persuasive in their intent?
- What is your general reaction to text messages sent by companies who want your business?
- How likely are you to buy a product as a result of text message advertising?

FIGURE 8-5

Poor Example of a Persuasive Claim

Reader Response	
Hey! We worked hard on that production!	We've just reviewed the first draft of the Thunderbolt music video and find it totally unacceptable. It must be redone to our specifications.
Apparently, you weren't as clear as you think. You got what you paid for.	We made it clear that our target is the MTV set, which demands over-the-top entertainment, and indicated the sample clips from the Indigos were similar to what we wanted. Instead, you sent us a simplistic video of nothing more than live-concert footage of the band.
This is totally unreasonable! We may just be meeting in court.	Call us immediately to schedule reshooting of the entire video.

Two major changes would improve the poor example in Figure 8-5: (1) writing inductively (to reduce the chance of a negative reaction in the first sentence), and (2) stressing an appeal throughout the message (to emphasize an incentive for taking favorable action). In a persuasive claim, an appeal serves the same purpose that a central selling feature does in a sales message. Both serve as a theme; both remind the receiver of a benefit gained from doing as asked. Note the application of these techniques in the revision in Figure 8-6.

Knowledge of effective claim writing should never be used as a means of taking advantage of someone. Hiding an unjustifiable claim under a cloak of untrue statements is difficult and strictly unethical. Adjusters typically are fair-minded people who will give the benefit of the doubt, but they will not satisfy an unhappy customer simply to avoid a problem.

Your Turn 8-4
Electronic Café

INTERACTIVITY IS WEB'S THIRD WAVE

First it was cool to have a website. Then it became expected that you would. Now you're lagging behind if your site doesn't offer interactivity. Interactive sites make the visitor an active participant and can include discussion areas, password-protected zones, online price calculators, searchable databases, product directories with user reviews and comparison prices, and shopping baskets with secure checkouts. With an interactive site, every page can be tailored to particular customers. The following electronic activities will allow you to explore aspects of web interactivity:

TAKE ACTION:

Read more about interactive websites and their expanded applications. Access your companion website at www.cengage.com/bcomm/lehman to link to the readings.

FIGURE 8-6

Good Example of a Persuasive Claim

A leader in entertainment video production

3109 Overlook Terrace / Beverly Hills, CA 90213-8120 / (213) 333-3120 Fax (213) 555-3129

May 20, 2011

Mr. Shannon Horne
Creative Director
Harrelson Producers
3674 Elmhurst Avenue
Los Angeles, CA 90052-3674

Dear Shannon

Seeks attention by giving sincere compliment that reveals subject of message.

When Thunderbolt negotiated with your firm to produce our first music video, we were impressed with the clips of other Harrelson videos and your proven performance record. Especially intriguing to us was your video of the Indigos, with its subtle use of symbolism in the graphic images along with creative shots of the musicians.

Contains central appeal—commitment to creative production—while providing needed details.

In our meeting with your creative team, we focused on the methods used in the Indigos video and specifically asked for graphic symbolism juxtaposed with shots of the band. After viewing the first draft of our video, we find the level of artistic expression disappointing. This video closely resembles a concert tape, focusing primarily on live-concert footage of the band and will have little appeal with our customers, the MTV set, who demand innovative and exciting new approaches in entertainment.

Presents reasoning that leads to request and subtle reminder of central appeal.

Connects specific request with firm's commitment to develop creative productions.

With Harrelson's reputation for creative productions, we are confident the video can be revised to meet our expectations. The band will do its part to assist in reshooting footage and will meet with the creative director at a mutually convenient time to discuss the kind of graphic imagery appropriate for interpreting our music and its message. Please call me at 555-3920 to schedule this meeting.

Sincerely

Bryant Ammerman

Bryant Ammerman
General Manager

Legal and Ethical Constraints Issue

- Uses letter rather than less formal email format to add formality for contractual agreement.

Asking a Favor

Occasionally, everyone has to ask someone else for a special favor—action for which there is little reward, time, or inclination. For example, suppose a professional association wants to host its annual fund-raiser dinner at an exclusive private club. The program chair of the association must write the club's general manager requesting permission to use the facility. Will a deductive message be successful?

How might the receiver react to a persuasive message written in the deductive style?

When a deductive approach is used in a persuasive situation, chances of getting cooperation are minimal. For example, what might be a probable reaction to the following beginning sentence? *Please send me, without charge, your $450 interactive video training game on workplace safety.*

If the first sentence gets a negative reaction, a decision to refuse may be made instantly. Having thought "No," the receiver may not read the rest of the message or may hold stubbornly to that decision in spite of a well-written persuasive argument that follows the opening sentence. Note that the letter in Figure 8-7 asks the favor before presenting any benefit for doing so. The letter illustrated in Figure 8-8 uses an inductive approach and applies the principles discussed earlier. As this message shows, if the preceding paragraphs adequately emphasize a receiver's reward for complying, the final paragraph need not shout loudly for action.

Requesting Information

Requests for information are common in business. Information for research reports frequently is obtained by questionnaire, and the reliability of results is strongly influenced by the percentage of return. If a message inviting respondents to complete a questionnaire is written carelessly, the number of responses may be insufficient.

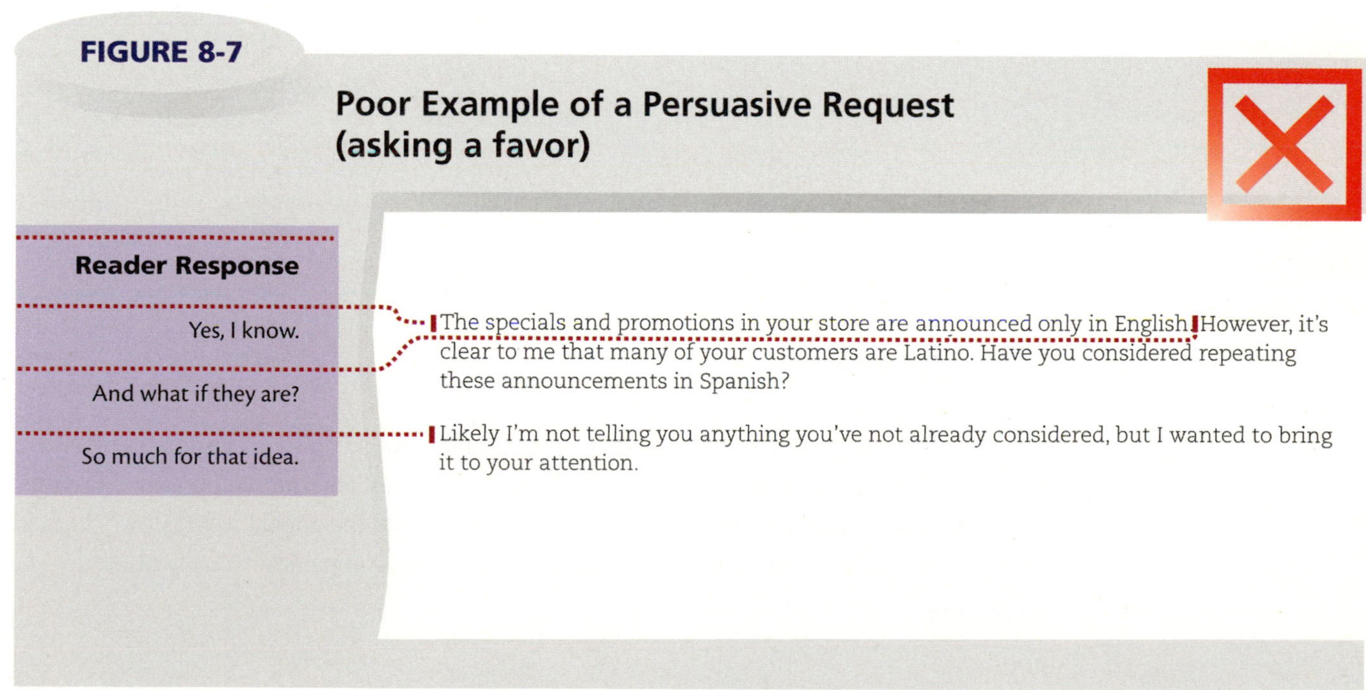

FIGURE 8-7
Poor Example of a Persuasive Request (asking a favor)
Reader Response
Yes, I know.
And what if they are?
So much for that idea.
The specials and promotions in your store are announced only in English. However, it's clear to me that many of your customers are Latino. Have you considered repeating these announcements in Spanish?
Likely I'm not telling you anything you've not already considered, but I wanted to bring it to your attention.

FIGURE 8-8

Good Example of a Persuasive Request (asking a favor)

Begins with a sincere compliment that sets stage for request that follows.

Explains rationale for request with discussion of benefits to store and its customers.

Connects specific action to rewards for taking action.

Audrey Ramirez

456 Bee Cave Drive • Austin, TX 39876-0456 • (512)555-3849

February 18, 2011

Ms. Angela Gilmer
General Manager
Fresh Foods
8976 Northeast Ninth Street
Austin, TX 39876-8976

Dear Ms. Gilmer:

As a regular customer of Fresh Foods grocery store, I have enjoyed and benefited from your store's practice of announcing price specials and promotions over your public address system. These announcements have saved me money and alerted me to specials I might have missed had the announcement not drawn my attention.

These announcements are currently made only in English. While I have no trouble understanding the English messages, many of your customers who live in the Latino community near your store have limited knowledge of spoken English and, therefore, do not benefit from these informative store announcements.

By providing both English and Spanish announcements for price specials and promotions, you could ensure that all your customers understand and can benefit from these announcements. Because these customers are now aware of your specials, they will be more likely to make additional purchases as well. It is a win for Fresh Foods and for the many customers patronizing your grocery store.

Sincerely,

Audrey Ramirez

Audrey Ramirez

The most serious weakness is asking for action too quickly and providing no incentive for action. Sometimes the reward for taking action is small and indirect, but the message needs to make these benefits evident. Note the reward and the appeal to Maslow's higher order of needs in the sample document provided at your companion website at www.cengage.com/bcomm/lehman.

© PRNEWSFOTO/HABITAT FOR HUMANITY INTERNATIONAL

SPOTLIGHT COMMUNICATOR: JONATHAN RECKFORD, CHIEF OPERATING OFFICER, HABITAT FOR HUMANITY.

Unique Leadership for a Not-for-profit Organization

When Jonathan Reckford became CEO of Habitat for Humanity International in 2005 at age 42, he had already built an impressive corporate résumé. After earning an MBA from Stanford, he held management positions with Goldman Sachs, Walt Disney, and Best Buy. Searching beyond his business success for personal fulfillment, Reckford was serving a Presbyterian church as a minister of business affairs when he was invited to apply for Habitat's head post. Since taking the helm at Habitat, Reckford has been successful in forming new partnerships and recruiting celebrity endorsements. Visit your companion website at www.cengage.com/bcomm/lehman to learn more about Reckford's leadership strategies at Habitat.

www.habitat.org

REFER TO SHOWCASE PART 3, ON PAGE 296
TO LEARN MORE ABOUT HOW HABITAT FOR HUMANITY PERSUADES POTENTIAL DONORS.

Persuading Within an Organization

Why are routine requests typically shorter than persuasive requests?

The majority of memos are of a routine nature and essential for the day-to-day operation of the business, for example, giving instructions for performing work assignments, scheduling meetings, providing project progress reports, and so on. In many organizations, such matters are handled through the use of email rather than paper memos. These routine messages, as well as messages conveying good news, are written deductively. However, some circumstances require that a supervisor write a persuasive message that motivates employees to accept a change in their jobs that might have a negative effect on the employees or generate resistance in some form (e.g., a job transfer, change in work procedures, software upgrade, etc.).

For example, Steak and Ale restaurant faced the challenge of communicating to its employees a significant change in service and style, accompanied by new uniforms. Rather than coercing or demanding that employees accept the change, a letter from Bob Mandes, president of Steak and Ale, emphasized reasons the changes were being made (benefits to guests, the company, and the employees) and the employee's important role in implementing the changes. Using a lighthearted, entertaining approach, the message and accompanying magazine provide (a) a visual model of the fresh, crisp, and professional look the company expected with the uniform change; and (b) helpful information on ways to achieve this look. Note the "you" orientation in the "style flashes" interwoven throughout the magazine excerpt that follows:

> Out of control hair is the biggest turnoff to Guests in restaurants—they don't want it wandering into their food. So pull your hair back and pull in a better tip.
>
> If you wear a lot of jewelry, Guests may think you don't need as large a tip.
>
> Your smile is the most important part of your appearance and it's the first signal to Guests that their Steak and Ale experience will be a memorable one. Your smile tells Guests, "I'm happy you're here!" But hey, don't take our word for it. Check out the recent study by Boston College which found that smiling suggests an awareness of the needs of others. Maybe that's the reason behind the phrase "winning smile."[19]

The detailed language leaves no doubt in an employee's mind as to what management considers clean, crisp, and professional. However, by continually emphasizing the benefits employees gain from the change, management garners support for the high standards being imposed.

Similarly, employees must often make persuasive requests of their supervisors. For example, they may recommend a change in procedure, acquisition of equipment or software, or attendance at a professional development program. They may justify a promotion or job reclassification or recommendation for policy changes, and so on. Persuasive memos and email messages are longer than most routine messages because of the extra space needed for developing an appeal and providing convincing evidence.

When preparing to write the memo in Figure 8-9, the human resources manager recognizes that productivity concerns could affect the president's reaction to his proposal to pilot-test substituting "e-breaks" for the traditional coffee break. Anticipating resistance, the manager writes inductively and builds a logical, compelling argument for her proposal.

In crafting a persuasive message for a product or service of your choice, what compelling reason can you offer the reader for taking the requested action?

Melissa Carter, the writer of the persuasive email at your companion website, www.cengage.com/bcomm/lehman, may have been one more burnout statistic had it not been for her initiative and, most importantly, her excellent writing skills. Managing her career and family had become increasingly difficult, and she decided to seek her supervisor's approval to telework —a work plan that would enable her to work from home on selected days.

The importance of effective persuasive strategies is relevant in all types of organizations, as discussed in ShowCase Part 3. Study carefully the overall suggestions for persuasive messages in the "General Writing Guidelines" available at your companion website at www.cengage.com/bcomm/lehman. After you have written a rough draft, compare your work with the "Check Your Communication" checklist at the end of this chapter and make any revisions.

FIGURE 8-9

Good Example of a Persuasive Message

To:	Jennifer Haupt
From:	Cadmon Volnecki
Subject:	Enhancing Employee Satisfaction
Attachments:	e-breaks.docx

Ms. Haupt,

Opens with reference to meeting discussion and company goal.

During our leadership team meeting last month, you mentioned concerns about declining employee morale and productivity. Providing our employees the best working environment possible is a high priority for all of us here at ICUP Enterprises. Asking the team members to consider ways to improve morale and productivity led me to poll employees about what would make them happier and more productive.

Presents a solution to an identified problem.

While employees indicate pay raises would increase their job satisfaction, many have shared a compelling reason for low morale. They feel that concern about taking care of personal business keeps them from being as productive as they could be. If they could occasionally handle personal business during the work day, they could accomplish more with a clear conscience.

Builds interest by describing benefits of proposed change.

They also have expressed a desire to "relax" at their desks during their coffee breaks rather than spending the time in the break room. Our employees sometimes want to spend their break time without the interaction required with the communal coffee break. The attached article highlights companies that allow employees to use their coffee break as an "e-break" to conduct personal business on their computers, connect with friends and family through email and FaceBook, or play short games like Solitaire and Minesweeper.

Alludes to benefits and closes with specific action to be taken.

Reduces potential resistance by tracking use and adhering to existing Internet usage policy.

With our goals for increasing employee morale and productivity in mind, would you allow me to test the "e-break" idea within the sales and marketing department during October? Employees participating in the pilot would be asked to log their "e-break" time and personal tasks and would be reminded of the company Internet policy that restricts web access to certain sites. At the end of the pilot, I will organize a complete report of the results, thereby allowing us to test the idea before expanding it to include all departments.

Later,

Cadmon

Cadmon Volnecki
Operations Manager
ICUP Enterprises
Oakland, CA 90053
213-555-7634, Ext. 45, Fax 213-555-9900
cvolnecki@ICUP.com

Your Turn 8-5
Career Portfolio

Email is used widely for sales solicitation messages. Assume you are employed in a position of your choice in your selected career field. As a part of your responsibilities, you are charged with increasing sales for your organization and plan to use an email communication as a persuasive outreach.

TAKE ACTION:

Beginning with an appropriate subject line, compose an email message designed to persuade clients, customers, or the public about the benefits of your organization's offerings. Focus on one particular product, service, or event you want to promote. Refer to Appendix A for appropriate business email format.

SHOWCASE PART 3

Habitat for Humanity Uses Website to Persuade Donors

"Shelter from rain, wind and sun is a basic human need. With your help, more deserving families can have decent places to call home . . . put your faith into action by clicking to donate online." As is typical for not-for-profit organizations, Habitat for Humanity uses its website to encourage donations. Before the advent of the Internet, donation requests were typically sent as direct mail. How do the two methods for distribution compare in terms of cost, convenience, audience, and probable response?

www.habitat.org

Activities

- Visit the Habitat site and review the "Donate to Habitat" link: www.habitat.org/getinv/default.aspx
- Locate the following article that discusses strategies for faith-based fundraising:

  Battistelli, M. (2006, April 1). Faith-based fundraising relies heavily on heartstrings. *Fund Raising Success Magazine.* Available at www.fundraisingsuccessmag.com/story/story.bsp?sid=31820&var=story

© PRNEWSFOTO/HABITAT FOR HUMANITY

- Summarize how the Habitat donation link effectively reflects the advice in the article and the steps in the AIDA formula.
- Following your instructor's directions, post an online comment that reflects your opinion as to the effectiveness of Habitat's call for action in convincing a web surfer to donate.

Summary

1. Develop effective outlines and appeals for messages that persuade.

The purpose of a persuasive message is to influence others to take a particular action or to accept your point of view. Effective persuasion involves understanding the product, service, or idea you are promoting; knowing your audience; presenting convincing evidence; and having a rational response to anticipated resistance to your arguments.

Effective persuasive communications build on a central selling point interwoven throughout the message. The receivers, rather than the product, serve as the subject of many of the sentences. Therefore, receivers can envision themselves using the product, contracting for the service, or complying with a request. Persuasive messages are written inductively.

2. Write effective sales messages.

A sales message is written inductively following the four-point AIDA steps for selling:

- **Gain attention.** Use an original approach that addresses one primary receiver's benefit (the central selling point) in the first paragraph.
- **Introduce the product, service, or idea.** Provide a logical transition to move the receiver from the attention-getter to information about the product, service, or idea. Hold the receiver's attention by using action-oriented sentences to stress the central selling point.
- **Provide convincing evidence.** Provide specific facts and interpretations that clarify features and quality. Include non-exaggerated, believable evidence and research and testimonials that provide independent support. De-emphasize price by presenting convincing evidence before the final paragraph, showing how money can be saved, stating price in small units, illustrating that the price is reasonable, or placing the price in a sentence that summarizes the benefits.
- **Motivate action.** State confidently the specific action to be taken and the benefits for complying. Present the action as easy to take, and provide a stimulus for acting quickly.

3. Write effective persuasive requests (claim, favor, and information requests, and persuasion within an organization).

A persuasive request is written inductively, is organized around a primary appeal, and is longer than a typical routine message because you must provide convincing evidence of receiver benefit.

- **Persuasive claim**—To convince an adjuster, gain the receiver's attention, develop a central appeal that emphasizes an incentive for making the adjustment, and end with the request for an adjustment you consider fair.
- **Request for a favor or information**—Gain the receiver's attention, build interest by emphasizing the reward for taking action, and encourage the receiver to grant the favor or send the information.
- **Persuasion within an organization**—When persuading an employee or supervisor to take specific actions, gain the receiver's attention, introduce and build interest and support for the proposed idea, address any major resistance, and encourage the receiver to take a specific action.

Chapter Review

1. List the writing principles that are important in writing an effective persuasive message. (Obj. 1)
2. What are the legal and ethical implications of persuasive messages? (Obj. 1)
3. Define "central selling feature." Where should it appear in a persuasive message? (Obj. 1)
4. What are the characteristics of a good attention-getter? List five techniques for getting receivers' attention. (Objs. 1, 2)
5. Why are sales messages normally longer than routine messages? What guidelines apply as to the recommended lengths for paragraphs? (Obj. 2)
6. What types of words and phrases are effective in persuasive messages? (Objs. 1–3)
7. In addition to the general guidelines for sales messages, what specific guidelines apply to sales-oriented email messages? (Objs. 1, 2)
8. How should price be handled in a sales message? (Obj. 2)
9. What is the principal difference between a persuasive claim and a routine claim? (Obj. 3)
10. What is meant by an "appeal" in a persuasive message? (Obj. 3)

Digging Deeper

1. Where does one cross the line between being persuasive and being coercive or overbearing?
2. How might a persuasive approach need to be modified when dealing with persons of other cultures?

Assessment

To check your understanding of the chapter, take the available online quizzes as directed by your instructor.

Check Your Communication
Persuasive Messages

Sales Messages

CONTENT

- ☐ Convince the reader that the product or service is worthy of consideration.
- ☐ Include sufficient evidence of usefulness to the purchaser.
- ☐ Reveal price (in the message or an enclosure).
- ☐ Make the central selling point apparent.
- ☐ Identify the desired specific action.
- ☐ Ensure that the message is ethical and abides by legal requirements.

ORGANIZATION

- ☐ Use an inductive sequence of ideas.
- ☐ Ensure that the first sentence is a good attention-getter.
- ☐ Introduce the central selling point in the first few sentences, reinforcing it throughout the message.
- ☐ Introduce price only after presenting receiver benefits.
- ☐ Associate price (what the receiver gives) directly with reward (what the receiver gets).
- ☐ End with a final paragraph that makes action easy and includes (a) specific action desired, (b) receiver's reward for taking action, and (c) incentive for quick action.

STYLE

- ☐ Use objective language.
- ☐ Ensure that active verbs and concrete nouns predominate.
- ☐ Keep sentences relatively short but varied in length and structure.
- ☐ Place significant words in emphatic positions.
- ☐ Make ideas cohere by avoiding abrupt changes in thought.
- ☐ Frequently call the central selling point to receiver's attention through repeated reference.
- ☐ Use original expression (sentences that are not copied directly from templates or sample documents). Omit clichés.
- ☐ Achieve unity by including in the final paragraph a key word or idea (central selling point) that was introduced in the first paragraph.

MECHANICS

- ☐ Ensure that keyboarding, spelling, grammar, and punctuation are perfect.

FORMAT

- ☐ Use correct document format.
- ☐ Ensure the document is appropriately positioned.
- ☐ Include standard document parts in appropriate position.
- ☐ Include special parts if necessary (subject line, enclosure, copy, etc.).

Persuasive Requests

CONTENT

- ☐ Convince the receiver that idea is valid, that the proposal has merit.
- ☐ Point out way(s) in which the receiver will benefit.
- ☐ Incorporate primary appeal (central selling feature).
- ☐ Identify the specific action desired.

ORGANIZATION

- ☐ Use an inductive sequence of ideas.
- ☐ Use a first sentence that gets attention and reveals the message's subject.
- ☐ Introduce the major appeal in first few sentences, reinforcing it throughout the message.
- ☐ Point out receiver benefits.
- ☐ Associate desired action with the receiver's reward for taking action.
- ☐ Include a final paragraph that makes reference to specific action desired and the primary appeal. Emphasize easy, quick action.

STYLE

- ☐ Use objective and positive language.
- ☐ Ensure that active verbs and concrete nouns predominate.
- ☐ Keep sentences relatively short, but vary them in length and structure.
- ☐ Place significant words in emphatic positions.
- ☐ Make ideas cohere by ensuring that changes in thought are not abrupt.
- ☐ Call primary appeal to receiver's attention frequently through repeated reference.
- ☐ Use original expression (sentences that are not copied directly from templates or model documents). Omit clichés.
- ☐ Achieve unity by including the primary appeal in the final paragraph.

MECHANICS

- ☐ Ensure that keyboarding, spelling, grammar, and punctuation are perfect.

Activities

1. Critique of Sales Letters and Persuasive Requests Produced by Real Companies

(Obj. 1–3)

Select an unsolicited sales message you (or a friend) have received. List (a) the principles it applies and (b) the principles it violates. Rewrite the message retaining its strengths and correcting its weaknesses.

2. Perfecting the Opening Statement (Obj. 1)

Decide which opening statement is preferable and describe why the others are less effective.

Version 1

You haven't lived until you've owned a Sony Blu-ray disc player!

Version 2

Are you serious about your home entertainment experience? Do you want to experience the full potential of your high definition television? Then, you're ready for the power of a Sony Blu-ray disc player that will change the way you watch movies.

Version 3

For a dollar a day for a year, you could own a Sony Blu-ray disc player.

3. Perfecting the Call to Action (Obj. 1)

Decide which call for action is preferable and describe why the others are less effective.

Version 1

It is a pleasure to share this cutting-edge business venture with you. If you have additional questions, please let me know.

Version 2

This could be your only chance to get into e-business services. Call me in the next 24 hours, or I'll have to move on in offering this opportunity to a competing hotel.

Version 3

Mark Thompson, our development specialist, will call you next week to schedule a personal consultation. He will share the details of setting up an e-business center in your hotel chains and answer questions about your becoming one of the first in your area to provide e-business services for business travelers.

4. Effective Opening Paragraphs (Objs. 1–3)

Analyze the effectiveness of each sentence as the opening for a persuasive message.

a. Instead of worrying about the starving in Africa, donate to the United Way and help the needy in your own neighborhood.
b. The enclosed folder shows our latest prices on our digital cameras and camcorders.
c. The merchandise you sent Mago Co. on May 3 is defective, and we refuse to pay for it. (persuasive claim)
d. I am requesting a promotion to regional sales manager because I have a proven track record of turning around sales revenues within two months. (persuasive request)

5. Convincing Evidence (Objs. 1–3)

Analyze the effectiveness of the convincing evidence included in the following sentences in a persuasive request.

a. I know you are extremely busy, but we would really like you to speak to us on effective investing in a bear market.
b. Southside Recycling has four regional offices located throughout Texas, with headquarters in Dallas. Our professional staff consists of 15 members at each location.
c. The touch screen interface available on your PDA phone is a must-have in today's information generation. Just sweep your finger across the screen, and you're on your way.
d. Reorganizing the loan department will help us serve our clients better and cut costs.

6. Document for Analysis: Sales Message

(Objs. 1, 2)

Analyze the following letter promoting services of a senior day services. Pinpoint its strengths and weaknesses, and then revise the message if directed by your instructor. Access a downloadable version of this activity from your companion website at www.cengage.com/bcomm/lehman.

The Senior Day Services Program at Forest View Hospital provides a safe place to leave elderly members of your family when you can't be home with them or just want to lead a normal life. Enclosed you will find a brochure that gives you more information.

Call us at 662-555-2345 to make an appointment to visit our facility. Our counselors will tell you about the different activities they plan each month. We also offer counseling, physical therapy, and many other typical services. Just tell us what you think your family member will need, and we'll tell you what our policies are.

We are located in the medical district of Harrisburg. Our hours are from 7 a.m. to 6 p.m., Monday through Friday. Other days and times are available by appointment for an additional fee. More information is posted at our website at http://seniorday.forestviewhospital.com.

7. Document for Analysis: Persuasive Claim

(Objs. 1, 3)

Analyze the following email persuading a video production house to reshoot a training video. Pinpoint its strengths and weaknesses, and then revise the message if directed by your instructor. Access a downloadable version of this activity from your companion website at www.cengage.com/bcomm/lehman.

We contracted with you to produce a video to teach our national service team how to perform the repairs required by our recent product recall. We've just reviewed the first draft of the video and find it totally unacceptable. It must be redone to our specifications.

It is imperative that our service team be able to precisely view every detail of the repair procedure. You failed to focus in on the most intricate steps of the procedure. The annoying blue tint of the video indicates that you also failed to white balance your camera.

Call us immediately to schedule reshooting of the entire video.

8. Document for Analysis: Persuasive Request (Objs. 1, 3)

Analyze the following message written by a human resources manager to persuade an employee to continue investing in the company's 403(b) plan despite unfavorable market conditions. Pinpoint the strengths and weaknesses of the memo, and then revise it if directed by your instructor. Access a downloadable version of this activity from your companion website at www.cengage.com/bcomm/lehman.

I just received your request to suspend the monthly contribution into your 403(b) plan. I think you are making a huge mistake. I understand that the decline in value of your account is disturbing, but this is not the time to abandon your long-term retirement investment strategy.

I know it may be hard to imagine now, but the stock market will recover. It may take a year or two, but the markets have always rebounded from these severe corrections. I think you should be increasing—not decreasing—your monthly contributions to take advantage of the depressed stock values.

I would be happy to meet with you to discuss your decision further. Years from now you will thank me.

9. Persuasive Claim: Your Dilemma (Objs. 1, 3)

Identify a situation in which you believe an adjustment is warranted but you doubt the company will comply without persuasion. Perhaps a retailer has already refused to make an adjustment, but you believe the manufacturer should be informed of your dissatisfaction.

Required: Write the claim letter to the appropriate recipient.

Applications

READ | THINK | WRITE | SPEAK | COLLABORATE

1. Communication Success Stories (Objs. 1–3)

Conduct an electronic search to locate an article that deals with the successful use of persuasive communication in a company or organization. Prepare an abstract of the article that includes the following parts: (1) article citation, (2) name of organization/company, (3) brief description of communication technique/situation, (4) and outcome(s) of the successful communication. As an alternative to locating an article, write about a successful communication situation in the organization/company for which you work.

Required: Submit your abstract to your instructor as an email attachment. Be prepared to give a short presentation in class.

2. Persuasive Message: Promoting Identify Theft Insurance (Objs. 1, 3)

You are an agent for a national insurance company that has begun offering identity theft insurance. Similar to protection against flood or earthquake damage, identity theft insurance would be an endorsement (option) on the client's homeowners policy. This coverage would help pay the legal and administrative fees of repairing credit information, establishing new credit cards and bank accounts, and removing any harmful software from computers. The insurance even covers lost wages incurred while attending to legal matters resulting from the theft. To promote this new coverage, you decide to send an email message to clients who have homeowners coverage with you and have subscribed to receive your regular email newsletters and electronic updates.

Required: In preparation for writing this message, use the Internet to expand your knowledge of identity theft insurance plans and your companion website, www.cengage.com/bcomm/lehman, to learn more about the design of effective permission marketing communication. Write an email message to your current clients persuading them to schedule an appointment or come by your office for an annual insurance checkup, including a short presentation on the benefits of identity theft insurance plans.

3. Persuasive Message: Improving Impact of Multimedia Presentations (Objs. 1, 3)

It happened again today. Your investor services proposal was far superior to your competition, but your presentation failed miserably. Your generic slide show made your team look incompetent when contrasted with your competitor's dazzling multimedia presentation. If the company is to win sizable contracts, you are convinced the company must invest in presentation media training and more advanced equipment. You are just as sure that the managing partner's resistance to technology will make for a hard sell. To win a pitch for the training, you must have cold, hard facts about the benefits of more advanced electronic presentations and be able to address any disadvantages associated with providing training and technology support. Begin your research by locating the following articles:

The big presentation went off without a hitch, but was it a winner or a washout? (2008). *Sales Insider, 2*(34), 1–4. Available from Business Source Complete database.

Gaskins, R. (2007). PowerPoint at 20: Back to basics. *Communication of the ACM, 50*(12), 15–17. Available from Business Source Complete database.

Required: Write a memo to Kim Macias, managing partner, persuading her to approve your proposal for investing in presentation media training, software, and projection equipment needed to enhance the company's presentation style. Prepare a short electronic presentation of your ideas to be presented to the class.

4. Designing Permission Marketing Communication (Obj. 2)

Permission (opt-in) marketing is a popular method used by advertisers to build an ongoing, personalized dialogue with customers who want to receive email offers and updates. Visit your companion website at www.cengage.com/bcomm/lehman to learn more about how to design permission marketing communication effectively.

Required: Respond to this communication issue as directed by your instructor:

1. Locate an additional article on the subject of permission marketing. Prepare a one-page abstract of the article that includes a bibliographic citation, an overview, important points, and application sections.
2. Print out a copy of an ineffective marketing email message you have received. Why was the selected message ineffective? What was your reaction to it? What is your current attitude toward the company?

READ | **THINK** | WRITE | SPEAK | COLLABORATE

5. Sales Message: Search for Potential Wyndham Associate (Objs. 1, 2)

Wyndham Vacation Resorts is continually expanding the selection of resorts available to its FairShare Plus members. One expansion method is to establish an alliance with an existing, independent resort, enabling FairShare Plus members to use their points to vacation there. Wyndham Vacation Resorts has even extended the "resort" concept by establishing an alliance with Carnival Cruise Lines.

Required: Use the Internet or advertisements to identify a potential associate location. Assume that Wyndham Vacation Resorts has just established an alliance with the resort. Write the script of a voice mail message that Wyndham Vacation Resorts could leave for its FairShare Plus members, inviting them to visit the new location. Provide the members with instructions for learning more about this resort by visiting the company's website at www.wyndhamworldwide.com.

6. Persuasive Message Promoting a Program: (Q) What Happens Every 15 Minutes? (A) Fatal Alcohol-Related Car Crash (Objs. 1, 3)

Educational efforts about the effects of drinking and driving have positively affected high school students in the last decade. One popular program, tailored to individual high schools, is "Every 15 Minutes" (EFM), named for a mid-1990s statistic that alcohol-related traffic collisions claimed a life every 15 minutes. EFM is a two-day program that challenges high school juniors and seniors to think about the consequences of drinking and driving. The program portrays the death of teens killed by teenage drunk drivers. Role-played by students, teachers, parents, police officers, emergency response personnel and coroners, the accidents and ensuing events of the accidents are realistically recreated.

Assume that the high school in your community offered the EFM program three years ago. More than 70 people from the community spent a year organizing this program. The EFM Steering Committee coordinated both emergency personnel and law-enforcement agencies, as well as students, school administrators, and faculty and parent volunteers. This year school administrators formed a new steering committee to coordinate the next EFM program. You are the chair of this committee and must recruit volunteers to assist you in planning the event.

Required: Respond to this communication issue as directed by your instructor:

1. Write a letter to community leaders promoting this important program and requesting their assistance.
2. Compose an email message to teachers in the high school and persuade them to help you identify potential volunteers.
3. Develop a script for the first meeting of volunteers explaining the importance of the EFM program.

For more information, read one of the following articles:

California Highway Patrol. (2006). Case studies. Program: Every 15 Minutes. Office of Traffic Safety, California Highway Patrol. Available at www.ots.ca.gov/Grants/Program_Information/Case_Study_3.asp

Turner, L. and Foley, E.V. (2001, September). Police stage death to promote life. Links: At the Schools. Available online from www.communitypolicing.org/publications/comlinks/cl16/cl16_chalu.htm

7. Persuasive Request: Turning Away Customers—Not Again (Objs. 1, 3)

Gordon's Deli is filled to capacity during the lunch hour because of its convenient location in the center of the downtown business district and its reputation for delicious specialty foods. As a summer employee, daily you watch small groups of office workers stand impatiently checking their watches as they wait for a table; other groups leave as soon as they see the long lines. While waiting for a table, numerous customers have told you they prefer your wide selection of healthy food choices over the other fast-food restaurants in the area. Often they cannot leave the office for lunch because of pressing deadlines and are forced to skip lunch or eat snacks from a vending machine. No space is available for expanding the dining room to shorten the waiting line. However, you believe customers who are eating on the run would react favorably to what you are calling a FaxFood Line: Customers would fax their orders, with delivery to their office guaranteed within a half hour. You realize that not all your menu items can be delivered effectively, and you cannot afford to deliver small orders. Other resistance includes the logistics of receiving and confirming orders, especially for those ordering as a group from the same office but wanting individual totals.

Required:

1. Write a memo to persuade the manager to introduce the FaxFood Line. Mention you are attaching a draft of a fax promoting the new service to downtown office workers and the order forms needed to expedite your plan.
2. Compose a fax with a creative message, including graphics, to promote this new service to downtown office workers. (Select a name for the service if you wish.)
3. Design an order form for the FaxFood Line and the confirmation form you will send after the order is received. Use your own creativity to generate a list of menu items or select them from the menu of your favorite deli.

READ | THINK | WRITE | SPEAK | COLLABORATE

8. Persuasive Request Promoting a Service: "Loaned Executives" Raise Funds (Objs. 1, 3)

United Way started in 1887 as an effort to coordinate fund-raising activities among local charitable organizations. Today, United Way helps many communities raise funds for local charitable needs by coordinating fund-raising activities among local health and human service organizations. Local businesses within communities play a significant role in United Way annual campaigns to raise funds for distribution to local charities. Many companies encourage employees to make annual pledges, and some companies even provide volunteers for the "loaned executive" program. In Goldsboro, North Carolina, 26 loaned executives from local businesses worked to raise more than $1.3 million by soliciting pledges during a recent United Way fall campaign. The loaned executive volunteered to lead employee coordinators from four or five businesses to plan the campaign within each company. These coordinators helped organize employee meetings and rallies, and arranged payroll deductions for donations.

Assume you are the United Way board president for Goldsboro, North Carolina. Fifteen loaned executives from last year's campaign have volunteered to help again for this year's campaign. You need 11 more executives.

Required: Respond to this communication issue as directed by your instructor:

1. Write a persuasive letter to local businesses asking them to designate a loaned executive for the upcoming United Way campaign. Address your letter to a business of your choice.
2. Develop a 30-second public service announcement (PSA) for your community's United Way campaign.
3. Develop an advertisement to appear in your local newspaper for this year's United Way campaign.

For more information, read the following article.

United Way and small business. (2006). United Way of Central Minnesota. Available at www.unitedwayhelps.org

9. Persuasive Claim: Look Who's Talking (Objs. 1, 3)

You recently paid $250 to Keller & Jenkins for adding a provision in your will to establish a scholarship endowment at your alma mater. While eating lunch in a crowded restaurant, Abigail Kemp, a clerk at Keller & Jenkins, stopped by your table to commend you on your planned generosity. Although no harm was intended, you were placed in the uncomfortable position of explaining the clerk's comments to your lunch guests. Keller & Jenkins provides its clients with a bill of rights that clearly states that client information will be kept strictly confidential.

Required: Write a letter to H. Daniel Keller, the lawyer who performed the legal work for you. Inform him of the situation and seek a full refund for the legal services.

10. Persuasive Claim: Seeking Refund for Unprofessional Practices (Objs. 1, 3)

For the past two years, your company has paid a technology consulting firm to perform regular maintenance on your computer systems. The maintenance contract requires monthly visits to service both hardware and software. You have been extremely satisfied with their service; their representatives are knowledgeable and professional and your computer systems have performed without incident during the contract period.

During a recent maintenance visit, you overheard a disturbing conversation. A representative of the consulting company admitted that most of your software would prompt users to install automatic updates every 90 days. You believe the consulting firm should have educated your employees how to install these automatic updates rather than charging your company to perform this service.

Required: Write a letter persuading the consulting firm to reimburse you for the fees you believe are attributed to this unnecessary service. Thomas Gatlin, GTR Technologies, 265 Gould Avenue, Boulder City, NV 89040-0265.

11. Persuasive Request: Trading in the Company Break Room for a Cool Video Lounge (Objs. 1, 3)

Although you enjoyed video games in your youth, you had not experienced modern video games until you attended a family reunion. Much to your surprise, relatives of all ages enjoyed the new interactive features of the games. You watched in amazement as the games eliminated interpersonal barriers that traditionally dominated the family reunion and also provided needed exercise following huge meals.

After returning home, you learned from a quick Internet search that some companies have installed "video rooms" that enable their employees to play video games during their lunch break. These companies cite benefits of the video game lounges, including creating a positive work culture, relieving stress, and promoting fitness. To learn more about this new office perk, read the following article and locate other articles of your choice:

Edelhauser, K. (2007, June 4). Video games at work? *Entrepreneur.com*. Available at www.entrepreneur.com/humanresources/managingemployees/article179274.html

Required: Respond to this communication issue as directed by your instructor:

1. Write an email message to your manager, John Berger, that identifies the potential benefits of installing a video room and seeks permission to make a formal presentation.
2. You receive a return email from John asking you to make a short presentation at next month's employee advisory group meeting. Prepare a 10-minute presentation that targets the diverse representation of the employee advisory group, from line employees and office staff to executive officers.
3. The employee advisory group was overwhelmingly in favor of your idea. Mary Sanchez, the chief financial officer, has asked you to prepare a detailed proposal to be presented to the company's board of directors. The proposal should address a cost/benefit analysis of the project and include policy statements for the room's use. Mary has stated that a little-used conference room would be an ideal location for the room and, therefore, your proposal must address only the cost of installing equipment and furniture in the room.

12. Persuasive Request: Applying Internet Best Practices to Online Banking (Objs. 1, 3)

When accessing your bank records online, you realized that you overdrafted your checking account nearly a week ago. Although your overdraft protection covered the overdrafts, you incurred daily transfer fees and a relatively high interest rate on the transferred funds. It is then that you realize your online bank service is not interactive. Why couldn't the bank email or text you whenever you overdraft your account? Better yet, couldn't the bank notify you when your account falls below an amount of your choice?

Required: Individually or as a group, develop a list of email alerts you would want to receive from your online banking system. Write a letter to Neal Mitchell, president of First National Bank, 2140 Foggy Grove Road, Kankakee, IL 60901-2140, persuading him to upgrade the online banking service to allow customers to select and customize email alerts.

13. Persuasive Request: Persuading Employees to Complete Community Service (Objs. 1, 3)

Your corporation strongly believes that it should give back to the community. Thus, each of the corporation's manufacturing plants is directed to select one community organization to sponsor. The corporation encourages but does not require its employees to donate one day each quarter in service to the organization and authorizes a $5,000 donation per year. Corporate policy requires that the sponsored organization be rotated every three years. By the slimmest margin, the employees at your plant recently voted to sponsor the local high school.

The athletic director at the high school has requested that your employees provide leadership in creating a field for the girls' softball team. The first workday would entail purchasing and installing pipe for a sprinkler system.

Required: Write an email message to the employees persuading them to participate in the workday, scheduled for the last Friday of this month. Lunch and refreshments will be served. Employees who do not participate in the workday must report to the plant to assist in regular maintenance of the production equipment.

READ | THINK | WRITE | SPEAK | COLLABORATE

14. Persuasive Claim for Replacement Product: No One Wants Another Bum Cell Phone (Objs. 1, 3)

Many families purchase a "family plan" from cell phone service providers. This plan is particularly convenient and cost effective for parents with college students. With the elimination of long-distance phone charges, family members can easily stay in touch with each other. You are a college student, and your family recently purchased the family cell phone plan from Radio Shack before you left for college. The contract is for a two-year period and includes an upgrade on phones within 18 months. A penalty of $150 is charged for cancellation of the contract.

The college student recently took the phone to a Radio Shack retail store for repair because the volume could not be adjusted high enough to hear conversations. Radio Shack shipped the phone to the service center, and the service center said that it cannot be repaired. The model is discontinued and not available for new contracts because "there were problems with the model." However, the corporate policy states that the defective phone cannot be replaced with a new model free of charge; the replacement phone must be the old model. The customer is infuriated, saying "It's unacceptable that the company would expect me to put up with another 'bum' phone."

Required: Respond to this communication issue as directed by your instructor:

1. Write a letter to Radio Shack asking for a phone replacement as an alternative to the upgrade that will be available to you in six months.
2. Develop a script for a phone conversation with (a) Radio Shack asking for a phone replacement and/or (b) your parents explaining the problem.

15. Sales Message: Practicing Sales Pitches (Objs. 1, 2)

Form groups of two and select a tangible item from a collection provided by your instructor or one of your own choice (your cell phone, purple stapler, nifty white-out pen, cool backpack, or favorite t-shirt or accessory, etc.).

Required:

1. Designate one member of the team as the buyer and one as the seller. The seller will present a compelling sales pitch for the item to the buyer focusing on an appropriate central appeal and convincing evidence. Following the sales pitch, the buyer will give friendly feedback for making the pitch more convincing. Reverse roles except the buyer will sell himself/herself as a potential employee of the company that makes the item. Again, share friendly feedback for improving the presentation and discuss differences you encountered in selling a product versus promoting yourself. Be prepared to share your experiences with the class.
2. Use the experience gained from the previous activity to deliver a one- to two-minute sales pitch on a pet project or idea you genuinely support. Choose at least three points that prove your case.

16. Persuasive Request: Calling for Continued Support (Objs. 1, 3)

As a business professional, you may be asked to serve on the board of directors of a philanthropic organization. Assume you are on the board of directors of the Pearson Foundation, an organization dedicated to providing scholarships to first-generation college students in your state. The Foundation has recently seen its endowment funds shrink as a result of a weak economy. As a result, the Foundation will be unable to fund the typical number of scholarships unless additional donations are received. You have been asked to assist in developing a plan to solicit the necessary funds.

Required: Write a voice script to be read by volunteers encouraging past donors to increase their annual contributions by 10 percent. In small groups, practice delivering your message as a conversation.

READ | THINK | WRITE | SPEAK | COLLABORATE

17. Persuasive Request: Selling Your Business Idea (Objs. 1, 3)

Despite having written what you consider an outstanding business proposal, you have not been successful in persuading any regional banks to finance the new venture. While attending a fund-raising dinner for a local charity, you had the good fortune to meet B. Stephen Richardson, a successful entrepreneur who you believed to be interested in your idea. He gave you his business card stating "Let me know if I can ever lend a helping hand." More importantly, you interpreted his nonverbal cues as clear interest in financing the project.

Required: Respond to the following communication issue as directed by your instructor:

1. In small groups, identify a retail business you believe would be successful in your community. Assuming you have written a business proposal, write a cover letter to B. Stephen Richardson seeking his financial support of the project. The letter should include a brief summary of the proposed business and your justification for its potential success.
2. Assuming you receive financing for the project, design a company logo that will serve as the centerpiece for advertising campaigns and developing consumer recognition. Be certain that your logo has a contemporary look and portrays the essence of your brand. Be prepared to present your recommended logo to the class in a brief presentation.

18. Persuasive Request: Reality Cooking Courses Build Team Spirit and More (Objs. 1, 3)

The size of your accounting firm is about to double as it plans to absorb a large number of accountants from another firm that is being dissolved. Having previous experience with a merger, you recognize the inherent problems with merging two former competitors into a single, cohesive team. To help with this transition, you want to plan a team building event that is more relaxing and creative than a boring out-of-town brainstorming retreat sitting around a table or another embarrassing outdoor excursion. You want to plan a reality cooking event that you understand is gaining popularity because of the widespread appeal of culinary arts to men and women. You must work out the details before presenting your proposal to the managing partner. How competitive or relaxing should the event be? Should we add a health-consciousness dimension to the event to complement our corporate wellness goals?

To learn more about the organizational benefits of culinary experiences, locate the following article:

Jacobson. L. (2007, January 24). Too many chefs in the kitchen can boost business. *Business Day, Health News Edition*. Available from LexisNexis Academic.

Required: Respond to the following communication issues as directed by your instructor.

1. In groups, develop a detailed plan for a culinary experience for your managers including logistics for the cook-off, required personnel, and budget.
2. Write a memo persuading Shannon Hassell, the managing partner, to organize the culinary experience that you planned.
3. Write an email promoting the culinary experience to the managers who will participate. Direct them to a video presentation about the event posted at the company intranet.
4. Develop a short video presentation to post on the company intranet encouraging managers to participate.

19. Developing a Creative Claim Strategy (Objs. 1, 3)

Sometimes creativity is more compelling than a complaint. Airline passenger David Carroll, wrote the song "United Breaks Guitar," an ode to his year-long battle with United Airlines who wouldn't pay for his $3,500 custom guitar that was broken when thrown by baggage handlers. After the video gained wide exposure on YouTube, a United Airlines spokesperson said the company was reviewing its policies and would use the video to train staff. "I'm not really looking for compensation anymore," said Carroll in referring to reaction from the song. "I just wanted change.[20]

You can view the David Carroll "United Breaks Guitars" video at www.youtube.com and read an article that discusses the baggage incident and resulting song:

McLean, J. (2009, July 10). Busted guitar blues is sweet YouTube revenge. *TheStar.com*. Available at www.thestar.com/news/canada/article/663869 Star.com

Respond to the following activities as directed by your instructor.

1. In class or in an online posting, discuss the legal and ethical implications of this type claim.
2. In teams, develop an effective claim strategy for a similar situation you have encountered. Be prepared to share your creation with the class.

20. Persuasive Request: Challenge Courses Build Team Leadership (Objs. 1, 3)

You are convinced that your managers could benefit from participating in a ropes challenge course conducted at the local Boy Scout camp. The ropes course challenges groups to perform a variety of activities that develop teamwork, communication, and imaginative thinking. For example, blindfolded and unable to speak, group members must place themselves in order by birthdate. Guided debriefing following each activity helps the participants evaluate and improve their team skills. To learn more about the organizational benefits of challenge courses, locate the following article:

Lovell, J. (2008, May 30). The EXCEL Group plans to reopen its ropes course. *Sun* (Yuma, AZ), p. NA. Available from General BusinessFile.

Required: Write a memo persuading Marina Nigel, the managing partner, to organize an outing for the firm centered around the challenge course.

CASES

© AP PHOTO/UNITED PARCEL SERVICE

1. Persuasive Message: Getting Paid to Volunteer Time and Talent (Obj. 1-3)

From vacations to health insurance, employers have sought to provide benefits to meet their employees' needs. Progressive employers recognize the genuine need of today's young executives to apply their profession skills in public service. In response, these employers are empowering their employees by paying them for all or part of the time they devote to skill-based volunteerism.

United Parcel Service Inc. is an example of a company supporting skills-based volunteerism. Jimmy Guadalupe, a logistics supervisor for UPS, provided supply-chain services to the Susan G. Komen Breast Cancer Foundation. Assisting with the logistics for the annual Race for a Cure event, approximately half of the 20 hours per week Jimmy worked with the Foundation was on company time.

Matching employees with volunteer assignments is critical to an effective skill-based volunteerism program. Robert Mallett, a senior vice president at Pfizer Inc., believes a good match helps develop employees' talent. "They come back with more substantial leadership skills and a better strategic sense of how to navigate in different types of environments."

Read the following article to learn more about skill-based volunteerism:

Needleman, S. E. (2008, April 29). The latest office perk: Getting paid to volunteer. *The Wall Street Journal, Eastern Edition*, pp. D1–5. Available from Business Source Complete.

Required: Individually or in groups, respond to the following communication issues as directed by your instructor.

1. Interview the director of a local government agency or nonprofit organization that could benefit from receiving pro bono professional services. Prepare a report that includes a description of specific assignments and a profile of the skills sets required by potential volunteers.
2. Prepare a persuasive cover letter to local businesses encouraging them to consider matching their young executives to the assignments presented in the report.
3. Prepare a letter to be sent by the government agency or not-for-profit organization to potential volunteers encouraging them to consider accepting the assignment.

© PRNEWSFOTO/STATE FARM/AP IMAGES

2. Sales Message Promoting a Product: Achieve Financial Goals with State Farm (Objs. 1, 2)

Many banks and insurance companies market a wide selection of customer services. This now requires bank officers and insurance agents to be well versed in marketing products other than traditional bank and insurance products. These employees need current, up-to-date information on all company products so that they can market them to customers. In fact, performance evaluation and employee income is frequently based on the number of products sold for the bank or insurance company.

State Farm Insurance is one of many insurance companies that offer products and services other than insurance policies. Insurance agents for State Farm may help customers plan for retirement, save for college, budget, plan their estate, develop savings strategies, and learn prevention/safety information. The State Farm mission, as noted on its website, is to "help people manage risks of everyday life, recover from the unexpected and realize their dreams."

State Farm Insurance offers its customers a free personalized Insurance and Financial Review to help them plan their financial future. Many customers who receive this personalized review choose State Farm products and services to help them achieve financial planning goals. Go to the official State Farm website www.statefarm.com for additional information.

Required: As a manager for State Farm, respond to the following communication issues as directed by your instructor:

1. Write a form letter to your current customers offering a free personalized Insurance and Financial Review. Address your letter to a fictitious customer.
2. Write an email message that can be sent to potential customers that discusses the range of services you provide.
3. Design an ad for your local newspaper promoting State Farm Insurance products and services.
4. Develop a phone script that responds to a customer's request for information on financial planning services.

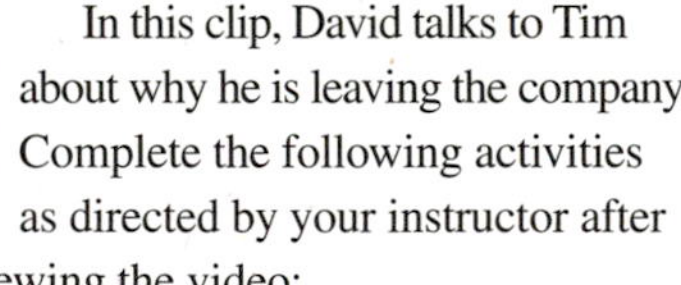

© BBC LTD./COURTESY: EVERETT COLLECTION

3. Video Case: The Office: Persuasion: It's Not All About Me

In this clip, David talks to Tim about why he is leaving the company. Complete the following activities as directed by your instructor after viewing the video:

1. In small groups, analyze David's use of persuasion in his "pep talk" with Tim. Does David's discussion follow the AIDA approach to persuasion? What does David do to put the receiver, Tim, in the spotlight?
2. If David actually wants Tim to stay, what could David offer Tim as part of the persuasive process to convince him to stay?

© DAWN HUDSON/SHUTTERSTOCK.COM

4. Inside View: Cyberclerking at Lands' End

Lands' End, a company that began in 1963 as a sailing supply mail order catalog, is known for its customer service. For example, the company will take back any item, anytime, from anywhere and refund 100 percent of the purchase price. Their products are "Guaranteed. Period." Lands' End continued success is due, in part, to its dedication to customer service provided on the Web.

Customer service is the emphasis in the Lands' End shopping experience. Think about what other companies do to provide online, face-to-face, and telephone customer service.

View the video segment online at your companion website at www.cengage.com/bcomm/lehman to learn more about enhancing the customer service experience.

Reflect

1. Go to your favorite Internet shopping website and analyze the shopping tools available (e.g., online help, cyberclerks, chat features). Discuss what you find. If the site offers no opportunities for human interaction, discuss what they might consider adding and why.
2. According to the video, two thirds of Internet shoppers end a transaction at the point of purchase. List reasons shoppers might spend time and effort assembling a shopping list and not complete the transaction.
3. From a communication standpoint, what do you see as the advantages and disadvantages of cyber-shopping vs. brick and mortar shopping?

React

Select a product you want to purchase and locate it on three or four different consumer websites. Prepare an outline that summarizes your web search. If price was not a factor, which website would you choose and why? Evaluate sites based on ease of use, customer service options, guarantees, and shipping information.

5. How to Get Off the Lists (Objs. 1–3)

The solicitation phone call interrupts dinner once again. The mailbox and the email inbox are stuffed with the usual array of junk mail. What can consumers do about these unwelcomed contacts? Nine out of ten households have received at least one telemarketing call, according to the American Teleservices Association, an industry trade group. By some estimates, telemarketers make 18 million calls a day, or 12,500 a minute. Additionally, consumer mailboxes are crowded with catalogs, sweepstakes offers, and credit card solicitations. The U.S. Postal Service reports that the average household gets 10 pieces of unsolicited third-class mail each week. All that is necessary to get on solicitation lists is to get a credit card, open a checking account, or complete a survey. But there are ways to get off the lists:

- **Opt out.** The first step in preventing unwanted calls and mail is to "opt out" of sales lists through the National Do Not Call Registry launched by the Federal Trade Commission in July 2003 and industry associations such as the Direct Marketing Association (DMA), which also operates a free nationwide name-removal service for mail. Once your request takes effect, it should drastically reduce the number of calls from publishers, credit card companies, telecommunications and utilities corporations, and major non-for-profit groups. To reduce phone calls, sign up for the national-do-not-call list by registering online at www.donotcall.gov. Register for the DMA's Mail Preference Service at www.dmachoice.org/MPS/proto1.php. Until a general opt-out procedure is developed for the Internet, you must opt out with each individual sender. The Can Spam law requires that senders provide an opt-out provision in every commercial email and that they have 10 days to remove the address of someone who has requested it.[21]

- **Maintain privacy.** Though you might enjoy ordering from home, remember that companies with whom you do business will keep you on their sales lists unless you tell them not to. Once you are pegged as a buyer, an organization will sell your name to other companies and the calls and mail will just keep coming. To reduce your exposure, never enter contests or complete surveys with your name and address or from your private email account, and use care when posting to newsgroups. Tell every company with which you do business not to sell your name. Set up a separate email account just for ordering purposes.
- **Be persistent.** Laws do not prevent a company from sending you mail, unless it is pornographic, sexually offensive, or involves fraud. In that case, contact your postmaster to launch an investigation. If you continue to receive other unwanted mail, write directly to the companies to tell them to stop. With first-class mail, you can print that request right on the envelope, along with "refused" or "return to sender." But since the post office won't return third-class mail, the more common rate for solicitations, you will have to use your own postage. Include the mailing label in your request so the company can find you on its sales list. Complain to your senator or representative about the need for laws to regulate unwelcomed solicitations.
- **Know the law.** Even after removing your name from sales lists, you may still get calls from telemarketers who simply dial random numbers. The Telephone Consumer Protection Act (TCPA) of 1991 restricts residential telemarketing calls to between 8 a.m. and 9 p.m. and requires that telemarketers keep a do-not-call list. You can also place your name on the "Do Not Call" national registry, which will enable you to be deleted from phone calling lists of most organizations. Telemarketers who disregard the registry can be fined. To file a telemarketing complaint or request information about the TCPA, write to Federal Communications Commission, Consumer Complaints, Washington, DC 20554, or file online at www.ftc.gov. Report repeat offenders to your state attorney general, who may take legal action against them.[22]
- **Follow through.** Keep a log near the phone to document calls. Write down the telemarketer's name, company, and time of call. If you haven't done business with them before, telemarketers are required to state their company's address or phone number during the solicitation, but most do not—a violation worth up to $500. After asking to be put on a company's do-not-call list, request a copy of its do-not-call policy. Failure to send the policy is an additional violation of up to $500. Check your log to see whether the same organization calls twice within 12 months after you've asked to be put on their no-call list. If so, that's another $500 violation, which can be tripled if the company is found to be willfully disregarding the law.
- **Protect yourself.** Legally speaking, salespeople are not allowed to lie. Under the Federal Trade Commission's Telemarketing Sales Rule, callers must disclose the company's identity, the purpose of the call, the product or service offered and any requirements for obtaining it. If a telemarketer won't do those things, hang up. To determine whether a telemarketer or mail offer is fraudulent, contact the NFIC at 800-876-7060 or visit them at www.fraud.org. You can also check with your local consumer protection agency or Better Business Bureau.[23]

Visit your companion website at www.cengage.com/bcomm/lehman to link to web resources related to this topic. As directed by your instructor, complete one or more of the following activities:

1. Prepare a presentation that describes current legal provisions that address the problem of unsolicited telephone calls, mailings, and email. Make recommendations for enforcement of existing laws and/or the passage of further legal requirements.
2. Discuss the challenges faced by telemarketers. Prepare a list of suggestions for phone solicitors to aid them in completing more successful contacts.
3. Prepare a short paper in which you argue for the right of sellers to offer products and services via telephone, mail, or email.

Part 4
Communication Through Reports and Business Presentations

9 Understanding the Report Process and Research Methods

10 Managing Data and Using Graphics

11 Organizing and Preparing Reports and Proposals

12 Designing and Delivering Business Presentations

Chapter 9
Understanding the Report Process and Research Methods

"Every day I read material on the Internet using key words to find a selection of articles and publications."

Novartis CEO, Daniel Vasella

Objectives When you have completed Chapter 9, you will be able to:

1. Identify the characteristics of a report and the various classifications of business reports.
2. Apply steps in the problem-solving process and methods for solving a problem.
3. Use appropriate printed, electronic, and primary sources of information.
4. Demonstrate appropriate methods of collecting, organizing, and referencing information.
5. Explain techniques for the logical analysis and interpretation of data.

SHOWCASE PART 1

Research and Development Strategies Offer Lifesaving Products at Novartis

Pharmaceutical companies spend billions of dollars annually to develop drugs that usually don't reach the market. Novartis International AG has an impressive track record of developing and marketing new products that save lives and relieve pain for many. Created in 1996 from the merger of two long-operating pharmaceutical firms, Novartis is a multinational pharmaceutical company based in Basel, Switzerland. In addition to internal research and development activities, the company is involved in joint research projects with the European Commission and various other health agencies.

While most drug manufacturers concentrate on products to treat highly visible diseases such as cancer and Alzheimer's, Novartis has taken a somewhat radical approach to its R&D. The company focuses on drugs that are backed by proven science, whether the diseases they treat are rare and the initial markets are miniscule. Once a drug has proven its effectiveness against one disease, it is tested against others. The strategy has paid off for the company in the development of Gleevec, a drug initially approved for the treatment of a rare blood cancer; Gleevec has since proven effective against six other life-threatening diseases.

Another important test for Novartis is its willingness to pursue treatment for an illness almost nobody has heard of and that affects just a few thousand people worldwide. This inflammatory disorder called Muckle-Wells syndrome results from a genetic mutation and results in the buildup of proteins that causes rashes, joint pain, and fatal kidney damage. Most drug makers would not bother with finding a cure or treatment for a condition that affects so few, but Novartis tested a drug to treat the rare disease. In early trials, four patients who received the drug showed dramatic improvement in the first 24-hours. Following successful clinical trials among patients suffering from Muckle-Wells syndrome, the drug is now marketed as Ilaris. Once FDA approval is obtained, Novartis hopes to seek approval of the drug for use against a variety of autoimmune diseases, including Type 2 diabetes and severe arthritis.[1]

In a field where most top executives have backgrounds in law, accounting, or marketing, Novartis CEO Daniel Vasella is a former physician. The company places a high premium on medical experience, with medically trained scientists holding down many of the company's senior positions. CEO Daniel Vasella speaks of the value of staying current about developments in his industry and in the scientific world: "Every day I read material on the Internet using key words to find a selection of articles and publications."[2]

Company research continues on an oral treatment for multiple sclerosis; and Afinitor, a drug approved to treat advanced kidney cancer, shows promise in six other forms of the disease.[3] Company plans include expansion into China, which has required a great deal of fact gathering, as well as visits with politicians and physicians.

Most managers are not in the lifesaving business. As a manager in your career field, however, you too will be faced with the challenge of maximizing results for your organization. Conducting successful research will provide you with the information needed to propose and implement effective solutions.

www.novartis.com

SEE SHOWCASE PART 2, ON PAGE 336
FOR SPOTLIGHT COMMUNICATOR DANIEL VASELLA, CEO, NOVARTIS.

Characteristics of Reports

"Hello, Emily. This is Ivan in customer service. The boss wants to know how things are going with the 400-case Duncan order. Are we going to make the 4 p.m. shipping deadline?"

"Oh hi, Ivan. We are going to make the deadline, with time to spare. We have about 250 cases on the loading dock, 100 on the box line, and 50 going through the labeling process. They'll all be ready for the loader at two o'clock."

This brief exchange illustrates a simple reporting task. A question has been posed; the answer given (along with supporting information) satisfies the reporting requirement. Although Emily may never have studied report preparation, she did an excellent job; so Ivan, in turn, can report to his supervisor. Emily's spoken report is a simple illustration of four main characteristics of reports:

- **Reports typically travel upward in an organization because they usually are requested by a higher authority.** In most cases, people would not generate reports unless requested to do so.
- **Reports are logically organized.** In Emily's case, she answered Ivan's question first and then supported the answer with evidence to justify it. Through your study of message organization, you learned the difference between deductive and inductive organization. Emily's report was deductively organized. If Emily had given the supporting evidence first and followed that with the answer that she would meet the deadline, the organization of her reply would have been inductive and would still have been logical.
- **Reports are objective.** Because reports contribute to decision making and problem solving, they should be as objective as possible; when nonobjective (subjective) material is included, the report writer should make that known.

How can receivers' needs be addressed in an organization's annual financial report?

- **Reports are generally prepared for a limited audience.** This characteristic is particularly true of reports traveling within an organization and means that reports, like letters, memos, and emails, can be prepared with the receivers' needs in mind.

Types of Reports

Based on the four characteristics, a workable definition of a ***report*** is an orderly, objective message used to convey information from one organizational area to another or from one organization to another to assist in decision making or problem solving. Reports have been classified in numerous ways by management and by report-preparation authorities. The form, direction, functional use, and content of the report are used as bases for classification. However, a single report might fit several classifications. The following brief review of classification illustrates the scope of reporting and establishes a basis for studying reports.

- **Formal or informal reports.** The formal/informal classification is particularly helpful because it applies to all reports. A ***formal report*** is carefully structured; it is logically organized and objective, contains much detail, and is written in a style that tends to eliminate such elements as personal pronouns. An ***informal report*** is usually a short

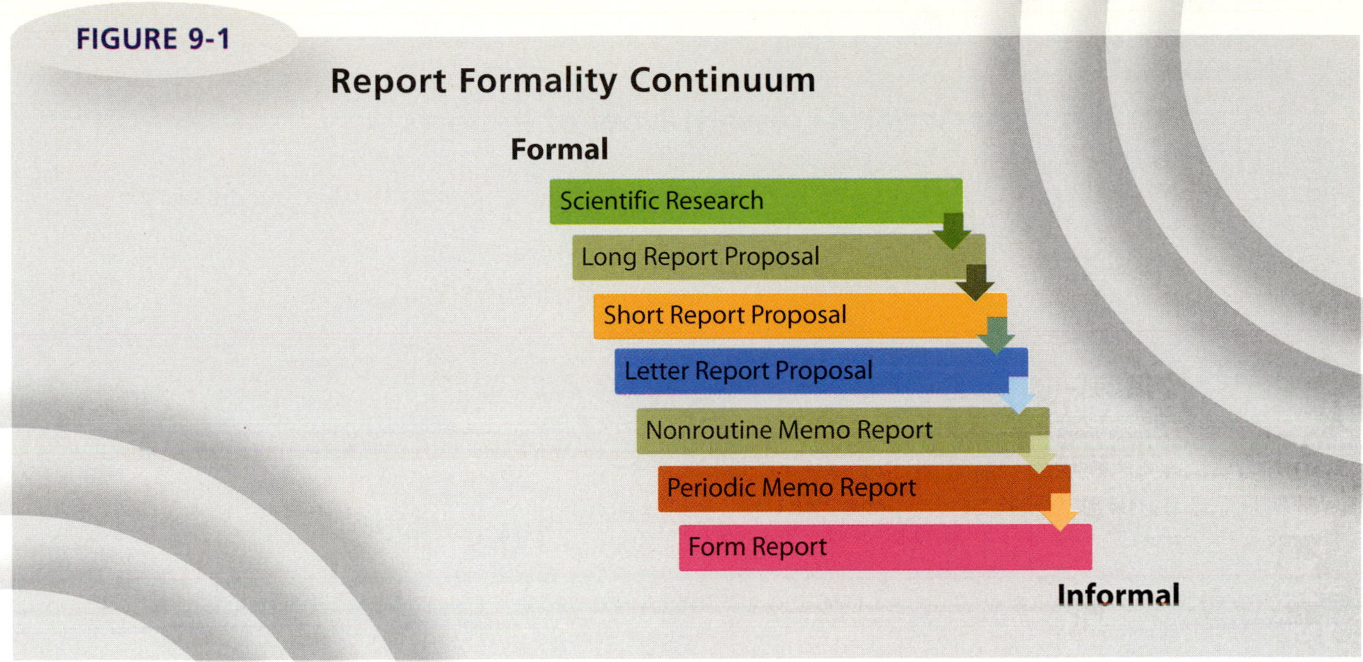

FIGURE 9-1

Report Formality Continuum

message written in natural or personal language. An internal memo generally can be described as an informal report. All reports can be placed on a continuum of formality, as shown in Figure 9-1. The distinction among the degrees of formality of various reports is explained more fully in Chapter 11.

- **Short or long reports.** Reports can be classified generally as short or long. A one-page memo is obviously short, and a report of 20 pages is obviously long. What about in-between lengths? One important distinction generally holds true: As it becomes longer, a report takes on more characteristics of formal reports. Thus, the classifications of formal/informal and short/long are closely related.

Why do organizations need information generated from both informational and analytical reports?

- **Informational or analytical reports.** An ***informational report*** carries objective information from one area of an organization to another. An ***analytical report*** presents suggested solutions to problems. Company annual reports, monthly financial statements, reports of sales volume, and reports of employee or personnel absenteeism and turnover are informational reports. Reports of scientific research, real estate appraisal reports, and feasibility reports by consulting firms are analytical reports.

- **Vertical or lateral reports**. The vertical/lateral classification refers to the directions reports travel. Although most reports travel upward in organizations, many travel downward. Both represent vertical reports and are often referred to as ***upward-directed*** and ***downward-directed*** reports. The main function of vertical reports is to contribute to management *control*, as shown in Figure 9-2. Lateral reports, on the other hand, assist in *coordination* in the organization. A report traveling between units on the same organizational level, as between the production department and the finance department, is lateral.

- **Internal or external reports**. An ***internal report***, such as a production or sales report, travels within an organization. An ***external report***, such as a company's annual report to stockholders, is prepared for distribution outside an organization.

FIGURE 9-2

The General Upward Flow of Reports

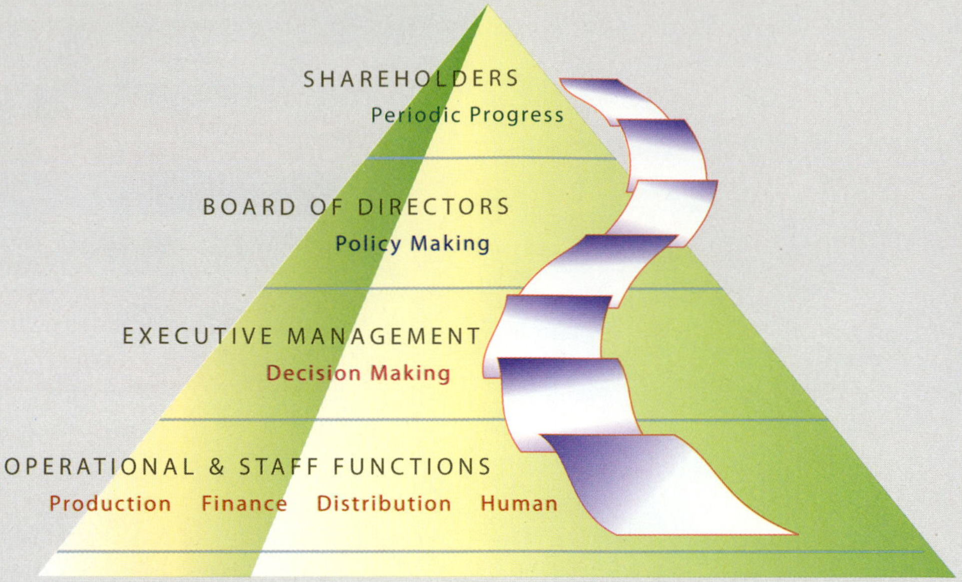

SHAREHOLDERS
Periodic Progress

BOARD OF DIRECTORS
Policy Making

EXECUTIVE MANAGEMENT
Decision Making

OPERATIONAL & STAFF FUNCTIONS
Production Finance Distribution Human

- **Periodic reports.** *Periodic reports* are issued on regularly scheduled dates. They are generally directed upward and serve management control purposes. Daily, weekly, monthly, quarterly, semiannual, and annual time periods are typical for periodic reports. Preprinted forms and computer-generated data contribute to uniformity of periodic reports.
- **Functional reports.** A *functional report* serves a specified purpose within a company. The functional classification includes accounting reports, marketing reports, financial reports, personnel reports, and a variety of other reports that take their functional designation from their ultimate use. For example, a justification of the need for additional personnel or for new equipment is described as a *justification report* in the functional classification.

Proposals

What types of proposals might you develop in your career field?

A ***proposal*** is a written description of how one organization can meet the needs of another; for example, provide products or services or solve problems. Businesses issue "calls for bids" that present the specifications for major purchases of goods and certain services. Most governmental agencies issue "requests for proposals," or RFPs. Potential suppliers prepare proposal reports telling how they can meet that need. Those preparing the proposal create a convincing document that will lead to their obtaining a contract.

In our information-intensive society, proposal preparation is a major activity for many firms. In fact, some companies hire consultants or designate employees to specialize in proposal writing. Chapter 11 presents proposal preparation in considerable detail.

As you review these report classifications, you will very likely decide—correctly—that almost all reports could be included in these categories. A report may be formal or informal, short or long, informational or analytical, vertically or laterally directed, internal or external, periodic or nonperiodic, functionally labeled, a proposal, or some other combination of these classifications. These report categories are in common use and provide necessary terminology for the study and production of reports.

Your Turn 9-1
You're the Professional

As employee relations manager for Ace Corporation, you have been asked to prepare a report for the vice president of operations on whether the company should offer an in-house daycare center for employees' children.

TAKE ACTION:

Discuss the merit of each of the following choices, describing your reasons. Your report will likely be:

a. informal, short, informational, lateral, and external.

b. formal, long, analytical, vertical, and external.

c. formal, long, informational, lateral, and internal.

d. formal, long, analytical, vertical, and internal.

Basis for Reports: The Problem-Solving Process

The upward flow of reports provides management with data that someone may use to make a decision. The purpose is to use the data to solve a problem. Some problems are recurring and call for a steady flow of information; other problems may be unique and call for information on a one-time basis. A problem is the basis for a report. The following steps are used for finding a solution:

1. Recognize and define the problem.
2. Select a method of solution.
3. Collect and organize the data and document the sources.
4. Arrive at an answer.

Only after all four steps have been completed is a report written for presentation. Reports represent an attempt to communicate how a problem was solved. These problem-solving steps are completed *before* the report is written in final form.

Recognizing and Defining the Problem

Problem-solving research cannot begin until the researchers define the problem. Frequently, those requesting a report will attempt to provide a suitable definition.

Lessons Learned from Online Customer Activity. What makes for a positive online transaction? That's what businesses of all types and sizes want to know. Wachovia Bank uses a variety of research methods to design an appealing website that customers will continue to use. When Wachovia's interactive design team doesn't know how to create the right experience, such as the proper sequence for resetting a password, they run a usability lab where engineers watch consumers complete various online tasks through a two-way mirror.[4] Online marketers of various companies track the screen habits of their web customers including the links they click, what they add to their shopping carts, and how many items are added to carts but never purchased.

Nevertheless, researchers should attempt to state the problem clearly and precisely to ensure they are on the right track.

Using Problem Statements, Statements of Purpose, and Hypotheses

The ***problem statement***, or statement of the problem, is the particular problem that is to be solved by the research. The ***statement of purpose*** is the goal of the study and includes the aims or objectives the researcher hopes to accomplish. Research studies often have both a problem statement and a statement of purpose. For example, a real estate appraiser accepts a client's request to appraise a building to determine its market value. The problem is to arrive at a fair market value for the property. The purpose of the appraisal, however, might be to establish a value for a mortgage loan, to determine the feasibility of adding to the structure, or to assess the financial possibility of demolishing the structure and erecting something else. Thus, the purpose may have much to do with determining what elements to consider in arriving at an answer. In other words, unless you know why something is wanted, you might have difficulty knowing what is wanted. Once you arrive at the answers to the *what* and *why* questions, you will be on your way to solving the problem.

Of what value is a research study in which the hypotheses are disproved?

A ***hypothesis*** is a statement to be proved or disproved through research. For example, a study of skilled manufacturing employees under varying conditions might be made to determine whether production would increase if each employee were part of a team, as opposed to being a single unit in a production line. For this problem, the hypothesis could be formulated in this way:

Hypothesis: Productivity will increase when skilled manufacturing employees function as members of production teams rather than as single units in a production line.

Write a statement of purpose for the study of teams.

Because the hypothesis tends to be stated in a way that favors one possibility or is prejudiced toward a particular answer, many researchers prefer to state hypotheses in the null form. The ***null hypothesis*** states that no relationship or difference will be found in the factors being studied, which tends to remove the element of prejudice toward a certain answer. The null hypothesis for the previous example could be written as follows:

Null hypothesis: No significant difference will be found in productivity between workers organized as teams and workers as individual production line units.

Using the problem/purpose approach and/or the hypothesis approach is a choice of the researcher. In many ways, the purpose of a study is determined by the intended use of its results.

Limiting the Scope of the Problem

How does the scope of a report serve a similar purpose as a scope on a rifle?

A major shortcoming that often occurs in research planning is the failure to establish or to recognize desirable limits. The ***scope*** of the report helps to establish boundaries in which the report will be researched and prepared. Assume, for instance, that you want to study salaries of customer service agents. Imagine the enormity of such a task. Millions of people are employed in customer jobs. Perhaps a thousand or so different types of jobs fall into this classification. To reduce such a problem to reasonable proportions, use the *what, why, when, where,* and *who* questions to limit the problem. Here are the limits you might derive as the human resources manager of an online travel booking company, such as Expedia:

What	A study of salaries of online customer service agents
Why	To determine whether salaries in our firm are competitive and consistent
When	Current
Where	United States
	Customer service agents in

Now you can phrase the problem this way:

Statement of purpose: The purpose of this study is to survey salaries of customer service agents for online travel booking sites working in the United States to determine whether our salaries are competitive and consistent.

Note that this process of reducing the problem to a workable size has also established some firm limits to the research. You have limited the problem to current salaries, the particular area, and a certain type of business. Note, too, how important the *why* was in helping to establish the limits. Limiting the problem is "zeroing in on the problem."

Why would a reader want to know about limitations and delimitations placed on a project?

In some reports, it is desirable to differentiate between the boundaries that were placed on the project outside the control of the researcher(s) and those that were chosen by the researcher(s). Boundaries imposed outside the control of the researchers are called ***limitations***; they may include the assignment of the topic, allotted budget, and time for completion of the report. These boundaries affect what and how the topic can be researched. Boundaries chosen by the researcher(s) to make the project more manageable are called ***delimitations***; they may include the sources and methods chosen for research.

Defining Terms Clearly

Words often have more than one meaning, and technical or special-use words may occur in the report that are not widely used or understood. Such terms would require a definition for the reader's understanding of the information presented. In the previously used example concerning the study of office support staff salaries, a comparison of one bank's salaries with those paid by others would be meaningful only if the information gathered from other banks relates to identical jobs. A job description defining the duties performed by an administrative assistant, for example, would help ensure that all firms would be talking about the same job tasks regardless of the job title. In addition, the term *salary* requires definition. Is it hourly, weekly, monthly, or yearly? Are benefits included?

Documenting Procedures

The procedures or steps a writer takes in preparing a report are often recorded as a part of the written report. This ***procedures*** section, or ***methodology***, adds credibility to the research process and also enables subsequent researchers to repeat, or replicate, the study in another setting or at a later time. Reports that study the same factors in different time frames are called ***longitudinal studies***.

The procedures section of a report records the major steps taken in the research, and possibly the reasons for their inclusion. It may, for instance, tell the types of printed and electronic sources that were consulted and the groups of people interviewed and how they were selected. Steps in the procedures section are typically listed in chronological order, so that the reader has an overall understanding of the timetable that existed for the project.

Your Turn 9-2
Miscue

Procedures in a research study must be carefully followed if the results are to be seen as credible, especially when the health and safety of participants are involved. In one particular medical study, an FDA inspection revealed that two subjects in a medical study were given the wrong medication for nearly three months. In this case, the patients were not deemed to have been harmed, but the error did distort the findings of the study.[5]

TAKE ACTION:

- What safeguards should have been taken to ensure accuracy in treatment procedures?
- What responsibility does the report writer have in ensuring that the procedures followed in a study are accurately reported?

Selecting a Method of Solution

After defining the problem, the researcher will plan how to arrive at a solution. You may use secondary and/or primary research methods to collect necessary information.

Secondary Research

Describe the proper balance between secondary research and primary research.

Secondary research provides information that has already been created by others. Researchers save time and effort by not duplicating research that has already been undertaken. They can access this information easily through the aid of electronic databases and bibliographic indexes. Suppose that a marketing manager has been asked to investigate the feasibility of implementing a strategic information system. The manager knows other companies are using this technology. By engaging in secondary research, the manager can determine the boundaries of knowledge before proceeding into the unknown.

Certain truths have been established and treated as principles reported in textbooks and other publications. However, because knowledge is constantly expanding, the researcher knows that new information is available. The job, then, is to canvass the literature of the field and attempt to redefine the boundaries of knowledge. Such secondary research accomplishes the following objectives:

- Establishes a point of departure for further research
- Avoids needless duplication of costly research efforts
- Reveals areas of needed research
- Makes a real contribution to a body of knowledge

Secondary research can be gathered by means of traditional printed sources or by using electronic tools.

Printed Sources

Major categories of published sources are books, periodicals, and government documents. Books are typically cataloged in libraries by call number, with larger libraries using the Library of Congress classification system. Traditional card catalogs in libraries have been replaced by online catalogs, which allow the user to locate desired books by author, title, subject, or key word. A wide assortment of reference books is typically available for use within libraries; these include dictionaries, encyclopedias, yearbooks, and almanacs. Some of these volumes contain general information on a wide array of topics, while others are designed for a specific field of study.

Periodicals, referred to as *serials* by librarians, include various types of publications that are released on a regular, periodic basis. Newspapers, magazines, and journals are all types of periodicals. Newspapers, which are usually published daily, are a good initial source for investigation, since they give condensed coverage of timely topics. Magazines may be published weekly, monthly, bimonthly, or in some other interval. They are typically written for a general readership, providing expanded coverage in an easy-to-read format. Journals, on the other hand, are written for more specialized audiences, and are more research oriented. Journal articles share the results of research studies and provide interpretive data that support their findings. They also provide bibliographies or citation lists that can be used to locate related materials. Articles on specific topics can be located using both published and online indexes. A noninclusive list of these sources is shown in Figure 9-3.

FIGURE 9-3

Useful Reference Sources

Printed Indexes

Business Periodicals Index
Education Index
The New York Times Index
Readers' Guide to Periodical Literature
Social Science and Humanities Index
The Wall Street Journal Index

Electronic Databases

ABI/INFORM
Academic Search Premier
Business & Company Resource Center
Business Source Complete
Business Dateline
DIALOG Information Services
ERIC
First Search
General BusinessFile ASAP
LexisNexis Academic Universe
FSI Online
Periodical Abstracts
ProQuest
Westlaw

Biography

Who's Who in America
Similar directories for specific geographic areas, industries, and professions

General Facts and Statistics

Statistical Abstract of the United States
Bureau of the Census publications
Dictionaries (general and discipline specific)
Encyclopedia (*Americana* or *Britannica*)
Fortune Directories of U.S. Corporations
World Atlas
LexisNexis Statistics
Almanacs

Report Style and Format

American Psychological Association. (2010). *Publication manual of the American Psychological Association*, (6th ed.). Washington, DC: Author. [www.apastyle.org]

Gibaldi, J. (2009). *MLA handbook for writers of research papers* (7th edition). New York: Modern Language Association. [www.mla.org/style_faq]

© ISTOCKPHOTO.COM/STUDIOVISION

Companies "Digg" and "Flickr" for Market Data. Social bookmarking is a method for saving and storing web pages, known as **tags**, in a single online location for future use from any computer. Social bookmarking websites, such as Flickr, Digg, and del.icio.us provide users with a place to store, categorize, annotate and share favorite web pages and files. Business, like individuals, can join a bookmarking site and then submit content links. As users vote by clicking links, submissions move up the list. Links that make the first page of a popular bookmarking site assure heavy traffic to the particular websites. Social bookmarking sites also track links each user accesses. Businesses can use this information to understand site visitor demography, which may confirm success with target markets or reveal new potential markets.

Electronic Sources

The availability of computer-assisted data searches has simplified the time-consuming task of searching through indexes, card catalogs, and other sources. Weekly and monthly updates keep electronic databases current, and they are easy to use. Databases such as LexisNexis Academic Universe have full-text retrieval capability, meaning you can retrieve the entire article for reviewing and printing. Other databases offer only some articles in full text, with citations or abstracts provided for others. Note the list of electronic databases for business users listed in Figure 9-3.

How have computer-assisted data searches revolutionized the research process?

The Internet and its subset, the World Wide Web, have made thousands of reference sources available in a matter of minutes. However, the vastness of this resource can be overwhelming to the novice researcher. Cautions related to the use of the Internet are discussed in the accompanying Strategic Forces feature, "Internet Sources Vary: Caution Advised." The following tips will help to make your Internet search more productive:

- **Choose your search engine or database appropriately.** A ***search engine*** is a cataloged database of websites that allows you to search specific topics. Several popular search engines exist, including Yahoo!, AltaVista, HotBot, and Excite. Megasearch engines such as Google and Bing, which index billions of web pages, search through a number of other engines to produce "hits."[8] (A ***hit*** is a located website that contains the word or words specified in the search.) You want to obtain a sufficient number of hits, but not thousands. Although the variety of these larger engines is greater, they pose more difficulty in narrowing a search.

To what databases does your campus library subscribe?

Electronic databases provide access to articles from newspapers, magazines, journals, and other types of publications. The database provider may charge to access articles either as a subscription fee or a document delivery fee. These types of databases are not accessible by a search engine and are often described as the ***hidden Internet***. Many libraries provide access to these databases. Some databases are suited for topic searches of general interest; others are geared toward specialized fields. A topic search will pro-

DIVERSITY CHALLENGES

STRATEGIC FORCES

Internet Sources Vary: Caution Advised

The Internet has been likened to a wild, untamed frontier, open to all who desire to exercise their right to free speech. In its decision to declare the Communications Decency Act unconstitutional, the Supreme Court said, "The interest in encouraging freedom of expression in a democratic society outweighs any theoretical but unproven benefit of censorship."[6] Because of the uncensored status of the Internet, the serious researcher has several reasons for exercising caution in using information found there.

- **Internet resources are not always accurate.**

  Because the Internet is not centrally patrolled or edited, postings come from a wide variety of sources. Some of these sources are reliable and credible; some are not.

© ISTOCKPHOTO.COM/ZSOLT NYULASZI

- **Certain uses of Internet sources may be illegal.**

  Some material available on the Internet is copyright protected and therefore not available for some uses by those who download the files. For instance, photograph files that are copyrighted may be viewed by Internet users but not incorporated into documents that have commercial use, unless permission is granted by the copyright holder. Such permission often involves a royalty fee.

- **Internet resources are not always complete.**

  Selected text of articles and documents are often available via the Internet, while full text may be available only in published form. Additionally, Internet resources are not always updated to reflect current information.

- **Electronic periodicals are not always subjected to a rigorous review process.**

  Because most traditional magazines and journal articles are reviewed by an editorial board or peer reviewers, they are considered to be of more value than an article prepared by one or a few individuals that is not critiqued by other experts before its publication. Articles available over the Internet may not have benefited from such a review process.

Because of these limitations, the Internet should not be seen as a substitute for traditional library research, but rather as a complementary search tool. To help you evaluate the credibility and value of web material, apply the following criteria:[7]

- Who wrote this, and who would believe it?
- Is the source educational, commercial, gossip, or solid research?
- What are the credentials of the writer or producer?
- When was it originally published or produced?
- How accurate, current, and organized is the information?
- Why was it done, and where might I get more accurate information?

Application

Select a business topic, if one is not assigned to you by your instructor, and search for resources related to that topic using the Internet.

- Locate at least one article you feel is a reliable source of valuable information for use in a business report on the assigned topic.
- Locate at least one article you feel would not be a good choice for use as a reference in a business report.
- Compose a brief explanation of the reasons for your selections; attach printouts of the selected articles and submit the assignment to your instructor.

duce a listing of references and abstracts for articles, or even full text of some. Databases available through your library might include Business Source Premier (an offering of EBSCO), Academic Search Elite, LexisNexis Academic Universe, ABI Inform First Search, Business and Company Resource Center, General Businessfile, and others.

How would the hits produced from linking two terms in a Boolean search with "and" differ from those produced by linking the same two terms with "or"?

- **Structure searches from broad to specific.** Use words for your topic that are descriptive and do not have multiple meanings. Once sites have been located for your general topic, you can use ***Boolean logic*** to narrow the selection. Boolean operands (*and, or, not*) serve to limit the identified sites. The following example shows how these delimiters can assist you in locating precisely what you want:
  - Using the key phrase *workplace productivity* will produce all sites that have either of the key words in the title or descriptors.
  - Placing "and" between key words will produce hits that have both words.
  - Keying *workplace productivity not United States* will eliminate hits that refer to the United States.
- **Use quotation marks when literal topics are desired.** Putting quotation marks around your topic words can drastically affect the number of hits. The quotation marks cause the search engine to look for the designated words as a phrase, thus producing only those sites that have the phrase present. Without the quotation marks, the search engine will treat the words individually and produce many more hits, most of which may not be useful. For instance, if you are looking for sites related to "international communication," placing quotation marks around the desired phrase would eliminate the sites that deal with international topics that are not communication oriented.
- **Look for web pages that have collections of links to other related topics.** Clicking on these hyperlinks will allow you to maximize your time investment in the data gathering phase of your research.
- **Be adaptable to the various access format requirements.** Each search engine and database has its own particular format and instructions for use. The method for specifying and narrowing your search will vary.

Primary Research

After reviewing the secondary data, you may need to collect primary data to solve your problem. ***Primary research*** relies on firsthand data, for example, responses from pertinent individuals or observations of people or phenomena related to your study. Recognized methods to obtain original information are observational studies, experimental research, and normative surveys.

Observational studies are those in which the researcher observes and statistically analyzes certain phenomena to assist in establishing new principles or discoveries. For example, market analysts observe buying habits of certain income groups to determine the most desirable markets. Internal auditors analyze expected patterns in expense reimbursement amounts to identify potential fraud activity. Developing an objective system for quantifying observations is necessary to collect valid data. For example, to gain insight on the effect of a comprehensive ethics program, a researcher might record the number of incidents of ethical misconduct reported or the number of calls made to an ethics help-line designed to provide advice about proper conduct. Observational studies typically involve no contact with the human subjects under study.

What are some challenges faced in experimental research?

Experimental research typically involves the study of two or more samples that have exactly the same components before a variable is added to one of the samples. Any differences observed are viewed as due to the variable. Like scientists, businesses use experimental research to solve various problems. For example, a company conducts new employee training with all new hires. Two training methods are presently used: New hires in one regional office receive their training in a traditional classroom setting with other new employees, while employees at the other regional office take a web-based training class. Management wants to determine whether one method is superior to the other in terms of learning success. During the period of the study, learning differences in the two study groups are noted. Because the training method is assumed to be the only significant variable, any difference is attributed to its influence. Experimental research involves very careful recordkeeping and can require informed consent from participants that are subjected to experimental methods.

Normative survey research is undertaken to determine the status of something at a specific time. Survey instruments such as questionnaires, opinion surveys, checklists, and interviews are used to obtain information from participants. Election opinion polls represent one type of normative survey research. The term normative is used to qualify surveys because surveys reveal "norms" or "standards" existing at the time of the survey. A poll taken two months before an election might have little similarity to one taken the week preceding the election.

Surveys can help verify the accuracy of existing norms. The U.S. Census is conducted every decade to establish an actual population figure, and each person is supposedly counted. In effect, the census tests the accuracy of prediction techniques used to estimate population during the years between censuses. A survey of what employees consider a fair benefits package would be effective only for the date of the survey. People retire, move, and change their minds often; these human traits make survey research of opinions somewhat tentative. Yet surveys remain a valuable tool for gathering information on which to base policy making and decision making.

Why are public opinion polls often inaccurate?

Researchers normally cannot survey everyone, particularly if the population is large and the research budget is limited. ***Sampling*** is a survey technique that eliminates the need for questioning 100 percent of the population. Sampling is based on the principle that a sufficiently large number drawn at random from a population will be representative of the total population; that is, the sample will possess the same characteristics in the same proportions as the total population. For example, a company collecting market research data before introducing a new low-fat food product would survey a small number of people. The data are considered *representative* if the sample of people surveyed has the same percentage of ages, genders, purchasing power, and so on as the anticipated target market. Other sampling methods are available that you can learn more about on your companion website at **www.cengage.com/bcomm/lehman**.

Can a sample be too small? Too large? Why?

As a researcher, you must be cautious about drawing conclusions from a sample and generalizing them to a population that might not be represented by the sample. For example, early-morning shoppers may differ from afternoon or evening shoppers; young adults may differ from senior citizens; men shoppers may differ from women shoppers. A good researcher defines the population as distinctly as possible and uses a sampling technique to ensure that the sample is representative.

Whether a survey involves personal interviewing or the distribution of items such as checklists or questionnaires, some principles of procedure and preplanning are common to both methods. These principles assure the researcher that the data gathered will reflect both validity (measure what the researcher intended to measure) and reliability (measure data accurately).

- **Validity** refers to the degree to which the data measure what you intend to measure. It generally results from careful planning of the questionnaire or interview questions or items. Cautious wording, preliminary testing of items to detect misunderstandings, and some statistical techniques are helpful in determining whether the responses to the items are valid. A ***pilot test*** of the instrument is often conducted prior to the full-scale survey so that a smaller number of participants can test the instrument, which can then be revised prior to wide-scale administration.

What steps can you take to ensure that your data are valid and reliable?

- **Reliability** refers to the level of consistency or stability over time or over independent samples; that is, reliable data are reasonably accurate or repeatable. Reliability results from asking a large enough sample of people so that the researcher is reasonably confident the results would be the same even if more people were asked to respond or if a different sample were chosen from the same population. For example, if you were to ask 10 people to react to a questionnaire item, the results might vary considerably. If you were to add 90 more people to the sample, the results might tend to reach a point of stability, where more responses would not change the results. Reliability would then be reasonably established.

Responses to surveys conducted by mail often represent only a small percentage of the total mailings. In some cases, a return of 3 to 5 percent is considered adequate and is planned for by researchers. In other cases, depending on the population, the sample, and the information requested, a return of considerably more than half the mailings might be a planned result. Selecting an appropriate data collection method and developing a sound survey instrument are crucial elements of an effective research study.

Your Turn 9-3
E-Research—An Expanding Internet Application

The Internet has accelerated the pace of business and has also given us e-research—research conducted online or using online databases. And unlike television, radio, or billboards, the Internet comes with not only the means to send and receive large volumes of information but also to identify and describe its audience. The following electronic activities will allow you to explore the e-research process in more depth:

TAKE ACTION:

- Learn about e-polling: Locate the following article about the pros and cons of online surveys:
  Pros and cons of online paid surveys. (2009, April 7). *Ecommerce Journal.* Available at www.ecommerce-journal.com/articles/14506_pros_and_cons_of_online_paid_surveys
- Compose a short report on ways to overcome challenges of online surveys and maximize their usefulness.

Collecting and Organizing the Data

Collecting the right data and ensuring that they are recorded appropriately is paramount to the success of a business report. Various techniques can assist in this process when collecting both secondary and primary research.

Collecting Secondary Data

When beginning to collect secondary data, beware of collecting too much information—one of the major deterrents to good report writing. Although you want to be thorough, you do not want to collect and record such a large amount of information that you will hardly know where to begin your analysis.

The availability of computer-assisted data searches has simplified the time-consuming task of searching through indexes, card catalogs, and other sources. For example, suppose you select an online database such as Business Source Premier or an Internet search engine such as Google to research the role of microblogging in the workplace. By inputting the key terms *microblogging* and *Twitter* in an online database, you receive the screen output in Figure 9-4. The screen output contains information that will facilitate your research.

FIGURE 9-4

Sample Computer Search Using an Online Database

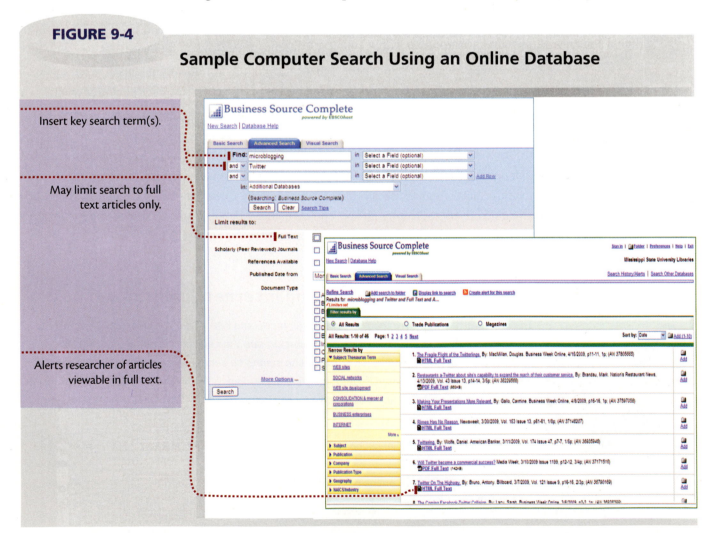

Insert key search term(s).

May limit search to full text articles only.

Alerts researcher of articles viewable in full text.

First, you can quickly evaluate the relevance of references by reading each article's title and abstract, if available, to determine appropriateness to your topic. Retrieved full-text articles can be read and analyzed for useful information, saved, and printed for later use. Be sure to record a full bibliographic citation for each reference you obtain to avoid the need to relocate the online source or revisit the library.

How does advice to become an expert before becoming an author apply to summarizing secondary research?

After you have located relevant sources, you can take notes using various methods. Because your aim is to *learn*, following technique for taking notes is effective: (1) read an article rapidly and put it aside, (2) list main and supporting points *from memory*, and (3) review the article to see whether all significant points have been included.

Rapid reading forces concentration, builds a strong understanding of the topic, and reveals relationships between ideas. Traditionally, researchers read the article and immediately wrote notes on cards. Currently, researchers typically prefer copying and pasting relevant information into a word processing file or highlighting important points on a photocopy or printout of the article; then from the selected passages, they compose notes at the keyboard.

When is an exact quote beneficial?

You can use two kinds of note-taking: direct quotation or paraphrase. The ***direct quotation method*** involves citing the exact words from a source. This method is useful when the exact words have specific impact or expert appeal. The ***paraphrase method*** involves summarizing information in your own words without changing the author's intended meaning. Put direct quotes in quotation marks, and indicate the page numbers, if available.

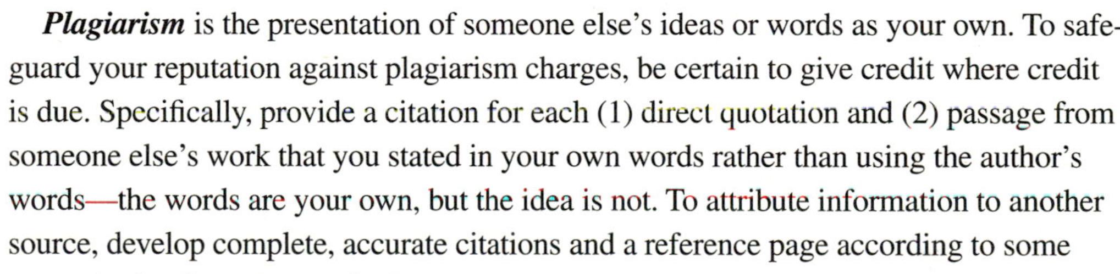

LEGAL AND ETHICAL CONSTRAINTS

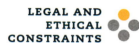

Plagiarism is the presentation of someone else's ideas or words as your own. To safeguard your reputation against plagiarism charges, be certain to give credit where credit is due. Specifically, provide a citation for each (1) direct quotation and (2) passage from someone else's work that you stated in your own words rather than using the author's words—the words are your own, but the idea is not. To attribute information to another source, develop complete, accurate citations and a reference page according to some recognized referencing method.

Plagiarism Charge Lands Coldplay in Hot Water. The British rock band Coldplay denied its song "Viva la Vida" had illegally copied portions of the song "If I Could Fly" by rock guitarist Joe Satriani. Satriani filed a copyright infringement lawsuit against Coldplay, who won the song-of-the-year Grammy Award for "Viva la Vida." When the suit was filed in 2009, Coldplay said the resemblance between the songs was "entirely coincidental" and that "Joe Satriani is a great musician." But in its legal filing, the band changed its tune, saying that "If I Could Fly" should not receive copyright protection because it "lacks originality."[9] Coldplay seemingly lost the case in the court of public opinion thanks to a video on YouTube. A clip titled "Did Coldplay Copy Joe Satriani?" was viewed more than 1.5 million times and answered its own question with a resounding "yes."[10]

© JEFFREY MAYER/WIREIMAGE/GETTY IMAGES

Your Turn 9-4
Assessment

Plagiarism deprives the true author of deserved recognition. It also represents an unearned boost to the plagiarizer's reputation achieved through false claims of authorship. Some individuals caught plagiarizing in academic or journalistic contexts claim they plagiarized unintentionally, by failing to include quotations or give the appropriate citation. The development of the Internet, where articles appear as electronic text, has made plagiarism more common due to the ease of copying and pasting the work of others and claiming it as one's own. How much do you know about plagiarism?

TAKE ACTION:

- Take the plagiarism quiz developed by the Pennsylvania State University's Teaching and Learning with Technology Center at www.dsa.csupomona.edu/judicialaffairs/plagquiz.asp, or go to your companion website at www.cengage.com/bcomm/lehman for updated links. You will receive instant feedback related to the accuracy of your answers.
- Print out a copy of the quiz and mark the correct answers for further discussion with your classmates or your instructor. Email your instructor with your results.

Collecting Data Through Surveys

The method of distribution and the makeup of the questionnaire are critical factors in successful survey research.

Selecting a Data Collection Method

Why might email polling lead to biased response data?

Selecting an appropriate data collection method is crucial to effective research. Researchers must consider various factors when selecting an appropriate method for collecting data, as illustrated in Figure 9-5. The Your Turn Electronic Cafe on p. 325 leads students to this content on the web.

Developing an Effective Survey Instrument

No matter which survey technique or combination of techniques is used, the way in which the survey instrument is designed and written has much to do with the validity and reliability of results, response rate, and quality of information received.

The construction of the survey instrument—usually a questionnaire or interview guide—is critical to obtaining reliable and valid data. Before developing items for a questionnaire or opinion survey, a researcher should visualize the ways responses will be compiled and included in a final report. Here are some suggestions for developing an effective questionnaire:

- **Provide brief, easy-to-follow directions.** Explain the purpose of the study in a cover message or in a brief statement at the top of the questionnaire so that the respondents understand your intent. While a screening question may be needed to determine whether the respondent is qualified to answer a set of questions, minimize confusing "skip-and-jump" instructions such as the following:

FIGURE 9-5

Selecting an Appropriate Data Collection Method

Method	Advantages	Limitations
Mailed surveys 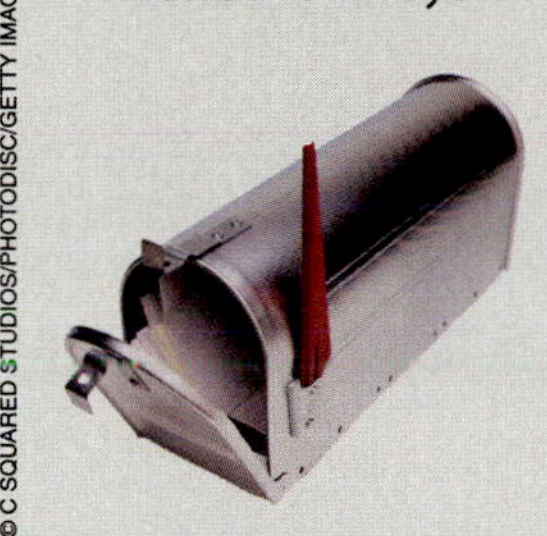 © C SQUARED STUDIOS/PHOTODISC/GETTY IMAGES	• Are relatively inexpensive to administer • Can reach a wide number of people who complete the survey at their convenience • Allow anonymity, which may produce more honest responses • Remove difference-in-status barriers	• Can be expensive if follow-up mailings are required • Yield a low response rate • Are not useful for obtaining detailed information
Telephone surveys  © RYAN MCVAY/PHOTODISC/GETTY IMAGES	• Provide inexpensive and rapid data collection • Allow personal contact between interviewer and respondent for clarification or follow-up questions	• Must be relatively short to minimize perceived intrusion and to increase typical small return rate • May exclude respondents with unlisted numbers and those without telephones
Personal interviews  © DUNCAN SMITH/PHOTODISC/GETTY IMAGES	• Are useful to obtain in-depth answers and explore sensitive topics • Allow personal contact between interviewer and respondent for clarification and follow-up questions	• Are time consuming and resource intensive • Require proper interviewer • Vary in value, depending on quality and consistency of interviewer
Email polling 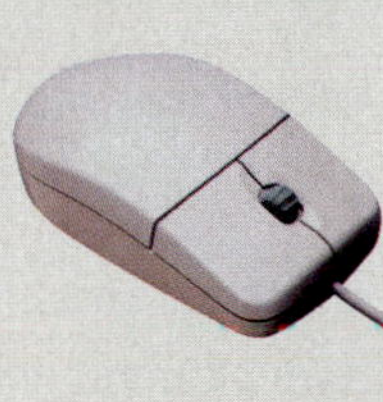 © SIEDE PREIS/PHOTODISC/GETTY IMAGES	• Is inexpensive • Provides for easy response • Yields quick results that can be updated electronically as responses are received	• Is limited to respondents with computer access

Ineffective Example 

If you answered Yes to item 4, skip directly to item 7; if you answered No, explain your reason in items 5 and 6.

Consider using electronic survey systems that advance respondents to the next question based on answers to screening questions.

- **Arrange the items in a logical sequence.** If possible, the sequence should proceed from easy to difficult items; simple, nonthreatening items involve respondents and encourage them to finish. You might group related items such as demographic data or those that use the same response options (multiple choice, rating scales, open-ended questions).

- **Create an appealing, easy-to-comprehend design.** Use typefaces, bold, underline, and italics to emphasize important ideas. Use text boxes and graphic lines to partition text so that the reader can identify and move through sections quickly.

- **Use short items that ask for a single answer to one idea.** Include only the questions needed to meet the objectives of your study, since long questionnaire length affects the return rate negatively.

- **Design questions that are easy to answer and to tabulate.** Participants may not take the time to answer numerous open-ended questions that require essay-style answers. When open-ended questions are included, provide enough space for respondents to answer adequately.

- **Strive to write clear questions that all respondents will interpret in the same way.** Avoid words with imprecise meanings (e.g., several, usually) and specialized terms and difficult words that respondents might not understand. Use accurate translations for each concept presented if other cultures are involved. Provide examples for items that might be difficult to understand.

- **Ask for factual information whenever possible.** Opinions may be needed in certain studies, but opinions may change daily. As a general rule, the smaller the sample, the less reliable are any conclusions based on opinions.

- **Ask for information that can be recalled readily.** Asking for "old" information may not result in sound data.

- **Provide all possible answer choices on multiple-choice items.** Add an "undecided" or "other" category so that respondents are not forced to choose a nonapplicable response.

- **Decide on an optimal number of choices to place on a ranking scale.** Ranking scales, also called Likert scales, allow participants to indicate their opinion on a numbered continuum. When deciding the numbers to place on the scale, consider the tendency of some groups to choose the noncommittal midpoint in a scale with an odd number of response choices (for instance, choosing 3 on a scale from 1 to 5).

- **Avoid questions that may be threatening or awkward to the respondent.** For sensitive issues, such as age and income, allow respondents to select among ranges if possible. Ensure that ranges do not overlap, and provide for all possible selections.

- **Consider the advisability of prompting a forced answer.** A forced answer question can be used to determine which single factor is most critical to a respondent, as shown in the following examples:

Of all the problems listed, which is the *single* most critical problem for you personally?

Should city taxes be levied to fund a city recreational complex?

☐ Yes ☐ No

When using forced choice items, avoid "leading questions" that cause people to answer in a way that is not their true opinion or situation. The following item is an example of such a question:

Ineffective Example

Have you stopped humiliating employees who question your management decisions?

☐ Yes ☐ No

- **Include a postage-paid envelope with a mailed questionnaire.** A higher response rate results when this courtesy is provided. Include your return information at the bottom of the questionnaire in the event the envelope is misplaced.

Various types of items can be used in questionnaire design, depending on your purpose and the characteristics of your participants. Figure 9-6 illustrates the principles of effective questionnaire design.

How does a pilot test help to validate a research instrument?

A final step in questionnaire design is to test the instrument by asking others to complete and/or critique the questionnaire. For surveys of major importance, researchers typically conduct a ***pilot test***, administering the questionnaire to a small group of the population involved. This process allows them to correct problems in clarity and design, and typically leads to better response and quality of answers. A pilot study may uncover factors affecting your results, which you can address in the final research design and before conducting the actual survey.

Researchers must select from among the several formats available the one best suited to the situation. Criteria for selecting one alternative over the others might include the following: Which format leaves the least chance for misinterpretation? Which format provides information in the way it can best be used? Can it be tabulated easily? Can it be cross-referenced to other items in the survey instrument?

FIGURE 9-6

Example of an Effective Questionnaire

Uses variety of items to elicit different types of responses.

Uses clear, concise language to minimize confusion.

Provides clear instructions for answering each item.

Provides additional lines to allow for individual opinions.

Provides even number of rating choices to eliminate "fence" responses.

Asks for easily recalled information.

Provides nonoverlapping categories of response and open-ended final category.

Format Pointers

- Provides adequate space for answering open-ended item.
- Keeps length as short as possible while meeting survey objectives.
- Includes instructions for submitting completed questionnaire.

1. Rank the following job factors in order of their importance to you. Add other factors important to you in the space provided.

	1	2	3	4	5	6	7
a. Wages	○	○	○	○	○	○	○
b. Health and retirement benefits	○	○	○	○	○	○	○
c. Job security	○	○	○	○	○	○	○
d. Ability to maintain balance between work and family life	○	○	○	○	○	○	○
e. Creativity and challenge of work assignment	○	○	○	○	○	○	○
f. Perceived prestige of work	○	○	○	○	○	○	○
g. ______	○	○	○	○	○	○	○
h. ______	○	○	○	○	○	○	○

2. Which of the following is the single job satisfaction factor that you feel needs more attention in our company? (Please select only one).

- ○ Wages
- ○ Health and retirement benefits
- ○ Job security
- ○ Ability to maintain balance between work and family life
- ○ Creativity and challenge of work assignment
- ○ Perceived prestige of work
- ○ Other (specify) ______

3. How would you rate your overall job satisfaction?

Very unsatisfied	Somewhat dissatisfied	Neutral	Somewhat satisfied		Very satisfied
1	2	3	4	5	6
○	○	○	○	○	○

4. How would you rate your overall job satisfaction 12 months ago?

Very unsatisfied	Somewhat dissatisfied	Neutral	Somewhat satisfied		Very satisfied
1	2	3	4	5	6
○	○	○	○	○	○

5. Indicate your age group.

- ○ 20–29
- ○ 30–39
- ○ 40–49
- ○ 50–59
- ○ 60–69
- ○ 70 years and over

6. Indicate your time with the company.

- ○ Less than one year
- ○ 1–3 years
- ○ 4–6 years
- ○ 7–10 years
- ○ Over 10 years

7. What could the company do to enhance your satisfaction as a company employee?

______

Thanks for your participation. Click to submit your questionnaire.

Submit

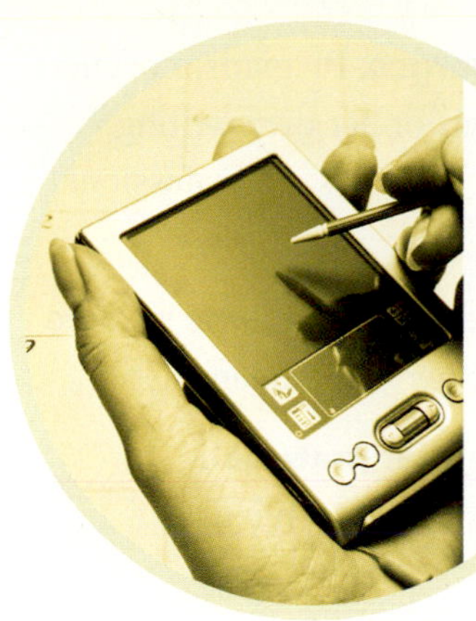

Your Turn 9-5
Career Portfolio

When you are involved in your career activities, you'll likely find yourself needing occasionally to solicit input from your clients or customers. A survey or poll will allow you to learn about overall opinions that will help you make appropriate decisions for improving your product or service.

TAKE ACTION:

Design a questionnaire appropriate for surveying your future clients/customers on a service-related issue. Limit your document to one page, include appropriate instructions and background information, and format for easy completion and tabulation. Your instructor may direct you to develop your questionnaire for online distribution.

Avoiding Data Gathering Errors

If acceptable data gathering techniques have been used, data will measure what they are intended to measure (have validity) and will measure it accurately (have reliability). Some common errors at the data gathering stage seriously hamper later interpretation:

LEGAL AND ETHICAL CONSTRAINTS

- Using samples that are too small
- Using samples that are not representative
- Using poorly constructed data gathering instruments
- Using information from biased sources
- Failing to gather enough information to cover all important aspects of a problem
- Gathering too much information (and then attempting to use all of it even though some may be irrelevant)

Hopefully, a carefully designed research process will yield useful data for analysis.

Sources of Information

A crucial part of ethical honest research writing is documenting or referencing sources fairly and accurately. Although time consuming and tedious, careful attention to documentation marks you as a respected, highly professional researcher.

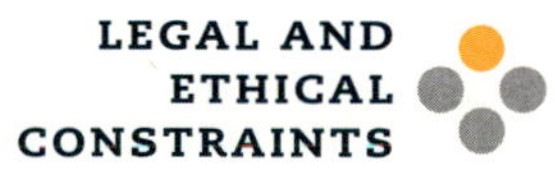

An important first step is to pledge that you will not, for any reason, present someone else's ideas as your own. Then, develop a systematic checklist for avoiding plagiarism. Carelessly forgetting to enclose someone else's words within quotation marks or failing to paraphrase another's words can cause others to question your ethical conduct. When you feel that the tedious work required to document sources fairly and accurately is not worth the time invested, remind yourself of the following reasons for documentation:

What are the legal and ethical consequences of failing to document sources for quoted and paraphrased material?

- **Citations give credit where it is due—to the one who created the material.** People who document demonstrate high standards of ethical conduct and responsibility in scholarship. Those exhibiting this professional behavior will gain the well-deserved trust and respect of peers and superiors.

- **Documentation protects writers against plagiarism charges.** Plagiarism occurs when someone steals material from another and claims it as his or her own writing. Besides embarrassment, the plagiarist may be assessed fines, penalties, or professional sanctions.
- **Documentation supports your statements.** If recognized authorities have said the same thing, your work takes on credibility; you put yourself in good company.
- **Documentation can aid future researchers pursuing similar material.** Documentation must be complete and accurate so that the researcher can locate the source.

Many style guides are available to advise writers how to organize, document, and produce reports and manuscripts. Figure 9-3 includes two of the most popular authoritative style manuals. The *Publication Manual of the American Psychological Association* has become the most-used guide in the social and "soft" sciences and in many scholarly journals. The *MLA Handbook for Writers of Research Papers* is another authoritative source used in the humanities. Style guides and format requirements are discussed further in Appendix B.

Citations and references that follow a specific style guide are easily created using word processing software; the documentation is automatically updated each time the report is revised. While technology simplifies this tedious process, you will likely need to edit automatically generated citations/references so that your style manual is followed accurately.

Follow these general suggestions for preparing accurate documentation:

- **Decide which authoritative reference manual to follow for preparing in-text parenthetical citations or footnotes (endnotes) and the bibliography (references).** Some companies and most journals require writers to prepare reports or manuscripts following a particular reference manual. Once you are certain you have selected the appropriate style manual, follow it precisely as you prepare the documentation and produce the report.
- **Be consistent.** If you are carefully following a format, you shouldn't have a problem with consistency. For example, one style manual may require an author's initials in place of first name in a bibliography; another manual requires the full name. The placement of commas and periods and other information varies among reference manuals. Consult the manual, apply the rules methodically, and proofread carefully to ensure accuracy and consistency. If you cannot locate a format for an unusual source in the reference manual you are using, use other entries as a guide for presenting information consistently.
- **Follow the rule that it is better to include more than enough than too little.** When you are in doubt about whether certain information is necessary, include it.

Citations

Two major types of citations are used to document a report: source notes and explanatory notes. Depending on the authoritative style manual used, these notes may be positioned in parentheses within the report, at the bottom of the page, or at the end of the report.

- **Source notes** acknowledge the contributions of others. These citations might refer readers to sources of quotations, paraphrased portions of someone else's words or ideas, and quantitative data used in the report. Source notes must include complete and accurate information so that the reader can locate the original source if desired.
- **Explanatory notes** are used for several purposes: (1) to comment on a source or to provide information that does not fit easily in the text, (2) to support a statistical table, or (3) to refer the reader to another section of the report. The following sample footnote describes the mathematics involved in preparing a table:

  *The weighted opinion was derived by assigning responses from high to low as 5, 4, 3, 2, 1; totaling all respondents; and dividing by the number of respondents.

In this case, the asterisk (*) was used rather than a number to identify the explanatory footnote both in the text and in the citation. This method is often used when only one or two footnotes are included in the report. If two footnotes appear on the same page, two asterisks (**) or numbers or letters are used to distinguish the second from the first. An explanatory note that supports a graphic or a source note that provides the reference from which data were taken appears immediately below the graphic.

Referencing Methods

Why do numerous referencing methods exist?

Various reference methods are available for the format and content of source notes: in-text parenthetical citations, footnotes, and endnotes. Note the major differences among the methods in the following discussion.

- **In-text parenthetical citations.** The *APA Publication Manual, MLA Handbook,* and some other documentation references eliminate the need for separate footnotes or endnotes. Instead, an in-text citation, which contains abbreviated information within parentheses, directs the reader to a list of sources at the end of a report. The list of sources at the end contains all publication information on every source cited. This list is arranged alphabetically by the author's last name or, if no author is provided, by the first word of the article title.

The in-text citations contain minimal information needed to locate the source in the complete list. In-text citations prepared using APA include the author's last name and the date of publication; the page number is included if referencing a direct quotation. An MLA citation includes the author's last name and the page number but not the date of publication.

- **Footnote citation method.** Placing citations at the bottom of the page on which they are cited is the footnote citation. The reader can conveniently refer to the source if the documentation is positioned at the bottom of the page. Alternatively, a list of footnotes can be collected at the end of the document in the order they appeared in an *endnotes page*. Footnotes and endnotes are not used in APA and MLA referencing, as these styles permit the use of in-text citations only.
- **References (or Works Cited).** This document is an alphabetized list of the sources used in preparing a report. Each entry contains publication information necessary for locating the source. In addition, the bibliographic entries give

SHOWCASE PART 2

© FABRICE COFFRINI/AFP/GETTY IMAGES

SPOTLIGHT COMMUNICATOR: DANIEL VASELLA, CEO, NOVARTIS

Thorough Research Results in Effective Decisions

According to consultant Ram Charan, Novartis CEO Daniel Vasella "is able to anticipate and visualize radical change much the same way Steve Jobs did at Apple, Andy Grove did at Intel, and Sam Walton did at Walmart."[11] Described as confident, direct, and searingly honest, Vasella is also obviously passionate about the pharmaceutical business. When asked about his success in business forecasting, he speaks of the various ways he accesses information, including the Internet and competitors' blogs: "One has to be careful when reading such 'information,' but one always learns something from it, even if it is only the political agenda of certain activists." Refer to your companion website at www.cengage.com/bcomm/lehman for information on Daniel Vasella's ideas on R&D.

www.novartis.com

SEE SHOWCASE PART 3, ON PAGE 341
TO LEARN ABOUT NOVARTIS' PROMISING DRUG DEVELOPMENT PROJECTS.

evidence of the nature of sources the author consulted. *Bibliography* (literally "description of books") is sometimes used to refer to this list. A researcher often uses sources that provide information but do not result in citations. To acknowledge that you may have consulted these works and to provide the reader with a comprehensive reading list, you might include them in the list of sources. The APA and MLA styles use different terms to distinguish between these types of lists. See Appendix B for additional information on preparing references.

Arriving at an Answer

Even the most intelligent person cannot be expected to draw sound conclusions from faulty information. Sound conclusions can be drawn only when information has been properly organized, collected, and interpreted.

Analyzing the Data

Follow a step-by-step approach to the solution of your research problem. Plan your study and follow the plan. Question every step for its contribution to the objective, and keep a record of actions. In a formal research study, the researcher is expected to make a complete report. Another qualified person should be able to make the same study, use the same steps, and arrive at the same conclusion.

Suppose you have conducted a survey and collected several hundred replies to a 20- or 30-item questionnaire in addition to many notes from printed and electronic sources. What do you do next? Notes must be carefully considered for relevance and organized for relationships among ideas. Appropriate statistical analysis must be applied to interpret survey results. ***Tabulation*** techniques should be used to reduce quantitative data such as numerous answers to questionnaire items. For instance, you may want to tabulate the number of males and females participating in the study, along with the appropriate percentages for each gender.

For many kinds of studies, ***measures of central tendency*** may help in describing distributions of quantitative data. The ***range*** assists the researcher in understanding the distribution of the scores. The ***mean***, ***median***, and ***mode*** are descriptions of the average value of the distribution. For information about how to compute the measure of central tendency, visit your companion website at www.cengage.com/bcomm/lehman.

What other statistical techniques are you aware of that could be useful in data analysis? Explain.

Other statistical techniques may be used. For example, ***correlation analysis*** might be used to determine whether a relationship existed between how respondents answered one item and how they answered another. Were males, for example, more likely to have chosen a certain answer to another item on the survey than were females?

The report process is one of reducing the information collected to a size that can be handled conveniently in a written message, as shown in Figure 9-7. Visualize the report process as taking place in a huge funnel. At the top of the funnel, pour in all the original information. Then, through a process of compression within the funnel, take these steps:

1. Evaluate the information for its usefulness.
2. Reduce the useful information through organization of notes and data analysis.
3. Combine like information into understandable form through the use of tables, charts, graphs, and summaries. (See Chapter 10.)
4. Report in written form the information that remains. (See Chapter 11.)

Interpreting the Data

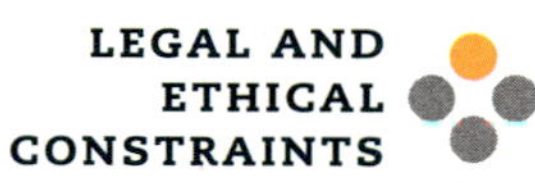

Your ethical principles affect the validity of your interpretations. Through all steps in the research process, you must attempt to maintain the integrity of the research. Strive to remain objective, design and conduct an unbiased study, and resist any pressure to slant research to support a particular viewpoint (e.g., ignoring, altering, or falsifying data). Some common errors that seriously hinder the interpretation of data include the following:

- **Trying, consciously or unconsciously, to make results conform to a prediction or desire.** Seeing predictions come true may be pleasing, but objectivity is much more important. Facts should determine conclusions.
- **Hoping for spectacular results.** An attempt to astonish supervisors by preparing a report with revolutionary conclusions can have a negative effect on accuracy.
- **Attempting to compare when commonality is absent.** Results obtained from one study may not always apply to other situations. Similarly, research with a certain population may not be consistent when the same research is conducted with another population.

FIGURE 9-7

The Report Process

RESEARCH

Primary
- Surveys
- Observations
- Experiments

© iStockphoto.com/ Edyta Pawlowska

Secondary
- Review of printed and online sources
- Company records

© iStockphoto.com/ Soren Pilman

CONDENSATION

Compiling using notes, cards or inputting into a computer
- Direct quotations
- Paraphrased citations

© iStockphoto.com/ DNY59

COMBINATION
- Charts
- Tables
- Graphs
- Summaries

© iStockphoto.com/ Paweł Tałajkowski

ASSIMILATION

Analysis
- Findings
- Conclusions
- Recommendations

© iStockphoto.com/ Alexandra Draghici

WRITING
- Finished report

© iStockphoto.com/ Jan Tyler

The men's basketball team has won a conference playoff every year since you began college. Is this record likely an example of correlation or causation?

- **Assuming a cause–effect relationship when one does not exist.** A company president may have been in office one year, and sales may have doubled. However, sales might have doubled in spite of the president rather than because of the president.

- **Failing to consider important factors.** For example, learning that McDonald's was considering closing its restaurants in Kassel, Germany, a manager of an industrial supply company recommended that his firm reconsider its plans to expand its operation into Germany. The manager failed to recognize that the adverse impact of a new tax on disposable containers, not an unfavorable German economy or government, was the reason McDonald's was considering closing its restaurants.[12] Other diversity issues that affect research are explored in the accompanying Strategic Forces feature, "International Marketing Research" on page 340.

© AP IMAGES/RENE MACURA

- **Basing a conclusion on lack of evidence.** "We have had no complaints about our present policy" does not mean that the policy is appropriate. Conversely, lack of evidence that a proposed project will succeed does not necessarily mean that it will fail.

Do you agree with the statement that statistics can be used to prove just about anything? Why?

- **Assuming constancy of human behavior.** A survey indicating 60 percent of the public favors one political party over the other in March does not mean the same will be true in November. Because some people paid their bills late last year does not mean a company should refuse to sell to them next year since reasons for slow payment may have been eliminated.

If you avoid common data collection errors, you are more likely to collect valid and reliable data and reach sound conclusions. However, if you interpret valid and reliable data incorrectly, your conclusions will still *not* be sound. Keep in mind the differences in meaning of some common research terms as you analyze your material and attempt to seek meaning from it.

- **Finding:** A specific, measurable fact from a research study
- **Conclusion:** Summation of major facts and evidence derived from findings
- **Recommendation:** A suggested action based on your research

Consider the following examples of conclusions and recommendations generated by analyzing research findings:

Example 1	*Example 2*
Finding: Nearly 75 percent of responding recruiters indicated they were more likely to hire a candidate who was involved in extracurricular activities.	**Finding:** Only 16 percent of the consumers interviewed knew that Hanson's Toy Company sells educational computer software.
Conclusion: Active involvement in extracurricular activities is an important job-selection criterion.	**Conclusion:** Few consumers are knowledgeable of our line of educational software.
Recommendation: Students should be involved in several extracurricular activities prior to seeking a job.	**Recommendation:** An advertising campaign focusing on educational software should be launched.

Visit your companion website at www.cengage.com/bcomm/lehman for additional information about interpreting data and arriving at conclusions and recommendations.

STRATEGIC FORCES

International Marketing Research

Cautious interpretation should be given to the results of research conducted within particular cultural settings as to their appropriateness for other groups. For instance, concluding that a certain product would sell well in Canada or Mexico because it sold well in the United States is risky.

Disney executives presumed company policies successful in the United States would be equally as successful at their French theme park, EuroDisney. This *faulty logic* caused immediate problems. Employees resisted Disney's disregard for national customs—the unpopular dress code prohibiting facial hair and limiting makeup and jewelry. Visitors to the park were also unhappy with the no-alcohol-in-the-park policy, as the French generally include wine with most meals.[13]

Coldwater Creek, a U.S. firm that began selling in Japan, found through research that Japanese favor clothing in brighter colors than the dark palette popular in the United States. They also found it necessary to add petite sizes to Japanese catalogs. When Gerber first started selling baby food in Africa, they used the same packaging as here in the USA— with the cute baby on the label. The company soon learned an important reason for sagging sales in Africa; since most people on the continent can't read, advertisers typically put pictures on the label of what is inside.[14] Hence the first rule of international marketing: Never assume what works in one country will work in another.

While information about related populations may serve as a basis for study, effort should be made to conduct research within the particular group that will be affected by the business decision. A good source for secondary research on international markets is the Columbus, Ohio–based Trade Point, USA, a non-for-profit online and print information service that was established in cooperation with the United Nations (http://tpusa.com).

© AP IMAGES/STEVEN SENNE

Secondhand information, however, can take you only so far. In many cases, a more desirable approach is to visit the target country yourself or hire an outside firm with solid experience in the particular culture to complete grassroots primary research in the country. Some products will be unsuitable or unattractive to certain nations of people because of differences in culture, lifestyle, or preferences.

Experts recommend thorough country-by-country testing before a product launch to help identify problems inherent in cross-cultural marketing. Testing provides insights into potential market sizes and responses and uncovers the extent to which language and consumer preference will be problematic. While such market research is expensive, it is justified when considering the essential information that results.[15]

Application

Conduct an online search to discover an example of a company whose product(s) experienced a negative reception in another country's consumer market. Be prepared to discuss the following questions in a class discussion:

(1) What issues were involved in the poor sales performance?

(2) How could the problem have been avoided?

Novartis Researches Ways to Cure and Treat Dreaded Diseases

Multiple sclerosis, kidney cancer, and lymphoma . . . threatening diseases that Novartis offers promise in curing and treating. With 93 drug candidates in the R&D pipeline, and with a record 80 percent of tested drugs advancing to late stage development, other drug miracles may be just around the corner. Drugs to treat high blood pressure, attention deficit disorder, and muscle pain are also the result of Novartis research efforts.

www.novartis.com

© SEBASTIEN BOZON/AFP/GETTY IMAGES

Activities

- Visit the R&D link on the Novartis website at www.novartis.com to learn more about the company's promising drug development projects.
- Locate the following article that discusses various medical conditions that Novartis offers promise in curing, treating, or alleviating symptoms.

  Capell, K. (2009, June 22). Novartis: Radically remaking its drug business. *BusinessWeek*, 30–35. Available from Business Source Complete database.

  Write a short report that summarizes the contribution of Novartis to the alleviation of human suffering.
- Following directions from your instructor, post an online comment that reflects your opinions of consumer drug pricing.

Summary

1. Identify the characteristics of a report and the various classifications of business reports.

The basis of a report is a problem that must be solved through data collection and analysis. Reports are usually requested by a higher authority, are logically organized and highly objective, and are prepared for a limited audience. Reports can be classified as formal/informal, short/long, informational/analytical, vertical/lateral, internal/external, or a proposal.

2. Apply steps in the problem-solving process and methods for solving a problem.

The four steps in the problem-solving process must be followed to arrive at a sound conclusion: (a) Recognize and define the problem; (b) select an appropriate secondary and/or primary method for solving the problem; (c) collect and organize data, using appropriate methods; and (d) interpret the data to arrive at an answer. Research methods in report preparation involve locating information from appropriate secondary sources to identify research that has already been done on the topic and then collecting primary data needed to solve the problem. Primary data collection may include observation, experimental, or survey research processes.

3. Use appropriate printed, electronic, and primary sources of information.

Location of secondary sources of information involves appropriate use of printed indexes and application of electronic search techniques that can lead the researcher to books, periodicals, and other documents needed for topic exploration. Methods for collecting survey data include mailed questionnaires, email polling, telephone surveys, personal interviews, and participant observation. Collecting data through a survey involves selecting a sample that is representative of the entire population. Effective survey design and un-biased data collection are essential to assuring the validity and reliability of the data reported.

4. Demonstrate appropriate methods of collecting, organizing, and referencing information.

Information from published sources should be carefully read and interpreted. To avoid plagiarism, both direct quotes and paraphrases must be referenced using an acceptable method. Surveys are a common method for collecting data. Instruments should be carefully designed to solicit needed information, avoid ambiguity and confusion, and reflect accurate information. The researcher must work to avoid various data gathering pitfalls including using small or unrepresentative samples, using biased sources or irrelevant information, and excluding relevant information.

5. Explain techniques for the logical analysis and interpretation of data.

Arriving at an answer in the research process involves proper analysis using appropriate statistical techniques. To maintain the integrity of the research, the interpretation of data should be objective and unbiased. Carefully presented findings give way to sound conclusions that lead to logical recommendations.

Chapter Review

1. A bank's internal auditing division performs semiannual audits of each branch. The audit reports are sent to the bank's chief executive officer and chief financial officer and to the manager of the audited branch. The purpose of the audits is to determine whether policies and practices are followed properly. Into what report classifications might the audit report fall? Explain. (Obj. 1)
2. How might a null hypothesis be stated for a research study attempting to determine whether television or magazine advertising has greater influence on athletic shoe sales? (Obj. 2)
3. How are observational and experimental research different? (Obj. 3)
4. What techniques can help make the Internet search process more efficient? (Obj. 4)
5. Distinguish between reliability and validity. How are both important to quality research? (Obj. 3)
6. What purpose do quotes and paraphrases serve in the findings of a report? (Obj. 4)
7. Why should a research study document information taken from other sources? (Obj. 4)
8. What questions might you ask of someone who wants assistance in planning a questionnaire survey to determine automobile owner satisfaction with certain after-the-sale services provided by dealers? (Obj. 4)
9. Gathering so much information that the researcher is "snowed under" by the amount is often a barrier to good reporting. How might researchers protect themselves against this possibility? (Obj. 5)
10. How does the assumption that human beings behave in consistent ways over time present a danger in data interpretation? (Obj. 5)

Digging Deeper

1. How has the process of research changed in recent years? How have the changes been both beneficial and detrimental?
2. What communication skills should an effective researcher possess?

Assessment

To check your understanding of the chapter, take the available online quizzes as directed by your instructor.

Check Your Communication
Report Process and Research Methods

PROBLEM FORMATION

- ☐ Decide what type of report is required.
- ☐ Formulate the problem statement.
- ☐ Determine boundaries for the research.
- ☐ Define specialized terms used in the report.

RESEARCH METHODOLOGY

- ☐ Select appropriate methods of solution, including relevant secondary and primary resources.
- ☐ Gather appropriate published and electronic sources.
- ☐ Plan appropriate primary research, using observational, experimental, or normative techniques.

DATA COLLECTION AND ORGANIZATION

- ☐ Document all quoted and paraphrased information using appropriate referencing method.
- ☐ Develop effective data collection instruments; pilot test and refine prior to conducting research.
- ☐ Avoid data collection errors that can minimize your research effort.

DATA INTERPRETATION

- ☐ Analyze data accurately and ethically.
- ☐ Interpret data to reach logical conclusions.
- ☐ Make recommendations that are well supported by the data presented.
- ☐ Avoid overgeneralizing results of research conducted in one setting to another group or setting.

Activities

1. Classifying Business Reports (Obj. 1)

Working in small groups, classify each of the following reports in one or more of the ways described in this chapter.

a. Your company's two-year study of traditional classroom training versus distance-learning instruction is to be written for publication in an industrial training journal.

b. You have surveyed company personnel on their perceptions of the need for a company-sponsored wellness program. You are preparing a report for the president that conveys the results.

c. You have completed your department's weekly time sheets to send to payroll.

d. As department head, you have sent a report to the vice president for finance requesting additional funding for equipment acquisition.

e. You have prepared an article on strategies for enhancing customer satisfaction for publication in your online employee newsletter.

f. As director of end-user computing, you have prepared a report for circulation to all departments. The report summarizes technology and human relations training offerings available through your department.

2. Writing a Hypothesis (Obj. 2)

Write a positive hypothesis and then restate it as a null hypothesis for each of the following research topics. Hypotheses for topic (a) are given as an example.

a. A study to determine functional business areas from which chief executive officers advanced in their organizations. Functional areas include legal, accounting, marketing, etc.
Positive Hypothesis: Chief executives advanced primarily through the legal background area.
Null Hypothesis: No relationship exists between chief executives' advancement and their functional field backgrounds.

b. A study to determine whether listening to music using mp3 player ear buds contributes to hearing loss.

c. A study to determine whether a person's career success is related to mentoring experiences.

d. A study to determine the relationship between college students' gender and their final grades in the business communication course.

3. Limiting the Scope of the Problem (Obj. 2)

What factors might limit or influence your findings in any of the studies in Activity 2? Could you apply the findings of the Activity 2 studies to a broader population than those included in the studies? Why or why not?

4. Selecting a Research Method (Obj. 3)

What research methods would you use for each of the research problems identified in Activity 2?

5. Outlining a Search Strategy (Obj. 3)

Outline a secondary search strategy for one of the topics in Activity 2. What printed indexes would you use? What electronic search techniques would you use?

6. Using Sampling Techniques (Obj. 4)

You are to conduct a survey of residents' attitudes toward recycling in a town of 35,000 people. Describe how you might construct a sampling procedure to avoid having to survey the entire population.

7. **Collecting and Documenting Secondary Data** (Obj. 4)

Select one of the research problems in Activity 2. Locate four related articles using both printed and electronic sources. As directed by your instructor, prepare a Reference page using APA style or another style specified by your instructor. (See Appendix B.)

8. **Developing Questionnaire Items** (Obj. 4)

In teams of three or four, develop a customer satisfaction questionnaire for a restaurant of your choice.

9. **Computing Measures of Central Tendency and Preparing a Table** (Obj. 4,)

Refer to your companion website at www.cengage.com/bcomm/lehman for information about measures of central tendency. The following figures represent the value of stock options in thousands of dollars issued to executive management of 25 local high-tech firms. Access a downloadable version of this activity at your companion website at www.cengage.com/bcomm/lehman.

a. Compute the range, mean, median, and mode of the following distribution.

50	91	164	217	425
60	130	170	260	596
65	139	170	283	600
70	143	170	350	650
78	159	204	390	690

b. Tally the scores in Part a in seven classes beginning with 0–99, 100–199, and so on to 700–799. When you have tallied the scores, compute the mean, median, and mode for each class.

c. Prepare a table for the data and indicate the appropriate percentages for each class. Write a sentence to introduce the table in a report.

Applications

READ | THINK | WRITE | SPEAK | COLLABORATE

1. **Identifying Challenges Posed by Human Subjects** (Obj. 3)

Using an online database, locate and read an article related to challenges associated with experimental research. What legal and ethical challenges do researchers face when conducting experimental research with human subjects? How can they be managed?

2. **Performing an Electronic Search** (Obj. 3)

Conduct an electronic search of a business research topic selected by you or assigned by your instructor. Topics might include challenge education, social networking, diversity training, electronic privacy, electronic meeting management, or translation software.

Required:

a. Research your topic, using two of the following search engines/databases and print out appropriate pages from the sites you identify.

Google (http://google.com)
Yahoo! (www.yahoo.com)
AltaVista (www.altavista.com)
Bing (http://bing.com)
Go.com (http://go.com)
Dogpile (www.dogpile.com)

b. Using your campus library database selection, select one or more online databases to research your topic. Refer to the list of available electronic databases in Figure 9-3.

c. Locate and bookmark one or more appropriate articles on your topic.

Send your instructor an email message explaining how you located the articles. How did the information you gathered using the search engine approach differ from the information gained from the database search? Attach a copy of one of the articles to your email message.

READ | THINK | WRITE | SPEAK | COLLABORATE

3. **Gathering Research Information** (Objs. 3, 4)

Visit your companion website at www. cengage.com/bcomm/lehman and read the enrichment content "Interpreting Research Data." To learn more about the research process and using various types of printed and electronic resources, complete the TILT tutorial at http://tilt.lib.utsystem.edu. Submit your scores for each module to your instructor according to the directions provided in TILT. Then develop a list of possible sources of information for a topic of your choice or one assigned by your instructor. For each item on your list, indicate the type of information that the source will likely yield (background facts, latest figures, theoretical base, expert opinions, etc.).

4. **Designing a Research Study** (Objs. 1–5)

Prepare a one-page description of your plan to solve the problem for each of the following research studies. Use the following headings for the problem assigned: (1) Statement of the Problem, (2) Research Method and Sources of Information,

(3) Nature of Data to Be Gathered and Analyzed, and (4) Hypothesis or Hypotheses to Be Proved or Disproved (if feasible). Access a downloadable version of this activity at your companion website at www.cengage.com/bcomm/lehman.

a. Investigate a problem occurring on your campus (elimination of common computer labs, declining enrollment in a selected major, increasing tuition, delayed financial aid payments, high cost of textbooks, or closed classes) or in a job or student organization position you hold.
b. Superior Foods, Inc., is considering adding organic versions of its frozen vegetables in an effort to establish itself as a leader in this fast growing market. To increase its available supply of organic produce, management recognizes the need to assist local growers in adopting organic farming methods. The first step in this process is to recruit experts in organic farming to design and implement a training program.
c. Rainbow Pool and Spas initiated a website to provide answers to frequently asked questions and product-update information. Customer response has been outstanding, freeing up the company's toll-free telephone lines for calls about more technical, nonrecurring problems—a primary goal of the service. As marketing manager, you are considering the possibility of starting a corporate blog and a microblogging site on Twitter to strengthen your relationship communication with customers.
d. As branch manager of a bank, you are faced with the task in a sagging economy of reassuring customers of the solvency of your institution. Your current strategies for casting a positive light on negative performance indicators don't seem to be effective.
e. For the first time, Greenwood Consulting Group held an all-company retreat that included customer service training, team-building sessions, and numerous social activities. Eight months following the conference, neither customer service nor employee morale seem to have had any noticeable improvement, and you must decide whether to schedule the retreat for the coming year.

READ | THINK | WRITE | SPEAK | COLLABORATE

5. Focus Groups Provide Research Findings (Objs. 1-5)

A **focus group** is a form of qualitative research in which a group of people are asked about their attitude toward a product, service, concept, advertisement, idea, or packaging. Questions are asked in an interactive group setting where participants are free to talk with other group members. For marketers, focus groups are an important tool for acquiring feedback regarding product development, such as product name, features, and packaging. Information from the focus group can provide invaluable information about the potential market acceptance of a product.

Required:

a. Select an existing product that could be improved or a product you can envision. Write five questions that could be asked of a focus group to elicit needed response for the product improvement or creation.
b. Ask for volunteers for the focus group, selecting participants who are knowledgeable about the type of focus product you have selected.
c. After conducting your focus group with the questions you developed, compile a report of your findings to submit to your instructor as directed.

READ | THINK | WRITE | SPEAK | COLLABORATE

6. Overcoming Problems in Data Collection and Interpretation (Objs. 4, 5)

Locate an article from a periodical that addresses a problem that has occurred for some organization when it failed to realize that research findings that were true for one country or culture were not accurate for another. Make a brief presentation to the class about your findings.

READ | THINK | WRITE | SPEAK | COLLABORATE

7. Developing a Survey Instrument (Obj. 4)

In teams of three, design a survey instrument for one of the research studies you analyzed in Application 4.

8. Enhancing Research with a Bookmark Manager (Obj. 4)

Social bookmarking sites, such as Delicious, Digg, and Flickr are gaining in popularity. Rather than saving on their computer the addresses of websites to revisit, social bookmarking allows users to store and efficiently share links to collections of web pages with friends and coworkers—without having to email or instant message everyone as new resources are located.

Required: In small groups, complete the following activities as directed by your instructor:

1. Learn more about the concept of social bookmarking by viewing the following video that illustrates the concept of social bookmarking using Delicious: www.commoncraft.com/bookmarking-plain-english.

2. Conduct an online search related to social bookmarking, beginning with the following article:

   Educause learning initiative. (2008, April). 7 things you should know about social bookmarking. Available from http://net.educause.edu/ir/library/pdf/ELI7036.pdf

   Write a brief written report providing information such as (a) explanation of the concept of social networking, (b) business significance and potential negative impacts, and (c) projections for future development of this technology. Be prepared to share your ideas with the class.

3. Register with a social bookmarking site such as Delicious (http://delicious.com) and create a collection of bookmarks on a topic of your choice or one assigned by your instructor (e.g., guidelines for business dress, job search advice) and share your collection with your team members. Prepare an attractive handout or web page posting that captures your collaborative efforts. Be prepared to share with the class.

CASES

COURTESY OF SURVEYMONKEY.COM

1. Survey Research Is Not Just Monkey Business

SurveyMonkey.com is an online survey tool that enables people of all experience levels to create their own surveys quickly and easily. Headquartered in Portland, Oregon, USA, and owned by Ryan Finley, SurveyMonkey.com is the leading survey tool on the Web, with over 80% of Fortune 100 companies currently using the service. Started in 1999, the site currently boasts over four million users a month. Every day, SurveyMonkey.com gives thousands of people the feedback they need to make more informed decisions.

SurveyMonkey.com members can create custom web surveys and view real-time statistical results of their posted surveys. A free trial membership allows members to send out limited surveys at no charge. For a subscription fee, members can send out unlimited surveys. Members select from a variety of question formats, templates, languages, and themes. After setting up the survey, members can also specify collection options for responses. A number of analysis options are also available, including filtering, real-time results, and browsing of individual responses. Users can download results, save results to PDF format, or share reports with other interested stakeholders.

Research about SurveyMonkey.com usage reveals that the top 250 site averages more than 5.2 million U.S. visitors each month. The demographics of usage, however, reveal a significant skew. The site attracts a more educated, fairly wealthy, slightly more female than male, older audience, with 85% of visitors being Caucasian.[16]

Applications: Complete one or more of the following activities as directed by your instructor.

1. Visit the Survey Monkey.com website at surveymonkey.com to learn more about the site's survey capabilities. Subscribe for a free trial membership.
2. Read the following article about the demographics of U.S. visitors to surveymonkey.com:

   SurveyMonkey.com (2009, March). *Quantcast*. Available at www.quantcast.com/surveymonkey.com
3. Read the following article on how to create effective online surveys:

   Ten tips for creating effective online surveys. (2009). *Cvent*. Available at www.cvent.com/resources/ten-tips.shtml
4. Using SurveyMonkey.com, design a survey to gather information on a topic specified by your instructor. Identify your target audience and send email invitations for participation in the SurveyMonkey.com survey you designed. Following participation, view your data analysis and report to the class on your findings.

© BBC LTD./COURTESY: EVERETT COLLECTION

2. Video Case: The Office: Researching Using Interviews: The Good, The Bad, The Ugly

In this clip, Gareth interviews Tim and Dawn to gain information about a risqué picture circulating around the office.

Complete the following activities as directed by your instructor after viewing the video:

1. What data collection method is Gareth using in his research? Is it effective in the given situation?
2. In Gareth's research process, what errors is he committing? How will they affect his research findings?
3. Design a research method for Gareth to use to discover the information he needs. Include in your plan the type of data gathering, appropriate survey instrument, and method for collecting the data.

3. Coping with Information Overload

The greatest challenge of our times is to reduce information, not to increase it. Until about 50 years ago, more information was always a good thing. Now we can't see our way through the "data smog." An ever-growing universe of information translates to masses of data through which people must search to find what is useful and meaningful to them. Consider the following statistics:

- Office workers average sending more than 160 messages and check their inboxes more than 50 times a day.[17]
- Managers report that email demands an average of two hours a day.
- A typical manager reads about a million words a week.
- Senior managers report spending an average of three-quarter hours per day accessing information on the Internet.[18]

While the original intent of advanced communication technologies was to make communication faster and more efficient, the result has been a communications gridlock and heightened stress for many workers. According to noted neurologist Barry Gordon, virtually everyone in today's environment suffers from some degree of information overload. He points out that people's memories do not work as well as needed because our brains were not built for the modern world. In the Stone Age there were no clocks, papers, or news flash as contrasted with everything individuals are expected to remember today.[19]

Some companies are going so far in battling information overload as hiring people whose job it is to filter and sort through the communications gridlock. These "information architects" are the translators and traffic controllers who help to bridge the communication gaps in the organization and deliver usable information in a concise way. The information architect reorganizes information for more effective communication, gives structure and order to pertinent information, and maps out the best way for the organization's people to access it.[20]

Whether for improved job performance, a better product, or increased productivity, more and more organizations are recognizing that good information means good business. And good information must somehow be made available in spite of increasing information overload.

Visit your companion website at www.cengage.com/bcomm/lehman to link to electronic resources related to this topic. As directed by your instructor, complete one or more of the following:

1. In teams, visit the listed sites and prepare a presentation on information overload (IO). The presentation should include the following elements: (1) seriousness of the problem, (2) suggestions for reducing IO in email usage, (3) suggestions for reducing IO in Internet usage, and (4) suggestions for reducing stress that results from IO.
2. "The information age has brought about a reduction in the quality of life." Choose to either support or defend the statement; write a one- to two-page paper that explains your position and gives supporting evidence and/or examples.
3. Select a personal example from your academic or work life in which you have experienced information overload. Prepare a written analysis that (1) describes the situation, (2) identifies the reasons for the IO that occurred, and (3) outlines strategies for reducing your IO.

Chapter 10
Managing Data and Using Graphics

"We never anticipated when we started this site we would have such a profound effect on popular culture . . ."
YouTube CEO, Chad Hurley

© RICHARD LEVINE/ALAMY

Objectives

When you have completed Chapter 10, you will be able to:

1. Communicate quantitative information effectively.
2. Apply principles of effectiveness and ethical responsibilities in the construction of graphic aids.
3. Select and design appropriate and meaningful graphics.
4. Integrate graphics within documents.

SHOWCASE PART 1  

YouTube at Center of Digital Media Revolution

A significant shift in digital media has occurred in just a few short years, and users are now in control of what they watch as well as when. YouTube allows videos to be uploaded and viewed by others on their TiVos, iPhones, PCs, or mobile devices. As it becomes increasingly easy to upload from phone, YouTube serves as a repository of every captured moment in a person's life. According to CEO Chad Hurley, "We never anticipated when we started this site we would have such a profound effect on popular culture . . . we're really just enabling so many more people to express their views, not only their talents, but to get a message out there."[1]

YouTube was founded in 2005 by Chad Hurley, Steve Chan, and Jwed Karim, all of whom had been employees of PayPal. Like many technology startups, YouTube began in a garage and with minimal funding. The company's tremendous growth in its first few months enabled it to attract significant investments and expand its staff. In late 2006, YouTube was sold to Google, though YouTube continues to operate independently.[2]

Currently, users upload more than 35,000 videos per day, with 100 million video clips viewed daily. The website averages nearly 20 million visitors per month, with an audience of 56 percent male and 44 percent female. While young people initially made up most of the audience, viewership is rather equitably distributed across the age brackets now.[3]

Copyright is one of the greatest challenges facing YouTube, with copyright holders notifying the company of unauthorized posted videos through the Digital Millennium Copyright Act notification process. "We comply with the DMCA and remove videos when we have knowledge that they are posted by users without permission of the copyright owners," says Hurley. YouTube policies prohibit inappropriate content, and users can flag content they feel is not acceptable. Accounts of repeat offenders are disabled. Agreements have been reached with NBC, Warner Music Group, and others to allow YouTube to host their videos while sharing a portion of the advertisement income.[4]

YouTube is not just for entertainment, however, as businesses are cashing in on its popularity as well. Videos promoting a product or service can be produced with very little cost and viewed by a wide audience. Organizations post short video segments of corporate addresses, product updates, and corporate officer profiles. Job applicants have discovered video résumés and have posted thousands of entries to YouTube. To date, few employers are looking to video résumés for potential employees, in part because of fears of discrimination claims resulting from the revealing of gender, race, and age. It's expected, however, that once the YouTube generation infiltrates the workplace, video résumés will be as popular as iPods.[5]

In much the same way that Yahoo! successfully exploits the capabilities and appeal of the Internet, you can use creative and engaging graphics to relate complex data and highlight important ideas in your business reports and presentations. Your success in these activities depends largely on how successful you are at organizing and interpreting your data and gaining and keeping audience interest.

www.youtube.com

SEE SHOWCASE, PART 2, ON PAGE 354, FOR SPOTLIGHT COMMUNICATOR CHAD HURLEY, CEO OF YOUTUBE.

Communicating Quantitative Information

Before you can interpret quantitative data, the elements must be classified, summarized, and condensed into a manageable size. This condensed information is meaningful and can be used to answer your research questions. For example, assume that you have been given 400 completed questionnaires from a study of employee needs for financial planning. This large accumulation of data is overwhelming until you tabulate the responses for each questionnaire item by manually inputting or compiling responses received through an online survey or optically scanning the responses into a computer. Then, you can apply appropriate statistical analysis techniques to the tabulated data.

The computer generates a report of the total responses for each possible answer to each item. For example, the tabulation of responses from each employee about his or her most important need in financial planning might appear like this:

Retirement Annuities	128
Traditional and Roth IRA	104
Mutual Funds	80
Internet Stock Trading	52
Effective Charitable Giving	36
	400

The breakdown reduces 400 responses to a manageable set of information. The tabulation shows only five items, each with a specific number of responses from the total of 400 questionnaires. Because people tend to make comparisons during analysis, the totals are helpful. People generally want to know proportions or ratios, and these are best presented as percentage parts of the total. Thus, the numbers converted to percentages are as follows:

Personal Development Need	*Number*	*Percentage*
Retirement Annuities	128	32
Traditional and Roth IRA	104	26
Mutual Funds	80	20
Internet Stock Trading	52	13
Effective Charitable Giving	36	9
	400	100

Now analyzing the data becomes relatively easy. Of the survey participants, 13 percent selected Internet stock trading, and only 9 percent selected effective charitable giving. Other observations, depending on how exactly you intend to interpret percentages, could be that a fifth of the employees selected mutual funds. Combining data in two categories allows you to summarize that slightly more than one half of the employees selected retirement annuities and individual retirement accounts.

What are the clearest terms for presenting your exam score of 112 points out of a possible 150?

When tabulating research results of people's opinions, likes, preferences, and other subjective items, rounding off statistics to fractions helps paint a clear picture for readers. In actuality, if the same group of people were asked this question again a day or two later, a few probably would have changed their minds. For example, an employee who had not indicated a desire for retirement planning may have learned of the benefits of a Roth IRA during a civic club meeting. The next day, the employee might indicate a desire for training in IRAs and retirement annuities.

Fractions, ratios, and percentages are examples of ***common language***. In effect, common language reduces difficult figures to the "common denominators" of language and ideas. Although "104 of 400 prefer traditional and Roth IRAs" is somewhat easy to understand, "26 percent prefer . . ." is even easier, and "approximately one out of four indicate a preference for traditional and Roth IRAs" is even more understandable.

Using common language, how would you describe to a computer novice the storage capacity of a USB flash drive and a DVD?

Common language also involves the use of indicators other than actual count or quantity. The Dow Jones Industrial Average provides a measure of stock market performance and is certainly easier to understand than the complete New York Stock Exchange figures. Similarly, oil is counted in barrels rather than in the quart or gallon sizes purchased by consumers. Because of inflation, dollars are not accurate items to use as comparisons from one year to another in certain areas; for example, automobile manufacturers use "automobile units" to represent production changes in the industry. The important thing for the report writer to remember is that reports are communication media, and everything possible should be done to make sure communication occurs.

© NYSE/HO/AP PHOTO

Your Turn 10-1
You're the Professional

Companies frequently poll their employees to involve them in the decision-making process. Your company has conducted a survey to determine if its 49 employees are interested in a participating in a mentoring program. The results are as follows:

If the company were to offer a mentoring program,

15 I would definitely be interested in participating

23 I might possibly be interested in participating

11 I would not be interested in participating

If I were to participate in a mentoring program, I would be interested in being

14 a mentor

15 a mentee

9 both a mentor and a mentee

11 N/A—I'm not interested in participating

TAKE ACTION:

Which of the following is the most effective statement concerning the results of the survey?

a. Most employees supported the idea of a mentoring program, and the majority of those were interested in being a mentee.

b. *Strong support was expressed among employees for a mentoring program, with 78 percent saying they were definitely or possibly interested. Responses were divided approximately equally between those wanting to serve as a mentor and those wanting to be a mentee; some were interested in both roles.*

c. *In answering the mentoring survey, 15 employees expressed a definite interest, and another 23 were possibly interested; 14 were interested in being a mentor, 15 in being a mentee, and 9 were interested in being both. Eleven employees were not interested in the idea.*

d. *Over three fourths of the employees were interested in the mentoring program, while somewhat less than one fourth were not. Of those who were interested, somewhat over one third were interested in the mentor role, and approximately the same number were interested in serving as a mentee. The remainder were interested in both roles.*

Using Graphics

Imagine trying to put in composition style all the information available in a financial statement. Several hundred pages might be necessary to explain material that could otherwise be contained in three or four pages of balance sheets and income statements. Even then, the reader would no doubt be thoroughly confused! To protect readers from being overwhelmed or simply bored with data, report writers must design a visually appealing graphic that is appropriate for the data being presented. Data reported in a table, graph, or picture will make your written analysis clearer to the reader.

Discuss the adage "A picture is worth a thousand words" from a business perspective.

The term ***graphics*** is used in this chapter to refer to all types of illustrations used in written and spoken reports. The most commonly used graphics are tables, bar charts, line charts, pie charts, pictograms, maps, flowcharts, diagrams, and photographs.

Effective and Ethical Use of Graphics

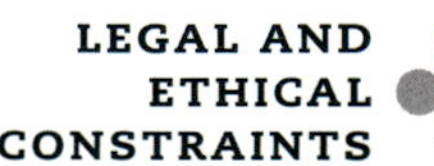

Graphics go hand in hand with the written discussion for three purposes: to clarify, to simplify, or to reinforce data. As you read this chapter, ask yourself if the discussion would be effective if the accompanying graphic figures were not included. Use the following questions to help you determine whether using a graphic element is appropriate and effective in a written or spoken report.

- Is a graphic needed to clarify, reinforce, or emphasize a particular idea? Or can the material be covered adequately in words rather than in visual ways? To maintain a reasonable balance between words and graphics, save graphics for data that are difficult to communicate in words alone.
- Does the graphic presentation contribute to the overall understanding of the idea under discussion? Will the written or spoken text add meaning to the graphic display?
- Is the graphic easily understood? Does the graphic emphasize the key idea and spur the reader to think intelligently about this information? Follow these important design principles:

- ▷ Avoid *chartjunk*. This term, coined by design expert Edward Tufte, describes decorative distractions that bury relevant data.[6] Extreme use of color, complicated symbols and art techniques, and unusual combinations of typefaces reduce the impact of the material presented.
- ▷ Develop a consistent design for graphics. Arbitrary changes in the design of graphics (e.g., use of colors, typefaces, three-dimensional or flat designs) within a written or spoken report can be confusing as the receiver expects consistency in elements within a single report.
- ▷ Write meaningful titles that reinforce the point you are making. For example, a receiver can interpret data faster when graphics use a talking title; that is, a title that interprets the data. Consider the usefulness of the following graphic titles for a physician browsing through a complex table at the hospital in the middle of the night:[7]

  Descriptive Title: White-Cell Counts During April
  Talking Title: White-Cell Count Has Fallen Throughout April

  The talking title saves the physician time in understanding the report and also ensures the accuracy of the physician's interpretation, proper diagnosis, and treatment of the patient. Similarly, poor business decisions may be averted if graphic titles reveal key information. You will learn more about the appropriate use of descriptive and talking headings as you study the preparation of informational and analytical reports in Chapter 11.

When would an informational handout to each audience member be appropriate during a presentation?

- ▷ Is the graphic honest? Visual data can be distorted easily, leading the reader to form incorrect opinions about the data. The Strategic Forces feature "Ethical Implications in Creating Graphs" provides directions for preparing ethical graphics.
- ▷ Can a graphic used in a presentation be seen by the entire audience? Electronic presentations, flip charts, whiteboards, and overhead transparencies are the visual means most often used to accompany presentations. You will learn more about designing graphics for a visual presentation in Chapter 12.

The key to preparing effective graphics is selecting an appropriate graphic for the data and developing a clean, simple design that allows the reader or audience to quickly extract needed information and meaning. Visit your companion website at www.cengage.com/bcomm/lehman to learn about other design techniques that enhance the professional appearance of graphics.

Your Turn 10-2
Miscue

In a case of mistaken identity, the "Today" show aired the photo of the wrong person when reporting on the trial of Senator Hillary Clinton's financial advisor David Rosen. A photo was inadvertently used of another man named David Rosen. The erroneous photo also appeared on the MSNBC website, and while a correction was issued on MSNBC, the "Today" show did not air it. The correction did not erase the fact that millions had viewed the wrong image and associated the investigation with someone in no way involved.[8]

TAKE ACTION:

Answer each of the following questions:

- What safeguards should be exercised to prevent such cases of mistaken identity?
- What are some potential repercussions of such errors in the use of graphic images?
- What legal responsibilities does a businessperson have when using the photo of another in print or electronic publications?

Types of Graphic Aids

Using powerful software programs, managers can perform data management functions discussed in this chapter to produce highly professional graphics. The information can be reproduced in a variety of ways for integrating into reports and for supporting highly effective presentations.

Selecting the graphic type that will depict data in the most effective manner is the first decision you must make. After identifying the idea you want your receiver to understand, you can choose to use a table, bar chart, line chart, pie chart, flowchart, organization chart, photographs, models, and so on. Use Figure 10-1 to help you choose the graphic type that matches the objective you hope to achieve.

Figures 10-2 through 10-8 illustrate a variety of graphics commonly used in reports. The figures show acceptable variations in graphic design, including placement of the caption (figure number and title), inclusion or exclusion of grid lines, proper labeling of the axes, proper referencing of the source of data, and other features. When designing

SHOWCASE PART 2

"Broadcast Yourself"

SPOTLIGHT COMMUNICATOR CHAD HURLEY

"YouTube and other sites will bring together all the diverse media which matters to you, from videos of your family and friends to news, music, sports, cooking and much, much more."

YouTube's motto "Broadcast Yourself" emphasizes the digital media revolution where everyone can be a star. According to Chad Hurley, CEO, "Our goal is to allow every person on the planet to participate . . . this new video content will be available on any screen—in your living room, or on your device in your pocket. YouTube and other sites will bring together all the diverse media which matters to you, from videos of your family and friends to news, music, sports, cooking and much, much more."[11] Go to your companion website at www.cengage.com/bcomm/lehman to read more about Hurley's vision for YouTube.

www.youtube.com

SEE SHOWCASE PART 3, ON PAGE 368
TO LEARN MORE ABOUT HOW TO ADAPT PRESENTATIONS FOR YOUTUBE.

FIGURE 10-1

Choosing the Appropriate Graphic to Fit Your Objective

GRAPHIC TYPE	OBJECTIVE	GRAPHIC TYPE	OBJECTIVE
Table 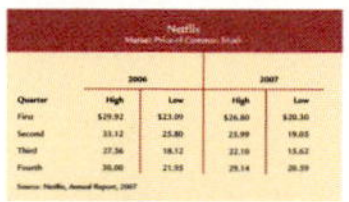	To show exact figures	Gantt chart 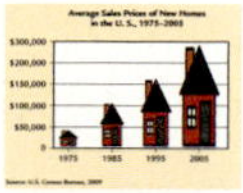	To track progress toward completing a project
Bar chart 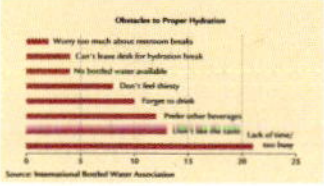	To compare one quantity with another	Map 	To show geographic relationships
Line chart 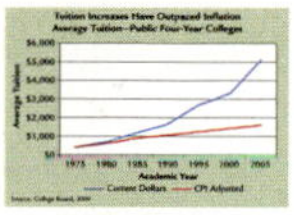	To illustrate changes in quantities over time	Flow chart 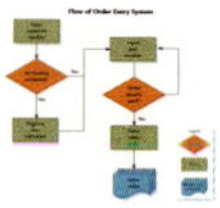	To illustrate a process or procedure
Pie chart 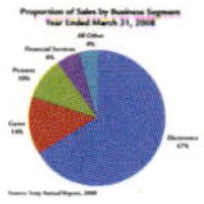	To show how the parts of a whole are distributed	Photograph 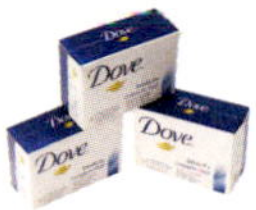	To provide a realistic view of a specific item or place

graphics, adhere to the requirements in your company policy manual or the style manual you are instructed to follow. Then be certain that you design graphics for a particular document or presentation consistently. When preparing a graphic for a slide show or mounted chart, remove the figure number and include the title only.

Tables

A ***table*** presents data in columns and rows, which aid in clarifying large quantities of data in a small space. Proper labeling techniques make the content clear. Guidelines for preparing an effective table follow and are illustrated in Figure 10-2:

Can a graphic figure be overly labeled?

- **Number tables and all other graphics consecutively throughout the report.** This practice enables you to refer to "Figure 1" rather than to "the following table" or "the figure on the following page."
- **Give each table a title that is complete enough to clarify what is included without forcing the reader to review the table.** Table titles may be quite long as they may contain sources of data, numbers included in the table, and the subject, as shown in Figure 10-2. Titles may be written in either all capitals or upper- and lowercase letters. Titles that extend beyond one line should be arranged on the page so that they are balanced.
- **Label columns of data clearly enough to identify the items.** Usually, column headings are short and easily arranged. If, however, they happen to be lengthy, use some ingenuity in planning the arrangement.

FIGURE 10-2

Effective Table Layout, Identifying Information, Labels, and Source

Netflix Market Price of Common Stock				
	2006		2007	
Quarter	High	Low	High	Low
First	$29.92	$23.09	$26.80	$20.30
Second	33.12	25.80	25.99	19.05
Third	27.56	18.12	22.10	15.62
Fourth	30.00	21.95	29.14	20.59

Source: Netflix, Annual Report, 2007

- **Indent the second line of a label for the rows (horizontal items) two or three spaces.** Labels that are subdivisions of more comprehensive labels should be indented, as should summary labels such as *total*.
- **Place a superscript beside an entry that requires additional explanation and include the explanatory note beneath the visual.**
- **Document the source of the data presented in a visual by adding a source note beneath the visual.** If more than one source was used to prepare a visual, use superscripts beside the various information references and provide the sources beneath the figure.

Bar Charts

How does a grouped bar chart differ from a simple bar chart?

A ***bar chart*** is an effective graphic for comparing quantities. The length of the bars, horizontal or vertical, indicates quantity. The vertical bars in Figure 10-3a (left) show changes in the number of subscribers to Netflix, a popular mail movie-rental business. Because of the lengthy labels, horizontal bars are ideal for depicting the top objections to drinking water shown in Figure 10-3a (right). Variations of the simple bar chart make it useful for a variety of purposes:

- **Grouped Bar Charts** (also called *clustered bar charts)* are useful for comparing more than one quantity. Figure 10-3b shows changes in the average inflation-adjusted prices in three major housing markets.

Should specific quantities be included in bar charts? Justify with an example.

- **Segmented Bar Charts** (also called *subdivided*, *stacked bar*, or *100 percent bar charts*) show how components contribute to a total figure. The segments in Figure 10-3c illustrate that sales outside of Sony's three primary market areas (Japan, U.S., and Europe) steadily are becoming a large portion of the company's total sales.

©AP IMAGES/PRNEWSFOTO/SONY

More Not Always Better. Absorption and retention of information are unquestionably enhanced by the use of graphics. We remember more of what we both see and hear than what we receive through only one sensory channel. When text and graphics are combined, retention goes up an average of 42 percent.[9] Placing text near graphics rather than farther apart also improves retention and recall of information.[10] Website designers would do well to remember, though, that there is such a thing as "too much." Overuse of graphic and text animation can irritate the user, obscure important information, and slow download time to a crawl. "Eye candy" can also cause eyestrain, headaches, and confusion for the viewer.

What icon would you choose to illustrate the number of households with Internet access?

- **Pictograms** use pictures or symbols to illustrate objects, concepts, or numerical values. A simple use of pictogram is a picture of an envelope used to represent an email message. Pictograms are common in everyday life, such as on signs in public places or roads, whereas the term "icon" is specific to interfaces on computers or other electronic devices. An image of a house is used in Figure 10-3d to depict home sales in the United States over a twenty-year period. Pictograms can be misleading if designed improperly as you'll learn in the Strategic Forces feature on page 359.

Describe a work activity in your career field that could be depicted in a Gantt chart.

- **The Gantt chart**, another variation of the bar chart, is useful for tracking progress toward completing a series of events over time. The Gantt chart in Figure 10-3e, prepared using Microsoft® Project, plots the output on the y-axis (activities involved in planning and implementing a research study) and the time (days planned to complete the activity) on the x-axis. This version of the Gantt chart not only schedules the important activities required to complete this research but also plots the *actual* progress of each activity along with the *planned* progress. Simple Gantt charts can be created using a spreadsheet program such as *Excel*.

In addition to the suggestions for developing tables, here are further suggestions related to constructing bar charts:

- **Avoid visual distortion that could exaggerate the data.** Begin the quantitative axis at zero, divide the bars into equal increments, and use bars of equal width.
- **Position chronologically or in some other logical order.**
- **Use color to convey meaning such as *using variations in color to distinguish among the bars when the bars represent different data.*** Avoid large surfaces of bright colors that may be tiring to the audience and detract from the data.
- **Avoid fancy formatting such as 3D that makes values more difficult to distinguish.**

How effective is a three-dimensional bar chart? Why?

- **Keep the labeling simple to reduce clutter and increase readability.** Exclude nonessential information such as data labels, gridlines, and explanatory notes if the meaning is understood. To determine labeling needs, consider the audience's use of the data. Omit actual amounts if a visual estimate is adequate for understanding the relationships presented in the chart. Include the data values above the bars or as a data table for an audience who expects specific data.

FIGURE 10-3

Variety of Bar Chart Formats

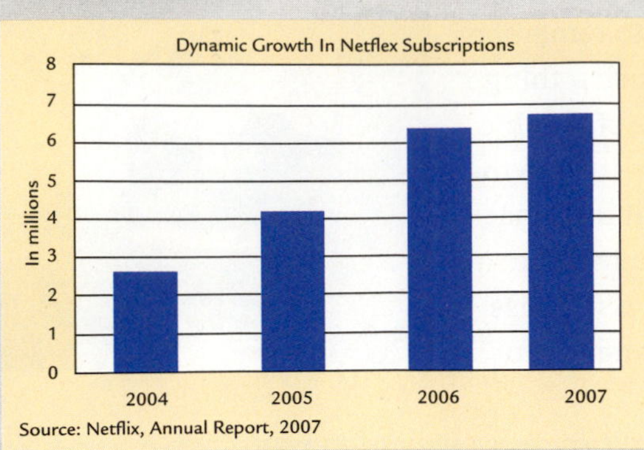

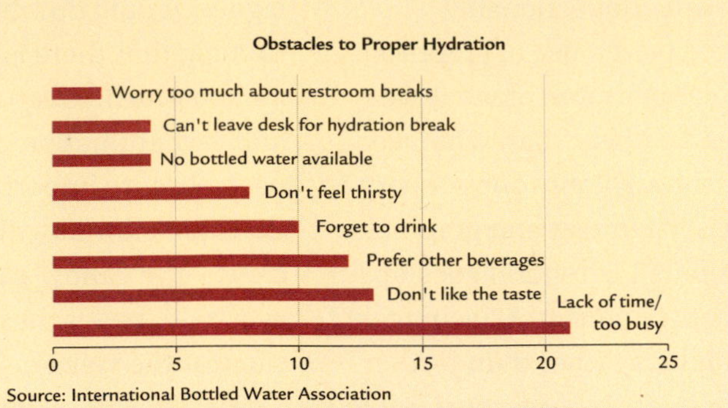

(a) Simple vertical bar chart with gridlines (left) and simple horizontal bar with data table and no gridlines (right)

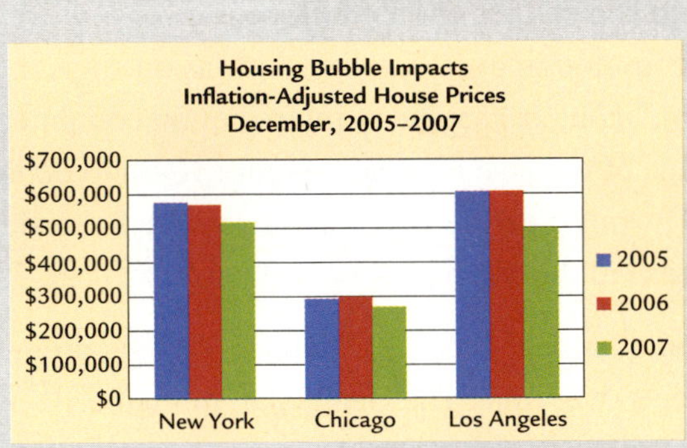

(b) Grouped bar chart

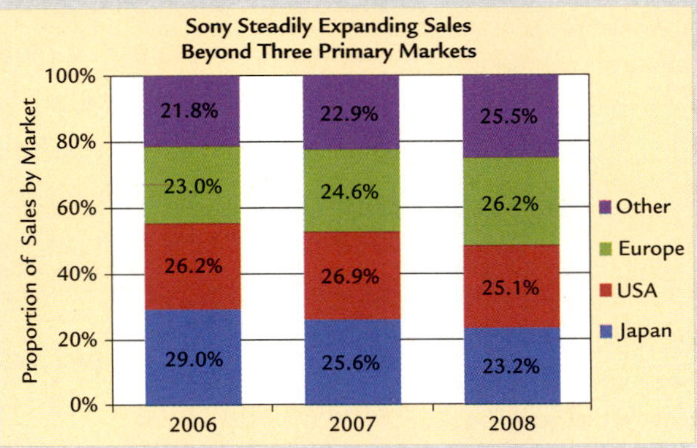

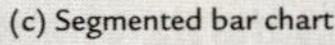
(c) Segmented bar chart

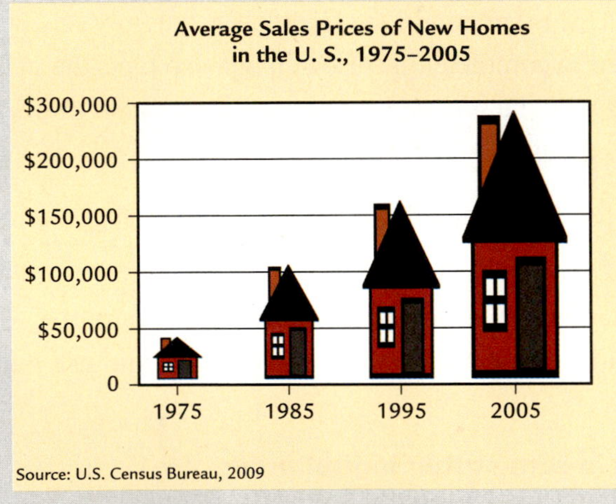

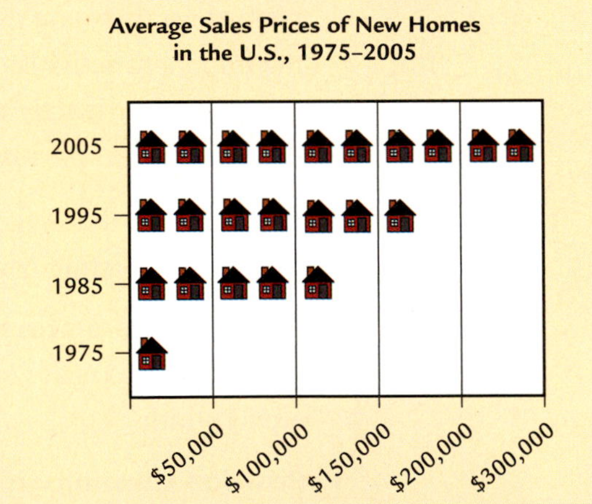

(d) Pictograms: Poor example (left) and good example (right)

ID	Task Name	Duration
1	Conduct secondary research	3 days
2	Obtain database	2 days
3	Construct mail questionnaire	5 days
4	Conduct pilot study/revise	3 days
5	Design mock graphics	3 days
6	Mail questionnaire	2 days
7	Draft selected report sections	4 days
8	Mail second requests	2 days
9	Tabulate and analyze data	5 days
10	Complete report draft	4 days
11	Revise report	5 days
12	Print and distribute copies	2 days

'11 | Feb. 3, '11 | Feb. 10, '11 | Feb
T W T F S S M T W T F S S M T W T F S S

(e) Gantt chart

LEGAL AND ETHICAL CONSTRAINTS

STRATEGIC FORCES

Ethical Implications in Creating Graphics

Creators of visuals can mislead their audience just as surely as can creators of text. In fact, visuals can sometimes have more impact than their accompanying text, for three reasons:

- Visuals have an emotional impact that words often lack.
- Skimmers of items will see visuals even when they don't read text.
- Readers remember visuals longer.

Ethical considerations become an issue in visual communication because graphic designers mislead their audiences either through lack of expertise or deliberate ambiguity. Today's professionally oriented communicators will need to defend themselves from unethical uses of visuals and determine what choices are ethical in the design of their own visuals.

Visual distortion can occur in a number of ways. For instance, distortion can occur in bar charts when the value scale starts at some point other than "0," as illustrated in the accompanying chart. The left bar chart seems to indicate a much greater improvement in test scores over the covered time period than actually occurred. This distortion could lead a student, parent, taxpayer, or employee to form a false impression about the schools' performance.

Another type of distortion can occur in bar charts when increments on the y-axis that are visually equal are used to represent varying values. For instance, if intervals are set at 100, then each additional increment must also represent an increase of 100. When graphic placement or eye appeal would be jeopardized by including all intervals, a break line can be used to show that intervals have been omitted. This technique makes accurate reader interpretation more likely.

Other visual distortions, such as the misuse of symbols in pictograms, can also confuse or mislead a reader. In a study of people from outside the U.S., many confused the symbol for ticket counter developed by the U.S. Department of Transportation with a sign indicating currency exchange.[12] Creators of visuals have a responsibility to report information as clearly and accurately as possible and should be able to answer the following questions favorably:[13]

© ISTOCKPHOTO.COM/DAN TERO

- Does the visual actually do what it seems to promise to do? Does the design cause false expectations?
- Is it truthful? Does it avoid implying lies?
- Does it avoid exploiting or cheating its audience?
- Does it avoid causing pain and suffering to members of the audience?
- Where appropriate, does it clarify text? Does the story told match the data?
- Does it avoid depriving viewers of a full understanding? Does it hide or distort information?

Application

Construct a bar chart for data you select with intervals of unequal value on the y-axis; then construct the same chart using intervals of equal value. Describe the difference in interpretation that the reader might have in viewing the two visuals.

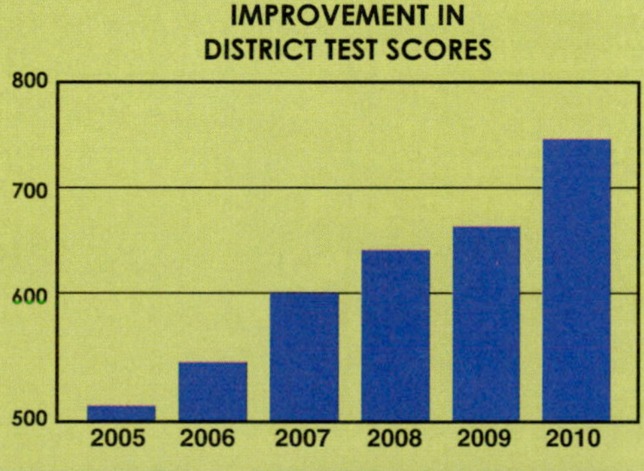

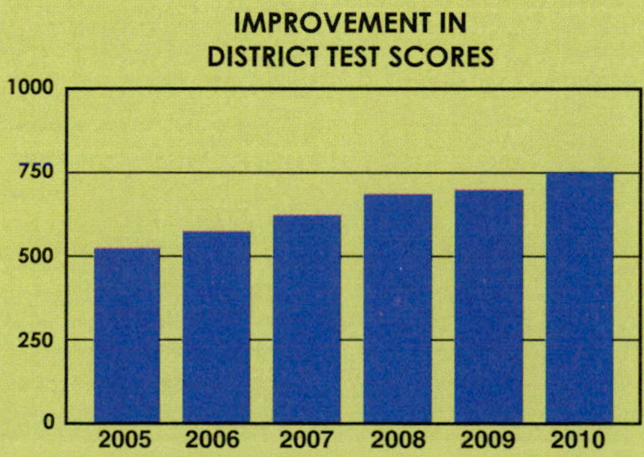

Line Charts

A ***line chart*** depicts changes in quantitative data over time and illustrates trends. The line chart shown in Figure 10-4 shows the degree to which college tuition increases have outpaced inflation. When constructing line charts, keep these general guidelines in mind:

- **Use the vertical axis for amount and the horizontal axis for time.**
- **Begin the vertical axis at zero.**
- **Divide the vertical and horizontal scales into equal increments.** The vertical or quantity increments, however, need not be the same as the horizontal or time increments so that the line or lines drawn will have reasonable slopes. Unrealistic scales might produce startling slopes that could mislead readers.

An ***area chart***, also called a *cumulative line chart* or a *surface chart*, is similar to a segmented bar chart because it shows how different factors contribute to a total. An area chart is especially useful when you want to illustrate changes in components over time. For example, the area chart in Figure 10-5 illustrates changes in the actions of visitors to a company's website. A company decision maker can easily recognize the growth in the number of hits and orders placed. The cumulative total of the number of hits, registrations, and orders is illustrated by the top line on the chart. The amount of each component can be estimated by visual assessment.

Can the information in a pie chart also be represented in a bar chart? Is the opposite true? Explain.

Pie Charts

A ***pie chart***, like segmented charts and area charts, shows how the parts of a whole are distributed. Pie charts are effective for showing percentages (parts of a whole), but they

FIGURE 10-4

Line Chart

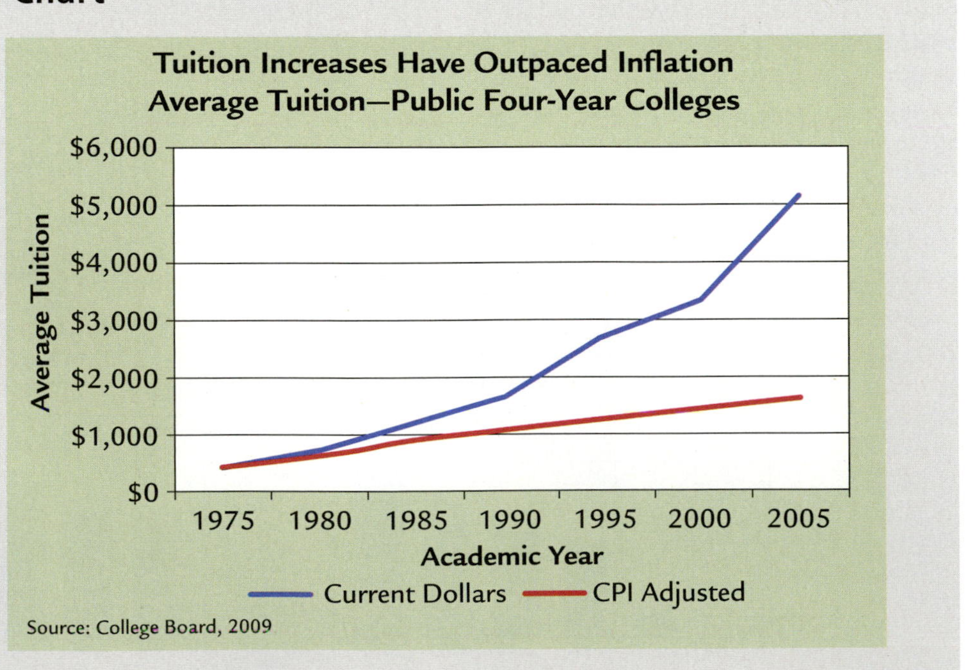

FIGURE 10-5

Area Chart

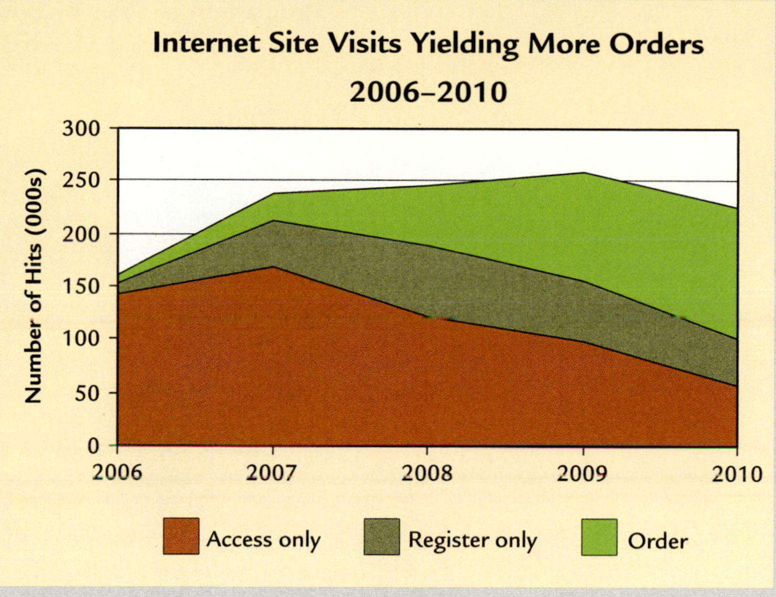

are ineffective in showing quantitative totals or comparisons. Bars are used for those purposes. The pie chart in Figure 10-6 shows the proportion of sales Sony earned from its various business segments.

Here are some generally used guidelines for constructing pie charts:

- **Position the largest slice or the slice to be emphasized at the twelve o'clock position.** Working clockwise, place the other slices in descending order of size or some other logical order of presentation.
- **Label each slice and include information about the quantitative size (percentage, dollars, etc.) of each slice.** If you are unable to attractively place the appropriate labeling information beside each slice, use a legend to identify each slice. Note the labeling in Figure 10-6.
- **Draw attention to one or more slices for desired emphasis.** Special effects include exploding the slice(s) to be emphasized (that is, removing it from immediate contact with the pie) or displaying or printing only the slice(s) to be emphasized.
- **Avoid using 3D-type formatting that makes values more difficult to distinguish.**

Your software may limit your ability to follow rules explicitly, and the nature of the data or the presentation may require slight deviations. For example, if you intend to explode the largest pie slice, placing it in the twelve o'clock position may not be desirable because the slice is likely to intrude into the space occupied by a title positioned above the graphic. Other deviations are discussed in the Strategic Forces feature "Presentation Software and Graphic Design Principles." on p. 363.

FIGURE 10-6

Pie Chart

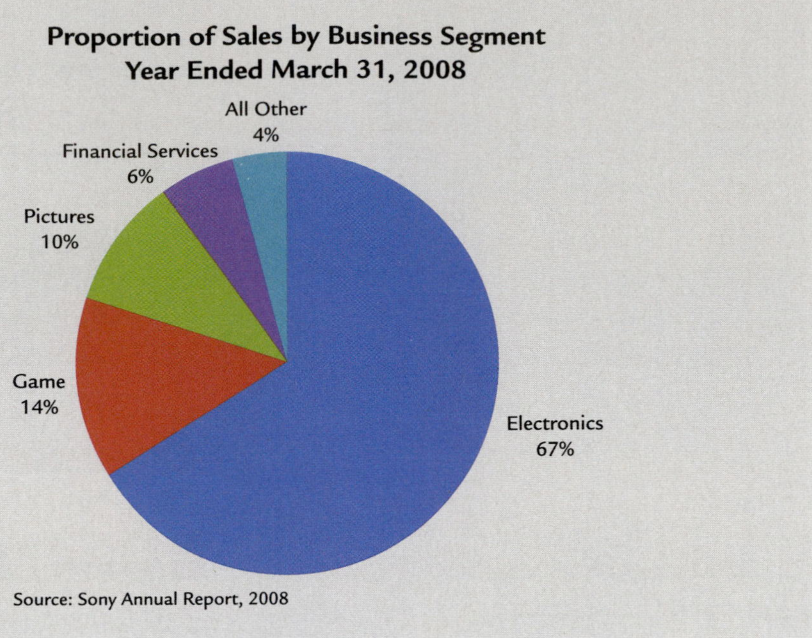

Your Turn 10-3
Electronic Café

DIGITAL COLLABORATION OVERCOMES GEOGRAPHICAL BARRIERS

Digital collaboration refers to the use of technology to enhance and extend the abilities of individuals and organizations to collaborate, independent of their geographical location. While collaboration has traditionally occurred in the same physical place, digital collaboration involves the creation of a "virtual place" that participants share. Various software applications are available that enable the technology for collaboration using both text and graphics to exchange information.

TAKE ACTION:

- **Participate in electronic collaboration.** Your instructor will give you instructions about how to access your online course and join an electronic meeting involving collaboration on a graphics document posted to the whiteboard.
- **Learn more about digital meetings.** Access your companion website at www.cengage.com/bcomm/lehman for information on advantages and disadvantages of digital collaboration and how to maximize its effectiveness.

Maps

A ***map*** shows geographic relationships. This graphic type is especially useful when a receiver may not be familiar with the geography discussed in a report. The map shown in Figure 10-7 effectively presents the distribution of electoral votes by political party in the 2008 U.S. presidential campaign. The map gives the information visually and thus eliminates the difficulty of explaining the information in words. In addition to being less confusing, a map is more concise and interesting than a written message.

CHANGING TECHNOLOGY

STRATEGIC FORCES

Presentation Software and Graphic Design Principles

In the early days of software development, some businesspeople made the mistake of assuming that because technical capabilities existed for creating a variety of graphic materials, everyone could perform the job of designer. This was not, and still is not, the case. Fortunately, the latest generation of presentation software does guide the user away from the worst errors of taste and judgment. For instance, Office 2007® offers themes and pre-built designs to assist in the design process. Other software developers have inserted relevant rules, such as incorporating graphic design principles in presentation applications.

In spite of ongoing improvements in presentation software applications, developers still often do not reflect good rules for formation of graphic aids in the default settings. For instance, many programs automatically arrange pie slices in random-size order; if the pie contains many slices, the program may intersperse the small with the larger slices to increase readability of labels that would otherwise appear very close together. Some programs also do not start pie charts at the twelve o'clock position. Applications often include an unnecessary series legend indicator for charts, even when only one value is represented.

With a little work on your part, you can usually achieve accurate depictions when using presentation and graphics applications. You can create, customize, and save a custom chart design that arranges the graphic according to appropriate rules. For example, the pie chart customized to follow design rules (shown at right, below) is much more effective than the default pie chart (shown at the left). Three minor format changes simplified the design and interpretation: (a) beginning the largest slice at the twelve o'clock position and positioning the remaining slices in descending order of size, (b) positioning the labels and percentages beside the slice to enhance readability, and eliminating the unnecessary legend. To ensure clarity and appeal, a competent designer never assumes the software application will produce the desired arrangement automatically.

Application

1. Select two different presentation software products (PowerPoint®, Impress®, Keynote®, Harvard Graphics®, etc.). Using the following data and the default settings of the application, construct a simple bar chart and a simple pie chart using both products.

   Operating Budget for Administrative Support Department, XYZ Company: salaries & benefits, 62%; training & development, 11%; supplies & materials, 12%; and operating chargeback, 15%

2. Print your results. What differences did you find in the output of each product? How did the outcomes deviate from and comply with the rules in this chapter?

Projected Expenses by Department

Production
Marketing
Human Resources
Finance
Accounting

Chart built with default values

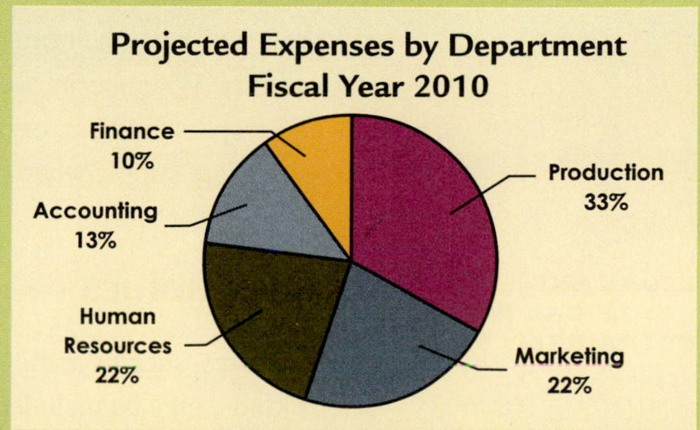

Chart enhanced for optional appeal and readability

FIGURE 10-7

Map Conveying Statistical Data

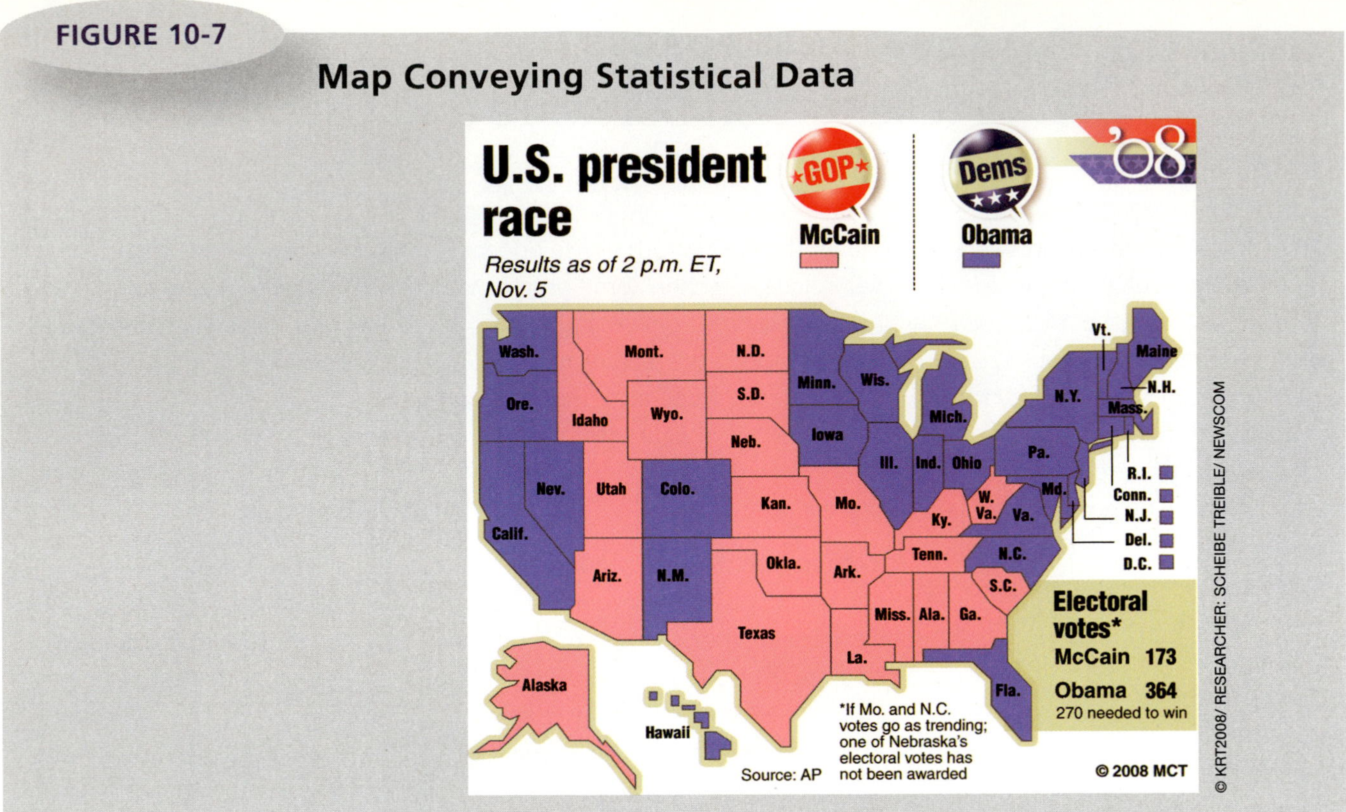

Sketch a flowchart outlining the procedure for shipping packages. Decisions may include priority of package, destination, and package weight.

Flowcharts

A ***flowchart*** is a step-by-step diagram of a procedure or a graphic depiction of a system or organization. A variety of problems can be resolved by using flowcharts to support written analyses. For example, most companies have procedure manuals to instruct employees in certain work tasks. Including a flowchart with written instructions minimizes the chance of errors. The flowchart in Figure 10-8 illustrates the procedures for processing a telephone order in a series of simple steps. If this information had been presented only in a series of written steps, the customer service manager would have to rely not only on the input operators' reading ability but also on their willingness to study the written procedures.

Organization charts, discussed in Chapter 1, are widely used to provide a picture of the authority structure and relationships within an organization. They provide employees with an idea of what their organization looks like in terms of the flow of authority and responsibility. When businesses change (because of new employees or reorganization of units and responsibilities), organization charts must be revised. Revisions to organizational charts are simple when prepared using word processing or graphics software.

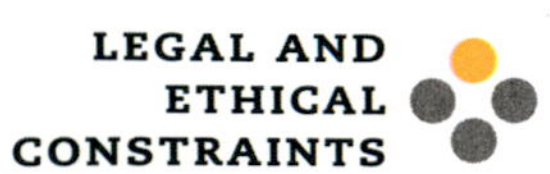

What legal precautions should be taken when scanning photographs and other artistic items for use in a business document?

Other Graphics

Other graphics, such as architectural plans, photographs, cartoons, blueprints, and lists of various kinds, may be included in reports. The availability of graphics and sophisticated drawing software facilitate inclusion of these more complex visuals in reports and spoken presentations. Photographs are used frequently in annual reports to help the general audience understand complex concepts and to make the documents more appealing to

FIGURE 10-8

Flowchart Simplifying Understanding of Tasks

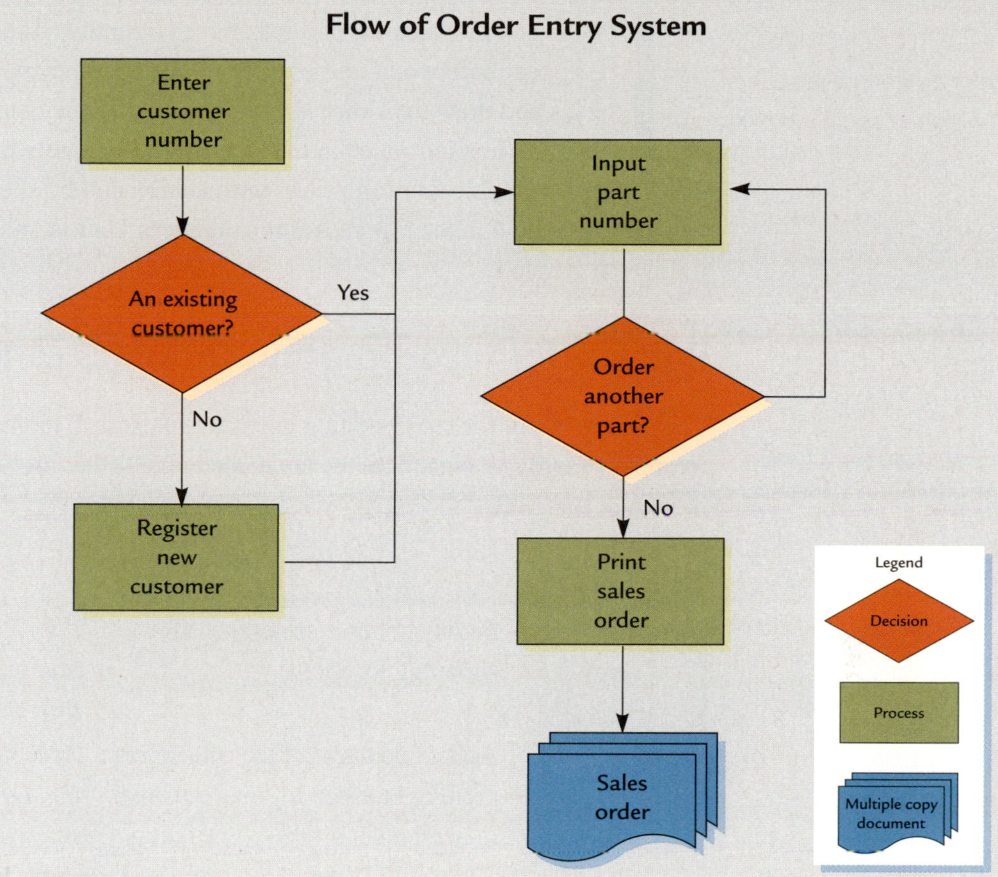

Flow of Order Entry System
Enter customer number
An existing customer?
Yes
No
Register new customer
Input part number
Order another part?
No
Print sales order
Sales order
Legend
Decision
Process
Multiple copy document

read. Frequently, you must include some graphic material in a report that would make the narrative discussion otherwise unwieldy. In this case, the material might be placed in an appendix and only referred to in the report.

MyPyramid.gov
STEPS TO A HEALTHIER YOU
© USDA

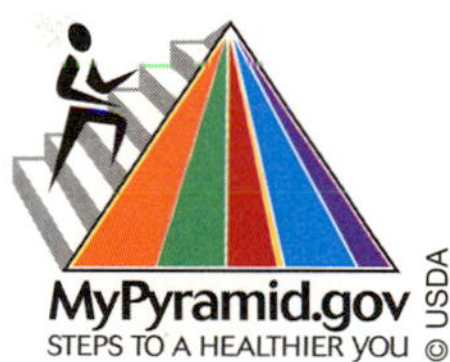

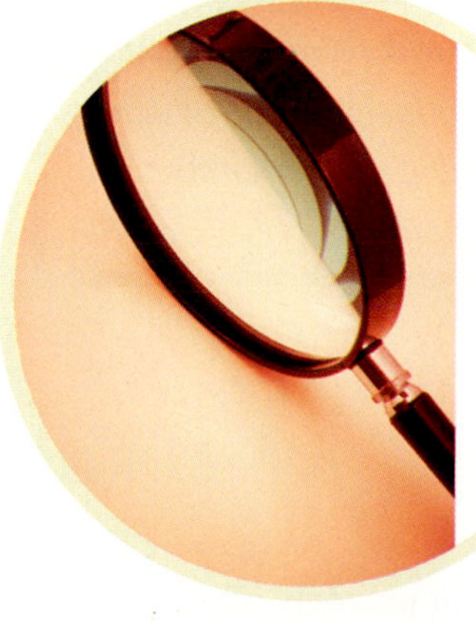

Your Turn 10-4
Assessment

Effective use of graphics requires understanding of basic mathematical concepts. Visit the following website sponsored by the creators of the SAT to review and test your knowledge of percentage and data interpretation:[14] http://www.bestsamplequestions.com/sat-sample-questions/data-interpretation/data-interpretation.html

You may link to this URL or other updated sites from your companion website at www.cengage.com/bcomm/lehman for updated sites.

TAKE ACTION:

- After reviewing the tutorial, take the 13-item quiz.
- Be prepared to discuss your results in class, taking note of any questions that caused problems for you.

Including Graphics in Text

Text and graphics are partners in the communication process. If graphics appear before readers have been informed, they will begin to study the graphics and draw their own inferences and conclusions. For this reason, always give a text introduction to a graphic immediately preceding the positioning of the graphic. A graphic that follows an introduction and brief explanation will supplement what has been said in the report. Additional interpretation and needed analysis should follow the graphic.

Pattern for Incorporating Graphics in Text

The pattern, then, for incorporating graphics in text is (1) introduce, (2) show, and (3) interpret and analyze. Note how the language in the following sentences introduces graphic or tabular material:

Poor:	Figure 1 shows preferences for shopping locations.	*Poor because it tells the reader nothing more than would the title of the figure.*
Acceptable:	About two thirds of the consumers preferred to shop in suburban areas rather than in the city. (See Figure 1.)	*Acceptable because it interprets the data, but it places the figure reference in parentheses rather than integrating it into the sentence.*
Better:	As shown in Figure 1, about two thirds of the consumers preferred to shop in suburban areas rather than in the city.	*Better than the previous examples but puts reference to the figure at the beginning, thus detracting from the interpretation of the data.*
Best:	About two thirds of the consumers preferred to shop in suburban areas rather than in the city, as shown in Figure 1.	*Best for introducing figures because it talks about the graphic and also includes introductory phrasing, but only after stressing the main point.*

Positioning of Graphics in Text

If a graphic will not fit on the page where it is introduced, what should be done with the blank space, and where should the graphic be positioned?

Ideally, a graphic should be integrated within the text material immediately after its introduction. A graphic that will not fit on the page where it is introduced should appear at the top of the following page. The previous page is filled with text that would have ideally followed the graphic. In this chapter, figures are placed as closely as possible to their introductions in accordance with these suggestions. However, in some cases, several figures may be introduced on one page, making perfect placement difficult and sometimes impossible.

When interpreting and analyzing the graphic, avoid a mere restatement of what the graphic obviously shows. Instead, emphasize the main point you are making. Contrast the boring style of the following discussion of graphic data with the improved revision:

Obvious Restatement of Data:	Among the respondents, 35 percent are pleased with their rate of return from online investing, 12 percent are not pleased with their rate of return from online investing, 31 percent are not investing online but plan to begin, 8 percent only invest using a broker, and 15 percent do not trade stocks.
Emphasis on Main Point:	Over one third of the respondents are pleased with their rate of return on online investing.

Your analysis may include summary statements about the data, compare information in the figure to information obtained from other sources, or extend the shown data into reasonably supported speculative outcomes. Strive to transition naturally from the discussion of the graphic into the next point you wish to make.

Which numbering system for report graphics would you use if you were writing a report for your supervisor?

Throughout the discussion of tables and graphics, the term *graphics* has been used to include all illustrations. Although your report may include tables, graphs, maps, and even photographs, you will find organizing easier and writing about the illustrations more effective if you label each item as a "Figure" followed by a number; then number the items consecutively. Some report writers prefer to label tables consecutively as "Table 1," etc., and graphs and charts consecutively in another sequence as "Graph 1," etc. When this dual numbering system is used, readers of the report may become confused if they come upon a sentence saying, "Evidence presented in Tables 3 and 4 and Graph 2 supports. . . ." Both writers and readers appreciate the single numbering system, which makes the sentence read, "Evidence presented in Figures 3, 4, and 5 supports. . . ."

Your Turn 10-5
Career Portfolio

The U.S. government publishes annual information about job opportunities in various fields throughout areas of the country. Using the *Occupational Outlook Handbook* (www.bls.gov/oco) or other sources, obtain information about salaries and career opportunities for your chosen career position in three regions of the United States.

TAKE ACTION:

Prepare a short report that compares the findings for the three regions, including at least two different types of graphs or charts. Supply appropriate references.

SHOWCASE PART 3

Adapting Your Presentation for YouTube

YouTube is a great potential resource for a business and can be used to distribute your sales message or training material to a wide audience. The easily accessed site can be a great avenue for sharing business presentations; however, some adaptation is necessary for best effect.

- **Keep it short.** According to CEO Chad Hurley, the average viewing time for a YouTube clip is 2.5 minutes. If you must stay with a longer presentation format, divide it into several short segments posted as separate videos.
- **Make it loud and clear.** Use an external microphone rather than relying on one built in the camera. Your audio quality will be much improved.
- **Avoid bulleted PowerPoint slides.** Bullet points will appear blurry on YouTube and be next to impossible to read. Edit your content and change it to full-screen slides before uploading.

Viewers don't have the time or inclination to struggle through a long, poorly prepared video. Make sure your postings on social media sites are "online compatible."[15]

www.youtube.com

© RICHARD LEVINE/ALAMY

Activities

1. View a business presentation posted to YouTube on the companion website at www.cengage.com/bcomm/lehman.
2. Explain how well the posted presentation reflects the suggested principles for YouTube presentations.
3. Make suggestions for improving the viewed presentation.

Summary

1. Communicate quantitative information effectively.

Graphics complement text by clarifying complex figures and helping readers visualize major points. Tabulating data and analyzing data using measures of central tendency aid in summarizing or classifying large volumes of data into manageable information you can interpret. You can then communicate this meaningful data using common language—fractions, ratios, and percentages—that the reader can easily understand.

2. Apply principles of effectiveness and ethical responsibilities in the construction of graphic aids.

A graphic aid should clarify, reinforce, or emphasize a particular idea and should contribute to the overall understanding of the idea under discussion. It should be uncluttered and easily understood and depict information honestly. Graphic aids used in spoken presentations should be large enough to be seen by the entire audience.

3. Select and design appropriate and meaningful graphics.

The type of graphic presentation should be chosen based on the ability to communicate the information most effectively. Tables present data in systematic rows and columns. Bar charts (simple, grouped, and stacked) compare quantities for a specific period. Line charts depict changes in quantities over time and illustrate trends. Pie charts, pictograms, and segmented and area charts show the proportion of components to a whole. Gantt charts track progress toward completing a series of events over time. Maps help readers visualize geographical relationships. Flow charts visually depict step-by-step procedures for completing a task; organization charts show the organizational structure of a company. Floor plans, photographs, cartoons, blueprints, and lists also enhance reports.

4. Integrate graphics within documents.

A graphic should always be introduced in text before it is presented. The graphic will then reinforce your conclusions and discourage readers from drawing their own conclusions before encountering your ideas. An effective introduction for a graphic tells something meaningful about what is depicted in the graphic and refers the reader to a specific figure number. The graphic should be placed immediately after the introduction if possible or positioned at the top of the next page after filling the previous page with text that ideally would have followed the graphic. Analysis or interpretation follows the graphic, avoiding a mere repetition of what the graphic clearly shows.

Chapter Review

1. In what ways does managing data help protect researchers and readers from being overwhelmed by information? (Obj. 1)
2. What is meant by *common language*? Provide several examples. (Obj. 1)
3. What is meant by the term *chartjunk*? Provide suggestions for eliminating chartjunk. (Obj. 2)
4. What are potential pitfalls of using presentation software to create graphics? What advice do you suggest for producing an effective graphic using presentation software? (Obj. 2)
5. Discuss the major principles involved in preparing effective tables. (Obj. 3)
6. Why should increments on the vertical axis of a graphic be equal? Is variation in the sizes of horizontal increments acceptable? (Obj. 3)
7. Under what conditions can data be represented in either a pie chart or a bar chart? When is that not possible? (Obj. 3)
8. When would a pictogram be preferred to a bar chart? Why? (Obj. 3)
9. Should every graphic be introduced before it appears in a report? Is interpreting a self-explanatory graphic necessary? Explain. (Obj. 4)
10. Discuss the appropriate way to introduce and to interpret a graphic in a report. (Obj. 4)

Digging Deeper

1. A poorly designed electronic slideshow can detract from the effectiveness of your presentation. Compose a list of blunders to avoid in designing effective slideshows.
2. How much is "too much" when considering the use of graphics in a business document?

Assessment

To check your understanding of the chapter, take the available online quizzes as directed by your instructor.

Activities

1. Selecting Appropriate Graphics (Obj. 3)

Select the most effective graphic means of presenting the following data. Justify your decision.

a. Data showing the growth in the number of companies offering employees paid time for volunteerism over a five-year period
b. Data showing the number of downloads from iTunes by media type (music, books, and TV segments) for the past quarter
c. Data showing percentage of organizational projects that are delayed, on time, or ahead of schedule
d. Growth in credit card debt over the past four years by state
e. Data showing the relationship of the functional areas of a company from the CEO to the vice presidents to the line supervisors
f. Predicted unemployment rate in regions of the U.S. for the year 2015
g. Instructions for conducting interrogations of employees suspected of committing fraud
h. Figures comparing the percentage of warranty claims of a company's three product lines for the past four quarters
i. Data showing the number of people utilizing the portfolio option of a financial investment firm's website. The data should depict the number of portfolios opened by investors in five age categories during each of the past four quarters.
j. Graphic tracking the progress of a product development team working on a new refrigeration product for a 2013 launch date

2. Improving Graphics (Obj. 3)

Decide which graphic design is preferable and describe why the others are less effective.

Version 1

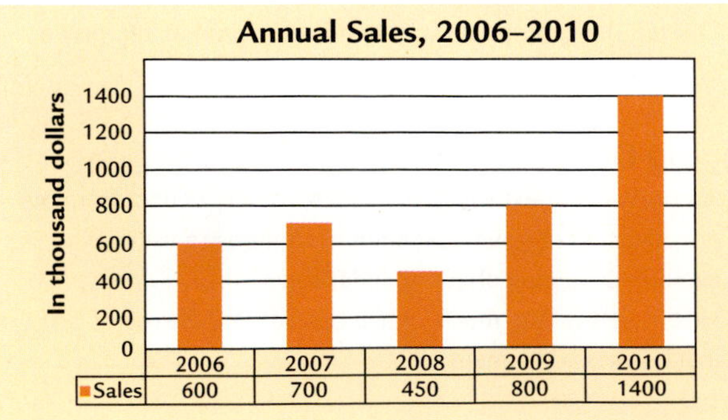

Version 2

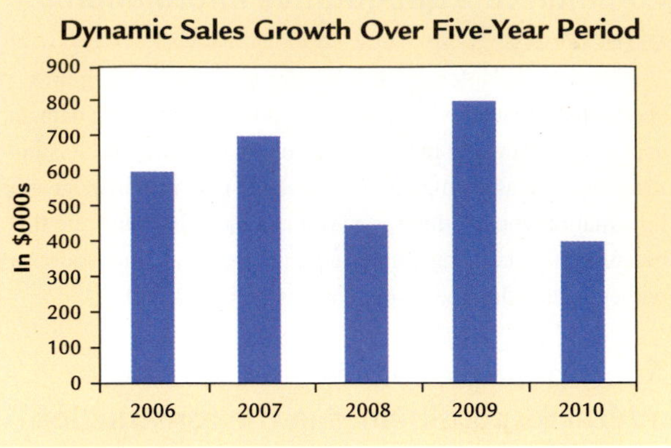

Version 3

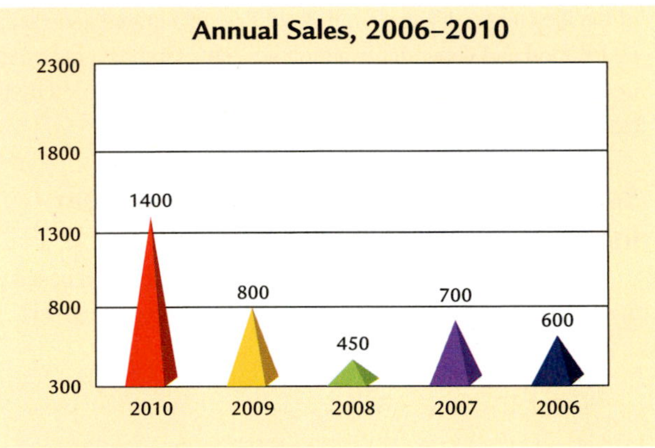

3. Evaluating Graphics (Objs. 2–3)

Evaluate each of the following graphics for its ethical presentation of the data and the effectiveness of its design. Be prepared to discuss your critique in class. Your instructor may ask you to revise each of the graphics, incorporating your suggestions for improvement. Write a descriptive or talking title and a sentence to introduce each graphic and emphasize the most important idea(s) in each graphic. Access a downloadable version of this activity at your companion website at www.cengage.com/bcomm/lehman.

a. Number of stores opened during 2011 by region of a national restaurant chain.

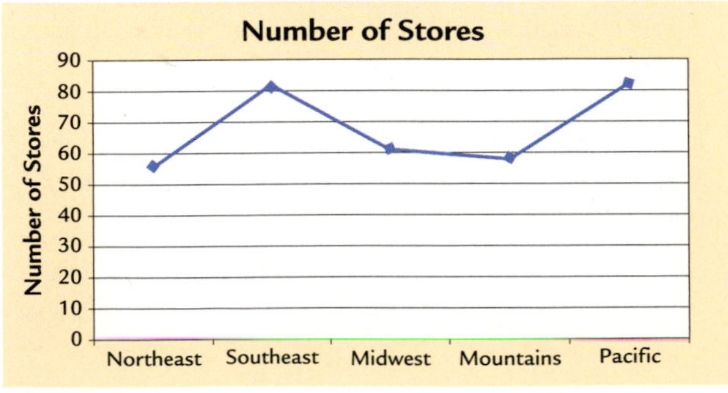

b. Profile of online customers of a professional clothing store, third quarter, 2011.

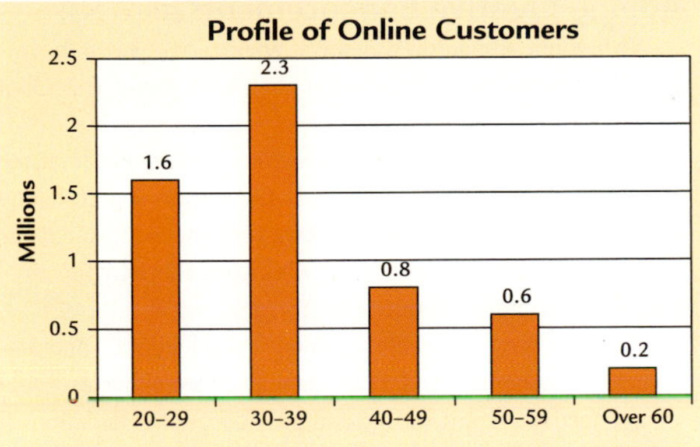

c. The most important factor affecting employee loyalty, according to a 2011 survey of employees of a regional distribution company.

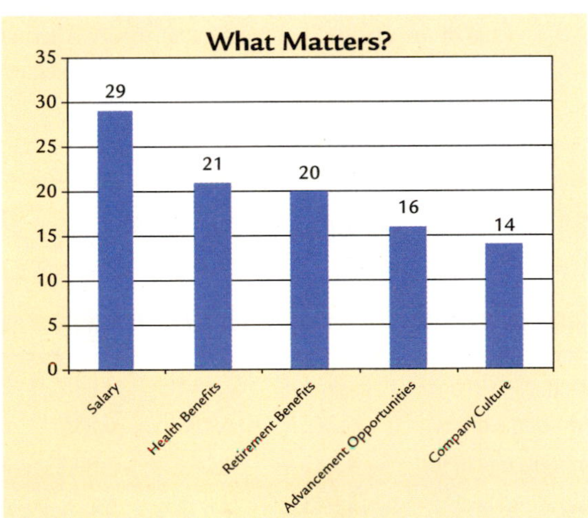

4. Improving Introductions to Graphics (Obj. 3)

Decide which graphic introduction is preferable and describe why the others are less effective.

Version 1

The data reveal (Figure 4) that only 7 out of 10 customers are satisfied with our service department.

Version 2

Take a look at Figure 4, where only 7 out of 10 customers are satisfied with our service department.

Version 3

Only 7 out of 10 customers are satisfied with our service department, as shown in Figure 4.

5. Improving Graphic Interpretations (Obj. 4)

Improve the discussion of a graphic taken from a report:

Figure 1 summarizes data related to college students' investment patterns. Of the college students surveyed, 45 percent believe their companies' pension plan will adequately fund their retirement, 25 percent plan to begin investing for retirement after their children complete college, 15 percent plan to begin investing in their 30s, 10 percent plan to begin investing in their 20s, and 5 percent have already begun their retirement investment plans.

Applications

READT | THINK | WRITE | SPEAK | COLLABORATE

1. Learning How to "Show the Numbers" (Objs. 1-3)

Business professionals are responsible for communicating quantitative information but many are unfamiliar with design practices that make them effective. Locate the following articles that discuss design strategies for effective charts and graphs:

Royston, R. A. (2007, November/December). Book review: Show me the numbers: Designing tables and graphs to enlighten. *The Value* Examiner, 11-14. Available from Business Source Complete database.

Jorge Cameos' Charts. (2008, October). 14 Misconceptions about charts and graphs. Available from http://charts.jorge-camoes.com/misconceptions-charts-graphs/

Required: Select three design techniques from these readings that were not covered in this chapter. Be prepared to share your insights with the class. Prepare a visual to support your presentation.

2. Mastering Graphic Design: Tufte Style (Obj. 2)

Locate the following information related to Edward Tufte's principles of information:

Graphics and web design based on Edward Tufte's principle. Available from www.washington.edu/computing/training/560/zz-tufte.html

Conduct an online search to locate other articles that discuss and apply Tufte's concepts or obtain a copy of one of Tufte's three books on information design: (a) *Visual Explanations: Images and Quantities, Evidence and Narrative;* (b) *Envisioning Information;* and (c) *The Visual Display of Quantitative Information.*

Prepare a presentation explaining Tufte's principles of information design for print and web pages. Include at least one of Tufte's classic examples that illustrates the importance of data design in proper decision making. Compile a list of basic principles for presenting data clearly and attractively following Tufte's theory.

READ | THINK | WRITE | SPEAK | COLLABORATE

3. Analyzing a Published Pictogram (Objs. 1–3)

Clip a pictogram from *USA Today* or the *Wall Street Journal* and share it with groups in class. Discuss the effectiveness of the symbols used and the ethical presentation of the data.

4. Selecting and Drawing an Appropriate Graphic (Objs. 2–4)

Create the graphic that would most effectively aid a human resources manager in identifying potential areas for personal enrichment for its employees. Write a descriptive or a talking title that interprets the data depicted in the chart and a sentence to introduce the graphic and emphasize its most important idea(s).

Interest by Age Group
January 2011

Age Group	Identity Security	Wireless Networking	Digital Photography	Online Investing
21-35	87	35	45	23
36-50	74	55	54	56
51-65	22	18	67	88

5. Adding Creative Enhancements (Objs. 2–4)

Visit your companion website at www.cengage.com/bcomm/lehman and read the enrichment content for Chapter 10, "Giving Graphics a Contemporary Look."

Required: As directed in the reading, analyze the creative techniques used in graphics appearing in various sources: annual reports, corporate websites, and news publications (printed and online), and television broadcasts. Complete the activities as directed by your instructor:

- Prepare a brief list of the techniques you identified and discuss the benefits and drawbacks of each technique as it relates to effective graphic design and provide recommendations for effective information design.
- Select one graphic that violates the principles presented in the web enrichment content; revise incorporating your suggestions for improvement. Be prepared to give a short report to the class that includes a summary of your analysis. Use a visual of the graphic to support your report. Alternatively, your instructor may require you to revise a graphic using a contemporary format.

READ | THINK | WRITE | SPEAK | COLLABORATE

6. Preparing a Table (Objs. 2–4)

Prepare a table to show the *total* revenue Scottsdale Fitness earned from membership fees for a fiscal period. Fees were collected by type of membership: single, $25; double, $40; family (3+ members), $50; corporate, $22.50; senior, $20. Scottsdale Sports Connection has 1,439 single memberships, 642 double, 543 family, 3,465 corporate, and 786 senior memberships.

7. Drawing a Bar Chart (Objs. 2–4)

The KPMG Fraud Report is completed annually to identify the common means of fraud detection. Using the following data from the 2008 survey, prepare a horizontal bar chart. Include a descriptive or a talking title that interprets the data and a source note. Write a sentence to introduce the graphic and emphasize the most important idea(s) in the graphic.

Tip (46%), by accident (20%), internal audit (19%), internal controls (23%), external audit (9.1%), and notification by police (3%)

8. Drawing a Segmented Chart (Objs. 2–4)

The director of the Scottsdale Sports Connection to compare the usage rate of various activities offered to its members over the past four quarters. Using the data provided in the following table, prepare a segmented chart that makes comparison of these usage rates easier to understand. Write a descriptive or talking title that interprets the data depicted in the chart; then write a sentence to introduce the graphic and emphasize its most important idea(s).

Activity	1st Q	2nd Q	3rd Q	4th Q
Group activities	2,451	2,315	2,248	2,258
Cardio machines	6,245	6,458	6,835	6,994
Strength machines	4,212	4,259	3,805	3,613
Free weights	5,945	5,845	6,258	6,789
Swimming pool	894	374	348	645

9. Drawing a Line Chart (Objs. 2–4)

The information technology group of First National Bank has prepared estimates on the number of customers expected to actively use its Internet banking site. Prepare a line chart showing the actual number of customers for 2006–2009 with the estimates for 2010–2012. To distinguish projected data from actual data, create a dashed line or add an explanatory note below the graph (e.g., Projected Data for ___). Write a descriptive or talking title that clearly identifies the data depicted in the chart. Write a sentence to introduce the graphic and emphasize its most important idea(s).

2006	645	2010	7,500
2007	1,247	2011	9,000
2008	2,456	2012	10,000
2009	5,119		

10. Drawing an Area Chart (Objs. 2–4)

Prepare an area chart showing how the various sources shown in the chart below contributed to the total revenue of a college football program over a seven-year period. Write a descriptive or talking title that clearly identifies the data depicted in the chart. Write a sentence to introduce the graphic and emphasize its most important idea(s).

11. Drawing a Pie Chart (Objs. 2–4)

Prepare a pie chart showing the percentage of operating income The Walt Disney Company generated in the following categories during 2010: media networks (56.2%), parks and resorts (22.4%), studio entertainment (12.9%), and consumer products (8.5%).Write a descriptive or talking title that interprets the data depicted in the chart; then write a sentence to introduce the graphic and emphasize its most important idea(s). If directed by your instructor, locate, graph, and interpret the same data for a business of your choice.

AREA CHART DATA FOR APPLICATION 10

Revenue Source ($ thousands)	2004	2005	2006	2007	2008	2009	2010
Ticket sales	10,815	10,921	9,869	12,801	14,736	15,647	15,568
Media contracts	8,210	9,601	9,715	10,004	11,071	13,170	15,288
Booster scholarships	—	—	—	600	640	720	2,865
Equipment/apparel contracts	1,200	1,200	1,200	1,400	1,400	1,600	1,600
Concessions	1,436	1,443	1,451	1,463	1,475	1,522	1,596

READ | THINK | WRITE | SPEAK | COLLABORATE

12. Evaluating Graphics in Annual Reports (Objs. 2–4)

Locate a recent annual report of a company of your choice. Prepare a short summary of effective graphic elements you observe; these could include photos, charts, and graphs, as well as the use of color, fonts, positioning, and spacing. In your summary, describe how the graphic elements reflect the message the company wishes to convey. In addition, identify a graphic that violates design principles and revise the graphic incorporating your suggestion. In your summary, include the revised graphic and a list of your suggestions for improving it. Be prepared to present your analysis to the class.

READ | THINK | WRITE | SPEAK | COLLABORATE

13. Drawing a Gantt Chart (Objs. 2–4)

In teams assigned by your instructor, prepare a Gantt chart to schedule the activities involved in completing a team project assigned by your instructor. The chart should include timelines that comp are the actual progress with the planned progress.

Your instructor will designate the software that should be used for preparing the Gantt chart or you may download a trial version of Microsoft Project®. Refer to *Building High-Performance Teams* (your team handbook) and your instructor's guidelines for identifying the activities and time requirements for the project.

14. Maximizing Movie Theater Ticket Sales (Objs. 1–3)

A movie theater must determine the genre of films to show on each screen during its 7:00, 9:00, and midnight show times. For example, a G-rated animation historically sells 60% of the available seats at 7:00 while selling only 25% of the available seats at 9:00. Theaters usually consider 80% capacity to be sold out.

Assume you are working with a software company developing a management information system targeted specifically to movie theaters. Using hypothetical data, create the reports the system should generate to enable theaters to manage their screens efficiently. For example, given a limited number of screens, a theater may elect to show an animated film on two screens at 7:00 but switch one of the screens to an action film at 9:00.

CASES

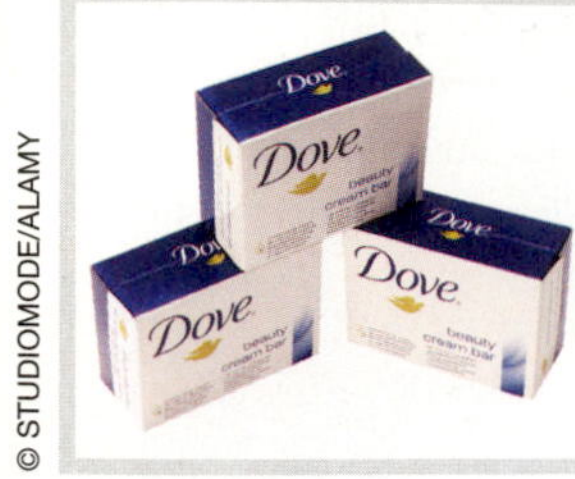

© STUDIOMODE/ALAMY

1. "Real Beauty" Not So Real

In 2004, Unilever launched a worldwide marketing campaign for its Dove beauty product line entitled "Campaign for Real Beauty." The campaign featured normal females who are nonprofessional models and of different ages, shapes, and sizes. The inspiration of the idea of the "Dove Beauties" is to change the Western concept of beauty from ultra-thin models with perfect features to making every little girl and woman feel positive about her looks. The campaign, which won several awards and recognitions in marketing circles, has included magazine spreads, television advertisements, and short films. A dashing blow to the "Campaign for Real Beauty" was levied in 2008 from reports that the company retouched the faces and bodies of women in their 50s, 60s, and 70s who modeled in their undergarments for an ad shoot. Accusations were levied that retouching contradicted the intent of the program to depict normal females as beautiful. A Unilever spokesperson responded that retouching was used only to remove dust and for color correction and that both the integrity of the photos and the women's natural beauty were maintained. The photographer involved in the photo shoot, however, indicated in interviews that signs of age were minimized and veins were removed from the images of the women. Unilever declined to make the original proofs or digital renderings available for inspection.

Application

1. Read more about the "Campaign for Real Beauty" and the retouching incident from the following sources:

   Dove campaign for real beauty to help foster self-esteem in girls. (2006, January 27). Dove Campaign for Real Beauty. Unilever. Available at www.campaignforrealbeauty.com/press.asp?id=4737§ion=news&target=press

   Neff, J. (2008, May 12). Retouching ruckus leaves Dove flailing. *Advertising Age, 79*(19). Available from Business Source Complete database.
2. Complete the following activities as directed by your instructor:
   a. Craft a statement suitable for placement on the Unilever/Dove website addressing the "realness" of models used in the "Campaign for Real Beauty" and decisions of the company concerning image enhancements.
   b. Write a short report on the ethical responsibilities involved in photo retouching. Address the issue of who wins and loses in such situations. Include other publicized examples in which photos were altered or enhanced and the resulting response from specific groups and the public in general.

© BBC LTD./COURTESY: EVERETT COLLECTION

2. Video Case: The Office: Diversity: To Point Out or Not To Point Out

In this clip, David introduces Ricky to Sange, an employee of Pakistani descent.

Complete the following activities as directed by your instructor after viewing the video:

1. In small groups, discuss the proper way to introduce colleagues in an office setting. Conduct research to locate information about introduction etiquette among those of a culture other than your own. Prepare an electronic slideshow that contrasts proper etiquette in making formal introductions among people from your culture and the selected cultural group. Give a presentation to the class, using your slideshow or post it electronically.
2. Considering the concepts of diversity discussed throughout the text, what mistakes does David make in his cross-cultural interaction? What tips can you provide to aid him in effective communications with those of other cultural backgrounds?

3. Lying Statistics

Three kinds of lies are possible, according to Benjamin Disraeli, a British prime minister in the nineteenth century—lies, damned lies, and statistics. A related notion exists that "you can prove anything with statistics." Such statements bolster the distrust that many people have for statistical analysis. On the other hand, many nonmathematicians hold quantitative data in awe, believing that numbers are, or at least should be, unquestionably correct. Consequently, it comes as a shock that various research studies can produce very different, often contradictory, results. To solve this paradox, many naive observers conclude that statistics must not really provide reliable indicators of reality after all, and if statistics aren't "right," they must be "wrong." It is easy to see how even intelligent, well-educated people can become cynical if they don't understand the concepts of statistical reasoning and analysis.

Consider, for instance, the frequent reporting of a "scientific discovery" in the fields of health and nutrition. The United States has become a nation of nervous people, ready to give up eating pleasures at the drop of a medical report. Today's "bad-for-you" food was probably once good for you, and vice versa. Twenty years ago, many consumers were turned away from consuming real butter to oily margarine, only to learn that the synthetically solidified oils of margarine, trans-fatty acids, are worse for our arteries than any fat found in nature. In the year following the publication of this finding, margarine sales dropped 8.2 percent and butter sales rose 1.4 percent.

Distrust also arises concerning studies that link exercise to health. Numerous studies have established statistically that people who exercise live longer. But the conclusion that exercise is good for you may put the cart before the horse. Are people healthy because they exercise? Or do they exercise because they are healthy? Correlation, once again, does not establish causation.

How do such incorrect and partial research findings become published and consequently disseminated through the media? Some of the responsibility should probably be cast upon researchers who may overstate the significance or the generalizability of their findings. The media should also shoulder some blame, as preliminary findings of small or limited studies are often reported as foregone conclusions. Consumers should also assume some responsibility in the interpretation of reported research. Questions such as the following should be asked when considering the value of reported findings:

- Is the study sample representative of the population involved?
- Were the statistical procedures used appropriate to the data?
- Has the research involved a sample of significant size and a sufficient time period of study?
- Were adequate controls applied to assure that outcomes are actually the result of the studied variable?
- Has the margin for error been taken into account in interpreting the results?
- Has any claim of causation been carefully examined using appropriate approaches?

The statement that "you can prove anything with statistics" is true only if statistics are used incorrectly. Understanding the basics of statistics is becoming increasingly important. With the prevalence of computers, vast amounts of data are available on every subject; and statistical packages allow analysis of these data with the press of a button, regardless of whether the analysis makes sense. Our professional and business lives thrive on numbers and our ability to interpret them correctly.

Visit your companion website at www.cengage.com/bcomm/lehman **to link to web resources related to this topic.** As directed by your instructor, complete one or more of the following:

1. Compile a list of behaviors or practices that can lead to the reporting of "lying statistics." For each item on your list, indicate whether the behavior or practice is likely an intentional or unintentional attempt to distort.
2. Write a one- to two-page analysis of the researcher's ethical responsibilities in reporting statistical results of a study versus the consumer's responsibilities in reading and interpreting the results.
3. Prepare a short spoken report in which you describe some of the issues that arise when reporting international economic statistics.

Chapter 11
Organizing and Preparing Reports and Proposals

"Our shareholders are our most valuable customers, and we believe that effective communication with our customers is crucial to the success of our business."

Aflac CEO Dan Amos

get the Aflacts SM
#5
Aflac belongs to you, not your company.
So make sure you take it with you.
M1485
4/09

© AP Images/PRNewsFoto/Aflac

Objectives When you have completed Chapter 11, you will be able to:

1. Identify the parts of a formal report and the contribution each part makes to the report's overall effectiveness.
2. Organize report findings.
3. Prepare effective formal reports using an acceptable format and writing style.
4. Prepare effective short reports in memorandum, email, and letter formats.
5. Prepare effective proposals for a variety of purposes.

SHOWCASE PART 1

Aflac Incorporated: Capitalizing on the Communication Power of the Annual Report

Of all the documents corporations publish, none receives as much attention as the annual report. Offering a valuable glimpse into the workings and financial performance of companies, these annual scorecards guide investors' decisions. Furthermore, annual reports serve as an ideal public relations mechanism to influence various stakeholders, including employees and the general public. Many managers are seizing the apparent opportunity to articulate effectively their company's corporate personality and philosophy.

One company that is successfully capitalizing on the communication power of its annual report is American Family Life Assurance Company (Aflac). A Fortune 500 company, Aflac insures more than 40 million people worldwide and is the largest life insurer in Japan. It has made its marketing fame as a leading underwriter of supplemental insurance.

According to the Aflac website, the company's mission is to combine innovative strategic marketing with quality products and services at competitive prices to provide the best insurance value for consumers. The company's motto is "Aflac pays you cash when you get hurt and miss work." While the Aflac duck catapulted the company's brand recognition from 12 percent to nearly 90 percent following its introduction in 2000, research has shown that consumers want to learn more about the company's products and services.[1]

The annual report is an important tool Aflac is using to convey its positive message. The company's annual reports have been honorably recognized every year since the inception of *Chief Executive* magazine's rating system of the best annual reports. Aflac's reports have consistently been assigned "World-Class" status by scoring at least 100 of a potential 135 points on the evaluation system. Commenting on the outstanding recognition, CEO Dan Amos said: "We are extremely pleased to see Aflac's annual report at the top of the list of the best annual reports. Our shareholders are our most valuable customers, and we believe that effective communication with our customers is crucial to the success of our business."[2]

The annual report rating is based on a 135-point copyrighted evaluation system that factors in elements ranging from extensive CEO involvement to more financial disclosure than is required by the Securities and Exchange Commission. According to Sid Cato, contributing editor and judge for *Chief Executive's* annual report listing, Aflac's annual reports feature strong writing, is externally focused, and celebrates the work of employees from the line worker all the way up to the CEO.[3]

Careful design and organization of Aflac's annual report have led to positive public recognition and likely improved the company's competitive edge. Similarly, you will want the reports you produce to be effective for their desired purpose. Each part must be carefully crafted and reviewed to make sure it is as perfect as possible and contains all necessary support and documentation. Finally, your skills in combining all the various parts into a clear, concise whole will assure that your report receives a "number one" rating.

www.aflac.com

SEE SHOWCASE PART 2, ON PAGE 393 FOR SPOTLIGHT COMMUNICATOR SID CATO, CONTRIBUTING EDITOR FOR *CHIEF EXECUTIVE* AND AUTHOR OF THE OFFICIAL ANNUAL REPORT WEBSITE.

Parts of a Formal Report

As you learned in Chapter 9, reports serve a variety of purposes. The type of report you prepare depends on the subject matter, the purpose of the report, and the readers' needs. The differences between a formal report and an informal report lie in the format and possibly in the writing style. At the short, informal end of the report continuum described in Chapter 9, a report could look exactly like a brief memorandum. At the long, formal extreme of the continuum, the report might include most or all of the parts shown in Figure 11-1.

A business report rarely contains all of the parts shown but may include any combination of them. The preliminary parts and addenda are organizational items that support the body of a report. The body contains the report of the research and covers the four steps in the research process. The organization of the body of a report leads to the construction of the contents page.

What factors determine the parts of a report that are desirable to include?

Because individuals usually write to affect or influence others favorably, they often add report parts as the number of pages increases. When a report exceeds one or two pages, you might add a cover or title page. When the body of a report exceeds four or five pages, you might even add a finishing touch by placing the report in a binder or binding in a professional manner. Reports frequently take on the characteristics of the formal end of the continuum simply by reason of length. First, note how the preliminary parts and addenda items shown in Figure 11-2 increase in number as the report increases

FIGURE 11-1

Parts of a Formal Report: Preliminary Parts, Report Text, and Addenda

Preliminary Parts

Half-title page (Title Fly)	Title page	Authorization	Transmittal	Table of contents	Table of figures	Executive summary
Contains report title; adds formality.	Includes title, author, and date; adds formality.	Provides written authorization to complete report.	Presents report to reader and summarizes main points or analysis.	Provides overview of report and order in which information will be presented; contains headings and page numbers.	Includes number, title, and page number of tables and graphics.	Summarizes essential elements in report.

Report Text

Introduction	Body	Analysis
Orients reader to topic and previews major divisions.	Presents information collected.	Reviews main points presented in body and may include conclusions and recommendations.

Addenda

References	Appendixes	Index
Includes alphabetical list of sources used in preparing report.	Contains supplementary information that supports report, but placing this information in report would make report bulky and unmanageable.	Includes alphabetical guide to subjects in report.

FIGURE 11-2

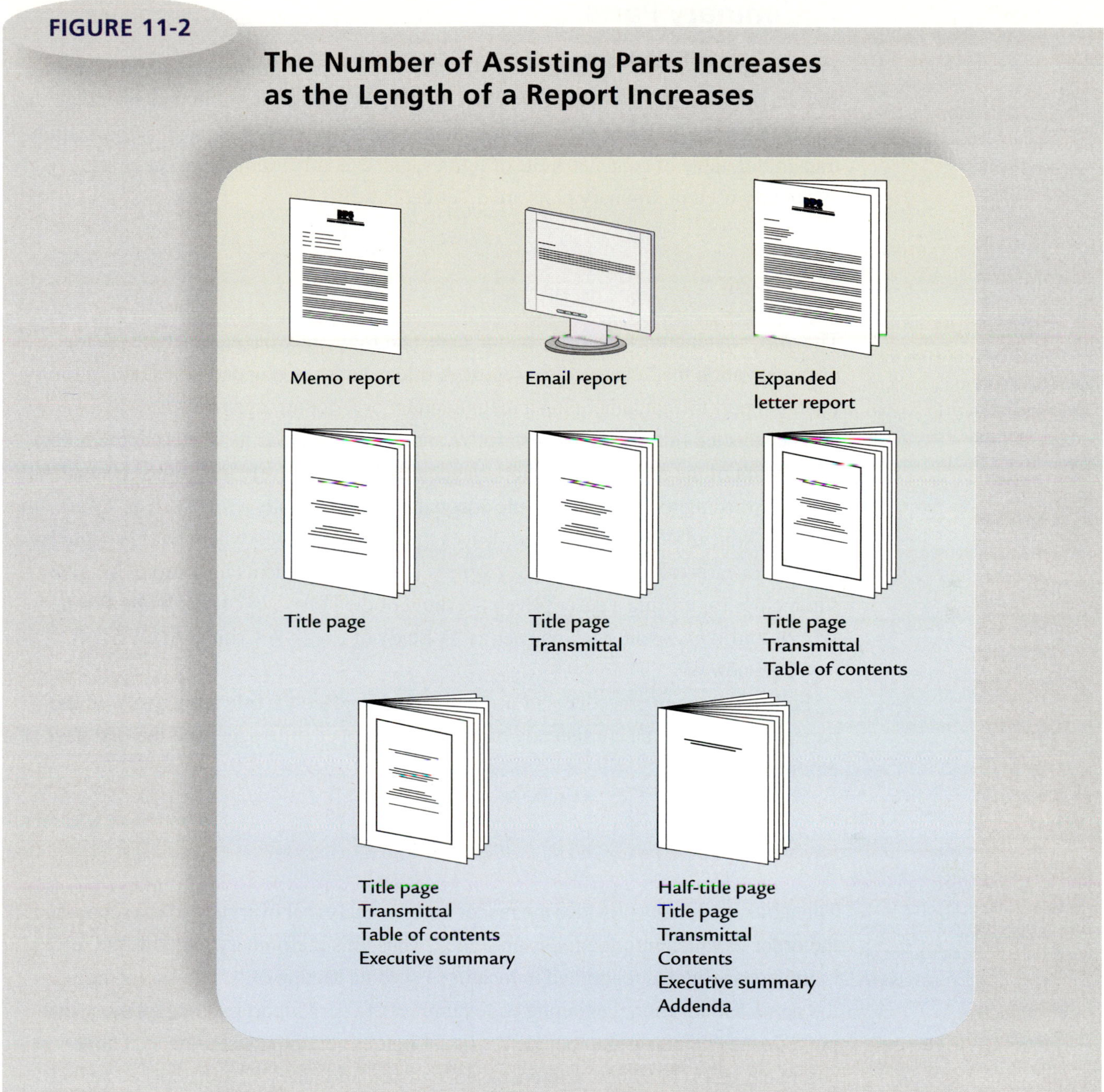

The Number of Assisting Parts Increases as the Length of a Report Increases

in length. Second, notice the order in which report parts appear in a complete report and the distribution of reports in print and electronic forms.

Memo and letter reports are often one page in length, but they can be expanded into several pages. As depicted, long reports may include some special pages that do not appear in short reports. The format you select—long or short, formal or informal—may help determine the supporting preliminary and addenda items to include.

To understand how each part of a formal report contributes to reader comprehension and ease of access to the information in the report, study the following explanations of each part shown in Figure 11-1. The three basic sections—preliminary parts, report text, and addenda—are combined to prepare a complete formal report.

Preliminary Parts

Preliminary parts are included to add formality to a report, emphasize report content, and aid the reader in locating information in the report quickly and in understanding the report more easily. These parts might include a half-title page, title page, authorization, transmittal, table of contents, table of figures, and executive summary. The most frequently used preliminary parts are described here.

Title Page

Write an effective title for a report to select a mobile phone carrier and rate plan for a pharmaceutical sales force.

The ***title page*** includes the title, author, date, and frequently the name of the person or organization that requested the report. A title page is often added when opting for a formal report format rather than a memorandum or letter arrangement.

The selected title should be descriptive and comprehensive; its words should reflect the content of the report. Avoid short, vague titles or excessively long titles. Instead, use concise wording to identify the topic adequately. For example, a title such as "Marketing Survey: Noncarbonated Beverages" leaves the reader confused when the title could have been "Noncarbonated Beverage Preferences of College Students in Boston." To give some clues for writing a descriptive title, think of the "Five Ws": *Who, What, When, Where,* and *Why*. Avoid such phrases as "A Study of . . . ," "A Critical Analysis of . . . ," or "A Review of . . . ."

Follow company procedures or a style manual to place the title attractively on the page. Arrange the title consistently on the half-title page, title page, and the first page of a report.

Table of Contents

How does the contents page contribute to the coherence of a formal report?

The table of contents provides the reader with an analytical overview of the report and the order in which information is presented. Thus, this preliminary part aids the reader in understanding the report and in locating a specific section of it. The list includes the name and location (beginning page number) of every report part except those that precede the contents page. Include the list of figures and the transmittal, executive summary, report headings, references, appendixes, and index. Placing spaced periods (leaders) between the report part and the page numbers helps lead the reader's eyes to the appropriate page number.

Word processing software simplifies the time-consuming, tedious task of preparing many of the preliminary and addenda report parts, including the contents. Because the software can generate these parts automatically, report writers can make last-minute changes to a report with updated preliminary and addenda parts.

Table of Figures

To aid the reader in locating a specific graphic in a report with many graphics, the writer might include a list of figures separate from the contents. The list should include a reference to each figure that appears in the report, identified by both figure number

and name, along with the page number on which the figure occurs. The contents and the figures can be combined on one page if both lists are brief. Word processing software can be used to generate the list of figures automatically.

Executive Summary

The executive summary (also called the *abstract*, *overview*, or *précis*) summarizes the essential elements in an entire report. This overview simplifies the reader's understanding of a long report and is positioned before the first page of the report.

Typically, an executive summary is included to assist the reader in understanding a long, complex report. Because of the increased volume of information that managers must review, some managers require an executive summary regardless of the length and complexity of a report. The executive summary presents the report in miniature: the introduction, body, and summary as well as any conclusions and recommendations. Thus, an executive summary should (1) introduce briefly the report and preview the major divisions, (2) summarize the major sections of the report, and (3) summarize the report summary and any conclusions and recommendations. Pay special attention to topic sentences and to concluding sentences in paragraphs or within sections of reports. This technique helps you write concise executive summaries based on major ideas and reduces the use of supporting details and background information.

An executive summary, or abstract, serves the immediate reader as well as "distant readers." Explain.

To assist them in staying up-to-date professionally, busy executives frequently request assistants to prepare executive summaries of articles they do not have time to read and conferences and meetings they cannot attend. Many practitioner journals include an executive summary (abstract) of each article. The executive summary provides the gist of the article and alerts the executive to articles that should be read in detail. The executive summary is prepared with the needs of specific executive readers in mind. For instance, a technically oriented executive may require more detail; a strategist, more analysis. An executive summary should "boil down" a report to its barest essentials, without making the overview meaningless. Top executives should be able to glean enough information and understanding to feel confident making a decision.

Preliminary pages are numbered with small Roman numerals (i, ii, iii, and so on). Figure 11-1 provides more information about the purpose of each preliminary part. To learn more about other preliminary pages and their format and function, visit your companion website at www.cengage.com/bcomm/lehman.

Report Text

The report itself contains the introduction, body, summary, and any conclusions and recommendations. Report pages are numbered with Arabic numerals (1, 2, 3, and so on).

Introduction

The introduction orients the reader to the problem. It may include the following items:

- what the topic is
- why it is being reported on

- the scope and limitations of the research
- where the information came from
- an explanation of special terminology
- a preview of the major sections of the report to provide coherence and transitions:
  - how the topic is divided into parts
  - the order in which the parts will be presented

Body

The ***body***, often called the heart of the report, presents the information collected and relates it to the problem. To increase readability and coherence, this section contains numerous headings to denote the various divisions within a report. Refer to "Organization of Formal Reports" in this chapter for an in-depth discussion of preparing the body.

Analysis

How do an informational and an analytical report differ? How is each used in business?

A good report ends with an analysis of what the reported information means or how it should be acted upon. An informational report ends with a brief ***summary*** that adds unity to a report by reviewing the main points presented in the body. A summary includes only material that is discussed in a report. Introducing a new idea in the summary may suggest that the study was not completed adequately or that the writer did not plan the report well before beginning to write.

An ***analytical report*** is designed to solve a specific problem or answer research questions. It will end with an "analysis," which may include a summary of the major research findings, particularly if the report is lengthy. Reviewing the major findings prepares the reader for the ***conclusions***, which are inferences the writer draws from the findings. If required by the person/organization authorizing the report, recommendations follow the conclusions. ***Recommendations*** present the writer's opinion on a possible course of action based on the conclusions. Review the examples of findings, conclusions, and recommendations presented in Chapter 9.

For a long report, the writer may place the summary, the conclusions, and the recommendations in three separate sections or in a section referred to as "Analysis." For shorter reports, all three sections are often combined.

Addenda

What addenda parts might be added to a report making a health care plan recommendation for company personnel?

The ***addenda*** to a report may include materials used in the research that are not appropriate to be included in the report itself. The three basic addenda parts are the references, appendixes, and index. Addenda parts continue with the same page numbering system used in the body of the report.

References

The ***references*** (also called *works cited* or *bibliography*) section is an alphabetical listing of the sources used in preparing the report. Because the writer may be influenced by any information consulted, some reference manuals require all sources consulted to be included in the reference list. When the reference list includes sources not cited in the report, it is referred to as a ***bibliography*** or a list of ***works consulted***. If a report includes endnotes rather than in-text parenthetical citations (author and date within the text), the endnotes precede the references. Using word processing software to create footnotes and endnotes reduces much of the effort of preparing accurate documentation. Refer to "Documenting Referenced Material" in Chapter 9, Appendix B, or a style manual for specific guidelines for citations.

Appendix

An ***appendix*** contains supplementary information that supports the report but is not appropriate for inclusion in the report itself. This information may include questionnaires and accompanying transmittal letters, summary tabulations, verbatim comments from respondents, complex mathematical computations and formulas, legal documents, and a variety of items the writer presents to support the body of the report and the quality of the research. Placing supplementary material in an appendix helps prevent the report body from becoming excessively long.

What criteria would you use to decide whether to place material in the body of the text or in an appendix?

If the report contains more than one appendix, label each with a capital letter and a title. For example, the two appendixes (or appendices) in a report could be identified as follows:

Appendix A: Cover Letter Accompanying Customer Satisfaction Survey
Appendix B: Customer Satisfaction Survey

Each item included in the appendix must be mentioned in the report. A reference within the report to the two appendixes mentioned in the previous example follows:

The cover message (Appendix A) and the customer satisfaction survey (Appendix B) were distributed by email to 1,156 firms on February 15, 2011.

Index

The ***index*** is an alphabetical guide to the subject matter in a report. The subject and each page number on which the subject appears are listed. Word processing software can generate the index automatically. Each time a new draft is prepared, a new index with revised terms and correct page numbers can be generated quickly and easily.

Your Turn 11-1
Electronic Café

EXTRANETS—INTRANETS' CYBERSPACE COUSINS

Extranets can be thought of as cyberspace cousins to intranets. Whereas intranets allow only internal colleagues to communicate with each other, extranets typically include on their guest lists selected business partners, suppliers, and customers. This selective sharing is in addition to the company's public website, which is accessible to everyone. Extranets are an increasingly important means of delivering services and communicating efficiently. The following electronic activities will allow you to learn more about the role of extranets in companies' external communications:

TAKE ACTION:

- *Read about how a company is using its extranet to expand global business.* Access the following article:

  Brown, J. (2006, February 9). Enterprise: Office technology company deploys European extranet. *Computing, 12*. Available from www.accessmylibrary.com/coms2/summary_0286-12668712_ITM.

Write a brief summary of the advantages the extranet provides for both Pitney Bowes and its European dealers.

- Visit your companion website, www.cengage.com/bcomm/lehman, for more information on how organizations use intranets.

Organization of Formal Reports

The authors of certain types of publications known as tabloids typically have no valid documentation to support their claims, so they make up their own support. Hopefully, absolutely no one believes them. The purpose of such publications is to entertain, not to inform. The writer of a bona fide report, however, must do a much more convincing and thorough job of reporting.

Writing Convincing and Effective Reports

Complete the following analogy: Outline is to report as ________ is to __________.

As discussed in Chapter 9, reports often require you to conduct research to find quotes, statistics, or ideas from others to back up the ideas presented. This support from outside sources serves to bolster the research as well as your credibility. Doing research and taking notes, however, are only parts of the process of putting together a well-documented, acceptable report. Careful organization and formatting ensure that the reader will understand and comprehend the information presented. While many companies have their own style manuals that give examples of acceptable formats for reports, this section presents some general organization guidelines.

Outlining and Sequencing

Why is an outline considered to be a "penciled" document?

The content outline serves as a framework on which to build the report. In the development of the outline, the writer identifies the major and minor points that are to be covered and organizes them into a logical sequence. Outlining is an essential

Finding Meaning in Financial Analysis. Stockholders, creditors, and other parties want and need to know about a company's financial position. The primary purpose of an annual report is to communicate relevant, useful, and reliable financial information about a company. Annual report requirements were tightened by the Securities and Exchange Commission (SEC) following significant business scandals and failures. Current SEC guidelines require that companies' annual reports include comprehensive and detailed financial information, as well as thorough analysis. Publicly-held companies spend thousands of dollars and hundreds of hours each year preparing the annual report, yet many reports go unopened as they include more financial information than the average investor desires to receive or can comprehend. An effectively written annual report can reduce stockholder uncertainty about the firm.

© AP IMAGES/MANUEL BALCE CENETA

prerequisite to writing the report. The outline is a planning document and is thus subject to modification as the writer develops the report.

Developing an outline requires the writer to think about the information to be presented and how it can best be organized for the clear understanding of the reader. Assume, for instance, that you must select a smartphone (integrates a cell phone with wireless email and web access and rich-media capabilities) from among three comparable brands—Palm, Apple iPhone, and Blackberry. You must choose the smartphone that will best serve the portable computing needs of a small office and present your reasons and recommendations in a ***justification report***.

You gather all available information from the suppliers of the three smartphones, operate each device personally, and compare the three against a variety of criteria. Your final selection is the Blackberry. Why did you select it? What criteria served as decision guides? When you write the report, you will have to tell the reader—the one who will pay for the equipment—how the selection was made so that he or she is "sold" on your conclusion.

© AP IMAGES/PRNEWSFOTO/ MEZEO SOFTWARE CORPORATION

If you organize your report so that you tell the reader everything about the Palm, the Apple iPhone, and the Blackberry each in a separate section, the reader may have trouble making comparisons. Your content outline might look like this:

Ineffective Example ☒

I. Introduction
  A. The Problem
  B. The Method Used
II. Palm
III. Apple iPhone
IV. Blackberry
V. Conclusion

Note that this outline devotes three Roman numeral sections to the findings, one to the introduction that presents the problem and the method, and one to the conclusion. This division is appropriate because the most space must be devoted to the findings. However, the reader may have difficulty comparing the expansion capacity of the smartphones because the information is in three different places. Would discussing the expansion capacity of all three in the same section of the report be better? Would prices be compared more easily if they were all in the same section? Most reports should be divided into sections that reflect the criteria used rather than into sections devoted to the alternatives compared.

If you selected your computer based on cost, service/warranties, expandability, and availability of applications, these criteria (rather than the smartphone options themselves) might serve as divisions of the findings. Then your content outline would appear this way:

I. Introduction
   A. The Problem
   B. The Methods Used
II. Product Comparison
   A. Palm Is Least Expensive
   B. Service/Warranties Favor Blackberry
   C. Expandability Is Best on Blackberry
   D. Availability of Applications Is Equal
III. Conclusion: Blackberry Is the Best Buy

The outline now has three major sections, with the product comparison consisting of four subsections. When the report is prepared in this way, the features of each smartphone (the evaluation criteria) are compared in the same section, and the reader is led logically to the conclusion.

Note the headings used in Sections II and III. These are called ***talking headings*** because they talk about the content of the section and even give a conclusion about the section. Adding page numbers after each outline item will convert the outline into a contents page. Interestingly, the headings justify the selection of the Blackberry. As a result, a knowledgeable reader who has confidence in the researcher might be satisfied by reading only the content headings.

What organizational plan would you use for outlining a report on a corporate office relocation to another state?

In addition to organizing findings for analytical reports by criteria, report writers can also use other organizational plans. When a report is informational and not analytical, you should use the most logical organization. A report on sales might be divided by geographic sales region, by product groups sold, by price range, or by time periods. A report on the development of a product might use chronological order. By visualizing the whole report first, you can then divide it into its major components and perhaps divide the major components into their parts.

A final caution: Beware of overdividing the sections. Too many divisions might make the report appear disorganized and choppy. On the other hand, too few divisions might cloud understanding for the reader.

When developing content outlines, some report writers believe that readers expect the beginning of the body to be an introduction, so they begin the outline with the first heading related to findings. In our example, then, Section I would be "Product Comparison." Additionally, when they reach the contents page, readers may eliminate the Roman numeral or other outline symbols.

What relation does a report outline have to the final report document?

The research process consists of inductively arranged steps as shown in Figure 11-3: (1) Problem, (2) Method, (3) Findings, and (4) Conclusion. Note how the four steps of research have been developed through headings in the Roman numeral outline and to a contents page for a report. When the report is organized in the same order, its users must read through the body to learn about the conclusions—generally the most important part of the report to users. To make the reader's job easier, report writers may organize the report deductively, with the conclusions at the beginning. This sequence is usually achieved by placing a synopsis or summary at the beginning:

Report Title in Deductive Sequence Reveals the Conclusion

I. Conclusion Reported in the Synopsis
II. Body of the Report
  A. Problem
  B. Method
  C. Findings
III. Conclusion

This arrangement permits the reader to get the primary message early and then to look for support in the body of the report. The deductive arrangement contributes to the repetitious nature of reports, but it also facilitates understanding.

FIGURE 11-3

The Basic Outline Expands into a Contents Page

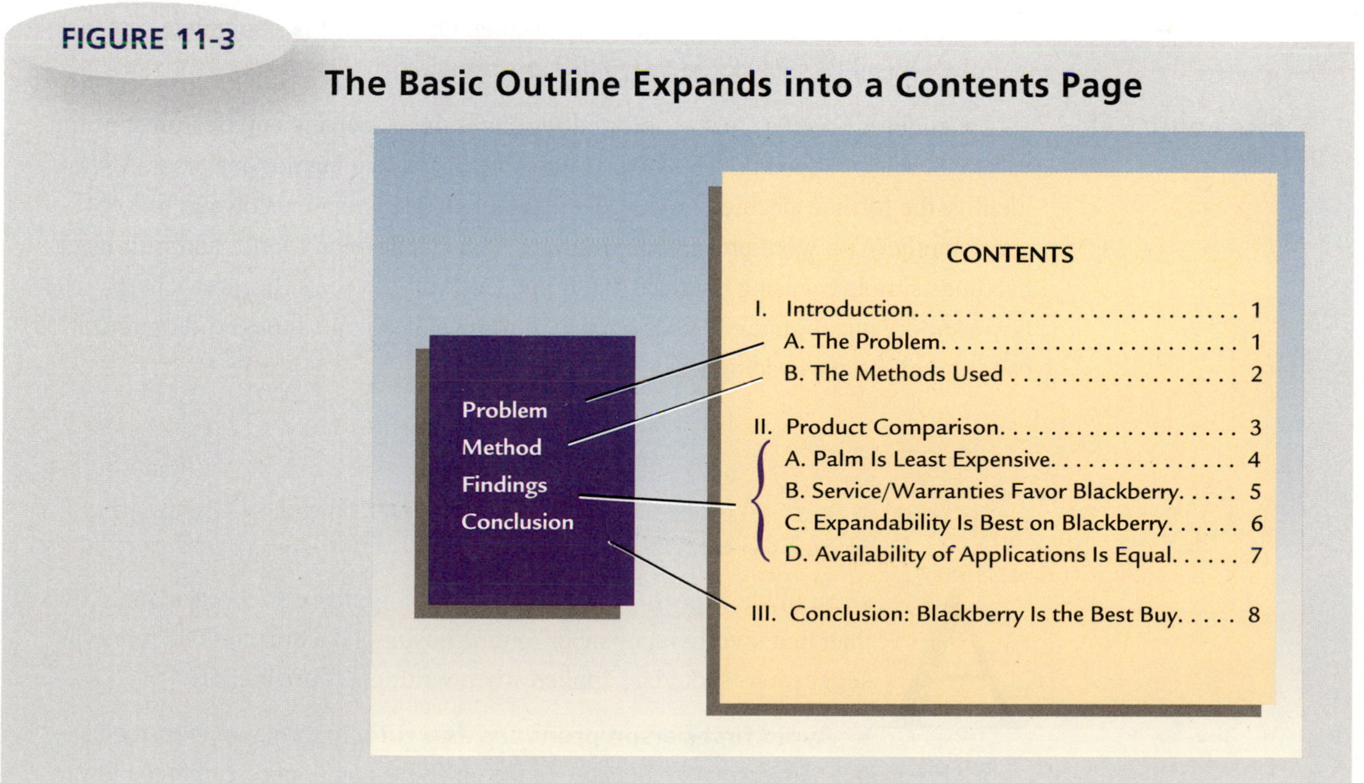

Problem
Method
Findings
Conclusion
CONTENTS
I. Introduction. 1
A. The Problem. 1
B. The Methods Used 2
II. Product Comparison. 3
A. Palm Is Least Expensive. 4
B. Service/Warranties Favor Blackberry. 5
C. Expandability Is Best on Blackberry. 6
D. Availability of Applications Is Equal. 7
III. Conclusion: Blackberry Is the Best Buy. 8

Using Headings Effectively

What formatting techniques can be used to differentiate levels of headings?

Headings are signposts informing readers about what text is ahead. Headings take their positions from their relative importance in a complete outline. For example, in a Roman numeral outline, "I" is a first-level heading, "A" is a second-level heading, and "1" is a third-level heading:

I. First-Level Heading
  A. Second-Level Heading
  B. Second-Level Heading
    1. Third-Level Heading
    2. Third-Level Heading
II. First-Level Heading

Two important points about the use of headings also relate to outlines:

Make the following headings from a sales analysis parallel: Sales in Northeast Are Flat, Sales Increase Dramatically in Southwest, Increasing Sales in West, Midwest Experienced No Change in Sales.

- **Because second-level headings are subdivisions of first-level headings, you should have at least two subdivisions (A and B).** Otherwise, the first-level heading cannot be divided—something divides into at least two parts or it is not divisible. Thus, in an outline, you must have a "B" subsection if you have an "A" subsection following a Roman numeral, or you should have no subsections. The same logic applies to the use of third-level headings following second-level headings.
- **All headings of the same level must be treated consistently.** Consistent elements include the physical position on the page, appearance (type style, underline), and grammatical construction. For instance, if Point A is worded as a noun phrase, Point B should be worded in the same manner. Or if Point I is a complete sentence, Points II and III should also be worded as sentences.

Appendix A provides further information about the placement and treatment of the various levels of headings. The method illustrated is typical but not universal. Always identify the format specified by the documentation style you are using and follow it consistently. With word processing programs, you can develop fourth- and fifth-level headings simply by using boldface, underline, and varying fonts. In short reports, however, organization rarely goes beyond third-level headings; thoughtful organization can limit excessive heading levels in formal reports.

3 OBJECTIVE

Choosing a Writing Style for Formal Reports

As you might expect, the writing style of long, formal reports is more formal than that used in many other routine business documents. The following suggestions should be applied when writing a formal report:

- **Avoid first-person pronouns as a rule.** In formal reports, the use of *I* is generally unacceptable. Because of the objective nature of research, the fewer personal references you use the better. However, in some organizations the first person is acceptable. Certainly, writing is easier when you can use yourself as the subject of sentences.

- **Use active voice.** "Authorization was received from the IRS" might not be as effective as "The IRS granted authorization." Subjects that can be visualized are advantageous, but you should also attempt to use the things most important to the report as subjects. If "authorization" were more important than "IRS," the writer should stay with the first version.
- **Use tense consistently.** Because you are writing about past actions, much of your report writing is in the past tense. However, when you call the reader's attention to the content of a graphic, remember that the graphic *shows* in the present tense. If you mention the study *will convince* the reader, use a future-tense verb.
- **Avoid placing two headings consecutively without any intervening text.** For example, always write something following a first-level heading and before the initial second-level heading.
- **Use transition sentences to link sections of a report.** Because you are writing a report in parts, show the connection between those parts by using transition sentences. "Although several advantages accrue from its use, the incentive plan also presents problems" may be a sentence written at the end of a section stressing advantages and before a section stressing problems.

Compose a transition sentence to move from a discussion of Company A's phone plan to Company B's phone plan as the better choice for employees.

Time Connectors	Contrast Connectors
at the same time	although
finally	despite
further	however
initially	in contrast
next	nevertheless
since	on the contrary
then	on the other hand
while	yet

Similarity Connectors	Cause-and-Effect Connectors
for instance/example	alternately
in the same way	because
just as	but
likewise	consequently
similarly	hence
thus	therefore

- **Use a variety of coherence techniques.** Just as transition sentences bind portions of a report together, certain coherence techniques bind sentences together: repeating a word, using a pronoun, or using a conjunction. If such devices are used, each sentence seems to be joined smoothly to the next. These words and phrases keep you from making abrupt changes in thought.

Additional ideas about transitional wording are covered in Chapter 4, "Link Ideas to Achieve Coherence" and "Apply Visual Enhancements to Improve Readability." Other ways to improve transition include the following:

- **Use tabulations and enumerations.** When you have a series of items, bullet them or give each a number and list them consecutively. This list of writing suggestions is easier to understand because it contains bulleted items.
- **Define terms carefully.** When terms are not widely understood or have specific meanings in the study, define them. Definitions should be written in the term-family-differentiation sequence: "A dictionary (*term*) is a reference book (*family*) that contains a list of all words in a language (*point of difference*)." "A sophomore is a college student in the second year." Refer to Chapter 9 for additional information on defining terms in a research study.
- **Check for variety.** In your first-draft stage, most of your attention should be directed toward presenting the right ideas and support. When reviewing the rough draft, you may discover certain portions with a monotonous sameness in sentence length or construction. Changes and improvements in writing style at this stage are easy and well worth the effort.

Your Turn 11-2
Miscue

Readability analyses of 60 financial privacy notices found that they are written at a third- to fourth-year college level, instead of the junior high school level recommended for the general public. Consumers will have a hard time understanding the notices because the writing style uses too many complicated sentences and uncommon words. Recent census data indicated that about 85 percent of adults have a high school diploma, and about 25 percent have college degrees. Despite these findings, research shows that many people read three to five grade levels below their education level, and for many, English is not their primary language.[6] For such individuals, privacy notices and other documents often are not understood.

TAKE ACTION:

- Search online for a privacy notice or other consumer notice posted by a financial institution, health agency, etc. Using cut and paste commands, move the document into your word processing software and run a grammar check to determine the reading level.
- How appropriate is the reading level to the intended audience? How could the document be rewritten for better impact?

Enhancing Credibility

Readers are more likely to accept your research as valid and reliable if you have designed the research effectively and collected, interpreted, and presented the data in an objective, unbiased manner. The following writing suggestions will enhance your credibility as a researcher:

- **Avoid emotional terms.** "The increase was fantastic" doesn't convince anyone. However, "The increase was 88 percent—more than double that of the previous year" does convince.
- **Identify assumptions.** Assumptions are things or conditions taken for granted. However, when you make an assumption, state that clearly. Statements such as "Assuming all other factors remain the same . . ." inform the reader of an important assumption.
- **Label opinions.** Facts are preferred over opinion, but sometimes the opinion of a recognized professional is the closest thing to fact. "In the opinion of legal counsel, . . ." lends conviction to the statement that follows and lends credence to the integrity of the writer.
- **Use documentation.** Citations and references (works cited) are evidence of the writer's scholarship and honesty. These methods acknowledge the use of secondary material in the research.

How can the report writer "dignify" an included opinion?

Effective writing requires concentration and the removal of distractions. A writing procedure that works well for one person may not work for another. However, some general guidelines for creating an environment conducive to effective writing are available on your companion website, www.cengage.com/bcomm/lehman.

Cultural variances, as well as legal and business requirements in some countries, may dictate the content and style of reports, as discussed in the Strategic Forces feature "Disclosure in Annual Financial Reports of International Firms."

Analyzing a Formal Report

A sample long report following APA style is available at the companion website at www.cengage.com/bcomm/lehman. The notations next to the text will help you understand how effective presentation and writing principles are applied.

DIVERSITY CHALLENGES

STRATEGIC FORCES

Disclosure in Annual Financial Reports of International Firms

The annual financial report is the basic tool used by investors to compare the performance of various companies. While U.S. firms must comply with Security and Exchange Commission (SEC) requirements for disclosure, the extent to which information is reported by companies based abroad varies.

For the most part, companies in English-speaking countries do a good job with disclosure. Annual reports of American and British firms provide much more than just a balance sheet and a profit-and-loss statement; they typically provide a comprehensive set of notes giving additional information—for instance, on how a firm's pension liabilities are calculated or whether assets have been sold and leased back. Passage in the United States of the Sarbanes-Oxley Act of 2002 heightened requirements for disclosure in response to widely publicized corporate scandals. These changes represent solid progress in enhancing user's understanding of the choices and judgments that underlie a set of financial statements. On the other hand, some information published in the annual report must be limited in detail to prevent competitors and possible takeover bidders from gaining useful but damaging knowledge of the organization.[4]

In some countries such as Germany, any information beyond the basic annual report is often nonexistent, in published form or otherwise. National requirements vary, as do voluntary responses of individual companies within a given country. More and more international firms, however, are reporting their financial results according to the International Financial Reporting Standards (IFRS) issued by the International Accounting Standards Board. While the board has no authority to require compliance with its standards, many countries require financial statements of publicly-traded companies to comply.[5] In the United States, the SEC requires international firms wishing to list their shares on an American exchange to comply with the United States' Generally Accepted Accounting Principles (GAAP).

Currently, in the United States and some other countries, a firm's annual financial report is recognized as communicating much more than just the accounting summary of the organization's performance. Management realizes this single communication document is scrutinized by three groups of vital partners: the customers, the owners, and the employees. In addition to projecting profitability, many U.S. firms see the annual report as a vehicle for illuminating management philosophy, projecting corporate charisma, and humanizing themselves to their publics.

Application

Using the Internet or a published source, obtain the annual financial report for a company based abroad. Write a short report that analyzes your responses to the following questions:

- Did the report contain the company's mission statement?
- Was the company's code of ethics, or credo, included?
- Was information provided about the company directors, officers, and/or executives?
- Were the major shareholders reported?
- What currency was used in the financial reporting (dollars, yen, pounds, etc.)?
- Was evidence provided of company concern for the environment or charities?
- How extensive and sophisticated were the graphics and photos?

CHANGING TECHNOLOGY

APA style requires that reports be double-spaced and that the first line of each paragraph be indented a half inch; however, a company's report-writing style manual may override this style and stipulate single or default spacing without paragraph indents. The sample report illustrates contemporary spacing with 1.15 spaces between lines and 10 points between paragraphs and paragraphs are not indented to save space and give a more professional appearance. The report may be considered formal and contains the following parts:

- Title Page
- Transmittal
- Table of Contents
- Table of Figures
- Executive Summary
- Report Text (Introduction, Body, Analysis)
- References
- Appendix

This sample should not be considered the only way to prepare reports, but it is an acceptable model. The "Check Your Communication" section at the end of the chapter provides a comprehensive checklist for use in preparing effective reports.

SHOWCASE PART 2

Promoting Annual Reports that Make the Grade

As contributing editor and the judge for *Chief Executive* magazine's annual report listing, Sid Cato is recognized by many as the world's foremost authority on annual reports. The annual listing, which has appeared in the magazine's November issue for over 20 years, is based on evaluations of reports submitted from around the world, according to a 135-point copyrighted evaluation system. Cato says the annual report is "the number one document a company can produce. It's the key corporate communiqué. It indicates how the company feels about itself."[7] Cato feels that the worst thing that can happen in an annual report is for management not to explain the numbers.

www.aflac.com
www.sidcato.com

© CATO COMMUNICATIONS

SPOTLIGHT COMMUNICATOR: SID CATO, CONTRIBUTING EDITOR, *CHIEF EXECUTIVE* AND AUTHOR OF THE OFFICIAL ANNUAL REPORT WEBSITE

REFER TO SHOWCASE PART 3, ON PAGE 410
TO LEARN ABOUT THE EFFECTIVE USE OF A THEME IN ANNUAL REPORTS.

Short Reports

Short reports incorporate many of the same organizational strategies as do long reports. However, most ***short reports*** include only the minimum supporting materials to achieve effective communication. Short reports focus on the body—problem, method, findings, and conclusion. In addition, short reports might incorporate any of the following features:

- personal writing style using first or second person
- contractions when they contribute to a natural style
- graphics to reinforce the written text
- headings and subheadings to partition portions of the body and to reflect organization
- memorandum, email, and letter formats when appropriate

Memorandum, Email, and Letter Reports

Besides the difference in length, how do short reports differ from long, formal reports?

Short reports are often written in memorandum, email, or letter format. The memorandum report is directed to an organizational insider, as are most email reports. The letter report is directed to a reader outside the organization. Short reports to internal and external readers are illustrated in Figures 11-4 and 11-5. The commentary in the left column will help you understand how effective writing principles are applied.

The memo report in Figure 11-4 communicates the activity of a company's child care services during one quarter of the fiscal period. The periodic report is formatted as a memorandum because it is prepared for personnel within the company and is a brief, informal report. An outside consultant presents an audit of a company's software policy in the short report in Figure 11-5. A concise, professional email will serve as a transmittal for this one-page report sent to the client as an email attachment.

The report in Figure 11-6 is written deductively. Implementation of cross-cultural virtual teams is described in an expanded letter report written by a consultant to a client (external audience). The consultant briefly describes the procedures used to analyze the problem, presents the findings in a logical sequence, and provides specific recommendations.

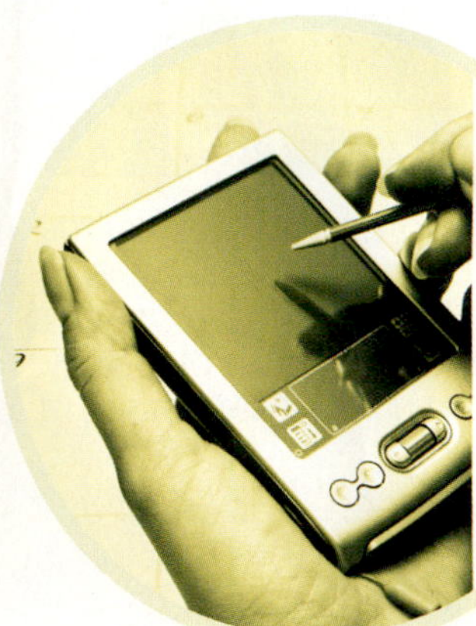

Your Turn 11-3
Career Portfolio

Choosing a career involves researching and comparing opportunities available to you. While the investment of time and energy is significant, the results are worth the effort.

TAKE ACTION:

Prepare a three-page report on career outlook and opportunities for your chosen career field based on research from government handbooks, yearbooks, and online materials that project the outlook of your career. Divide your report into the following sections: (1) the career you have chosen, with reasons; (2) the relative demand for that career over the next five to ten years; and (3) the pay scale and other benefits that are typical of that career. Include references from at least four sources, using APA style (or another style, as directed by your instructor). Supply appropriate title and reference pages.

FIGURE 11-4

Short, Periodic Report in Memorandum Format

Includes headings to serve formal report functions of transmittal and title page.

Uses deductive approach to present periodic report requested by management on quarterly basis.

Uses headings to highlight standard information; allows for easy update when preparing subsequent report.

Includes primary data from survey completed by parents.

Attaches information page that would be appendix item in a formal report.

THE PLAY STATION *(Child Care and Learning Center)*

1560 Kingsbury Lane / Arlington, VA 22922 / 703-555-6413 FAX 703-555-0919

TO: Alyssa Foster, Director, Human Resources

FROM: Connor Klasson, Coordinator, Child Care Services *CK*

DATE: September 14, 2011

SUBJECT: Quarterly Report on In-House Child Care Center, Second Quarter, 2011

The in-house child care center experienced a successful second quarter. Data related to enrollment and current staffing follow:

Enrollment: 92 children, up from 84 at end of first quarter.

Staff: Ten full-time staff members, including six attendants, three teachers, and one registered nurse.

Registration for the upcoming school year is presently underway and is exceeding projected figures. Current staff size will necessitate an enrollment cap of 98. Further increases in enrollment will be possible only if additional personnel are hired.

The payroll deduction method of payment, instituted on January 1, has ensured that operations remain profitable. It has also eliminated the time and expense of billing. Parents seem satisfied with the arrangement as well.

Full license renewal is expected in August as we have met and/or exceeded all state and county requirements for facilities, staff, and programs.

Favorable results were obtained from the employee satisfaction poll, which was administered to parents participating in the child care program. Ninety-one percent indicated that they were very satisfied or extremely satisfied with our in-house child care program. The most frequently mentioned suggestion for improvement was the extension of hours until 7 p.m. This change would allow employees time to run necessary errands after work, before picking up their children. We might consider this addition of services on a per-hour rate basis. A copy of the survey instrument is provided for your review.

Call me should you wish to discuss the extended service hours idea or any other aspects of this report.

Attachment

Format Pointer

- Uses a memorandum format for brief periodic report prepared for personnel within company.

FIGURE 11-5

Audit Report in Short Report Format

Introduces overall topic and leads into procedures and findings.

Uses side heading to denote beginning of body.

Uses bulleted list to add emphasis to important information.

Summarizes major point in table and refers reader to it. Does not number this single figure.

Formats data in four-column table to facilitate reading and uses clear title and column headings.

Uses side heading to denote beginning of recommendation section.

Uses enumerations to emphasize recommendations.

Computer Software Audit for Spectrum Analysis

The personal computer software audit for Spectrum Analysis has been completed according to the procedures recommended by Software Publishers Association. These procedures and our findings are summarized below.

PROCEDURES

Specific procedures involved

- Reviewing the software policy of the organization and its implementation and control.
- Reviewing the organization's inventory of software resources, including a list of all personal computers by location and serial number. Using Visual Audit X4, we obtained a list of all the software on the hard disk of each computer.
- Matching purchase documentation with the software inventory record we had established. This procedure included reviewing software purchase records, such as invoices, purchase orders, check registers, canceled checks, manuals, installation media, license agreements, and registration cards.

FINDINGS

In the area of software policy and controls, we found that the organization owns a total of 432 copies of 11 applications from seven vendors. No record of registration with the publisher was available for 81 of the programs owned. In addition, we identified 65 copies of software programs for which no corresponding purchase records existed. These copies appear to be illegal. Of the 113 personal computers, we found 14 machines with software that had been brought from home by employees. A summary of the software license violations identified follows:

Identified Software License Violations

Total Copies	Total Copies Found	Legal Copies Found	Copies in Violation
Microsoft Office	110	100	10
Windows 7	115	75	40
Norton AntiVirus	90	75	15

We have deleted all copies in excess of the number of legal copies, and you are now in full compliance with applicable software licenses. We have also ordered legal software to replace the necessary software that was deleted.

CONCLUSIONS AND RECOMMENDATIONS

While some departments had little or no illegal software, others had significant violations. Therefore, the following recommendations are made:

1. Institute a one-hour training program on the legal use of software and require it for all employees. Repeat it weekly over the next few months to permit all employees to attend. Additionally, require all new employees to participate in the program within two weeks of their start date.
2. Implement stricter software inventory controls, including semi-annual spot audits.

Thank you for the opportunity to be of assistance to you with your software compliance needs.

GSI Technology Consulting Group April 3, 2011

Format Pointers

- Uses short format for report prepared by outside consultant.
- Uses email channel to transmit formatted document as attachment for quick, convenient delivery.
- Summarizes ideas succinctly in one-page report for easy read.

FIGURE 11-6

Short Report in Expanded Letter Format, Page 1

STRATEGIC SOLUTIONS
761 Westgate Avenue Atlanta, GA 30319-8718 (404)555-1768 Fax (404)555-6221

Management Consulting and Corporate Training

Letterhead and letter address function as title page and transmittal.

January 23, 2011

Mr. Jose Ferantino, President
TechSense, Inc.
1660 Fremont Street
Dickinson, TX 77539

Dear Mr. Ferantino:

RECOMMENDATIONS FOR IMPLEMENTING CROSS-CULTURAL VIRTUAL TEAMS

Uses deductive approach to present main idea to president.

Thank you for allowing us to assist you in outlining a plan for successful implementation of cross-cultural virtual (CCV) teams for TechSense, Inc. This trend is gaining wide support throughout the business community as more companies go international and as budgets for employee travel shrink.

Procedures

Provides research methods and sources to add credibility.

In preparing this report, a variety of resources were consulted, including paper and online resources. Additionally, interviews were conducted with 20 businesspersons from a variety of organizations in Texas that have utilized CCV teams. Their perceptions, along with published research, led to the recommendations in this report. Published resources, as well as firsthand interviews, generally support the use of well-managed CCV teams.

Uses centered heading to denote major division of body.

Findings

Uses transition sentence to move reader smoothly to minor section.

Research revealed useful information concerning the unique challenges faced by cross-cultural virtual teams.

Uses side heading to denote minor section.

Challenges Faced by Cross-Cultural Virtual Teams

Virtual teams have various challenges, even when their membership is homogeneous. Virtual teams can lack cohesion, members may feel isolated, and coordination of work is more challenging. Special leadership skills are required to manage the challenges of virtual teams. An effective team leader must be able to skillfully leverage team talent, include all members, provide the team with necessary information, promote trust, encourage healthy discussions, and help manage conflict. Unless teams can effectively deal with interpersonal communication challenges, members quickly face burnout. Research indicates that virtual team performance typically peaks and then declines after the first year (Hawkrigg, 2007).

Format Pointer

- Uses subject line to introduce topic of letter report.

(*continued on next page*)

FIGURE 11-6

Short Report in Expanded Letter Format, Page 2 *continued*

Includes second page heading to show continuation; appears on plain matching paper.

Mr. Jose Ferantino
Page 2
January 23, 2011

Culturally heterogeneous groups have the potential for greater conflict than in groups where members are culturally similar (Thomas, 1999). Obviously, a certain degree of fluency in the common language used by the team is a requisite to effective communication. Beyond the basic language consideration, team members must recognize other challenges of cultural diversity and adapt their behavior accordingly. Recognition of cultural patterns and expectations and adaptations to spoken and written messages can improve CCV team interactions (Nawati & Craig, 2006).

Uses side heading and transition sentence to move reader smoothly to minor section.

Recommendations for Effective Cross-Cultural Virtual Teams

Culturally diverse virtual teams do have a greater potential for conflict than do teams that are homogeneous and are able to meet face to face. While variations in beliefs, behaviors, and expectations occur within all cultural groups, certain generalities about a person based on his or her cultural group can be useful for others seeking better understanding. "Given little or no other information about an individual's values and behaviors, culture provides a good first impression of that person" (Maznevski & Peterson, 1997).

Neyer & Harzing (2008) found that experiences in cross-cultural interactions do serve to improve one's abilities to adapt in such situations. One advantage gained through experience is the overcoming of cultural stereotypes which often stand in the way of effective communication. Cross-cultural experience also leads to the establishment of norms that support interaction among individuals and to the development of mutual consideration for people (Neyer & Harzing, 2008). Several studies have established that individuals who learn a foreign language also gain appropriate culturally determined behavior and are thus better able to adapt to specific characteristics of the other culture (Harzing & Feely, 2008; Yang & Bond, 1980).

Provides APA citations for direct quotes and paraphrased information.

Some individuals are better suited than are others for membership in CCV teams due to their temperament and experiences. In addition to possessing strong technical skills, qualities that are important to successful membership in cross-cultural virtual teams include the following (Adler & Gundersen, 2008; Hurn & Jenkins, 2000):

Uses bullets to highlight qualities important to virtual teams.

- Flexibility and adaptability
- Strong interpersonal skills
- Ability to think both globally and locally
- Linguistic skills
- Listening (interpretive) skills
- Initiative
- Enthusiasm
- Consensus building skills
- Patience and empathy
- Nonjudgmental attitude

FIGURE 11-6

Short Report in Expanded Letter Format, Page 3

Mr. Jose Ferantino
Page 3
January 23, 2011

A primary goal of CCV teams should be to harmonize differences between cultures so that normal business activity can occur. Some suggestions for building harmony include the following:

- Provide cross-cultural training to increase ability to identify and cope with potential conflicts (Dunkel & Meierewert, 2004).
- Select a skillful leader who can perceive and facilitate handling of potential cultural misunderstandings (Hurn & Jenkins, 2000).
- Strive for transparency in all stages of activity, which aids in the development of trust.
- Set clear, specific agenda with no surprises that could be seen as hidden agendas (Hurn & Jenkins, 2000).
- Encourage the use of questions to solicit input and check for understanding.

Success in CCV teams is largely dependent on the formation of a group culture that supersedes the individual cultural norms of the various members.

Summary

In the global business environment, the success of many organizations depends on the effective functioning of cross-cultural virtual teams, and individuals possessing the specific skill set to be successful in CCV teams are highly marketable to a wide variety of organizations. Obviously, teams cannot pay constant attention to cross-cultural differences. However, virtual teams whose members recognize, respect, and respond to cultural expectations for behavior enhance their prospects for achieving high levels of performance. Education about other cultures and experience in cross-cultural exchange will serve to strengthen team members' ability to interact effectively in cross-cultural virtual teams.

Thank you for the opportunity to provide this information concerning cross-cultural virtual teams development. Please let us know how we can assist you further with this project or with other related matters.

Sincerely,

Paige Lorimer

Paige Lorimer, Consultant

ksm

Enclosure: Reading list

Uses bulleted list to highlight strategies for virtual team development.

Combines summary with recommendation as is typical in short reports.

Closes with courteous offer to provide additional service.

Includes enclosure notation to alert reader to enclosed reading list.

Format Pointer

- Includes complimentary close and signature to comply with letter format.

(*continued on next page*)

FIGURE 11-6

Short Report in Expanded Letter Format, Page 4 *continued*

Mr. Jose Ferantino
Page 3
January 23, 2011

Reading List

Adler, N. J., & Gundersen, A. (2008). *International dimensions of organizational behavior.* Boston: Kent.

Dunkel, A., & Meierewert, S. (2004). Cultural standards and their impact on teamwork: An empirical analysis of Austria, German, Hungarian and Spanish culture differences. *Journal for East European Management Studies, 9,* 147-174.

Harzing, A. W., & Feely, A. J. (2008). The language barrier and its implications for HQ-subsidiary relationships. *Cross Cultural Management, 15*(1), 49-61.

Hawkrigg, J. (2007, March 12). Virtual teams need human touch. *Canadian HR Reporter, 20*(5), 16.

Hurn, B. F., & Jenkins, M. (2000). International peer group development. *Industrial and Commercial Training, 32*(4), 128-131.

Maznevski, M. L., & Peterson, M. F. (1997). Societal values, social interpretation, and multinational teams. *Cross-cultural workgroups.* C. Granrose, Ed. Thousand Oaks, CA: Sage.

Nawati, D. A., & Craig, A. (2006, March). Behavioral adaptation within cross-cultural virtual teams. *IEEE Transactions, 49*(1), 44-56. doi: 10.1109/TPC.2006.870459

Neyer, A., & Harzine, A. (2008). The impact of culture on interactions: Five lessons learned from the European Commission. *European Management Journal, 26*(5), 325-334. doi: 10.1016/j.emj.2008.05.005

Thomas, D. C. (1999). Cultural diversity and work group effectiveness: An experimental study. *Journal of Cross Cultural Psychology, 30*(2), 242-263.

Yang, K. S., & Bond, M. H. (1980). Ethnic affirmation by Chinese bilinguals. *Journal of Cross-Cultural Psychology, 11*(4), 411-425.

Format Pointer

- Uses Readings List instead of References as the title to comply with employing company preference.
- Includes alphabetical listing of all cited sources using APA 6th edition referencing style to comply with employing company preference.
- Includes digital object identifier (DOI) for electronic resources when available.

Form Reports

What form reports are you familiar with?

Form reports meet the demand for numerous, repetitive reports. College registration forms, applications for credit, airline tickets, and bank checks are examples of simple form reports. Form reports have the following benefits:

- When designed properly, form reports increase clerical accuracy by providing designated places for specific items.

Least-Liked Form Report?
As one of America's least-liked reports, the federal tax return stirs fear and consternation in the minds of many citizens. Several forms are available, depending on the taxpayer's income situation. For those reluctant to undertake their returns on their own, tax software products are available that guide the user through preparation of the appropriate forms and worksheets. Individuals and businesses can also pay tax preparer services to prepare their returns. Once the forms are completed, they can be submitted electronically or on paper, with the shortest form also submittable via phone. Taxpayers expecting refunds are typically more highly motivated to meet the annual April 15 deadline than those who expect to have to pay.

- Forms save time by telling the preparer where to put each item and by preprinting common elements to eliminate the need for narrative writing.
- In addition to their advantages of accuracy and time saving, forms make tabulation of data relatively simple. The value of the form is uniformity.

Most form reports, such as a bank teller's cash sheet, are informational. At the end of the teller's work period, cash is counted and totals entered in designated blanks. Cash reports from all tellers are then totaled to arrive at period totals and perhaps to be verified by computer records.

In addition to their informational purpose, form reports assist in analytical work. A residential appraisal report assists real estate appraisers in analyzing real property. With this information, the appraiser is able to determine the market value of a specific piece of property.

CHANGING TECHNOLOGY

Many form reports are computer generated. For example, an automated hospital admission process expedites the repetitive patient reports that must be created. The admission clerk inputs the patient information using the carefully designed input screen. If the patient has been admitted previously, the patient's name, address, and telephone number are displayed automatically for the clerk to verify. When the clerk inputs the patient's date of birth, the computer calculates the patient's age, eliminating the need to ask a potentially sensitive question and ensuring accuracy when patients cannot remember their ages. All data are stored in a computer file and retrieved as needed to generate numerous reports required during a patient's stay: admissions summary sheet, admissions report, pharmacy profile, and even the addressograph used to stamp each page of the patient's record and the identification arm band.

Using the computer to prepare each report in the previous example leads to higher efficiency levels and minimizes errors because recurring data are entered only once. Preparing error-free form reports is a critical public relations tool because even minor clerical errors may cause patients or customers to question the organization's ability to deliver quality service.

Proposals

Managers prepare ***internal proposals*** to justify or recommend purchases or changes in the company; for instance, installing a new computer system, introducing telecommuting or other flexible work schedules, or reorganizing the company into work groups. An ***external proposal***, as described in Chapter 9, is a written description of how one organization can meet the needs of another; for example, provide products or services. Written to generate business, external proposals are a critical part of the successful operation of many companies.

Proposals may be solicited or unsolicited. ***Solicited proposals*** are invited and initiated when a potential customer or client submits exact specifications or needs in a bid request or a request for proposal, commonly referred to as an ***RFP***. Governmental agencies such as the Department of Education solicit proposals and place orders and contracts based on the most desirable proposal. The bid request or RFP describes a problem to be solved and invites respondents to describe their proposed solutions.

Give examples of situations in your career field for which a proposal may need to be prepared.

An ***unsolicited proposal*** is prepared by an individual or firm who sees a problem to be solved and submits a proposal. For example, a business consultant is a regular customer of a family-owned retail store. On numerous occasions she has attempted to purchase an item that was out of stock. Recognizing that stock shortages decrease sales and profits, she prepares a proposal to assist the business in designing a computerized perpetual inventory with an automatic reordering system. For the business to accept the proposal, the consultant must convince the business that the resulting increase in sales and profits will more than offset the cost of the computer system and the consulting fee.

Structure

When would price be the only deciding factor for distinguishing between competing proposals?

A proposal includes (1) details about the manner in which the problem would be solved and (2) the price to be charged or costs to be incurred. Often the proposal is a lengthy report designed to "sell" the prospective buyer on the ability of the bidder to perform. However, a simple price quotation also constitutes a proposal in response to a request for a price quotation.

The format of a proposal depends on the length of the proposal and the intended audience:

FORMAT	PROPOSAL LENGTH AND INTENDED AUDIENCE
Memo or email report	Short; remains within the organization
Letter report	Short; travels outside the organization
Formal report	Long; remains within the organization or travels outside the organization

How can the writer make the proposal more successful in the competitive process?

Most work resulting from proposals is covered by a working agreement or contract to avoid discrepancies in the intents of the parties. In some cases, for example, users of outside consultants insist that each consultant be covered by a sizable general personal liability insurance policy that also insures the company. Many large firms and governmental organizations use highly structured procedures to ensure understanding of contract terms.

The following general parts, or variations of them, may appear as headings in a proposal: (1) Problem or Purpose, (2) Scope, (3) Methods or Procedures, (4) Materials and Equipment, (5) Qualifications, (6) Follow-Up and/or Evaluation, (7) Budget or Costs, (8) Summary, and (9) Addenda. In addition to these parts, a proposal may include preliminary report parts, such as the title page, transmittal message, and contents as well as addenda parts, such as references, appendix, and index.

Your Turn 11-4
You're the Professional

In your role as a freelance motivational speaker, you recently had the opportunity to meet and converse with Gene Stephens, president of a local bank. He is interested in sponsoring a seminar to motivate and inspire his employees to higher performance and has invited you to submit a proposal as to what you can offer.

TAKE ACTION:

Discuss which of the following proposals would be most appropriate, explaining the reason for your choice.

a. External, solicited, and in letter form.

b. External, unsolicited, and in memo form.

c. Internal, solicited, and in email form.

d. Internal, unsolicited, and in letter form.

What other elements should your proposal reflect?

Problem and/or Purpose

Problem and purpose are often used as interchangeable terms in reports. Here is the introductory purpose statement, called "Project Description," in a proposal by a firm to contribute to an educational project:

Project Description: Bartlett Community College has invited business and industry to participate in the creation of *Business Communication*, a television course and video training package. These materials will provide effective training in business communication skills to enhance the performance of individuals in business and contribute to organizational skills and profitability. In our rapidly evolving information society, skill in communication is integral to success.

Note how the heading "Project Description" has been used in place of "Purpose." In the following opening statement, "Problem" is used as the heading:

Problem: The Board of Directors of Oak Brook Village Association has requested a proposal for total management and operation of its 1,620-unit permanent residential planned development. This proposal demonstrates the advantages of using Central Management Corporation in that role.

How can a good purpose statement be written so that it is ambitious, yet attainable?

The purpose of the proposal may be listed as a separate heading (in addition to "Problem") when the proposal intends to include objectives of a measurable nature. When you list objectives such as "To reduce overall expenses for maintenance by 10 percent," attempt to list measurable and attainable objectives and list only enough to accomplish the purpose of selling your proposal. Many proposals are rejected simply because writers promise more than they can actually deliver.

Scope

When determining the scope of your proposal, you can place limits on what you propose to do or on what the material or equipment you sell can accomplish. The term *scope* need not necessarily be the only heading for this section. "Areas Served," "Limitations to the Study," and "Where (*specify topic*) Can Be Used" are examples of headings that describe the scope of a proposal. Here is a "Scope" section from a consulting firm's proposal to conduct a salary survey:

What the Study Will Cover: To assist Sun Valley Technologies in formulating its salary and benefits program for executives, Patterson Consulting will include an analysis of compensation (salary and benefits) for no fewer than 20 of Sun Valley's competitors in the same geographic region. In addition to salaries, insurance, incentives, deferred compensation, medical, and retirement plans will be included. Additionally, Patterson Consulting will make recommendations for Sun Valley's program.

Another statement of scope might be as follows:

Scope: Leading figures in business will work with respected academicians and skilled production staff to produce fifteen 30-minute interactive video training courses that may be used in courses for college credit or as modules dealing with discrete topics for corporate executives.

Methods and/or Procedures

How do the introductory sections build credibility for the proposal and the writer?

The method(s) used to solve the problem or to conduct the business of the proposal should be spelled out in detail. In this section, simply think through all the steps necessary to meet the terms of the proposal and write them in sequence. When feasible, you should include a time schedule for implementation of the project.

Materials and Equipment

For large proposals, such as construction or research and development, indicate the nature and quantities of materials and equipment to be used. In some cases, several departments will contribute to this section. When materials and equipment constitute a major portion of the total cost, include prices. Much litigation arises when clients are charged for "cost overruns." When contracts are made on the basis of "cost plus XX percent," the major costs of materials, equipment, and labor/personnel must be thoroughly described and documented.

Qualifications

Assuming your proposal is acceptable in terms of services to be performed or products to be supplied, your proposal must convince the potential buyer that you have the expertise to deliver what you have described and that you are a credible individual or company. Therefore, devote a section to presenting the specific qualifications and special expertise of the personnel involved in the proposal. You may include past records of the bidder and the recommendations of its past customers, and the proposed cost. Note how the brief biography of the principal member in the following excerpt from a proposal contributes to the credibility of the proposer:

Principals: Project Director: Charles A. McKee, M.B.A., M.A.I., Partner in Property Appraisers, Inc., consulting appraiser since 1984. Fellow of the American Institute of Appraisers, B.A., M.B.A., Harvard University. Phi Kappa Phi and Beta Gamma Sigma honorary societies. Lecturer and speaker at many realty and appraisal conferences and at the University of Michigan.

In another related section, the proposal might mention other work performed:

Major Clients of Past Five Years: City of Tulsa, Oklahoma; Dade County, Florida; City of San Francisco, California; City of Seattle, Washington; Harbor General Corporation, Long Beach, California; Gulf Houston, Incorporated, Houston, Texas. Personal references are available on request.

Your Turn 11-5
Assessment

Each employer seeks a different mix of skills and experience from a prospective employee, but one thing they all look for is soft skills. Soft skills include your ability to communicate, solve problems, and get along well with others.

TAKE ACTION:

- Assess your soft skills by taking the MonsterTrak quiz found at http://www.proprofs.com/quiz-school/story.php?title=communication-test-soft-skills, or go to your companion website, www.cengage.com/bcomm/lehman, for updated links.
- Send your instructor an email message or post your response, as directed, that summarizes what you learned from taking the soft skills quiz and what you plan to do to improve your soft skills quotient.

Follow-Up and/or Evaluation

Although your entire proposal is devoted to convincing the reader of its merit, clients are frequently concerned about what will happen when the proposed work or service is completed. Will you return to make certain your work is satisfactory? Can you adjust your method of research as times change?

If you propose to conduct a study, do not promise more than you can deliver. Not all funded research proves to be successful. If you propose to prepare a study in your firm's area of expertise, you may be more confident. A public accounting firm's proposal to audit a company's records need not be modest. The accountant follows certain audit functions that are prescribed by the profession. However, a proposal that involves providing psychological services probably warrants a thoughtful follow-up program to evaluate the service.

Budget or Costs

The budget or cost of the program should be detailed when materials, equipment, outside help, consultants, salaries, and travel are to be included. A simple proposal for service by one person might consist of a statement such as "15 hours at $200/hour, totaling $3,000, plus mileage and expenses estimated at $550." Present the budget or costs section after the main body of the proposal.

Summary

You might conclude the proposal with a summary. This summary may also be used as the initial section of the proposal if deductive sequence is desired.

Addenda

What other types of items might appear in a proposal addendum?

When supporting material is necessary to the proposal but would make it too bulky or detract from it, include the material as addenda items. A bibliography and an appendix are examples of addenda items. References used should appear in the bibliography or as footnotes. Maps, questionnaires, letters of recommendation, and similar materials are suitable appendix items.

FIGURE 11-7

Short Proposal, Page 1

PROPOSAL FOR STAFF DEVELOPMENT SEMINAR: PROMOTING PRODUCTIVE CROSS-CULTURAL TEAMS

for TechSense, Inc.

by Paige Lorimer, Communications Consultant

September 14, 2011

Purpose

Describes problem and presents proposed plan as solution to problem.

After careful study, the management of TechSense has implemented cross-cultural virtual (CCV) teams with members representing the 28 various metropolitan bank locations. The proposed training course is designed to help participants understand the purposes of the decision and ensure appropriate participation in the CCV teams.

Uses headings to aid reader in understanding proposal's organization. Boldface font adds emphasis.

Proposed Course of Instruction

The training course will be delivered by Claire Massey, a dynamic associate with more than 10 years of business experience in CCV instruction. Because behavior in CCV teams is a reflection of one's personality and cultural understanding, the program will actively involve participants and facilitate personal application of the new strategy.

Divides "Proposed Course of Instruction" into six minor divisions for easier comprehension. Describes course content, instructional method, and design in detail.

Teaching/Learning Methods

This activity-oriented training program will involve response to videos, role playing, and case discussion. The trainer will act as a facilitator to assist each participant in assessing CCV behaviors and expectations and planning effective strategies for improving overall effectiveness.

Program Content

The following topics constitute the content core of the program:

Uses bulleted lists to highlight course components and learning materials.

- History and background of CCV teams
- Challenges faced by CCV teams
- Issues CCV teams face in the stages of team development
- Strategies for CCV teams

Learning Materials

The following materials will be provided to facilitate learning:

- Copies of current published articles on the importance and function of CCV teams
- Consultant-developed workbook for each participant

1 Paige Lorimer Consultants

Format Pointer

- Incorporates page design features to enhance appeal and readability (e.g., headings styles including color; crisp, open fonts and wide linespacing for easy onscreen reading or print copy; bulleted lists; and appealing table).

(*continued on next page*)

FIGURE 11-7

Short Proposal, Page 2

Includes informational header to identify second page and client.

TechSense, Inc.	September 14, 2011	Page 2

Length of Course

As requested by management, this course will consist of three two-hour sessions held on a selected day of the week for three consecutive weeks.

Number of Participants

The seminar will serve all 67 TechSense employees involved in CCV team activity.

Cost

Itemizes costs so reader understands exactly how figure was calculated. Disclosing detailed breakdown gives reader confidence that cost is accurate.

All teaching-learning materials will be provided by the consulting firm and include workbooks, videos, and video camera and recorder. Exact cost figures are as follows:

Workbooks and other materials for 67 participants	$ 835.00
Equipment lease fees	100.00
Professional fees (6 hours' instruction @ $250/hour)	1,500.00
Travel/meals	75.00
Total	$2,510.00

A short, informal proposal that includes several of the parts previously discussed is shown in Figure 11-7. This proposal consists of three major divisions: "The Problem," "Proposed Course of Instruction," and "Cost." The "Proposed Course of Instruction" section is divided into six minor divisions to facilitate understanding. Wanting to increase the chances of securing the contract, the writer made sure the proposal was highly professional and had the impact needed to get the reader's attention. To add to the overall effectiveness of the proposal, the writer incorporated appealing, but not distracting, page design features. Printing the proposal with a laser printer using fonts of varying sizes and styles resulted in a professional appearance and an appealing document. The reader's positive impression of the high standards exhibited in this targeted proposal is likely to influence his or her confidence in the writer's ability to present the proposed seminar.

Preparation

What message does Aesop's Fable about the tortoise and the hare have for the writer of a report or proposal?

Writers have much flexibility in preparing proposals. When they find a particular pattern that seems to be successful, they no doubt will adopt it as their basic plan. The ultimate test of a proposal is its effectiveness in achieving its purpose. The task is to assemble the parts of a proposal in a way that persuades the reader to accept it.

As with most report writing, first prepare the pieces of information that you will assemble later as the "whole" report. Determine the parts to include, select one part that will be easy to prepare, prepare that part, and then go on to another. When you have completed the parts, you can arrange them in whatever order you like, incorporate the transitional items necessary to create coherence, and then put the proposal in finished

Aflac/Sid Cato: Capitalizing on the Communication Power of the Annual Report

Annual reports guide investor decisions by offering a valuable glimpse into a company's workings and financial performance as well as articulating its personality and philosophy. Organizing the report's information around a theme and providing attractive visual elements assist in reading comprehension.

www.aflac.com

www.sidcato.com

get the Aflacts
Aflac belongs to you, not your company.
So make sure you take it with you.

© AP IMAGES/ PRNEWSFOTO/AFLAC

Activities

- Visit the Aflac website at www.aflac.com to identify the theme used in the award-winning Aflac report and the strategies for reflecting company values throughout the report.
- Visit Sid Cato's website at www.sidcato.com to read about his view of what makes a good annual report.
- Locate the following article that offers further advice for maximizing the impact of the annual report:

  Ambler, T., & Neely, A. (2008). Narrating the real corporate story. *Business Strategy Review, 19*(2), 28–32. Available from Business Source Complete database.

Consider the tips offered in the Ambler and Neely article to improve annual reports and those offered by Cato at his website. As a company stockholder, compose a letter to a company on Cato's "worst" list, making suggestions for improving the firm's annual report. Following instructions given by your instructor, electronically post your response to this question: While Cato recommends full explanation of financial information, how much is too much?

form. Allow adequate time after completing the research and writing for proofreading and editing. Figures should be checked carefully for accuracy, since underreporting costs can lead to a financial loss if the proposal is accepted, and overreported costs may lead to refusal of the proposal. If you fail to allow sufficient time for proposal completion, you may miss the required deadline for proposal submission.

TEAM
ENVIRONMENT

If you become part of a collaborative writing team producing a proposal of major size, you probably will be responsible for writing only a small portion of the total proposal. For example, a proposal team of 16 executives, managers, and engineers might be required to prepare an 87-page proposal presenting a supplier's plan to supply parts to a military aircraft manufacturer. After the group brainstorms and plans the proposal, a project director delegates responsibility for the research and origination of particular sections of the proposal. Finally, one person compiles all the sections, creates many of the preliminary and addenda parts, and produces and distributes the final product.

Additional information about writing in teams is provided in the accompanying Strategic Forces feature "Collaborative Skills for Team Writing."

TEAM ENVIRONMENT

STRATEGIC FORCES

Collaborative Skills for Team Writing

Many problems faced by organizations cannot be solved by an individual because no one person has all the experience, resources, or information needed to accomplish the task. Team writing produces a corporate document representing multiple points of view. Group support systems (GSSs) are interactive computer-based environments that support coordinated team efforts. Numerous GSS products have been developed, and the style of the team-editing process dictates which GSS application will be most appropriate:

- **Sequential editing.** Collaborators divide the task so the output of one stage is passed to the next writer for individual work. Software supporting markup tools are used in the process.
- **Parallel editing.** Collaborators divide the task so that each writer works on a different part of the document at the same time. Then the document is reassembled in an integration stage.
- **Reciprocal editing.** Collaborators work together to create a common document, mutually adjusting their activities in real time to incorporate each other's changes.

Early attempts at collaborative writing typically used an unstructured process that often proved to be dysfunctional and frustrating to participants. Successful collaborative writing projects typically involve a multistage process:

1. **Open discussion.** Collaborators develop the objectives and general scope of the document using brainstorming or parallel-discussion software.
2. **Generation of document outline.** Collaborators develop main sections and subsections that will provide the structure for the document.
3. **Discussion of content within outline.** Collaborators interactively generate and discuss document content in each section using parallel discussions.
4. **Composing by subteams.** Subteams may consist of a few people (or sometimes only one person) who take the content entries from a section and organize, edit, and complete the section as a first draft.
5. **Online feedback and discussion.** The team reviews each section and makes suggestions in the form of annotations or comments. The section editors accept, reject, or merge suggestions to improve their own sections.
6. **Verbal walkthrough.** Using a collaborative writing tool, the team does a verbal walkthrough of the document.

© ISTOCKPHOTO.COM/ANDREY POPOV

Stages 1 through 3 are sequential and are undertaken only once. Stages 4 through 6 are circular in nature, and in some cases multiple loops are carried out before the document is finalized. As synchronous group time may be limited and valuable, it is used to add and refine document content. Formatting can be accomplished later by team members or an outside editor.

Disputes can arise when collaborative team members have conflicting information or different philosophical approaches to an issue. In such cases, the disputing team members can be assigned to work together as a subteam, negotiating their differences without an audience. When the subteam returns to the group with compromised text, the group can accept it, knowing multiple points of view went into its composition.[8]

Application

In teams, research a GSS product. Prepare a five-minute oral report about the product that includes the following: (1) description of the product, (2) applications for which it is suited, (3) requirements and specifications for use, and (4) limitations of the product.

Summary

1. Identify the parts of a formal report and the contribution each part makes to the report's overall effectiveness.

As reports increase in length from one page to several pages, they also grow in formality with the addition of introductory and addenda items. As a result, reports at the formal end of the continuum tend to be repetitious. These report parts and their purposes are summarized in Figure 11-1 on page 378.

2. Organize report findings.

Organizing the content of a report involves seeing the report problem in its entirety and then breaking it into its parts. After the research or field work has been completed, the writer may begin with any of the report parts and then complete the rough draft by putting the parts in logical order. Short reports that don't require the many supporting preliminary and addenda parts usually are written in memorandum, email, or letter format. Although reports grow in formality as they increase in length, writers determine whether to prepare a report in formal style and format before they begin writing. As they organize and make tentative outlines, writers determine the format and style best able to communicate the intended message.

3. Prepare effective formal reports using an acceptable format and writing style.

In preparing effective long reports, outlining assists the writer with logical sequencing. Appropriate headings lead the reader from one division to another. The writing style should present the findings and data interpretation clearly and fairly, convincing the reader to accept the writer's point of view, but in an unemotional manner. Opinions should be clearly identified as such. The writer should lay the first draft aside long enough to get a fresh perspective, then revise the report with a genuine commitment to making all possible improvements.

4. Prepare effective short reports in memorandum, email, and letter formats.

Short reports are typically written in a personal writing style and in memorandum, email, or letter format. Form reports provide accuracy, save time, and simplify tabulation of data when a need exists for numerous, repetitive reports.

5. Prepare effective proposals for a variety of purposes.

Proposals can be written for both internal and external audiences. Proposals call for thorough organization and require writing methods that will be not only informative but convincing. Because they have discrete parts that can be prepared in any order and then assembled into whole reports, they are conducive to preparation by teams.

Chapter Review

1. How does a report writer decide the best organization for a formal report and determine which preliminary or addenda parts to include in a report? (Objs. 1, 3)
2. Briefly discuss the primary principles involved in writing an executive summary. What is the significance of other names given to this preliminary report part? (Obj. 1)
3. What purposes are served by the findings, conclusions, and recommendations sections? How are they related, yet distinctive? (Obj. 1)
4. Give two or three examples of emotional terms that should be avoided in a formal report. Why is impersonal, third person style frequently used in formal reports? How is it achieved? (Obj. 2)
5. Explain the relationship between the content outline of a report and the placement of headings within the body of a report. (Obj. 2)
6. In addition to length, what are the differences between long and short reports? (Objs. 3, 4)
7. How are memorandum, letter, and email reports similar? In what ways are they different? (Obj. 4)
8. What is the primary purpose of a proposal, and what can the writer do to ensure that the purpose is achieved? (Obj. 5)
9. What is meant by RFP? Why is it important to the preparation of a proposal? (Obj. 5)
10. How does team preparation of a proposal differ from preparation by an individual? How can technology assist in team writing? (Obj. 5)

Digging Deeper

1. How do diversity considerations impact the choices made in report style and format?
2. Considering general trends in society toward more informality in many situations, how might the style of reports be impacted?

Assessment

To check your understanding of the chapter, take the available practice quizzes as directed by your instructor.

Check Your Communication
Formal Reports

The following checklist provides a concise, useful guide as you prepare a report for proposal.

TRANSMITTAL LETTER OR MEMORANDUM

(Use a letter-style transmittal in reports going outside the organization. For internal reports, use a memorandum transmittal.)

The transmittal letter or memo should:

- ☐ Transmit a warm greeting to the reader.
- ☐ Open with a "Here is the report you requested" tone.
- ☐ Establish the subject in the first sentence.
- ☐ Follow the opening with a brief summary of the study. Expand the discussion if a separate summary is not included in the report.
- ☐ Acknowledge the assistance of those who helped with the study.
- ☐ Close the message with a thank-you and a forward look.

TITLE PAGE

The title page should:

- ☐ Include the title of the report, succinctly worded.
- ☐ Provide full identification of the authority for the report (the person or organization for whom the report was prepared).
- ☐ Provide full identification of the preparer(s) of the report.
- ☐ Provide the date of the completion of the report.
- ☐ Use an attractive layout.

TABLE OF CONTENTS

For a contents page:

- ☐ Use *Table of Contents* or *Contents* as the title.
- ☐ Use indention to indicate the heading degrees used in the report.
- ☐ List numerous figures separately as a preliminary item called *Table of Figures* or *Figures*. (Otherwise, figures should not be listed because they are not separate sections of the outline but only supporting data within a section.)

EXECUTIVE SUMMARY

In an executive summary or abstract:

- ☐ Use a descriptive title, such as *Executive Summary, Synopsis*, or *Abstract*.
- ☐ Condense the major report sections.
- ☐ Use effective, generalized statements that avoid detail available in the report itself. Simply tell the reader what was done, how it was done, and what conclusions were reached.

REPORT TEXT

In writing style, observe the following guidelines:

- ☐ Avoid the personal *I* and *we* pronouns in formal writing. Minimize the use of *the writer, the investigator*, and *the author*.
- ☐ Use active construction to give emphasis to the *doer* of the action; use passive voice to give emphasis to the *results* of the action.
- ☐ Use proper tense. Tell naturally about things in the order in which they happened, are happening, or will happen. Write as though the reader were reading the report at the same time it is written.
- ☐ Avoid ambiguous pronoun references. (If a sentence begins with *This is*, make sure the preceding sentence uses the specific word for which *This* stands. If the specific word is not used, insert it immediately after *This*.)
- ☐ Avoid expletive beginnings such as *There is, There are*, and *It is that* present the verb before the subject.
- ☐ Use bulleted or enumerated lists for three or more items if listing will make reading easier. For example, a list of three words such as *Growth, Adaptability*, and *Cost* need not be bulleted; but a list of three long phrases, clauses, or sentences would probably warrant bulleting or enumeration.
- ☐ Incorporate transition sentences to ensure coherence.

In physical layout, observe the following guidelines:

- ☐ Use headings to assist the reader by making them descriptive of the contents of the section. Talking headings are preferred.
- ☐ Maintain consistency in the mechanical placement and design of headings of equal degree.
- ☐ Use parallel construction in headings of equal degree in the same report section.
- ☐ Incorporate the statement of the problem or purpose and method of research as minor parts of the introduction unless the research method is the unique element in the study.
- ☐ Use the picture-frame layout for all pages, with appropriate margins that allow for bindings.
- ☐ Number all pages appropriately.

In using graphics or tabular data, observe the following guidelines:

- ☐ Number consecutively figures (tables, graphics, and other illustrations) used in the report.
- ☐ Give each graph or table a descriptive title.
- ☐ Refer to the graph or table within the text discussion that precedes its appearance.

- ☐ Place the graph or table as close to the textual reference as possible and limit the text discussion to analysis. (It should not merely repeat what can be seen in the graph or table.)
- ☐ Use effective layout, appropriate captions and legends, and realistic vertical and horizontal scales that help the table or graph stand clearly by itself.

In reporting the analysis, observe the following guidelines:

- ☐ Question each statement for its contribution to the solution of the problem. Is each statement either descriptive or evaluative?
- ☐ Reduce large, unwieldy numbers to understandable ones through a common language, such as units of production, percentages, or ratios.
- ☐ Use objective reporting style rather than persuasive language; avoid emotional terms. Identify assumptions and opinions. Avoid unwarranted judgments and inferences.

In drawing conclusions:

- ☐ State the conclusions carefully and clearly, and be sure they grow out of the findings.
- ☐ Repeat the major supporting findings for each conclusion if necessary.
- ☐ Make sure any recommendations grow naturally from the stated conclusions.

CITATIONS

If citations are used:

- ☐ Include a citation (in-text reference, footnote, or endnote) for material quoted or paraphrased from another source.
- ☐ Adhere to an acceptable, authoritative style or company policy.
- ☐ Present consistent citations, including adequate information for readers to locate the source in the reference list.

REFERENCES

If a reference list is provided:

- ☐ Include an entry for every reference cited in the report.
- ☐ Adhere to an acceptable, authoritative style or company policy.
- ☐ Include more information than might be necessary in cases of doubt about what to include in an entry.
- ☐ Include separate sections (e.g., books, articles, and nonprint sources) if the references section is lengthy and your referencing style allows it.

APPENDIX

If an appendix is provided:

- ☐ Include cover messages for survey instruments, maps, explanations of formulas used, and other items that provide information but are not important enough to be included in the report body.
- ☐ Subdivide categories of information beginning with Appendix A, Appendix B, and so on.
- ☐ Identify each item with title.

Activities

1. Outlining an Analytical Report (Obj. 2)

In small groups, develop an outline for a report that would explain the criteria for choosing a college major or a topic assigned by your instructor.

2. Critiquing a Report Outline (Obj. 2)

Analyze the following table of contents. What suggestions do you have for improving it? A downloadable version of this activity is available at your companion website, www.cengage.com/bcomm/lehman.

Table of Contents

3. Identifying a Writing Environment that Works (Obj. 2)

Visit your companion website, www.cengage.com/bcomm/lehman, and read the "Guidelines for Creating an Effective Environment for Writing." Add three or more additional suggestions to those given.

Applications

READ | THINK | WRITE | SPEAK | COLLABORATE

1. Researching the Importance of Readability in Reports (Objs. 1–3)

Locate and read the following article on the how to write a report that is readable and achieves your desired purpose:

Raman, B. (2004, April). How to write a good report. Available at www.cse.iitk.ac.in/users/braman/students/good-report.html

Although the article deals specifically with technical reports, much of the information is appropriate to all professional reports. Prepare a detailed outline of the article, including major and minor points related to readability.

2. Gathering Background Information for a Report (Objs. 2, 4)

Using databases available through your campus library, locate and read three articles on social media marketing as a means of promoting a business. Mark the main points of each article and prepare a bibliographic citation for each

READ | THINK | WRITE | SPEAK | COLLABORATE

3. Developing a Report Outline (Objs. 1, 2)

Select one of the report topics listed in Application 12. Develop an outline for the described report. Identify possible sources for locating the necessary information.

4. Summarizing a Professional Meeting (Objs. 2, 4)

Attend a professional meeting of a campus or community organization. Take notes on the program presented, the issues discussed, and so on. Submit a short report to your instructor summarizing the events of the meeting, and include a section that describes the benefits that might be derived from membership in that organization.

READ | THINK | WRITE | SPEAK | COLLABORATE

Informational Reports

5. Auditing a Computer Lab (Objs. 2, 4)

Visit the computer lab on your campus. Through observation and interviews, prepare an audit report of the lab's offerings. Include the following items in your report: (1) the types of equipment available (e.g., PCs, Macs, mainframe terminals), (2) the quantity of each type, and (3) the operating systems and applications software available (product, version). Attach a table that summarizes your analysis. Submit the letter report to your instructor.

6. Evaluating the Performance of a Stock Portfolio (Objs. 2, 4)

Create a stock portfolio of 10 stocks on a financial website (e.g., www.stockmaster.com, http://moneycentral.msn.com/content/P58723.asp). Assume that you will purchase 100 shares of each of the 10 stocks at the prices listed at the market close on a particular day. The stock portfolio will record the changes in each of the ten stocks for each trading day. Print this report for five trading days.

Required: Submit a memorandum report to your instructor on the purchase date reporting your 10 stocks according to the following format:

Name of Stock | *Price per Share* | *Total Cost (× 100)*

At the end of the trading period, submit another memorandum to your instructor detailing how your investments fared during the week. Record the Dow Jones Industrial Average for both your purchase date and the end of the five-day period. Compare your total performance—percentage gain or loss—with that of the Dow Jones average.

7. Promoting International Understanding (Objs. 2, 4)

Research the cultural differences between business executives in the United States and China; write a memorandum report communicating this information to U.S. managers working in China. Write another memo to Jeanne Pitman, director of international assignments, persuading her to develop other ways to promote international understanding in the company. You may vary this case by selecting a country of your choice.

8. Communicating Concern for Employees (Objs. 2, 4)

Review research related to cell phone safety and identify ways to solve businesses' problems resulting from accidents among workers. Write a short informational report. To make the case more meaningful, address the issue in an employee group or environment with which you are familiar.

9. Communicating During a Crisis (Objs. 2, 4)

Review research and write an informational report related to crisis communication and the sharing of information with employees about a financial, ethical, health, or environmental crisis. Your instructor may vary this assignment so that your report will be directed to stockholders, the public, or another specified group.

Analytical Reports

10. Comparing the Merits of Franchising Versus Starting an Independent Business (Objs. 2, 4)

You and a silent partner plan to open a business establishment in your city. You are unsure whether to obtain a franchise for such an establishment or to start your own independent restaurant. Select a franchise opportunity of your choice and research it. Include in your findings the initial investment cost, start-up expenses, franchise requirements and fees, and success and failure rate. Compare the franchise opportunity to the option of an independent business.

Required: Prepare a report for your intended silent partner that compares the options of franchising versus independent ownership. Make a recommendation as to the more desirable action to take.

11. Assessing the Feasibility of Constructing a Recreational Complex (Objs. 2, 4)

Oakdale University has established a committee to study the feasibility of constructing a recreational center for students, faculty, and staff. To help determine the interest of faculty and staff, the committee has administered a questionnaire. The findings will be combined with other aspects of the feasibility study in a presentation to the president. The committee believes the 668-person sample is representative of the faculty and staff. The results of the survey follow:

1. On average, how often do you exercise each week?
   - 136 0–1 day
   - 274 2–3 days
   - 197 4–5 days
   - 61 6–7 days
2. During a week, in which of the following activities do you participate? Check all that apply.
   - 171 Aerobic exercise
   - 157 Jogging
   - 147 Weightlifting
   - 299 Walking
   - 67 Tennis
   - 42 Other
3. If you had access, in which of the following activities would you participate? Check all that apply.
   - 196 Racquetball
   - 361 Swimming
   - 72 Basketball
   - 126 Running or walking on an indoor track
   - 165 Weight machines
4. If a recreation center were constructed for employees, what is the maximum amount you would be willing to pay per month to provide use of the center to your immediate family members?
   - 125 $0–$10
   - 69 $11–$20
   - 156 $21–$30
   - 261 $31–$40
   - 57 $41–$50

Required: As a member of the committee, prepare a short report for the president, Michelle Karratassos. You asked respondents to estimate the amounts they would be willing to pay a month for their families to use the center as $0 to $10, $11 to $20, and so on. If you were to do mathematical computations, you would probably use midpoints such as $5, $15.50, $25.50, and so on as values for each class. In this case, however, write in generalities simply using percentages.

12. Preparing an Analytical Report (Objs. 2, 4)

In teams of three or four, prepare a short report on *one* of the following cases. Make any assumptions and collect any background information needed to make an informed decision. Reviewing this list may help you identify a business-related problem you have encountered that you would like to investigate; evaluate possible alternative solutions, and make a recommendation.

a. Recommend a digital camera for your regional quality assurance inspectors of a national convenience store chain. The inspectors will use the camera to enhance the quality of periodic reports documenting each store's adherence to company policies (e.g., visibility of company signage, friendliness of staff, cleanliness of restrooms).

b. Recommend one of three laptop computers for use by the company's sales staff. The computer must have wireless capability for transmitting and retrieving data from the central office.

c. Investigate whether allowing employees to take "e-breaks" at their computer rather than the traditional coffee break in the employee lounge would improve productivity and employee morale.

d. Numerous studies cite obesity as a major health problem affecting company productivity. Study the issue and make a recommendation to the company as to how to respond. If directed by your instructor, search an online database or the Internet and choose another health problem.

e. After suffering catastrophic losses following Hurricane Ike, an insurance company is seeking your advice on its plan to withdraw coverage from Texas counties within the devastated areas. Provide the insurance company with an analysis of the significant issues and any ethical and legal implications of the decision.

f. As director of human resources, investigate the merits of adopting a corporate policy banning cell phone usage by employees driving company vehicles. The legislature of your state has not banned cell phone usage while driving.

g. A local orchard has sold its line of jellies and jams only to specialty retailers. Consider the feasibility of launching a website with online ordering capability for individual consumers.

h. A national study suggests that employees who participate regularly in formal fitness programs file fewer health insurance claims than those who do not. As a member of the board of directors, weigh alternatives and present a plan that would provide employees an incentive to participate actively in a fitness program.

13. Studying the Merits of Mentoring (Objs. 2, 3)

Your company, Ultron Oil, is considering implementing a formal mentoring program as a means for developing managerial talent. Your supervisor, the division director, has commissioned you to prepare a report on the effectiveness of mentoring. As a part of the study, you have surveyed 70 managers representing a variety of businesses; 44 were male, and 26 were female. They ranged in age from 22 to 69, with the median age being 45. Their responses follow:

1. In your career development, have you ever had a mentor?
   - 66 Yes. Answer all items.
   - 4 No. Skip to Item 6.
2. Which of the following describes your mentoring relationship(s)?
   - 6 Formal; my mentor(s) was/were appointed or assigned to me.
   - 38 Informal; the relationship(s) just evolved.
   - 22 One or more was formal, and one or more was informal.
3. How long did the typical mentoring relationship last?
   - 10 Less than one year
   - 12 One to two years
   - 16 Three to five years
   - 14 More than five years
   - 14 Varying lengths of time (answers varied from one month to life)
4. Did you perceive that you benefited from the mentoring relationship?
   - 63 Yes
   - 3 No
5. Did you perceive that your mentor benefited from the relationship?
   - 60 Yes
   - 6 No
6. Have you ever been a mentor to another person?
   - 54 Yes
   - 16 No
7. Does your company have a mentoring program in place?
   - 32 Yes
   - 38 No

Required: Prepare the report for the division director. Present your findings, draw conclusions, and make recommendations. Prepare any preliminary and addenda parts you believe will enable the reader to understand the report.

14. Solving a Business Problem (Objs. 2, 3)

Select one of the following problems to solve. Provide the necessary assumptions and background data. Then write a formal report of your analysis, conclusions, and recommendations. Include preliminary and ending parts you believe appropriate. You may need to design a questionnaire and administer it to an appropriate sample. Reviewing this list may help you identify a business-related problem you have encountered during your employment or cooperative education and intern experiences. If you choose to solve your own problem, provide the necessary assumptions and background data.

a. Choose from the five research studies presented in Chapter 9, Application 4.

b. Your president is concerned about the increasing incidence among employees of visible tattoos and other types of body art. Conduct research about company policies that prohibit or limit the display of body art by employees. Write a company policy for review by the president.

c. Investigate the feasibility of your company becoming the corporate sponsor of a professional athletic team located in the same city as the company's corporate headquarters. The stadium would be named for the company and the company would control all advertising rights within the stadium.

d. You have read articles about the advantages of having global positioning satellite (GPS) trackers in automobiles to help stranded motorists. Propose how GPS trackers could be used to monitor the movement of remote employees and investigate the implications of this action.

e. Your human resources department is considering the implementation of a full criminal background check in the selection of employees. Study the advisability of this practice.

f. Your department handles highly sensitive information and, as a result, requires extremely reliable user identification. You are considering ocular scanning or perhaps some other type of biometric identification. Investigate the advantages and disadvantages of such a system and recommend whether your organization should pursue it.

g. Since its inception, your company has paid full employee health insurance premiums. Because of spiraling premiums, the company is considering requiring a 20 percent co-payment from employees for each medical claim. Investigate the implications of this action.

h. Investigate the possibility of enlisting senior citizen volunteers to staff a city welcome center scheduled to open next year.

i. A committee of employees has recommended that the company establish a hazardous waste depository where employees can discard items not accepted in the landfill (e.g., paint, batteries, and insecticides). The president has asked you to think the idea through and present a report of the cost, public relations implications, employee relations, and logistics of operating the depository.

j. You have received reports that several of your major competitors have installed electronic auditing procedures to monitor employees' computer usage. Investigate the implications of using technology to monitor employees' computer activities. Will employees consider this procedure an invasion of privacy? Anticipate all possible problems and present strategies for dealing with them.

k. Although no employees have made formal complaints of sexual harassment in the workplace, information from the grapevine has convinced you that the company needs a formal policy concerning sexual harassment. To develop this company policy, research the legalities related to this issue and gather information (strategies) from other companies with sexual harassment policies.

Proposals

15. Bidding for a Convention Site (Obj. 5)

The National Insurance Appraisers Association is planning an upcoming convention. This association of 500 members conducts a three-day conference during late October that includes at least one general session and as many as five breakout groups of 50–75 participants. The chair of this group's convention site committee has invited your city (instructor will assign) to submit a proposal bidding for the convention's 2011 national convention.

Required: As executive director of the Economic Development Council, write a proposal including specific information to convince the group that your city (choose a location) can provide the needed meeting facilities, hotel accommodations, economical transportation from major U.S. cities, and a variety of social and recreational activities for members and guests. Obtain your information via the Internet.

16. Applying for a Franchise to Open a 24/7 Fitness Center (Obj. 5)

Interested in opening a fitness center, Emily Pearson wrote 24/7 Energy, a popular franchiser of fitness centers, to solicit franchise information. In answer to his request, Holland received an extremely receptive letter requesting standard information designed to help 24/7 Energy determine the economic viability of the proposed location. After analyzing this preliminary information, 24/7 Energy will decide whether to accept Pearson's franchise application.

24/7 Energy has requested preliminary information regarding the economic and social environment of the proposed site. Specifically, Pearson must provide valid, objective data concerning the population of the service area, the economic status of the population, accessibility of the proposed site, the nature and extent of competing fitness franchises that offer patrons round-the-clock access, and any other information that would support the economic success of the proposed franchise.

Required: As Emily Pearson, prepare a letter report to the franchiser. Address it to 24/7 Energy, 700 Gulfside Drive, Pensacola, FL 32501-9700.

17. Proposing Additional Employee Benefit to Management (Obj. 5)

As human resources manager at Innovative Solutions, you are preparing a proposal to be submitted to company management that would institute a company sponsored volunteer program for employees.

Required: Write a proposal that includes the following information: (1) an explanation of how the volunteer program described in your proposal would benefit employees and the company, (2) a complete explanation of how the program would work, and (3) a budget for anticipated costs.

READ | THINK | WRITE | SPEAK | COLLABORATE

18. Analyzing an Organization's Report (Objs. 1, 2)

Obtain a copy of a report prepared by an organization and analyze it in the following ways:

a. Purpose
b. Intended audience
c. Degree of formality
d. Use of graphic support
e. Parts included (see Figure 11-1)
f. Referencing method

Make a brief presentation to your class about your findings.

19. Responding to Problem of Computer Virus Hoaxes (Objs. 2, 4)

Prepare an oral report on computer virus hoaxes and the appropriate response to them. Include the following parts in your report outline: (1) Why are virus hoaxes problematic for individuals and organizations? (2) What are some common virus hoaxes? (3) How can virus hoaxes be "checked out"? Prepare appropriate visuals for your presentation. End your report with a recommendation as to how to best respond to virus hoaxes. Submit your report outline and a copy of your visuals to your instructor after delivering your presentation.

READ | THINK | WRITE | SPEAK | COLLABORATE

20. Writing as a Team (Objs. 1–4)

Your instructor has provided detailed instructions for completing a long or short report or proposal in teams. *Building High-Performance Teams* (your team handbook) contains instructions, sample formats, and guidelines for electronically communicating with your instructor in the following ways:

a. Send your instructor a weekly progress report via email. The report should contain the following information about each meeting held during the week: date, place, and duration of meeting; members present; report of work accomplished since the last meeting; brief description of work accomplished during the current meeting; and work allocated to be completed before the next meeting. (See *Building High-Performance Teams* for format.)
b. About midway in your report preparation, or when you are instructed, send your instructor an email message containing your evaluation of each member of the group. Assign a percentage indicating the contribution each member has made

to the group thus far. Ideally each member should contribute his or her fair share of 100 percent. However, assume that a group consisted of four members; one person contributed more than his or her equal share, and one person contributed less. You might assign these two members 30 percent and 20 percent, respectively, and rank the other two members 25 percent each. Note the total percentages awarded must equal 100 percent. Write a brief statement justifying the rating you assigned each member; provide specific, verifiable evidence. (A form for completing this evaluation is included in *Building High-Performance Teams.*)

c. After your report is completed, fill out the team member evaluation provided in your team handbook. Email a debriefing memo to your instructor that describes your perceptions about your team's performance. (See *Building High-Performance Teams* for details of this assignment.)

CASES

© ISTOCKPHOTO.COM/FOTEK

1. Financial Reporting Goes Multimedia

Hoovers was established as The Reference Press in 1990 by Gary Hoover, who was convinced that there was a need for a directory that provided in-depth information about businesses. The first publication was called "Hoover's Handbook 1991: Profiles of Over 500 Major Corporations." As years passed additional titles were offered, and eventually in 1995, a CD-ROM product containing the company profiles was marketed. That same year a web-based product was also introduced called Hoover's Online.

Hoover's Online, owned by Hoover's Inc. of Austin, Texas, is an excellent resource for business researchers. It provides core financial and operating information on important public and private U.S. and foreign companies. The Video Center found on the Hoover's website allows viewers to access information on a variety of topics. Subscribers have access to a variety of financial reports including income statements, balance sheets, liabilities, shareholders equity, and cash flow statements for 28 million companies. Reports can be downloaded into Excel or CSV format and are supplemented by business information that includes company executives, competitors, and other operational insights that may be of interest to a potential customer, investor, or competitor. Hoover's podcast series provides access to various business topics related to the latest business news, trends, and advice. Podcasts are updated frequently and can be listened to directly from the website, downloaded to an MP3 player, or subscribed to as a RSS feed.

Application:

1. Explore the video and podcast features of the Hoover's Online site at www.hoovers.com. Prepare a short report on how quantitative data reporting can be enhanced with video and audio elements.
2. Select a current business issue to research. Prepare a 2-minute podcast on the topic that follows the style of the Hoover's business podcasts. Following your instructor's directions, post your podcast online for your classmates to access.
3. In memo report form, provide a critique of the podcast created by a classmate as to its effectiveness in reporting on the selected topic. Comment on the scope of content, organization, and audience appeal. In your summary, make suggestions as to what would the creator do differently if the same information is to be presented in a written report?

2. Cybertheft: It's a Big Deal

One of the World Wide Web's most attractive features, easy access to a universe of information and data, is also one of its greatest vulnerabilities. Computer users can easily access, download, copy, cut, paste, and publish any of the text, pictures, video, sound, program code, and other data forms available on the Internet. An inherent conflict of interest prevails because of the consumer's appetite for data and the creator's right to remuneration for original work.

Copyrights provide an economic incentive for the development of creative works in literature, computer applications, and the performing arts. For instance, songwriters in the United States are paid royalties by radio stations for broadcasting their copyrighted musical works. Because of copyrights, it is illegal to make and sell an authorized duplicate of a commercial CD, video, or DVD. The law assures that creators receive remuneration from sales for their investment of time, talent, and energy. The information superhighway, however, crosses borders where U.S. copyright laws do not apply. With proper equipment and the aid of file sharing websites, cyberfans can make high-quality digital copies of downloaded music and movies, effectively bypassing copyright requirements.

Passage of the Patriot Act gave the FBI easier access to information about cyberspace theft by allowing examination of Internet databases without search warrants. Internet service providers have been compelled to turn over the names of subscribers traced by the music industry to their IP addresses. The Recording Industry Association has also targeted college campuses in its aggressive campaign to curtail unauthorized music downloading. In 2003, for example, four students agreed to fines of $12,000 to $17,500 each and promised to stop illegally downloading music on their campus computer servers as part of an out-of-court settlement. Some universities are also denying Internet access to students who download films and music illegally.[9]

Web pages are another type of creative expression falling victim to cybertheft. Dealernet, an organization that helps car dealers sell vehicles over the Internet, was shocked to discover that a Southern California company had downloaded Dealernet web pages and reproduced them on its own website. The competing site deleted the pages when Dealernet threatened legal action.

Cybertheft deprives musicians, artists, and other creative parties from the income that would otherwise result from the sale and licensing of their artistic works. The World Intellectual Property Organization, sponsored by the United Nations, is working to ensure copyright protection worldwide. Representatives of the United States and 183 other countries who are members of the group have signed treaties that extend copyrights to the Internet and strengthen copyright laws in many of the world's nations. On the home front, various representatives of the computer industry have joined entertainment groups such as the Recording Industry Association of America and the Motion Picture Association of America to form the Creative Incentive Coalition; a major activity of the group is to lobby Congress for legislation and treaties that would provide better copyright protection.[10]

Every business entity has a responsibility to avoid situations of copyright infringement and to ensure that its employees do so as well. Companies are legally responsible for violations if the copyright owner can prove that they knew or should have known about the infringement. Google News, for example, was found by a Belgian court to have violated copyright when it posted extracts from Belgian newspaper stories on its website.[11] While it is rare for employees to be taken to court for copyright violation, it does occur and carries heavy penalties. Such liability makes it advisable for organizations to develop policies against copyright violation and to provide training to employees about the risks and responsibilities.

Visit your companion website, www.cengage.com/bcomm/lehman, to link to web resources related to this topic. As directed by your instructor, complete one or more of the following:

1. Visit the listed sites to determine current international copyright issues or cases. Provide a one-page written summary to your instructor that describes the issue and the country(ies) involved.
2. Write a short, informative report describing how a company's website can violate the copyrights of others and giving advice to organizational web page developers for avoiding possible copyright infringement.
3. "The nature of cyberspace defies copyright enforcement." In a one- to two-page report, justify or refute this statement, giving reasons and/or examples.

© BBC LTD./COURTESY: EVERETT COLLECTION

3. Video Case: The Office: Delivering Bad News at a Team Briefing? NOT!

In this clip, David gives an oral report to his employees about his meeting with the board concerning the future of the office.

Complete the following activities as directed by your instructor after viewing the video:

1. In small groups, consider how David should have handled his oral briefing differently. Compose a short skit that redesigns the oral briefing using an inductive outline and focuses on the most important positive news from the employees' perspectives. Deliver your skit to the class, focusing on delivery that projects an empathetic, compassionate tone.
2. As David's supervisor, consider ways to help him deliver this information to his employees. Compose a short report to give to him at the meeting that outlines the specific information to be shared and provides him tips for delivering bad news to employees.

Chapter 12
Designing and Delivering Business Presentations

The Java platform is "touching nearly every business system on earth" and "powering billions of consumers on mobile handsets and consumer electronics."

Microsoft CEO Scott McNealy

Objectives

When you have completed Chapter 12, you will be able to:

1. Plan a business presentation that accomplishes the speaker's goals and meets the audience's needs.
2. Organize and develop the three parts of an effective presentation.
3. Select, design, and use presentation visuals effectively.
4. Deliver speeches with increasing confidence.
5. Discuss strategies for presenting in alternate delivery situations such as culturally diverse audiences, team, and distance presentations.

SHOWCASE PART 1

Sun Microsystems: Technology Advancements Revolutionize Business Presentations

While Sun Microsystems was originally involved with the manufacture of computer workstations, it is most associated with Java, one of the most well-known Internet-based programming languages. Because of the capabilities of Java, Internet sites, cell phones, and home game players can effectively offer splashy graphics, animation, and real-time data updates.

One of Java's most noticeable abilities is the delivery of small programs, called applets, over the Web. Java applets have wide applicability because they are system independent and can be used by Windows, Mac, or Unix computers. This flexibility has attracted many developers around the globe to use Java to enhance their websites and wireless communication capabilities. In Japan, Java-enabled cell phones allow users to access calendars, expense reports, email, and more. In Brazil, Java offers doctors instant access to the medical records of 12 million people, ensuring accurate information wherever residents need care.

Following Oracle's acquisition of Sun in 2009, a new online Java Store was launched to showcase applications to the 800 million desktop Java technology users worldwide. Developers can submit applications to the store's Java Warehouse and, if selected by Sun, their software is offered for distribution in the Java Store.[1]

Java-enabled webcams let you see the world in real time from the comfort of your home or office. The Java website illustrates this technology by allowing you to view live shots of London, Moscow, Tokyo, and other exciting locations. Java runs virtually everywhere, across networked technologies, servers, and handheld devices. In speaking about the wide popularity of the Java platform, Sun Microsystem board chairman Scott McNealy said it is "touching nearly every business system on earth" and "powering billions of consumers on mobile handsets and consumer electronics."[2]

Before the Web was widely regarded as a viable business tool, presentations were created with smaller audiences in mind. Presentation choices came in the form of slides, handouts, or an automated slide show that could be saved to a single computer. Now, however, you can upload your presentation to a website and let viewers watch at their leisure.

A special consideration in posting presentations to the Web is to keep graphics small, since the larger the image, the longer it will take to appear. In addition, using universally available fonts such as Cambria and Calibri ensures that your audience is able to view what you intended. No matter how nice your presentation looks on your own PC, you will want to visit the site and view the show, ideally on different computers and using different browsers.[3]

Whether designing visual presentations for the Web or developing face-to-face presentations for delivery to your staff or customers, you will want to relate your ideas clearly and effectively. This chapter provides guidelines for refining your presentation skills—skills for which no amount of innovative technology can substitute. You will learn how to plan and organize your presentation, develop dynamic presentation media, refine your delivery, and adapt your presentation for an intercultural audience or alternate delivery methods, such as team and distance presentations.

www.java.sun.com

SEE SHOWCASE PART 2, ON PAGE 454 FOR SPOTLIGHT COMMUNICATOR SCOTT MCNEALY, BOARD CHAIRMAN, SUN MICROSYSTEMS.

1 OBJECTIVE Planning an Effective Business Presentation

The simplicity of writing email and talking on the phone has deterred many workers from learning to communicate in front of people with authority and authenticity.[4] Being a skilled business communicator requires skill in both written and verbal form. A business presentation is an important means of exchanging information for decision making and policy development, relating the benefits of the services offered, and sharing our goals, values, and vision. Because multiple people receive the message at the same time and are able to provide immediate feedback for clarification, presentations can significantly reduce message distortion and misunderstanding.

Many of the presentations you give will be formal, with sufficient time allowed for planning and developing elaborate visual support. You may present information and recommendations to external audiences such as customers and clients whom you've never met or to an internal audience made up of coworkers and managers you know well. You can also expect to present some less formal presentations, often referred to as ***oral briefings***. An oral briefing might entail a short update on a current project requested during a meeting without advance notice or a brief explanation in the hallway when your supervisor walks past. Sales representatives give oral briefings daily as they present short, informal pitches for new products and services.

Which is the most critical component of a presentation: content, quality of visual support, or delivery?

Regardless of the formality of the presentation, the time given to prepare, the nature of the audience (friends or strangers), or the media used (live, distant, Web, or DVD delivery on demand) your success depends on your ability to think on your feet and speak confidently as you address audience needs. Understanding the purpose you hope to achieve through your presentation and conceptualizing your audience will enable you to organize the content in a way the audience can understand *and* accept.

Identify Your Purpose

Determining what you want to accomplish during a presentation is a fundamental principle of planning an effective presentation. Some speech coaches recommend completing the following vital sentence to lay the foundation for a successful presentation: "At the end of my presentation, the audience will ________." In his book, *Do's and Taboos of Public Speaking*, Axtell provides two excellent mechanisms for condensing your presentation into a brief, achievable purpose that will direct you in identifying and supporting the major points:[5]

- Ask yourself, "What is my message?" Then, develop a phrase, a single thought, or a conclusion you want the audience to take with them from the presentation. This elementary statement likely may be the final sentence in your presentation—the basic message you want the audience to remember.
- Imagine a member of your audience has been asked to summarize your message. Ideally, you want to hear them describe your central purpose.

Know Your Audience

How is preparation of written messages and presentations similar in terms of empathy for the audience?

A common mistake for many presenters is to presume they know the audience without attempting to find out about them. If you expect to get results, you must commit the time to know your audience and focus your presentation on them—from planning your speech to practicing its delivery.

As a general rule, audiences *do* want to be in tune with a speaker. Yet people listen to speeches about things of interest to them. "What's in it for me?" is the question most listeners ask. A speech about global warming to a farm group should address the farmers' problems, for example, and not focus on theories of global warming. Additionally, different strategies are needed for audiences who think and make decisions differently. For instance, different strategies are needed for making a successful presentation to sell software to a group of lawyers than to a group of doctors. Lawyers typically think quickly and are argumentative and decisive while doctors are often cautious, skeptical, and don't make quick decisions.[6]

To deliver a presentation that focuses on the wants and expectations of an audience, you must determine who they are, what motivates them, how they think, and how they make decisions. Helpful information you can obtain about most audiences includes ages, genders, occupations, educational levels, attitudes, values, broad and specific interests, and needs. In addition, you should also consider certain things about the occasion and location. Patriotic speeches to a group of military veterans will differ from speeches to a group of new recruits, just as Fourth of July speeches will differ from Veterans Day speeches. Seek answers to the following questions when you discuss your speaking engagement with someone representing the group or audience:

1. *Who* is the audience and *who* requested the presentation? General characteristics of the audience should be considered, as well as the extent of their knowledge and experience with the topic, attitude toward the topic and you as a credible speaker, anticipated response to the use of electronic media, and required or volunteer attendance.

2. *Why* is this topic important to the audience? What will the audience do with the information presented?

3. *What* environmental factors affect the presentation?
   - How many will be in the audience?
   - Will I be the only speaker? If not, where does my presentation fit in the program? What time of day?
   - How much time will I be permitted? Minimum? Maximum?
   - What are the seating arrangements? How far will the audience be from the speaker? Will a microphone or other equipment be available?

What other questions would you ask when planning a presentation?

Answers to these questions reveal whether the speaking environment will be intimate or remote, whether the audience is likely to be receptive and alert or nonreceptive and tired, and whether you will need to use additional motivational or persuasive techniques.

To illustrate the planning stage of a presentation, assume that you are a promotional representative for Project COPE (Challenging Outdoor Personal Experiences), a personal development program. Through a weekend of mentally and physically challenging events, participants develop self-confidence, trust, communication, and teamwork. Participants build these valuable managerial skills as they attempt to do things they have never done and work together to develop creative ways to overcome various obstacles. The "trust fall" (falling backwards to be caught by a team member) and climbing a 30-foot tower and leaning out to catch a bar being held by team members are examples of these demanding events. Several senior executives of a large multinational company are sold on your program as a means to develop a trust-based corporate culture, and you have been invited to speak during the company's annual two-day management retreat. You are scheduled to speak at 10 a.m. and will have 30 minutes to present your message to 300 managers of various ages, genders, and cultures. Your analysis of the purpose and your audience follows:

Purpose: To guide participants in the use of COPE techniques to facilitate development of self-confidence, communication, and teamwork.

Audience: Managers desiring to improve the corporate culture in the organization and in their units. Audience should be alert for this early morning presentation and experience minimal mental distractions in a retreat environment. Managers will likely welcome a captivating electronic presentation with realistic images of the described activities.

Your Turn 12-1
Assessment

Your professional success may well depend on the ability to make successful presentations. While many fear public speaking, you can hone your presentation skills by first assessing your current abilities and then targeting areas for improvement.

TAKE ACTION:

- Assess your presentation abilities by responding to the *Are You a Good Presenter? Questionnaire©* at www.fripp.com/cgi-bin/alltest/alltest.cgi. You may link to this URL or go to your companion website at www.cengage.com/bcomm/lehman for updated links.
- Print out the results and highlight the tips you find most useful for perfecting your presentation skills.

Communicating Your Message During a Brief Ride. An "elevator speech" is an overview of an idea for a product, service, or project that could conceivably be delivered in the time span of an elevator ride. Whether in an elevator or elsewhere, we often have brief encounters with important people with whom we want to share our message. Your elevator speech must grab attention and say a lot in a few words. By relating your central message, you market yourself or your business in a way that will make others want to know more about you. Memorize your two-minute presentation and make it such a part of you that you can share it confidently and without hesitation. Your elevator speech will serve as your introduction to others, so it has to be good!

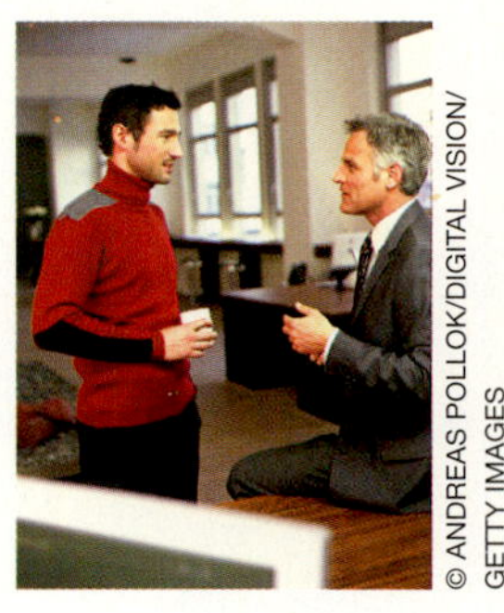

OBJECTIVE 2

Organizing the Content

With an understanding of the purpose of your business presentation—why you are giving it and what you hope to achieve—and a conception of the size, interest, and background of the audience, you are prepared to outline your presentation and identify appropriate content. First introduced by famous speech trainer Dale Carnegie and still recommended by speech experts today, the simple but effective presentation format includes an introduction, a body, and a close. In the introduction, tell the audience what you are going to tell them; in the body, tell them; and in the close, tell them what you told them.

How can the speaker avoid redundancy in the delivery of the three parts of the presentation?

This design may sound repetitive; on the contrary, it works quite well. The audience processes information verbally and cannot slow the speaker down when information is complex. Thus, repetition aids the listener in processing the information that supports the speaker's purpose.

Introduction

What you say at the beginning sets the stage for your entire presentation and initiates your rapport with the audience. However, inexperienced speakers often settle for unoriginal and overused introductions, such as "My name is . . . , and my topic is . . ." or "It is a pleasure . . . ," or negative statements, such as apologies for lack of preparation, boring delivery, or late arrival, that reduce the audience's desire to listen. An effective introduction accomplishes the following goals:

How would you gain attention for a presentation on your firm's entry into the Latin American market?

- **Captures attention and involves the audience.** Choose an attention-getter that is relevant to the subject and appropriate for the situation. Attention-getting techniques may include:
  - a shocking statement or startling statistic.
  - a quotation by an expert or well-known person.

- a rhetorical or open-ended question that generates discussion from the audience.
- an appropriate joke or humor.
- a demonstration or dramatic presentation aid.
- an anecdote or timely story from a business periodical.
- a personal reference, compliment to the audience, or a reference to the occasion of the presentation.

To involve the audience directly, ask for a show of hands in response to a direct question, allow the audience time to think about the answer to a rhetorical question, or explain why the information is important and how it will benefit the listeners. Consider the following examples.

A drug awareness speech to young people might begin with a true story:

"I live in a quiet, middle-class, comfortable neighborhood. That is, until just a few months ago—when four young people from three different families were killed in an automobile accident following a party at which drugs were used."

A report presenting an information systems recommendation could introduce the subject and set the stage for the findings (inductive sequence) or the recommendation (deductive sequence):

Inductive: "When we were granted approval to adopt enterprise resource planning, a team immediately began work identifying the optimal software to meet our information needs."

Deductive: "By investing in enterprise resource planning, we can manage our information needs and support the future growth of our company."

- **Establishes rapport.** Initiate rapport with the listeners; convince them that you are concerned that they benefit from the presentation and that you are qualified to speak on the topic. You might share a personal story that relates to the topic but reveals something about yourself, or discuss your background or a specific experience with the topic being discussed.

How can the speaker effectively guide the audience from one major section of the presentation to another?

- **Presents the purpose statement and previews the points that will be developed.** To maintain the interest you have captured, present your purpose statement directly so that the audience is certain to hear it. Use original statements and avoid clichés such as "My topic today is . . ." or "I'd like to talk with you about . . ." Next, preview the major points you will discuss in the order you will discuss them. For example, you might say,

"First, I'll discuss . . . , then . . . , and finally. . . ."

"The acquisition and construction cost of all three sites were comparable. The decision to locate the new distribution facility in Madison, South Carolina, is based on the quality of living, transportation accessibility, and an adequate work force."

Revealing the presentation plan will help the audience understand how the parts of the body are tied together to support the purpose statement, thus increasing their understanding. For a long, complex presentation, you might display a presentation visual that lists the points in the order they will be covered. As you begin each major point, display a slide that contains that point and perhaps a related image. These section slides partition your presentation just as headings do in a written report, and thus move the listener more easily from one major point to the next.

Body

What factors affected the success of a presentation you have heard?

In a typical presentation of 20 to 30 minutes, limit your presentation to only a few major points (typically three to five) because of time constraints and your audience's ability to concentrate and absorb. Making every statement in a presentation into a major point—something to be remembered—is impossible, unless the presentation lasts only two or three minutes.

Once you have selected your major points, locate your supporting material. You may use several techniques to ensure the audience understands your point and to reinforce it:

- **Provide support in a form that is easy to understand.** Two techniques will assist you in accomplishing this goal:

  1. **Use simple vocabulary and short sentences that the listener can understand easily and that sound conversational and interesting.** Spoken communication is more difficult to process than written communication; therefore, complex, varied vocabulary and long sentences often included in written documents are not effective in a presentation.

  2. **Avoid jargon or technical terms that the listeners may not understand.** Instead, use plain English that the audience can easily comprehend. Make your speech more interesting and memorable by using word pictures to make your points. Matt Hughes, a speech consultant, provides this example: If your message is a warning of difficulties ahead, you might say: "We're climbing a hill that's getting steeper, and there are rocks and potholes in the road."[7]

  3. **Use a familiar frame of reference.** Drawing analogies between new ideas and familiar ones is another technique for generating understanding. For example, noting that the U.S. blog-reading audience is already one half the size of the newspaper-reading population helps clarify an abstract or complex concept. Saying that "infodumping" is the verbal equivalent of email spam explains well the expected consequences of overloading an audience with too many details.[8] When it became apparent that many Mississippi Gulf Coast residents intended to weather Katrina, a category 5 hurricane, Mississippi Governor Haley Barbour

instructed the news media to stress that this hurricane was predicted to be worse than Hurricane Camille, a destructive hurricane that most Mississsippians still remember or have heard of in their families' stories.

- **Provide relevant statistics.** Provide statistics or other quantitative measures available to lend authority and credibility to your points. In your presentation about COPE, you could (1) locate evidence to support your thesis that trust environments can be created, and (2) obtain statistics from companies that have participated in COPE (e.g., reduced turnover and absenteeism, improved internal communication, stronger relationships with customers/clients, and other measures of increased effectiveness).

Unless there is a need for precision, do not overwhelm your audience with excessive statistics. Instead, round off numbers and use broad terms or word pictures that the listener can remember. Instead of "68.2 percent" say "over two thirds"; instead of "112 percent rise in production" say "our output more than doubled." Hearing that a high capacity flash drive holds as much data as 800 CDs is less confusing and more memorable than hearing the exact number of gigabytes for each medium.[9] In a message to persuade customers to replace their energy-draining light bulbs with compact-fluorescent lights (CFLs), California energy company PG&E used the following comparisons to ensure that customers understood the implications: "If 12 traditional light bulbs are replaced throughout a home with CFLs, over the lifetime of the bulbs, it would save approximately $900 in energy costs . . . in such a case, you would reduce greenhouse gases by 2,900 pounds, as much as taking one car off the road for four months."[10]

What comparison could you use to explain a complex concept or overwhelming statistics in your field?

- **Use quotes from prominent people.** Comments made by other authorities are helpful in establishing credibility. In the case of the COPE presentation, comments from top management of leading companies represent a credible source of quotations.
- **Use interesting anecdotes.** Audiences like and remember anecdotes or interesting stories that tie into the presentation and make strong emotional connections with the audiences. In her book *Who Ever Tells the Best Story Wins*, Annette Simmons stresses that stories allow the audience to feel a presenter's presence, to show a trace of humanity, is vital for understanding, influence, and strong relationships. She encourages leaders to craft personal stories into specific, intentional messages that communicate values, vision, and important lessons.[11] While communicating their values, leaders communicate the values they expect from employees. Like jokes, be sure you can get straight to the point of a story. In the COPE presentation, you might include stories about leading companies that have participated in COPE and relate their firsthand experiences.
- **Use jokes and humor appropriately.** A joke or humor can create a special bond between you and the audience, ease your approach to sensitive subjects, disarm a nonreceptive audience, or make your message easier to understand and remember. Plan your joke carefully so that you can (1) get the point across as quickly as possible, (2) deliver it in a conversational manner with interesting inflections and effective body movements, and (3) deliver the punch line effectively. If you cannot tell a joke well, use humor instead—amusing things that happened to you or someone you know, one-liners, or humorous quotations that relate to your presentation. Refrain from any

humor that may reflect negatively on race, color, religion, gender, age, culture, or other personal areas of sensitivity.

For the COPE presentation, you could incorporate a few amusing incidents that occurred during a COPE session. Each incident should be relevant to your speech and appropriate to your audience. You believe these humorous accounts will make the audience more receptive to the idea of a weekend of intense activities.

- **Use presentation visuals.** Presentation visuals, such as handouts, whiteboards, flip charts, transparencies, electronic presentations, and demonstrations, enhance the effectiveness of the presentation. Develop presentation visuals that will enable your audience to see, hear, and even experience your presentation. A simple demonstration by Apple founder Steve Jobs made numbers related to the processing power of two networks relevant to the lives of his customers. A website loaded on the Apple iPhone 3G in 21 seconds took 59 seconds to load on the AT&T's EDGE network.[12]

- **Encourage audience involvement.** Skilled presenters involve their audiences through techniques such as asking reflective questioning, role playing, directing audience-centered activities, and incorporating current events or periodicals that tie directly to the message. One communications coach's advice for getting an audience "to sit up and listen" is to make the presentation contemporary by working Twitter, texting, video, and other technologies into the speech.[13] Some presenters provide relevant responses to text messages received from the audience during and after a presentation. An audience member too shy to ask a question in a live setting may be an active participant in electronic Q&A.

Why do audiences generally respond positively to the use of statistics, human interest stories, quotes, and humor?

Although stories, statistics, quotations, and the like may seem trivial, they are critical to effective speaking. They retain listener interest, provide evidence to support major points, and often provide the humor that turns an otherwise dreary topic into a stimulating message. They are among the professional speaker's most important inventory items. You can begin accumulating these items from reading about your topic, accessing quotations from prominent people, and observing techniques for speaking effectively from commercial media. Develop a system for collecting materials that seem worth remembering.

Close

The close provides unity to your presentation by "telling the audience what you have already told them." The conclusion should be "your best line, your most dramatic point, your most profound thought, your most memorable bit of information, or your best anecdote."[14] Because listeners tend to remember what they hear last, use these final words strategically. Develop a close that supports and refocuses the audience's attention on your purpose statement.

- **Commit the time and energy needed to develop a creative, memorable conclusion.** An audience is not impressed with endings such as "That's all I have" or "That's it." Useful concluding techniques include summarizing the main points that have been made in the presentation and using anecdotes, humor, and illustrations.

When closing an analytical presentation, state your conclusion and support it with the highlights from your supporting evidence: "In summary, we selected the Madison, South Carolina, location because it had. . . ." In a persuasive presentation, the close is often an urgent plea for the members of the audience to take some action or to look on the subject from a new point of view.

- **Tie the close to the introduction to strengthen the unity of the presentation.** For example, you might answer the rhetorical question you asked in the opening, refer to and build on an anecdote included in the introduction, and so on. A unifying close to a drug awareness presentation might be "So, my friends, make your community drug free so you and your friends can grow up to enjoy the benefits of health, education, family, and freedom."

How can the speaker make a smooth transition from the body to the close?

- **Use transition words that clearly indicate you are moving from the body to the close.** Attempt to develop original words rather than rely on standard statements such as "In closing," or "In conclusion."
- **Practice your close until you can deliver it without stumbling.** Use your voice and gestures to communicate this important idea clearly, emphatically, and sincerely rather than fade out at the end as inexperienced speakers often do.
- **Smile and stand back to accept the audience's applause.** A solid close does not require a "thank you"; instead wait confidently for the audience spontaneous applause to thank you for a worthwhile presentation. Appear eager to begin a question-and-answer period or walk with assurance to your seat.

As you formulate ideas about the introduction, body, and close, a working outline of your presentation about COPE might take this form:

COPE (Challenging Outdoor Personal Experiences):
Skills for Creating Trust Environments in Today's Dynamic Workplace

I. Introduction
   A. Attention-getter that involves the audience and establishes credibility
   B. Purpose statement
   C. Preview of three major points

II. Body
   A. Self-confidence
   B. Communication skills
   C. Team-building skills

III. Close: Restatement of primary benefits to be derived or statement that refocuses the audience's attention to the purpose in a memorable way

Visit your companion website at www.cengage.com/bcomm/lehman to download a Presentation Planning Guide. This planning guide will simplify your preparation for future presentations as you follow a systematic process of selecting a topic, analyzing your audience and speaking environment, and organizing a logical, concise presentation.

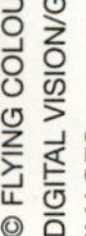

Your Turn 12-2
Miscue

Opening your mouth on behalf of your company can be risky. That's because companies and their spokespeople can be held liable for information shared with coworkers, customers, investors, or other audiences, either in speech or in writing. Nike was charged with presenting false and deceptive advertising due to incomplete reporting of a company study reported in a series of press releases and presentations to the media. The court ruled against Nike, stating that since Nike's public statements about its operations might persuade consumers to buy its products, that communication should be treated as commercial advertising and fall under consumer protection laws. Nike's settlement cost the company $1.5 million.[15]

TAKE ACTION:

- *Discuss the ramifications of this court decision on press releases, televised interviews with corporate leaders, and conversations with clients and customers.*
- *Develop a brief electronic presentation outlining how a company can safeguard itself against possible legal charges related to public statements.*

Designing Compelling Presentation Visuals

Speakers who use presentation visuals are considered better prepared and more interesting, and achieve their goals more often than speakers without visuals. Presentation visuals support and clarify a speaker's ideas and help the audience visualize the message. A speaker using presentation visuals reaches the receiver with double impact—through the eyes and the ears—and achieves the results quoted in an ancient Chinese proverb: "Tell me, I'll forget. Show me, I may remember. But involve me and I'll understand." Research studies confirm that using visuals enhances a presentation. The effective use of presentation visuals provides several advantages:[16]

- clarifies and emphasizes important points.
- increases retention from 14 to 38 percent.
- reduces the time required to present a concept.
- results in a speaker's achieving goals 34 percent more often than when presentation visuals are not used.
- increases group consensus by 21 percent when presentation visuals are used in a meeting.

How can visuals become a negative rather than a positive factor in a presentation?

Types of Presentation Visuals

A speaker must select the appropriate medium or combination of media to accomplish the purpose and to meet the needs of a specific audience. The most common presentation visuals are illustrated in Figure 12-1. Visit your companion website at www.cengage.com/bcomm/lehman for additional explanation about each type.

FIGURE 12-1

Selecting an Appropriate Presentation Visual

VISUAL	ADVANTAGES	LIMITATIONS
Handouts  (© FENG YU/SHUTTERSTOCK.COM)	• Provide detailed information that audience can examine closely • Extend a presentation by providing resources for later use • Reduce the need for note taking and aid in audience retention	• Can divert audience's attention from the speaker • Can be expensive
Boards and flip charts  (© ALEX KALMBACH /SHUTTERSTOCK.COM)	• Facilitate interaction • Are easy to use • Are inexpensive if traditional units are used	• Require turning speaker's back to audience • Are cumbersome to transport, can be messy, and not professional looking • Are not reusable, provide no hard copy, and must be developed on-site if traditional units are used
Overhead transparencies  (© ISTOCKPHOTO.COM/SEAN O'RIORDAN)	• Are simple to prepare and use • Allow versatile use; prepare beforehand or while speaking • Are inexpensive and readily available	• Are not easily updated and are awkward to use • Must have special acetate sheets and markers unless using a document camera • Pose potential for equipment failure
Electronic presentations  (© GOYGEL-SOKOL DMITRY/ SHUTTERSTOCK.COM)	• Meet audience expectations of visual standards • Enhance professionalism and credibility of the speaker • Provide special effects to enhance retention, appeal, flexibility, and reuse	• Can lead to poor delivery if misused • Can be expensive, require highly developed skills, and are time-consuming • Pose technology failure and transportability challenges
35mm slides  (© JAMES STEIDL/ SHUTTERSTOCK.COM)	• Are highly professional • Depict real people and places	• Require darkened room • Creates a formal environment not conducive to group interaction • Lacks flexibility in presentation sequence
Objects  (© TACU ALEXEI/ SHUTTERSTOCK.COM)	• Are useful to demonstrate an idea	• Can compete with the speaker for attention

Design of Presentation Visuals

Computer technology has raised the standards for presentation visuals; however, inexperienced designers often use too many visuals and make them overly complex and difficult to understand. Not only are live audiences subjected to "PowerPoint poisoning," but "docu-points" are often sent when a different type of communication is called for. An "electability" PowerPoint slideshow the 2008 Hillary Clinton Campaign emailed to all House Democrats contained nine slides, 275 words, one table, three bar charts, and two pie charts. Such "docu-points" are usually less effective than a concise, well-designed handout or summary report.[17]

Your goal is to create an appealing, easy-to-read design that supports your main points without overwhelming the audience. Presentation visuals should possess the same degree of professionalism as your delivery and personal appearance. You can create dynamic and useful presentation visuals, including slides, handouts, and notes pages, by following these simple guidelines:

How does the advice "more is not necessarily better" apply to the design of presentation visuals?

- **Limit the number of visual aids used in a single presentation.** While audiences value being able to "see" your points, they also welcome the variety provided by listening and the break from concentrating on visuals. Design compelling visuals that direct the audience's attention to major points and clarify or illustrate complex information. Use precise, vivid language that will involve the audience and enrich your message and delivery style.
- **Limit slide content to key ideas presented in as few words as possible.** Well-organized, crisp slide content enhances the audience's ability to grasp the speaker's meaning and find immediate value in the information. Good content also leads to an extemporaneous delivery rather than a speaker's monotonous reading of scripted slides. Short text lines also are easier for the eye to follow and open up the slide with appealing white space.

Best practices for presentation design are exactly what the doctor ordered to end the death-by-PowerPoint diagnosis.

What additional suggestions do you have for avoiding "death by PowerPoint" for your audience?

- **Develop only one major idea using targeted keywords the audience can scan quickly, understand, and remember.** Full sentences may be used for a direct quotation; otherwise, less is more. William Earnest, author of *Save Our Slides*, offers a cure for verbalitis: PowerPoint is not a word processor — it is a visual medium in which fewer words are always more.[18]
  - Keep type sizes large enough to read when projected and to discourage crowding slides with text. Strive for these targets: slide titles, 44 points; main bullets, 32; sub-bullets, 24 points. Do not use text smaller than 18 points as it is unreadable when projected.
  - Limit slide titles and headings to four words and follow the 7 × 7 rule, which limits text to 7 lines per slide and 7 words per line. Eliminate articles (*a*, *an*, *the*), understood pronouns/possessives (*we*, *you*, *your*), simple verbs and infinitive beginnings (are, to), and repetitive phrasing.[19]
  - Develop powerful bulleted lists that are easy to follow and remember. For easy recall, limit the list to three to five main bullets, but absolutely no more than seven. To eliminate confusion and rereading, use bulleted lists that are grammatically parallel. One item appearing out of place weakens the emphasis given to each item and may distract audience attention from the message. Be certain each major point relates to the key concept presented in the slide title and each subpoint relates to its major point. Unless sequence is important, use bullets as they add less clutter and are easier to follow than numbers.
- **Choose an effective template and powerful images to reinforce ideas, illustrate complex ideas, and enliven boring content.** Images and shapes are more visually appealing and memorable than words, and enable audiences to grasp information more easily. Today's audiences expect media-rich, dynamic visuals, not a speaker's dense crutch notes displayed on screen. Although photographs and clip art available in your presentation software gallery are acceptable, avoid images that are overused, outdated, grainy, and convey an unprofessional tone. Instead search for or create high-quality, professional images that convey the desired message and can project onscreen without distortion.
- **Choose an effective color scheme.** The colors you choose and the way you combine them determine the overall effectiveness of your presentation and add a personal touch to your work. Follow these simple rules to plan a non-distracting, complementary color scheme that has unity with the template graphics:

What colors do you consider to be complementary?

  - **Limit colors to no more than three colors on a slide to avoid an overwhelming feel.**
  - **Begin by selecting a background color that conveys the appropriate formality and tone.** Choose cool colors (blue and green) in muted shades for formal presentations; choose warm colors (red, orange, and yellow) or brighter shades of cool colors for a less formal and perhaps trendy look. Think carefully about whether your color selection has a natural association with your topic or organization. For example, a presentation on environmental friendly policies might incorporate colors naturally associated with nature and cleanliness (earth tones, white and blue);

Give examples of other colors associated with certain themes or ideas.

a presentation to Coca-Cola likely would be designed around the company colors of red and white.

- **Choose complementary foreground (text) colors that have high contrast to the background to ensure readability.** To ensure high contrast, choose either dark text on a light background or light text on a dark background. For example, the often-used color scheme of yellow slide title text and white bulleted list with a blue background is a good choice because the colors are complementary and have high contrast. Choose a slightly brighter color for the slide title that distinguishes it from the color chosen for the bullet list.

Black text against a white background has the greatest contrast. A blue background with yellow text contrasts well, but a light blue background with white text would be difficult to read because of low contrast. Evaluate the readability of the following contrast variations.

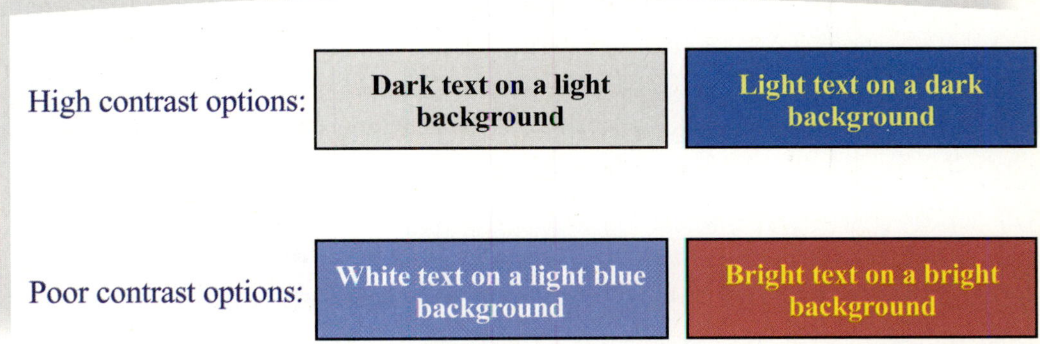

Because the lower resolution of projectors can wash out colors making them less vibrant than what is seen on a printed page or computer screen, choose options with very high—not minimally high—contrast. Project your presentation ahead of time in the room where you are to present so you can assess the color scheme. You can also double check for readability and typographical errors at the same time.

- **Choose the accent colors that complement the color scheme.** Accent colors are used in small doses to draw attention to key elements: bullet markers; bars/slices in graphs, backgrounds (fills) of shapes and lines, selected text; or drawings that are color coded for emphasis. Avoid red and green when differentiating important points as almost 10 percent of the population is color impaired and cannot distinguish between red and green. The red and green bars in a graph would be seen as one large area.

Which font would be effective for a presentation to your board of directors? to a potential client? to your department staff?

- **Choose an appealing font that can be read onscreen easily.** *Generally,* avoid delicate, decorative, or condensed choices that are difficult to read when projected. The clean, simple lines of a sans serif font, such as Calibri, Tahoma, or Verdana, is ideal for projecting on a large screen, newspaper headline, sign, or billboard. *A sans serif font,* has no short cross-strokes, known as ***serifs***, which provides extra detail that helps guide the eye on print media. Examples of serif fonts are Cambria, Times New Roman and Garamond.

- **Follow these keyboarding rules for easy reading.** Use capital letters sparingly as they are difficult to read from a distance. Capitalize the first letter of important words in slide titles (initial caps) and the first letter of the first word and proper nouns in a bulleted list (sentence case). Omit hard-to-see punctuation at the end of bulleted lists and elsewhere, and avoid abbreviations and hyphenations that may cause confusion.

- **Reflect legal and ethical responsibility in the design of presentation visuals.** Like the graphics you developed in Chapter 10, presentation visuals should be uncluttered, easily understood, and depict information honestly. You will learn about the perils of copyright violations in the Strategic Forces feature "Copyright Violations: A Presenter's Peril."
- **Proofread the visual carefully following the same systematic procedures used for printed letters and reports and electronic communication.** Misspellings in visuals are embarrassing and diminish your credibility. Double-check to be certain that names of people, companies, and products are spelled correctly.

Figure 12-2 offers a review of slide design guidelines. The poor example (left) includes many common slide design errors that are corrected in the good example (right).

FIGURE 12-2

Designing Compelling Slides: Poor (left) and Good (right) Examples

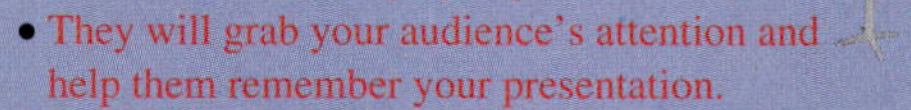

Compelling stories enhance a presenter's ability to present effectively
• Stories are an important strategy for today's business presenters who want to stand apart from other presenters.
• This strategy allows you to genuinely show you're a human being and create a strong bond with your audience.
• When stories are told well and with enough detail, they transport the people you want to influence into incredible life-changing experiences.
• They will grab your audience's attention and help them remember your presentation.
• They also give the audience a break from so many slides.
© ISTOCKPHOTO.COM/CURVABEZIER

Value of Storytelling
□ Displays presenter's genuine personality
□ Leads audience to life-changing experiences
□ Focuses audience attention and increases retention
□ Provides change of pace
© ISTOCKPHOTO.COM/NEUSTOCKIMAGES

The revised slide

- Includes short descriptive title that captures major idea of slide.
- Limits slide content to meet the 7 × 7 criteria:
  - Omits items unrelated to value of strategy and explanations presenter will make verbally.
  - Enlarges type size to increase white space and readability.
  - Eliminates articles, understood pronouns/possessives, simple verbs and infinitive; and repetitive phrasing
  - Collapses remaining content into a few memorable bullet points using parallel structure for clarity and grammatical accuracy (singular action verbs).
- Uses a simple, but appealing template with high-quality, relevant image that is large enough for audience to see and has not been overused.
- Uses high-contrast background and sans serif fonts to assure legibility. Color choices are complementary and convey a professional tone.
- Uses initial caps in slide title, capitalizes the first word in bulleted list, and omits period at end of bulleted items.
- Proofreads carefully to avoid misspellings that damage credibility.

LEGAL AND ETHICAL CONSTRAINTS

STRATEGIC FORCES

Copyright Violations: A Presenter's Peril

When preparing presentations, you will at times want to use copyrighted materials to support your ideas. Your informed use may save you embarrassment and your company the cost of an expensive lawsuit.

Under the Copyright Act of 1976, copyright is automatic when an original work is first "fixed" in a tangible medium of expression (including electronic files, Internet postings, and email) regardless of whether a notice of copyright appears with the material. To protect their ability to obtain commercial benefit from the work and control what is done with the work by others, copyright owners have five rights:

- to reproduce the copyrighted work;
- to distribute copies of a copyrighted work to the public;
- to prepare derivative works, or creations based on the original;
- to perform the copyrighted work publicly; and
- to display copyrighted work publicly.

Statutory damages for infringing on copyright can be as much as $100,000 in cases of willful violation, and commercial copyright violation of more than 100 copies is a felony in the United States.[20]

Presenters are often tempted to commit copyright infringements as a result of scanning and duplicating technologies and the wealth of high quality, downloadable graphics, sound, and video. Copyright owners and watchdog organizations, however, are becoming more aggressive, using new methods to enforce their rights. Recent court cases, such as the highly publicized Napster trial regarding music copyrights, indicate strong support for copyright owners.[21]

To avoid copyright abuse when preparing presentation materials:

- **Commit to learning the basics of copyright law.** Don't gamble that you won't get caught or that you will be safe if you plead ignorance.
- **Assume that any pre-existing work is copyrighted and requires permission from the copyright owner to use or copy.** Plan ahead so you will have plenty of time to secure permissions and negotiate a fair price with the copyright owner.
- **Note the precautions that relate to fair use.** The "fair use" defense is generally applicable in education, research, and scholarly uses, and rarely applies in for-profit settings.[22]
- **Acquire your own library of multimedia content by purchasing royalty-free multimedia content.** Royalty-free multimedia content provides unlimited use for a one-time fee, because all copyrights have been cleared for the purchased content. However, be wary of advertisers that sell "royalty-free" content but fail to clear the copyrights.
- **Stay current on changes in the copyright law.** Lawmakers will continue to devise ways to make the copyright law work in an electronic environment.

Application

1. Test your knowledge of copyright law by taking the quiz at http://literacy.kent.edu/Oasis/Workshops/copyquizinteractive.html
2. Locate the following website that describes the 10 common myths related to copyright: www.templetons.com/brad/copymyths.html
   - Write a short report that explains the discussed myths related to copyright law.
   - Prepare a handout that effectively conveys this information for office staff.

Design Tips for Audience Handouts and Notes Pages

Audience handouts should add value for individual audience members; otherwise, the information can better be conveyed in a projected format for group benefit. An effective handout can help audience members remember your message, serve as a reference for later consideration or action, and encourage involvement when space is provided for note taking or response. You can prepare useful presenter notes on small index cards or on pages generated by electronic presentation software. Visit your companion website at www.cengage.com/bcomm/lehman for guidelines on preparing well-designed, highly professional handouts and effective notes pages.

Refining Your Delivery

After you have organized your message, you must identify the appropriate delivery method, refine your vocal qualities, and practice your delivery.

Delivery Method

What delivery methods are used most often by professionals in your chosen career field?

Four presentation methods can be used: memorized, scripted, impromptu, and extemporaneous. Impromptu and extemporaneous styles are generally more useful for business presentations.

Memorized presentations are written out ahead of time, memorized, and recited verbatim. Memorization has the greatest limitations of the speech styles. Speakers are almost totally unable to react to feedback, and the speaker who forgets a point and develops a mental block may lose the entire speech. Memorized speeches tend to sound monotonous, restrict natural body gestures and motions, and lack conviction. For short religious or fraternal rites, however, the memorized presentation is often impressive.

Manuscript, or scripted, delivery involves writing the speech word for word and reading it to the audience. For complex material and technical conference presentations, manuscript presentations ensure content coverage. Additionally, this style protects speakers against being misquoted (when accuracy is absolutely critical) and fits into exact time constraints, as in television or radio presentations. Speeches are sometimes read when time does not permit advance preparation, or several different presentations are given in one day (e.g., the speaking demands of the President of the United States and other top-level executives). Manuscript presentations limit speaker–audience rapport, particularly when speakers keep their eyes and heads buried in their manuscripts. Teleprompters that project the manuscript out of view of the audience allow the speaker to appear to be speaking extemporaneously.

CHANGING TECHNOLOGY

Impromptu delivery is frightening to many people because the speaker is called on without prior notice. Experienced speakers can easily analyze the request, organize supporting points from memory, and present a simple, logical response. In many cases, businesspeople can anticipate a request and be prepared to discuss a particular idea when requested (e.g., status report on an area of control at a team meeting). Because professionals are expected to present ideas and data spontaneously on demand, businesspeople must develop the ability to deliver impromptu presentations.

Extemporaneous presentations are planned, prepared, and rehearsed but not written in detail. Brief notes prompt the speaker on the next point, but the words are chosen spontaneously as the speaker interacts with the audience and identifies this audience's specific needs. Extemporaneous presentations include natural body gestures, sound conversational, and can be delivered with conviction because the speaker is speaking "with" the listeners and not "to" them. The audience appreciates a warm, genuine communicator and will forgive an occasional stumble or groping for a word that occurs with an extemporaneous presentation. Learning to construct useful notes will aid you in becoming an accomplished extemporaneous speaker; guidelines are provided at your companion website at www.cengage.com/bcomm/lehman.

Vocal Qualities

How do the "voice of experience" and the "voice of authority" sound?

The sound of your voice is a powerful instrument used to deliver your message and to project your professional image. To maximize your vocal strengths, focus on three important qualities of speech—phonation, articulation, and pronunciation.

Phonation involves both the production and the variation of the speaker's vocal tone. You project your voice and convey feelings—even thoughts—by varying your vocal tones. Important factors of phonation are pitch, volume, and rate. These factors permit us to recognize other people's voices over the phone.

- **Pitch** is the highness or lowness of the voice. Pleasant voices have medium or low pitch; however, a varied pitch pattern is desirable. The pitch of the voice rises and falls to reflect emotions; for example, fear and anger are reflected in a higher pitch; sadness, in a lower pitch. Lower pitches for both men and women are perceived as sounding more authoritative; higher pitches indicate less confidence and suggest pleading or whining. Techniques discussed later in this section can help you lower the pitch of your voice.

- **Volume** refers to the loudness of tones. Generally, good voices are easily heard by everyone in the audience but are not too loud. Use variety to hold the audience's attention, emphasize words or ideas, and create a desired atmosphere (energetic, excited tone versus dull, boring one).

- **Rate** is the speed at which words are spoken. Never speak so quickly that the audience cannot understand your message or so slowly that they are distracted or irritated. Vary the rate with the demands of the situation. For example, speak at a slower rate when presenting a complex concept or emphasizing an important idea. Pause to add emphasis to a key point or to transition to another major section of the presentation. Speak at a faster rate when presenting less important information or when reviewing.

An inherent problem related to speaking rate is verbal fillers—also called *nonwords*. Verbal fillers, such as *uhhh*, *ahhh*, *ummm*, and *errr*, are irritating to the audience and destroy your effectiveness. Many speakers fill space with their own verbal fillers; these include *you know*, *I mean*, *basically*, *like I said*, *okay*, and *as a matter of fact*. Because of the conversational style of impromptu and extemporaneous presentations, a speaker will naturally struggle for a word or idea from time to time. Become aware of verbal fillers you frequently use by critiquing a recording of yourself and then focus on replacing fillers with a three- to five-second pause. This brief gap between thoughts gives you an opportunity to think about what you want to say next and time for your audience to absorb your idea. Presenting an idea (sound bite) and then pausing briefly is an effective way to influence your audience positively. The listener will not notice the slight delay, and the absence of meaningless words will make you appear more confident and polished. Also avoid annoying speech habits, such as clearing your throat or coughing, that shift the audience's attention from the speech to the speaker.

The following activities will help you achieve good vocal qualities: medium to low pitch and audible, steady pace, with variations to reflect mood:

- **Breathe properly and relax.** Nervousness affects normal breathing patterns and is reflected in vocal tone and pitch. The better prepared you are, the better your phonation will be. Although relaxing may seem difficult to practice before a speech, a few deep breaths, just as swimmers take before diving, can help.
- **Listen to yourself.** A recording of your voice reveals much about pitch, intensity, and duration. Most people are amazed to find their voices are not quite what they had expected. "I never dreamed I sounded that bad" is a common reaction. Nasal twangs usually result from a failure to speak from the diaphragm, which involves taking in and letting out air through the larynx, where the vocal cords operate. High pitch may occur from the same cause, or it may be a product of speaking too fast or experiencing stage fright.
- **Develop flexibility.** The good speaking voice is somewhat musical, with words and sounds similar to notes in a musical scale. Read each of the following sentences aloud and emphasize the *italicized* word in each. Even though the sentences are identical, emphasizing different words changes the meaning.

I am happy you are here.	Maybe I'm the only happy one.
I *am* happy you are here.	I really am.
I am *happy* you are here.	Happy best describes my feeling.
I am happy *you* are here.	Yes, you especially.
I am happy you *are* here.	You may not be happy, but I am.
I am happy you are *here*.	Here and not somewhere else.

What words do you use incorrectly or enunciate poorly?

Articulation involves smooth, fluent, and pleasant speech. It results from the way in which a speaker produces and joins sounds. Faulty articulation is often caused by not carefully forming individual sounds. Common examples include

- dropping word endings—saying *workin'* for *working*.
- running words together—saying k*inda* for *kind of, gonna* for *going to*.
- imprecise enunciation—saying *dis* for *this*, *wid* for *with*, *dem* for *them*, *pin* for *pen*, or *pitcher* for *picture*.

These examples should not be confused with dialect, which people informally call an accent. A dialect is a variation in pronunciation, usually of vowels, from one part of the country to another. Actually, everyone speaks a dialect; speech experts can often identify, even pinpoint, the section of the country from where a speaker comes. In the United States, common dialects are New England, New York, Southern, Texan, Mid-Western, and so forth. Within each of these, minor dialects may arise regionally or from immigrant influence. The simple fact is that when people interact, they influence each other even down to speech sounds. Many prominent speakers have developed a rather universal dialect, known as Standard American Speech or American Broadcast English, that seems to be effective no matter who the audience is. This model for professional language is widely used by newscasters and announcers and is easily understood by those who speak English as a second language because they likely listened to this speech pattern on television as they learned the language. The case "Now About That Accent . . ." allows you to further explore the impact of accents on your potential for advancement.

Of what region is your accent typical? Is your accent stronger or more beneficial at certain times?

You can improve the clarity of your voice, reduce strain and voice distortion, and increase your expressiveness by following these guidelines:

- **Stand up straight with your shoulders back and breathe from your diaphragm rather than your nose and mouth.** If you are breathing correctly, you can then use your mouth and teeth to form sounds precisely. For example, vowels are always sounded with the mouth open and the tongue clear of the palate. Consonants are responsible primarily for the distinctness of speech and are formed by an interference with or stoppage of outgoing breath.
- **Focus on completing the endings of all words, not running words together, and enunciating words correctly.** To identify recurring enunciation errors, listen to a recording and seek feedback from others.
- **Obtain formal training to improve your speech.** Pursue a self-study program by purchasing recordings that help you reduce your dialect and move more closely to a universal dialect. You can also enroll in a diction course to improve your speech patterns or arrange for private lessons from a voice coach.

Pronunciation involves using principles of phonetics to create accurate sounds, rhythm, stress, and intonation. People may articulate perfectly but still mispronounce words. A dictionary provides the best source to review pronunciation. Two pronunciations are often given for a word, the first one being the desired pronunciation and the second an acceptable variation. An American adopting a pronunciation commonly used in England, such as *shedule* for *schedule* or *a-gane* for *again,* could be seen negatively. In some cases, leeway exists in pronunciation. The first choice for pronouncing *data* is to pronounce the first *a* long, as in *date*; but common usage is fast making pronunciation of the short *a* sound, as in *cat*, acceptable. Likewise, the preferred pronunciation of *often* is with a silent *t*. Good speakers use proper pronunciation and refer to the dictionary frequently in both pronunciation and vocabulary development.

What does a dictionary show as the preferred pronunciation of status, often, economics, and envelope?

When your voice qualities combine to make your messages pleasingly receptive, your primary concerns revolve around developing an effective delivery style.

Delivery Style

Speaking effectively is both an art and a skill. Careful planning and practice are essential for increasing speaking effectiveness.

Before the Presentation

Follow these guidelines when preparing for your presentation:

What are the causes and symptoms of public speaking anxiety?

- **Prepare thoroughly.** You can expect a degree of nervousness as you anticipate speaking before a group. This natural tension is constructive because it increases your concentration and your energy and enhances your performance. Even Kara DioGuardi, a fourth judge added to the 2009 *American Idol* season, admitted being nervous as she adjusted to giving short, meaningful advice in front of 30 million people on the most-watched TV show in the nation.[23]

  Being well prepared is the surest way to control speech anxiety. Develop an outline for your presentation that supports your purpose and addresses the needs of your audience and take advantage of every opportunity to gain speaking experience. Additionally, John Davis, a successful speech coach, warned: "Never, never, never give a speech on a subject you don't believe in. You'll fail. On the other hand, if you prepare properly, know your material, and *believe* in it . . . your audience will not only hear but *feel* your message."[24]

- **Prepare effective presentation support tools.** Follow the guidelines presented in the prior section to select and design visuals, handouts, and notes pages appropriate for your audience and purpose. Additionally, develop a contingency plan in the event of technical difficulties with computer equipment, such as hard copies of the slides or a backup computer pre-loaded and ready. Arrive early so you can troubleshoot unexpected technological glitches. Despite your degree of planning, however, technical problems may occur during your presentation. Remain calm and correct them as quickly and professionally as you can. Take heart in the fact that Bill Gates' computer once crashed when he introduced a new version of Windows!

- **Practice, but do not rehearse.** Your goal is to become familiar with the key phrases on your note cards so that you can deliver the presentation naturally as if you are

Present or perish! Are poor speaking skills jeopardizing your career success? To improve your presentation skills, begin by taking every opportunity to practice your speaking skills in public.

talking with the audience—not reciting the presentation or acting out a role. Avoid overpracticing that may make your presentation sound mechanical and limit your ability to respond to the audience.

What personal "verbal potholes" must you seek to eliminate?

- **Practice the entire presentation.** This practice will allow you to identify (1) flaws in organization or unity, (2) long, complex sentences or ineffective expressions, and (3) "verbal potholes." Verbal potholes include word combinations that could cause you to stumble, words you have trouble pronouncing ("irrelevant" or "statistics"), and words that accentuate your dialect ("get" may sound like "git" regardless of the intention of a Southern speaker).
- **Spend additional time practicing the introduction and conclusion.** You will want to deliver these important parts with finesse while making a confident connection with the audience. A good closing leaves the audience in a good mood and may help overcome some possible weaknesses during the speech. Depending on the techniques used, consider memorizing significant brief statements to ensure their accuracy and impact (e.g., direct quotation, exact statistic, etc.).

- **Practice displaying presentation visuals so that your delivery appears effortless and seamless.** Your goal is to make the technology virtually transparent, positioned in the background to support *you* as the primary focus of the presentation. First, be sure you know basic commands for advancing through your presentation without displaying distracting menus. Develop skill in returning to a specific slide in the event of a computer glitch or an audience question.
- **Seek feedback on your performance that will enable you to polish your delivery and improve organization.** Critique your own performance by practicing in front of a mirror and evaluating a recording of your presentation. If possible, present to a small audience ahead of time for feedback and to minimize anxiety when presenting to the real audience.
- **Request a lectern to hold your notes and to steady a shaky hand, at least until you gain some confidence and experience.** Keep in mind, though, that weaning yourself from the lectern will eliminate a physical barrier between you and the audience. Without the lectern, you will speak more naturally. If you are using a microphone, ask for a portable microphone so that you can move freely.
- **Request a proper introduction if the audience knows little about you.** An effective introduction will establish your credibility as a speaker on the subject and will make the audience eager to hear you. You may prepare your own introduction as professional speakers do, or you can provide concise, targeted information that answers these three questions: (1) Why is the subject relevant? (2) Who is the speaker? and (3) What credentials qualify the speaker to talk about the subject? Talk with the person introducing you to verify any information, especially the pronunciation of your name, and to review the format of the presentation (time limit, question-and-answer period, etc.). Be certain to thank the person who made the introduction as you begin your presentation. "Thank you for your kind introduction, Ms. Garcia" is adequate. Then, follow with your own introduction to your presentation topic.

- **Dress appropriately to create a strong professional image and to bolster your self-confidence.** An audience's initial impression of your personal appearance, your clothing and grooming, affects their ability to accept you as a credible speaker. Because first impressions are difficult to overcome, take time to groom yourself immaculately and to select clothing that is appropriate for the speaking occasion and consistent with the audience's expectations.

- **Arrive early to become familiar with the setup of the room and to check the equipment.** Check the location of your chair, the lectern, the projection screen, light switches, and electrical outlets. Check the microphone and Internet connection and ensure that all equipment is in the appropriate place and working properly. Project your electronic presentation so you can adjust the color scheme to ensure maximum readability. Finally, identify the technician who will be responsible for resolving any technical problems that may occur during the presentation.

During the Presentation

The following are things you can do during your presentation to increase your effectiveness as a speaker:

What can you do as a speaker to build rapport with the audience? How do you know when you have succeeded?

- **Communicate confidence, warmth, and enthusiasm for the presentation and the time spent with the audience.** "Your listeners won't care how much you know until they know how much you care," is pertinent advice.[25]
    - **Exhibit a confident appearance with alert posture.** Stand tall with your shoulders back and your stomach tucked in. Stand in the "ready position"—no slouching, hunching over the lectern, or rocking. Keep weight forward with knees slightly flexed so you are ready to move easily rather than rooted rigidly in one spot, hiding behind the lectern.
    - **Smile genuinely throughout the presentation.** Pause as you take your place behind the lectern, and smile before you speak the first word. Smile as you finish your presentation and wait for the applause.
    - **Maintain steady eye contact with the audience in random places throughout the room.** Stay with one person approximately three to five seconds—long enough to finish a complete thought or sentence to convince the listener you are communicating individually with him or her. If the audience is large, select a few friendly faces and concentrate on speaking to them rather than a sea of nondescript faces.
    - **Refine gestures to portray a relaxed, approachable appearance.** Vary hand motions to emphasize important points; otherwise, let hands fall naturally to your side. Practice using only one hand to make points unless you specifically need two hands, such as when drawing a figure or showing dimensions or location. Eliminate any nervous gestures that can distract the audience (e.g., clenching your hands in front or behind your body, steepling your hands, placing your hands in your pockets, jingling keys or change, or playing with a ring or pen).

- **Move from behind the lectern and toward the audience to reduce the barrier created between you and the audience.** You may stand to one side and casually present a relaxed pose beside the lectern. However, avoid methodically walking without a purpose.

- **Exercise strong vocal qualities.** Review the guidelines provided for using your voice to project confidence and credibility.

- **Watch your audience.** They will tell you how you are doing and whether you should shorten your speech. Be attentive to negative feedback in the form of talking, coughing, moving chairs, and other signs of discomfort.

- **Use your visuals effectively.** Many speakers will go to a great deal of effort to prepare good presentation visuals—and then not use them effectively. Inexperienced speakers often ignore the visual altogether or fall into the habit of simply nodding their heads toward the visual. Neither of these techniques is adequate for involving the audience with the visual. In fact, if the material is complex, the speaker is likely to lose the audience completely.

  - **Step to one side of the visual so the audience can see it.** Use a pointer if necessary. Direct your remarks to the audience, so that you can maintain eye contact and resist the temptation to look over your shoulder or turn your back to read the information from the screen behind you.

  - **Paraphrase the visual rather than reading it line for line.** To increase the quality of your delivery, develop a workable method of recording what you plan to say about each graphic. Detailed guidelines for preparing useful notes are provided at your companion website at www.cengage.com/bcomm/lehman.

- **Handle questions from the audience during the presentation.** Questions often disrupt carefully laid plans. At the same time, questions provide feedback, clarify points, and ensure understanding. When people ask questions that will be answered later in the presentation, say, "I believe the next slide will clarify that point; if not, we will come back to it." If the question can be answered quickly, you should do so while indicating that it will also be covered more later.

Anticipate and prepare for questions that might be raised. You may generate presentation visuals pertaining to certain anticipated questions and display them only if the question is posed. An audience will appreciate your thorough and complete explanation and your ability to adjust your presentation to their needs—this strategy is much more professional than stumbling through an explanation or delaying the answer until the information is available. Speakers giving electronic presentations have ready access to enormous amounts of information that can be displayed instantly for audience discussion. Hyperlinks created within a presentation file will move a speaker instantaneously to a specific slide, another file, or an embedded music or video file.

- **Keep within the time limit.** Be prepared to complete the presentation within the allotted time. In many organizations, speakers have one or more rehearsals before delivering reports to a group such as a board of directors. These rehearsals, or dry runs, are made before other executives, and are critiqued, timed, revised, and rehearsed again. Presentation software makes rehearsing your timing as simple as clicking a button and advancing through the slides as you practice. By evaluating the total presentation time and the time spent on each slide, you can modify the presentation and rehearse again until the presentation fits the time slot.

After the Presentation

How you handle the time following a presentation is as important as preparing for the presentation itself:

How will you prepare for the question-and-answer period?

- **Be prepared for a question-and-answer period.** Encourage the audience to ask questions, recognizing an opportunity to ensure that your presentation meets audience needs. Paraphrasing the question allows you time to reflect on what was asked, ensures that everyone heard the question, and assures the questioner that he or she was understood. You may ask the questioner if your answer was adequate. Be courteous even to hostile questioners so you will maintain the respect of your audience. Stay in control of the time by announcing that you have time for one or two more questions and then invite individual questions when the presentation is over.
- **Distribute handouts.** Distribute the handout when it is needed rather than at the beginning of the presentation. Otherwise, the audience may read the handout while you are explaining background information needed to understand the written ideas. If you expect the audience to take notes directly on the handout or if the audience will need to refer to the handout immediately, distribute the handout at the beginning of the presentation or before it begins. To keep control of the audience's attention, be sure listeners know when they should be looking at the handout or listening to you. If the handout is intended as resource material only, post the handout to a web page or place it on a table at the back of the room and at the front for those who come by to talk with you after the presentation.

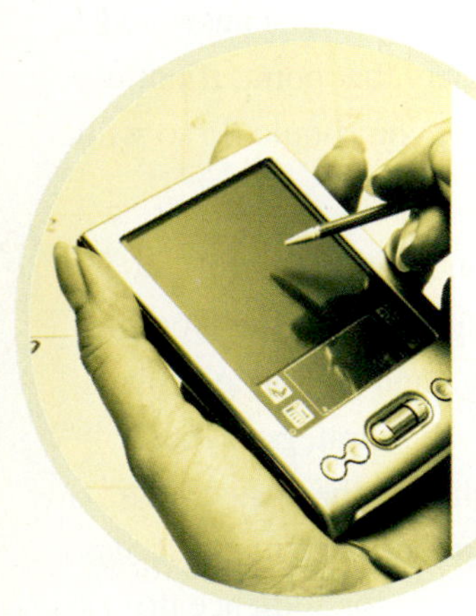

Your Turn 12-3
Career Portfolio

Having a clear, concise, compelling explanation of what your company does often is called an elevator speech because it should be something you can explain during a short elevator ride. Unfortunately, it may take a rather long elevator ride—and a translator—to figure out exactly what some companies are up to. Elevator speeches are the verbal application of a company's printed messages. They help executives and salespeople explain exactly what their company does in about 30 seconds, and more importantly, what the information means to investors, prospects, or customers.

TAKE ACTION:

- Visit the following website to learn more about elevator speeches and to view good and poor examples: www.elevatorspeech.com/. You may link to this URL from your companion website at www.cengage.com/bcomm/lehman.
- Prepare your own elevator speech that explains what you have to offer a prospective employer. Read through the speech several times to gain familiarity, and then video record yourself delivering the speech in one minute or less.

- Prepare a short slide show presentation that highlights your employment qualifications. Using this content, produce a video presentation to be distributed electronically. A demo copy of Camtasia Studio, video production software, can be downloaded from http://techsmith.com.

Adapting to Alternate Delivery Situations

As you've learned, presenting a dynamic presentation that focuses on the audience's needs and expectations is the fundamental principle in presenting effectively. Along with the solid foundation you've set for spoken communication, you'll also need to adapt your presentation style to the ever-changing business environment and the special needs of culturally diverse audiences. Delivering team presentations and presenting in distance formats are other common situations you'll need to master.

Culturally Diverse Audiences

When speaking to a culturally diverse audience, you will want to be as natural as possible, while adjusting your message for important cultural variations. Using empathy, you can effectively focus on the listener as an individual rather than a stereotype of a specific culture. Be open and willing to learn, and you will reap the benefits of communicating effectively with people who possess a variety of strengths and creative abilities. Additionally, follow these suggestions for presenting to people from outside your own culture:

- **Speak simply.** Use simple English and short sentences. Avoid acronyms and expressions that may be confusing to nonnative English speakers, namely, slang, jargon, figurative expressions, and sports analogies. The Strategic Forces feature "Did I Make Myself Clear???" provides more information about avoiding confusion in terminology.

- **Avoid words that trigger negative emotional responses such as anger, fear, or suspicion.** Such "red flag" words vary among cultures; thus, try to anticipate audience reaction and choose your words carefully.

- **Enunciate each word precisely and speak somewhat slowly.** Clear, articulate speech is especially important when the audience is not familiar with various dialects and vocabulary. Avoid the temptation to speak in a loud voice, a habit considered rude in any culture and especially annoying to the Japanese who perceive the normal tone of North Americans as too loud.

- **Be extremely cautious in the use of humor and jokes.** Cultures that prefer more formality may think you are not serious about your purpose or find your humor and jokes inappropriate. Asians, for instance, do not appreciate jokes about family members and the elderly.

- **Learn the culture's preferences for a direct or indirect presentation.** While North Americans tend to prefer directness, with the main idea presented first, people

DIVERSITY CHALLENGES

STRATEGIC FORCES

Did I Make Myself Clear???

Even though English is the generally recognized international business language, presenting in English is not without its problems. Non-native speakers may be fairly fluent in English, but they may have difficulty with common expressions such as these:

Acronyms: FYI, ASAP, USB, O&M, TARP, HMO

Slang: Referring to a dollar as a *buck* or a law enforcement officer as a *cop*, using *cool* and *bad* to indicate approval, and *a slide* for an easy course.

Figurative expressions: Held hostage, bent out of shape, thrown under the bus, a lot on my plate, playing a bad hand, flying under the radar, tipping point, toxic, bail out, cutting edge, train wreck, time crunch, dead ringer, brainstorm

Sports analogies: Batting a thousand, struck out, out of the ballpark, drop back and punt, touch base, on target, right on line, up to par, kick off, shot down, springboard, caught off guard

To ensure understanding, substitute dictionary terms for each of the following expressions:

After that marketing pitch, you are so *off the box*.

You're playing on the varsity team now.

The company is facing a *perfect storm*.

Going green placed the company *ahead of the curve*.

Your analysis was *right on the money*.

The employee was *caught red-handed*.

I blew it.

Go for it.

Mastering a large vocabulary in a second language is a daunting task, and Simplified English, or Simplified Technical English, was developed to aid in communicating with diverse audiences. A joint project of the Aerospace and Defense Industries, Association of Europe and the Aerospace Industries Association, the language has a core vocabulary of 1,500 words and a set of approximately 40 rules of style and grammar. With few exceptions, each word has only one meaning and can be used as only one part of speech. For instance, the word *close* can be used in the phrase "Close the door" but not in "do not go close to the landing gear." Necessary technical words can be added to the core vocabulary. Although developed initially for use in aircraft maintenance, Simplified English has generated wide interest because of its potential for other communication situations.[26]

© RYAN MCVAY/PHOTODISC/GETTY IMAGES

Application

1. Visit the following website for detailed information about the rules and vocabulary of Simple English: www.userlab.com/SE.html
2. Using Simple English, translate the following excerpt from a presentation using digital images in a PowerPoint slide show:

Two methods will allow you to convert images into digital files that can be imported into a presentation: Use a graphics scanner to scan photographs taken with a regular camera or a digital camera to capture the photograph directly onto disk without developing the film. Using a digital camera saves time and money and eliminates the use of chemicals that are not environmentally friendly.

Submit your translation to your instructor, along with a short summary of your effort. Is your translation longer or shorter than the original? What is the reading level of the original? Of the revision? Did you encounter any problems?

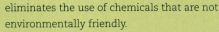

from many cultures, such as Japanese, Latin American, and Arabic, consider a straightforward approach tactless and rude. The Strategic Forces feature "Basic Cultural Values Influence Communication Styles" in Chapter 6 explores this practice in greater detail.

- **Adapt to subtle differences in nonverbal communication.** The direct eye contact expected by most North Americans is not typical of Asian listeners who often keep their eyes lowered and avoid eye contact to show respect. Arab audiences may stare into your eyes in an attempt to "see into the window of the soul." Cultures also vary on personal space and degree of physical contact (slap on the back or arm around the other as signs of friendship).
- **Adapt your dress and presentation style to fit the formality of the culture.** Some cultures prefer a higher degree of formality than the casual style of North Americans. To accommodate, dress conservatively; strive to connect with the audience in a formal, reserved manner; and use highly professional visuals rather than jotting ideas on a flip chart.
- **Seek feedback to determine whether the audience is understanding your message.** Observe listeners carefully for signs of misunderstanding, restating ideas as necessary. Consider allowing time for questions after short segments of your presentation. Avoid asking "Is that clear?" or "Do you understand?" as these statements might elicit a "Yes" answer if the person perceives saying "No" to be a sign of incompetence.

How can you become more comfortable when speaking to culturally diverse audiences?

Potential frustrations can also occur when presentations or meetings bring together people of cultures who are not time conscious and who believe that personal relationships are the basis of business dealings (e.g., Asian, Latin American) with North Americans who see "time as money." When communicating with cultures that are not time driven, be patient with what you may consider time-consuming formalities and courtesies and lengthy decision-making styles when you would rather get right down to business or move to the next point. Recognize that the presentation may not begin on time or stay on a precise schedule. Allow additional time at the beginning of the presentation to establish rapport and credibility with the audience, and perhaps provide brief discussion periods during the presentation devoted to building relationships.

Be patient and attentive during long periods of silence; in many cultures people are inclined to stay silent unless they have something significant to say or if they are considering (not necessarily rejecting) an idea. In fact, some Japanese have asked how North Americans can think and talk at the same time. Understanding patterns of silence can help you feel more comfortable during these seemingly endless moments and less compelled to fill the gaps with unnecessary words or to make concessions before the other side has a chance to reply.

Other significant points of difference between cultures are the varying rules of business etiquette. Should you use the traditional American handshake or some other symbol of greeting? Is using the person's given name acceptable? What formal titles should be used with a surname? Can you introduce yourself, or must you have someone else who knows the other person introduce you? Are business cards critical, and what rules should you follow when presenting a business card? Should you have business cards that are printed in two languages?

Gift-giving can be another confusing issue. When you believe a gift should be presented to your event host, investigate the appropriateness of gift giving, types of gifts considered appropriate or absolutely inappropriate, and colors of wrapping to be avoided in the speaker's culture. Liquor, for example, is an inappropriate gift in Arab countries.

Gaining competence in matters of etiquette will enable you to make a positive initial impression and concentrate on the presentation rather than agonizing over an awkward, embarrassing slip in protocol. Your audience will appreciate your willingness to learn and value their customs. Being sensitive to cultural issues and persistent in learning specific differences in customs and practices can minimize confusion and unnecessary embarrassment.

Your Turn 12-4
You're the Professional

You are presenting to an audience that speaks a language other than your own. Which of the following best describes effective communication with your audience through an interpreter?

TAKE ACTION:

Discuss which of the following actions would be most appropriate, justifying your response.

a. Make eye contact with the interpreter when you are speaking, then look at the audience while the interpreter is telling them what you said.

b. Speak slowly, pausing between each word.

c. Ask the interpreter to further explain any of your ideas he/she feels is necessary for the audience to understand.

d. None of the above.

Team Presentations

Because much of the work in business today is done in teams, many presentations are planned and delivered by teams of presenters. Well-conducted team presentations give an organization an opportunity to showcase its brightest talent while capitalizing on each person's unique presentation skills. Email, collaborative software, and other technologies make it easy to develop, edit, review, and deliver impressive team presentations.

The potential payoff of many team presentations is quite high—perhaps a $200,000 contract or a million-dollar account. Yet, according to experts, team presentations fail primarily because presenters don't devote enough time and resources to develop and rehearse them.[27] Resist the sure-to-fail strategy of "winging" a team presentation rather than taking the time to do it correctly. Instead, adapt the skills you already possess in planning and delivering an individual presentation to ensure a successful team presentation. Follow these guidelines as you plan and prepare your team presentation:

What personal characteristics, abilities, and strengths do you bring to a team presentation?

- **Select a winning team.** Begin by choosing a leader who is well liked and respected by the team, is knowledgeable of the project, is well organized, and will follow through. Likewise, the leader should be committed to leading the team in the development of a cohesive strategy for the presentation as well as the delegation of specific responsibilities to individual members. Frank Carillo, president of Executive Communications Group, warns team presenters that a frequent problem with "divvying up" work into pieces is that the "pieces don't fit together well when they come back."[28]

  The core team members, along with management, should choose a balanced mix of individuals who each has something important to contribute to the team. Use these questions to guide team selection: What are this member's complementary strengths and style (e.g., technical expertise, personality traits, and presentation skills)? Can this member meet the expectations of the audience (e.g., a numbers person, technical person, person with existing relationship with the audience)? Is this member willing to support the team strategy and commit to the schedule?[29]

- **Agree on the purpose and schedule.** The team as a whole should plan the presentation using the same process used for an individual presentation. Agreeing on the purpose to be achieved and selecting content that focuses on a specific audience will prevent the challenges caused by an individual's submitting off-target material. The quality of the presentation deteriorates when material must be redone hurriedly in the final days before the deadline or when unacceptable material is included just because the team worked so hard on it. Mapping out a complete presentation strategy can also minimize bickering among team members because of uneven workloads or unfavorable work assignments.

  The team will also need to agree on a standard design for presentation visuals to ensure consistency in the visuals prepared by individual presenters. Assign a person to merge the various files, to edit for consistency in design elements and the use of jargon and specialized terminology, and to proofread carefully for grammatical accuracy.

  Developing a rehearsal schedule ensures adequate time for preparation and practice. Many experts recommend five practice sessions to produce team presentations that are delivered with a unified look. Planning time in the schedule to present before a review team is especially useful for obtaining feedback on team continuity and adjustments needed to balance major discrepancies in the delivery styles of individual presenters.

- **Practice ahead of time.** The team must be well prepared which will require several rehearsals. Member must know what others will say to avoid repetition and to fit the time slot and must work out logistical details such as where people will stand, who will run the slides, when handouts will be distributed, etc. A great deal of your rehearsal time for a team presentation should be spent planning and rehearsing appropriate verbal and physical transitions between team members. The transitions serve to introduce each part of the presentation and make the whole presentation cohesive. This continuity makes your team look polished and conveys team commitment.

Follow these suggestions for delivering seamless, impressive team presentations:

- **Decide who will open and conclude the presentation.** The team member who knows the audience and has established rapport is a logical choice for these two critical sections of a presentation. If no one knows the audience, select the member with the strongest presentation skills and personality traits for connecting well with strangers. This person will introduce all team members and give a brief description of the roles they will play in the presentation.

What behaviors demonstrate that the presenters are functioning as an effective team?

- **Build natural bridges between segments of the presentation and presenters.** A lead presenter must build a bridge from the points that have been made that will launch the following presenter smoothly into what he or she will discuss. If a lead presenter forgets to make the connection to the next section clear, the next person must summarize what's been said and then preview his or her section. These transitions may seem repetitive to a team that has been working extensively with the material; however, audiences require clear guideposts through longer team presentations. Also, courtesies such as maintaining eye contact, thanking the previous speaker, and clearing the presentation area for the next speaker communicate an important message that the presenters are in sync and work well together.

- **Deliver as a team.** You must present a unified look and communicate to the audience that you care about the team. Spend your time on the "sideline" paying close attention to the current presenter, monitoring the audience for feedback, and being ready to assist the presenter with equipment malfunctions, handouts, and so on. Avoid side conversations and reading notes, yawning, or coughing. To keep an audience engaged in a team presentation, Frank Carillo recommends that team members not presenting should focus on the presenter at least two thirds of the time. "It may be the 27th time you've heard it, but for that audience it's the first time. Keep it fresh for the listeners."[30]

- **Field questions as a team.** Decide in advance who will field questions to avoid awkward stares and silence that erode the audience's confidence in your team. Normally, the person presenting a section is the logical person to field questions about that section. You may refer questions to team members who are more knowledgeable, but avoid pleading looks for someone else to rescue you. Rather, check visually to see if the person wants to respond and ask if he or she would like to add information. Tactfully contradict other presenters *only* when the presenter makes a mistake that will cause misunderstanding or confusion. While you should be ready to help presenters having difficulty, resist the urge to tack on your response to a presenter's response when the question has already been answered adequately.

Distance Presentations

Videoconferencing has been used for some time for large, high-exposure activities, such as quarterly executive staff presentations, companywide addresses, new product launches, and crisis management. The technology's lower cost, improved quality, and increased ease of use have opened videoconferencing to many settings.

Presentations on the Go! Mobile presentations are easier than ever. Software available for most dataphones converts and stores presentation files in a compressed format. All you need to do is connect your phone by cable or wireless connection to a projector, turn on the application, and begin presenting. Podcasting has also become a popular way for companies to make web presentations portable by distributing multimedia files over the Internet for playback on mobile devices. At their website, Ford Motor Company offers downloadable podcasts that promote their various vehicles, including the Fusion hybrid. Rather than a dealership salesperson conducting a walk-around on a showroom floor, the podcost provides similar kick-the-tires information about the Fusion's interior and exterior features, fuel performance, and reliability.[32]

Substantial cost savings from reduced travel is a compelling reason for companies to use videoconferencing. Additionally, threats of terrorism and contagious disease provide more reasons for companies to restrict business travel and look for alternative delivery methods. Videoconferencing also leads to important communication benefits that result from[31]

- improving employee productivity by calling impromptu videoconferences to clear up issues.
- involving more people in key decisions rather than limiting important discussions to those who are allowed to travel.
- involving expertise critical to the mission, regardless of geographic boundaries.
- creating a consistent corporate culture rather than depending on memos to describe company policy.
- improving employees' quality of life by reducing travel time that often cuts into personal time (e.g., Saturday night layovers for a reasonable airfare).

Why has the Internet been referred to as a virtual presentation auditorium?

Internet conferencing or ***webcasting*** allows companies to conduct a presentation in real time over the Internet simultaneously with a conference telephone call. Because it runs on each participant's Internet browser, a presentation can reach hundreds of locations at once. While listening to the call, participants can go to a designated website and view slides or a PowerPoint presentation that is displayed in sync with the speaker's statements being heard on the phone. Participants key comments and questions in chat boxes or press a keypad system to respond to an audience poll, thus giving valuable feedback without interrupting the speaker.

Companies deliver live web presentations on issues ranging from internal briefings on new developments and organizational and procedural changes to product strategy and training presentations. Ernst & Young uses web presentations to announce organizational changes and has found it to be an effective alternative to memos and emails that weren't always remembered or understood. People most affected by an organizational change are able to interact with leaders announcing the change.

SHOWCASE PART 2

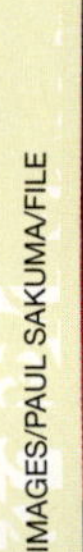

© AP IMAGES/PAUL SAKUMA/FILE

SPOTLIGHT COMMUNICATOR: SCOTT MCNEALY CHAIRMAN OF THE BOARD, SUN MICROSYSTEMS

Don't Lose the Forest in the Trees

Some companies have declared electronic presentations as too formal for internal communications; others have offered guidelines to limit the number of slides used in a presentation, or even dictated what colors could or could not be used. Scott McNealy, Board Chairman of Sun Microsystems, once went so far as to ban the use of PowerPoint by his 25,000 employees. McNealy's reasoning for prohibiting slide usage was that Sun employees were spending too much time preparing slides, presumably at the expense of other kinds of preparation. While the ban was reportedly not enforced, it provided wide exposure to the problem with overuse and abuse of slide presentations. Read more about McNealy's reasons for downplaying the use of PowerPoint at your companion website at www.cengage.com/bcomm/lehman.

REFER TO SHOWCASE PART 3, ON PAGE 457
TO LEARN HOW SUN MICROSYSTEMS DISTRIBUTES PRESENTATIONS TO VIRTUAL AUDIENCES.

Follow these guidelines for adapting your presentation skills to videoconferences and web presentations:

What challenges are faced by the audience in a distance presentation?

- **Determine whether a distance delivery method is appropriate for the presentation.** Is the presentation purpose suited to the technology? Can costs in time, money, and human energy be justified? Are key people willing and able to participate? For example, a videoconference for a formal presentation such as an important speech by the CEO to a number of locations justifies the major expense and brings attention to the importance of the message. Distance delivery formats are inappropriate for presentations that cover highly sensitive or confidential issues, for persuasive or problem-solving meetings where no relationship has been established among the participants, and whenever participants are unfamiliar with and perhaps unsupportive of the technology.

What are some other ways to build rapport with a virtual audience?

- **Establish rapport with the participants prior to the distance presentation.** If possible, meet with or phone participants beforehand to get to know them and gain insights about their attitudes. This rapport will enhance your ability to interpret subtle nonverbal cues and to cultivate the relationship further through the distance format. Emailing or faxing a short questionnaire or posting presentation slides with a request for questions is an excellent way to establish a connection with participants and to ensure that the presentation is tailored to audience needs. Some enterprising distance presenters engage participants in email discussions before the presentation and then use this dialogue to develop positive interaction during the presentation.
- **Become proficient in delivering and participating through distance technology.** Begin by becoming familiar with the equipment and the surroundings.

While technical support staff may be available to manage equipment and transmission tasks, your goal is to concentrate on the contribution you are to make and not your intimidation with the delivery method.

- **Concentrate on projecting positive nonverbal messages.** Keep a natural, friendly expression; relax and smile. Avoid the tendency to stare into the camera. Instead, look naturally at the entire audience as you would in a live presentation. Speak clearly with as much energy as you can. If a lag occurs between the video and audio transmission, adjust your timing to avoid interrupting other speakers. Use gestures to reinforce points, but avoid fast or excessive motion that will appear blurry. Avoid side conversations and coughing and throat clearing that could trigger voice-activated microphones. Pay close attention to other presenters to guard against easy distraction in a distance environment and to capture subtle nonverbal cues. You will need to judge the vocal tone of the person asking a question because you may not see faces.

- **Adjust camera settings to enhance communication.** Generally, adjust the camera so that all participants can be seen, but zoom in more closely on participants when you wish to clearly observe nonverbal language. Project a wide-angle shot of yourself during rapport-building comments at the presentation's beginning and zoom in to signal the start of the agenda or to emphasize an important point during the presentation. While some systems accommodate a split screen, others allow participants to view either you or your presentation visuals only. You will want to switch the camera between a view of you and your visuals, depending on what is needed at the time.

How do television news broadcasts or video presentations provide relief from the "talking head?"

Develop high-quality graphics appropriate for the particular distance format. Even more than in a live presentation, you will need graphics to engage and maintain participants' attention. Graphics are a welcome variation to the "talking head"—you—displayed on the screen for long periods. Some companies provide assistance from a webmaster or graphics support staff in preparing slide shows specifically for distance presentations. Also, e-conferencing companies will develop and post presentation slides and host live web presentations including managing email messages and audience polling. Regardless of the support you receive, you should understand basic guidelines for preparing effective visuals for videoconferencing and web presentations.

- **Videoconferences.** Readability of text will be a critical issue when displaying visuals during a videoconference because text becomes fuzzy when transmitted through compressed video. Select large, sturdy fonts and choose a color scheme that provides high contrast between the background and the text. Stay with a tested color scheme such as dark blue background, yellow title text, and white bulleted list text to ensure readability. Projecting your visuals ahead of time so you can adjust the color scheme, font selections, and other design elements is an especially good idea.

- **Web presentations.** In addition to considering overall appeal, clarity, and readability, web presentations must be designed for minimal load time and compatibility with various computers. For your first presentation, consider using a web template in your electronic presentations software and experiment with the appropriateness of other designs as you gain experience.

Stand-alone presentations designed specifically for web delivery require unique design strategies to compensate for the absence of a speaker.[33]

- Consider posting text-based explanations in the notes view area or adding vocal narration.
- Develop interactive slide formats that allow viewers to navigate to the most useful information in your presentation. For example, design an agenda slide that includes hyperlinks to the first slide in each section of the presentation.
- Select simple, high-quality graphics that convey ideas effectively.
- Plan limited animation that focuses audience attention on specific ideas on the slide.
- Consider adding video if bandwidth is not an issue.

Additional information related to developing web content is included in Chapter 5. Before planning a business presentation and designing effective presentation visuals, study carefully the specific suggestions in the "Check Your Communication" checklist in this chapter. Practice your delivery at least once, and then compare your style with the points listed in the delivery section of the checklist. Make necessary improvements as you continue to polish your presentation skills.

Your Turn 12-5
Electronic Café

COMMUNICATING THROUGH SECURE ELECTRONIC DOCUMENTS

What happened to the concept of the paperless office? Firms have been interested in the idea of a paperless work environment since personal computers were introduced. Eliminating the space needed to store documents, reduced time spent handling and looking for information, and making better use of documents are all promising outcomes. However, studies show that offices continue to increase their paper output each year. Securely storing documents, conveniently locating information, and reliably retrieving desired information are ongoing challenges of paperless information management.

TAKE ACTION:

- Read the following article to learn why people and organizations often still prefer paper documents:

  Tomlinson, C. (2006, April 25). The ideal of the paperless office—it only looks good on paper. *The Birmingham Post* (England), p. 22. Available from Business & Company Resource Center database.
- Prepare a chart showing the types of documents you prefer to receive on paper and those you prefer to access on a computer screen.
- Visit your companion website at www.cengage.com/bcomm/lehman to complete other activities related to paperless business activity.

Sun Microsystems: Presenting to a Virtual Audience

Why limit a presentation to the number of people that can fit in a conference room? Companies can now expand their training program or sales pitch to appeal to thousands or even millions. By distributing your presentation via the Web, you can extend it to a widely scattered audience.

The Web has made it possible for presenters to reach a wide audience while offering customized viewing options. Special considerations in design help assure that graphics are delivered quickly, accurately, and effectively. As with face-to-face delivery, the web presenter must relate ideas clearly and remember that less can be more. Scott McNealy, chairman of the board at Sun Microsystems, characterizes the current consumer phase as "The Participation Age," emphasizing that consumers not only desire information but also the ability to interact with it.[34] Java has played a major part in the development of interactive technologies.

www.java.sun.com

Activities

- Visit the Java site at **www.java.sun.com.** Read about applets and how they are being used to enhance visual communication on the Web.
- Locate and read the following article:

  Gallo, C. (2009, April 8). Making your presentations more relevant. *Business Week Online*, p. 16. Available from Business Source Complete database.

Following your instructor's directions, prepare a short oral or written report that presents guidelines for effective presentations for today's technology-centered audiences.

© RICK WILKING/REUTERS/LANDOV

Summary

1. Plan a business presentation that accomplishes the speaker's goals and meets the audience's needs.

First, determine what you want to accomplish in your presentation. Second, know your audience so you can direct your presentation to the specific needs and interests of the audience. Identify the general characteristics (age, gender, experience, etc.), size, and receptiveness of the audience.

2. Organize and develop the three parts of an effective presentation.

An effective presentation has an introduction, body, and close. The introduction should capture the audience's attention, involve the audience and the speaker, present the purpose statement, and preview major points. The body is limited to a few major points that are supported and clarified with relevant statistics, anecdotes, quotes from prominent people, appropriate humor, presentation visuals, and so forth. The close should be a memorable idea that supports and strengthens the purpose statement.

3. Select, design, and use presentation visuals effectively.

Using visual aids reduces the time required to present a concept and increases audience retention. Available aids include handouts, models and physical objects, whiteboards, flip charts, overhead transparencies, electronic presentations, videotapes, and audiotapes. Each type provides specific advantages and should be selected carefully. Guidelines for preparing visual aids include limiting the number of visuals, presenting one major idea in a simple design large enough for the audience to read, selecting fonts and color schemes that convey appropriate tone and can be read easily, and proofreading to eliminate all errors. Permissions should be obtained for the use of copyrighted multimedia content. Effective visual aid use includes paraphrasing rather than reading the visual and stepping to one side so the audience can see the visual.

4. Deliver speeches with increasing confidence.

Business speakers use the impromptu and extemporaneous speech methods more frequently than the memorized or scripted methods. Professional vocal qualities include a medium or low voice pitch, adequate volume, varied tone and rate, and the absence of distracting verbal fillers. Articulate speakers enunciate words precisely and ensure proper pronunciation. Before your presentation, prepare thoroughly, develop any presentation visuals needed to support your presentation, prepare useful notes to aid your delivery, request a lectern to hold notes but not to hide behind, request a proper introduction, dress appropriately, and arrive early to check last-minute details. During the presentation, communicate confidence and enthusiasm for the audience, watch your audience for feedback, answer questions politely, and stay within your time limit. After the presentation answer questions from the audience, and distribute handouts at the appropriate time.

5. Discuss strategies for presenting in alternate delivery situations such as culturally diverse audiences, team, and distance presentations.

When communicating with other cultures, use simple, clear speech. Consider differences in presentation approach, nonverbal communication, and social protocol that may require flexibility and adjustments to your presentation style. To deliver an effective team presentation, select an appropriate leader and team members with complementary strengths and styles. Plan the presentation as a team, and agree on a schedule to ensure a cohesive presentation focused on audience needs. Rehearse thoroughly to ensure a coordinated, cohesive, and uniform team presentation. When delivering a videoconference or live web presentation, determine whether a distance delivery method is appropriate for the presentation, attempt to establish rapport with the participants prior to the distance presentation, become proficient in delivering and using distance technology, and develop high-quality graphics appropriate for the distance format.

Chapter Review

1. How does the purpose of a presentation affect the process of planning a presentation? What two techniques can you use to condense the purpose of a presentation into a brief statement? **(Obj. 1)**
2. What important facts should a speaker know about the audience when planning a presentation? **(Obj. 1)**
3. What is the basic three-part structure of an effective presentation? What are the purposes of each part? **(Obj. 2)**
4. What does a speaker hope to accomplish in the close? What suggestions will help a speaker accomplish this goal? **(Obj. 2)**
5. Discuss general guidelines for preparing an effective presentation visual. **(Obj. 3)**
6. Briefly explain the provisions of the Copyright Law of 1976 as it applies to multimedia content (graphics, sound, and video). What steps can presenters take to ensure they are complying with copyright law? **(Obj. 3)**
7. Which delivery methods are used most often by business speakers? What are the advantages and limitations of each? **(Obj. 4)**
8. What ethical responsibility does a speaker have when planning and delivering a presentation? **(Objs. 1, 4)**
9. What can a speaker do to ensure that a presentation is understood and not offensive to audience members of various cultures? **(Obj. 5)**
10. What strategies are recommended for delivering an effective team presentation or broadcasted presentation? **(Obj. 5)**

Digging Deeper

1. What is the single most important piece of advice you would give for making an effective business presentation?
2. With current advancements in technology, how has the business presenter's role been simplified? How has it become more difficult?
3. How does the advice "communicate a lot, using as little as possible" relate to the design of presentation visuals? Provide an example to support your point.

Assessment

To check your understanding of the chapter, take the available practice quizzes as directed by your instructor.

Activities

1. Preparing a Top 10 List for Effective Business Presentations (Objs. 1–5)

Generate a list of the top 10 mistakes presenters make based on your experience as a speaker and listener. In small groups, discuss the points listed by each student and compile your ideas into a top 10 list reflecting group consensus. Next, discuss strategies team members have used to avoid each of the mistakes you've listed. Be prepared to share your valuable advice with the class in an informal presentation. As directed by your instructor, continue contributing your thoughts to a blog related to business presentation success strategies.

2. Focusing on an Effective Introduction and Close (Objs. 1, 2)

In a small group, develop a captivating introduction and memorable close for the COPE presentation discussed in this chapter or for a topic your instructor provides. Be prepared to present to the class and discuss the techniques you applied in each of these important sections of a presentation.

Check Your Communication
Presentation Skills

PLANNING AND ORGANIZING A PRESENTATION

- ☐ **Identify your purpose.** Know what you hope to accomplish and choose supporting content.
- ☐ **Analyze your audience.** Identify common characteristics, number in audience, seating arrangements, and time of day.
- ☐ **Develop an effective opening.** Assure that the opening captures attention, initiates rapport with audience, presents the purpose, and previews the main points.
- ☐ **Develop the body.** Select a few major and supporting points: statistics, anecdotes, quotes, and appropriate humor. Use simple, nontechnical language and understandable sentences. Avoid excessive statistics and use word pictures when possible. Use jokes or humor appropriately.
- ☐ **Develop an effective close.** Call for the audience to accept your idea or provide a strong conclusion with recommendations.

SELECTING AN APPROPRIATE PRESENTATION VISUAL

- ☐ Select a presentation visual appropriate for the audience and topic.
- ☐ Use whiteboards and flip charts for small audiences in an informal setting and when no special equipment is available. Prepare flip charts in advance when possible.
- ☐ Use overhead transparencies for small, informal audiences.
- ☐ Use slides for presentations requiring photography; sequence appropriately and show in a darkened room.
- ☐ Use electronic presentations for large audiences and to enliven the topic with multimedia. Make needed last-minute changes; use as a supplement to the presentation, not a replacement.
- ☐ Use models and physical objects to convey the idea presented.

DESIGNING AND USING PRESENTATION VISUALS

- ☐ Limit the number of visual aids to avoid overload.
- ☐ Clear all copyrights for multimedia content.
- ☐ Write descriptive titles and parallel bulleted lists.
- ☐ Create a standard design for each visual following these slide design principles:
  - Include only the major idea to be remembered.
  - Make the design concise, simple, and readable.
  - Choose fonts and a color scheme that convey the formality and tone. Avoid graphics that distort facts.
  - Proofread the visual carefully to eliminate errors.
- ☐ Use presentation visuals effectively. Paraphrase rather than reading and step to one side for audience viewing.

Delivering a Presentation

BEFORE THE PRESENTATION

- ☐ Prepare thoroughly to minimize natural nervousness.
- ☐ Prepare easy-to-read note cards or pages to prompt recall.
- ☐ Practice to identify organizational flaws or verbal potholes; do not rehearse.
- ☐ Use a lectern for steadiness but not to hide behind.
- ☐ Request a proper, impressive introduction.
- ☐ Dress appropriately to create a professional image.
- ☐ Arrive early to check out the room and last-minute details.

DURING THE PRESENTATION

- ☐ Use clear, articulate speech and proper pronunciation.
- ☐ Use vocal variety and adjust volume and rate to emphasize ideas.
- ☐ Avoid verbal fillers and annoying speech habits.
- ☐ Maintain steady eye contact with audience members in various places.
- ☐ Smile genuinely and use gestures naturally to communicate confidence and warmth.
- ☐ Watch your audience for important feedback and adjust your presentation accordingly.
- ☐ Handle questions from the audience politely.
- ☐ Keep within the time limit.

AFTER THE PRESENTATION

- ☐ Be prepared for a question-and-answer period.
- ☐ Distribute handouts at the appropriate time.

ADAPTING TO A CULTURALLY DIVERSE AUDIENCE

- ☐ Use simple English and short sentences and avoid abbreviations, slang, jargon, figurative expressions, etc.
- ☐ Enunciate precisely and speak slowly. Observe the audience carefully for signs of misunderstanding.
- ☐ Consider the appropriateness of jokes and humor.
- ☐ Use a straightforward, direct approach.
- ☐ Adjust to differences in nonverbal communication, preference for formality, gift-giving practices, and social protocol.

DELIVERING A TEAM PRESENTATION

- ☐ Select a leader to lead in developing a cohesive presentation strategy and team members with complementary strengths and styles.
- ☐ Plan the presentation as a team and agree on a schedule to ensure a cohesive, audience-centered presentation.
- ☐ Rehearse thoroughly for cohesion, uniformity, smooth transitioning, and fielding of questions.

DELIVERING A DISTANCE PRESENTATION

- ☐ Determine whether a distance delivery method is appropriate for the presentation.
- ☐ Establish rapport with participants prior to the presentation.
- ☐ Become proficient in using distance technology.
- ☐ Develop high-quality, appropriate graphics.

3. Presenting an Impromptu Presentation for Self-Critique (Objs. 1, 2, 4)

In groups of four assigned by your instructor, select four topics from the following list of questions provided by your instructor. A group leader may randomly assign a topic to each member or allow the members to select a topic. Following a brief preparation time, each member will give a one- to two-minute presentation to the group. After all presentations are given, the group will briefly discuss the strengths and weaknesses of each presentation and strive to provide each member with a few specific suggestions for improvement.

a. Choose one of the following thought-provoking questions from *The Conversation Piece* by Nicholaus and Lowrie:[35]
   - What is one of the simple pleasures of life you truly enjoy?
   - What is something you forgot once that you will never forget again?
   - What thought or sentiment would you like to put in one million fortune cookies?
   - Almost everyone has something that he/she considers a sure thing. What is your "ace in the hole"?
   - Most people have a story or experience they love to share. What's your story?

b. What is the best career advice you've received?

c. What communication abilities are especially important during uncertain times?

d. How do social networking sites such as MySpace and Twitter affect your marketability?

e. What are the top three goofs made by [new hires, student interns, job applicants, presenters, or others].

f. Who is the CEO you admire most and why?

g. Why is being a team player (or global thinker) important in today's economy?

h. Which technology has had the most effect on your day-to-day life? Which do you expect to have the most impact on your worklife?

i. What do you consider to be the distinction between management and leadership?

4. Improving Presentation Visuals (Obj. 3)

Evaluate the effectiveness of the following slide and offer suggestions for improvement following the design principles presented in the text. Be prepared to present your analysis to the class. Your instructor may ask you to revise or build slides. A downloadable version is available at your companion website at www.cengage.com/bcomm/lehman.

a. Revise the slide content shown on page 461 and select an appropriate template and graphics to support the topic.

b. In groups, brainstorm strategies for preparing an effective team presentation. Collapse your ideas into five memorable points that capture key success ideas. Revise the list for parallel wording, clarity, and brevity. Display your list on a slide using a format that includes more than a basic bulleted list; add an engaging title and an appropriate template and graphics. Be prepared to present your slide to the class for critique; incorporate suggestions received and submit to your instructor as an email attachment.

c. In groups, design slides to support one of the following topics or as directed by your instructor. Include a title slide, at least one bulleted list, and one direct quotation. Be prepared to share the slides with another small group and then revise, incorporating suggestions received.
   - Present an argument for the continued use of electronic presentations in your company. Include succinct advice for using the communication tool effectively.
   - Present an argument for the importance of a highly demanded workplace skill and strategies for developing it. You might choose a key team skill such as trust or collaboration, or a new technology skill such as social networking or social bookmarking. Conduct a search of an online database or the Internet for assistance in selecting a topic of value to the class.

d. Design one slide to support the personal story you are asked to develop in Application 1. Follow the 7×7 rule, and include a powerful image related to the key point being made.

5. How Not to Use PowerPoint (Obj. 3)

View Comedian Don McMillan's YouTube video, "How Not to Use PowerPoint," that humorously illustrates common faux pas in using PowerPoint effectively. In small groups, generate a list of additional faux pas that you have observed in the design and use of presentation visuals. Develop a two- to three-minute presentation conveying this information in a workplace setting.

How well are you handling stress in the workplace?

<u>*Five Foolproof Ways to Keep You Stress Levels Under Control:*</u>

1. Begin by keeping your expectations realistic. Don't set unrealistic goals that you know you can't reach.
2. Avoid working unnecessary long hours that will only reduce your productivity in the long run.
3. Don't be afraid to turn down requests that require you to take on additional responsibility, if you don't have the time.
4. Plan and take regular short breaks that allow you to relax, even if it's just a simple stretch at your desk.
5. Taking advantage of all your holidays is important as you need this time to recharge and energize yourself.

Applications

READ | THINK | WRITE | SPEAK | COLLABORATE

1. Build Your Leadership with a Collection of Good Stories (Objs. 1–2, 4)

Read the following selections about the importance of crafting personal and hypothetical stories to convey inspiring messages and extend your influence as a leader.

Simmons, A. (2007). *Whoever tells the best story wins: How to use your own stories to communicate with power and impact*. New York: Amacon.

Heath, D. (2009, April). The story whisperer: Seize the power of stories. *Chief Learning Officer*, 58. Available from Business Source Complete database.

Required: Complete the following activities as directed by your instructor:

1. Using information from these sources and others that you locate, prepare a short report that includes (a) a summary of the benefits of storytelling in spoken and written business communication, (b) discussion of a story you've heard with explanation of its strengths and weaknesses, and (c) examples of how storytelling could be used effectively in your field.
2. In small groups, practice your storytelling techniques by telling one of the stories that Simmons recommends and following her format for receiving feedback on your story. Share a time you shined; a time you blew it; the impact of an important person in your life; or a scene from a movie, book, or current event that illustrates a point. To refine your story, ask the listeners to answer these questions: (a) "What your story tells me about you is . . . ," "What I like about your story is . . . ," "What your story helps me remember is . . . ," and "The impact I see your story having in a specific situation (describe) is . . ."
3. Write a brief introduction of yourself to appear on the company website along with the "bios" of other new hires. Be creative and integrate a story line that tells "who I am," "why I'm here," and "what key values I hold."

2. Selecting Appropriate Presentation Visuals (Obj. 3)

A speaker must select the appropriate medium or combination of media to accomplish the speech's purpose and to meet the needs of a specific audience. Visit your companion website at www.cengage.com/bcomm/lehman to learn about the most common types of presentation visuals and design guidelines for effective presentation visuals.

Required: Develop a standard slide layout for a slideshow that (a) displays the advantages and disadvantages of each type of presentation visual and (b) provides tips for using each type of effectively. For easier comparison, collapse the information into four categories: (a) electronic presentations, (b) boards and flipcharts, (c) still projection objects (overheads), and (d) hard copy visuals (handouts). Be prepared to present your slideshow to the class.

3. Adapting Presentations for International Audiences (Objs. 1, 5)

Locate the following article that offers suggestions for developing business presentations for an international audience:

St. Amant, K. R. (2005, May). Presentations for international audiences, *Intercom*, 13–15. Available from Business Source Complete database.

Required: Prepare a grid that compares presentation practices appropriate for audiences of the same culture as compared to international audiences. Research further as necessary to complete your informational comparison.

4. Creating Presentations for On-Demand Access (Objs. 3, 5)

Thousands of podcasts are available via the Internet that entertain, raise brand exposure, and ultimately increase revenues. Video presentations, or podcasts, convey information, increase retention, and compel action better than static web pages or PowerPoint slides. Easy-to-use software allows users with no video training to produce professional presentations at a reasonable cost. The corporate communication applications for this rich communication medium are endless with powerful messages available on demand.

Required: Complete the following activities as directed by your instructor:

1. Write a memo to your instructor summarizing the benefits of video presentations in enhancing business communications.
2. Locate the following article:

   Eastman, D. (2006, August 28). Podcast best practices. Available from http://debeastman.blogspot.com/2006/08/podcast-best-practices.html
3. Go to the BusinessWeek podcast series at www.businessweek.com/search/podcasting.htm and choose a podcast from the series. Write a critique that includes (a) a summary of the overall effectiveness of the podcast as compared to reading the related article, (b) your impression of the effectiveness of the delivery, and (c) suggestions for improving the overall impact of the podcast.
4. Take a product tour, view video samples, and download a trial version of Camtasia Studio, video production software at http://techsmith.com. Then, produce a 1–2 minute audio podcast or vodcast that provides advice on making presentations relevant to Generation Y audiences, or present on a topic assigned by your instructor.

READ | THINK | WRITE | SPEAK | COLLABORATE

5. Evaluating a Presenter (Objs. 1–5)

Evaluate the speaking skill of a well-known television newscaster, political figure, or a recognized speaker on your campus. You may choose to locate a web or podcast of your most admired CEO or company spokesperson at the company website or at the *Wall Street Journal Online* or *BusinessWeek Online*. Use the "Check Your Communication" checklist to direct your attention to the various components of effective speaking. Offer suggestions for improving the person's presentation abilities related to content, organization, visuals, and delivery style.

6. Analyzing an Executive Speech (Objs. 1–5)

Locate the following article and complete the following activities as directed by your instructor:

Wilson, A. B. (2005). Crafting a winning speech. *Vital Speeches of the Day, 71*(22), 685–689. Available from EBSCOhost database.

1. Describe a presentation that you have heard that depicts one or more of the cardinal principles Wilson presents. If necessary, conduct an online search for a video or printed presentation given by an executive or politician that you admire.
2. Locate an executive speech using YouTube or a web search. Prepare a short report that includes the following elements:
   - Who was the speaker and what is his or her professional affiliation?
   - Who was the audience and what goal did the presenter intend to accomplish through this presentation?
   - What three techniques set this presentation apart from a typical presentation? Justify your choices.
   - What advice would you offer for improving the presentation?

7. Developing Vocal Power (Objs. 1, 2, 4)

Strong vocal skills are especially critical in today's environment in which much communication takes place via phone, computer, or fax, rather than face-to-face. Mispronunciations, mumbling, and distracting regional accents can interfere with clear understanding. Complete the following activities to begin your vocal makeover.

Required:

a. Visit www.greatvoice.com/speaker/index.html. Read this speech coach's advice including "Play Your Voice Like a Finely Tuned Instrument" and "Leave Voicemail that Gets Results." Practice the exercises at "My Favorite Vocal Warmup."

b. Prepare a recording of your voice for analysis using an article from a newspaper or magazine. Listen to your recording and seek constructive feedback from friends or classmates, especially those from other regions or cultures who can help you identify speech problems affecting understandability and impression.

c. Write a memo to your instructor that includes an honest critique of your voice and a description of the modifications needed to develop a professional voice. Use the checklist at your companion website at www.cengage.com/bcomm/lehman as a guide for your analysis

d. As an owner/operator of a home business, (1) record an outgoing voice mail message for a home business that sounds professional, enthusiastic, and articulate; and (2) leave a voice mail message on a prospective customer/client's phone that you're confident will be returned.

8. Evaluating Your Speaking Style (Objs. 1, 2, 4, 5)

Videotape your delivery of a presentation on one of the topics listed in Activity 3 or a topic of your choice. Use the "Check Your Communication" checklist to direct your attention to the various components of effective speaking as you review the videotape.

Required: Complete the following activities; be prepared to discuss with your instructor and to incorporate changes.

- What was your overall impression of your performance after you completed the presentation?
- List at least three strengths and three weaknesses in your delivery style.
- Ask two other people in your class to view the videotape and critique your performance; they should provide at least two strengths and two suggestions for improvement.
- What is your overall impression of your performance after you analyzed the videotape and received feedback from class members? Does this impression differ from your impression before viewing the videotape? Explain.

READ | THINK | WRITE | SPEAK | COLLABORATE

9. Embracing a Presenter's Code of Conduct (Objs. 1–5)

Locate and read the following professional code of ethics for professional communicators and a related article:

International Association of Business Communicators (IABC): www.iabc.com/about/code.htm

Zielinski, D. (2002, August 10). The presenter's pledge: Do presenters need a code of conduct? *Presentations*, *16*(8), 24+. Available at www.allbusiness.com/services/business-services-advertising/4246997-1.html

Required: Consider the ethical challenges presenters face and the behavioral guideposts presented in these readings. Write your own presenter's pledge to ensure honesty and integrity in your professional presentations. Be prepared to explain to the class your rationale for the actions included.

10. Critiquing a Slide Show Prepared to Support a Written Report (Objs. 1–3)

Visit your companion website at www.cengage.com/bcomm/lehman to download a slide show developed to support a consultant's presentation about cross-cultural virtual teams at TechSense, Inc. Compare the slide show to the consultant's written report shown in Figure 11-6 in your text.

Required: Write a memo to your instructor (a) analyzing the overall effectiveness of the slides in supporting the consultant's purpose and (b) summarizing the use of key multimedia elements (e.g., template, images, animation, and sound).

READ | THINK | WRITE | SPEAK | COLLABORATE

11. Preparing an Extemporaneous In-House Presentation (Objs. 1–5)

Your instructor has provided specific instructions for presenting a proposal to management. Select a topic from the following list of suggested proposal topics or use them as a springboard for other in-house presentations. Obtain your instructor's approval for your topic before beginning work.

a. Proposal to develop a policy that provides up to five paid days annually for volunteer work.
b. Proposal to implement an in-house recycling program.
c. Proposal to a local business to enhance the customer experience without increasing costs.
d. Proposal to the board of directors to forge a strategic alliance with another company. Choose two likely companies and present the concept and the benefits that could be derived for each company.
e. Proposal to extend your company's domestic retail market into an international market of your choice.
f. Proposal to management for creating a joint venture with another company to offer a business-to-business (B2B) exchange for online commerce and supply chain services. Choose two feasible companies that could take advantage of the benefits of supply chain management (e.g., HomebuildersXchange links suppliers, distributors, and trade contractors and builders to bring efficiencies to every participant in the construction process).

12. Preparing an Extemporaneous Presentation on a Chosen Topic (Objs. 1, 2, 4, 5)

Your instructor has provided specific instructions for preparing a presentation of approximately five to ten minutes. Select a topic from the following list or from the expanded list at your companion website at www.cengage.com/bcomm/lehman, or suggest a different relevant business topic. Obtain your instructor's approval for your topic before beginning work.

a. Strategies for assuring employability in a faltering or recovering economy.
b. Effects of blogging on writing style and how a business professional can capture the best of blogging for more formal business communication.
c. Business professionals' use of technology to increase the reach, timeliness, and interactivity of their communication.
d. The benefits and potential problems with the trend to replace the traditional coffee break with "e-breaks," giving employees approved time for personal computer use.
e. Benefits derived from company-sponsored volunteer programs.

f. Efforts of corporate leaders to increase employees' sensitivity toward diversity (cultures, genders, ages of coworkers, and potential markets).
g. Changes in preferences for communication channels over the past five years, especially in the younger generation and effects on the workplace.
h. Benefits of working cooperatively in diverse work groups.
i. Key issues leading companies to expand their computer usage policies to include social networking sites.
j. Effects of body art in the workplace and businesses' response to the issue.

READ | THINK | WRITE | SPEAK | COLLABORATE

13. Developing a Presentation Plan (Objs. 1–5)

The foundation of an effective presentation is selecting an appropriate topic, one that is narrow in scope, fits the time slot, appeals to the speaker's interests, and meets audience needs. Following the process outlined in the Presentation Planning Guide will direct you in planning an effective presentation. A downloadable version of the guide is available at your companion website at www.cengage.com/bcomm/lehman.

a. In preparation for a 10-minute presentation, select a topic from this list or one approved by your instructor:
   - Implementing environmentally friendly workplace policies
   - Communicating confidently in uncertain times
   - Enhancing the productivity of virtual teams
   - Increasing financial literacy
   - Networking in the cyber age
   - Enhancing the customer experience with limited resources
   - Coping with an ethical dilemma in your profession
   - Ways Web 2.0 (wikis and social media) is changing business
   - Attracting and retaining talented employees
   - Communication and the generation gap
   - Identity theft or fraud detection
b. Complete the "Topic and Purpose" section of the Presentation Planning Sheet as you develop a purpose statement and preview statement (points to be covered in the presentation). In groups of two or three, critique each member's topic and preview statements; revise your own work, and submit the original and revised statements to your instructor. Be prepared to discuss your improvements in an informal presentation to the class.

14. Preparing a Team Presentation (Objs. 1–5)

Develop one of the topics in Application 13 into a team presentation for delivery to the class. Prepare a detailed action plan for the preparation and delivery of the team presentation following the guidelines for team presentations in your textbook. Complete the Presentation Planning Sheet (available at your companion website, www.cengage.com/bcomm/lehman), making your own assumptions about the audience and logistics or following those assigned by your instructor. To support your ideas, use at least two periodicals, a newspaper, a book, an electronic source, and a government publication. List the sources in a references page formatted in APA style. Following the team presentation, prepare a debriefing memo to your instructor outlining the strengths of the team's work and planned improvements for future presentations.

15. Preparing an Oral Briefing (Objs. 1, 2, 4, 5)

In small groups assigned by your instructor, give a one- to three-minute oral briefing regarding progress completed on an assigned team project. Alternately, each member may present a one- to two-minute presentation explaining a key concept or new development in his or her career field. A *brief* preparation time will be provided; however, the purpose of the activity is to prepare for impromptu spoken presentations. After all presentations are given, the group will briefly discuss the strengths and weaknesses of each presentation and provide each member with a few specific suggestions for improvement in delivering an impromptu presentation.

CASES

© AP IMAGES/ JACK ARENT

1. Learning from Steve Jobs' Life Stories

Steve Jobs is the CEO of Apple, which he co-founded in 1976. Apple leads the industry in innovation with its award-winning Macintosh computers, OS X operating system, and consumer and professional applications software. Apple is most known for its blockbuster iPhone product and its leadership role in the digital music revolution, having sold almost 200 million iPods and over six billion songs from its iTunes online store.

While the charismatic Jobs has been asked to speak at numerous college commencements, he himself never graduated from college. According to Jobs, he dropped out of college after six months and then began dropping back in on the classes that were of interest to him. By the age of 20, Jobs and his college roommate had started Apple Computers in his parents' garage. Jobs philosophically explains his eventual firing from the company he started as the best thing that ever happened to him.

His work with other technology enterprises convinced him even more solidly of the importance of following your heart. "Your time is limited, so don't waste it living someone else's life," says Jobs. Jobs eventually would return to lead Apple, though weathering various health problems including pancreatic cancer and a liver transplant.

In Jobs' commencement address at Stanford, he related three stories from his life experiences that shaped his outlook on life and that relate in a very personal way the value of pursuing one's dreams.

View Steve Jobs' 2005 commencement address to the graduating class at Stanford University or read the script of the speech:

Video: YouTube: "Steve Jobs Stanford Commencement Speech 2005"

Script: Stanford Report. (2005, June 14). 'You've got to find what you love,' Jobs says. Available from http://news-service.stanford.edu/news/2005/june15/jobs-061505.html

1. Discuss how Jobs establishes and sustains his credibility as a speaker and the audience's interest throughout the presentation.
2. Based on current information about Apple Computers, what are other points that Jobs could have made that would be relevant in a similar presentation given today? Prepare an outline of Jobs' speech that reflects your additional points.
3. Assume that Jobs has asked you to create an electronic slide show for the speech he will give at Stanford. Prepare the slide show based on the script he has provided, and share it with the class.

© TERRI MILLER/ E-VISUAL COMMUNICATIONS, INC.

2. Yoplait Appeals to Health, Convenience, and Great Taste

As the top-selling yogurt maker in the United States, Yoplait is committed to making products that consumers love. According to Bob Waldron, president of Yoplait-Colombo USA, "We're in a very favorable category. It's on-trend, it tastes great, it's convenient, and it's healthy—kind of the trifecta of food for us."[36] Designed to maximize health and nutritional benefits, Yoplait's product innovations are aimed at increasing the percentage of households eating yogurt, attracting a wider mix of yogurt lovers (kids and males), and increasing the shelf space allotted to yogurt. Yoplait Healthy Heart, a yogurt containing plant sterols that are clinically proven to reduce cholesterol, is leading a proactive health market segment; consumers are enticed to eat two servings of yogurt each day to reduce LDL or "bad" cholesterol by an average of 6 percent. New products include a variety of convenient tasty treats for kids, fat-free yogurt as a vital part of a weight-loss plan, and Chocolate Mousse Style, a proprietary recipe for a great-tasting chocolate-flavored yogurt with live and active yogurt cultures consumers have demanded for years. The success of Yoplait's R&D team could prove healthy for Yoplait.

For more information about Yoplait's products and activities, visit the company's website at www.generalmills.com and read the following articles:

Latest study Shows Yoplait YoPlus improves digestive health. (2009, June 20). *Neutraceuticals World*. Available at www.nutraceuticalsworld.com/news/2009/06/05/Latest%20Study%20Shows%20Yoplait%20YoPlus%20Improves%20Digestive%20Health

Dudlicek, J. (2005, November). Team spirit: Yoplait strives to feel small but do things big through team work and leveraging the strengths of parent General Mills. *Dairy Field, 188*(11), 20(7). Available from General Businessfile database.

In teams prepare the following communications as directed by your instructor:

1. As members of the Yoplait management team, present a five-minute presentation outlining key issues facing the company, an overview of strategies the company has adopted to address them, and projections for the company's future direction. Then prepare a 1- to 2-minute speech promoting additional shelf space for Yoplait products in a leading retail chain. You may choose to produce your presentation as a podcast to be distributed on the company's website or intranet.
2. As members of a marketing team for Yoplait, brainstorm various strategies for addressing the disparity of yogurt consumption between male and female consumers. Develop a print advertisement and a 30-second commercial to attract male consumers. Based on team interactions, write a brief report summarizing what your team learned about differences in communication preferences of men and women—thinking, organizing ideas, persuasive appeals, etc.
3. Develop a flyer that can be sent electronically to doctors' offices that touts the value of yogurt in overall good health. Design the flyer so that it will have appeal to patients who visit the doctors' offices.

© BBC LTD./COURTESY: EVERETT COLLECTION

3. Video Case: The Office: Presenter's Promises: Can You Deliver?

In this clip, David presents sobering news to office personnel and responds to staff concerns. Complete the following activities as directed by your instructor after viewing the video:

1. What presentation style does David use in this clip? Is the style appropriate for the information he has to deliver? Explain.
2. How does David handle his employees' questions? How could he have responded more appropriately?

3. Now About That Accent . . .

Most individuals "pick up" the accent spoken in the region in which they live, and those who learn English as a second language typically retain some elements of pronunciation that are indicative of their first language. When you leave your native area, your accent may be a subject of interest, humor, or even ridicule.

Studies have indicated that salespersons with a standard accent or dialect are often perceived more favorably by customers than foreign-accented salespersons.[37] The U.S. media promotes the acceptance of "general American standard dialect," and the seeming lack of accent among public broadcasters is often the result of extensive retraining in vocal delivery. Corporations often also desire to enhance universal acceptance by cultivating "standard English" among their management. Corporate accent-reduction speech clients have included executives from Beech Aircraft, Mitsubishi Bank, NCR Corporation, Union Carbide, and Wells Fargo Bank.[38]

Not everyone, however, feels that accents are detrimental. A countering opinion is that an accent may at times serve as an asset to the speaker. It reflects personhood and adds dimension and interest to the individual. Furthermore, the "best English" is often dictated by audience expectation and the circumstances in which a speaker functions. Regardless of the charm value of an accent, your audience must be able to understand you. The following guidelines are suggested when the speaker's dialect is different from that of the audience:

- Speak more slowly and distinctly than usual during the opening minutes of your presentations, to allow the audience to adjust to your speech patterns and style.
- Don't apologize for your accent. The audience will likely not find it offensive once they can understand your speech patterns.
- To avoid emphasizing the wrong syllables, ask someone fluent in the dialect of the audience to pronounce unfamiliar words, names, etc. Devise a kind of shorthand for marking the pronunciation and accented syllables in your notes.
- Try not to let your concern over dialect interfere with your interaction with the audience. Be enthusiastic and let your personality show through.

Visit your companion website at www.cengage.com/bcomm/lehman to link to web resources related to this topic. As directed by your instructor, complete one or more of the following:

- Locate at least one additional website on the subject of accents that you found interesting. What is the URL of the site? Summarize the important aspects of the information in outline form.
- Analyze your own accent, responding to the following questions: Of what region is it typical? What distinguishes your accent from others? Is your accent stronger at certain times? If so, why? Email your instructor with your self-analysis.
- How are accent and dialect different yet related? Prepare a chart that illustrates the relationship.
- What are the advantages and disadvantages of a regional accent? How can accent work either to enhance or worsen a businessperson's communication? Write a one- to two-page summary of your position on the issue.

5. Inside View: Speech Jitters

Earthquake! Experiencing such a traumatic event certainly creates high levels of stress; and doctors tell us that such heightened stress increases the incidence of heart damage. What many don't know is that the fear of public speaking can cause the same stress reaction in the body as living through an earthquake. Is there a pill in our future that speakers will take to prevent potential stress damage to their bodies? What do surviving an earthquake and giving a speech have in common? More than you might think. Significant mental stress, like physical stress, can cause serious physiological problems in the body.

View the "Speech Jitters" video segment online at your companion website, www.cengage.com/bcomm/lehman, to learn more about stress and public speaking.

Reflect:

1. What types of physical problems can result from high levels of stress?
2. Some doctors suggest that taking medication before an anticipated high stress situation might protect a person from potential physical complications. What are the implications of such a measure?
3. The risk of social embarrassment makes public speaking the number one fear of many. How can that fear be minimized?
4. On a scale of 1 to 10 with 10 being the highest level, how do you rate your own public speaking anxiety?

React:

Locate the following article that provides further information about public speaking anxiety and how to minimize it:

McMaster, M. (2002). Performance anxiety: How can a fretful sales rep with a fear of speaking in public become a knock-'em-dead company pitchman? Take a lesson from three execs who overcame presentation panic with the help of hypnotists, hostile crowds, and some time in prison. *Sales & Marketing Management, 154*(8), 48–50. Available from Business Source Complete database.

Develop a list of the coping strategies discussed in the article that can help in minimizing the unpleasantness of public speaking anxiety. Highlight those you feel will be most beneficial as you plan an upcoming presentation.

Part 5
Communication for Employment

Chapter 13 Preparing Résumés and Application Messages

"One of their keys to success is that they hire very well. It's such a generous place, such a high-trust place, that employees love it. They hire people with the same values as the leaders."

Leonard Berry, Texas A & M

© MELANIE STETSON FREEMAN/THE CHRISTIAN SCIENCE MONITOR/GETTY IMAGES

Objectives When you have completed Chapter 13, you will be able to:

1. Prepare for employment by considering relevant information about yourself as it relates to job requirements.
2. Identify career opportunities using traditional and electronic methods.
3. Prepare an organized, persuasive résumé that is adapted for print and electronic postings.
4. Utilize employment tools other than the résumé that can enhance employability.
5. Write an application message that effectively introduces an accompanying print (designed) or electronic résumé.

SHOWCASE PART 1

The Container Store: Hiring Well Results in Stable Employee Base

One great person is equal to three good people. That's a Foundation Principle and employment philosophy at The Container Store. The Dallas-based firm that specializes in storage and organization products for the home employs over 3,200 people in its 47 retail locations. With operations in 17 states, a large portion of the company's revenues come from its large catalog and website operations. Annual sales of $600 million suggest that the company is doing some things well.[1]

In addition to its continued financial success and steady expansion, The Container Store has consistently been named in *Fortune* magazine's list of "100 Best Companies to Work for in America." The company believes that the first step in forging a great workforce is to hire only employees willing and able to use their creativity, enthusiasm, and intuition to devote themselves to customer service. All employees assist in the recruitment process and carry gold job interview invitations to give to friends, relatives, and even store customers who they feel would be great additions to the company.

Once a great employee is found, ample training is a vital factor in turning that worker into someone who can reach his or her potential. The Container Store invests 241 hours of formal training in every first-year employee, while the retail industry average is a measly 7 hours. High-quality employees are paid high-quality salaries, with The Container Store paying its workers 50 to 100 percent more than the retail average.[2]

Extensive training and enviable salaries are not the only ways that The Container Store empowers its people. Another Foundation Principle is to openly and fully communicate what is going on at the company with everyone who works there. Instead of tightly guarding financial information, The Container Store opens its ledger to all employees. The outcome is an annual turnover rate that is a fraction of the industry average, with the company losing just 8 percent of its full-time salespeople to voluntary turnover.

In his book *Discovering the Soul of Service*, Texas A & M Professor Leonard Berry explains the reasons for The Container Store's success: "One of their keys to success is that they hire very well. It's such a generous place, such a high-trust place, that employees love it. They hire people with the same values as the leaders."[3]

The successful job search process involves matching the needs and values of the individual with those of the organization. A careful match results in a long-lasting, satisfying relationship that is mutually beneficial. This chapter presents the employment process you will need to follow to land your "ideal" job. From the careful self-analysis and identification of prospective employers to the preparation of a powerful résumé and application message, each step in the employment process is important to you in obtaining the right position with the right organization.

http://www.containerstore.com

SEE SHOWCASE, PART 2, ON PAGE 502
FOR SPOTLIGHT COMMUNICATOR MELISSA REIFF, PRESIDENT, THE CONTAINER STORE.

Preparing for the Job Search

Managing your career begins with recognizing that securing a new job is less important than assessing the impact of that job on your life. Work isn't something that happens from 8 to 5, with life happening after 5 p.m. Life and work are interconnected, and true satisfaction comes from being able to fully express yourself in what you do. This means merging who you are—your values, emotions, capabilities, and desires—with the activities you perform on the job.[4]

Have you set your career goals? What is your plan for reaching them?

An ideal job provides satisfaction at all of Maslow's need levels, from basic economic to self-actualizing needs. The right job for you will not be drudgery; the work itself will be satisfying and give you a sense of well-being. Synchronizing your work with your core beliefs and talents leads to enthusiasm and fulfillment. You will probably work 10,000 days of your life, not including time spent commuting and on other related activities. Why spend all this time doing something unfulfilling when you could just as easily spend it doing what you enjoy?

Your ***résumé*** is a vital communication tool that provides a basis for judgment about your capabilities on the job. In preparing this document, your major tasks will be gathering essential information about yourself and the job using traditional and electronic resources, planning and organizing the résumé to showcase your key qualifications, and adapting the résumé for various types of delivery. You may also need to supplement your résumé with examples of your accomplishments and abilities. Finally, you'll prepare persuasive application messages appropriate for the delivery of your résumé.

Your Turn 13-1
Electronic Café

USE OF TIME SPEAKS VOLUMES

Time is a language, and how we spend our 1,440 minutes a day speaks much about our interests, priorities, and commitment. In addition, how we use other people's time and attention communicates our attitudes about them. While we can't increase the total minutes in a day, we can do much to improve our use of the available time we have so that our goals are met.

TAKE ACTION:

Locate the following article:

Gahrmann, N. (2009). Top ten time wasters. *Mom MD*. Available at www.mommd.com/toptentimewasters.shtml

- Make a list of the time management suggestions offered in the article. Star those that you most need to put into practice. Send an email to your instructor, explaining your course of action for improving your time management through eliminating time wasters.
- Visit your companion website at www.cengage.com/bcomm/lehman for more information and activities related to time management.

Gathering Essential Information

The job search begins with research—collecting, compiling, and analyzing information—in order to assess your marketability. The career planning guides available at your companion website (www.cengage.com/bcomm/lehman) will help you identify key qualifications as they relate to an employer's needs, ensure that you have selected the right career, and compare your qualifications to the duties and responsibilities of the job you are seeking. The key accomplishments that surface from this thoughtful analysis will be the main ideas touted in a résumé or an interview. The research phase of the job search involves the steps shown in Figure 13-1 and are summarized as follows:

1. **Gather relevant information for decision making.** Complete (a) a self-assessment to identify your own job-related qualifications, and (b) an analysis of the career field that interests you and a specific job in that field. Follow up with an interview of a career person in your field to acquire additional information.

2. **Prepare a company/job profile.** Compile the information you gathered into a format that allows you to compare your qualifications with the company and job requirements. This organized information will help you determine a possible match between you and the potential job.

3. **Identify unique selling points and specific support.** Determine several key qualifications and accomplishments that enhance your marketability. These are the key selling points you'll target in your résumé and later in a job interview.

What reasons account for the fact that most entry-level employees are in the job market again within six months?

Take a look at the company/job profile for an entry-level audit accountant employed in an international public accounting firm shown at your companion website at www.cengage.com/bcomm/lehman. Comparing the job requirements and the applicant's basic qualifications and expectations for salary and advancement uncovers some incompatibility in the work style and travel/overtime requirements the applicant desires and weaknesses in several relevant job skills.

Identifying Potential Career Opportunities

Plan to begin your job search for prospective employers months beforehand. Waiting too long to begin and then hurrying through the job search process could affect your ability to land a satisfying job.

Before you begin, take the time to develop an organized strategy for your search efforts. You might download a template such as Microsoft's job search log (http://office.microsoft.com/en-us/results.aspx?qu=job+search+log) or invest in software such as Winway Résumé and Résumé Maker Deluxe to simplify the task of tracking your contacts. You'll need a record of the name, address, email address, and telephone number of each potential employer. Later, record the date of each job contact you make and receive (along with what you learned from the contact), the name of the contact person, the date you sent a résumé, and so on.

Your search for potential career opportunities likely will involve traditional and electronic job search sources.

FIGURE 13-1

Process of Applying for a Job

STEP 1	STEP 2	STEP 3	STEP 4	STEP 5
Conduct research and analysis of self, career, and job	Identify a job listing using traditional and electronic sources	Prepare targeted résumé and application message in required formats	Consider supplementing the résumé: Portfolio (print or electronic) or video recording	Interview with companies

© ISTOCKPHOTO.COM/PALI RAO

© ISTOCKPHOTO.COM/YINYANG

© ISTOCKPHOTO.COM/JIM JURICA

© ISTOCKPHOTO.COM/LEIGH SCHINDLER

© COMSTOCK IMAGES/ JUPITERIMAGES

RÉSUMÉ PRESENTATION AND DELIVERY OPTIONS

© TERRI MILLER/ E-VISUAL COMMUNICATIONS, INC.

Print (Designed)

- Mailing to company accompanied by application letter
- Mailed follow up to electronic submission

© ISTOCKPHOTO.COM/PALI RAO

Scannable

- Print résumé formatted for computer scanning

© ISTOCKPHOTO.COM/JOSELITO BRIONES

Electronic Postings

- Email to network contacts, career and corporate sites, and career service centers
- Online form
- Electronic portfolio at personal website
- Beamer to PDA or cell phone

Using Traditional Sources

Traditional means of locating a job include printed sources, networks, career services centers, employers' offices, employment agencies and contractors, and professional organizations.

Printed Sources

Numerous printed sources are useful in identifying firms in need of employees. Responses to advertised positions in the employment sections of newspapers should be made as quickly as possible after the ad is circulated. If your résumé is received early and is impressive, you could get a favorable response before other applications are received. If an ad invites response to a box number without giving a name, be cautious. The employer could be legitimate but does not want present employees to know about the ad or does not want applicants to phone or drop by. However, you have a right to be suspicious of someone who wants to remain obscure while learning everything you reveal in your résumé. Print job listings can also be found in company newsletters, industry directories, and trade and professional publications, which may also be available on the Internet. Visit your companion website at www.cengage.com/bcomm/lehman to review a list of useful resources available in print form.

Networks

Who would you include in a list of network contacts who might assist you in your job search?

The majority of job openings are never advertised. Therefore, developing a network of contacts may be the most valuable source of information about jobs. Your network may include current and past employers, guest speakers in your classes or at student organization meetings, business contacts you met while interning or participating in shadowing or over-the-shoulder experiences, and so on. Let these individuals know the type of job you are seeking and ask their advice for finding employment in today's competitive market.

Career Services Centers

Visit your campus career services center. What services and materials are available?

You will want to register with your college's career services center at least three semesters before you graduate. Typically, the center has a website and a browsing room loaded with career information and job announcement bulletins. Career counseling is available, including workshops on résumé writing, interviewing, etiquette, mock interviews, "mocktail" parties for learning to mingle in pre-interview social events, and more. Through the center, you can attend job fairs to meet prospective employers and schedule on campus and phone and video interviews with company recruiters.

Most career services centers, like companies, use electronic tracking systems. Rather than submitting printed résumés, students input their résumés into a computer file following the specific requirements of the tracking system used by the college or university. A search of the résumé database generates an interview roster of the top applicants for a campus recruiter's needs. Some centers assist students in preparing electronic portfolios to supplement the résumé, as discussed in a later section of this chapter.

Employers' Offices

Employers who have not advertised their employment needs may respond favorably to a phone or personal inquiry. The receptionist may be able to provide useful information, direct you to someone with whom you can talk, or set up an appointment.

Employment Agencies and Contractors

City, county, state, and federal employment agencies provide free or inexpensive services. Some agencies offer online listings or phone recordings so that applicants can get information about job opportunities and procedures for using their services. The fee charged by private agencies is paid by either the employee or the employer and usually is based on the first month's salary and due within a few months. Some agencies specialize in finding high-level executives or specialists for major firms. Employment contractors specialize in providing temporary employees and may be able to place you in a position on a temporary basis until you find a full-time job.

Professional Organizations

Officers of professional organizations, through their contacts with members, can be good sources of information about job opportunities. Much job information is exchanged at meetings of professional associations. In response to job listings in journals or organization websites, interviews are sometimes conducted at conference locations.

In addition to the professional growth that comes from membership in professional organizations, active participation is a good way to learn about jobs. Guest speakers share valuable information about the industry, career, and job opportunities. Employers are often favorably impressed when membership and experiences gained are included on the résumé and discussed during an interview. They are even more impressed if the applicant has been an officer in the organization, indicating leadership, community commitment, and willingness to serve without tangible reward, social acceptance, or high level of aspiration. By joining and actively participating in professional, social, and honorary organizations, you increase your opportunities to develop rapport with peers and professors and get an edge over less involved applicants.

Using Electronic Job Searches

An increasing number of companies and job hunters are using the Internet to assist in various stages of the job search process. Convenience, speed, and accessibility are all reasons for the popularity of electronic job searches among human resources managers. The cost of electronic recruiting is lower than traditional methods, and applicants and employers can respond more quickly. Job seekers can use the Internet to complement rather than replace the traditional methods previously discussed.

Numerous printed sources and excellent online assistance are available for learning to tap into the power of online job hunting. For a list of some of these resources, visit your companion website at www.cengage.com/bcomm/lehman. In this chapter, you'll explore the vast availability of useful career information and job postings on job banks and corporate home pages that match your qualifications. Later, you'll apply effective techniques for online job searching, including ways to protect your privacy while job hunting in cyberspace.

Do you agree that electronic recruiting impersonalizes the employment process? Explain?

Locating Career Guidance Information

According to one career consultant, "Most people in the old days could go into an organization [during a job interview] and not really know about it and hope for the best. Now, people can understand the organization before they even apply."[5] The Internet places at your fingertips a wealth of information that will prepare you for the job interview if you use it as a research tool. Suggestions follow for effectively using the career guidance information you can locate on the Internet:

How does online recruiting benefit the employer? the applicant?

- **Visit career sites for information related to various phases of the job search.** You'll find a wide range of timely discussions at career sites: planning a job search, finding a job you love, researching employers, working a career fair, crafting winning résumés and cover letters, negotiating a salary, and so on. Visit your companion website at www.cengage.com/bcomm/lehman to link conveniently to the top career sites and begin exploring career topics of interest to you.
- **Visit corporate websites to learn about the company.** You can locate information online for targeting your résumé appropriately and to prepare for the job interview. Read mission statements or descriptions of services to see how the organization describes itself, and review the annual report and strategic plan to learn about the financial condition and predicted growth rates. Search for sections promoting new developments on "What's New" or "News" links and career opportunities and job postings. Evaluating the development and professional nature of the website will give you an impression of the organization. Supplement this information with independent sources to confirm the company's stability and status, as negative news will likely not be posted on the website.
- **Identify specific skills companies are seeking.** Study the job descriptions provided on corporate home pages and job sites to identify the skills required for the job and the latest industry buzzwords. Use this information to target your résumé to a specific job listing and to generate keywords for an electronic résumé.

- **Network electronically with prospective employers.** It's easy to network online by attending electronic job fairs, chatting with career counselors, participating in news groups and listservs applicable to your field, and corresponding by email with contacts in companies. The value of these electronic networking experiences is to learn about an industry and career, seek valued opinions, and uncover potential job opportunities. By applying effective communication strategies for an online community, you can make a good impression, create rapport with employment contacts online, and polish your interviewing skills.

Identifying Job Listings

You can use the Internet to locate job opportunities in several ways:

- Look in the employment section of companies' corporate web pages to see if they are advertising job openings.

How has the employment process in your career field changed as a result of electronic technologies?

- Search the electronic databases of job openings of third-party services such as those listed at your companion website at www.cengage.com/bcomm/lehman.
- Access online job classifieds from daily and trade newspapers. CareerBuilder (www.careerbuilder.com) offers the classifieds of a number of major newspapers.

- Subscribe to a newsgroup through UseNext (www.usenext.com) that gives you access to jobs by geographic location and specific job categories.
- Subscribe to services such as America Online (www.aol.com) that provide job search sites and services by keying "Career."

Online and printed sources will help you learn to search particular databases. The following general suggestions will help you get started:

What words describe your skills?

- Input words and phrases that describe your skills rather than job titles because job titles vary by company.
- Use specific phrases such as "entry-level job" or "job in advertising" rather than "job search."
- Start with a wider job description term, such as "pharmaceutical sales jobs," then narrow down to the specific subject, geographic region, state, and so forth.
- Don't limit yourself to one search engine. Try several and bookmark interesting sites.
- Stay focused on your goal and don't get distracted as you go.

Searching for useful career sites among the hundreds available can be quite time consuming. CareerBuilder, JobCentral, and Monster.com are major career sites offering a wide array of information and services.

© AP GRAPHICS BANK

Your Turn 13-2
Assessment

Many people dream of owning their own business. But not everyone is cut out to be an entrepreneur. Take the quiz at the following website to determine your entrepreneurial potential: www.midwest-brokers.com/quiz.html. You may link to this URL or to your companion website at www.cengage.com/bcomm/lehman for updated sites.

TAKE ACTION:

Prepare a short oral presentation that summarizes your entrepreneurial score and what you learned about yourself through taking the quiz.

Planning a Targeted Résumé

In order to match your interests and qualifications with available jobs, you'll need an effective résumé. To win a job interview in today's tight market where job seekers outnumber positions, you need more than a general résumé that documents your education and work history. The powerful wording of a ***targeted résumé*** reflects the requirements of a specific job listing that you have identified through traditional and electronic job search methods.

What decisions must you make when planning a résumé? Which requires the most time?

An employer typically scans résumés quickly looking for reasons to reject the applicant, schedule an interview, or place in a stack for rereading. This initial scan and a second brief look for those who make the cut give little time to explain why you are the best person for the job. To grab an employer's attention, you must selectively choose *what to say*, *how to say it*, and *how to arrange it* on the page so that it can be read quickly but thoroughly. A concise, informative, easy-to-read summary of your relevant qualifications will demonstrate that you possess the straightforward communication skills demanded in today's information-intensive society.

LEGAL AND ETHICAL CONSTRAINTS

The goal of the résumé is to get an interview, so ask yourself this question: "Does including this information increase my chances of getting an interview?" If the answer is "Yes," include the information; if the answer is "No," omit the information and use the space to develop your qualifications. When selecting information to be included, you must also be cautious of the temptation to inflate your résumé to increase your chances of being hired. This chapter's Strategic Forces feature "Inflated Résumés: High Price of Career Lies" discusses the consequences of inflating résumés.

Your Turn 13-3
Miscue

Lies on a résumé can be extremely costly. Former RadioShack CEO David Edmondson was found to have lied on his résumé, claiming he had earned a bachelor's degree in theology and psychology from a small religious-affiliated college. He later said that he had completed a three-year correspondence course, though the school said he had attended only two semesters of classes. Edmondson's resignation over the discrepancy resulted in his forfeiting a $1.5 million yearly salary and additional millions in stock options.[6]

TAKE ACTION:

- What other examples point out the need to be truthful on a résumé?
- Do you agree that a résumé should "tell the truth, the whole truth, and nothing but the truth" concerning the job applicant?

RÉSUMÉ

- Identification
- Objective
- Career Summary
- Qualifications
- Personal Information
- References

Standard Parts of a Résumé

A winning résumé contains standard parts that are adapted to highlight key qualifications for a specific job. An in-depth explanation of each standard part and sample résumés provided in Figures 13-2 to 13-5 will prepare you for preparing a résumé that describes your qualifications best.

Identification

Your objective is to provide information that will allow the interviewer to reach you. Include your name, current address, and phone number and email address. Provide a clear, benign email address that reflects a positive impression (e.g., no mustangsally). You may also include your Internet address to provide access to more detailed information.

LEGAL AND ETHICAL CONSTRAINTS

STRATEGIC FORCES

Inflated Résumés: High Price of Career Lies

Increase in unemployment rates and a weakened economy have created intense competition for fewer jobs, and desperate job seekers are increasingly more willing to "enhance" their résumés. Applicants may feel lying is necessary to get past the initial screening and to stand out in a crowded market. Some rationalize their actions by saying, "Who will ever know?"; "Everyone does it"; or "I deserve it."

According to a CareerBuilder.com's survey, only 8 percent of job-seekers admitted to bending the truth. However, nearly half of hiring managers reported they detected a lie on a résumé.[7] Similarly, Accu-Screen, Inc., a background checking company, reports that 43 percent of all résumés and job applications contain lies, with the falsification increasing during economic downturns.[8]

High-profile people have lost jobs after fudging on their academic credentials. Robert Irvine, "Dinner: Impossible" chef star, lost his contract with the FoodNetwork by claiming that he had cooked for the royal family.[9] The damaging effects of résumé lies can surface when applying for promotions and awards, underscoring the importance of honesty.

Common ways that applicants lie on résumés include the following:

- **Fabricating or embellishing academic experience and professional licensure.** Applicants claim they earned degrees only partially completed or from institutions they never attended. Applicants also fudge on grade-point averages and professional certifications and may list fictitious honors and activities.
- **Fudging employment dates to hide gaps in employment.** Rather than lying, applicants should answer honestly: "Yes, I was laid off at Company X and spent six months looking for the right employer, so there is a gap in my employment dates."
- **Overinflating salary, job title, and job duties.** A job seeker might report a job title as "supervisor" rather than "senior clerk" or write "facilitated daily production of casualty documentation" when "input and processed 200 insurance forms a day" would be more truthful.

Murphy's Law No. 2
The *one* little exaggeration on your résumé is the one they check!
PERSONNEL
HELLO... IS THIS THE WHITE HOUSE?
C86-4 The Drawing Board™ Box 660429 Dallas, Texas © Wheeler Group, Inc., 1985

THAYER PUBLISHING

According to the Society of Human Resource Management, a trade group, 96 percent of businesses now conduct background checks on job applicants. This spark is fueled by companies' increasing concern about data security, fraud prevention, potential security or workplace violence, and protection of the organization's reputation and culture of ethical behavior.[10] Also, "there's a lot of evidence that those who cheat on job applications also cheat in school and life," says Richard Griffith, director of industrial and organizational psychology program at the Florida Institute of Technology. "If someone says they have a degree and they don't, I'd have little faith that person would tell the truth when it came to financial statements, and so on."[11]

Generally a company will not hire an applicant who submits false information and will terminate employment when the deception is discovered. Deceptive employees who are retained face negative consequences for their unethical action. Loss of trust may prevent advancement, and job performance will eventually suffer if an employee lacks appropriate skills.

When preparing your résumé, ask yourself, "Does this information present my qualifications honestly and ethically, or does it inflate my qualifications to increase my chances of getting the job?" If you sense you're stretching the truth, omit the item. What you believe is a "career booster" could raise a red flag about your overall ethics and end your career.

Application

Review your résumé carefully. Is it truthful? Does it promote your accomplishments in a direct, simple, and accurate way?

To ensure that the interviewer can quickly locate the identification information, center it on the page or use graphic design elements to target attention to your name. You may also include a permanent address (parent's or other relative's address) if you are interviewing when classes are not in session. Leave a clear, straightforward greeting on your phone that portrays you as a person serious about securing a job. Eliminate music, clever sayings, or background noise.

Job and/or Career Objective

What are the characteristics of a good job/career objective?

Following the "Identification" section, state your job/career objective—the job you want. Interviewers can see quickly whether the job you seek matches the one they have to offer. A good job/career objective must be specific enough to be meaningful yet general enough to apply to a variety of jobs. The following example illustrates a general objective that has been revised to describe a specific job.

GENERAL OBJECTIVE	SPECIFIC OBJECTIVE
A position that offers both a challenge and a good opportunity for growth.	Entry into management training program with advancement to commercial lending.
A responsible position with a progressive organization that provides opportunity for managerial development and growth commensurate with ability and attitudes.	Enter a challenging management position with special interest in mergers and acquisitions.

Some experts argue that a statement of your job or career objective may limit your job opportunities. Your objective should be obvious from your qualifications, they say. In general, however, making your objective clear at the beginning assures the interviewer that you have a definite career goal.

Career Summary

To survive the interviewer's 40-second scan, you must provide a compelling reason for a more thorough review of your résumé. Craft a persuasive introductory statement that quickly synthesizes your most transferable skills, accomplishments, and attributes and place it in a section labeled "Summary" or "Professional Profile."

What statement would capture your major qualifications and convince an employer to hire you?

In this synopsis of your key qualifications, communicate why you should be hired. Your answer should evolve naturally from the career objective and focus on your ability to meet the needs of the company you have identified from your extensive research. Combining the career objective with the career statement is an acceptable strategy as noted in the following examples.

SEPARATE OBJECTIVE AND CAREER SUMMARY

Objective	Obtain a challenging entry-level sales position for a high-growth consumer products company. Desire advancement into international sales management.
Career Summary	Honors graduate with a bachelor's degree in marketing with strong international emphasis including study abroad; three semesters of related co-op experience with a large retail store; effective team worker and communicator.

COMBINED OBJECTIVE WITH CAREER SUMMARY

Professional Profile	Sales position, leading to sales management. International sales/marketing manager with three years' experience in pharmaceutical sales, advertising, and contract negotiation with international suppliers. Strong technology, presentation, and interpersonal skills.

LINKED OBJECTIVE AND CAREER SUMMARY

Profile Position as sales representative where demonstrated commission selling and hard work bring rewards.

Accomplishments:

- three years' straight commission sales
- average of $35,000–$55,000 a year in commissioned earnings
- consistent success in development and growth of territories

A high-impact career summary, once considered optional, has become a standard section of résumés in today's fast-paced information age. Develop your résumé that skillfully targets the requirements of a specific position; then compose a career summary sure to interest any interviewer who instantly sees an applicant with exactly the skills needed.

Qualifications

The "Qualifications" section varies depending on the information identified in the self-, career, and job analyses. This information is used to divide the qualifications into appropriate parts, label them appropriately, and arrange them in the best sequence.

Please Don't View My Public Information! Your Facebook or MySpace profile, photos, and "innermost" thoughts create a shadow résumé that may hurt your employment opportunities far into your future. A recent employer survey indicated that 44 percent of employers use social networking sites to examine the profiles of job candidates, and 39 percent have looked up the profile of a current employee.[12]

While some feel that "online background checks" are unfair and invasive, employers argue that applicants who post information about themselves in a public domain forfeit their right to privacy. Use good judgment when participating in social networks, and use privacy settings carefully. Your carelessness could damage your chances of landing or keeping a job.

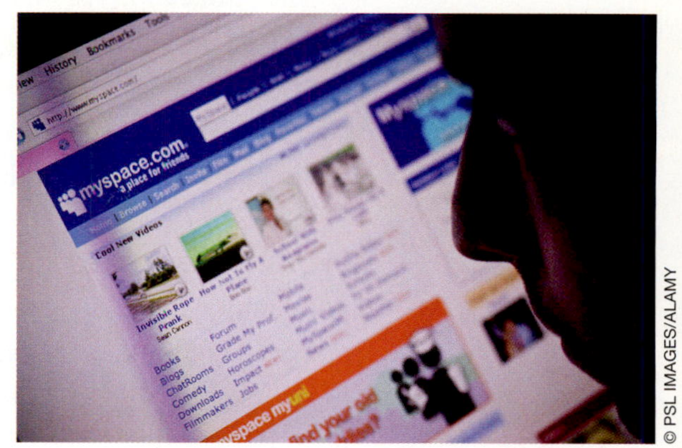

© PSL IMAGES/ALAMY

Is your education or your work experience the stronger factor?

Usually, qualifications stem from your education and work experience (words that appear as headings in the résumé). Order these categories according to which you perceive as more impressive to the employer, with the more impressive category appearing first. For example, education is usually the chief qualification of a recent college graduate. However, a sales representative with related work experience might list experience first, particularly if the educational background is inadequate for the job sought.

Education. Beginning with the most recent, list the degree, major, school, and graduation date. Include a blank line between schools for easy reading. The interviewer will probably want to know first whether you have the appropriate degree, then the institution, and then other details. Recent or near college graduates should omit high school activities because that information is "old news." However, include high school activities if they provide a pertinent dimension to your qualifications. For example, having attended high school abroad is a definite advantage to an applicant seeking employment in an international firm. In addition, high school accomplishments may be relevant for freshmen or sophomores seeking cooperative education assignments, scholarships, or part-time jobs. Of course, this information will be replaced with college activities when the résumé is revised for subsequent jobs or other uses.

Include overall and major grade-point averages if they are B or better—but be prepared to discuss any omissions during an interview. Some recruiters recommend that every candidate include grade-point average, since an omission may lead the reader to assume the worst. Honors and achievements that relate directly to education can be incorporated in this section or included in a separate section. Listing scholarships, appearance on academic lists, and initiation into honor societies is common; but consider also including business-relevant skills you've developed including client projects, team building, and field experiences. If honors and achievements are included in the "Education" section, be sure to include plenty of white space or use bullets to highlight these points (see Figures 13-2 and 13-4 later in this chapter).

What educational experiences do you have other than degrees earned?

The "Education" section could also include a list of special skills and abilities such as foreign language and computer competency. A list of courses typically required in your field is unnecessary and occupies valuable space. However, you should include any courses, workshops, or educational experiences that are not usual requirements, such as internships, cooperative education semesters, "shadowing," and study abroad.

Work Experience. The "Work Experience" section provides information about your employment history. For each job held, list the job title, company name, dates of employment, primary responsibilities, and key accomplishments. The jobs may be listed in reverse chronological order (beginning with the most recent) or in order of job relatedness. Begin with the job that most obviously relates to the job being sought if you have gaps in your work history, if the job you are seeking is very different from the job you currently hold, or if you are just entering the job market and have little, if any, related work experience.

Arrange the order and format of information about each job (dates, job title, company, description, and accomplishments) so that the most important information is emphasized—but format all job information consistently. If you have held numerous jobs in a short time, embed dates of employment within the text rather than surround them with white space. Give related job experience added emphasis by listing it first or surrounding it with white space.

Employers are interested in how you can contribute to their bottom line, so a winning strategy involves concentrating on accomplishments and achievements. Begin with the job title and company name that provides basic information about your duties, and then craft powerful descriptions of the quality and scope of your performance. These bullet points will provide deeper insight into your capability, ambition, and personality and set you apart from other applicants who take the easy route of providing only a work history.

How can you most effectively summarize your work experience?

Return to the in-depth analysis you completed at the beginning of the job search process to recall insights as to how you can add immediate value to this company. Consider the following questions to spur your recognition of marketable skills from your education, work, and community experiences.[13]

- How does my potential employer define success for the job I'm applying for? How do I measure up?
- What is my potential employer's bottom line (money, attendance, sales, etc.)? When have I shown that I know how to address that bottom line?
- What project am I proud of that demonstrates I have the skill for my job objective?
- What technical or management skills do I have that indicate the level at which I perform?
- What problem did I solve, how did I solve it, and what were the results?

Because interviewers spend such a short time reading résumés, the style must be direct and simple. Therefore, a résumé should use crisp phrases to help employers see the value of the applicant's education and experiences. To save space and to emphasize what you have accomplished, use these stylistic techniques:

1. Omit pronouns referring to yourself (*I*, *me*, *my*).
2. Use subject-understood sentences.
3. Begin sentences with action verbs as shown in the following examples:

INSTEAD OF	USE
I had responsibility for development of new territory.	***Developed*** new territory.
My duties included designing computer systems and writing user documentation manuals.	***Designed*** computer programs to monitor accounting systems including writing user documentation that enabled users to operate systems efficiently.
I was the store manager and supervised employees.	***Managed*** store operations with $1 million sales volume and supervised eight employees.
My sales consistently exceeded sales quota.	***Earned*** average of $35,000 a year in commissioned earnings. ***Received*** service award for exceeding sales quota two of three years employed.
I was a member of the Student Council, Society for the Advancement of Management, Phi Kappa Phi, and Chi Omega social sorority.	***Refined*** interpersonal skills through involvement in student organizations such as the Student Council . . . .

What experiences have you gained from a previous job that can be transferred to a job you might seek after graduation?

Because employers are looking for people who will work, action verbs are especially appropriate. Note the subject-understood sentences in the right column of the previous example: Action words used as first words provide emphasis. The following list contains action verbs that are useful in résumés:

achieved	drafted	participated
analyzed	increased	planned
assisted	initiated	recruited
compiled	managed	streamlined
developed	organized	wrote

To give the employer a vivid picture of you as a productive employee, you may find some of the following adjectives helpful as you describe your work experience:

adaptable/flexible	dependable	resourceful
analytical	efficient/productive	sensitive
conscientious	independent	sincere
consistent	objective	tactful
creative	reliable	team oriented

To avoid a tone of egotism, do not use too many adjectives or adverbs that seem overly strong. Plan to do some careful editing after writing your first draft.

What section titles will you include on your résumé to reflect your unique job qualifications?

Honors and Activities. Make a trial list of any other information that qualifies you for the job. Divide the list into appropriate divisions and then select an appropriate label. Your heading might be "Honors and Activities." You might include a section for "Activities," "Leadership Activities," or "Memberships," depending on the items listed. You might also include a separate section on "Military Service," "Civic Activities," "Volunteer Work," or "Interests." If you have only a few items under each category, use a more general term and combine the lists. If your list is lengthy, divide it into more than one category as interviewers prefer "bite-size" pieces that are easy to read and remember.

Resist the urge to include everything you have ever done; keep in mind that every item you add distracts from other information. Consider summarizing information that is relevant but does not merit several separate lines—for example, "Involved in art, drama, and choral groups." To decide whether to include certain information, ask these questions: How closely related is it to the job being sought? Does it provide job-related information that has not been presented elsewhere?

Personal Information

Because a résumé should contain primarily information that is relevant to an applicant's experience and qualifications, you must be selective when including personal information (not job related). The space could be used more effectively to include more about your qualifications or to add more white space. Personal information is commonly placed at the end of the résumé just above the "References" section because it is less important than qualifications (education, experience, and activities).

LEGAL AND ETHICAL CONSTRAINTS

Under the 1964 Civil Rights Act (and subsequent amendments) and the Americans with Disabilities Act (ADA), employers cannot make hiring decisions based on gender, age, marital status, religion, national origin, or disability. Employers prefer not to receive information that provides information about these protected areas because questions could be raised about whether the information was used in the hiring decision.

This topic is explored further in the Strategic Forces feature "Diversity Issues Affecting Employability." Follow these guidelines related to personal information:

- **Do not include personal information that could lead to discriminatory hiring.** Exclude height, weight, and color of hair and eyes, and a personal photograph on the résumé.

- **Reveal ethnic background (and other personal information) only if it is job related.** For example, certain businesses may be actively seeking employees in certain ethnic groups because the ethnic background is a legitimate part of the job description. For such a business, ethnic information is useful and appreciated.
- **Include personal information (other than information covered by employment legislation) that will strengthen your résumé.** Select information that is related to the job you are seeking or that portrays you as a well-rounded, happy individual off the job. Typically, include interests, hobbies, favorite sports, and willingness to relocate. You can also include the following topics if you have not covered them elsewhere in the résumé: spoken and written communication skills, computer competency, foreign-language or computer skills, military service, community service, scholastic honors, job-related hobbies, and professional association memberships.

What personal information will you include on your résumé?

- **Consider whether personal information might be controversial.** For example, listing a sport that an interviewer might perceive to be overly time consuming or dangerous would be questionable. An applicant seeking a position with a religious or political organization may benefit from revealing a related affiliation.

References

Providing potential employers a list of references (people who have agreed to supply information about you when requested) complements your employment credentials. Listing names, addresses, phone numbers, and email addresses of people who can provide information about you adds credibility to the résumé. Employers, former employers, and college instructors are good possibilities. Friends, relatives, and neighbors are not (because of their perceived bias in your favor). Some career experts recommend including a peer to document your ability to work as a member of a team, an important job skill in today's team-oriented environment.[17] According to Bob Daugherty, who heads U.S. recruiting for PricewaterHouseCoopers, the best references are people who work for the organization you are looking to join.[18] You'll gain these employee referrals through strong relationships developed through proactive and professional networking through traditional and electronic means. Update your reference list often to be certain that your choices remain relevant and credible (e.g., none are deceased or dismissed for embezzlement).

Who could serve as a positive work reference for you?

References can be handled on the résumé in several ways. As the closing section of your résumé, you can provide a list of references, include a brief statement that references are available on request or from a career services center, or omit any statement regarding references assuming that references are not needed until after an interview. You might list references directly on the résumé if you have limited qualifications to include, if you know a company interviews applicants *after* references are contacted, or when you believe the names of your references will be recognizable in your career field. You may include a statement such as "For references . . ." or "For additional information . . ." and

DIVERSITY CHALLENGES

STRATEGIC FORCES

Diversity Issues Affecting Employability

The objective of a responsible employer's recruitment policy and selection process should be to find the most suitable person to fill a particular job in terms of skills, experience, aptitude, and other qualifications. Employers may face claims of discrimination if they deny equality of opportunity by relying on selection criteria such as sex, race, ethnic origin, marital status, age, or disability. While gender discrimination in employment has been illegal in the United States for nearly 50 years, it still persists in some instances, often subtly.

Recent research suggests that employers may be selecting or overlooking prospective job candidates for interviews based on their assumed race as suggested by names. Researchers submitted 5,000 bogus résumés in response to job ads, with half the résumés bearing stereotypical African-American names such as LaTonya and Tyrone and the other half sporting traditionally Anglo names such as Kristin and Brad. Of the candidates with Caucasian-sounding names, 10 percent were contacted, in contrast to only 6.7 percent of those with a presumed ethnic identity and identical résumés.[14] After the September 11 tragedy, frequent reports surfaced of Muslims and Arabs shortening or changing their foreign-sounding names to English ones to gain more favorable employment opportunities.[15]

Women, too, continue to report dissimilar treatment in employment situations. Consider the following situations:

- **Marital status:** A man who includes marital status on the résumé may enhance his desirability as an applicant. For instance, indication of "married" may be associated with stability. A woman who indicates "married" may be viewed as unreliable or temporary because she may have children who could interfere with her job performance. She may also be seen as likely to leave the company if her husband is transferred or relocates. Indicating "single" is not necessarily a plus for a woman either, as she may be viewed as seeking temporary work until she marries.
- **Physical appearance:** When qualifications among candidates are equal, physical attraction has been found to be positively correlated with job offers and with total lifetime earning potential. However, physical attractiveness has been found in some cases to work against women. While unattractive men and women are rejected by potential employers about equally, a woman who is very attractive may be bypassed because a feeling still persists in some camps that a woman cannot be both beautiful and smart. Thus, a woman can be too attractive for employment.

© ISTOCKPHOTO.COM/JACOB WACKERHAUSEN

Employers should be aware that illegal discrimination can have negative repercussions, not only from the courts but in terms of lower productivity resulting from selection of less capable employees. Businesspeople who have overcome discriminatory situations frequently say that networking with friends, former teachers, college alumni, and other acquaintances has helped them break the glass, or concrete, ceilings they encountered to land better jobs.[16]

Application

In small groups, brainstorm a list of other ways that discrimination may occur in employment.

- For each incidence of possible discrimination, propose an action that the applicant may take to minimize or eliminate it.
- Compose a class list that summarizes the small group discussions.

give the address of the career services center of your college or university, the job bank posting your credentials, or the URL of your electronic portfolio.

What are the advantages and disadvantages of including a list of references in your résumé?

Withholding references until they are requested prevents unnecessary or untimely requests going to your present employer. This action also conveys genuine courtesy to the references. Even the most enthusiastic references may become apathetic if required to provide recommendations to endless interviewers. For this same reason, be sure to communicate with references regularly if your job search continues longer than expected. Suggestions for communicating with references are discussed in Chapter 14.

When preparing a separate list of references to be given after a successful interview, place the word *References* and your name in a visible position as shown in Figure 13-3. Balance the list (name, address, phone number, and relationship of reference to applicant) attractively on the page and use the same paper used for printing the résumé. Whether it is handed to the interviewer personally or mailed, the references page professionally complements your résumé. Confident that you have a good message, you are now ready to put it in writing—to construct a résumé that will impress an employer favorably.

Appropriate Organizational Plan

The general organization of all résumés is fairly standard: identification (name, address, phone number, and email address), job objective, qualifications, personal information, and references. The primary organizational challenge is in dividing the qualifications section into parts, choosing labels for them, and arranging them in the best sequence. When you review your self-, career, and job analyses data and company/job profile, you will recognize that your qualifications stem mainly from your education and your experience. Your task is to decide how to present these two categories of qualifications. Résumés usually are organized in one of three ways: reverse chronological order (most recent activity listed first), functional order (most important activity listed first), or a chrono-functional, which combines the chronological and functional orders as the name implies. To determine which organizational plan to use, draft your résumé in each.

Chronological Résumé

The ***chronological résumé*** is the traditional organizational format for résumés. Two headings normally appear in the portion that presents qualifications: "Education" and "Experience." Which one should appear first? Decide which one you think is more impressive to the employer, and put that one first. Within each section, the most recent information is presented first. Reverse chronological order is easier to use and is more common than functional order; however, it is not always more effective.

The chronological résumé is an especially effective format for applicants who have progressed up a clearly defined career ladder and want to move up another rung. Because the format emphasizes dates and job titles, the chronological résumé is less effective for applicants who have gaps in their work histories, are seeking jobs different from the job currently held, or are just entering the job market with little or no experience.[19]

Five years after graduation, would education or experience likely appear first on your résumé? Why?

If you choose the chronological format, look at the two headings from the employer's point of view, and reverse their positions if doing so is to your advantage. Under the

"Experience" division, jobs are listed in reverse order. Assuming you have progressed typically, your latest job is likely to be more closely related to the job being sought than the first job held. Placing the latest or current job first will give it the emphasis it deserves. Include beginning and ending dates for each job.

Functional Résumé

How do functional résumés report experience and education?

In a ***functional résumé*** points of primary interest to employers—transferable skills—appear in major headings. These headings highlight what an applicant can *do* for the employer—functions that can be performed well. Under each heading, an applicant could draw from educational and/or work-related experience to provide supporting evidence.

A functional résumé requires a complete analysis of self, career, and the job sought. Suppose, for example, that a person seeking a job as an assistant hospital administrator wants to emphasize qualifications by placing them in major headings. From the hospital's advertisement of the job and from accumulated job appraisal information, an applicant sees this job as both an administrative and a public relations job. The job requires skill in communicating and knowledge of accounting and finance. Thus, headings in the "Qualifications" section of the résumé could be "Administration," "Public Relations," "Communication," and "Budgeting." Under "Public Relations," for example, an applicant could reveal that a public relations course was taken at State University, from which a degree is to be conferred in May, and that a sales job at ABC Store provided abundant opportunity to apply principles learned. With other headings receiving similar treatment, the qualifications portion reveals the significant aspects of education and experience.

Order of importance is the best sequence for functional headings. If you have prepared an accurate self- and job analysis, the selected headings will highlight points of special interest to the employer. Glancing at headings only, an employer can see that you understand the job's requirements and have the qualities needed for success.

Having done the thinking required for preparing a functional résumé, you are well prepared for a question that is commonly asked in interviews: "What can you do for us?" The answer is revealed in your major headings. They emphasize the functions you can perform and the special qualifications you have to offer.

If you consider yourself well qualified, a functional résumé is worth considering. If your education or experience is scant, a functional résumé may be best for you. Using "Education" and "Experience" as headings (as in a chronological résumé) works against your purpose if you have little to report under the headings; the format would emphasize the absence of education or experience.

Chrono-Functional Résumé

The ***chrono-functional résumé*** combines features of chronological and functional résumés. This format can give quick assurance that educational and experience requirements are met and still use other headings that emphasize qualifications. More information on the chrono-functional résumé can be found at your companion website at www.cengage.com/bcomm/lehman.

Adapting Résumés for Alternate Presentation and Delivery Options

Format requirements for résumés have changed significantly in recent years. Whether presented on paper or electronically, the arrangement of a résumé is just as important as the content. If the arrangement is unattractive, unappealing, or in poor taste, the message may never be read. Errors in keyboarding, spelling, and punctuation may be taken as evidence of a poor academic background, lack of respect for the employer or carelessness. Recognize that résumés serve as your introduction to employers and indicate the quality of work you'll produce.

How do spelling and punctuation errors in a résumé counteract superior content, organization, and style?

As in preparing other difficult documents, prepare a rough draft as quickly as you can and then revise as many times as needed to prepare an effective résumé that sells you. After you are confident with the résumé, ask at least two other people to check it for you. Carefully select people who are knowledgeable about résumé preparation and the job you are seeking and can suggest ways to present your qualifications more effectively. After you have incorporated those changes, ask a skillful proofreader to review the document.

To accommodate employers' preferences for the presentation and delivery of résumés, you'll need three versions of your résumé as shown in Figure 13-1: a designed résumé printed on paper, a scannable résumé to be read by a computer, and designed résumé accessible through email and websites.

Preparing a Print (Designed) Résumé

Your print (designed) résumé is considered your primary marketing document, and appearance is critical. To win out among hundreds of competing résumés, it must look professional and reflect current formatting and production standards while maintaining a distinctive conservative tone. Follow these guidelines for designing and producing a highly professional résumé:

What is your reaction to "I'll just use the format and style my friend used on her résumé; she got a job with it"?

- **Develop an appealing résumé format that highlights your key qualifications and distinguishes your résumé.** Use the power of your word processing software for style enhancements rather than settle for overused, inflexible templates. Study the example résumés in this chapter and models from other sources for ideas for enhancing the style, readability, and overall impact of the document. Then create a custom design that best highlights your key qualifications.

- **Format information for quick, easy reading.** To format your résumé so that it can be read at glance,
  - Use attention-getting headings to partition major divisions, and add graphic lines and borders to separate sections of text.
  - Use an outline format when possible to list activities and events on separate lines, and include bullets to emphasize multiple points.
  - Use font sizes no smaller than 10 point to avoid reader eye strain.

- ▷ Use type styles and print attributes to emphasize key points. For example, to draw attention to the identification and headings, select a bold sans serif font (e.g., Calibri or Arial) slightly larger than the serif font (e.g., Cambria or Times New Roman) used for the remaining text. Capitalization, indention, and print enhancements (underline, italics, bold), are useful for adding emphasis. Limit the number of type styles and enhancements, however, so the page is clean and simple to read.
- ▷ Include identification on each page of a multiple-page résumé. Place your name and a page number at the top of the second and successive pages with "Continued" at the bottom of the first page. The interviewer is reexposed to your name, and pages can be reassembled if separated.

Create an appealing output to produce top professional quality.

- ▷ Check for consistency throughout the résumé. Consistency in spacing, end punctuation, capitalization, appearance of headings, and sequencing of details within sections will communicate your eye for detail and commitment to high standards.
- ▷ Balance the résumé attractively on the page with approximately equal margins. Allow generous white space so the résumé looks uncluttered and easy to read.

What kinds of creative résumé features might be well received by a prospective employer in your career field?

Consider adding a statement of your creativity and originality. Be certain that your creativity will not be construed as gimmicky and distract from the content of the résumé. Demonstrating creativity is particularly useful for fields such as advertising, public relations, graphic design, and those requiring computer proficiency.

- ▷ Select paper of a standard size (8 1/2″ by 11″) neutral color (white, buff, or gray), and high quality (preferably 24-pound, 100-percent cotton fiber). Review Appendix A for additional discussion of paper quality. Consider using a mailing envelope large enough to accommodate the résumé without folding. The unfolded documents on the reader's desk may get favorable attention and will scan correctly if posted to an electronic database.
- ▷ Print with a laser printer that produces high-quality output. Position paper so the watermark is read across the sheet in the same direction as the printing.

What is the ideal length for a résumé for your career field?

Some employers insist that the "best" length for a résumé is one page, stating that long résumés are often ignored. However, general rules about length are more flexible. Most students and recent graduates can present all relevant résumé information on one page. However, as you gain experience, you may need two or more pages to format an informative, easy-to-read résumé. A résumé forced on one page will likely have narrow margins and large blocks of run-on text (multiple lines with no space to break them). This dense format is unappealing and complicates the interviewer's task of skimming quickly for key information.

The rule about length is simple. Be certain your résumé contains only relevant information presented as concisely as possible. A one-page résumé that includes irrelevant information is too long. A two-page résumé that omits relevant information is too short.

The résumés illustrated in Figures 13-2 and 13-4 demonstrate the organizational principles for the chronological and functional résumés; the chrono-functional résumé, an alternate chronological résumé is illustrated at your companion website at www.cengage.com/bcomm/lehman. A references page is illustrated in Figure 13-3. Study the various layouts to decide on one that will highlight your key qualifications most effectively.

FIGURE 13-2

Chronological Résumé

Includes email address that reflects professional image.

Reveals position sought and powerful summary of qualifications.

Positions education as top qualification for recent graduate. Includes high GPA and describes value-added experiences.

Edges out competition by expanding on related experience and work achievements.

Emphasizes activities that reflect service attitude, high level of responsibility, and people-orientation.

Uses separate sections to emphasize proficiencies listed in job requirements.

Lists academic recognitions and highlights relevant skills.

Omits references to use space for additional qualifications; references furnished when requested.

Jacob Raneri
59 Tuscany Court
Germantown, TN 38183-0059
901-555-4918
jraneri@netdoor.com

OBJECTIVE Challenging position in logistics management with international promotion opportunities

CAREER SUMMARY
- Honor student pursuing bachelor's degree in logistics with a minor in Chinese
- Related work and multicultural experiences developed through a two-semester study abroad program and a co-op position with an international delivery company
- Willingness to relocate

EDUCATION Bachelor of Arts, Garner College; expected graduation, December 2011
Major in logistics, minor in Chinese
GPA 3.6 on a 4.0 scale
Included an intensive study abroad program with total cultural immersion in Korea, Summers 2007 and 2008

RELATED EXPERIENCE *Assistant to Transportation Manager*, Cooperative Education Program, FedEx, Memphis, Tennessee, three semesters, 2009–2010
- Assisted writing operations documentation for supply chain system to new international hubs
- Collected and evaluated data on carrier productivity
- Received commendation for developing project management checklist for transportation of sensitive government documents

VOLUNTEER WORK Cumberland Food Bank, Memphis local affiliate, 2008 to present
Coordinate delivery of bulk shipments to five local distribution centers

LANGUAGES Native fluency in English
Fluent in Mandarin dialect (speaking, reading, writing, comprehension)

SKILLS Lived and traveled extensively in China and Korea
Proficient in Microsoft Office Suite

HONORS AND ACTIVITIES Dean's List (3.6 GPA or higher)
Beta Gamma Sigma (business honor society, upper 10% of senior class)
International Business Club
- Elected vice president of public relations; coordinated guest speakers at monthly meetings
- Organized overnight field trip to FedEx distribution center and First National Bank in Memphis

Format Pointers

- Places name at top center for easy viewing (top right is also acceptable). Uses bold font to distinguish identification section and headings from remaining text.
- Uses two-column format for easy location of specific sections.
- Creates visual appeal through custom format rather than commonly used template, short readable sections focusing on targeted qualifications, and streamlined bulleted lists.

Diversity Challenges Constraint

- Follows standard format and rules for résumés for application with U.S. company. Specific formats vary for specific countries and federal government.

FIGURE 13-3

References Page

Jacob Raneri
59 Tuscany Court
Germantown, TN 38183-0059
901-555-4918
jraneri@netdoor.com

Includes professor and immediate supervisors as references, but excludes friends, relatives, or clergy to avoid potential bias.

Ms. Olivia D. Walther
Transportation Manager
FedEx
P.O. Box 555
Memphis, TN 38101-1801
901-555-9000
owalther@fedex.com
Relationship: Immediate supervisor during three-semester cooperative education program, 2009–2010

Dr. Aiden Byrne, Professor
Logistics and Marketing Department
Garner College
P.O. Box 5937
Nashville, TN 38132-5937
615-555-4382
abyrne@gu.edu
Relationship: Academic adviser, professor in three upper-level logistics management courses, and chapter adviser of International Business Club

Includes for each reference full contact information, including email address if available, and relationship to job applicant.

Mr. Logan A. Shultz
Cumberland Food Bank
Treasurer, Memphis Affiliate
2150 North Bailey Avenue
Memphis, TN 38101-2150
865-555-4385
logan_shultz@cumberlandfoodbank.net
Relationship: Immediate supervisor of volunteer office staff

Format Pointers

- Prepares reference page at same time as résumé and makes available immediately after successful interview. Paper (color, texture, and size) and print type match résumé.
- Balances references attractively.

Preparing Electronic Résumé Submissions

To this point you have focused on the preparation of a print résumé. However, in the digital age of instant information, you'll use various online methods to apply for a job and present your qualifications to prospective employers.

FIGURE 13-4

Functional Résumé

Includes clear objective and descriptive summary statement to grab attention and invite close reading.

Arranges qualifications into sections that emphasize applicant's relevant skills and accomplishments.

Uses headings that show applicant knows what skills are needed to succeed in sales.

Uses employers' names and dates to match skills with work history.

Limits education and work history as quick overview of basic qualifications and to accommodate employers' preference for chronological format.

Lists references for employer convenience and to strengthen résumé.

Emma Kennedy
225 Kilby Lane
Houston, TX 77001-0025
713-555-1396
ekennedy@hotmail.com

OBJECTIVE Position in retail clothing sales with advancement to sales management.

CAREER SUMMARY

- Honor student majoring in marketing with four years' related part-time experience in sales and promotions.
- Highly dependable and proven record of initiative and creativity.
- Exceptional communication and interpersonal skills; commitment to customer satisfaction.

RELEVANT SKILLS

MARKETING AND PROMOTIONS

- Created unique seasonal displays and developed script and graphics for television commercials for Lavenders Boutique.
- Designed original tee shirt designs for university and community organizations for Creative Designs.
- Designed a company website and marketing campaign in an Internet marketing class.

CUSTOMER SERVICE

- Received consistently high performance evaluations at Lavenders Boutique for superior customer service. Selected by management as employee of the month, February 2011.
- Gained experience working with diverse groups while volunteering as a camp counselor at Camp Choctaw for three summers.

TECHNOLOGY PROFICIENCIES

- Proficient in Microsoft Office Suite, InDesign, and DreamWeaver.
- Keep accurate electronic records of tee shirt and dye inventory at Creative Designs.
- Enrolled in elective class related to computerized accounting systems.

INITIATIVE AND DEPENDABILITY

- Proposed and launched Twitter site at Lavenders Boutique that has led to increased communication between customers and employees in other store locations; received commendation from management for initiative and innovation.
- Achieved Dean's List for the last two semesters. Earned 3.3 grade-point average (on a 4.0 scale) in major courses to date.

EMPLOYMENT HISTORY Sales associate, Lavenders Boutique, August 2007 to present (part time).
Production staff, Creative Designs, Summers 2007–2011.

EDUCATION B.S., Marketing, West State College, Expected graduation, May 2011.

REFERENCES Dr. Kirk Baxter, Advisor, Marketing Department, West State College, P.O. Box 4293, Temple, TX 76501-3293, 817-555–2746.

Ms. Ruth Lucas, Camp Director, Camp Seminole, 1493 Dunlap Drive, Kingsville, TX 78363-1493, 512-555-8934.

Ms. Vicki Abrams, Manager, Lavenders Boutique, 151 Woodlake Street, Corpus Christi, TX 78469-7310, 512-555-6789.

Format Pointers

- Places name at top center where it can be easily seen.
- Uses bold font to distinguish identification section and headings from remaining text.
- Creates visual appeal with easy-to-read columnar format and balanced page arrangement.

The easiest and most common method of putting your résumé online is through emailing a résumé to a job bank for posting or to a networking contact who asked you to send a résumé. Many job banks, corporate sites, and career services centers require you to respond to specific openings by completing an online form that may require you to paste your résumé into a designated section of the form. Frequently, you may input information directly on the website or download the form to be submitted by email, fax, or mail. You may also choose to post your résumé on your personal web page as part of an electronic portfolio that showcases evidence of your qualifications. You may also need to develop a **beamer,** or **beamable résumé,** a quick version of your résumé designed in a format suitable for broadcasting on smartphone. Recruiting professionals predict that millions of these electronic résumés will be exchanged silently at conferences, business meetings, and power lunches similar to exchanging business cards.[20]

Electronic submissions are quick and easy but present new challenges and many opportunities to jeopardize your employment chances and compromise your privacy. Just consider recent struggles you may have faced in dealing with viruses and unwelcomed emails, attempting to access nonworking links, and more. Before sending your résumé into cyberspace, follow these suggestions to ensure that your electronic submission is both professional and technically effective:

- **Choose postings for your résumé with purpose.** Online résumé postings are not confidential. Once your résumé is online, anyone can read it, including your current employer. You may also begin to receive junk mail and cold calls from companies who see your résumé online; even more seriously, you could become a victim of identity theft. To protect your privacy online, limit personal information disclosed in the résumé and post only to sites with password protection allowing you to approve the release of your résumé to specific employers. Dating your electronic résumé will also prevent embarrassment should your employer find an old version of your résumé, which could occur as result of exchange of résumés between career sites and delays in updating postings.

Protect your references' privacy by omitting their names when posting online. Withholding this information will prevent unwelcomed calls by recruiters and other inappropriate contacts and threats to privacy. Although technology allows broadcast of your résumé to all available positions on a career site, read postings carefully and apply only to those that match your qualifications. This action improves the efficiency of the job selection process for the company and the applicant and depicts fair, ethical behavior.

How can online job searching offer benefit and risk to both the applicant and the employer?

- **Don't get in a hurry.** The speed, convenience, and informality of filling in online boxes or composing an email cover letter for an attached résumé can lead to sloppiness that reflects negatively on your abilities and attitude. Make sure every aspect of your electronic submission is top-notch just as you would for a print résumé. Provide all information exactly as requested, write concise, clear statements relevant to the job sought, and proofread carefully for grammatical and spelling errors. If you direct an employer to an electronic portfolio, devote necessary time to make it attractive, informative, and technically sound. Double-check your files to ensure they can be opened and retain an appealing format. Finally, read the posting carefully to learn how long your résumé will remain active, how to update it, and how to delete it from the site.

- **Include your résumé in the format requested by the employer or job bank.** You may be instructed to send the résumé as an attachment to the message or include it in the body of an email message, known as an ***inline résumé***. The inline résumé is becoming the preferred choice as fear of computer viruses and daily email overload prevent employers from opening attachments.

Unless instructed to send your attachment in a specific format such as Word, save your résumé and cover letter in one file beginning with the cover letter as an ASCII or Rich Text Format file with line length limited to 65 characters and spacing. This plain text version, referred to as a ***text résumé***, removes formatting and lacks the appeal of your designed résumé; however, you can be confident that an employer can open the file and won't have to spend time "cleaning up" your résumé if it doesn't transmit correctly. For this reason, you'll also paste the text version of your résumé below your email message when sending an inline résumé.

As an added safeguard, send yourself and a couple of friends a copy of the résumé and see how it looks on different computers before sending it out to an employer. If you wish, follow up with a print résumé and cover letter on high-quality paper.

- **Include a keyword summary after the identification section.** You'll want to grab the employer's attention by placing the keywords on the first screen (within the first 24 lines of text). Providing this relevant information will motivate the employer to keep scrolling down to see how the keywords are supported rather than click to the next résumé.

- **Email a cover message to accompany an online résumé.** Some companies consider this cover email message to be prescreening for a job interview. Write a formal, grammatically correct message just as you would if you were sending an application letter in the mail.

What are the advantages and disadvantages of an electronic tracking system?

Some print résumés become electronic files when they are scanned by the employer into an electronic database where they can be read and sorted by a computer. Companies of all sizes are using ***electronic applicant-tracking systems*** to increase efficiency of processing the volumes of résumés received in a competitive market. Such systems store scanned résumés in an electronic database where they can be sorted by keywords with a resulting ranking of applicants. The system can also automatically prepare letters of rejection and interview offers and store the résumés of hired applicants for future promotion consideration.

When seeking a job with a company that scans résumés into an electronic database, you will need to submit a ***scannable résumé*** as well as a print résumé that will be read by a person. If you are unsure whether a company scans résumés, call and ask. If still in doubt, take the safe route and submit your résumé in both formats.

To ensure that the scanner can read your résumé accurately and clearly, you must prepare a plain résumé with no special formatting. Follow these guidelines to prepare an electronic résumé that can be scanned accurately:

- **Use popular, nondecorative typefaces.** Typefaces such as Cambria and Times New Roman are clear and distinct and will not lose clarity in scanning.

- **Use 10- to 14-point font.** Computers cannot read small, tight print well. With a larger font, your résumé may extend to two pages, but page length is not an issue because a computer is reading the résumé.

- **Do not include italics, underlining, open bullets, or graphic lines and boxes.** Use boldface or all capitals for emphasis. Italicized letters that touch and underlining that runs into the text result in a garbled scanned image. Design elements, such as graphic lines, shading, and shadowing effects, can confuse equipment. Use solid bullets (•) because open bullets (•) may be read as o's.
- **Use ample white space.** Use at least one-inch margins. Leave plenty of white space between the sections of a résumé so that the computer recognizes the partitions.
- **Print on one side of white, standard-size paper with sharp laser print.** Colored and textured paper scans poorly, and the scanner may pick up dirty specks on a photocopy.
- **Use a traditional résumé format.** Complex layouts that simulate catalogs or newspaper columns can confuse scanners.
- **Do not fold or staple your résumé.** If you must fold, do not fold on a line of text.

You have two concerns in preparing a scannable résumé. You want to (1) be certain information is presented in a manner the computer can read, and (2) maximize the number of "hits" your résumé receives in a computerized résumé search. Follow these guidelines for making your print résumé searchable:

- **Position your name as the first readable item on the page.** Follow with your address, phone number, fax number, and email below your name on separate lines.

What keywords from your print résumé should appear in the electronic version?

- **Add powerful keywords in a separate section called "Keywords" or "Keyword Summary" that follows the identification.** To identify key words, ask yourself what words best describe your qualifications. Make maximum use of industry jargon and standard, easily recognizable abbreviations (B.A., M.S.) in the keyword summary and the body of the résumé as these buzzwords will likely be matches with the computer's keywords.
- **Format the keyword summary to maximize hits.** Capitalize the first letter of each word and separate each keyword with a period. Position keywords describing your most important qualifications first and move to the least important ones. Order is important as some systems stop scanning after the first 80 keywords. The usual order is (a) job title, occupation, or career field, (b) education, and (c) essential skills for a specific position. Be certain to include keywords that describe interpersonal traits, such as *adaptable, flexible, sensitive, team player, willing to travel, ethical, industrious, innovative, open minded,* and *detail oriented*.

What are some industry jargon terms for your profession, as well as their synonyms?

- **Support your keywords with specific facts in the body of the résumé.** Use synonyms of your keywords in the body in the event the computer does not recognize the keyword (e.g., use M.B.A. in the keyword summary and Master of Business Administration in the body; use presentation graphics software in the keyword summary and a specific program in the body). One unfortunate applicant reported using "computer-assisted design" consistently throughout his résumé when the computer was searching for "CAD." Also, use a specific date of graduation in the education section. Some computer programs read two dates beside an institution to mean the applicant did not earn the degree (e.g., 2007–2011).

FIGURE 13-5

Scannable Résumé

Positions name as first readable item.

Identifies position sought and reason to hire in separate section.

Includes "Keyword Summary" section listing qualifications that match job description.

Supports keywords with specific facts.

Uses synonyms of keywords in body to ensure match with database.

ISABELLA STEWART
89 Lincoln Street
San Antonio, TX 78285-9063
512-555-9823
jfulton@netdoor.com
www.netdoor/istewart

Professional Profile

- First-year audit staff in an international accounting firm with an interest in forensic accounting
- Technical proficiency in ERP systems, ACL, database, and spreadsheet software
- Realistic forensic and audit experience through an internship with a regional CPA firm
- Superior leadership and team orientation developed through student organizations; strong written and spoken communication skills
- Fluency in Spanish

Keywords

Entry-level audit position. Master's and bachelor's degrees in accounting. Sam Houston State University. 3.8 GPA. Beta Alpha Psi. Professional internship. Forensic accounting. Spanish fluency. Traveled Mexico. Analytical ability. Computer proficiency. Communication skills. Team player. Ethical. Adaptable. Willing to relocate. Software applications. Word, Excel, Access, PowerPoint. ACL. ERP Systems. Web design.

Education

M.P.A., Accounting, Systems Emphasis, Sam Houston State University, August 2011, GPA 3.8

B.B.A., Accounting, Sam Houston State University, May 2010, GPA 3.6

- President's Scholar, 2007–2010
- Beta Alpha Psi (honorary organization for financial information students)
- Lloyd Markham Academic Scholarship

Technical Skills

- Proficient in database, spreadsheet, ERP systems, ACL, and web design
- Fluent Spanish; have traveled to Mexico

Related Employment

Professional Internship, Smith & Lewis, CPAs, Dallas, Texas, June–August, 2010

- Participated in a litigation support engagement related to an alleged embezzlement
- Involved in audits of companies in the oil and gas and retail sectors
- Developed time management, team building, and communication skills while completing independent projects with diverse work teams
- Demonstrated ability to accept and respond to criticism, learn job tasks quickly, and perform duties with minimal supervision

FIGURE 13-5

Scannable Résumé (continued)

Extends beyond one page without concern because computer will read full résumé.

Emphasizes willingness to provide professional, more impressive document.

Includes date of last revision to avoid confusion or embarrassment if résumé is accessed after hiring.

ISABELLA STEWART Page 2

Leadership Activities
Beta Alpha Psi, 2008–2011
- Served as local chapter president; chapter earned superior chapter designation
- Managed activities of the chapter and planned meetings and service activities
- Received commendation from chapter advisor for strong organizational skills and excellent written and spoken communication

An attractive and fully formatted hard copy version of this document is available upon request

Last revised 10/15/11

Format Pointers

- Keeps résumé simple and readable by computer: ample white space especially between sections; easy-to-read font of 10 to 14 points; solid bullets and no italics, underlining, or graphic lines or borders.
- Mails cover letter and print résumé unfolded and unstapled in large envelope.

The scannable résumé Isabella Stewart prepared when seeking an entry-level audit position in a public accounting firm appears in Figure 13-5. Note how she presents qualifications that correspond to the company/job profile posted at your companion website at www.cengage.com/bcomm/lehman. The scannable résumé is formatted for scanning into an electronic database to be matched with employer requirements.

Supplementing a Résumé

Some candidates may feel their career accomplishments are not appropriately captured in a standard résumé. Two additional tools for communicating your qualifications and abilities are the portfolio and the employment video.

Professional Portfolios

The professional portfolio (also called the ***electronic*** or ***e-portfolio*** when presented in a digital format) can be used to illustrate past activities, projects, and accomplishments. It is a collection of artifacts that demonstrate your communication, people, and technical skills. Although portfolios were once thought of as only for writers, artists, or photographers, they are now seen as appropriate for other fields of work when the applicant wants to showcase abilities.

Many portfolios are now presented in digital format, making the portfolio easier to organize and distribute to prospective employers via a website or burned to a CD or other media. With the availability of user-friendly software, college campuses are offering e-portfolio systems that aid students in reflecting on their experiences and producing e-portfolios. Just as students currently are not asked if they have an email account, predictions are that soon they will also be expected to have "a web space that represents their learning and their assessment."[21]

What items would you include in your professional portfolio?

A clear understanding of your audience's needs and your qualifications will allow you to develop a logical organizational structure for your portfolio. You may find the planning forms available at your companion website at www.cengage.com/bcomm/lehman helpful for planning your showcase of accomplishments. Some possible items for inclusion are

- sample speeches with digitized audio or video clips of the delivery.
- performance appraisals.
- awards.
- certificates of completion.
- reports, proposals, or written documents prepared for classes or on the job.
- brochures or programs describing workshops attended.
- commendation messages, records, or surveys showing client or customer satisfaction with service.

After selecting the items for inclusion in your portfolio, select the appropriate software or binder you will use to showcase your accomplishments. Once you're organized, you can add items that demonstrate you have the characteristics the employer is seeking. Maintain your portfolio even after you are hired because it can demonstrate your eligibility for promotion, salary increase, advanced training, or even justify why you should not be laid off.

What work samples might Isabella include?

For illustration purposes, take a look at Isabella Stewart's electronic portfolio shown in Figure 13-6 that was created using a Microsoft web template and posted to her personal web page.

Employment Videos

What additional items would you link to your electronic portfolio résumé?

A video recording may be used to extend the impact of the printed résumé visually. A video can capture your stage presence and ability to speak effectively and add a human dimension to the written process. Current technology enables applicants to embed video segments into ***multimedia résumés*** created with presentation software such as Camtasia Studio and sent to prospective employers on CD or DVD or posted on the applicant's personal web page.

YouTube ***video résumés*** are the latest trend in developing creative job qualifications. You can learn some important lessons for your video project by taking a look at

FIGURE 13-6

Electronic Portfolio Posted to an Applicant's Personal Website

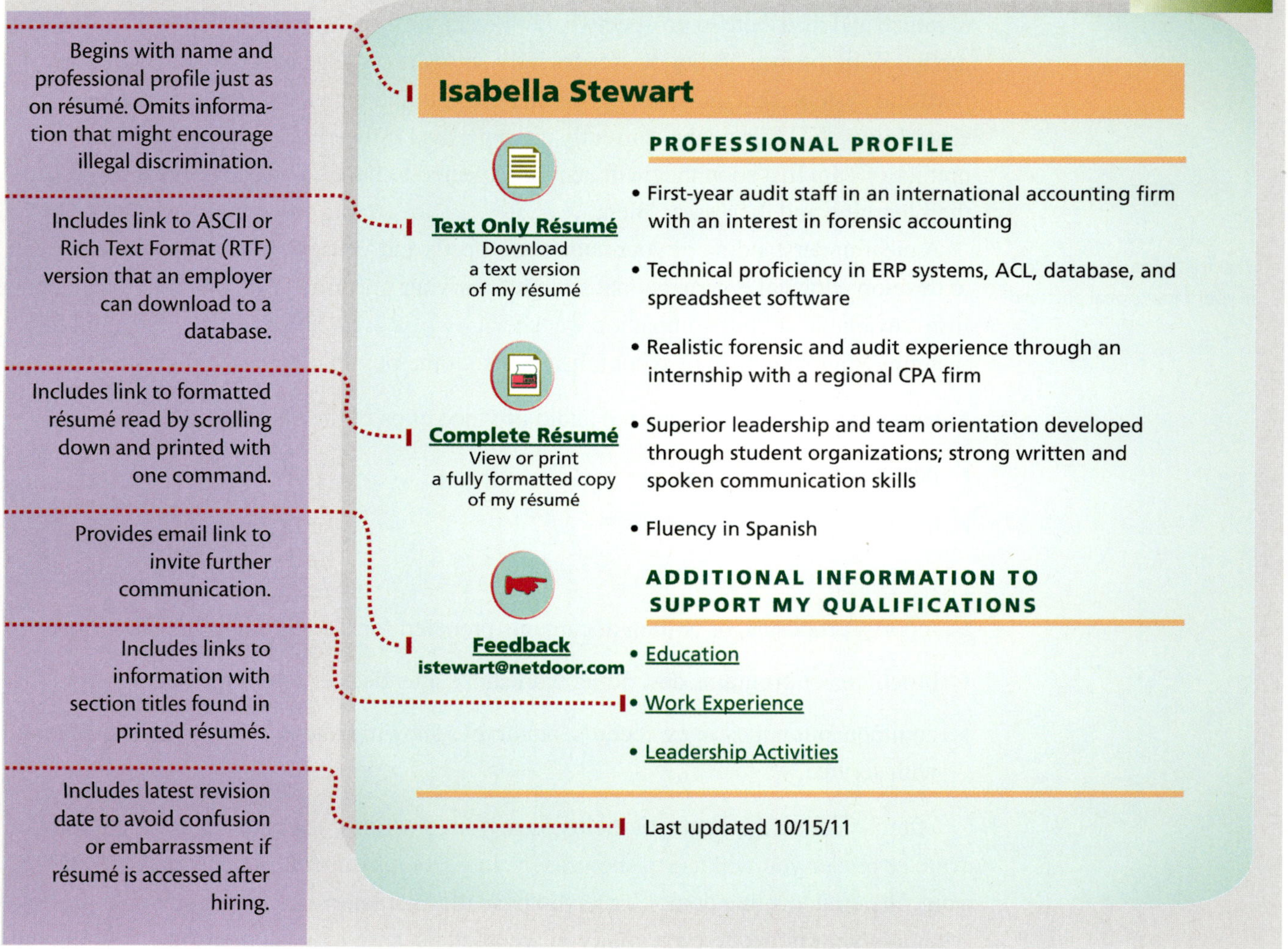

Begins with name and professional profile just as on résumé. Omits information that might encourage illegal discrimination.

Includes link to ASCII or Rich Text Format (RTF) version that an employer can download to a database.

Includes link to formatted résumé read by scrolling down and printed with one command.

Provides email link to invite further communication.

Includes links to information with section titles found in printed résumés.

Includes latest revision date to avoid confusion or embarrassment if résumé is accessed after hiring.

Isabella Stewart

Text Only Résumé
Download a text version of my résumé

Complete Résumé
View or print a fully formatted copy of my résumé

Feedback
istewart@netdoor.com

PROFESSIONAL PROFILE

- First-year audit staff in an international accounting firm with an interest in forensic accounting
- Technical proficiency in ERP systems, ACL, database, and spreadsheet software
- Realistic forensic and audit experience through an internship with a regional CPA firm
- Superior leadership and team orientation developed through student organizations; strong written and spoken communication skills
- Fluency in Spanish

ADDITIONAL INFORMATION TO SUPPORT MY QUALIFICATIONS

- Education
- Work Experience
- Leadership Activities

Last updated 10/15/11

the abundance of good and bad examples already posted. If possible, solicit the help of someone with film experience and follow these simple suggestions for creating a visually enhanced résumé that is brief, showcases your key qualifications, and reflects your personality:[22]

- Keep your video simple with one stationary shot using a good camera and tripod. Avoid gimmicky effects and excessive panning that distract from the message.
- Use proper lighting, making sure that the employer can see your face. Avoid light behind you that casts shadows.
- Invest in a good quality microphone and speak clearly and at an appropriate pace for easy listening.

© AP IMAGES/ROSS D. FRANKLIN

Move Over Résumés—"Vésumés" Are Here. The growth in the number of video résumés, or "vésumés" illustrates a growing trend away from the traditional paper résumé. Before creating your own vésumé, study others that are available online. It will be clear to you whether the candidate edited the video for content and clarity and whether the creator made critical errors such as an undesirable background distraction. Effective vésumés are typically three to five minutes in length. Perhaps the best thing about a vésumé is the creativity that you can reveal to gain the employer's attention. Since employers typically don't have time to troll the web for candidates, online services have sprung up that search for interesting vésumés and then send online "postcards" of job candidates to a network of subscribing employers.[23]

- Choose clothing appropriate for the job you are seeking. Video yourself wearing different clothing and watch the video to select the ideal choice. Avoid clothing that gaps and bunches when you sit, as well as bright colors and close patterns that tend to vibrate when filmed.
- Edit your video to eliminate dead air and other imperfections that detract from a professional image.

Employment videos are more commonly used to obtain employment in career fields for which verbal delivery or visual performance is a key element. These fields include broadcasting and the visual and performing arts. The following guidelines apply when preparing an employment video:

- Be sure the video makes a professional appearance and is complimentary to you. A "home movie" quality recording will be a liability instead of an asset to your application.
- Avoid long "talking head" segments. Include segments that reflect you in a variety of activities; shots that include samples of your work are also desirable.

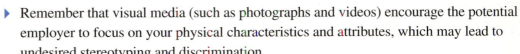

- Remember that visual media (such as photographs and videos) encourage the potential employer to focus on your physical characteristics and attributes, which may lead to undesired stereotyping and discrimination.

Be sure to advertise the availability of your portfolio and employment video to maximize its exposure. List your URL address in the identification section of your résumé. In your application letter, motivate the prospective employer to view your portfolio or video by describing the types of information included. Talk enthusiastically about the detailed supplementary information available during your job interview and encourage the interviewer to view it when convenient. Note Isabella Stewart's promotion of her e-portfolio when you read her application letter later in this chapter (Figure 13-7).

Would a video enhance employability in your career field? If so, what elements would you include in your video?

SHOWCASE PART 2

Open Employee Communication Fosters Superior Productivity

SPOTLIGHT COMMUNICATOR:
MELISSA REIFF
PRESIDENT,
THE CONTAINER STORE

"Melissa is the most effective communicator I've seen in my career, driving every day our whole-brained approach to business."[24] That's how The Container Store CEO Kip Tindall describes President Melissa Reiff. Reiff believes in setting high goals and continuing to meet or exceed them—an important reason The Container Store has averaged 20 percent growth per year since its inception in 1978. The company's remarkable success can be attributed largely to its impeccable customer service, extensive employee training, and open communication. Reiff actively practices the belief that information is power. Read more at your companion website at www.cengage.com/bcomm/lehman about Reiff's shared leadership and The Container Store's success formula built on effective communication.

www.containerstore.com

REFER TO SHOWCASE PART 3, ON PAGE 511
TO LEARN ABOUT THE COMPANY'S CREATIVE EMPLOYEE INCENTIVES.

Composing Application Messages

When employers invite you to send either a print or electronic résumé, they expect you to include an ***application*** or ***cover message***. A mailed paper résumé should be accompanied by an application letter. When a résumé is submitted electronically, the application "letter" can take the form of an email message. As you have learned, a résumé summarizes information related to the job's requirements and the applicant's qualifications. An application message complements a résumé by (1) introducing the applicant, (2) attracting interest to the résumé, and (3) interpreting the résumé in terms of employer benefits. When mailed, the application message is placed on top of the résumé so it can be read first by the employer.

What does an application message have in common with a sales message?

Because it creates interest and points out employer benefits, the application message is persuasive and, thus, written inductively. It is designed to convince an employer that qualifications are adequate just as a sales message is designed to convince a buyer that a product will satisfy a need. Like sales messages, application messages can be either solicited or unsolicited. Job advertisements *solicit* applications. Unsolicited application messages have greater need for attention-getters; otherwise, solicited and unsolicited application messages are based on the same principles.

Unsolicited application messages are the same basic message (perhaps with slight modifications) sent to many prospective employers. By sending unsolicited messages, you increase your chances of locating potential openings and may alert employers to needs they had not previously identified for someone of your abilities. However, sending unsolicited messages has some disadvantages. Because the employer's specific needs are not known, the opening paragraph will likely be more general (less targeted to a specific position) than the opening paragraph in solicited messages. The process could also be time consuming.

Isabella Stewart wrote the letter in Figure 13-7 to accompany a chronological résumé she prepared after completing the company/job profile of an entry-level auditor posted at your companion website at www.cengage.com/bcomm/lehman. The time Isabella devoted to analyzing the job, the company, and her qualifications was well spent.

Persuasive Organization

A persuasive message is designed to convince the reader to take action, which in this case is to read the résumé and invite you to an interview. Because an application message is persuasive, organize it as you would a sales message:

SALES MESSAGE	APPLICATION MESSAGE
Gets attention	Gets attention
Introduces product	Introduces qualifications
Presents evidence	Presents evidence
Encourages action	Encourages action
(sells a product, service, or idea)	(results in an interview)

What central appeal could you use to get hired? How might you introduce it in the attention-getting paragraph?

Like a well-written sales message, a well-written application message uses a central selling feature as a theme. The central selling feature is introduced in the first or second paragraph and stressed in paragraphs that follow. Two to four paragraphs are normally sufficient for supporting evidence. Consider order of importance as a basis for their sequence, with the most significant aspects of your preparation coming first.

Gain the Receiver's Attention

To gain attention, begin the message by identifying the job sought and describing how your qualifications fit the job requirements. This information will provide instant confirmation that you are a qualified applicant for an open position. An employer required to read hundreds of application letters and résumés will appreciate this direct, concise approach.

For an announced job, you may indicate in the first paragraph how you learned of the position—for example, employee referral, customer referral, executive referral, newspaper advertising, or job fair. Your disclosure will confirm you are seeking an open job as well as facilitate evaluation of the company's recruiting practices. Note that the opening of the letter in Figure 13-7 indicates the applicant learned of the position through a referral from a professor.

FIGURE 13-7

Example of an Application Letter

Addresses letter to specific person using correct name and job title.

Identifies how applicant learned of position, specific position sought, and background.

Discusses how education relates to job requirements.

Uses bulleted list to highlight qualifications corresponding to job requirements.

Introduces résumé and website for additional information.

Encourages employer to take action without sounding pushy or apologetic.

Isabella Stewart | 89 Lincoln Street | San Antonio, TX 78285-9063 | 512.555.9823

October 15, 2011

Mr. Ethan Blanc, Partner
Brown & Donavon, CPAs
1000 Plaza Court
Austin, TX 78710-1000

Dear Mr. Blanc:

Dr. Dunn, an accounting professor at Sam Houston State University, told me that Brown & Donavon has an auditing position available. A systems emphasis in my master's degree and related work experience qualify me for this auditing position.

Because of my interest in fraud investigation, I enhanced my credentials with an emphasis in forensic accounting. Courses in fraud examination and criminology have given me the skills to extract data from ERP systems and detect evidence of fraud using ACL, Excel, and Access. Unstructured, often ambiguous problems that require creative solutions are among my favorite assignments.

My internship at Smith & Lewis has prepared me for audit assignments in your firm by providing:

- Firsthand interaction with practicing auditors and clients, often working long, irregular hours.
- A proven ability to work effectively as a member of an audit team, building trust and credibility with clients and a diverse staff.
- Excellent performance ratings with commendations for superior technical proficiency and strong written and spoken communication skills.

Please review the enclosed résumé for additional information about my accounting education and related work experience. Work samples and further details are available in my electronic portfolio at www.netdoor/istewart. I look forward to talking with you about how my skills and experiences can benefit Brown & Donavon.

Sincerely,

Isabella Stewart

Isabella Stewart

Enclosure

Format Pointers

- Formats as formal business letter since message is accompanying print résumé. Abbreviated email message including online résumé in ASCII or RTF format would be appropriate for electronic submission.
- Uses same high-quality, standard size paper as for résumé in neutral color; includes writer's address and contact information.

How does an unsolicited application message differ from one responding to an announced position? How are they similar?

An opening for an unsolicited message must be more persuasive: You must convince the interviewer to continue to read your qualifications even though a job may not exist. As in the opening of a solicited message, indicate the type of position sought and your qualifications but be more creative in gaining attention. The following paragraph uses the applicant's knowledge of recent company developments and an intense interest in the company's future to gain receiver attention.

> During the past few years, TelCom has experienced phenomenal growth through various acquisitions, mergers, and market expansion. With this growth comes new opportunities, new customers, and the need for new team players to work in sales and marketing. While following the growth of TelCom, I have become determined to join this exciting team and am eager to show you that my educational background, leadership abilities, and internship experience qualify me for the job.

Provide Evidence of Qualifications

How can a job applicant ensure that the application message is not just a "rehash" of the résumé?

For graduates entering the world of full-time work for the first time, educational backgrounds usually are more impressive than work histories. They can benefit from interpreting their educational experiences as meaningful, job-related experiences. An applicant for an auditor's trainee program should do more than merely report having taken courses in auditing theory and practice:

> In my auditing theory and practice class, I could see specific application of principles encountered in my human relations and psychology classes. Questions about leadership and motivation seemed to recur throughout the course: What really motivates executives? Why are auditors feared at many levels? How can those fears be overcome? How can egos be salvaged? The importance of the human element was a central focus of many courses and my research report, "The Auditor as a Psychologist."

Your application message may not necessarily refer to information learned in a class. Recognizing that auditors must be tactful (a point on which the person reading the message will surely agree), the applicant included some details of a class. That technique is a basic in persuasion: Do not just say a product or idea is good; say what makes it good. Do not just say that an educational or work experience was beneficial; say what made it so.

By making paragraphs long enough to include interpretation of experiences on the present or previous job, you show an employer that you are well prepared for your next job. For example, the following excerpt from an applicant whose only work experience was at a fast-food restaurant is short and general: *For three months last summer, I worked at Marketplace Bagel. While the assistant manager was on vacation, I supervised a crew of five on the evening shift. Evaluations of my work were superior.*

Added details and interpretation could make the value of the work experience more convincing:

> In my summer job at Marketplace Bagel, I learned the value of listening carefully when taking orders, making change quickly and accurately, offering suggestions when customers seemed hesitant, and keeping a cheerful attitude. Supervising a crew of five while the assistant manager was on vacation, I appreciated the importance of fairness and diplomacy in working with other employees.

The applicant has called attention to qualities that managers like to see in employees: willingness to listen, speed, accuracy, concern for clients or customers, a positive attitude, fairness, and tact. As a *learning* experience, the Marketplace Bagel job has taught or reinforced principles that the employer sees can be transferred to the job being sought.

How can an applicant give the impression of confidence in the application message without appearing arrogant?

In this section, you can discuss qualifications you have developed by participating in student organizations, student government, athletics, or community organizations. Be specific in describing gained skills that can be applied directly on the job—for example, organizational, leadership, spoken and written communication skills, and budgeting and financial management. You can also use your involvement as a channel for discussing important personal traits vital to the success of a business—interpersonal skills, motivation, imagination, responsibility, team orientation, and so forth.

> For the past year, I have served as state president of Phi Beta Lambda, a national business student organization. By coordinating various statewide meetings and leadership seminars, I have refined communication, organizational, and interpersonal skills.

Finally, end this section with an indirect reference to the résumé. If you refer to it in the first or second paragraph, readers may turn from the message at that point and look at the résumé. Avoid the obvious statement "*Enclosed please find my résumé*" or "*A résumé is enclosed.*" Instead, refer indirectly to the résumé while restating your qualifications. The following sentence emphasizes that references can confirm applicant's qualifications:

> References listed on the enclosed résumé would be glad to comment on my accounting education and experience.

Encourage Action

How does a successful application message lead the reader to the desired action?

Once you have presented your qualifications and referred to your enclosed résumé, the next move is to encourage the receiver to extend an invitation for an interview. The goal is to introduce the idea of action without apologizing for doing so and without being demanding or "pushy." If the final paragraph (action closing) of your message is preceded by impressive paragraphs, you need not press hard for a response. Just mentioning the idea of a future discussion is probably sufficient. If you have significant related experience that you have developed as a central selling feature, mentioning this experience in the action closing adds unity and stresses your strongest qualification one last time. Forceful statements about *when* and *how* to respond are unnecessary and irritating. Do avoid some frequently made errors:

- **Setting a date.** "May I have an appointment with you on March 14?" The date you name could be inconvenient; or even if it is convenient for the employer, your forwardness in setting it could be resented.
- **Expressing doubt.** "If you agree," "I hope you will," and "Should you decide" use subjunctive words that indicate lack of confidence.
- **Sounding apologetic.** "May I take some of your time" or "I know how busy you are" may seem considerate, but an apology is inappropriate when discussing ways you can contribute to a company.
- **Sounding overconfident.** "I will call you next week to set an appointment time that works for both of us." This statement is presumptuous and egotistical.
- **Giving permission to call.** "You may call me at 555-6543." By making the call sound like a privilege ("may call") you could alienate the reader. Implied meaning: You are very selective about the calls you take, but the employer does qualify.

The following sentences are possible closing sentences that refer to an invitation to interview. They are not intended as model sentences that should appear in your message. Because finding the right job is so important, you will be well rewarded for the time and thought invested in original wording.

- **"When a date and time can be arranged, I would like to talk with you."** The statement does not indicate who will do the arranging, and the meeting place and the subject of the conversation are understood.
- **"I would appreciate an opportunity to discuss the loan officer's job with you."** The indirect reference to action is not forceful. However, if the applicant has impressive qualifications, the reader will want an interview and will not need to be pushed.
- **"I look forward to talking with you about how my skills and experiences can benefit Hannover Industries."** The statement asks for the interview and re-emphasizes the applicant's strong qualifications.

Is an employer's busy schedule a valid argument for keeping an application message short?

General Writing Guidelines

An excellent application message may be the most difficult message you ever attempt to write. It's natural to feel uncomfortable writing about yourself; however, your confidence will increase as you study the wealth of model documents available through your career services center and other sources and writing principles you've been introduced to in this chapter. Then, commit to writing a thoughtful, original message that impresses the interviewer. Instead of standard verbiage included in dozens of models, your self-marketing connects *your* experiences to your future with a specific company and reflects *your* personality and values. The following writing techniques will help distinguish your application message from the competition:

What other "filler statements" can you identify that add no real content to the application letter?

- **Substitute fresh, original expressions that reflect contemporary language.** Overly casual expressions and overused statements will give your message a dull, unimaginative tone. Obvious ideas such as "This is an application," "I read your ad," and "I am writing to apply for," are sufficiently understood without making direct statements. With the application message *and* résumé in hand, a reader learns nothing from "I am enclosing my résumé for your review." Observe caution in choosing overused words such as *applicant, application, opening, position, vacancy,* and *interview*.
- **Avoid overuse of "I" and writer-focused statements.** Because the message is designed to sell your services, some use of "I" is natural and expected; but restrict the number of times "I" is used, especially as the first word in a paragraph. Focus on providing specific evidence that you can meet the company's needs. The employer is not interested in reading about your need to earn more income, to be closer to your work, to have more pleasant surroundings, or to gain greater advancement opportunities.
- **Avoid unconvincing generalizations that may sound boastful.** Self-confidence is commendable, but overconfidence (or worse still, just plain bragging) is objectionable. Overly strong adjectives, self-judgmental terms, and unsupported generalizations damage your credibility. Instead of labeling your performance as "superior" or "excellent," or describing yourself as "an efficient, technically skilled team player" give supporting facts that show the interviewer you can deliver on what you're selling.
- **Tailor the message to the employer's need.** To impress the interviewer that your message is not a generic one sent to everyone, provide requested information and communicate an understanding of the particular company, job requirements, and field.

How would you respond to a requirement listed in a job ad that you do not meet?

- **Provide requested information.** Job listings often request certain information: "Must provide own transportation and be willing to travel. Give educational background, work experience, and salary expected." Discuss these points in your application message. Preferably, the question of salary is left until the interview, allowing you to focus your message on your contributions to the company—not what you want from the company (money). Discussion of salary isn't meaningful until after a mutually successful interview; however, if an ad requests a statement about it, the message should address it. You may give a minimum figure or range, indicate willingness to accept a figure that is customary for work of that type, or indicate a preference for discussing salary at the interview.

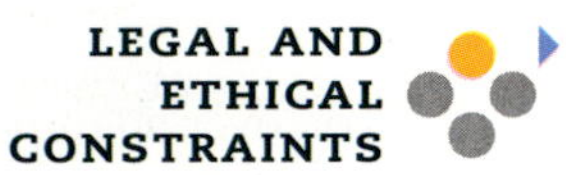

- **Communicate knowledge of the company, job requirements, and language of the field.** Your statements about a company's rapid expansion or competitive advantage show you really are interested in the company, read widely, do more than you are required to do, and gather information before making decisions. However, phrase these statements carefully to avoid the perception of insincere flattery. For example, referring to the employer as "*the* leader in the field," "*the* best in the business," or "a great company" may appear as an attempt to get a favorable decision as a reward for making a complimentary statement. To reflect your understanding of the job requirements, use indirect statements that are informative and tactful. Direct statements such as "The requirements of this job are . . ." presents information the employer presumes you already know; "An auditor should be able to . . ." and "Sales personnel should avoid . . ." sound like a lecture and may be perceived as condescending. Discussing experiences related to a specific job requirement or your preference for work that requires this skill reveals your understanding without a direct statement. Including terminology commonly used by the profession allows you to communicate clearly in terms the reader understands; it also saves space and implies your background in the field.

How is your presentation in the résumé and application message a "one-sided balance sheet"?

- **Focus on strengths and portray a positive attitude.** Concentrate on the positive aspects of your education or experience that have prepared you for the particular job. Apologizing for a shortcoming or admitting failure only weakens your case and raises questions about your self-esteem. Do not discuss your current employer's shortcomings. Regardless of how negatively you perceive your present employer, that perception has little to do with your prospective employer's needs. Also, if you speak negatively of your present employer, you could be perceived as someone who would do the same to the next employer.

Your Turn 13-4
You're the Professional

You are submitting a résumé and application letter in response to a job ad you read in the local newspaper. After describing the position to be filled, the ad requests that applicants "send résumé, salary history, and reason for leaving current job to . . ." Your main reason for seeking a new position is to raise what you feel to be a below-market salary and to escape a boss who is impossible to work with. How will you respond in your application letter?

Discuss the merit of each of the following choices, describing your reasons:

TAKE ACTION:

a. Mention the salary you are now earning, and state that your main reason for leaving is to increase your income.

b. State that you look forward to discussing your qualifications for the position, along with salary, at the interview. Do not mention your current salary or reason for wanting to leave your job.

c. Mention the salary you are now earning, pointing out that it is below market average. State your desire to work for a supervisor that is more competent and fair than your current one.

d. Say that your salary expectations would start with the market average and can be negotiated. State that your reason for leaving your present job is to seek more opportunity for advancement.

Finishing Touches

The importance of professional formatting and careful proofreading of a print document is generally understood. However, proofing and formatting a "real" résumé and letter appears more important to some applicants than producing quality email submissions. Employers frequently voice concern with the sloppiness and unprofessional appearance and content of electronic submissions. To survive the skeptical eye of an interviewer scanning for ways to reject an applicant, allow yourself time to produce a professional-looking document regardless of the presentation or delivery option you've chosen. Include these steps in your finishing phase:

- Regardless of your delivery option, address your application letter or email message to the specific individual who is responsible for hiring for the position you are seeking rather than sending the document to the "Human Resources Department" or "To Whom It May Concern." If necessary, consult the company's annual report or website, or call the company to locate this information.
- Verify the correct spelling, job title, and address, and send a personalized message to the appropriate individual.
- Keep the message short and easy to read. A one-page letter is sufficient for most applications from students and graduates entering the job market.
- Apply visual enhancements learned previously to enhance the appeal and readability of the message and to draw attention to your strengths.
- Definitely keep the paragraphs short and consider listing your top four or five achievements or other important ideas in a bulleted list.

What color paper is best for an application letter in your career field?

- Use paper that matches the résumé (color, weight, texture, and size). The watermark should be readable across the sheet in the same direction as the printing. Since you're using plain paper, include your street address and city, state, and ZIP Code above the date or formatted as a letterhead at the top of the page.
- Include "Enclosure" below the signature block to alert the employer that a résumé is enclosed. The proper letter format is shown in the example in Figure 13-7. Refer to Appendix A for more on professional letter layouts and to this chapter's tips for formatting print résumés that also relate to the accompanying letter.
- Get opinions from qualified individuals and make revisions where necessary.

CHANGING TECHNOLOGY

When preparing an application message for email submission, career experts recommend formatting it as a business letter with the complete address of the company exactly as presented in a letter sent by mail and a formal closing such as "Sincerely." To help people reach you, include a full signature file with your mailing and email addresses, and phone number(s). The recipient can easily contact you without opening your attachments. While seemingly unnecessary, the email address is useful when a recipient forwards your email to someone else who may want to reply to you but cannot see your email address. Exclude quotes from your signature file that might be misunderstood or offensive. Add an enclosure notation drawing attention to your résumé attachment provided as requested by the employer (Résumé attached as Word document).

To compete with the high volumes of junk mail, daily messages, and fear of computer viruses, you must provide a motive for an interviewer to open an unexpected message from an unknown person. Messages with missing or vague subject lines may be ignored or deleted immediately. To bring attention to your message, include the name of the person referring you to the position directly in the subject line or mention your email is a follow-up to a conversation (RE: Follow-up: Résumé for . . .).

Attracting Employees Through Creative Incentives

The Container Store, named repeatedly by *Fortune* magazine as one of the best companies to work for in America, attributes its favorable recognition to its worker-centered philosophy. The Container Store impressed *Fortune* magazine with its employee perks such as the Colorado Get Away, in which a dozen employees are selected from nominations to spend a week at the founder's cabin in the mountains. The company also offers a paid sabbatical from work after 10 years. Other companies that have made the list also offer creative incentives to attract and retain employees in a tight labor market:

- NetApp and Umpqua Bank give employees five paid days for volunteer work.
- MBNA, a credit card company, gives its newly married employees a week off and a limo on their wedding day.
- SAS, a leading software supplier, provides fresh fruit every Monday, M&Ms on Wednesdays, and breakfast goodies on Fridays.
- Microsoft managers maintain "morale budgets" to stage fun events such as team dinners and outings to sports events or plays.
- BMC software washes its employees' cars and changes the oil.
- The pharmaceutical company Pfizer's employees receive free drugs, including Viagra.
- In addition to monthly performance bonuses, employees at Continental Airlines can win a Ford Explorer for perfect attendance.

www.containerstore.com

Activities

Locate the issue of *Fortune* that includes the latest "best company" award winners. Prepare a short report that summarizes incentives and rewards offered by award-winning companies in an effort to attract qualified employees. Conclude with the incentives you personally find most appealing.

© MELANIE STETSON FREEMAN/THE CHRISTIAN SCIENCE MONITOR/GETTY IMAGES

LEGAL AND ETHICAL CONSTRAINTS

If the message is totally "cold," describe the specific value you can add to the company (Résumé for Forensics Accountant with Extensive ACL Skills). Stay away from tricks such as marking an email "urgent" or adding "re" to pass your message off as a reply to an earlier message.

Check any instructions provided by the prospective employer and follow them precisely. Typically, however, you will want to send a complete letter and copy of your résumé by regular mail as a follow-up to the email submission. These suggestions are illustrated in Figure 13-8, a sample application letter an applicant sent after talking with a prospective employer at a career fair.

Before writing a résumé and application message, study carefully the overall suggestions in the "General Writing Guidelines" at your companion website at www.cengage.com/bcomm/lehman. Then study the specific suggestions in the "Check Your Communication" checklist. Compare your work with this checklist again after you have written a rough draft and make any necessary revisions.

FIGURE 13-8

Example of Application Message Sent by Email

To:	ckelsey@tropicalimporters.com
From:	jraneri@netdoor.com
Subject:	Career Fair Followup: Resume for Jacob Raneri
Attached:	Jacob_Raneri_resume

October 15, 2011

Mr. Caleb Kelsey
Human Resources Manager
Tropical Importers
1240 Coastal Lane
Miami, FL 33140-1000

Dear Mr. Kelsey:

It was a pleasure meeting you at the career fair this morning. The opportunities offered in logistics management identify your company as a leader in today's international marketplace.

My experience and knowledge of logistics management enable me to be a valuable asset to your company:

- Realistic international experience with a delivery company.
- Demonstrated commitment to developing an appreciation for international cultures and business practices.
- Excellent performance evaluations, including special recognition for developing a project management checklist for transportation of sensitive government documents.

After you have reviewed the attached résumé that you requested for additional information about my education and related work experience, please message me so we can discuss my joining Tropical Importers.

Sincerely,

Jacob Raneri
Jacob Raneri
59 Tuscany Court
Germantown, TN 38183-0059
901 555-4918
jraneri@netdoor.com

Résumé text included in email below and attached as MS Word document.

Provides specific subject line that ensures message will be opened.

Names attachment logically for the recipient.

Reveals how applicant learned of position and confirms knowledge of and interest in company.

Condenses persuasive application message to one screen. Avoids tendency to send impersonal message stating résumé is attached.

Introduces résumé and reminds interviewer that submission was requested.

Encourages employer to take action without sounding pushy or apologetic.

Includes email address in .sig file to simplify access to all contact information without opening attached résumé.

Includes enclosure notation pointing out that résumé is sent as required by the company.

Format Pointer

- Formats as formal business letter with complete address exactly as done when job credentials are sent by mail. Complete letter and printed copy of résumé will be sent as follow-up to email.

Your Turn 13-5
Career Portfolio

Job listings can be found through both print and electronic sources. When applying for a position in response to a posted ad, pay close attention to the stated requirements of the job and skills sought in the successful applicant. Your résumé should address those stated needs as closely as possible.

TAKE ACTION:

- Select a job ad or posting for a position in your career field. Prepare a résumé that effectively reflects your qualifications and skills for the position.
- Following your instructor's directions, compose an appropriate application message in either letter or email format.

Summary

1. Prepare for employment by considering relevant information about yourself as it relates to job requirements.

As a job candidate, you should complete systematic self-, career, and job analyses. Gather information to make wise career decisions, asking questions about yourself, about a possible career, and about a specific job in the chosen field. Interview people already working. Recording and analyzing this information will aid in selecting a satisfying career and preparing an effective résumé and application message.

2. Identify career opportunities using traditional and electronic methods.

You can widen employment opportunities by using traditional and electronic methods for the employment search. Names and addresses of possible employers may be obtained from networks, career services centers at schools, employers' offices, employment agencies and contractors, online databases and printed sources, and professional organizations. Information is available via the Internet about how to conduct a successful electronic job search and available job vacancies. Network with prospective employers through electronic job fairs, news groups, and chat sessions.

3. Prepare an organized, persuasive résumé that is adapted for print and electronic postings.

A résumé typically includes identification, objective, career summary, qualifications, personal information, and references. The most effective résumé for a particular candidate could be a chronological, functional, or chrono-functional résumé.

- Chronological résumés have headings such as "Education" and "Experience" and list experiences in reverse chronological order; they are appropriate for applicants who have the apparent qualifications for the job.
- Functional résumés show applicant qualifications as headings; this format is especially effective for applicants who lack the appropriate education and experience.
- The chrono-functional résumé lists education and experience as headings and uses functional headings that emphasize qualifications.

Effective print (designed) résumés concisely highlight key qualifications and are formatted for quick, easy reading. Electronic résumé posting varies considerably, with popular options including a job bank posting, a website entry, a link to a personal web page, an email attachment, and an inline résumé within the body of an email message. Scannable résumés are designed so that information can be scanned and processed by an applicant-tracking system. An effective keyword section summarizes qualifications and helps ensure that the résumé is identified during a search for matching requirements.

4. Utilize employment tools other than the résumé that can enhance employability.

The résumé may be supplemented with other employment tools that include a professional portfolio and a video recording of the applicant. Content for a portfolio or video should be carefully chosen to reflect skills necessary for effective job performance and should complement information in the résumé.

5. Write an application message that effectively introduces an accompanying print (designed) or electronic résumé.

An application message, which may be in the form of a printed letter or email communication, effectively introduces an accompanying résumé. The purposes of the application message are to introduce the applicant and the résumé, create interest in the information given on the résumé, and assist an employer in seeing ways in which the applicant's services would be desirable. As such, it is a persuasive message—beginning with an attention-getter, including a central appeal and convincing evidence, and closing with an indirect reference to the enclosed résumé and desired action (invitation to an interview).

Chapter Review

1. Where can you obtain information about the responsibilities, compensation, and career potential of a certain job? (Obj. 1)
2. List five sources from which prospective employers' names and addresses may be obtained; include traditional and electronic sources. (Obj. 2)
3. How can a job applicant conduct a successful job search without leaving home? (Obj. 2)
4. What are the standard parts of a résumé? What are some optional parts? How does a job candidate decide which parts to include? (Obj. 3)
5. Under what conditions might you choose to include or not include references on a résumé? Is obtaining permission from references necessary? (Obj. 3)
6. Describe the three organizational patterns of résumés and explain under what circumstances each would be effective. (Obj. 3)
7. How does the format and content of an electronic résumé differ from a print résumé? (Obj. 3)
8. What safeguards should be taken when posting a résumé electronically? (Obj. 3).
9. Describe a job for which a portfolio or video recording might be an effective résumé enhancement. What should be included? (Obj. 4)
10. List techniques for effective persuasion that should be applied in application messages. Refer to Chapter 8 for ideas if necessary. (Obj. 5)

Digging Deeper

1. Explain the rise in popularity of the "Career Summary" section on résumés. How else have résumés changed in recent years?
2. Is it possible for a candidate to "try too hard" when preparing a résumé? Explain your answer.

Assessment

To check your understanding of the chapter, take the available online quizzes as directed by your instructor.

Activities

1. Preparing to Harness the Monster (Objs. 1–3)

Browse the career sites available at your companion website at www.cengage.com/bcomm/lehman. Select the one that provides career guidance that you believe would be most useful in your job search. Register to receive the site's free online newsletter for timely job search information. Your instructor may also require you to prepare a brief summary of the information that you found especially timely or relevant to your needs. Below the last summary, write a brief statement describing the effectiveness of the information provided and the presentation of these email updates. Refer to the discussion for email marketing in Chapter 8 if necessary to review criteria important to effective campaigns. Be prepared to share in small groups or with the class.

2. Document for Analysis: Chronological Résumé (Objs. 1–3)

In your position as a career counselor, review the narrative of qualifications available at your companion website that you have received from Shane Austin, who is seeking a position as a senior loan officer in a major banking firm. In small groups, discuss the following questions and be prepared to present a short report to the class: (a) What information is relevant to Shane's career objective and thus should be included in his résumé? (b) Which of the three organizational plans for résumés would present Shane's qualifications most effectively? Explain. (c) What details could be included in a "Career Summary" section to strengthen Shane's résumé? (d) How should Shane communicate information about his references? Which of the references would you recommend he use? If directed by your instructor, prepare Shane's résumé incorporating your decisions. Provide fictitious information if needed. Access downloadable version of this application at your companion website at www.cengage.com/bcomm/lehman.

3. Document for Analysis: Application Message (Obj. 5)

Analyze the following message. Pinpoint its strengths and weaknesses and then revise as directed by your instructor. Access

Check Your Communication
Résumés and Application Messages

PRINT (DESIGNED) RÉSUMÉ

CONTENT

- ☐ Include relevant qualifications compatible with the job requirements generated from analyses of self, career, and the job.
- ☐ Present qualifications truthfully and honestly.

ORGANIZATION

- ☐ Choose organizational pattern that highlights key qualifications: chronological, functional, or chrono-functional.
- ☐ Arrange headings in appropriate sequence.
- ☐ Place significant ideas in an emphatic position.
- ☐ List experiences consistently, either in time sequence or in order of importance.

STYLE

- ☐ Omit personal pronouns.
- ☐ Use action verbs.
- ☐ Use past tense for previous jobs; present tense for present job.
- ☐ Place significant words in emphatic positions.
- ☐ Use parallelism in listing multiple items.
- ☐ Use positive language.
- ☐ Use simple words (some jargon acceptable).

MECHANICS

- ☐ Ensure there are *no* keying, grammar, spelling, or punctuation errors.
- ☐ Balance elements on the page.
- ☐ Use ample margins even if a second page is required.
- ☐ Include a page number on all pages except the first and "continued" at the bottom of the first page to indicate a multiple-page document.
- ☐ Position and format headings consistently throughout.
- ☐ Use an outline format or a bulleted list to emphasize multiple points.
- ☐ Use indention, underlining, capitalization, font changes, and graphic lines and borders to enhance overall impact.
- ☐ Laser print on high-quality (24-pound, 100-percent cotton-fiber content), neutral-colored paper.

ELECTRONIC RÉSUMÉS

CONTENT

- ☐ Adapt general guidelines for résumé preparation to fit the particular requirements of the submission.
- ☐ Place "Keyword Summary" on first screen (first 24 lines of text) listing qualifications that match the job description.
- ☐ Support keywords with specific facts
- ☐ Include link or reference to electronic portfolio.
- ☐ For scannable résumés, position name as the first readable item on each page.

MECHANICS

- ☐ Save résumé in appropriate format for transmitting as an attachment, or paste into email message.

PROFESSIONAL PORTFOLIO

CONTENT

- ☐ Include items that showcase abilities and accomplishments.

MECHANICS

- ☐ Choose an appropriate traditional or electronic format.
- ☐ Organize logically to assist in ease of use.
- ☐ For electronic formats, include links to print résumé, plain text version of résumé, email address, and appropriate supplementary documents.

APPLICATION MESSAGE

CONTENT

- ☐ Identify the message as an application for a certain job.
- ☐ Include valid ideas (statements are true).
- ☐ Emphasize significant qualifications and exclude nonessential ideas.
- ☐ Make reference to enclosed or attached résumé.
- ☐ End with action closing that is neither apologetic nor pushy.

ORGANIZATION

- ☐ Begin by revealing the job sought in the attention-getter.
- ☐ Present paragraphs in most appropriate sequence (order of importance is possibly best).
- ☐ End with a reference to action employer is to take (call or write to extend an invitation for an interview).

STYLE

- ☐ Use simple language; some jargon is justified.
- ☐ Use relatively short sentences with sufficient variety.
- ☐ Place significant words and ideas in emphatic positions.

MECHANICS

- ☐ Ensure that there are no keying, grammar, spelling, or punctuation errors.
- ☐ Include the writer's address above the date or format as a letterhead since the letter is presented on plain paper that matches the résumé.
- ☐ Include equal side margins (approximately one inch) and balance on the page.
- ☐ Keep first and last paragraphs relatively short; hold others to six or seven lines.

a downloadable version of this application at your companion website at www.cengage.com/bcomm/lehman.

April 5, 2011

Bailey Stores Incorporated

Roanoke VA 24022

Dear Sirs:

I am looking for an opportunity for advancement with a new employer. My background is in retail management and I fell well qualified for the Store Manager position in the Bailey's West location you advertised on your website. I would like to be considered as an applicant for the position. The primary advantage I would have as a manager is my heavy educational background. Among the courses I have taken are advertising, internet marketing, marketing research, public relations, and advertising. I am sure you realize the many ways in which these courses can prepare one for a career in sales management.

In addition to my classes, my educational background includes work in the university bookstore, service on the school yearbook, and president of my fraternity. I will be receiving my degree on May 5, 2011. I will appreciate you studying the résumé which you will find inclosed. If you can use an energetic young man with my educational background as I hope, will you grant me an interview at your earliest convenience. So I can put my educational background to work for you. I will followup this email with a mailed letter and phone call so we can talk more about the position.

4. Locating Employment Opportunities (Objs. 1–3)

Mallory Schilling, a graduating senior in computer information systems, has sought your advice as to how to locate job opportunities in her field. Outline a course of action for her that includes traditional and electronic methods that may help her locate the right job.

Applications

READ | THINK | WRITE | SPEAK | COLLABORATE

1. Making Yourself More Marketable (Obj. 1)

Locate the following article from an online database that offers suggestions for increasing marketability as a job seeker and dedicated professional:

Scivicque, C. (2008, January 22). How to sell yourself: Effective tips for self-promotion. *Suite 101.com*. Available at http://job-interview-skills.suite101.com/article.cfm/how_to_sell_yourself

After reflecting on your job skills and the ideal job you wish to obtain, prepare an action plan for increasing your market potential. Include steps you will take in your application process, companies/organizations you will contact, and references you will include. Research further as necessary to develop a viable plan.

2. Surfing Cyberspace to Land a Job (Objs. 1, 2)

Visit one of the career sites using the links provided at your companion website at www.cengage.com/bcomm/lehman and note the types of career guidance information available. Print the page of a resource that you believe will be beneficial to you as you search for a job. Summarize the results of your exploration in a short report to your instructor. Your instructor may ask you to complete the activities in the Holistic Assessment Case related to Internet recruiting.

3. Creating Your Own Vésumé (Objs. 3, 4)

Read the following article that provides tips for preparing your own vésumé to post online and shows video examples of pitfalls to avoid:

YouTube résumé tips: You can learn from others' mistakes. (2007, August 1–7). *Time Out New York*. Available at http://newyork.timeout.com/articles/features/9523/youtube-resume-tipsa

Prepare your own vésumé for a job posting in your career field. Post your vésumé to YouTube and share with your instructor and your class.

READ | THINK | WRITE | SPEAK | COLLABORATE

4. Assessing Career Interests (Obj. 1)

Various career, or vocational, tests are available that can help you assess your areas of job interest. Visit the following site that discusses the value and use of such assessments and links you to some representative examples of career tests: www.jobhuntersbible.com/counseling/sec_page.php?sub_item=048

After considering the six rules about taking career tests, take the Career Values Test. Write a one-page summary of what your test results revealed and how you will use the information in your career planning.

5. Getting Essential Information to Make a Wise Career Decision (Obj. 1)

Select a job listing for a job for which you wish to interview (full- or part-time, internship or co-op position). Complete the planning forms available at your companion website, www.cengage.com/bcomm/lehman, to direct your reflection on your interests and abilities and understanding of your career and job sought. To validate your career and job analyses, interview a person currently working in your career field. Give honest, insightful answers to each question; add additional questions that you deem appropriate for a complete analysis in the planning form for each part of the analysis. Access a downloadable version of this application at your companion website at www.cengage.com/bcomm/lehman.

6. Preparing a Company/Job Profile (Obj. 1)

Use information obtained from completing Application 5 to prepare a company/job profile for the company/job in which you expect to be interviewing. Using the sample profile posted at your companion website at www.cengage.com/bcomm/lehman complete these steps:

a. Review the completed profile and note the degree of compatibility between your qualifications and the company and job requirements.
b. Compile a list of strengths and weaknesses (lack of a match between your qualifications and job requirements) as they relate to the job requirements.
c. Consider carefully the deficiencies you must overcome before your qualifications fully match the job requirements. What are possible strategies for overcoming these deficiencies? Are any of these strategies feasible, or is overcoming these deficiencies out of your control?
d. Analyze the final comparison and decide whether interviewing for this job would be wise.

7. Critiquing a Peer's Résumé (Obj. 3)

Exchange a rough draft of your résumé with another class member. Critique the document's effectiveness using the guidelines and the examples provided in the chapter. Send an email message to the student giving your overall impression of the résumé and specific suggestions for improving it. Print a copy of your message and submit it to your instructor with a copy of the student's résumé.

READ | THINK | **WRITE** | SPEAK | COLLABORATE

8. Applying for a Job of Your Choice: Résumé with Accompanying Application Letter (Objs. 1, 3, 5)

Prepare a print version of your résumé and an application letter for a job of your choice using information compiled in Applications 5 and 6. Assume you are applying for an immediate part-time job, a full-time job for the summer, a cooperative education assignment or internship, or a full-time job immediately after you graduate. Look at the list of courses you plan to take and write as though you had taken them and satisfied the requirements for a degree. Follow the guidelines for preparing a print résumé, and then incorporate the valid comments of at least two others competent in proofreading and résumé design. Produce a highly effective, professional document.

9. Mastering Electronic Submissions (Obj. 5)

Assume one of your networking contacts asked you to email your résumé for a potential opening in his firm. Prepare an abbreviated version of the application letter you prepared in Application 8. Email the application message with an inline résumé positioned below the application "letter." Email the document to your instructor using a subject line that stands out in an overloaded mailbox as an expected message from a known person.

10. Designing an Electronic Portfolio (Obj. 4)

Sketch the information you would include on the first page of an electronic portfolio posted at your personal website. Brainstorm about the types of information you might include in links to additional qualifications. Consider materials you have prepared for your career portfolio while completing the Your Turn applications in this text. Create your electronic résumé if your instructor directs you to do so. Post to your student home page in your online course or your personal web page. Send your instructor an email message providing the URL address if posted to your personal webpage.

READ | THINK | WRITE | **SPEAK** | COLLABORATE

11. Analyzing Résumé Critiques Made by Experts (Obj. 3)

Study the résumé blunders and "before and after" versions of résumés, including recommendations from career experts, available at major career sites. Compile a list of suggestions that reinforce and/or supplement the information related to résumé construction presented in the chapter. Share your suggestions for an effective résumé in a short presentation to the class. You may link to career sites from your companion website at www.cengage.com/bcomm/lehman.

12. Presenting Your Career Portfolio (Objs. 3–5)

Prepare a class presentation that will showcase your employment strengths through the materials you have prepared for your career portfolio while completing the Your Turn applications in the text. Emphasize your preparation, experiences, and skills that have prepared you for your ideal career position.

13. Launching a Newsletter to Boost Career Skills (Objs. 1–5)

A student organization that you're a member of is initiating an online monthly recruiting newsletter available to members at the organization's home page. The vision is to create a fresh, personalized approach to career information specifically related to the needs of the members of your group and the current competitive market. Each newsletter will include at least one article addressing specific job search skills, highlights of special recruiting events and previews of upcoming events, and an interview providing insights from an employer, returning co-op students, campus recruiters, etc. In small groups choose an organization and generate a one-page issue of the newsletter. Consider using a newsletter template from a word processing program to assist you in generating the document. Email your newsletter to your instructor; distribute to the class through email or an electronic posting to the student home page in your online course or a personal web page.

CASES

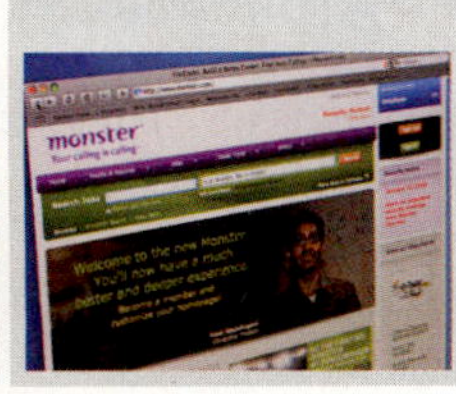

© ERIC CARR/ALAMY

1. Avoiding Online Job Scams

Careerbuilder.com, Monster.com, and JobCentral are three of the largest online job banks. They offer various advantages to both employers and applicants as they cover a broad array of industries and occupations, reach a large audience, and allow for easy job posting and application submission. Online recruiting has become extremely popular, due in part to its very low cost as compared to traditional media efforts used to hire candidates, such as newspapers and television job listings.

Even the big three job banks, however, have been used by scammers to take advantage of unsuspecting job applicants. The con artist typically uses a job ad to lure unsuspecting job seekers, or they may use information from a résumé they have found online. Such scammers can be quite convincing and may even steal company names and corporate logos to convince victims that they are legitimate employers.

After the con artist has won the job seeker's trust, the scammer tricks the job seeker into giving up bank account numbers or other personal information. The reasons given for requesting personal information can be clever, including setting up electronic salary payments. Using such information, the scammer can steal the applicant's money or identity. Legitimate employers do not usually need applicants' social security numbers and bank account numbers prior to hire. Once an applicant has met in person with the employer and has received a job offer, then the disclosure of such private information is more likely in order. "Work from home" and telecommuting jobs are most at risk when agreeing to direct deposit, especially from brand new employers. The applicant should use caution and good sense.[25]

Application:

- Read the following article that details the crime of online job scamming:

  Dixon, P. (2008). A year in the life of an online job scam. *World Privacy Forum*. Available at www.worldprivacyforum.org/jobscamreportpt1.html
- Develop an electronic slide show presentation to share with the class that outlines safeguards for online job applicants so that they are not duped by a scam employer.
- Assume that you are employed by one of the leading job banks and have received a letter from a registered job applicant complaining that a job listed on your site turned out to be a scam. Contact with the scammer resulted in identity theft for the applicant who is now attempting legal action against the scammer. Compose a letter to the job applicant that expresses your regret and eagerness to work to eliminate bogus job postings from your site.

© BBC LTD./COURTESY: EVERETT COLLECTION

2. Video Case: The Office: Job Qualifications: Who Really Cares, Anyway?

In this clip, David calls a "friend" in the warehouse to secure a job for an applicant.

Complete the following activities as directed by your instructor after viewing the video:

1. In small groups, discuss the ethical issues involved with lying about job qualifications, either in an interview or on a résumé. What might be the consequences for lying about being qualified, e.g., having passed the fork-lift driver's test?
2. Research information about well-known people who falsified information on a résumé or in an interview and the consequences that resulted. Prepare a short presentation for the class about such a case.

3. Employment Market Goes Cyber

The cyberspace employment market is here and advancing rapidly. What is being witnessed is nothing less than a transformation in the way people look for jobs and how organizations look for qualified employees. Those who do not engage in electronic employment searching may soon be left out entirely from the digital economy.

Employers and prospective employees traditionally carried on their mutual searching process in physical space. Now, information can be exchanged totally electronically. According to a 2009 report, there were over 3.1 million unduplicated jobs posted on over 1,200 job boards in the United States alone.[26] Large and small companies alike are realizing the advantages offered by online recruiting:

- Worldwide access to job postings increases the response rates to advertised job openings.
- More and better information on applicants is available since a résumé document can provide links to publications, reference letters, and other informational items.
- The ability to quickly scan files, looking for keywords that emphasize experience, knowledge, and abilities, is replacing the tedious task of sorting through volumes of paper résumés, thus reducing the number of days necessary to fill a vacant position.
- A company can instantly ask an applicant to supply additional or missing information.
- The search process can be programmed to run the necessary security, criminal, or credit checks on the applicant automatically.

In sum, the process by which organizations gather necessary information from and about applicants can be made much more efficient through the application of an Internet-based recruiting process. Likewise, the communications garnered through such an automated procedure can be gathered much more quickly—at the speed of light rather than the speed of bureaucratic action and snail mail delivery.

Making use of the Internet allows companies to expand their geographic reach greatly. The paradox, however, of the increasing use of the Internet for corporate recruiting is the potential for both less and greater diversity in organizations. Although an applicant's gender, race, and even physical disabilities play no role in the decision-making process, current statistics on the Internet community reflect a built-in bias. While the demographics are beginning to change to be more reflective of society as a whole, the Internet is currently overwhelmingly male and white. In fact, it has been speculated that employers who would rely solely on the Internet for recruiting might well be in violation of Title VII of the Civil Rights Act. Employers should thus be aware of the potential for discrimination inherent in Internet-based recruiting. The EEOC currently requires that companies with more than 100 employees store all submitted résumés for one year and compile demographic data on applicants; EEOC officials can use the data to look for discriminatory hiring practices.[27]

Complete one or more of the following activities as directed by your instructor:

1. Locate the web page of an organization for whom you would like to work. Print the page. Does the web page provide information about job vacancies? Does it invite résumé postings? How effectively is the company using its web page for recruiting applicants? Report your findings to the class.
2. Locate the online résumé of a job applicant in your chosen field. Is the résumé effectively designed? Are linked files used, and if so, do they enhance the candidate's appeal? What personal information is included? Does the information presented give rise to possible discrimination? Send an email to your instructor reporting what you found.
3. Visit the following website that presents information on recent Internet recruiting polls and statistics: www.recruitersnetwork.com. Write a short informative paper that describes the current status of Internet recruiting. Give examples to substantiate trends and practices.

Chapter 14
Interviewing for a Job and Preparing Employment Messages

"Choose something you love to do, make sure you're with people you like, and then give it your all."
Jack Welch

Objectives When you have completed Chapter 14, you will be able to:

1 Explain the nature of structured, unstructured, stress, group, and virtual interviews.

2 Explain the steps in the interview process.

3 Prepare effective answers to questions often asked in job interviews, including illegal interview questions.

4 Compose effective messages related to employment (application forms, follow-up, thank-you, job acceptance, job-refusal, resignation, and recommendation request).

SHOWCASE PART 1  

GE: Do You Have What It Takes?

Imagine, solve, build, and lead—four bold verbs that express what it is to be part of General Electric, better known as GE. Known for its demanding high-performance culture, GE also recognizes the value of work/life flexibility in helping employees feel fulfilled both professionally and personally. GE, headquartered in Fairfield, Connecticut, is made up of 11 technology, services, and financial businesses with more than 300,000 employees worldwide. The corporation heads the list of Top 20 Companies for Leaders and strives to create a balance between the value that employees contribute to the company and the rewards offered in return.[1] GE views its size as a strength, not a deterrent, in encouraging its employees to take risks and think outside the box.

At GE, its people are viewed as the company's greatest asset. From biochemists, to finance specialists, to wind energy engineers, GE employees are passionate about making life better for people in more than 140 countries. Good ideas and a strong work ethic are encouraged and rewarded, with company values based on three traditions: unyielding integrity, commitment to performance, and thirst for change. According to Steve Canale, a recruiting and staffing services manager, GE is "looking for individuals with high integrity, intelligence, and energy."[2]

GE seeks qualified applicants who are willing to learn the skills necessary for company success. Some candidates are hired directly into leadership development programs that combine work experience with education and training. The Risk Management Leadership Program develops risk management leaders through a combination of rotation in various risk management positions and education in state-of-the-art risk management techniques. The Global Leadership Development Program grooms international leaders through a combination of global assignments and management training.[3] In the company's commercial leadership program, new hires are rotated through a variety of positions over a two-year period to find the best fit for each individual's talents and interests.

Diversity isn't just a noble idea at GE but an ongoing initiative, evidenced by the fact that women make up 35 percent of those hired for entry-level full-time corporate training programs. Minorities make up about 30 percent of those programs.[4] GE recognizes the "power of the mix" and the strength that results from inclusiveness. In an atmosphere of inclusiveness, all employees are encouraged to contribute and succeed. Former CEO and business legend Jack Welch offers the following career advice to anyone looking for the right job: "Choose something you love to do, make sure you're with people you like, and then give it your all."[5]

At GE, "bringing good things to life" begins with offering opportunities to those who have a vision, as well as the energy and confidence to pursue it. Success for GE, as for every company, begins with hiring well. The interview process provides the prospective employer with the opportunity to observe your talents and abilities, as well as your people skills. The interview is also your opportunity to form an impression of the company, its culture, your future supervisors and coworkers. This knowledge will enable you, too, to make the right decision!

SEE SHOWCASE, PART 2, ON PAGE 539
FOR SPOTLIGHT COMMUNICATOR DEBORAH ELAM, GE VICE PRESIDENT & CHIEF DIVERSITY OFFICER.

http://www.ge.com

Understanding Types of Employment Interviews

Most companies conduct various types of interviews before hiring a new employee. While the number and type of interviews vary among companies, applicants typically begin with a screening interview often completed by phone or videoconferencing, an in-depth interview, an on-site interview with multiple interviewers, and sometimes a stress interview. Depending on the goals of the interviewer, interviews may follow a structured or an unstructured approach.

Structured Interviews

In what types of interviews have you participated?

In a ***structured interview*** the interviewer follows a predetermined agenda, including a checklist of questions and statements designed to elicit necessary information and reactions from the interviewee. Because each applicant answers the same questions, the interviewer has comparable data to evaluate. A particular type of structured interview is the behavior-based interview, in which you are asked to give specific examples of occasions in which you demonstrated particular behaviors or skills. The interviewer already knows what skills, knowledge, and qualities successful candidates must possess. The examples you provide will indicate whether you possess them.[7]

Many companies are finding computer-assisted interviews to be a reliable and effective way to conduct screening interviews. Applicants use a computer to provide answers to a list of carefully selected questions. A computer-generated report provides standard, reliable information about each applicant that enables an interviewer to decide whether to invite the applicant for a second interview. The report flags any contradictory responses (e.g., an applicant indicated he was terminated for absenteeism but later indicated that he thought his former employer would give him an outstanding recommendation), highlights any potential problem areas (e.g., an applicant responded that she would remain on the job less than a year), and generates a list of structured interview questions for the interviewer to ask (e.g., "Terrance, you said you feel your former employer would rate you average. Why don't you feel it would be higher?").

Let's Shake On It. Contestants on the popular television show *American Idol* must quickly impress the show's openly critical judges and then members of the viewing audience who vote for their favorite contestant. Similarly, you will have just a few minutes to impress an interviewer that you are the best candidate for the job. While clothing, appearance, and posture help to form a favorable first impression, research has shown that the initial handshake has a strong impact. Candidates who score high on handshakes are also seen as having more extroverted personalities and stronger social skills. The handshake has been found to be even more important for women than men in making a positive impression on interviewers.[6] Practice your winning handshake!

LEGAL AND ETHICAL CONSTRAINTS

Research has shown that applicants prefer computer interviews to human interviews and that they respond more honestly to a computer, feeling less need to give polite, socially acceptable responses. Because expert computer systems can overcome some of the inherent problems with traditional face-to-face interviews, the overall quality of the selection process improves. Typical interviewer errors include talking too much, forgetting to ask important questions, being reluctant to ask sensitive or tough questions, forming unjustified negative first impressions, obtaining unreliable and illegal information that makes an applicant feel judged, and using interview data ineffectively.[8] Regardless of whether the interview is face-to-face or computer assisted, you will need to provide objective, truthful evidence of your qualifications as they relate to specific job requirements.

Unstructured Interviews

Why have unstructured interviews decreased in popularity in recent years?

An ***unstructured interview*** is a freewheeling exchange and may shift from one subject to another, depending on the interests of the participants. Some experienced interviewers are able to make a structured interview seem unstructured. The goal of many unstructured interviews is to explore unknown areas to determine the applicant's ability to speak comfortably about a wide range of topics.

Stress Interviews

A ***stress interview*** is designed to place the interviewee in an anxiety-producing situation so an evaluation may be made of the interviewee's performance under stress. In all cases, interviewees should attempt to assess the nature of the interview quickly and adjust behavior accordingly. Understanding that interviewers sometimes deliberately create anxiety to assess your ability to perform under stress should help you handle such interviews more effectively. As the following discussion of different interviewer styles reveals, you can perform much better when you understand the interviewer's purpose.

TEAM ENVIRONMENT

Group Interviews

As organizations have increased emphasis on the team approach to management and problem solving, selecting employees who best fit their cultures and styles has become especially important. Involving key people in the organization in the candidate selection process has led to new interview styles. In a series interview, the candidate meets individually with a number of different interviewers. Each interviewer will likely ask questions from a differing perspective; for instance, a line manager may ask questions related to the applicant's knowledge of specific job tasks while the vice president of operations may ask questions related to the applicant's career goals. Some questions will likely be asked more than once in the process. A popular trend in organizations that desire a broad range of input in the hiring decision but want to avoid the drawn-out nature of series interviews is to conduct team interviews. The accompanying Strategic Forces feature, "The Team Interview: What to Expect When the Interviewer Turns Out to Be a Team," provides additional information about team interviews.

TEAM ENVIRONMENT

STRATEGIC FORCES

The Team Interview: What to Expect When the Interviewer Turns Out to Be a Team

Today, the hiring process is often a team effort. Once a hiring manager has identified a need, it is likely that Human Resources (HR) will pull together a team to fill it. A team of four to seven members is common, but teams can be larger, depending on the position to be filled. A team typically has an HR facilitator, employees who will work with the individual, the hiring manager, a peer of the hiring manager, subordinates of the position, and experts in the position's field. The team will likely meet to review the existing job description or develop a new one if necessary. After the job description is developed, the team meets to discuss other attributes of the job, such as leadership and interpersonal skills.

While HR screens the résumés using the job description and the desired attributes, the team develops questions to use in the team interviews. HR circulates the résumés that best match the job requirements to the hiring team, and the team reviews them individually and collaboratively to identify the candidates to be invited for a team interview.

Some or all of the hiring team may participate in the interview process. As the interview begins, the facilitator explains the interview process to the candidate; then the team spends several hours asking the questions that have been determined earlier. Each interviewer is likely to be armed with tailored questions designed to bring out information concerning specific competencies that have been identified as important for the job. The applicant is typically given the opportunity to ask questions as well, which can be directed to a particular member of the hiring team or to the team as a whole. Each member of the team takes notes for further discussion.

© DIGITAL VISION/GETTY IMAGES

After the interview, the hiring team discusses the candidate's performance and makes collective notes before moving to the next candidate. After all candidates have completed the interview process, the group discusses the results and determines to whom, if any, to offer the job or to ask back for an additional interview. Using the group selection process, the "right" person for the job usually emerges quickly.[9]

In some cases, a group of candidates may participate together in a team interview. The applicants may be brought in together and placed in teams to solve problems, while being observed directly or through two-way mirrors by company personnel. At the end of the day, each candidate participates in a traditional interview with one or more persons, who may ask questions based on the observations made of the candidate during the day's activities. Serious contenders may be asked to return for a second-round interview.

Application

In groups assigned by your instructor, search the Internet to learn more about the team interview; then complete the following activities as directed by your instructor.

- In small groups, compare and contrast the team interview and the traditional interview with one interviewer.
- Outline advice for the applicant for the following situations: (a) pre-interview preparation, (b) interview behaviors, and (c) the post-interview follow-up for both a traditional interview and a team interview.

Virtual Interviews

Technology is allowing much business activity, including job interviews, to be conducted virtually. Companies, such as IBM, Microsoft, Nike, and Hallmark Cards, save money and time by screening candidates through video interviews from remote locations. Virtual interviews conducted by videoconferencing allow positions to be filled quickly after interviewing applicants worldwide with a significant reduction in travel costs and access to a wider applicant pool. The consensus is that the video interview is excellent for screening applicants, but a "live interview" is appropriate whenever possible for the important final interview.

Why is a face-to-face interview preferred for the final selection interview?

Various companies have direct hookups with the career services centers of colleges and universities to interview students. These virtual interviews allow students to meet large companies whose representatives typically would not visit colleges with small applicant pools and to interview with companies whose representatives could not travel because of financial constraints or other reasons. Students simply sit in front of a camera, dial in, and interview with multiple interviewers; in some cases, several applicants are interviewed simultaneously. As you would imagine, some candidates who interview well in person may fail on camera or in a group conference call. Virtual interviewing is an excellent method for screening out candidates who are unable to communicate their competence, enthusiasm, and conviction in a technology-rich environment.

Would you feel more comfortable in a video interview or a face-to-face interview? Why?

You should prepare for a virtual interview differently than you would for a traditional interview. First, suggest a preliminary telephone conversation with the interviewer to establish rapport. Arrive early and acquaint yourself with the equipment; know how to adjust the volume and other camera functions for optimal performance after the interview begins. Second, concentrate on projecting strong nonverbal skills: speak clearly but do not slow down; be certain you are centered in the frame, sit straight; look up, not down; and use gestures and an enthusiastic voice to communicate energy and reinforce points while avoiding excessive motion that will appear blurry. Third, realize voices may be out of step with the pictures if there is a lag between the video and audio transmissions. You will need to adjust to the timing (e.g., slow down voice) to avoid interrupting the interviewer.

Your Turn 14-1
Electronic Café

COPING WITH TECHNOLOGY'S DOWNSIDE

For all of its advantages, technology poses some negative aspects. Pessimists argue that online activities pull people away from real-world interactions, making them less concerned about individual relationships and their communities. Productivity gains for businesses are questioned in light of computer viruses, web surfing during work hours, and information overload. The Internet is charged with creating opportunities for invasion of privacy by commercial interests and the government. The following electronic activities will allow you to explore these complex issues and consider how to use technology to its best advantage.

TAKE ACTION:

- **Read about how to avoid rude technology behaviors.** Locate the following article about how technology encourages rudeness and how to avoid it:

  Cortez, M. (2005, March 1). Technology is increasing while civility is decreasing. Deseret News (Salt Lake City). Available at http://findarticles.com/p/articles/mi_qn4188/is_20050301/ai_n11838477/

  Based on the author's discussion of technology abuses, develop a list of 10 "commandments" for using technology and include them in a technology policy that could be implemented in the firm you work for or hope to work for.

- Visit your companion website at www.cengage.com/bcomm/lehman for more information on appropriate online behavior.

Preparing for an Interview

College students frequently schedule on-campus interviews with representatives from various business organizations. Following the on-campus interviews, successful candidates often are invited for further interviews at the company location. The purpose of the second interview is to give executives and administrators other than the human resources interviewer an opportunity to appraise the candidate. Whether on campus or at the company location, interview methods and practices vary with the situation.

Pre-interview planning involves learning something about the company or organization, studying yourself, and making sure your appearance and mannerisms will not detract from the impression you hope to make.

Research the Company

What sources would you consult to gain information about a prospective company?

Nothing can hurt a job candidate more than knowing little about the organization. No knowledge indicates insincerity, and the interviewer does not want to waste precious interview time providing candidates with information they should have considered long before. Preparation will also arm candidates with information needed to develop pertinent qualifications and point their stories to solve an employer's specific problems.

Companies that have publicly traded stock are required to publish annual reports that are available in school libraries or online. Other information can be obtained from the printed and electronic sources you consulted when preparing the company/job profile discussed in the web enrichment content for Chapter 13. Be sure to read news items and blog posts and sign up to receive news alerts from the prospective company for current company information up until the day of the interview. Use social networking utilities such as LinkedIn and Hoovers.com to find profiles of company leaders and gain insights on the types of managers this company employs.

CHANGING TECHNOLOGY

Employees of the company or other applicants who have interviewed may be of help to the interviewee. Employee reviews of selected companies, salaries, and sample interview questions are available online, and some universities may share taped interviews with various company recruiters. Pertinent information about the company and the job sought needed for an interview includes the following:

Company Information

Be sure to research the following on the companies with which you interview:

- **Name.** Know, for example, that the publishing company Cengage Learning was so named to reflect the company's mission to be a "center of engagement" for its global customers.[10]

© AP IMAGES/PRNEWSFOTO/CENGAGE LEARNING

- **Status in the industry.** Know the company's share of the market, its Fortune 500 standing if any, its sales, and its number of employees.
- **Latest stock market quote.** Be familiar with current market deviations and trends.
- **Recent news and developments.** Read current business periodicals, news, and blogs for special feature articles on the company, its new products, and its corporate leadership.
- **Scope of the company.** Is it local, national, or international?
- **Corporate officers.** Know the names of the chairperson, president, and chief executive officer.
- **Products and services.** Study the company's offerings, target markets, and innovative strategies.

Job Information

Be sure to know the following about the job you are seeking:

- **Job title.** Know the job titles of typical entry-level positions.
- **Job qualifications.** Understand the specific knowledge and skills desired.
- **Probable salary range.** Study salaries in comparable firms, as well as regional averages.
- **Career path of the job.** What opportunities for advancement are available?

Study Yourself

What three points could you use to persuade an interviewer you are right for the job?

When you know something about the company, you will also know something about the kinds of jobs or training programs the company has to offer. Next, review your answers to the company/job profile. This systematic comparison of your qualifications and job requirements helps you identify pertinent information (strengths or special abilities) to be included in your résumé. If you cannot see a relationship between you and the job or company, you may have difficulty demonstrating the interest or sincerity needed to sell yourself.

Plan Your Appearance

An employment interviewer once said she would not hire a job applicant who did not meet her *extremities* test: fingernails, shoes, and hair, must be clean and well kept. This interviewer felt that if the candidate did not take care of those details, the candidate could not really be serious about, or fit into, her organization. Other important guidelines include avoiding heavy makeup and large, excessive jewelry. Select conservative clothes, and be certain clothing is clean, unwrinkled, and properly fitted. Additionally, avoid smoking, drinking, or wearing heavy fragrance.

You can locate a wealth of information on appropriate interview dress from numerous electronic and printed sources (many are listed in Chapter 13). Additionally, talk with professors in your field, professors of business etiquette and professional protocol, personnel at your career services center, and graduates who have recently acquired jobs in your field. Research the company dress code—real or implied—ahead of time. If you *look* and *dress* like the people who already work for the company, the interviewer will be able to visualize your working there as well.

Plan Your Time and Materials

What other materials would you take to an interview?

One of the worst things you can do is be late for an interview. If something should happen to prevent your arriving on time, phone an apology. Another mistake is to miss the interview entirely. Plan your time so that you will arrive early and can unwind and review mentally the things you plan to accomplish. Be sure to bring a professional briefcase or notebook that contains everything you will need during the interview. These items might include copies of your résumé, a list of references and/or recommendations, a professional-looking pen, paper for taking notes, highlights of what you know about the company, a list of questions you plan to ask, and previous correspondence with the company.

Practice

The job interview may be the most important face-to-face interaction you ever have. You will be selling yourself in competition with others. How you listen and how you talk are characteristics the interviewer will be able to measure. Your actions, your mannerisms, and your appearance will combine to give the total picture of how you are perceived. Added to the marketable skills you have acquired from your education, experience, and activities, your interview performance can give a skilled interviewer an excellent picture of you. Practicing for an interview will prepare you to handle the nervousness that is natural when interviewing. Practice is what you want to do; do not memorize verbatim answers that may sound rehearsed and insincere. Instead, think carefully about how your accomplishments match the job requirements and practice communicating these ideas smoothly, confidently, and professionally.

Prepare for standard interview questions and other interview issues following suggestions provided later in this chapter. Once you are satisfied you have identified your key selling points, have a friend ask you interview questions you have developed and surprise you with others. Participate in mock interviews with a friend or someone in your career services center, alternating roles as interviewer and interviewee. Then follow each practice interview with a constructive critique of your performance.

Your Turn 14-2
Miscue

Until they found topless photos online, Austin High School officials considered Tamara Hoover a model art teacher with a knack for helping students find their creative streaks. The photos, which were posted on Flickr.com by her partner, depicted Hoover in the shower, lifting weights, and engaged in other routine activities. While Hoover referred to the photos as art, the school district said they were inappropriate and violated the "higher moral standard" expected of public school teachers. Her abrupt dismissal highlights a new concern for employees: Your boss has Internet access, too.[11]

TAKE ACTION:

- Should those in certain leadership roles be held to differing standards in terms of their public behavior and communications?
- How can individuals protect themselves from repercussions that may result from the discovery of "digital dirt"?

Conducting a Successful Interview

The way you handle an interview will vary somewhat depending on your stage in the hiring process. Regardless of whether you are being screened by a campus recruiter in person, by phone or videoconference, or have progressed to an on-site visit, an interview will have three parts: the opening formalities, an information exchange, and the close.

The Opening Formalities

How can you "put your best foot forward" during the few minutes you have in a job interview?

According to management consultant Dan Burns, most candidates don't realize that in the first 60 seconds, interviewers typically decide whether the candidate will be moved to the top of the list or dropped from consideration. Burns emphasizes that skills missing during the interview are important because he assumes these same deficiencies will carry over during employment.[13] Clearly, since the impression created during the first few seconds of an interview often determines the outcome, you cannot afford to take time to warm up in an interview. You must enter the door selling yourself!

No Do-Overs in First Impressions. While many things can go wrong in the nerve-racking job interview process, the five most common faux pas candidates commit include (1) arriving late, (2) talking negatively about previous employers, (3) dressing down, (4) avoiding discussion of personal weaknesses, and (5) demonstrating ignorance of the company or the position sought.[12] As you plan for your interview, don't forget to pack one of the most powerful business tools available: ETIQUETTE. Employers increasingly complain of job applicants who take personal phone calls or text message during the interview. Play it safe by turning off electronic devices for the duration of the interview and stowing them out of sight. Your etiquette and people skills can make the difference between a mediocre performance and one that propels you in the hiring process.

Common courtesies and confident body language can contribute to a favorable first impression in the early few seconds when you have not yet had an opportunity to talk about your qualifications:

- **Use the interviewer's name and pronounce it correctly.** Even if the interviewer calls you by your first name, always use the interviewer's surname unless specifically invited to do otherwise.
- **Apply a firm handshake.** Usually, the interviewer will initiate the handshake, although you may do so. In either case, apply a firm handshake. You do not want to leave the impression that you are weak or timid. At the same time, you do not want to overdo the firm grip and leave an impression of being overbearing.
- **Wait for the interviewer to ask you to be seated.** If you aren't invited to sit, choose a chair across from or beside the interviewer's desk.
- **Maintain appropriate eye contact, and use your body language to convey confidence.** Sit erect and lean forward slightly to express interest. For a professional image, avoid slouching, chewing gum, and fidgeting.
- **Be conscious of nonverbal messages.** If the interviewer's eyes are glazing over, end your answer, but expand it if they are bright and the head is nodding vigorously. If the interviewer is from a different culture, be conscious of subtle differences in nonverbal communication that could affect the interviewer's perception of you. For example, a North American interviewer who sees eye contact as a sign of trust may perceive an Asian female who keeps her eyes lowered as a sign of respect to be uninterested or not listening.[14] Women should also be aware of typical "feminine behavior" during the interview. For instance, women nod more often than men when an interviewer speaks. Women also are likely to smile more and have a rising intonation at the end of sentences; such behaviors can convey a subservient attitude.[15]

Following the introductions, many interviewers will begin the conversation with non-business talk to help you relax and to set the stage for the information exchange portion of the interview. Other interviewers may bypass these casual remarks and move directly into the interview.

Your Turn 14-3
Assessment

What's your NVIQ? Your NVIQ—nonverbal interview quotient—reveals your ability to manage your nonverbal behaviors so that the messages you communicate in an interview are those you wish others to consciously and subconsciously perceive.

TAKE ACTION:

- Assess your nonverbal IQ by taking the quiz at www.winningthejob.com/page2.php3?ID=94&Item+23ll, or you may link to this URL or updated sites from your companion website at www.cengage.com/bcomm/lehman.
- Discuss the areas you will work on most to ensure you use favorable nonverbal communication.

The Information Exchange

Much of the information about you will appear on your résumé or application form and is already available to the interviewer. Thus, the interviewer most likely will seek to go beyond such facts as your education, work experience, and extracurricular activities. He or she will attempt to assess your general attitude toward work and the probability of your fitting successfully into the organization.

Presenting Your Qualifications

Your preparation pays off during the interview. Like a defense attorney ready to win a case, you are ready to present evidence that you should be hired. According to Joyce Kennedy & Thomas Morrow, leading career consultants, your case will have three major points: You must convince the interviewer that you (1) can do the job, (2) will do the job, and (3) will not stress out everyone else while doing the job.[16] That's an overwhelming task. Where do you begin? You learned during your study of persuasive writing that saying you're the best at what you do is not convincing. To convince an interviewer to allow you to continue to the next interview or to extend you a job offer, you must provide specific, concrete evidence that your qualifications match the job description and equip you to add immediate value to the company. Use the following guidelines to help you relate your skills and knowledge to the job.

What personal abilities and skills would you emphasize in a job interview?

- **List five or six key points that you want to emphasize.** Likely, you will want to present your education as a major asset. You should point out its relationship to the job sought. Even more important, the fact that you have succeeded in academics indicates that you have the ability and self-discipline to learn. Because most companies expect you to learn something on the job, your ability to learn and thus quickly become productive may be your greatest asset. Even lack of work experience may be an asset: You have acquired no bad work habits that you will have to unlearn.

  Additionally, be sure to provide evidence of your interpersonal skills. Unlike the candidate in the Dilbert cartoon on page 532, you will want to communicate that you can get along with others and are sensitive to diversity.

An effective interview reveals abilities beyond your technical qualifications.

- What did you do in college that helped you get along with others?
- Were you a member, an officer, or president of an organization? What did you accomplish? How did others perceive you? Were you a leader? How did your followers respond to your leadership style? to your commitment to ethical standards?
- Can you organize projects, motivate people to complete important goals, and deal with difficult people?

The extracurricular activities listed on your résumé give an indication of these traits, but how you talk about them in your interview helps. "I started as public relations vice president and was subsequently elected to higher office for four semesters, eventually becoming president" is a statement that may prove your leadership qualities. If you can show your organization moved to greater heights, you will appear successful as well. You can also use questions about your extracurricular activities to show that you have broad, balanced interests rather than a single, time-consuming avocation that could lead to burn-out and stress if carried to the job.

Is it possible for a candidate to interview too well?

What are other skills that graduating students need to succeed in a cross-cultural, interdependent workforce? While academic performance is weighted more heavily for some types of jobs than others, the ability to juggle a complicated schedule is weighed heavily by many employers as an important job-success factor. Additionally, a UNESCO report of employer views revealed certain skills to be essential for workers in today's business climate as shown in Figure 14-1.[17]

Consider these general job success traits and then use your knowledge of the job requirements and your own strengths to develop your "central selling features." These key points targeted to your audience are the central element of a winning argument: You are able and willing to become a contributing part of a high-performance team that will enhance the company's performance.

What is involved in being your "best self" in an interview?

- **Be prepared to answer standard interview questions.** These questions are designed to show (a) why you want the job, (b) why you want to work for this organization, and (c) why the company should want you. Practice concise but fully

FIGURE 14-1

Skills Needed: Balance of Soft and Hard Skills

B A L A N C E

SOFT SKILLS –	HARD SKILLS
Your Emotional Intelligence	Discipline-specific skills
Communication skills	Technical skills
Team skills	Skills related to the 3 Rs
Flexibility	
Creativity and entrepreneurial ability	
Ability to cope with responsibility	
Social sensitivity	
Interest in life-long learning	

developed answers that reflect your personality and your communication power. While one-word answers aren't adequate, long-winded answers may prevent interviewers from asking you other planned questions critical to making an informed decision. Many of the career sites and printed sources discussed in Chapter 13 include lists of frequently asked interview questions; some sources provide suggested answers to the more difficult questions. Research these sites thoroughly, and visit your companion website at www.cengage.com/bcomm/lehman for a sample of the types of questions you might be asked.

- **Be prepared to answer behavioral questions.** These questions are designed to challenge you to provide evidence of your skills or the behaviors required to perform the job. Rather than asking applicants how they feel about certain things, interviewers are finding that asking potential employees for specific examples to illustrate their answers is a more objective way to evaluate applicants' skills. Behavioral questions include the following:

  - Describe a time when you worked well under pressure, worked effectively with others, organized a major project, motivated and led others, solved a difficult problem, or used persuasion to convince someone to accept your idea.
  - What was the most difficult problem you had to overcome in your last job (or an academic or extracurricular activity)? How did you cope with it? What lesson did you learn from the situation? Share a time you applied the lesson learned.
  - Tell me about a time you had difficulty working with a supervisor or coworker (professor, peer in a team in a class setting). How did you handle the situation?

- ▷ Describe something you have done that shows initiative and willingness to work or required you to think on your feet to solve a problem.
- ▷ How have your extracurricular activities, part-time work experience, or volunteer work prepared you for work in our company?
- ▷ Tell me about a time you hit a wall trying to push forward a great idea.

How would you respond to one of the listed behavioral questions using the STAR method?

To prepare for answering behavioral questions, brainstorm to identify stories that illustrate how your qualifications fit the job requirements. These stories should show you applying the skills needed on the job. Career counselors recommend using the STAR method (Situation or Task/Action/Result) as a consistent format to help you present a complete answer to these open-ended questions. You first describe a situation or task you were involved in, the action you took, and finally the result of your effort.[18]

Even if the interviewer doesn't ask behavioral questions, you can use this approach when answering standard interview question. Take the initiative to make your interview stronger by planning "stories" that illustrate your knowledge of the company. For example, suppose news items and blog posts reveal customer service problems. An applicant prepares to focus discussion of his or her experiences toward solving problems in past roles, overcoming adversity, working with difficult people—all evidence the applicant can "reduce the pain" the employer is facing.[19]

- **Be prepared to demonstrate logical thinking and creativity.** Many interviewers ask applicants to solve brain teasers and riddles, create art out of paper bags, and solve complex business problems. Some are asked to "do the job before we give it to you"; for example, write a press release on the spot or field a tech-support call.[20] These techniques are used to gauge an applicant's ability to think quickly and creatively and observe an emotional response to an awkward situation. You cannot anticipate this type of interview question, but you can familiarize yourself with mind teasers that have been used. Most importantly, however, recognize the interviewer's purpose; relax, and do your best to showcase your logical reasoning, creativity, or your courage to even try.
- **Display a professional attitude.** First, communicate your sincere interest in the company; show that you are strongly interested in the company and not just taking an interview for practice. Reveal your knowledge of the company gained through reading published information, and refer to the people you have talked with about the working conditions, company achievements, and career paths.

  Second, focus on the satisfaction gained from contributing to a company rather than the benefits you will receive. What's important in a job goes beyond financial reward. All applicants are interested in a paycheck; any job satisfies that need—some will pay more, some less. Recognize that the paycheck is a part of the job and should not be your primary concern. Intrinsic rewards such as personal job satisfaction, the feeling of accomplishment, and making a contribution to society are ideas to discuss in the interview. You should like what you are doing and find a challenging job that will satisfy these needs.

How would you share a personal weakness with an interviewer without disqualifying yourself for the job?

Third, show your humanness. If you are being interviewed by a representative of a successful company, do not suggest that you can turn the company around. Similarly, telling an interviewer you have no weaknesses could make you sound shallow and deceptive. Instead, mention a weakness that can be perceived as a strength, preferably a "weakness" that a company wants. Indicate that you occasionally become overcommitted to extracurricular activities (assuming your résumé includes a high level of extracurricular participation *and* a strong academic record). If you're applying for a job that involves detail, confess that you are a perfectionist or that you are prone toward being a workaholic.

- **Be prepared to discuss salary and benefits.** For most entry-level positions, the beginning salary is fixed. However, if you have work experience, excellent scholarship records, or added maturity, you may be able to obtain a higher salary. The interviewer should initiate the salary topic. What you should know is the general range for candidates with your qualifications so that your response to a question about how much you would expect is reasonable. If your qualifications are about average for the job, you can indicate that you would expect to be paid the going rate or within the normal range. If you have added qualifications, you might say, "With my two years of work experience, I would expect to start at the upper end of the normal salary range."

  If you have other job offers, you are in a position to compare salaries, jobs, and companies. In this case, you may suggest to the interviewer that you would expect a competitive salary and that you have been offered X dollars by another firm. If salary has not been mentioned, and you really want to know about it, simply ask courteously how much the salary would be for someone with your qualifications. In any case, if you really believe the job offers the nonmonetary benefits you seek, do not attempt to make salary a major issue.

  Typically, an interviewer will introduce the subject of benefits without your asking about them. In some cases, a discussion of total salary and "perks" is reserved for a follow-up interview. If nothing has been said about certain benefits, you should take the liberty of asking, particularly when an item may be especially important to you. Dental and visual insurance, for example, may be very important when you have children.

LEGAL AND ETHICAL CONSTRAINTS

- **Be knowledgeable of interview questions and information on your social networking sites that might lead to discriminatory hiring practices.** You may face the dilemma of being asked an improper interview question because of an innocent slip by the interviewer or lack of training on the legalities of interviewing. The types of illegal (or potentially illegal) interview questions and ways to handle them are described in the Strategic Forces feature "Handling Illegal Interview Questions." Use this knowledge to remove any potentially discriminatory information from your Facebook or MySpace page.

STRATEGIC FORCES

Handling Illegal Interview Questions

The Equal Employment Opportunity Commission (EEOC) and Fair Employment Practices Guidelines make it clear that an employer cannot legally discriminate against a job applicant on the basis of race, color, gender, age, religion, national origin, or disability. Interviewers must restrict questions to an applicant's ability to perform specific job-related functions essential to the job sought. Generally, the following topics should not be introduced:

- **National origin and religion.** "You have an unusual accent; where were you born?" "What religious holidays will require you to miss work?"
- **Age.** "I see you attended Metro High School; what year did you graduate?" "Could you provide a copy of your birth certificate?"
- **Disabilities, health conditions, and physical characteristics not reasonably related to the job.** "Do you have a disability that would interfere with your ability to perform the job? "Have you ever been injured on the job?" "Have you ever been treated by a psychiatrist?" "How much alcohol do you consume each week?" "What prescription drugs are you currently taking?"
- **Marital status, spouse's employment, or dependents.** "Are you married?" "Who is going to care for your children if you work for us?" "Do you plan to have children?" "Is your spouse employed?" Additionally, employers may not ask the names or relationships of people with whom you live.
- **Arrests or criminal convictions that are not related to the job.** "Have you ever been arrested other than for traffic violations? If so, explain." Keep in mind that the arrest/conviction record of a person applying for a job as a law enforcement officer or a teacher could be highly relevant to the job, but the same information could be illegal for a person applying for a job as an engineer.

© RYAN MCVAY/PHOTODISC GREEN/GETTY IMAGES

Since interviewers may ask illegal questions because of lack of training or an accidental slip, you must decide how to respond. You can refuse to answer and state the question is improper, though you risk offending the interviewer. A second option is to answer the inappropriate question, knowing it is illegal and unrelated to job requirements. A third approach is to provide a low-key response such as "How does this question relate to how I will do my job?" or to answer the legitimate concern that likely prompted the question. For example, an interviewer who asks, "Do you plan to have children?" is probably concerned about how long you might remain on the job. An answer to this concern would be "I plan to pursue a career regardless of whether I decide to raise a family." If you can see no legitimate concern in a question, such as "Do you own your home, rent, or live with parents?" answer, "I'm not sure how that question relates to the job. Can you explain?"[21]

Application

- In small groups discuss illegal interview questions that group members may have been asked. How did the person handle the illegal question, and what were the consequences? Give suggestions for handling the questions effectively.
- What consequences does a company face when applicants believe illegal interview questions led to discriminatory hiring?

Mutual Selection. Just as a company must make the decision of whether to choose you as an employee, you must also decide whether to choose to work for the company. Salary is only one factor among many that may influence your satisfaction. You will want to ask yourself several important questions: Are the values of the company in keeping with your own? Does the company offer the type of work culture that will promote your comfort and sense of belonging? Will you have a reasonable opportunity for achieving your goals and aspirations? If you can honestly answer "yes" to all of these questions, the likelihood of your job satisfaction is significantly increased.

Asking Questions of the Interviewer

Both the interviewer and interviewee want to know as much as possible about each other before making a commitment to hire. A good way to determine whether the job is right for you is to ask pertinent questions.

Good questions show the interviewer that you have initiative and are interested in making a well-informed decision. Responses may provide insight to job requirements that you can then show you possess. Therefore, be sure not to say, "I don't have any questions." Focus on questions that help you gain information about the company and the job that you could not learn from published sources or persons other than the interviewer. Respect the interviewer's time by avoiding questions that indicate you are unprepared (for example, questions about the company's scope, products/services, job requirements, or new developments). Avoid questions about salary, required overtime, and benefits that imply you are interested more in money and the effort required than in the contribution you can make.

What other questions might you ask in a job interview?

To show further initiative, introduce questions throughout the interview whenever appropriate rather than waiting until you are asked whether you have questions. This approach will promote positive two-way interaction and should create a relaxed, unintimidating atmosphere. Just remember that the *interviewer* is in charge of the interview. Add your own questions to the typical interviewee questions that follow:

- How would you describe the ideal employee or what's the best background for this job?
- What is a typical day like in this job?
- What type of people would I be working with (peers) and for (supervisors)?
- Why do you need someone for this job (why can this job not be done by a current employee)?
- What circumstances led to the departure of the person I would be replacing? What is the turnover rate of people in this job? (or, How many people have held this job in the past five years?)

- Why do you continue to work for this company? (to an interviewer with several years' tenure with the company)
- Would you describe the initial training program for people in this position?
- What types of ongoing employee in-service training programs are provided?
- How much value does your firm place on a master's degree?
- How do you feel this field has changed in the past 10 years? How do you feel it will change in the next 10 years?
- What advice do you wish you had been given when you were starting out?
- When do you expect to make your decision about the position?

The Closing

The interviewer will provide cues indicating that the interview is completed by rising or making a comment about the next step to be taken. At that point, do not prolong the interview needlessly. Simply rise, accept the handshake, thank the interviewer for the opportunity to meet, and close by saying you look forward to hearing from the company. The tact with which you close the interview may be almost as important as the first impression you made. Be enthusiastic. If you really want the job, you might ask for it.

Your ability to speak confidently and intelligently about your abilities will help you secure a desirable job. Effective interviewing skills will be just as valuable once you begin work. You will be involved in interviews with your supervisor for various reasons: to seek advice or information about your work and working conditions, to receive informal feedback about your progress, to receive a deserved promotion, and to discuss other personnel matters. In addition, your supervisor will likely conduct a performance appraisal interview to evaluate your performance. This formal interview typically occurs annually on the anniversary of your start of employment. Visit your companion website at www.cengage.com/bcomm/lehman to learn how you can make the most of the performance appraisal process.

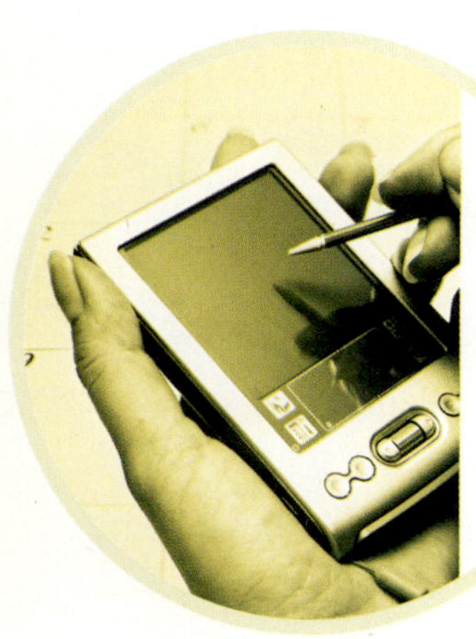

Your Turn 14-4
Career Portfolio

A job interview can be stressful, especially when the applicant is asked unexpected questions without obvious answers. Doing some research about possible questions that might be asked and practicing appropriate responses can help you feel more at ease during the interview and more likely to make a favorable impression.

TAKE ACTION:

- Read the following online article: "The 25 most difficult questions you'll be asked on a job interview," located at www.datsi.fi.upm.es/~frosal/docs/25mdq.html.
- Select a job advertisement from a newspaper or online source that would interest you following graduation. Then select 10 questions from among those covered in the article that you feel are most appropriate to the job you have selected. Compose an effective answer to each question.

Strength in the Diversity Mix

On its website, GE proclaims its firm commitment to diversity and team building: "We recognize the power of the mix, the strength that results from successful diversity. Our business and workforce diversity creates a limitless source of ideas and opportunities."[22] As vice president and chief diversity officer, Deborah Elam steers efforts to globally develop and execute GE's strategies that promote internal diversity, flexibility, and inclusion. The diversity culture at GE is advanced through a corporate leadership institute, business training centers, and leadership best practice sharing. The company believes that the best ways to stay competitive are to share intelligence across the organization and foster learning about the changing demands of the marketplace.[23] Visit your companion website at www.cengage.com/bcomm/lehman to learn more about how GE promotes internal diversity.

www.ge.com

© SCOTT WINTROW/GETTY IMAGES

SPOTLIGHT COMMUNICATOR: DEBORAH ELAM, GE VICE PRESIDENT & CHIEF DIVERSITY OFFICER

REFER TO SHOWCASE, PART 3, ON PAGE 546 TO EXPAND YOUR KNOWLEDGE ABOUT GE'S "AMERICA'S MOST ADMIRED" AWARDS.

Preparing Other Employment Messages

Preparing a winning résumé and application letter is an important first step in a job search. To expedite your job search, you may need to prepare other employment messages: complete an application form, send a follow-up message to a company that does not respond to your résumé, send a thank-you message after an interview, accept a job offer, reject other job offers, and communicate with references. A career change will require a carefully written resignation letter.

Application Forms

Before going to work on a new job, you will almost certainly complete the employer's application and employment forms. Some application forms, especially for applicants who apply for jobs with a high level of responsibility, are very long. They may actually appear to be tests in which applicants give their answers to hypothetical questions and write defenses for their answers. Increasing numbers of companies are designing employment forms as mechanisms for acquiring information about a candidate that may not be included in the résumé. Application forms also ensure consistency in the information received from each candidate and can prevent decisions based on illegal topics which may be presented in a résumé. Visit your companion website at www.cengage.com/bcomm/lehman for guidelines for completing application forms.

Follow-Up Messages

When an application message and résumé do not elicit a response, a follow-up message may bring results. Sent a few weeks after the original message, it includes a reminder that an application for a certain job is on file, presents additional education or experience accumulated and its relationship to the job, and closes with a reference to desired action. In addition to conveying new information, follow-up messages indicate persistence (a quality that impresses some employers). Figure 14-2 shows a good example of a follow-up letter.

Thank-You Messages

What purposes are served in sending a thank-you message, even though you expressed thanks in person after the interview or a discussion with a special employer at a career fair? After a job interview, a written message of appreciation is a professional courtesy and enhances your image within the organization. To be effective, it must be sent promptly. For maximum impact, send a thank-you message the day of the interview or the following day. Even if during the interview you decided you do not want the job or you and the interviewer mutually agreed that the job is not for

FIGURE 14-2

Example of a Follow-Up Letter

Dear Mr. Nolan:

States main idea and clearly identifies position being sought.

Recently I applied for an auditing position with Foster & Daniel and now have additional qualifications to report.

Refers to enclosed résumé; summarizes additional qualifications.

The enclosed, updated résumé shows that I attended the annual ACFE Fraud Conference and Exhibition sponsored by the Association of Certified Fraud Examiners. I attended sessions in the technology track and learned about a variety of tools used to detect fraudulent financial transactions. In a post-conference session, I was introduced to interrogation techniques.

Assures employer that applicant is still interested in job.

Mr. Nolan, I would welcome the opportunity to visit your office and talk more about the contributions I could make as an auditor with Foster & Daniel. Please write or call me at (512) 555-9823.

Format Pointers

- Uses template to design professional personal letterhead and matching envelope.
- Formats as formal business letter, but could have sent message electronically if previous communication with employer had been by email.
- Prints letter and envelope with laser printer on paper that matches résumé and application letter.

you, a thank-you message is appropriate. As a matter of fact, if you've made a positive impression, interviewers may forward your résumé to others who are seeking qualified applicants.

The medium you choose for sending this message depends on the intended audience. If the company you've interviewed with prefers a traditional style, send a letter in complete business format on high-quality paper that matches your résumé and application letter. If the company has communicated with you extensively by email, follow the pattern and send a professional email that can be read in a timely manner. Choosing to send an email rather than slower mail delivery can give you a competitive edge over other candidates whose mailed letters arrive several days later than yours.

After an interview has gone well and you think a job offer is a possibility, include these ideas in the message of appreciation: express gratitude, identify the specific job applied for, refer to some point discussed in the interview (the strength of the interview), and close by making some reference to the expected call or message that conveys the employer's decision. The tone of this business message should remain professional regardless of the personal relationship you may have developed with the interviewer and the informality encouraged by email. The message may be read by many others once it is placed in your personnel file as you complete annual appraisals and compete for promotions. Specific points to cover are outlined in Figure 14-3.

The résumé, application letter, and thank-you message should be stored in a computer file and adapted for submission to other firms when needed. Develop a database for keeping a record of the dates on which documents and résumés were sent to certain firms and answers were received, names of people talked with, facts conveyed, and so on. When an interviewer calls, you can retrieve and view that company's record while you are talking with the interviewer.

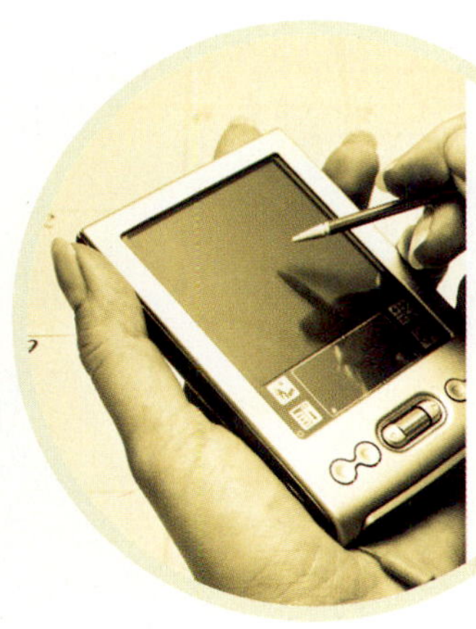

Your Turn 14-5
You're the Professional

You feel confident you aced the interview with Careers, Inc., and have followed up immediately with a dynamic thank-you letter. The interviewer told you a decision would be made within one week and that you should expect a phone call about the decision. That was last Friday; now it's Friday of the following week with no call from the company. What would you do?

TAKE ACTION:

Discuss which of the following actions would be most appropriate, explaining your reasoning:

a. Wait for the company to contact you; the "ball is in their court" at this point.

b. Call the company today (Friday) and inquire as to whether a decision has been made. If the interviewer is unavailable, leave a message asking her to return your call. Call back on Monday if you still have not received a call.

c. Wait and call the company on Monday to inquire as to whether a decision has been made. If the interviewer is unavailable, leave a message asking her to return your call. Assume you did not get the job if she does not call back.

FIGURE 14-3

Example of a Thank-You Message

To:	rmatawi@hcc.com
From:	msharma@hotmail.com
Subject:	Appreciation for Office Interview

Dear Mr. Atawi:

States main idea of appreciation for interview and information gained.

Thank you for the opportunity to visit the Hattiesburg Chamber of Commerce (HCC) for an interview yesterday. I enjoyed meeting you and your staff and the opportunity to learn about the exciting programs sponsored by the HCC.

Includes specific points discussed during interview, increasing sincerity and recall of applicant.

Having lived in Hattiesburg for over six years, I often read reports about how the HCC has influenced the development of our city. The office visit allowed me to learn the vast mission of the HCC, from welcoming new residents, hosting conferences, promoting legislative initiatives, to writing state and federal grants to fund infrastructure improvements.

Assures employer of continued interest in position.

After visiting your office on Monday, I am confident that my interest and previous experience working in the president's office at the University of Southern Mississippi would allow me to contribute to the HCC's important role as the economic and social ambassador for the city. I would also gain valuable real-world experience needed to enhance the public relations degree at the university.

Politely reminds employer that applicant is awaiting reply.

Mr. Atawi, I am eager to receive an offer from the HCC for the public relations position. If you need additional information in the meantime, please contact me.

Thanks,

Matt Sharma

Format Pointer

- Prepares as email message because previous communication with the company has been by email.

Job-Acceptance Messages

A job offer may be extended either by phone or in writing. If a job offer is extended over the phone, request that the company send a written confirmation of the job offer. The confirmation should include the job title, salary, benefits, starting date, and anything else negotiated.

Often, companies require a written acceptance of a job offer. Note the deductive sequence of the message shown in Figure 14-4: acceptance, details, and closing (confirms the report-for-work date).

FIGURE 14-4

Example of a Job-Acceptance Message

States main idea of the job acceptance.	I accept your employment offer as a market analyst. Thank you for responding so quickly after our discussion on Thursday.
Continues with any necessary details.	As you requested, I have signed the agreement outlining the specific details of my employment. Your copy is enclosed, and I have kept a copy for my records.
Confirms beginning employment date.	If you should need to communicate with me before I report to work on May 14, please call me at 555-6841.

Job-Refusal Messages

Should the job-refusal letter include the reason for refusing the job?

Like other messages that convey unpleasant news, job-refusal messages are written inductively: a beginning that reveals the nature of the subject, explanations that lead to a refusal, the refusal, and a pleasant ending. Of course, certain reasons (even though valid in your mind) are better left unsaid: questionable company goals or methods of operation, negative attitude of present employees, possible bankruptcy, unsatisfactory working conditions, and so on. The applicant who prefers not to be specific about the reason for turning down a job might write this explanation: *After thoughtfully considering job offers received this week, I have decided to accept a job in the actuarial department of an insurance company.*

You may want to be more specific about your reasons for refusal when you have a positive attitude toward the company or believe you may want to reapply at some later date. The letter in Figure 14-5 includes the reasons for refusal.

FIGURE 14-5

Example of a Job-Refusal Message

Begins with neutral but related idea to buffer bad news.	I appreciate your spending time with me discussing the loan officer's job.
Presents reasons diplomatically that lead to refusal.	Your candid comparison of my background and opportunities in finance and insurance was especially helpful. Having received job offers in both fields, I am now convinced that a career in insurance is more consistent with my aptitudes and goals. Today, I am accepting a job in the actuarial department of States Mutual.
Ends message on positive note that anticipates future association with company.	Thank you for your confidence demonstrated by the job offer. When I receive reports of Lincoln's continued success, I will think of the dedicated people who work for the company.

Resignations

Resigning from a job requires effective communications skill. You may be allowed to "give your notice" in person or be required to write a formal resignation. Your supervisor will inform you of the company's policy. Regardless of whether the resignation is given orally or in writing, show empathy for your employer by giving enough time to allow the employer to find a replacement. Because your employer has had confidence in you, has benefited from your services, and will have to seek a replacement, your impending departure *is* bad news. As such, the message is written inductively. It calls attention to your job, gives your reasons for leaving it, conveys the resignation, and closes on a positive note. A written resignation is shown in Figure 14-6.

A resignation is not an appropriate instrument for telling managers how a business should be operated. Harshly worded statements could result in immediate termination or cause human relations problems during your remaining working days. If you can do so sincerely, recall positive experiences you had with the company. Doing so will leave a lasting record of your goodwill, making it likely that your supervisor will give you a good recommendation in the future.

Recommendations

Companies seek information from references at various stages. Some prefer talking with references prior to an interview, and others, after a successful interview. Specific actions on your part will ensure that your references are treated with common courtesy and that references are prepared for the employer's call.

FIGURE 14-6

Example of a Resignation Message

SUBJECT: PLEASURE OF SERVING ARDEN ELECTRONICS

Begins with appreciative comments to buffer bad news.

My job as a Level 3 Internet Developer for the last two years has been a rewarding experience. It has taught me much about the development and maintenance of an effective retail Internet site.

Presents reasons that lead to main idea, the resignation.

Predicting customers' need for instant information has been challenging. From the time I declared a major in information systems, I have wanted to manage one of the sites where I regularly purchase merchandise. Before I accepted my present job, that goal was discussed. Now, that goal is becoming a reality, as I have accepted a job as the retail Internet manager for Franklin Cycles beginning one month from today. If satisfactory with you, I would like May 31 to be my last day in my position here.

States resignation, including additional details.

Conveys genuine appreciation for experience gained, and ends on cordial note.

Thank you for the confidence you placed in me, your positive rapport with the technology staff, and your expressions of appreciation for my work. As I continue my career, I will always recall pleasant memories of my position at Arden.

What individuals will you include as references for employment? What were the reasons for their selection?

- **Remind the reference that he/she had previously agreed to supply information about you.** Identify the job for which you are applying, give a complete address to which the message is to be sent, and indicate a date by which the prospective employer needs the message. By sharing information about job requirements and reporting recent job-related experiences, you may assist the reference in writing an effective message. Indicate your gratitude, but do not apologize for making the request. The reference has already agreed to write on your behalf and will likely take pleasure in assisting a deserving person.
- **Alert the reference of imminent requests for information, especially if considerable time has elapsed since the applicant and reference have last seen each other.** Enclosing a recent résumé and providing any other pertinent information (for example, name change) may enable the reference to write a message that is specific and convincing. To ensure on-target job references, politely explain the types of information you perceive relevant to the job sought: specific job skills, work ethic, attitude and demeanor toward work, leadership style, and so on. If the job search becomes longer than anticipated, a follow-up message to references explaining the delay and expressing gratitude for their efforts is appropriate.
- **Send a sincere, original thank-you message after a position has been accepted.** This thoughtful gesture will build a positive relationship with a person who may continue to be important to your career. The message in Figure 14-7 is brief and avoids clichés and exaggerated expressions of praise but instead gives specific examples of the importance of the reference's recommendation.

Visit your companion website at www.cengage.com/bcomm/lehman to learn how to provide recommendations for former employees or others in a professional capacity.

FIGURE 14-7

Example of a Thank-You Message to a Reference

States main idea of appreciation for recommendation. Informs reference of success in locating job.	Thank you so much for the letter of recommendation you prepared for my application to Ward & Cain. I learned today that I have been hired and will begin work next month.
Communicates sincere appreciation for assistance; uses specific examples and avoids exaggeration.	Because the position is in auditing, I believe your comments about my performance in your auditing and systems classes carried a great deal of weight. Mr. Copley commented he was impressed with the wealth of evidence and examples you provided to support your statements, unlike the general recommendations he frequently receives.
Restates main idea and anticipates continued relationship; is original and sincere.	Dr. Eshee, I appreciate your helping me secure an excellent position in a highly competitive job market. Thanks for the recommendation and your outstanding instruction. I look forward to talking with you about how I am faring in the real world when I return to campus for fall homecoming.

SHOWCASE PART 3

GE Earns Admiration and Applicants

"Bringing good things to life" at GE begins with offering opportunities to applicants who have the vision, energy, and confidence to strive for excellence. Success for GE, as for any other company, begins with hiring well and then developing employees effectively to pursue the vision of the organization. GE has repeatedly appeared among the top ten of Fortune magazine's "America's Most Admired."

Studies of the 10 most admired companies reveal that they attract far more applicants than they need, by an even greater ratio than *Fortune's* 100 Best Companies to Work For.[24] To find out why GE has repeatedly received the most admired designation, visit GE's career website and link to the information about the award:

www.gecareers.com

www.ge.com

Activities

- What assessment factors are considered in determining the "America's Most Admired" award winners?
- Using the assessment factors used in the award process as a guide, compose a list of questions that you might ask during an employment interview to determine the respectability of the company with which you are interviewing.

© FREDERICK FLORIN/AFP/GETTY IMAGES

Summary

1. Explain the nature of structured, unstructured, stress, group, and virtual interviews.

Interviewers and interviewees can be considered as buyers and sellers: Interviewers want to know whether job candidates can meet the needs of their firms before making a "purchase"; interviewees want to sell themselves based on sound knowledge, good work skills, and desirable personal traits. Structured interviews follow a preset, specific, format; unstructured interviews follow no standard format but explore for information. Computer-assisted interviews provide standard, reliable information on applicants during the preliminary interview stages. Stress interviews are designed to reveal how the candidate behaves in high-anxiety situations. Group interviews involve various personnel within the organization in the candidate interview process.

2. Explain the steps in the interview process.

Successful job candidates plan appropriately for the interview so that they will know basic information about the company, arrive on time dressed appropriately for the interview, and present a polished first impression following appropriate protocol. During the interview, the candidate presents his or her qualifications favorably and obtains information about the company to aid in deciding whether to accept a possible job offer.

3. Prepare effective answers to questions often asked in job interviews including illegal interview questions.

The successful job candidate effectively discusses key qualifications and skillfully asks questions that show initiative and genuine interest in the company. The candidate recognizes issues that fall outside the bounds of legal questioning. Refusing to answer an illegal question could be detrimental to your chances to secure a job, but answering the question may compromise your ethical values. An effective technique is to answer the legitimate concern behind the illegal question rather than to give a direct answer.

4. Compose effective messages related to employment (application forms, follow-up, thank-you, job-acceptance, job-refusal, resignation, and recommendation request).

The job applicant should:

- Complete application forms accurately, neatly, and completely.
- Send a follow-up message after a few weeks of no response to an application; include a reminder that an application has been made, present additional education or experience, and ask for action.
- Send a prompt thank-you message following an interview as a professional courtesy; express appreciation, refer to some point of discussion, and close with an expectation of the employer's decision.
- Write a deductive job-acceptance message that includes the acceptance, details, and a closing that confirms the date the employee will begin work.
- Write an inductive job-refusal message that includes a buffer beginning, reasons that lead to the refusal, a tactful decline to the offer, and a goodwill closing.
- Write a resignation notice that confirms that termination plans are definite and emphasizes positive aspects of the job.
- Prepare requests for recommendations that include specific information about the job requirements and the applicant's qualifications.

Chapter Review

1. What types of interviews are common in today's business environment and how do they differ from one another? (Obj. 1)
2. What information should you locate about a company with which you will interview? What means will you use to locate the information? (Obj. 2)
3. Write a brief statement that describes your unique value to an employer. Include information about your educational experiences, work experience, involvement in student organizations, and other pertinent information. (Obj. 2)
4. What nonverbal messages can an interviewee convey to favorably impress an interviewer? What negative nonverbal messages can be conveyed? (Obj. 2)
5. How do responses to direct and indirect interview questions differ? (Obj. 3)
6. What is a good strategy to use when you are asked about your major weakness? Provide a specific example you might use. (Obj. 3)
7. Discuss three ways an interviewee can handle an illegal interview question. What are the advantages and disadvantages of each? (Obj. 3)
8. How do the thank-you letter and the follow-up letter differ? What should each contain? (Obj. 4)
9. What guidelines should be followed in requesting a recommendation letter? (Obj. 4)
10. Which would be written deductively: (a) an acceptance letter, (b) a refusal letter, or (c) a resignation letter? What ideas should be included in each of these letters? (Obj. 5)

Digging Deeper

1. How can a job applicant maximize the likelihood of accepting the "right" job?
2. Explain why communication skills are the universal job requirement.
3. How relevant are references when information about an applicant can be easily located through an online search of blogs, social networking sites, and news sources?

Assessment

To check your understanding of the chapter, take the available online quizzes as directed by your instructor.

Check Your Communication
Interviews and Employment Messages

INTERVIEWS

Planning Stage

- ☐ Learn as much as you can about the job requirements, range of salary and benefits, and the interviewer.
- ☐ Research the company with whom you are interviewing (products/services, financial condition, growth potential, etc.).
- ☐ Identify the *specific* qualifications for the job and other pertinent information about the company.
- ☐ Plan your appearance, including clean, well groomed, and appropriate clothing.
- ☐ Arrive early with appropriate materials to communicate promptness and organization.
- ☐ Try to identify the type of interview you will have (structured, unstructured, virtual, stress, or group).

OPENING FORMALITIES

- ☐ Greet the interviewer by name with a smile, direct eye contact, and a firm handshake.
- ☐ Wait for the interviewer to ask you to be seated.
- ☐ Sit erect and lean forward slightly to convey interest.
- ☐ Avoid distractions such as looking at your cell phone.

BODY OF THE INTERVIEW

- ☐ Adapt your responses to the type of interview situation.
- ☐ Explain how your qualifications relate to the job requirements using multiple specific examples.
- ☐ Identify illegal interview questions; address the concern behind an illegal question or tactfully avoid answering the question.
- ☐ Ask pertinent questions that communicate intelligence and genuine interest in the company. Introduce questions throughout the interview where appropriate.
- ☐ Allow the interviewer to initiate a discussion of salary and benefits. Be prepared to provide a general salary range for applicants with your qualifications.

CLOSING THE INTERVIEW

- ☐ Watch for cues the interview is ending; rise, accept the interviewer's handshake, and communicate enthusiasm.
- ☐ Express appreciation for the interview and say you are eager to hear from the company.

EMPLOYMENT MESSAGES

Application Forms

- ☐ Read the entire form before completing it and follow instructions precisely.
- ☐ Complete the form neatly and accurately.
- ☐ Respond to all questions; insert N/A for questions that do not apply.
- ☐ Retain a copy for your records.

FOLLOW-UP MESSAGES

- ☐ Remind the receiver that your application is on file and you are interested in the job.
- ☐ Present additional education or experience gained since previous correspondence; do not repeat information presented earlier.
- ☐ Close with a courteous request for an interview.

THANK-YOU MESSAGES

- ☐ Express appreciation for the interview and mention the specific job for which you have applied.
- ☐ Refer to a specific point discussed in the interview.
- ☐ Close with a reference to an expected call or document conveying the interviewer's decision.

JOB-ACCEPTANCE MESSAGES

- ☐ Begin by accepting the job offer; specify position.
- ☐ Provide necessary details.
- ☐ Close with a courteous ending that confirms the date employment begins.

JOB-REFUSAL MESSAGES

- ☐ Begin with a neutral, related idea that leads to the explanation for the refusal.
- ☐ Present the reasons that lead to a diplomatic statement of the refusal.
- ☐ Close positively, anticipating future association with the company.

RESIGNATION MESSAGES

- ☐ Begin with a positive statement about the job to cushion the bad news.
- ☐ Present the explanation, state the resignation, and provide any details.
- ☐ Close with an appreciative statement about experience with the company.

RECOMMENDATION REQUESTS

- ☐ Begin with the request for the recommendation.
- ☐ Provide necessary details including reference to an enclosed résumé to ensure a targeted message.
- ☐ End with an appreciative statement for the reference's willingness to aid in the job search.
- ☐ Send a follow-up letter explaining delays and expressing appreciation for extended job searches.

THANK-YOU FOR A RECOMMENDATION

- ☐ Begin with expression of thanks for the recommendation.
- ☐ Convey sincere tone by avoiding exaggerated comments and providing specific examples of the value of the recommendation.
- ☐ End courteously, indicating future association with the reference.

Activities

1. Subscribing to a Career Newsletter (Objs. 1–4)

Subscribe to the career newsletter at the following link or to one of your choosing: www.quintcareers.com/QuintZine/. Create a career file that contains the following information about your selected career field:

a. Outlook for job openings
b. Typical starting salaries by region
c. Minimum requirements
d. Desired skills and experience
e. Networking opportunities
f. Recommended interview strategies
g. Potential for advancement

Submit your file to your instructor for review or use it as directed. A downloadable version of this application is available at your companion website at www.cengage.com/bcomm/lehman

2. Preparing to Answer Interview Questions Effectively (Objs. 2, 3)

Considering your career field, compose a list of potential questions you might be asked in a job interview. As directed by your instructor, complete one or more of the following:

a. Divide into groups of three and discuss appropriate answers to the interview questions.
b. Revise your answers, incorporating relevant feedback and being sure that the answers are truthful and reflect your individual personality.
c. Conduct mock interviews, with one person portraying the interviewer, the second person portraying the interviewee, and the third person performing a critique of the interview. Discuss the results of the critique.

3. Developing Appropriate Interview Questions (Objs. 2, 3)

Exchange a copy of your résumé with another student. Assume you are an employer who has received the résumé for one of the following positions:

a. A part-time job visiting high schools to sell seniors on the idea of attending your school.
b. A full-time summer job as a management intern in a local bank.
c. A campus job as an assistant in your school president's office.

Write several appropriate interview questions based on the résumé. With the other student, take turns playing the part of the interviewer and the interviewee. Critique each other's ability to answer the questions effectively.

4. Responding to Challenging Interview Questions (Objs. 2, 3)

Go to http://web.mit.edu/career/www/guide/star.html to review sample behavioral questions and a response prepared using the STAR method. Your instructor will then divide the class into pairs. One member will send an email message; the other will respond. The sender will compose an email message to the other member asking for a thoughtful response to five tough interview questions. At least one of the questions should be sensitive in nature (possibly illegal or quite close) and one should be a behavioral question. The team member receiving the message will email answers to the five questions. Send your instructor a copy of the original message and the answers to the questions. The instructor may ask that you reverse roles so that each of you has experience composing and answering difficult interview questions.

5. Cleaning Up that Home Page (Obj. 3)

Review the Facebook or MySpace page of another student in the class. Prepare a list of suggestions as to how to improve the impression the page might make on a prospective employer and reduce the likelihood of illegal questions in a job interview. Email the list to the student and to your instructor.

6. Critiquing a Job Application (Obj. 4)

Obtain a copy of a job application and bring it to class. In small groups, critique each application, commenting on the appropriateness of items included. Discuss how you would respond to each item. Share with the class any items you felt were inappropriate or illegal and how you would respond.

Applications

READ | THINK | WRITE | SPEAK | COLLABORATE

1. Rebounding from a Termination (Objs. 1–4)

Each year, many workers from every career field find themselves out of work. The process of becoming reemployed can be stressful, to say the least. Locate the following article that presents strategies for surviving a job termination and successfully becoming re-employed:

Lim, F. (2007, March 28). What to do after job termination. *Ezine Articles*. Available at http://ezinearticles.com/?What-to-Do-After-Job-Termination&id=506760

Using the information in the article, develop a checklist of strategies for locating and landing a desirable job. Add your own additional strategies. Submit your checklist to your instructor.

2. Investigating the Role of the Interviewer (Objs. 2, 3)

An interviewer's role is to hire the ideal employee for the company—the person with the skills, experience, and demeanor required for the position. Getting the necessary information to make the right decision requires knowledge and skill. Locate the following articles that provide advice to the interviewer for conducting a productive interview and avoiding legal liability:

Tips on conducting interviews. (2008). *Caterer & Hotelkeeper, 198*(4530), 49. Available from Business Source Complete database.

Willmer, D. (2007). Interviewers, you're on the hot seat, too. *Advertising* Age, 78(37), 63. Available from Business Source Complete database.

Prepare a short presentation on guidelines for interviewers. Include role playing that models appropriate interviewer behavior.

READ | THINK | WRITE | SPEAK | COLLABORATE

3. Researching a Company and Asking Questions of an Interviewer (Objs. 2, 3)

In small groups or individually, research a company of your choice. Use the chapter information in the "Study the Company" section as a guide for your research and locate the following article:

Daniel, L., & Brandon, C. (2006). Finding the right job fit: Asking the right questions—of yourself and a potential employer—can help ensure that you end up in the right place. *HRMagazine, 51*(3), 62–67. Available at http://findarticles.com/p/articles/mi_m3495/is_3_51/ai_n26804405/

Generate a list of 10 questions to ask an interviewer from the company you researched. Your original questions should communicate initiative, intelligence, and genuine interest in the company and the job. Submit a memo to your instructor that summarizes important facts about the organization and shows the rationale for the selection of your questions.

4. Understanding the Legality of Social Networking Profiles Sites in the Hiring Process (Obj. 3)

Employers typically understand the legal requirement to avoid unfair discrimination in the hiring process, and avoid eliciting information during an interview that could become grounds for a discrimination charge. Information that can be used in an unlawful discriminatory fashion is readily available on the social network profiles of many applicants. Locate the following article that discusses the practice of using social media profiles to gain information about job applicants:

Cook. J. (2008, December). Social gets legal. *Credit Union Management*, 58–59. Available from http://www.cues.org/pls/cuesp/!cues1.main?complex_id_in=3069489.3071923.3072774.12103209.page

Prepare a brief report describing the positives and negatives of using information from social media profiles to learn more about potential employees. Outline recommendations for appropriate actions.

5. Learning to Play Mind Games to Win an Interview (Objs. 2, 3)

Locate five brain teasers that could be incorporated into a job interview to identify an applicant's ability to think logically and creatively. Choose your brain teasers from the numerous brain teaser books, websites (such as http://amusingfacts.com/brain/), or share brain teasers that you know have been used during actual job interviews. Write a two-page report on the importance of logical and creative thinking to your chosen career field. Include the brain teasers you have selected as examples of how critical thinking can be assessed in an interview.

READ | THINK | WRITE | SPEAK | COLLABORATE

6. Following Up on a Job Application (Obj. 4)

Assume that you have applied for a position earlier in this current class term. Make the assumption you prefer about the position: You applied for (a) an immediate part-time job, (b) a full-time job for next summer, (c) a cooperative education assignment or internship, or (d) a full-time job immediately after your graduation. Mentioning the courses you have completed this term, write a follow-up letter for the position for which you have applied.

7. Saying "Thank-You" for an Interview (Obj. 4)

Assume that you were interviewed for the job for which you applied in Application 6. Write a thank-you email message to the interviewer; send it to your instructor or submit as directed.

8. Accepting a Job Offer (Obj. 4)

Write a letter of acceptance for the job (internship) for which you applied in Application 6. Assume you have been asked to start work in two weeks. Provide additional details concerning work arrangements, salary, etc. Supply an address.

9. Refusing a Job Offer Diplomatically (Obj. 4)

Assume that the job search identified in Application 6 was successful; you were offered positions with two firms. Write a letter refusing one of the job offers. Because you want to maintain a positive relationship with the company for whom you are refusing to work, provide specific reasons for your decision. Supply an address.

10. Resigning from a Job (Obj. 4)

Write a letter resigning from your current job. If you are not currently employed, supply fictitious information.

11. Contacting Job References (Obj. 4)

Write an email message requesting someone to serve as an employment reference. Your reference could be a professor, past or present employer, employee at the company you hope to join who referred you to the position, or other appropriate person. Provide specific information about how your qualifications relate to the job requirements and include a résumé. Now assume your job search is taking much longer than you had hoped. Because your references have been providing recommendations for six months now, you must write expressing your gratitude and updating them on the status of your job search. If your qualifications have changed, include an updated résumé. Compose an email to one of your references. Send your request and followup messages to your instructor or submit as directed.

READ | THINK | WRITE | SPEAK | COLLABORATE

12. Interviewing Tips from the Experts (Objs. 2, 3)

Interview a manager preferably in your field who conducts job interviews regularly. Discuss techniques that will improve your interviewing techniques. Share your findings with the class in a short presentation or contribute to a blog related to job interview strategies.

13. Sending the Right Nonverbal Signals (Obj. 3)

While what you say in an interview will obviously be important, you will also have to be careful to send the right unspoken signals. Your numerous nonverbal messages will also be noted by a prospective employer. Locate the following articles about nonverbal communication in interviews:

McCollum, K. (2009). Louder than words. *Office Pro, 69*(1), 18–20. Available from the Business Source Complete database.

Shepherd, L. C. (2007). Reading body language can offer insight to HR pros. *Employee Benefit News, 21*(6), 22. Available from the Business Source Complete database.

In teams of three or four, prepare a presentation on the topic of nonverbal communication in interviews; include demonstrations of appropriate and inappropriate nonverbal messages.

READ | THINK | WRITE | SPEAK | COLLABORATE

14. Organizing an Employer Panel (Objs. 1–4)

Working with a small group, organize an employer panel for a class session on successful interviewing. Include the following elements in your panel activity:

a. Contact employers who would be willing to serve on the panel and share their views about successful job interviewing.
b. In advance of the panel presentation, prepare a list of questions to be asked of the panel.
c. Select a team member to serve as moderator for the panel discussion.
d. As part of the panel discussion, solicit questions from the class for response by the guest employers.

15. Conducting a Live or Virtual Job Interview (Objs. 1–3)

Visit your companion website at www.cengage.com/bcomm/lehman for information about the types of questions typically asked in a job interview. Identify another student in your class with similar career goals, and together select a related job listing from a newspaper or web posting. Using that job listing, develop a set of questions for an employment interview. Submit your set of questions to your instructor for approval. Stage an interview, with one of you portraying the role of the interviewer and one the interviewee. Be prepared to conduct your interview in a class session or follow your instructor's directions for recording it or conducting it by phone or videoconferencing.

CASES

© ALEX SEGRE/ALAMY

1. Volunteerism Is Alive and Well in Corporate America

Thousands of employees of Deloitte & Touche USA LLP (Deloitte) annually set aside their regular work to make their communities their clients through the company's IMPACT Day, a one-day example of the firm's year-round commitment to volunteer service. Deloitte's nearly 40,000 employees are encouraged to engage in a variety of projects, many of which involve the contribution of their business knowledge and experience to help nonprofits deal with strategic, operational, and financial business challenges.

"Whether you're leading a multi-billion dollar enterprise or a grassroots nonprofit organization, the management challenges are similar. How do you operate with greater efficiency? How do you stretch a finite budget? How do you motivate and develop people?" said Barry Salzberg, chief executive officer of Deloitte & Touche USA. "Deloitte professionals help our clients deal with these challenges every day. So we can have the greatest impact in the community when we draw upon our experiences and insights to help nonprofits in the same ways we advise our clients."[25] Evan Hochberg, Deloitte's, national director of community involvement, points to research the organization conducted that shows a need among nonprofits for skills-based contributions from corporate volunteers. He noted that more than three-quarters of nonprofit leaders think their organization's business practices could improve significantly if volunteers were to donate their professional skills. Yet, only 12 percent of nonprofits say they actually work with such volunteers.

IMPACT benefits not only the local communities served but also Deloitte itself. Company benefits derived from the IMPACT program include enhancements in employee recruiting, workplace morale, and professional development, as well as the favorable publicity gained from showcasing employees' knowledge and experience. According to Hochberg, "People enjoy working for and with companies whose mission, vision and values align with their own."[26] Deloitte research has indicated that such satisfaction is especially important for younger, Gen Y employees, with 97 percent of Gen Y volunteers believing companies should provide opportunities for their employees to volunteer their work-related skills or talents to nonprofits. More than three out of five of those surveyed (62 percent) said they would prefer to work for companies that offer them skills-based volunteer opportunities.

Application:

1. Read more about Deloitte's IMPACT program:
   Welch, S, B, (2009, June 1). Deloitte workshop to help non-profits survive recession. *Crain's Detroit Business*. Available at www.crainsdetroit.com/article/20090601/FREE/906019936
2. Select another business firm of your choice and study its product or services, along with its mission and vision statement. Outline a volunteer service plan by which company employees could contribute professional skills and knowledge to address community needs.
3. Design an electronic slide show presentation to share your volunteer service plan with the class.

© BBC LTD./COURTESY: EVERETT COLLECTION

2. Video Case: The Office: Interviewing: The Wrong Way

In this clip, David interviews two candidates for an administrative support position.

Complete the following activities as directed by your instructor after viewing the video:

1. In small groups discuss the problems encountered because of David's interview style. What interview style does David use? How does he handle the candidates differently? What problems might result from his interview techniques?
2. As David's supervisor, compose an email to all managers with hiring capacity outlining effective interviewing strategies. Your message should include a list of standard questions to ask, illegal questions to avoid, and suggestions for creating a productive interview environment.

3. To Tell or Not to Tell: Disclosure of Potentially Damaging Information in an Employment Reference

Highly publicized and widespread business scandals have led to a significant increase in reference checking. While some firms do their own checking, others turn to the expertise of reference-checking services. Until recently, the rule for employers for responding to reference checks about their employees was fairly simple: The less said, the better. The risk of providing employment references to prospective employers is that former employees may sue if your references are unfavorable and lead to job rejection or if they constitute invasion of privacy. The employers may be liable to a former employee for defamation if the employer communicates to a prospective employer or other person a false statement that results in damage to the former employee's reputation. Defamation is commonly referred to as "slander" if the communication is verbal and as "libel" if the communication is written. Employers have traditionally been cautioned about relating information that is not formally documented or for which no objective evidence exists. Thus, the more information provided, the greater the likelihood of a defamation or privacy invasion suit by the former employee. Awards in successful suits may include damages for lost earnings, mental anguish, pain and suffering, and even punitive damages.

Recent court decisions may have changed all of that or at least created confusion for employers about what to disclose. If an employer gives a positive reference for a fired employee, the employee could sue for wrongful termination. In situations where the employer knows that a former employee has a history of criminal violence or extremely aggressive behavior, the employer may have a legal obligation to provide such information to a prospective employer. Questions arise as to what to do if you are not sure that the information about the previous employee is true. The risk of remaining silent is that you could be sued for negligently failing to disclose the information if the former employee were to harm someone on the next job. On the other hand, you could be sued for defamation if you do disclose the information and the former employee can successfully establish that it is not true.[27]

Some attorneys recommend that companies have employees who are leaving the organization sign a form releasing the employer from any liability for responding truthfully during the course of giving references. All inquiries for references should be handled through an established point of contact, and only written requests for references should be considered. Only accurate and verifiable information should be reported.[28]

Visit your companion website at www.cengage.com/bcomm/lehman to link to web resources related to this topic. As directed by your instructor, complete one or more of the following.

1. Make a list of types of statements that a former employer should generally avoid making when giving employment references.
2. Write an organizational policy that addresses the appropriate guidelines for giving employee references. Include statements concerning appropriate content and the manner in which such information should be issued.
3. Formulate a legal argument that presents the conflict between the potential employer's right to know and the previous employer's right to avoid possible defamation charges. Present both sides in a short written report or presentation.

4. Inside View: The Job Interview

In today's diverse world, employers interview job candidates from various cultures. Cross-cultural interviewing can increase the chances for misunderstanding or rejecting a talented candidate. Handshakes, eye contact, body language, and dress are among the culturally related factors that may influence an interviewer's success. How can you avoid making a negative impression during a job interview? As an employer, how will you avoid making false assumptions during a cross-cultural interview?

All recruiters want to hire the best candidates, but cross-cultural misunderstandings during the interview may lead to rejection of qualified individuals. Candidates from different nationalities and cultures can be discriminated against through misperceptions and poor judgments in cross-cultural interviews.

View the "The Job Interview" video segment at your companion website at www.cengage.com/bcomm/lehman to learn more about the problem of cultural barriers in job interviews.

Reflect:

1. How can an interviewer's assumptions about what should or should not happen in an interview create cultural misperceptions?
2. What elements of body language and physical appearance can cause cultural misunderstandings?
3. How can eye contact, tone of voice, posture, showing emotions, the giving of information, and the use of language vary depending on cultural background?

React:

Locate the following article that provides suggestions on cross-cultural interviewing and the difficulties managers can encounter when interviewing applicants of various cultures.

Cross-cultural interviews. (2009). *Kwintessential.* Available at www.kwintessential.co.uk/cultural-services/articles/cross-cultural-interviews.html

- List several types of behavior that could confuse a job interviewer who is not aware of cultural differences.
- Conduct a mock interview with a classmate of another culture. How can an expression of your surprise about the candidate's response to a question say something about your assumptions?

Appendices

Appendix A
Document Format and Layout Guide

First impressions are lasting ones, and the receiver's first impression of your document is its appearance and format. This section presents techniques for producing an appealing document as well as standard formats for letters, envelopes, memos, email messages, and reports.

Document Appearance

To convey a positive, professional image, a document should be balanced attractively for visual appeal, proofread carefully, and, when appropriate, printed on high-quality paper. Other factors that affect the overall appearance of your document are justification of margins, spacing after punctuation, abbreviations, and word division. Review the following guidelines to ensure that your documents are accurate in these areas.

Paper. The quality of paper reflects the professionalism of the company and allows a company to control communication costs effectively. Paper quality is measured by cotton-fiber content and weight. High-cotton bond paper has a crisp crackle, is firm to the pencil touch, is difficult to tear, and ages without deterioration or chemical breakdown. The heavier the paper, the higher the quality. Another characteristic of high-quality paper is the watermark, a design incorporated into the paper that can be seen clearly when held up to the light. For a professional appearance, the watermark is positioned so that it can be read across the sheet in the same direction as the printing.

The standard paper size for business documents is 8½ by 11 inches in the United States, but this standard varies from country to country. Most business letters are produced on company letterhead printed on 16- or 20-pound bond paper. Extremely important external documents such as reports and proposals may be printed on 24-pound bond paper with 100-percent cotton content. Memorandums, business forms, and other intercompany documents may be printed on lighter-weight paper with lower cotton-fiber content. Envelopes and plain sheets used for second and successive pages of multiple-page documents should be of the same weight, cotton-fiber content, and color as the letterhead.

Justification of Margins. For a professional, personalized look, most business documents are printed with ragged right margins, referred to as **left justified margins.**

The uneven margins give the document a personalized look that is easier to read than justified copy. Justified margins can give a highly professional appearance to formal documents such as newsletters, reports, and proposals.

Special Symbols. To give documents the appearance of a professionally typeset document, use special symbols available in your word processing software. For example, insert an em dash (—) rather than keying two hyphens (--) to show an abrupt change of thought; insert the symbol for ½ rather than keying 1/2. Some word processors automatically make these changes when letters and symbols are keyed.

Revision Marks. When proofreading documents for editing by yourself or others, mark revisions to your documents using the standard proofreaders' marks included at the companion website for Chapter 4 at www.cengage.com/bcomm/lehman.

Word Division. Word division is necessary at times to avoid extreme variations in line length but should be avoided when possible. If words must be divided, follow acceptable word division rules that are available at the companion website, www.cengage.com/bcomm/lehman. Word processing software can automatically hyphenate based on accepted word division rules, or you make the decisions manually.

Letter and Punctuation Styles

Decisions about page format impact the effectiveness of the message. Many companies have policies that dictate the page layout, letter and punctuation style, and other formatting issues. In the absence of company policy, make your format choices from among standard acceptable options illustrated in this appendix.

Page Layout. The default margins set by word processing software typically reflect standard line length to increase the efficiency of producing business correspondence. Letters typically begin two inches from the top of the page or at least one-half inch below the letterhead. Short letters (one or two paragraphs) are centered on the page.

CHANGING TECHNOLOGY

Current word processing software has increased the default line spacing to 1.15 spaces between lines and the space between paragraphs to 10 points for easier on-screen reading. If you prefer the tighter, traditional spacing, simply adjust the line spacing to 1.0 and eliminate the automatic space after paragraphs. To conserve space but keep the fresh, open look, try reducing the line spacing in the letter address or the signature block but retain the wider line and paragraph spacing in the body of the letter. Another new default is the crisp, open Calibri font (replacing the common Times New Roman), designed for easy reading on computer screens.

NEW DOCUMENT LOOK	TRADITIONAL SPACING
July 24, 2011 ↓2 Mr. Alex Starr 125 Forrest Avenue Naperville, IL 60565-0125 ↓1 Dear Mr. Starr ↓1 The downturn in the housing market has presented appraisers with unprecedented challenges. New strategies are required in today's environment to identify objective comparable sales for estimating current home values. ↓1 The Society of Real Estate Appraisers is rising to meet this challenge . . .	July 24, 2011 ↓4 Mr. Alex Starr 125 Forrest Avenue Naperville, IL 60565-0125 ↓2 Dear Mr. Starr ↓2 The downturn in the housing market has presented appraisers with unprecedented challenges. New strategies are required in today' s environment to identify objective comparable sales for estimating current home values. ↓2 The Society of Real Estate Appraisers is rising to meet this challenge . . .

Punctuation Styles. Two punctuation styles are customarily used in business letters: mixed and open. Letters using mixed punctuation style have a colon after the salutation and a comma after the complimentary close. Letters using open punctuation style omit a colon after the salutation and a comma after the complimentary close. Mixed punctuation is the traditional style; however, efficiency-conscious companies have increasingly adopted the open style (and other similar format changes), which is easier to remember.

Letter Styles. Business letters are typically formatted in either block or modified block letter styles. Review Figures A-1 and A-2 to observe the differences in each style.

- **Block.** Companies striving to reduce the cost of producing business documents adopt the easy-to-learn, efficient block format. All lines (including paragraphs) begin at the left margin.
- **Modified block.** Modified block is the traditional letter format still used in many companies. The dateline, complimentary close, and signature block begin at the horizontal center of the page. Paragraphs may be indented one-half inch if the writer prefers or the company policy requires it. However, the indention creates unnecessary keystrokes that increase the production cost. All other lines begin at the left margin.

Standard Letter Parts. Business professionals expect to see seven standard letter parts arranged in the proper sequence. Other parts are optional and may be included when necessary. The proper placement of these parts is shown in the model letters in

FIGURE A-1

Block Letter Style with Open Punctuation

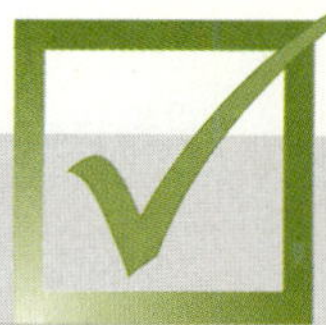

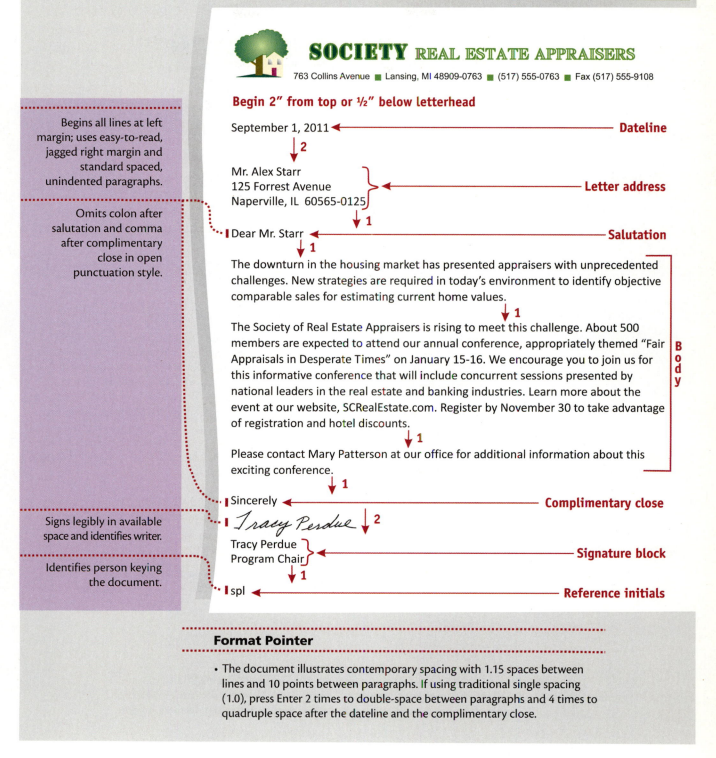

Begins all lines at left margin; uses easy-to-read, jagged right margin and standard spaced, unindented paragraphs.

Omits colon after salutation and comma after complimentary close in open punctuation style.

Signs legibly in available space and identifies writer.

Identifies person keying the document.

SOCIETY REAL ESTATE APPRAISERS
763 Collins Avenue ■ Lansing, MI 48909-0763 ■ (517) 555-0763 ■ Fax (517) 555-9108

Begin 2" from top or ½" below letterhead

September 1, 2011 ← **Dateline**

↓ 2

Mr. Alex Starr
125 Forrest Avenue
Naperville, IL 60565-0125 ← **Letter address**

↓ 1

Dear Mr. Starr ← **Salutation**

↓ 1

The downturn in the housing market has presented appraisers with unprecedented challenges. New strategies are required in today's environment to identify objective comparable sales for estimating current home values.

↓ 1

The Society of Real Estate Appraisers is rising to meet this challenge. About 500 members are expected to attend our annual conference, appropriately themed "Fair Appraisals in Desperate Times" on January 15-16. We encourage you to join us for this informative conference that will include concurrent sessions presented by national leaders in the real estate and banking industries. Learn more about the event at our website, SCRealEstate.com. Register by November 30 to take advantage of registration and hotel discounts.

↓ 1

Please contact Mary Patterson at our office for additional information about this exciting conference.

Body

↓ 1

Sincerely ← **Complimentary close**

Tracy Perdue ↓ 2

Tracy Perdue
Program Chair ← **Signature block**

↓ 1

spl ← **Reference initials**

Format Pointer

- The document illustrates contemporary spacing with 1.15 spaces between lines and 10 points between paragraphs. If using traditional single spacing (1.0), press Enter 2 times to double-space between paragraphs and 4 times to quadruple space after the dateline and the complimentary close.

Figures A-1 and A-2; a discussion of each standard part follows. Once you're familiar with these standard parts, explore the word processing feature referred to in Word 2007 as *Quick Parts*, that allows you to format and save these standard elements for insertion in a document as needed.

FIGURE A-2

Modified Block Letter Style with Mixed Punctuation

Tiger Lanes Entertainment Center
1245 Curry Street
Myrtle Beach, SC 29572-1245
843.555.9750

Begin 2″ from top or ½″ below letterhead

April 3, 2011 ← **Dateline**

↓ 2

Mr. Brent Cox
1240 Coastal Lane
North Myrtle Beach, SC 29258-1240 ← **Letter address**

↓ 1

Dear Mr. Cox: ← **Salutation**

↓ 1

Thank you for choosing Tiger Lanes for your family's recent evening of bowling. The facilities, equipment, and service areas were designed to provide you with the finest bowling experience available today.

↓ 1

The current bowling fee structure was developed to limit the time spent waiting for a bowling lane. Research conducted by the bowling industry indicates charging by the minute maximizes the usage of bowling lanes which limits the amount of time customers must wait for a lane. Because the demand for lanes is not as great during the weekday, the rate charged per minute is adjusted to a lower per minute charge.

↓ 1

To make certain our customers are aware of the charges, signs identifying fee structures are posted throughout our facility. A minute counter appears on each lane's scoring monitor to indicate the total charge customers should expect to pay on checkout. The $180 fee you paid last Saturday night for three hours of bowling on two lanes was based on the peak hour rate of $.50 per minute.

↓ 1

Mr. Cox, please visit Tiger Lanes, the next time your family is looking for bowling entertainment. A bowling lane and many amenities will be available for your enjoyment.

Body

↓ 1

Sincerely, ← **Complimentary close**

Lauren Peattie ↓ 2

Lauren Peattie ← **Signature block**

Begins dateline, complimentary close, and signature block at horizontal center.

Includes colon after salutation in mixed punctuation style.

Uses standard spaced, unindented paragraphs, but indentions are acceptable with modified block style.

Includes comma after complimentary close in mixed punctuation style.

Signs legibly in available space and identifies writer.

Omits reference initials since writer keyed document.

Format Pointer

- The document illustrates contemporary spacing. If using traditional spacing (1.0) between lines, press Enter 2 times to double-space between paragraphs and 4 times to quadruple space after the dateline and the complimentary close.

Heading. When the letterhead shows the company name, address, phone and/or fax number, and logo, the letter begins with the dateline. Use the month-day-year format (September 2, 2011) for documents prepared for U.S. audiences. When preparing government documents or writing to an international audience, use the day-month-year format (2 September 2011). Company policy may require another format.

Letter Address. The ***letter address*** includes a personal or professional title (e.g., Mr., Ms., or Dr.), the name of the person and company receiving the letter, and the complete address. United States Post Service (USPS) official abbreviations for states, districts, and provinces are available at the companion website at www.cengage.com/bcomm/lehman or from the USPS website (www.usps.com/). Space two times between the official abbreviations and the zip code.

Salutation. The ***salutation*** is the greeting that opens a letter. To show courtesy for the receiver, include a personal or professional title (for example, Mr., Ms., Dr., Senator). Refer to the *first line* of the letter address to determine an appropriate salutation. "Dear Ms. Henson" is an appropriate salutation for a letter addressed to Ms. Donna Henson (first line of letter address). "Ladies and Gentlemen" is an appropriate salutation for a letter addressed to "Wyatt Enterprises," where the company name is keyed as the first line of the letter address.

Body. The ***body*** contains the message of the letter. Because extra space separates the paragraphs, paragraph indention, which requires extra setup time, is not necessary. However, for organizations that require paragraph indention as company policy, the modified block format (Figure A-2) with indented paragraphs is the appropriate choice.

Complimentary Close. The ***complimentary close*** is a phrase used to close a letter in the same way that you say good-bye at the end of a conversation. To create goodwill, choose a complimentary close that reflects the formality of your relationship with the receiver. Typical examples are "Sincerely," "Cordially," and "Respectfully." Using "yours" in the close has fallen out of popularity (as in "Sincerely yours" and "Very truly yours"). "Sincerely" is considered neutral and is thus appropriate in a majority of business situations. "Cordially" can be used for friendly messages, and "Respectfully" is appropriate when you are submitting information for the approval of another.

Signature Block. The ***signature block*** consists of the writer's name keyed below the complimentary close, allowing space for the writer to sign legibly. A woman may include a courtesy title to indicate her preference (e.g., Miss, Ms., Mrs.), and a woman or man may use a title to distinguish a name used by both genders. (e.g., Shane, Leslie, or Stacy) or initials (E. M. Goodman). A business or professional title may be placed on the same line with the writer's name or directly below it as appropriate to achieve balance.

Title on the Same Line	*Title on the Next Line*
Ms. Leslie Tatum, President	Ms. E. M. Goodman Assistant Manager
Perry Watson, Manager	Richard S. Templeton Human Resources Director

Reference Initials. The ***reference initials*** consist of the keyboard operator's initials keyed in lowercase below the signature block. The reference initials and the signature block identify the persons involved in preparing a letter in the event of later questions. Reference initials are frequently omitted when a letter is keyed by the writer. However, company policy may require that the initials of all people involved in preparing a letter be placed in the reference initials line to identify accountability. For example, the following reference initials show the indicated level of responsibility. The reference line might also include department identification or other information as required by the organization.

SF:lm:cd

Person who signed document | **Person who wrote document** | **Person who keyed document**

Optional Letter Parts. Other letter parts may be added depending on the particular situation. Proper placement is illustrated in Figure A-3.

Delivery and Addressee Notations. A ***delivery notation*** provides a record of how a letter was sent. Examples include *Air Mail*, *Certified Mail*, *Federal Express*, *Registered Mail*, and *Fax Transmission*. Addressee notations such as *Confidential* or *Personal* give instructions on how a letter should be handled.

Attention Line. An ***attention line*** is used for directing correspondence to an individual or department within an organization while still officially addressing the letter to the organization. The attention line directs a letter to a specific person (*Attention Ms. Laura Ritter*), position within a company (*Attention Human Resources Director*), or department (*Attention Purchasing Department*). Current practice is to place the attention line in the letter address on the line directly below the company name and use the same format for the envelope address. The appropriate salutation in a letter with an attention line is "Ladies and Gentlemen."

Reference Line. A ***reference line*** (*Re: Contract No. 983-9873*) directs the receiver to source documents or to files.

Subject Line. A ***subject line*** tells the receiver what a letter is about and sets the stage for the receiver to understand the message. For added emphasis, use initial capitals or all capitals, or center the subject line if modified block style is used. Omit the word *subject* because its position above the body clearly identifies its function.

Second-Page Heading. The second and succeeding pages of multiple-page letters and memorandums are keyed on plain paper of the same quality as the letterhead. Identify the second and succeeding pages with a ***second-page heading*** including the name of the addressee, page number, and the date. Place the heading one inch from the top edge of the paper using either a vertical or horizontal format as illustrated. The horizontal format looks attractive with the modified block format and may prevent the document from requiring additional pages. In word processing software, the header feature with convenient pre-built formats simplifies the addition of this element.

CHANGING TECHNOLOGY 

Vertical Format

Communication Systems, Inc.

Page 2

January 19, 2011

Horizontal Format

Communication Systems, Inc.	2	January 19, 2011

FIGURE A-3

Optional Letter Parts

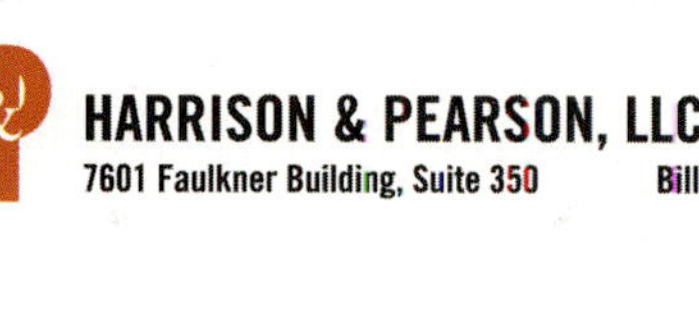

HARRISON & PEARSON, LLC, CPAs
7601 Faulkner Building, Suite 350 Billings, MT 59101-7601 Telephone: (406) 555-3400 Fax: (406) 555-6874

March 1, 2011
↓1
FAX TRANSMISSION ← **Delivery notation** — Identifies method of delivery.
↓1
Communication Systems, Inc.
Attention Ms. Margaret Daniel ← **Attention line** — Directs document addressed to a company to a specific person.
250 North Lexington Street
Atlanta, GA 30311-5309
↓1
Re: Engagement No. 39-29-3773 ← **Reference line** — Identifies account number.
↓1
Ladies and Gentlemen:
↓1
Engagement Agreement for Communication Systems, Inc. ← **Subject line** — Provides useful subject line.
↓1
Harrison & Pearson is pleased to confirm arrangements to audit the financial statements of Communication Systems, Inc., for the year ended June 30, 2011.

Begin 1" from top of page

Communication Systems, Inc.
Page 2
March 1, 2011
} ← **Second-page heading** — Identifies second page.
↓1
Please submit the documents listed in the enclosed pre-audit checklist by March 15, 2011, to facilitate an efficient audit and minimize your audit fee. Please let us know if you have questions prior to our arrival.
↓1
Sincerely,
↓1
HARRISON & PEARSON, LLC, CPAS ← **Company name in signature block** — Emphasizes document is written on behalf of company.
Stephen P. Numez ↓2
Stephen P. Numez
Audit Partner
↓1
Enclosure ← **Enclosure notation** — Alerts reader that item is included.
↓1
c Mr. David Banks ← **Copy notation** — Indicates courtesy copy was sent.
↓1
C:/communicationsystems/engagement.doc ← **Computer file notation** — Adds computer file notation for file copy.

Enclosure Notation. An ***enclosure notation*** indicates that additional items (brochure, price list, résumé) are included in the same envelope. Key the plural form (Enclosures) if more than one item is enclosed. You may identify the number of enclosures (Enclosures: 3) or the specific item enclosed (Enclosure: Bid Proposal). Avoid abbreviations (Enc.) that may give the impression that your work is hurried and careless. Some companies use the word "Attachment" on memorandums when the accompanying items may be stapled or clipped and not placed in an envelope.

Copy Notation. A ***copy notation*** indicates that a courtesy copy of the document was sent to the person(s) listed. Include the person's personal or professional title and full name, after keying "c" for copy or "cc" for courtesy copy. Key the copy notation below the enclosure notation, reference initials, or signature block (depending on the optional letter parts used).

Computer File Notation. A ***computer file notation*** provides the path and file name of the letter. Some companies require this documentation on the file copy to facilitate revision. Place the computer file notation a line space below the last keyed line of the letter.

Envelopes

An envelope should be printed on the same quality and color of paper as the letter and generated using the convenient envelope feature of your word processing program. Adjust defaults as needed to adhere to the recommendations of the United States Postal Service (USPS). To increase the efficiency of mail handling, use the two-letter abbreviations for states, territories, and Canadian provinces. USPS official state abbreviations are available at the USPS website (www.usps.com/).

Most companies today do not follow the traditional USPS recommendation to key the letter address in all capital letters with no punctuation. The mixed case format matches the format used in the letter address, looks more professional, and allows the writer to generate the envelope automatically without rekeying text. No mail handling efficiency is lost as today' s optical character readers that sort mail can read both upper- and lowercase letters easily. Proper placement of the address on a large envelope generated using an envelope template is shown here.

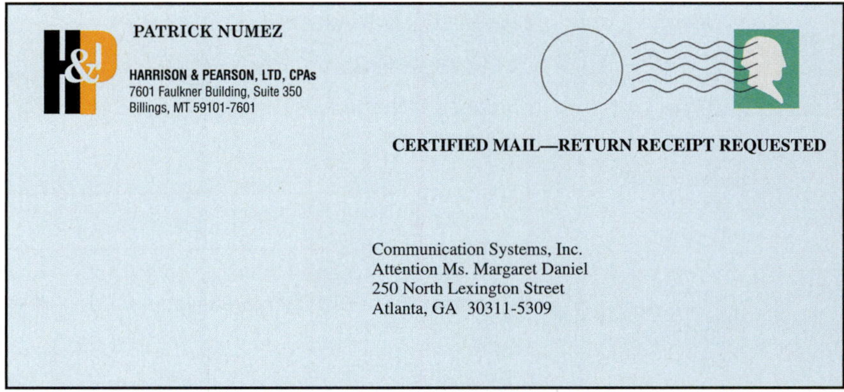
PATRICK NUMEZ

HARRISON & PEARSON, LTD, CPAs
7601 Faulkner Building, Suite 350
Billings, MT 59101-7601

CERTIFIED MAIL—RETURN RECEIPT REQUESTED

Communication Systems, Inc.
Attention Ms. Margaret Daniel
250 North Lexington Street
Atlanta, GA 30311-5309

Additionally, to create a highly professional image, business communicators should fold letters to produce the fewest number of creases. The proper procedures for folding letters for large and small and envelopes appear on the companion website at www.cengage.com/bcomm/lehman.

Memorandum Formats

To increase productivity of memorandums (memos), which are internal messages, companies use formats that are easy to input and that save time. Most companies use customized or standard memo templates found in most word processing software that include the basic headings (TO, FROM, DATE, SUBJECT) to guide the writer in providing the needed transmittal information. Memos may be printed on memo forms, plain paper, or letterhead depending on the preference of the company. Follow the guidelines for formatting a memo illustrated in Figure A-4.

FIGURE A-4

Memo Format

Davis Metal Buildings
172 Binford Drive — Long Beach, MS 39566
(800) 555-5291 — Fax: (218) 555-9214

Begin 2″ from top or ½″ below letterhead

TO: Jacob Bivins, President

FROM: Hannah Robertson, Vice President of Sales *HR*

DATE: April 4, 2011

SUBJECT: Customer Support Proposal

Heading

↓ 1

Taking advantage of video technology can provide our company with a competitive advantage by enhancing technical support to today's technology-oriented consumers.

↓ 1

Assembly Podcasts

↓ 1

Transforming hundreds of parts delivered in a box into a storage building requires thorough instructions and close attention to detail. Because these buildings are assembled outdoors on site, our customers have been limited to following long, often confusing written instructions. By downloading a free podcast including a video of the assembly process, customers can have the video with them, on site, providing specific instructions and pictures of every required assembly procedure. With the high resolution of today's digital screen iPods, our customers will have clear pictures of even the most minute assembly details.

Live Chat Feature

Customers calling our current support line receive the best personal service available. However, after the call is ended, their ability to correct the problem depends on how well they recall or have made notes of the support rep's advice. Unlike a phone call, an online chat feature at our website would allow our reps to integrate explanatory text and useful diagrams in a format that customers could view from their cell phones while assembling our product.

Call me when you are available to discuss the attached cost projections and projected timeline for developing the instructional podcasts.

Body

Attachments ← **Enclosure notation**

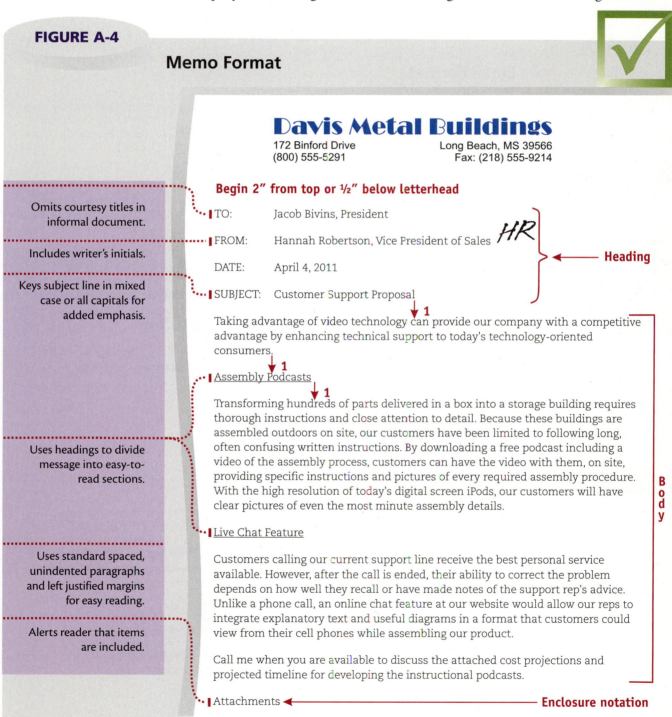

Omits courtesy titles in informal document.

Includes writer's initials.

Keys subject line in mixed case or all capitals for added emphasis.

Uses headings to divide message into easy-to-read sections.

Uses standard spaced, unindented paragraphs and left justified margins for easy reading.

Alerts reader that items are included.

Email Format

While certain email formats are standard, some degree of flexibility exists in formatting email messages. Primarily, be certain your message is easy to read and represents the standards of formality that your company has set. The following guidelines and the model email illustrated in Figure A-5 will assist you in formatting professional email messages:

FIGURE A-5

Email Format

Includes descriptive subject line.

Includes appropriate salutation for group of coworkers.

Uses email abbreviation and emoticon in informal message to a familiar audience.

Includes signature file that identifies writer.

Includes quote to communicate company culture.

To:	All professional staff
From:	Lyndsey Steele
Subject:	Ethan Keller Joins the Firm

Everyone,

I'm pleased to announce that Ethan Keller will join us soon to establish a forensic accounting unit within the firm. FYI, Ethan brings over 20 years of investigative experience with several branches of government, most recently with the FBI.

Initially Ethan will provide litigation support for local lawyers and data analysis for our existing assurance clients. Once Ethan's reputation in the business community is established, we anticipate that this unit will be engaged to investigate alleged frauds, particularly embezzlement and money laundering.

Ethan merits your full support. Please extend him a sincere welcome when he arrives on July 1. :-)

Thanks,

Lyndsey

Lyndsey Steele, Managing Partner
Franklin Corporation
875 Marshall Freeway, Suite 4500
San Diego, CA 92101
(858) 555-3000, Ext. 6139 Fax: (853) 555-9759
lyndsey.steele@franklin.com

"People don't care how much you know, until they know how much you care."
– John C. Maxwell

Format Pointers

- Email message includes mixed case for easy reading. It illustrates single spaced, unindented paragraphs and short lines for complete screen display.
- Keeps format simple for quick download and compatibility.

- **Include an appropriate salutation and closing.** You might write "Dear" and the person's name or simply the person's first name when messaging someone for the first time. Casual expressions such as "Hi" and "Later" are appropriate for personal messages but not serious business email. A closing of "Sincerely" is considered quite formal for email messages; instead, a simple closing such as "Best wishes" or "Thank you" provides a courteous end to your message.
- **Include a signature file at the end of the message.** The signature file (known as a *.sig*) contains a few lines of text that include your full name and title, mailing and email addresses, phone and fax numbers, and any other information you want people to know about you.
- **Format for easy readability.**

Following these suggestions for email message creation:

- Limit each message to one screen to minimize scrolling. If you need more space, consider a short email message with a lengthier message attached as a word processing file. Be certain the recipient can receive and read the attachment.
- Limit the line length to 60 characters so that the entire line is displayed on the monitor without scrolling.
- Use short, unindented paragraphs. Separate paragraphs with an extra space.
- Use mixed case for easy reading. Typing in all capital letters is perceived as shouting in email and considered rude online behavior.
- Emphasize a word or phrase by surrounding it with quotation marks or keying in uppercase letters when email has limited word processing functions such as color, highlighting, or alternate font styles.

- **Use emoticons or email abbreviations in moderation when you believe the receiver will understand and approve.** *Emoticons*, created by keying combinations of symbols to produce "sideways" faces, are a shorthand way of lightening the mood, adding emotion to email messages, and attempting to compensate for nonverbal cues lost in one-way communication:

:-)	smiling, indicates humor or sarcasm	%-(	confused
:-(	frowning, indicates sadness or anger	:-0	surprised

Alternately, you might put a "g" (for grin) or "smile" in parentheses after something that is obviously meant as tongue-in-cheek to help carry the intended message to the receiver. Abbreviations for commonly used phrases save space and avoid unnecessary keying. Popular ones include BCNU (be seeing you), BTW (by the way), FYI (for your information), FWIW (for what it's worth), HTH (hope this helps), IMHO (in my humble opinion), and LOL (laugh out loud).

Some email users feel strongly that emoticons and abbreviations are childish or inappropriate for serious email and decrease productivity when the receiver must take time for deciphering. Before using them, be certain the receiver will understand them and that the formality of the message and your relationship with the receiver justify this type of informal exchange. Then, use only in moderation to *punctuate* your message. Similarly, some individuals and companies add an engaging quote to the end of emails as a means of promoting the company culture. Critics believe that these add-ons distract from the focus of the message.

Formal Report Format

Page arrangement for reports varies somewhat, depending on the documentation style guide followed or individual company preferences. Take advantage of your software's automatic formatting features for efficient formatting and generating report parts. Portions of a sample report are shown in Figure A-6.

Margins. For formal reports, use one-inch side margins. If the report is to be bound, increase the left margin by one-half inch. Use a two-inch top margin for the first page of each report part (table of contents, executive summary) and a one-inch top margin for all other pages. Leave at least a one-inch bottom margin on all pages.

Spacing. While documentation style guides typically specify double spacing of text, company practice is often to single-space reports. Double spacing accommodates editorial comments and changes but results in a higher page count. Even if you choose to double-space the body of a report, you may opt to single-space some elements, such as the entries in your references page and information in tables or other graphic components. Many companies have moved toward using the new wider line and paragraph spacing software defaults rather than formatting reports in traditional single or double spacing.

A multiple-page document should contain no single lines of a paragraph at the top or bottom of a page. The widow-orphan protection default feature of your word processing software eliminates widow lines (line of a paragraph left at the top of a page) and orphan lines (first line of a paragraph left at bottom of a page).

Headings. Several levels of headings may be used throughout the report and are typed in different ways to indicate level of importance. Suggested formatting guidelines for a report divided into three levels are illustrated in Figure A-7. Develop fourth- and fifth-level headings simply by using boldface, underline, and varying fonts. In short reports, however, organization rarely goes beyond third-level headings. However, because this format is not universal, be sure to identify the format specified by the documentation style you are using and follow it consistently.

This document illustrates Word 2007 Style Set with style formats applied for the report title, the three heading levels, and the enumerated list. Creating a custom style set allows businesses to create a report style that is consistent with their company image and brand. It also uses the wider line and paragraph spacing defaults for an open, readable format that allows space for editorial comments and eliminates the need for paragraph indention.

FIGURE A-6

Formal Report Parts

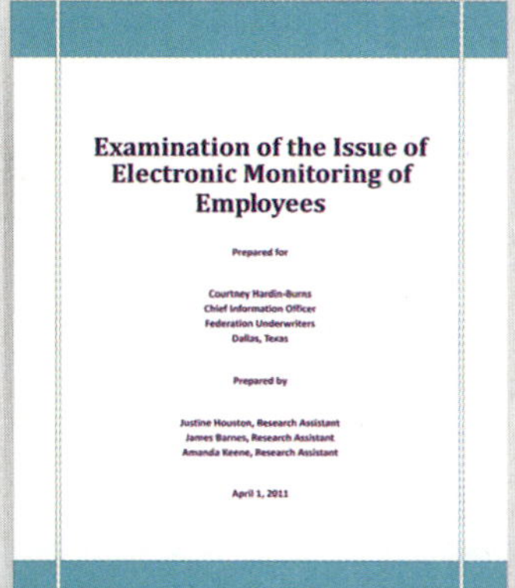

Examination of the Issue of Electronic Monitoring of Employees

Prepared for

Courtney Hardin-Burns
Chief Information Officer
Federation Underwriters
Dallas, Texas

Prepared by

Justine Houston, Research Assistant
James Barnes, Research Assistant
Amanda Keene, Research Assistant

April 1, 2011

Title page

Transmittal document

Table of contents

Executive summary

First page of report

Page with graphic

References in APA style

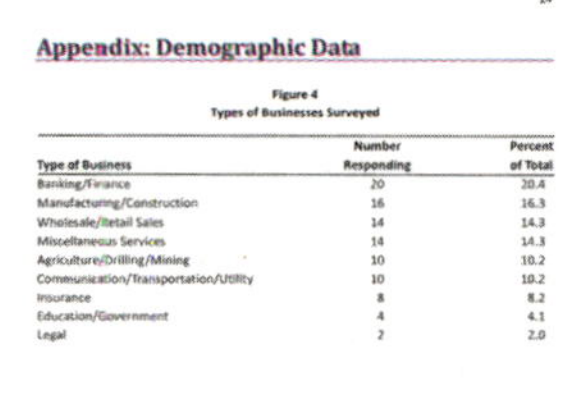

14

Appendix: Demographic Data

Figure 4
Types of Businesses Surveyed

Type of Business	Number Responding	Percent of Total
Banking/Finance	20	20.4
Manufacturing/Construction	16	16.3
Wholesale/Retail Sales	14	14.3
Miscellaneous Services	14	14.3
Agriculture/Drilling/Mining	10	10.2
Communication/Transportation/Utility	10	10.2
Insurance	8	8.2
Education/Government	4	4.1
Legal	2	2.0

Appendix

FIGURE A-7

Report Format Using Preset Styles

2″ top margin

REPORT TITLE

Title style (26-point Cambria font)

1

xxx xxxxxx xxxxxxxx xxxxx xxxxxxx xxxxxx xxxxxxx xxxxxx xxxx xxxxxx xxxxxxxxx xxx x xxxxxx xxx x xxxxxxxxx xxx x xxxxxx xxxx xxxxxxxxx xxx xxxxxxx.

1

First-Level Heading

Heading 1 (14-point Cambria font)

1

xxxx xxxxxxxx xxxx xxxx xxxxxxx xxxxxx xxxxxx xxxxx xxxxxxx xxx xxxxxxxx xx xxxxxxx x xxxxxx xxxxx xxxxxx xxxxxx xxxxxx xxxx.

1

Second-Level Subheading

Heading 2 (13-point Cambria font)

1

xxx xxxxxx xxxx xxx xxxxxxx xxxxx xx xxxx xxxxx xxxxxxx xxx x xxxx xxxxxx x xxxxxxxx xxxx x xxxxxx xxxxxxxxx xxxxxxx. xxxxxxxx xxxxxxx. xxxxxxxx xx:

1

1. xxxxx. xxxxxxxx xxxxxxx. xxxxxxxx xxxxxxx. xxxxxxxx xxxxxxx. xxxxxxxx xxxxxxx. xxxxxxxx. **Space automatically reduced between enumerated items**
2. xxx xxxxxx xxxx xxx xxxxxxx xxxxx xx xxxx xxxxx xxxxxxx xxx x xxxx xxxxxx x xxxxxxxx xxxx x xxxxxx xxxxxxxxx xxxxxxx. Xxxxxxxx.

Second-Level Subheading

x xxxx xxxxxxxxx xxxx xxxx xxxx xxxx xxxx xxxx xxx xxxxxx xxx xxx xxxxxx xxx xxxxxxx xxxxxx xxxxxxx xxxxxxxx xxxxxxxxxx xxxxxxxx xxxxx.

Heading 3 (11-point Cambria font) 1

Third-level subheading. xxxxxx xx xxxx xxxxxxxx xxxxx xxx xxx x xxxxx xxx xxxx xxxxxx xxxx xxx xxxx xxxx xxxx xxxxxx xxxx xxx xxxxxx xxxx xxx xxxxxx xxxx xxx xxxxxx xxxx xxx xxxxxx xxxx xxx.

Third-level subheading. x xxxxxxx xxxxxxx xxx xxxxxx xxxxx xxxx xxxx xxx xxxxxxxx xxxxxxx xxx xxx xxxxxxxxxx xxxxxxxxx. xxxxx xxxxxx xxxx xxx xxxxxx xxxx xxx xxxxxx xxxx xxx xx.

Capitalizes all letters in report title.

Places first- and second-level headings at left margin and capitalizes initial letters. Larger font size makes the first level stand out.

Includes intervening text between first- and second-level headings.

Uses default indentation and decreased spacing between enumerated and bulleted items.

Places third-level subheadings at left margin and capitalizes first letter.

Format Pointers

- The report document illustrates Word 2007 Style Set with style formats applied for report title, three heading levels, and enumerated list.
- The increased spacing after each paragraph eliminates the need for indented paragraphs.

Appendix B
Referencing Styles

A number of widely used reference styles are available for documenting the sources of information used in report writing. Two of the more popular style manuals for business writing are as follows:

Publication Manual of the American Psychological Association, 6th ed., Washington, DC: American Psychological Association, 2010.

MLA Handbook for Writers of Research Papers, 7th ed., New York: Modern Languages Association of American, 2009.

The *MLA Handbook* is designed for high school and undergraduate college students; the *MLA Style Manual and Guide to Scholarly Publishing*, 3rd ed. (2009) is designed for graduate students, scholars, and professional writers.

These sources, commonly referred to as the APA and MLA styles, provide general rules for referencing and give examples of the citation formats for various types of source materials. Whenever you are not required to use a particular documentation style, choose a recognized one and follow it consistently. Occasionally, you may need to reference something for which no general example applies. Choose the example that is most like your source and follow that format. When in doubt, provide more information, not less. Remember that a major purpose for listing references is to enable readers to retrieve and use the sources. This appendix illustrates citation formats for some common types of information sources and refers you to online support that provides further detailed guidelines for preparing citations for both print and electronic sources.

In-Text Parenthetical Citations

While some referencing styles use footnotes at the bottom of each page to document the source of numbered citations, both the MLA and APA referencing styles support the use of ***in-text citations***. Abbreviated information within parentheses in the text directs the reader to a list of sources at the end of a report. The list of sources at the end contains all bibliographic information on each source cited in a report. This list is arranged alphabetically by the author's last name or, if no author is provided, by the first word of the title.

References

The *references*, or works cited page, located at the end of your document contains an alphabetized list of the sources used in preparing a report, with each entry containing publication information necessary for locating the source. A researcher often uses sources that provide information but do not result in citations. If you want to acknowledge that you have consulted these works and provide the reader with a comprehensive reading list, include these sources in the list of references and refer to your list as a *bibliography*. Your company guidelines may specify whether to list only works that were cited or all works consulted. If you receive no definitive guidelines, use your own judgment. If in doubt, include all literature cited and read, and label the page with the appropriate title so that the reader clearly understands the nature of the list.

To aid the reader in locating sources in lengthy bibliographies, you may include subheadings denoting the types of publications documented; for example, books, articles, unpublished documents and papers, government publications, and websites. Check your reference manual to determine if subheadings are allowed.

Formats for Print and Recorded References. A number of useful online resources are available that provide information about citations of print and recorded materials. One of the more comprehensive sites is the OWL website developed by Purdue University, which provides general guidelines for using APA style and MLA style for referencing various types of sources. You can access this site at http://owl.english.purdue.edu/.

Formats for Electronic References. Referencing Internet and other electronic sources can be somewhat challenging, since electronic information and publication environments continue to evolve. The Purdue OWL site includes examples of citing electronic references in the latest versions of the APA and MLA styles.

When referencing an electronic source, include as many of the following items as possible:

1. Author (if given)
2. Date of publication
3. Title of article and/or name of publication
4. Electronic medium (such as CD or DVD)
5. Volume; series; page, section, or paragraph
6. Internet address (URL) and database if applicable
7. Direct object identifier (doi) if available. The doi is a permanent identifier for online resources.

Some current word processing programs include features to assist in the creation of reference pages, and several free-standing referencing software programs are available that work in conjunction with word processors to aid in providing adequate referencing. Figure B-1 illustrates a sample page from a report prepared in APA style, along with an accompanying reference page.

You may also review a formal report with in-text citations and a reference page that is part of the Chapter 11 content on the companion website (www.cengage.com/bcomm/lehman).

FIGURE B-1

Sample Report and References Pages in APA (6th Edition) Style

Cross-Cultural Virtual Teams 4

Culturally diverse virtual teams do have a greater potential for conflict than do teams that are homogeneous and are able to meet face to face ("Collaborative Teams," 2008). While variations in beliefs, behaviors, and expectations occur within all cultural groups, certain generalities about one based on his or her cultural group can be useful for others seeking better understanding. "Given little or no other information about an individual's values and behaviours, culture provides a good first impression of that person" (Maznevski & Peterson, 1997, p. 37).

Neyer and Harzing (2008) found that experiences in cross-cultural interactions do serve to improve one's abilities to adapt in such situations. One advantage gained through experience is the overcoming of cultural stereotypes which often stand in the way of effective communication (Williams & O'Reilly, 1998). Cross-cultural experience also leads to the establishment of norms that support interaction among individuals and to the development of mutual consideration for others (Neyer & Harzing, 2008). Studies have established that individuals who learn a foreign language also gain appropriate culturally determined behavior and are thus better able to adapt to specific characteristics of the other culture (Harzing & Feely, 2008).

In addition to possessing strong technical skills, qualities that are important to successful membership on cross-cultural virtual teams include the following (Adler, 1991; Hurn & Jenkins, 2000):

- Flexibility and adaptability
- Strong interpersonal skills
- Ability to think both globally and locally
- Linguistic skills

Cross Cultural Virtual Teams 5

References

Adler, N. J. (1991). *International dimensions of organizational behavior*. Boston: PWS Kent.

Collaborative teams. (2008, June). *Bulletpoint*, 152, 3–5.

Hurn, B. F., & Jenkins, M. (2000). International peer group development. *Industrial and Commercial Training*, 32(4), 128–131. doi: 10.1108/00197850010372205

Maznevski, M. L. & Peterson, M. F. (1997). Societal values, social interpretation, and multinational teams. In C. Granrose (Ed.), *Cross-cultural workgroups* (pp. 27–29). Thousand Oaks, CA: Sage.

Neyer, A., & Harzine, A. (2008). The impact of culture on interactions: Five lessons learned from the European Commission. *European Management Journal*, 26(5), 325–334. doi: 10.1016/j.emj .2008.05.005

Williams, K. Y., & O'Reilly, C. A. (1998). Demography and diversity in organizations. In B. M. Staw & R. M. Sutton (Eds.), *Research in organizational behavior* (pp. 77–140). Stamford, CT: JAI.

Appendix C
Language Review and Exercises

Polishing your language skills will aid you in preparing error-free documents that reflect positively on you and your company. This text appendix is an abbreviated review that focuses on common problems frequently encountered by business writers and offers a quick "refreshing" of key skills. Complete the online pretest and post-test available at your companion website (www.cengage.com/bcomm/lehman) to assess your understanding of principles before and after your complete the printed tutorials.

Other resources are available to assist you in improving your language skills:

- **Interactive Language Review.** Complete the language review available in your online course as directed by your instructor.
- **Reference books.** For more thorough reviews, consult standard reference books on language usage.

Grammar

Sentence Structure

1. ***Rely mainly on sentences that follow the normal subject-verb-complement sequence for clarity and easy reading.***

   Jennifer and I withdrew for three reasons.
   (subject) (verb) (complement)

Original	*Better*
There are two reasons for our withdrawal.	Two reasons for our withdrawal are . . . .
	Jennifer and I withdrew for two reasons.
It is necessary that we withdraw.	We must withdraw.
Here is a copy of my résumé.	The enclosed résumé outlines . . .

There, it, and *here* are *expletives*—filler words that have no real meaning in the sentence.

2. ***Put pronouns, adverbs, phrases, and clauses near the words they modify.***

Incorrect	*Correct*
Angie put a new type of gel on her hair, which she had just purchased.	Angie put a new type of gel, which she had just purchased, on her hair.
He works only in the call center during peak periods.	He works in the call center only during peak periods.
The clerk stood near the fax machine wearing a denim skirt.	The clerk wearing a denim skirt stood near the fax machine.

3. ***Do not separate subject and predicate unnecessarily.***

Incorrect	*Clear*
She, hoping to receive a bonus, worked rapidly.	Hoping to receive a bonus, she worked rapidly.

4. ***Place an introductory phrase near the subject of the independent clause it modifies.*** Otherwise, the phrase dangles. To correct the dangling phrase, change the subject of the independent clause, or make the phrase into a dependent clause by assigning it a subject.

Incorrect	*Correct*
When a young boy, my mother insisted I learn a second language. [Implies that the mother was once a young man.]	When I was a young boy, my mother insisted I learn a second language.
Working at full speed every morning, fatigue overtakes me in the afternoon. [Implies that "fatigue" was working at full speed.]	Working at full speed every morning, I become tired in the afternoon. Because I work at full speed every morning, fatigue overtakes me in the afternoon.
To function properly, you must oil the machine every hour. [Implies that if "you" are "to function properly," the machine must be oiled hourly.]	If the equipment is to function properly, you must oil it every hour. To function properly, the equipment must be oiled every hour.

5. ***Express related ideas in similar grammatical form (use parallel construction).***

Incorrect	*Correct*
The machine operator made three resolutions: (1) to be punctual, (2) following instructions carefully, and third, the reduction of waste.	The machine operator made three resolutions: to be punctual, to follow instructions carefully, and to reduce waste.
The human resources manager is concerned with the selection of the right worker, providing appropriate orientation, and the worker's progress.	The human resources manager is concerned with selecting the right worker, providing appropriate orientation, and evaluating the worker's progress.

6. ***Do not end a sentence with a needless preposition.***

Where is the new sushi bar to be located (not *located at*)?

The applicant did not tell us where he was going (not *going to*).

End a sentence with a preposition if for some reason the preposition needs emphasis.

I am not concerned with what he is paying for. I am concerned with what he is paying with.

The prospect has everything—a goal to work toward, a house to live in, and an income to live on.

7. ***Avoid split infinitives.*** Two words are required to express an infinitive: *to* plus a *verb*. The two words belong together. An infinitive is split when another word is placed between the two.

Incorrect	*Correct*
The superintendent used to occasionally visit the offices.	The superintendent used to visit the offices occasionally.
I plan to briefly summarize the report.	I plan to summarize the report briefly.

Exercise 1

Identify the weakness in each sentence and write an improved version.

1. It is essential that you learn to design spreadsheets that make financial information meaningful to users.
2. There are many online tools available that build relationships with customers.
3. I am submitting an employee testimonial to the company website, which I first posted to a presentation blog.
4. More companies are videoconferencing because of the need to significantly reduce travel costs.
5. To operate efficiently, you must perform periodic maintenance on your computer.
6. Planned store improvements include widening the aisles, improved lighting, and lower shelves for a sophisticated feel.

Pronoun Reference

1. *Make a pronoun agree in number with its antecedent (the specific noun for which a pronoun stands).*

a. Use a plural pronoun when it represents two or more singular antecedents connected by *and*.

The secretary and the treasurer will take their vacations.

["The" before "treasurer" indicates that the sentence is about two people.]

The secretary and treasurer will take his vacation.

[Omitting "the" before "treasurer" indicates that the sentence is about one person who has two sets of responsibilities.]

b. Parenthetical remarks (remarks that can be omitted without destroying the basic meaning of the sentence) that appear between the pronoun and its antecedent have no effect on the form of the pronoun.

President Ritter, not the managers, is responsible for his strategic goals.

[Because "his" refers to President Ritter and not to "managers," "his" is used instead of "their."]

c. Use a singular pronoun with *each*, *everyone*, *no*, and their variations.

Each student and each team member will perform his or her own data collection.

Everyone is responsible for her or his work.

d. Use a singular pronoun when two or more singular antecedents are connected by *or* or *nor*.

Neither Brandon nor Will can complete his work.

Ask either Mallory or Suzanne about her in-service training.

e. Use pronouns that agree in number with the intended meaning of collective nouns.

The team has been asked for its contributions. ["Team" is thought of as a unit; the singular "its" is appropriate.]

The team have been asked for their contributions. ["Team" is thought of as more than one individual; the plural "their" is appropriate.]

2. *Place relative pronouns as near their antecedents as possible for clear understanding.* A *relative* pronoun joins a dependent clause to its antecedent.

Ambiguous	***Clear***
The members were given receipts who have paid.	The members who have paid were given receipts.
The agreement will enable you to pay whichever is lower, 6 percent or $50.	The agreement will enable you to pay 6 percent or $50, whichever is lower.

Restate a noun instead of risking a *vague* pronoun reference.

Vague	***Clear***
The officer captured the suspect even though he was unarmed.	The officer captured the suspect even though the officer was unarmed.

3. ***Do not use a pronoun by itself to refer to a phrase, clause, sentence, or paragraph.*** A pronoun should stand for a noun, and that noun should appear in the writing.

Incorrect	***Correct***
He expects to take all available accounting courses and obtain a position in a public accounting firm. This appeals to him.	He expects to take all available accounting courses and obtain a position in a public accounting firm. This plan appeals to him.

Exercise 2

Correct the error in pronoun use.

1. Conversation skills and good listening (affect, affects) a leader's effectiveness.
2. Each sales rep (was, were) trained to encourage customers to buy more than one size or color since shipping is free.
3. The production manager, not the controller, presented (her, their) strongly opposing views.
4. Neither Stephen nor Lydia (was, were) recognized for their contribution.
5. The company restructured (its, their) recreation event to avoid a frivolous perception.
6. The committee will present (its, their) recommendation at the next staff meeting.
7. Jenna forgot to retain her receipts; (this, this oversight) caused a delay in reimbursement.

Pronoun Case

1. ***Use the correct case of pronouns.*** *Case* tells whether a pronoun is used as the subject of a sentence or as an object in it.

   a. Use nominative-case pronouns (also known as subjective-case pronouns) (*I, he, she, they, we, you, it, who*) as subjects of a sentence or clause.

   You and I must collaborate. ["You" and "I" are subjects of the verb "collaborate."]

   Those who work will be paid. ["Who" is the subject of the dependent clause "who work."]

   b. Use objective-case pronouns (*me, him, her, them, us, you, it, whom*) as objects of verbs and prepositions.

   His mother texted him about the family emergency. ["Him" is the object of the verb "texted."]

   The customer feedback survey was sent to the project manager and them. ["Them" is the object of the preposition "to."]

   To whom should we send the analysis? ["Whom" is the object of the preposition "to."]

   Tip: Restate a subordinate clause introduced by who or whom to determine the appropriate pronoun.

   She is the type of manager whom we can promote. [Restating "whom we can promote" as "We can promote her (whom)" clarifies that "whom" is the object.]

   She is the type of manager who can be promoted. [Restating "who can be promoted" as "She (who) can be promoted" clarifies that "who" is the subject.]

   Tip: Change a question to a statement to determine the correct form of a pronoun.

   Whom did you call? [You did call *whom*.]

   Whom did you select for the position? [You did select *whom* for the position.]

   c. Use the nominative case when forms of the linking verb *be* require a pronoun to complete the meaning.

   It was he who received credit for the sale.

   It is she who deserves the award.

["It was he" may to some people sound just as distracting as the incorrect "It was him." Express the ideas in a different way to avoid the error and an expletive beginning.]

He was the one who received credit for the sale.

She deserves the award.

d. Use the possessive form of a pronoun before a gerund (a verb used as a noun).

We were delighted at his (not *him*) assuming a leadership role.

["Assuming a leadership role" is used here as a noun. "His" in this sentence serves the same purpose it serves in "We were delighted at his initiative."]

Exercise 3

Correct the error in pronoun case.

1. The professor agreed to award (we, us) partial credit for the confusing question.
2. Stacey requested that the tasks be divided equally between Addison and (her, she).
3. It was (her, she) (who, whom) recommended revising the company's technology policy to include social networking sites.
4. The manager seemed unaware of (him, his) inability to relate to younger employees.
5. Emma is a leader in (who, whom) we have great confidence.

Verb Agreement

1. Make subjects agree with verbs.

a. Ignore intervening phrases that have no effect on the verb used.

Good material and fast delivery are (not *is*) essential.

You, not the carrier, are (not *is*) responsible for the damage. [Intervening phrase, "not the carrier," does not affect the verb used.]

The attitude of these investors is (not *are*) deep concern. [The subject is "attitude"; "of these investors" is a phrase coming between the subject and the verb.]

b. Use a verb that agrees with the noun closer to the verb when *or* or *nor* connects two subjects.

Only one or two questions are (not *is*) necessary.

Several paint brushes or one paint roller is (not *are*) necessary.

c. Use singular verbs with plural nouns that have a singular meaning or are thought of as singular units.

The news is good. Economics is a required course.

Twenty dollars is too much. Ten minutes is sufficient time.

d. Use a singular verb for titles of articles, firm names, and slogans.

"Etiquette in the Age of Social Media" is an interesting article.

Forestieri and Chaudrue is the oldest firm in the city.

"Eat Smart for Hearts" is a campaign slogan directed at better nutrition for senior adults.

2. Choose verbs that agree in person with their subjects.

Person indicates whether the subject is (1) speaking, (2) being spoken to, or (3) being spoken about.

First person: I am, we are. [Writer or speaker]

Second person: You are. [Receiver of message]

Third person: He is, she is, they are. [Person being discussed]

She doesn't (not *don't*) eat well or exercise regularly.

They don't recognize the value of strong networking skills.

Verb Tense and Mood

1. ***Use the appropriate verb tense.*** *Tense* indicates time. Tense can be either simple or compound.

   Simple tenses:

   Present: I see you. [Tells what is happening now.]

   Past: I saw you. [Tells what has already happened.]

   Future: I will see you. [Tells what is yet to happen.]

   Compound tenses:

   Present perfect: I have seen you. [Tells of past action that extends to the present.]

   Past perfect: I had seen you. [Tells of past action that was finished before another past action.]

   Future perfect: I will have seen you. [Tells of action that will be finished before a future time.]

   a. Use present tense when something was and still is true.

      The speaker reminded us that Rhode Island is (not *was*) smaller than Wisconsin.

      The consultant's name is (not *was*) Ryan Abrams.

   b. Avoid unnecessary shifts in tense.

      The carrier brought (not *brings*) my package but left without asking me to sign for it.

      Verbs that appear in the same sentence are not required to be in the same tense.

      The contract that was prepared yesterday will be signed tomorrow.

2. ***Use subjunctive mood to express situations that are untrue or highly unlikely.*** Be sure to use *were* for the present tense of to *be* to indicate the subjunctive mood. Use *was* when the statement could be true.

   I wish the story were (not *was*) true.

   If I were (not *was*) you, I would try again.

Verb Voice

See Chapter 3 for a detailed explanation of active- and passive-voice verbs.

Exercise 4

Select the correct word.

1. Only one of the free smartphone applications (has, have) value to me.
2. Taxpayers, not the government, (are, is) held accountable for paying the national debt.
3. Neither the manager nor the employees (was, were) aware of the policy change.
4. Both Josh and Krystal (was, were) notified of the impending layoffs.
5. The news from the rescue mission (is, are) encouraging.
6. *Good to Great* (has, have) been placed in the company library.
7. The sales manager announced that Portsmouth, South Carolina, (is, was) the site for the annual sales meeting.
8. Taylor (don't, doesn't) expect preferential treatment.
9. The client studied the financial analysis for a minute and (starts, started) asking questions.
10. If the applicant (was, were) experienced with databases, she would have been hired.

Adjectives and Adverbs

1. Use an adjective to modify a noun or pronoun and an adverb to modify a verb, an adjective, or another adverb.

Adjective: Bryan gave an impressive sales pitch.

Adverb: The new employee looked enthusiastically at the sales prospect. [The adverb "enthusiastically" modifies the verb "looked."]

The team leader was really visionary. [The adverb "really" modifies the adjective "visionary."]

Worker A progressed relatively faster than did Worker B. [The adverb "relatively" modifies the adverb "faster."]

2. Use an adjective after a linking verb when the modifier refers to the subject instead of to the verb. (A linking verb connects a subject to the rest of the sentence. "He is old." "She seems sincere.")

The man entering the building looked suspicious. [The adjective "suspicious" refers to "man," not to "looked."]

3. Use comparatives (to compare two) and superlatives (to compare three or more) carefully.

She is the faster (not *fastest*) of the two workers.

Edwin is the better (not *best*) writer of the two team members.

Exclude a person or thing from a group with which that person or thing is being compared.

He is more observant than anyone else (not *anyone*) in his department. [As a member of his department, he cannot be more observant than himself.]

"The X-60 is newer than any other machine (not *any machine*) in the plant." [The X-60 cannot be newer than itself.]

Exercise 5

Select the correct word.

1. Despite the dangers, employees change their computer passwords (infrequent, infrequently).
2. Daniel looked (impatient, impatiently) at the new production assistant.
3. The server moved (quick, quickly) from table to table.
4. Of the several people I met during the speed networking event, Olivia made the (better, best) impression.
5. The Chicago plant has a higher safety record than (any, any other) plant.

Punctuation

Commas

1. Use a comma

a. Between coordinate clauses joined by *and, but, for, or,* and *nor*.

He wanted to pay his bills on time, but he did not have the money.

b. To separate introductory clauses and certain phrases from independent clauses. Sentences that begin with dependent clauses (often with words such as *if, as, since, because, although,* and *when*) almost always need a comma. Prepositional phrases and verbal phrases with five or more words require commas.

Dependent clause:	If you can postpone your departure, the research team will be able to finalize its proposal submission. [The comma separates the introductory dependent clause from the independent clause.]
Infinitive:	To get the full benefit of our insurance plan, complete and return the enclosed card. [A verb preceded by "to" ("to get").]
Participial:	Believing that her earnings would continue to increase, she requested a higher credit card limit. [A verb form used as an adjective: "believing" modifies the dependent clause "she requested."]
Prepositional phrase:	Within the next few days, you will receive written confirmation of this transaction. [Comma needed because the phrase contains five words.]
	Under the circumstances we think you are justified. [Comma omitted because the phrase contains fewer than five words and the sentence is clear without the comma.]

c. To separate three or more words in a series.

You have a choice of gray, green, purple, and white.

Without the comma after "purple," no one can tell for sure whether four choices are available, the last of which is "white," or whether three choices are available, the last of which is "purple and white."

You have a choice of purple and white, gray, and green. [Choice is restricted to three, the first of which is "purple and white."]

d. Between two or more independent adjectives that modify the same noun.

New employees are given a long, difficult examination. [Both "long" and "difficult" modify "examination."]

We want quick, factual news. [Both "quick" and "factual" modify "news."]

Do not place a comma between two adjectives when the second adjective modifies the adjective and noun as a unit.

The supervisor is an excellent team player. ["Excellent" modifies the noun phrase "team player."]

e. To separate a nonrestrictive clause (a clause that is not essential to the basic meaning of the sentence) from the rest of the sentence.

Kent Murray, who is head of customer resource management, has selected Century Consulting to oversee the product launch. [The parenthetical remark is not essential to the meaning of the sentence.]

The man who is head of customer resource management has selected Century Consulting to oversee the product launch. [Commas are not needed because "who is head of customer resource management" is essential to the meaning of the sentence.]

f. To set off or separate dates, address, geographical names, degrees, and long numbers:

On July 2, 2011, Jason Kennedy made the final payment. [Before and after the year in month-day-year format.]

I saw him in Tahoe City, California, on the 12th of October. [Before and after the name of a state when the name of a city precedes it.]

Jesse Marler, President [Between the printed name and the title on the same line beneath a signature or in a letter address.]

Tristan A. Highfield [No comma is used if the title is on a separate line.]
President of Academic Affairs

g. To separate parenthetical expressions or other elements interrupting the flow from the rest of the sentence.

Ms. Watson, speaking in behalf of the entire department, accepted the proposal. [Set off a parenthetical expression]

Cole, I believe you have earned a vacation. [After a direct address]

Yes, you can count on me. [After the words *No* and *Yes* when they introduce a statement.]

Arun Ramage, former president of the Jackson Institute, spoke to the group. [Set off appositives when neutral emphasis is desired.]

The job requires experience, not formal education. [Between contrasted elements.]

Exercise 6

Insert needed commas. Write "correct" if you find no errors.

1. The employee who is featured in our latest television commercial is active in the community theatre.
2. Emoticons which are created by keying combinations of symbols to produce "sideway faces" communicate emotion in electronic messages.
3. Sean Cohen a new member of the board remained silent during the long bitter debate.
4. Top social networking sites include Facebook MySpace and Flickr.
5. The entire population was surveyed but three responses were unusable.
6. If you tag websites in a social bookmarking site you can locate them easily for later use.
7. To qualify for the position applicants must have technology certification.
8. We should be spending less money not more.
9. On May 9 2011 the company's Twitter site was launched.
10. Yes the president approved a team-building event to replace our annual golf outing.

Semicolons and Colons

1. Use a semicolon

a. To join the independent clauses in a compound sentence when a conjunction is omitted.

Your voice counts; email us with your ideas and concerns.

b. To join the independent clauses in a compound-complex sentence.

As indicated earlier, we prefer delivery on Saturday morning at four o'clock; but Friday night at ten o'clock will be satisfactory.

We prefer delivery on Saturday morning at four o'clock; but, if the arrangement is more convenient for you, Friday night at ten o'clock will be satisfactory.

c. Before an adverbial conjunction. Use a comma after the adverbial conjunction.

Adverbial conjunction: The shipment arrived too late for our weekend sale; therefore, we are returning the shipment to you.

Other frequently used adverbial conjunctions are however, otherwise, consequently, and nevertheless.

d. Before words used to introduce enumerations or explanations that follow an independent clause.

Enumeration with commas: Many factors affect the direction of the stock market; namely, interest rates, economic growth, and employment rates.

Explanation forming a complete thought: We have plans for improvement; for example, we intend . . . .

The engine has been "knocking"; that is, the gas in the cylinders explodes before the pistons complete their upward strokes.

Note the following exceptions that require a comma to introduce the enumeration or explanation:

Enumeration without commas: Several Web 2.0 tools are available, for example, blogs and wikis. [A comma, not a semicolon, is used because the enumeration contains no commas.]

Explanation forming an incomplete thought: A trend is to replace expensive employee networking events with purposeful recreation, for instance, community service events. [A comma, not a semicolon, is used because the explanation is not a complete thought.]

e. In a series that contains commas.

Some of our workers have worked overtime this week: Smith, 6 hours; Hardin, 3; Cantrell, 10; and McGowan, 11.

2. *Use a colon*

a. After a complete thought that introduces a list of items. Use a colon following both direct and indirect introductions of lists.

Direct introduction:	The following three factors influenced our decision: an expanded market, an inexpensive source of raw materials, and a ready source of labor. [The word "following" clearly introduces a list.]
Indirect introduction:	The carpet is available in three colors: green, burgundy, and blue.

Do not use a colon after an introductory statement that ends with a preposition or a verb (*are, is, were, include*). The list that follows the preposition or verb finishes the sentence.

Incomplete sentence:	We need to (1) expand our market, (2) locate an inexpensive source of materials, and (3) find a ready source of labor. [A colon does not follow "to" because the words preceding the list are not a complete sentence.]

b. To stress an appositive (a noun that renames the preceding noun) at the end of a sentence.

A majority of white collar criminals report that a single factor led to their crimes: pressure to achieve revenue targets.

Our progress is due to the efforts of one person: Brooke Keating.

Exercise 7

Insert semicolons and colons where needed. Write "correct" if you find no errors.

1. Some privacy concerns have become less important in recent years, however, most people feel extremely vulnerable to privacy invasion.
2. The following agents received bonuses Barnes, $750, Shelley, $800, and Jackson, $950.
3. Employees were notified today of the plant closing they received two weeks' severance pay.
4. This paint does have some disadvantages for example a lengthy drying time.
5. Soon after the applications are received, a team of judges will evaluate them, but the award recipients will not be announced until January 15.
6. The program has one shortcoming: flexibility.
7. The new bakery will offer: frozen yogurt, candies, and baked goods.
8. We are enthusiastic about the plan because: (1) it is least expensive, (2) its legality is unquestioned, and (3) it can be implemented quickly.

Apostrophes

1. *Use an apostrophe to form possessives.*

a. Add an apostrophe and *s* (*'s*) to form the possessive case of a singular noun or a plural noun that does not end with a pronounced *s*.

Singular noun:	Jenna's position	firm's assets
	employee's benefits	
Plural noun without a pronounced s:	men's clothing	children's games
	deer's antlers	

b. Add only an apostrophe to form the possessive of a singular or plural noun that ends with a pronounced *s*.

Singular noun with pronounced s:	Niagara Falls' site
	Ms. Jenkins' interview

Plural noun with pronounced s:	two managers' decision six months' wages	

Exception: An apostrophe and *s ('s)* can be added to singular nouns ending in a pronounced s if an additional s sound is pronounced easily.

Singular noun with additional s sound:	boss's decision Jones's invitation	class's party

c. Use an apostrophe with the possessives of nouns that refer to time (minutes, hours, days, weeks, months, and years) or distance in a possessive manner.

eight hours' pay	today's global economy	a stone's throw
two weeks' notice	ten years' experience	a yard's length

Exercise 8

Correct the possessives.

1. The new hires confidence was crushed by the managers harsh tone.
2. This companies mission statement has been revised since it's recent merger.
3. Employees who are retained may be asked to accept a reduction of one weeks pay.
4. Vendors' have submitted sealed bids for the construction contract that will be opened in two week's.
5. Younger workers must appreciate older employees extensive company knowledge.

Hyphens

1. Use a hyphen

a. Between the words in a compound adjective. (A *compound adjective* is a group of adjectives appearing together and used as a single word to describe a noun.)

An eye-catching design A two-thirds interest

Do not hyphenate a compound adjective in the following cases:

(1) When the compound adjective follows a noun.

A design that is eye catching.

Today's consumers are convenience driven.

Note: Some compound adjectives are hyphenated when they follow a noun.

The news release was up-to-date.

The speaker is well-known.

For jobs that are part-time, ...

(2) An expression made up of an adverb that ends in *ly* and an adjective is not a compound adjective and does not require a hyphen.

commonly accepted principle

widely quoted authority

(3) A simple fraction and a percentage.

Simple fraction: Two thirds of the respondents

Percentage: 15 percent sales increase

b. To prevent misinterpretation.

Recover a chair [To obtain possession of a chair once more]

Re-cover a chair [To cover a chair again]

Eight inch blades [Eight blades, each of which is an inch long]

Eight-inch blades [Blades eight inches long]

Exercise 9

Add necessary hyphens. Write "correct" if you find no errors.

1. The web based application was unavailable because of a denial of service attack.
2. State of the art computers provide quick access to timely business information.
3. A large portion of holiday orders are time sensitive.
4. A two thirds majority is needed to pass the 5-percent increase in employee wages.
5. Nearly one-half of the respondents were highly-educated professionals.

Quotation Marks and Italics

1. *Use quotation marks*

a. To enclose direct quotations.

Single-sentence quotation:	The supervisor said, "We will make progress."
Interrupted quotation:	"We will make progress," the supervisor said, "even though we have to work overtime."
Multiple-sentence quotation:	The manager said, "Have a seat, Seth. Please wait a moment while I complete this email." [Place quotation marks before the first word and after the last word of a multiple-sentence quotation.]
Quotation within quotation:	The budget director said, "Believe me when I say 'A penny saved is a penny earned' is the best advice I ever had." [Use single quotation marks to enclose a quotation that appears with a quotation.]

b. To enclose titles of songs, magazine and newspaper articles, lecture titles, and themes within text.

"Candle in the Wind" "Making an Impact" The chapter, "Online Presence," . . .

c. To enclose a definition of a defined term. Italicize the defined word.

The term *downsizing* is used to refer to "the planned reduction in the number of employees."

d. To enclose words used in humor, a word used when a different word would be more appropriate, slang expressions that need to be emphasized or clarified for the receiver, or nicknames. These words can also be shown in italics.

Humor/ Different Word:	Our "football" team. . . . [Hints that the team appears to be playing something other than football.]
	Our football "team" . . . . [Hints that "collection of individual players" would be more descriptive than "team."]
	. . . out for "lunch." [Hints that the reason for being out is something other than lunch.]
Slang:	The "tipping point" in the planned reorganization is securing support of union management.
Nicknames:	And now for some comments by Robert "Bob" Johnson.

2. *Use italics*

a. To indicate words, letters, numbers, and phrases used as words.

He had difficulty learning to spell *recommendation*.

b. To emphasize a word that is not sufficiently emphasized by other means.

Our goal is to hire the *right* person, not necessarily the most experienced candidate.

c. To indicate the titles of books, magazines, and newspapers.

Creating a Culture of Excellence *The New York Times* *Reader's Digest*

Exercise 10

Add necessary quotation marks and italics.

1. Cynthia Cooper's Extraordinary Circumstances is required reading in some forensic accounting classes.
2. The article How to Persuade People to Say Yes appeared in the May 2009 issue of Training Journal.
3. The consultant's accomplishments are summarized on her opening blog page. [Indicate that a word other than *accomplishments* may be a more appropriate word.]
4. Connie said I want to participate in a volunteer program that serves such a worthy cause. [direct quotation]
5. The term flame is online jargon for a heated, sarcastic, sometimes abusive message or posting to a discussion group.
6. Limit random tweets but focus on ideas and issues that are interesting and relevant.

Dashes, Parentheses, and Periods

1. Use a dash

a. To place emphasis on appositives.

His answer—the correct answer—was based on years of experience.

Compare the price—$125—with the cost of a single repair job.

b. When appositives contain commas.

Their scores—Chloe, 21; Tairus, 20; and Drew, 19—were the highest in a group of 300.

c. When a parenthetical remark consists of an abrupt change in thought.

The committee decided—you may think it's a joke, but it isn't—that the resolution should be adopted.

Note: Use an em dash (not two hyphens) to form a dash in computer-generated copy.

2. Use parentheses for explanatory material that could be left out.

Three of our employees (Kristen Hubbard, Alex Russo, and Mark Coghlan) took their vacations in August.

All our employees (believe it or not) have perfect attendance records.

3. Use a period after declarative and imperative sentences and courteous requests.

We will attend. [Declarative sentence.]

Complete this report. [Imperative sentence.]

Will you please complete the report today. [Courteous request is a question but does not require a verbal answer with requested action.]

Exercise 11

Add necessary dashes, parentheses, or periods.

1. Additional consultants, programmers and analysts, were hired to complete the computer conversion. [Emphasize the appositive.]
2. The dividend will be raised to 15 cents a share approved by the Board of Directors on December 1, 2011. [Deemphasize the approval.]
3. Would you link this YouTube video to my slide show?

Number Usage

1. *Use figures*

a. In most business writing because figures provide deserved emphasis and are easy for readers to locate if they need to reread for critical points. Regardless of whether a number has one digit or many, use figures to express dates, sums of money, mixed numbers and decimals, distance, dimension, cubic capacity, percentage, weights, temperatures, and chapter and page numbers.

May 10, 2011   165 pounds

$9 million   Chapter 3, page 29

5 percent (use % in a table)

over 200 applicants (or two hundred) [an approximation]

b. With ordinals (*th, st, rd, nd*) only when the number precedes the month.

The meeting is to be held on June 21.

The meeting is to be held on the 21st of June.

c. With ciphers but without decimals when presenting even-dollar figures, even if the figure appears in a sentence with another figure that includes dollars and cents.

Miranda paid $70 for the cabinet.

Miranda paid $99.95 for the table and $70 for the cabinet.

d. Numbers that represent time when a.m. or p.m. is used. Words or figures may be used with o'clock

Please meet me at 10:15 p.m.

Please be there at ten o'clock (or 10 o'clock).

Omit the colon when expressing times of day that include hours but not minutes, even if the time appears in a sentence with another time that includes minutes.

The award program began at 6:30 p.m. with a reception at 7 p.m.

2. *Spell out*

a. Numbers if they are used as the first word of a sentence.

Thirty-two people attended.

b. Numbers one through nine if no larger number appears in the same sentence.

Only three auditors worked at the client's office.

Send 5 officers and 37 members.

c. The first number in two consecutive numbers that act as adjectives modifying the same noun; write the second number in figures. If the first number cannot be expressed in one or two words, place it in figures also.

The package required four 44-cent stamps. [A hyphen joins the second number with the word that follows it, thus forming a compound adjective that describes the noun "stamps."]

We shipped 250 180-horsepower engines today. [Figures are used because neither number can be expressed in one or two words.]

Exercise 12

Correct the number usage in the following sentences taken from a letter or a report.

1. The question was answered by sixty-one percent of the respondents.
2. The meeting is scheduled for 10:00 a.m. on February 3rd.
3. These 3 figures appeared on the expense account: $21.95, $30.00, and $35.14.
4. The purchasing manager ordered 50 4-GB flash drives.
5. 21 members voted in favor of the $2,000,000 proposal.
6. Approximately 100 respondents requested a copy of the results.
7. Mix two quarts of white with 13 quarts of brown.
8. Examine the cost projections on page eight.

Capitalization

Capitalize

1. ***Proper nouns (words that name a particular person, place, or thing) and adjectives derived from proper nouns.*** Capitalize the names of persons, places, geographic areas, days of the week, months of the year, holidays, deities, specific events, and other specific names.

Proper nouns	***Common nouns***
Jessica Moore	An applicant for the management position
Bonita Lakes	A land development
Centre Park Mall	A new shopping center
Veteran's Day	A federal holiday
Information Age	A period of time
***Proper adjectives*:**	Irish potatoes, Roman shades, Swiss army knife, Chinese executives, British accent, Southern dialect

Do not capitalize the name of the seasons unless they are personified.

Old Man Winter

2. ***The principal words in the titles of books, magazines, newspapers, articles, compact disks, movies, plays, television series, songs, and poems.***

The Carrot Principle [Book]

"Smart Moves for New Leaders" [Article]

Video Producer [Magazine]

Encarta Encyclopedia [Compact disk]

3. ***The names of academic courses that are numbered, are specific course titles, or contain proper nouns.*** Capitalize degrees used after a person's name and specific academic sessions.

Addison Malone is enrolled in classes in French, mathematics, science, and English.

Students entering the MBA program must complete Accounting 6093 and Finance 5133.

Allison Ward, M.S., will teach International Marketing during Spring Semester 2011.

Professor O'Donnell earned a master's degree in business from Harvard.

4. ***Titles that precede a name.***

Mr. Ronald Moxley	Editor Deeden	Uncle Ian
Dr. Lauren Zolna	President Lopez	Professor Copley

Do not capitalize titles appearing alone or following a name unless they appear in addresses.

The manager approved the proposal submitted by the editorial assistant.

Jon Sharma, executive vice president, is responsible for that account.

Clint has taken the position formerly held by his father.

Address all correspondence to Colonel Michael Anderson, Department Head, 109 Crescent Avenue, Baltimore, MD 21208.

5. ***The main words in a division or department name if the official or specific name is known or the name is used in a return address, a letter address, or a signature block.***

Official or specific name known:	Return the completed questionnaire to the Public Relations Department by March 15.
Official or specific name unknown:	Employees in your information systems division are invited . . .
Return or letter address, signature block:	Mr. Blake Cain, Manager, Public Relations Department . . .

6. ***Most nouns followed by numbers (except in page, paragraph, line, size, and verse references).***

Policy No. 8746826	Exhibit A	Chapter 7
page 97, paragraph 2	Figure 3-5	Model L-379
Flight 340, Gate 22	size 8, Style 319 jacket	

7. ***The first word of a direct quotation.***

The placement officer warned, "Those with offensive email habits may be the first to lose their jobs during layouts."

Do not capitalize the first word in the last part of an interrupted quotation or the first word in an indirect quotation.

"We will proceed," he said, "with the utmost caution." [Interrupted quotation]

He said that the report must be submitted by the end of the week. [Indirect quotation]

8. ***The first word following a colon when a formal statement or question follows.***

Here is an important rule for report writers: Plan your work and work your plan.

Each sales staff should ask this question: Do I really look like a representative of my firm?

Exercise 13

Copy each of the following sentences, making essential changes in capitalization.

1. The first question professor Burney asked me during interviewing 101 was "why do you want to work for us?"
2. The remodeling will give the store a more sophisticated feel according to the Public Relations Director.
3. As the Summer Season arrives, gas prices are expected to rise.
4. We recently purchased digital juice, an excellent source of copyright-free animated images.
5. Thomas Frieden, Director of the Center for Disease Control, is the agency's key communicator.

Words Frequently Misused

Visit your companion website (**www.cengage.com/bcomm/lehman**) to view definitions and sentences containing these frequently misused words.

1. Accept, except
2. Advice, advise
3. Affect, effect
4. Among, between
5. Amount, number
6. Capital, capitol
7. Cite, sight, site
8. Complement, compliment
9. Continual, continuous
10. Credible, creditable
11. Council, counsel
12. Different from, different than
13. Each other, one another
14. Eminent, imminent
15. Envelop, envelope
16. Farther, further
17. Fewer, less
18. Formally, formerly
19. Infer, imply
20. Its, it's
21. Lead, led
22. Lose, loose
23. Media, medium
24. Personal, personnel
25. Principal, principle
26. Reason is, because
27. Stationary, stationery
28. That, which
29. Their, there, they're
30. To, too, two

Exercise 14

Select the correct word.

1. What (affect, effect) will the change have on us?
2. The consultant plans to (advice, advise) the company to eliminate the fourth shift for at least three months.
3. The (amount, number) of complaints from customers declined with the addition of online chat.
4. The (cite, sight, site) of the new 24/4 fitness center is being debated.
5. I consider your remark a (compliment, complement); I agree that the granite countertops (compliment, complements) the deep, earthy tones in the room.
6. The three panelists were constantly interrupting (each other, one another).
7. Generally staple merchandise is placed (farther, further) from the cashier than impulse items.
8. Limit your discussion to five or (fewer, less) points.
9. I (infer, imply) from Avanti's comments to the press that the merger will occur.
10. The hurricane seems to be (losing, loosing) (its, it's) force, which is (different from, different than) predictions.
11. The chemical engineer (lead, led) the research team's investigation to eliminate (lead, led) from gas emissions.
12. Employees may handle (personal, personnel) business during e-breaks beginning next week.
13. Customer perception is the (principal, principle) reason for the change.
14. (Their, There, They're) planning to complete (their, there, they're) strategic plan this week.
15. The (to, too, two) external auditors expect us (to, too, two) complete (to, too, two) many unnecessary reports.

SOLUTIONS TO EXERCISES IN APPENDIX C

Exercise 1—Sentence Structure

1. You must learn to design spreadsheets that make financial information meaningful to users.

2. Many online tools are available that build relationships with customers.

3. I am submitting an employee testimonial, which I first posted to a presentations blog, to the company website.

4. More companies are videoconferencing because of the need to reduce travel costs significantly.

5. You must perform periodic maintenance on your computer to keep it operating efficiently. [The introductory phrase dangles.]

6. Planned store improvements include widening the aisles, improving lighting, and lowering shelves for a sophisticated feel.

Planned store improvements include widened aisles, improved lighting, and lowered shelves for a sophisticated feel.

Exercise 2—Pronoun Reference

1. affect

2. was

3. her

4. was

5. its

6. its

7. this oversight

Exercise 3—Pronoun Case

1. us
2. her
3. she, who
4. his
5. whom

Exercise 4—Verb Agreement, Tense, and Mood

1. has
2. are
3. were
4. were
5. is
6. has
7. is
8. doesn't
9. started
10. were

Exercise 5—Adjectives and Adverbs

1. infrequently
2. impatient
3. quickly
4. best
5. any other

Exercise 6—Commas

1. Correct.
2. Emoticons, which are created by keying combinations of symbols to produce "sideway faces," communicate emotion in electronic messages.
3. Sean Cohen, a new member of the board, remained silent during the long, bitter debate.
4. Top social networking sites include Facebook, MySpace, and Flickr.
5. The entire population was surveyed, but three responses were unusable.
6. If you tag websites in a social bookmarking site, you can locate them easily for later use.
7. To qualify for the position, applicants must have technology certification.
8. We should be spending less money, not more.
9. On May 9, 2011, the company's Twitter site was launched.
10. Yes, the president approved a team-building event to replace our annual golf outing.

Exercise 7—Semicolons and Colons

1. Some privacy concerns have become less important in recent years; however, most people feel extremely vulnerable to invasion.
2. The following agents received bonuses: Barnes, $750; Shelley, $800; and Jackson, $950.
3. Employees were notified today of the plant closing; they received two weeks' severance pay.
4. This paint does have some disadvantages, for example, a lengthy drying time.
5. Soon after the applications are received, a team of judges will evaluate them; but the award recipients will not be announced until January 15.
6. Correct.
7. The new bakery will offer frozen yogurt, candies, and baked goods.
8. We are enthusiastic about the plan because (1) it is least expensive, (2) its legality is unquestioned, and (3) it can be implemented quickly.

Exercise 8—Apostrophes

1. hire's; manager's
2. company's; its
3. week's
4. Vendors; weeks
5. employees'

Exercise 9—Hyphens

1. web-based; denial-of-service attack
2. State-of-the-art
3. Correct
4. two-thirds; 5 percent
5. one half; highly educated

Exercise 10—Quotation Marks and Italics

1. Cynthia Cooper's *Extraordinary Circumstances* is required reading in some forensic accounting classes. [Italicizes a book title.]
2. The article "How to Persuade People to Say Yes" appeared in the May 2009 issue of *Training Journal*. [Encloses the name of an article in quotation marks and italicizes the title of a journal.]
3. The consultant's "accomplishments" are summarized on her opening blog page. [Uses quotation marks to introduce doubt about whether "accomplishments" is the right label. His undertakings may have been of little significance.]
4. Connie said, "I want to participate in a volunteer program that serves such a worthy cause." [Uses quotations marks in a direct quotation.]
5. The term *flame* is online jargon for "a heated, sarcastic, sometimes abusive message or posting to a discussion group." [Italicizes a word used as a word and enclose a definition of a defined term.]
6. Limit random "tweets" but focus on ideas and issues that are interesting and relevant. [Use quotation marks to emphasize or clarify a word for the reader.]

Exercise 11—Dashes, Parentheses, and Periods

1. Additional consultants—programmers and analysts—were hired to complete the computer conversion.
2. The dividend will be raised to 15 cents a share (approved by the Board of Directors on December 1, 2011).
3. Would you link this YouTube video to my slide show. [Uses a period to follow courteous request that requires no verbal response.]

Exercise 12—Number Usage

1. The question was answered by 61 percent of the respondents.
2. The meeting is scheduled for 10 a.m. on February 3.
3. These three figures appeared on the expense account: $21.95, $30, and $35.14.
4. The purchasing manager ordered fifty 4-GB flash drives.
5. Twenty-one members voted in favor of the $2 million proposal.
6. Approximately 100 respondents requested a copy of the results. [Approximations above nine that can be expressed in one or two words may be written in either figures or words, but figures are more emphatic.]
7. Mix 2 quarts of white with 13 quarts of brown.
8. Examine the cost projections on page 8.

Exercise 13—Capitalization

1. The first question Professor Burney asked me during Interviewing 101 was "Why do you want to work for us?"
2. The remodeling will give the store a more sophisticated feel according to the public relations director.
3. As the summer season arrives, gas prices are expected to rise.
4. We recently purchased Digital Juice, an excellent source of copyright-free animated images.
5. Thomas Frieden, director of the Center for Disease Control, is the agency's key communicator.

Exercise 14—Words Frequently Misused

1. effect
2. advise
3. number
4. site
5. compliment, complements
6. one another
7. farther
8. fewer
9. infer
10. losing, its, different from
11. led, lead
12. personal
13. principal
14. They're, their
15. two, to, too

References

Chapter 1

[1]Baer, S. (2002, July 3). Anthrax response leader to head CDC; AIDS expert became chief spokeswoman after agency came under fire. *The Baltimore Sun,* p. 1A.

[2]Centers for Disease Control. (2009). Campaigns and initiatives: Health communication strategies. National Prevention Information Network. Retrieved from **www.cdcnpin.org/scripts/campaign/strategy.asp**

[3]Koncz, A. (2007, March 15). Employers cite communication skills, honesty/integrity as key for job candidates. National Association of Colleges and Employers. Retrieved from **www.naceweb.org/press/display.asp?year=2007&prid=254**

[4]Koncz, A. (2007, March 15). Employers cite communication skills, honesty/integrity as key for job candidates. National Association of Colleges and Employers. Retrieved from **www.naceweb.org/press/display.asp?year=2007&prid=254**

[5]Tobin, T. C. (2005, February 15). Chain of errors led to bus death. *St. Petersburg Times,* p. 1A.

[6]O'Brien, J. M. (2009, February 2). Zappos knows how to kick It. *Fortune*, 55–60.

[7]Tapscott, D. (2008, December 8). Supervising Net Gen. *Business Week Online*, 5. Retrieved from Business Source Complete database.

[8]Hunt, V. D. (1993). *Managing for quality: Integrating quality and business strategy* (p. 37). Homewood, IL: Business One Irwin.

[9]Long, R., & Pearson, R. (2009, January 30). Impeached Illinois Gov. Rod Blagojevich has been removed from office. *Chicagotribune.com*. Retrieved from **http://www.chicagotribune.com/news/local/chi-blagojevich-impeachment-removal,0,5791846.story**

[10]Turner, T. (2009, March 16). Tax AIG executive bonuses, Dodd says. *FoxNews.com*. Retrieved from **http://www.foxnews.com/politics/2009/03/16/tax-aig-executive-bonuses-dodd-says/**

[11]Savage, C. (2008, September 10). Sex, drug use and graft cited in Interior Department. *The New York Times*. Retrieved from **http://www.nytimes.com/2008/09/11/washington/11royalty.html**

[12]Timmons, H., & Wassemer, B. (2009, January 7). Satyam chief admits huge fraud. *The New York Times*, Retrieved from **www.nytimes.com/2009/01/08/business/worldbusiness/08satyam.html**

[13]Slayton, M. (1980). *Common sense & everyday ethics*. Washington, DC: Ethics Resource Center.

[14]Slayton, M. (1991, May-June). Perspectives. *Ethics Journal*. Washington, DC: Ethics Resource Center.

[15]A question of ethics. (2000, January). *Communication World*, 17, 9.

[16]When something is rotten. (2002, July 27). *Economist*, 53+.

[17]A gift or a bribe? (2002, September). *State Legislatures*, *2*(8), 9.

[18]Mathison, D. L. (1988). Business ethics cases and decision models: A call for relevancy in the classroom. *Journal of Business Ethics, 10,* 781.

[19]Martha Stewart found guilty on all counts, vows appeal. (2004, March 8). *Ethics Newsline*. Retrieved from **www.globalethics.org**

[20]Jelly Belly Candy Company: Expanding internationally. (2007). *Talent Management*. Retrieved from **http://www.talentmgt.com/departments/application/54/**

[21]McGarry, M. J. (1994, June 9). Short cuts. *Newsday*, p. A50.

[22]Allen, M. (1996). NAFTA can't undo mistakes: Small businesses still find it hard to sell into Mexico, sidestep goofs. *Dallas Business Journal*, p. 1.

[23] Bazar, E., & Overberg, P. (2008, August 14). *USA Today*, p. 41. Retrieved from LexisNexis Academic database.

[24]U.S. workforce ages. (2005, July). *Journal of Accountancy*. Retrieved from www.journalofaccountancy.com/Issues/2005/Jul/USWorkforceAges.htm

[25]Jōyō Kanji. (2009). *Wikipedia*. Retrieved from http://en.wikipedia.org/wiki/Jōyō_kanji

[26]Marquardt, M. J., & Engel, D. W. (1993). HRD competencies for a shrinking world. *Training & Development, 47*(5), 59–64.

[27]Mason, R. O. (1986). Four ethical issues of the information age. In Dejoie, R., Fowler, G., & Paradice, D. (1991). *Ethical issues in information systems* (pp. 46–55). Boston: Boyd & Fraser.

[28]Harris Interactive. (2008, March 19). Harris Poll #17: Most people are "privacy pragmatists" who, while concerned about privacy, will sometimes trade it off for other benefits. Retrieved from www.harrisinteractive.com/harris_poll/index.asp?PID=365

[29]Nancherta, A. (2008, May). Surveillance increases in workplace. *T&D, 62(5)*, 12.

[30]Orwell, G. (1949). *1984.* (pp. 6–7). *New York:* Signet Classics.

[31]Brown, W. S. (1996). Technology, workplace privacy, and personhood. *Journal of Business Ethics, 15,* 1237–1248.

[32]Felts, C. (1995). Taking the mystery out of self-directed work teams. *Industrial Management, 37*(2), 21–26.

[33]Miller, B. K., & Butler, J. B. (1996, November/December). Teams in the workplace. *New Accountant*, 18–24.

[34]Ray, D., & Bronstein, H. (1995). *Teaming up*. New York: McGraw Hill.

[35]The trouble with teams. (1995, January 14). *Economist*, 61.

[36]Frohman, M. A. (1995, April 3). Do teams . . . but do them right. *IndustryWeek*, 21–24.

[37]Zuidema, K. R., & Kleiner, B. H. (1994). New developments in developing self-directed work groups. *Management Decision, 32*(8), 57–63.

[38]Barry, D. (1991). Managing the baseless team: Lessons in distributed leadership. *Organizational Dynamics, 20*(1), 31–47.

[39]O'Connor, S. (2009, May 15). Obama picks activist Frieden to head CDC. *FT.com*. Retrieved from www.ft.com/cms/s/0/237b84ac-416e-11de-bdb7-00144feabdc0.html

[40]Pounds, M. H. (1996, April 12). New breed of executive is ruthless, highly paid. *Sun-Sentinel* (Fort Lauderdale), p. 1F.

Chapter 2

[1]Whelan, D. (2007, September 17). This won't hurt a bit. *Forbes*. Retrieved from www.forbes.com/free_forbes/2007/0917/116.html

[2]O'Hara, K. J. (2007, September). Guided by principles: How Angela Braly leads WellPoint based on clear goals and a strong sense of purpose. *Smart Business*. Retrieved from www.sbnonline.com/Local/Article/12852/82/0/Guided_by_principles.aspx?Category=112

[3]Whelan, D. (2007, September 17). This won't hurt a bit. *Forbes.* Retrieved from www.forbes.com/free_forbes/2007/0917/116.html

[4]Braly, A. (2009). Diversity at WellPoint: Welcome statement. Retrieved from www.wellpointdiversity.com

[5]WellPoint, Inc. (2009). Mission, vision, & values. WellPoint, Inc. official website. Retrieved from www.wellpoint.com/business/about_mission.asp

[6]Delaney, S. (2008, October 28). Senn Delaney congratulates WellPoint on being named one of the best places to work in health care. Senn Delaney Leadership Consulting Group, LLC. Retrieved from http://www.senndelaney.com/news_WellPoint.html

[7]Interpersonal intelligence. (2009). My Personality. Retrieved from www.mypersonality.info/multiple-intelligences/interpersonal/

[8]Galpin, T. (1995, April). Pruning the grapevine. *Training & Development, 49*(4), 28+.

[9]Lampton, B. (2003, December 1). "My pleasure": The Ritz-Carlton Hotel part II. *ExpertMagazine.com.* Retrieved from www.expertmagazine.com/EMOnline/RC/part2.htm

[10]Hersey, P., & Blanchard, K. H. (1982). *Management of organizational behavior: Utilizing human resources* (4th ed.). Englewood Cliffs, NJ: Prentice-Hall.

[11]Felts, C. (1995). Taking the mystery out of self-directed work teams. *Industrial Management, 37*(2), 21–26.

[12]Mehrabian, A. (1971). *Silent messages*. Belmont, CA: Wadsworth.

[13]White, M. (2009, January 2). Proper attire for a professional image. *American Small Business News*. Retrieved from www.americanentrepreneurship.com/2009/01/02/proper-attire-for-a-professional-image/

[14]Axtell, R. E. (1997, April). Watch what you say: Hand gestures mean different things to different people. *Reader's Digest*, 71–72.

[15]Flannigan, T. (1990). Successful negotiating with the Japanese. *Small Business Reports, 15*(6), 47–52.

[16]Briggs, W. (1998, December). Next for communicators: Global negotiation. *Communication World*. Retrieved from http://findarticles.com/p/articles/mi_m4422/is_1_16/ai_53527378

[17]Briggs, W. (1998, December). Next for communicators: Global negotiation. *Communication World*, *16*(1), 12+.

[18]Tapscott, D. (2008, December 8). Supervising Net Gen. *Business Week Online*, 5. Retrieved from Business Source Complete database.

[19]Brooke, P. S. (2004). Legal questions: Cell phone orders. *Nursing, 34*(4), 12.

[20]Hillkirk, J. (1993, November 9). More companies reengineering: Challenging status quo now in vogue. *USA Today*, p. 1b.

[21]A structure that means business. (2007, December 1). *CIO, 21*(5), 80.

[22]O'Hara, K. J. (2007, September). Guided by principals: How Angela Braly leads WellPoint based on clear goals and a strong sense of purpose. *Smart Business*. Retrieved from www.sbnonline.com/Local/Article/12852/82/0/Guided_by_principles.aspx?Category=112

[23]Zuidema, K. R., & Kleiner, B. H. (1994, October). Self-directed work groups gain popularity. *Business Credit*, 21–26.

[24]Hunt, V. D. (1993). *Managing for quality: Integrating quality and business strategy* (p. 121). Homewood, IL: Business One Irwin.

[25]Electronic meetings. (2004). *EffectiveMeetings.com.* Retrieved from www.effectivemeetings.com/technology/mrtools/electronic_meetings.asp

[26]Chaney, L. H., & Lyden, J. A. (1998, May). Managing meetings to manage your image. *Supervision, 59*(5), 13–15.

[27]Munter, M. (1998, June). Meeting technology: From low-tech to high-tech. *Business Communication Quarterly, 61*(2), 80–87.

[28]Lawlor, C. (2006). Gender interactions in computer-mediated computer conferencing. *The Journal of Distance Education, 21*(2). Retrieved from www.jofde.ca/index.php/jde/article/viewArticle/63

[29]Munter, M. (1998, June). Meeting technology: From low-tech to high-tech. *Business Communication Quarterly*, *61*(2), 80-87.

[30]Matthews, C. S. (2008). Community service day. *Profiles in Diversity Journal, 10*(4), 42.

[31]NetApp ranked #1 on the "Best Companies to Work for" list by FORTUNE Magazine. (2009). News. Official website of NetApp. Retrieved from www.netapp.com/us/company/news/news-rel-20070108.html

[32]NetApp ranked #1 on the "Best Companies to Work for" list by FORTUNE Magazine. (2009). News. Official website of NetApp. Retrieved from www.netapp.com/us/company/news/news-rel-20070108.html

[33]NetApp: 100 best companies to work for. (2009). *Money.cnn.com*. Retrieved from http://money.cnn.com/magazines/fortune/bestcompanies/2009/snapshots/1.html

[34]Alter, A. (2008, March 6). Collaboration: Unlocking the power of teams. *CIO Insight*. Retrieved from www.cioinsight.com/c/a/Research/Collaboration-Unlocking-the-Power-of-Teams/

[35]Hughes, L. (2002). How to be a good listener. *Women in Business*, *54*, 17.

[36]Bruner, B. R. (2008). Listening: Communication & trust: Practitioners' perspectives of business/organizational relationships. *International Journal of Listening, 22,* 73–82.

Chapter 3

[1]Thiruvengadam, M. (2005, November 1). Hallmark and others adding cards for foreign holidays. *San Antonio Express News*. Retrieved from Business & Company Resource Center database.

[2]Mann, J. (2005, February 13). Hallmark greets fresh challenges. *The Kansas City Star*. Retrieved from LexisNexis database.

[3]About greeting cards: Trends. (2008, March 29). Greeting Card Association. Retrieved from www.greetingcard.org/about.php?ID=3

[4]Canavor, N., & Meirowitz, C. (2005). Good corporate writing: Why it matters, and what to do; poor corporate writing-in press releases, ads, brochures, websites and more—is costing companies credibility, and revenues. Here's how to put the focus back on clear communication. *Communication World, 22*(4), 30(4).

[5]Dennett, J. T. (1988, September). Not to say is better than to say: How rhetorical structure reflects cultural context in Japanese-English technical writing. *IEEE Transactions on Professional Communication, 31*(3), 116–119. doi 10.1109/47.7816

[6]Waxer, C. (2009, February 16). Clash of the generations: A twist of fate has technology vets and fresh talent vying for the same jobs. *Computerworld*, 16–18, 20.

[7]Saunderson, R. (February 2009). Is it really so hard to reward and recognize a multi-generational workplace. *Employee Benefit Plan Review*, 6–7.

[8]Shi, D. (1997, March 17). "We regret you'll be unbearable." *Christian Science Monitor*, 18.

[9]Jury sent message with huge reward in Vioxx drug case. (2005, August 24). *Gainesville Times.* Retrieved from www.gainesvilletimes.com.

[10]MacDonald, C. (2009, March 18). Madoff's accountant charged. The Business Ethics Blog. Retrieved from http://open.salon.com/blog/chris_macdonald/2009/03/18/madoffs_accountant_charged

[11]Goldberg, C., & Allen, S. (2005, March 18). Researcher admits fraud in grant data. Global Healing Center. Retrieved from www.ghchealth.com

[12]Another worker pays the price for fabricating resume. (2007, April 28). Retrieved from www.physorg.com/news96987628.html

[13]Reinemund, S. S. (1992). Today's ethics and tomorrow's work place. *Business Forum, 17*(2), 6–9.

[14]Telushkin, J. (1997). Avoid words that hurt. *USA Today*, p. 74.

[15]Lutz, W. (n.d.). Life under the chief doublespeak officer. Retrieved from www.dt.org/html/Doublespeak.html

[16]William Lutz talks about how doublespeak has taken over the business world. (1998, January 26). *Business News New Jersey, 11*(4), 13. Retrieved from Regional Business News (EBSCHO) database.

[17]Dolezalek, H. (2005). The clarity challenge: For too long, business writing has been a lifeless mass of jargon, obscurity, and unnecessary chatter. Can training help people to write more clearly? *Training, 42*(9), 28(5).

[18]Obama has apologized for Special Olympics quip. (2009, May 20). *USA Today.com*. Retrieved from http://news.yahoo.com/s/ap/20090320/ap_on_en_tv/obama_special_olympics

[19]Dysphemism. (2009, November 22). *Wikipedia.* Retrieved from http://en.wikipedia.org/wiki/Dysphemism

[20]Husted, B. (1999, November). Cyberscene; E-cards perfect for the forgetful. *Atlanta Constitution,* p. 3H.

[21]Connor, T. (2005, May 21). NYC TV reporter gets fired for using profanity on air unknowingly. *Sean Hannity: Tuned in to America*. Retrieved from www.hannity.com/forum/printthread.php?t=7987

[22]Horton, T. R. (1990, January). Eschew obfuscation. *Security Management, 34*(1), 22+.

[23]Mckenna, J. F. (1990, March 19). Tales from the circular file. *IndustryWeek,* 38.

[24]Baker, L. (2006, April 27). Yahoo Babel Fish translation tool. *Search Engine Journal.* Retrieved from www.searchenginejournal.com/yahoo-babel-fish-translation-tool/3335/

[25]Nobel, C. (2002, September 23). Industry capsule: Translator runs on pocket PCs. *EWeek, 18.*

Chapter 4

[1]Securities and Exchange Commission. (1998, August). *A plain English handbook: How to create clear SEC disclosure documents.* Retrieved from www.sec.gov/pdf/handbook.pdf

[2]Prudential, MetLife are first to speak clients' language (1999, July). *Best's Review, 100*(3), 93.

[3]Stucker, H. (1999). Annuity issuers hustling to speak 'plain English.' *National Underwriter, 103*(14), 7, 22.

[4]Fontaine, V. (2002, October). Receiving loud and clear: While it may appear that speech language technologies have not had the impact that many initially predicted, Vincent Fontaine, CEO of Babel Technologies, argues that recent developments are now starting to bear fruit. *Communicate*. Retrieved from the InfoTrac College Edition database.

[5]Fabrizio, L. (2009, February 18). Apology of the weak. *Spectator*. Retrieved from http://spectator.org/archives/2009/02/18/apology-of-the-weak/print

[6]Keown, T. (2009, February 13). A-Rod's weak apology is sadly the best one so far. *ESPN.com*. Retrieved from http://sports.espn.go.com/espn/page2/story?page=keown/090210

[7]Gordon, M. (2009, January 16). Schapiro pledges toughness at SEC. *The Washington Post*. Retrieved from http://www.washingtontimes.com/news/2009/jan/16/crisis-of-confidence/

[8]Is email making bosses ruder? (2005). *European Business Forum, 21*, 72.

[9]Rindegard, J. (1999). Use clear writing to show you mean business. *InfoWorld, 21*(47), 78.

[10]Dyrud, M. A. (1996). Teaching by example: Suggestions for assignment design. *Business Communication Quarterly*, *59*(3), 67-70.

[11]Redish, J. C. (1993). Understanding readers. In C. M. Barnum & S. Carliner (Eds.), *Techniques for technical communicators*. New York: Prentice Hall.

[12]Redish, J. C. (1993). Understanding readers. In C. M. Barnum & S. Carliner (Eds.), Techniques for *technical communicators*. New York: Prentice Hall.

[13]Wrong number. (1995). *Central New Jersey Business, 8*(13), 3.

[14]Neuwirth, R. (1998). Error message: To err is human, but darn expensive. *Editor & Publisher, 131*(29), 4.

[15]UCSD sends acceptance email to wrong list. (2009, April 2). *Eschool News*. Retrieved from http://www.eschoolnews.com/news/around-the-web/index.cfm?i=58045

[16]If you're going to impersonate Rachael Ray, be sure you can spell her name. (2009, March 29). Retrieved from http://terriblywrite.wordpress.com/2009/03/29/if-youre-going-to-impersonate-rachael-ray-be-sure-you-can-spell-her-name/

[17]To dye for. (2004, January 31). *World Magazine, 19*(4). Retrieved from LexisNexis database.

[18]Gamauf, M. (2004, December). The importance of good tech talk. *Business & Commercial Aviation, 95*(6), 66-69.

[19]Charlton, J. (Ed.) (1985). *The writer's quotation book*. Stamford, CT: Ray Freeman.

[20]Downing, C. E., & Clark, A. S. (1999). Groupware in practice. *Information Systems Management, 16*(2), 25.

[21]Weintraub, A. (2002, December 23). Privacy rights—In plain English. *BusinessWeek*, 10.

[22]Wolf, M. S., Davis, T. C., Tilson, H. H., Bass, P. F., & Parker, R. M. (2006, June 8). Misunderstanding of prescription drug warning labels among patients with low literacy. *Medscape*. Retrieved from http://www.medscape.com/viewarticle/5333483

[23]Plain English Campaign. (2003). Retrieved from http://www.plainenglish.co.uk

Chapter 5

[1]1500,000 and growing. (2005, July 1). *Lodging and Hospitality*, 22.

[2]Wyndham worldwide completed $450 million vacation ownership receivables securitization. (2008, June 30). *Internet Wire*. Retrieved from General Businessfile database.

[3]Fairfield Resorts. (2005, May 25). Fairfield Resorts celebrates major milestone reaching 500,000 owners. Retrieved from www.fairfieldresorts.com/ffr/href.co?id=NEWS-0000023

[4]Hear no evil, see no evil: Business email overtakes the telephone. (2007, August 20). *Network*. Retrieved from www.networkworld.com/community/node/18555

[5]McKay, D. R. (2008). Email etiquette. *About.com*. Retrieved from http://careerplanning.about.com/od/communication/a/email_etiquette.htm?p=1

[6]Silverman, D. (2009, April 14). Words at work: How to revise an email so that people will read it. Retrieved from http://blogs.harvardbusiness.org/silverman/2009/04/how-to-revise-an-email-so-that.html

[7]Silverman, D. (2009, April 14). Words at work: Is your email businesslike - or brusque? Retrieved from http://blogs.harvardbusiness.org/silverman/2009/05/is-your-email-businesslike-or.html

[8]New technology makes work harder. (1999, June 1). *BBC News.* Retrieved from http://news.bbc.co.uk/2/hi/science/nature/357993.stm

[8]Lacy, S. (2006, January 6). IM security one tough sell. *Business Week Online*, 11.

[10]Knapp, L. (2007, January 20). Switching to texting has pluses, minuses: Getting started. *The Seattle Times*, p. E6. Retrieved from General BusinessFile database.

[11]McGrath, C. (2006, January 22). The pleasures of the text. *The New York Times*, p. 15.

[12]Knapp, L. (2007, January 20). Switching to texting has pluses, minuses: Getting started. The *Seattle Times*, p. E6. Retrieved from General BusinessFile database.

[13]Electronic Privacy Information Center. (2008, September 15). Public opinion on privacy. Retrieved from www.epic.org/privacy/survey

[14]Circuit rules on text-message privacy. (2008, July 15). *Law.com*. Retrieved from www.law.com/jsp/legaltechnology/pubArticleLT.jsp?id=1202422970200

[15]Brown, P. B. (2005, December 31). Resolved: I will take good advice. *The New York Times.* Retrieved from http://www.nytimes.com/2005/12/31/business/31offline.html

[16]Mabrey, V., Scott, D. W., & Foster, M. (2008, Marcy 24). Charges filed in Detroit mayor scandal. *ABC News.* Retrieved from http://abcnews.go.com/print?id=4355795

[17]Varchaver, N. (2003). The perils of e-mail. *Fortune, 147*(3), 96+.

[18]Varchaver, N. (2003). The perils of e-mail. *Fortune, 147*(3), 96+.

[19]Adapted from Gaithersburg-Germantown Chamber of Commerce (2002). Retrieved from www.ggchamber.org/business/view_article.asp?id=32

[20]Mason, R. O. (1986). Four ethical issues of the information age. In R. Dejoie, G. Fowler, & D. Paradice (1991). *Ethical issues in information systems* (pp. 46-55). Boston: Boyd & Fraser.

[21]Laudon, K. C., & Laudon, J. P. (1994). *Management information systems: Organization and technology* (3rd ed.). New York: Macmillan.

[22]Downer, K. (2008). A great website in five steps. *Third Sector*, 9.

[23]Tierney, J. (2007, April). Ignore universal web design at your own peril. *Multichannel Merchant,* 8.

[24]Huettner, B. (2008, January 19). Web accessibility basics. Professional Communication Society. Retrieved from http://ewh.ieee.org/soc/pcs/index.php?q=node/124

[25]McAlpine, R. (2001). *Web word wizardry: A guide to writing for the Web and intranet*. Berkeley, CA: Ten Speed Press.

[26]Fichter, D. (2001, November/December). Zooming in: Writing content for intranets. *Online, 25*(6), 80+.

[27]How to write for the web. (2008, March 26). *Knight Digital Media Center.* Retrieved from www.ojr.org/ojr/wiki/writing

[28]Goodnoe, E. (2005, August 8). How to use wikis for business. *Information Week*. Retrieved from www.informationweek.com/news/management/showArticle.jhtml?articleID=167600331&pgno=3&queryText=&isPrev=

[29]Weblog. (2005). Loosely coupled. Retrieved from www.looselycoupled.com/glossary/weblog

[30]Quible, Z. K. (2005). Blogs and written business communication courses: A perfect union. *Journal of Education for Business, 80*(6), 327-332.

[31]Jones, D. (2005, May 10). CEOs refuse to get tangled up in messy blogs. *USA Today*. Retrieved from Academic Search Premier database.

[32]DeBare, I. (2005, May 5). Tips for effective use of blogs in business. *San Francisco Chronicle,* p. C6.

[33]Johnson, C. Y. (2008, July 7). Hurry up, the customer has a complaint: As blogs expand the reach of a single voice, firms monitor the Internet looking for the dissatisfied. *The Boston Globe*. Retrieved from Boston.com

[34]Brieger, P., & O'Shea, S. (2004, September 4). Employee fired by Starbucks over blog. *Blogcritics.org*. Retrieved from http://blockcritics.org/archives/2004/09/04/141004.php

[35]Hutchins, J. P. (2005, November 14). Beyond the water cooler. *Computerworld*, *39*(46), 45–46.

[36]Tough, P. (2005, December 11). The stream-of-consciousness newspaper. *New York Times Magazine*, 55, 93–94.

[37]Chase, N. (1999, April). Quality data on the Internet. *Quality, 38*(5), 122–126.

[38]Centric Software delivers first Apparel Suite with operational performance management. (2007, September 17). *Business Wire*. Retrieved from http://findarticles.com/p/articles/mi_m0EIN/is_2007_Sept_17/ai_n19521198

[39]USA: Centric Apparel Suite to propel LeCoq Sportif growth. (2007, September 17). *Fibre2Fashion*. Retrieved from www.fibre2fashion.com/news/printstory.asp?news_id=41159

[40]How to get the most out of voice mail (2000, February). *The CPA Journal, 70*(2), 11.

[41]Leland, K., & Bailey, K. (1999). *Customer service for dummies* (2nd ed.). New York: Wiley.

[42]Berkley, S. (2003, July). Help stamp out bad voicemail! *The Voice Coach Newsletter*. Retrieved from www.greatvoice.com/archive_vc/archiveindex_vc.html

[43]McCarthy, M. L. (1999, October). Email, voicemail and the Internet: How employers can avoid getting cut by the double-edged sword of technology. *Business Credit, 100*(9), 44+.

[44]Krotz, J. L. (2008). *Cell phone etiquette:* 10 dos and don'ts. *Microsoft Small Business Center.* Retrieved from www.microsoft.com/smallbusiness/resources/technology/communications/cell-phone-etiquette-10-dos-and-donts.aspx#Cellphoneetiquettedosanddonts

[45]Cell phone etiquette (2001, March). *Office Solutions, 18*(3), 13.

[46]Coustan, D., & Strickland, J. (n.d.). How smartphones work: The future of smartphones. Retrieved from http://communication.howstuffworks.com/smartphone5.htm

[47]Shellenbarger, S. (2007). A day without email is like . . . Career Journal (*The Wall Street Journal*). Retrieved from http://online.wsj.com/public/article/SB119205641656255234-tmvyaC6sQRWh4D2UINHEAJlbWdU_20071109.html

Chapter 6

[1]Kane, M. (2008, April 18). New Zappos: Shoes—and gadgets to boot. *CNET News*. Retrieved from http://news.cnet.com/8301-10784_3-9921188-7.html

[2]About Zappos.com. (2008). The Zappos story. Retrieved from http://www.zappos.com/about/zhtml

[3]Durst, S. (2007, March 15). Shoe in. *Business 2.0*. Retrieved from http://money.cnn.com/magazines/business2/business2_archive/2006/12/01/8394993/index.htm

[4]Hugenberg, L. W., LaCivita, R. M., & Lubanovic, A. M. (1996). International business and training: Preparing for the global economy. *Journal of Business Communication, 33*(2), 205–222.

[5]Oblander, P., & Daniels, E. (1997). International communication and the U.S.-Japan lumber trade: An exploratory study. *Forest Products Journal*, *47*(3), 38–44.

[6]Varner, I. I. (1987). Internationalizing business communication courses. *Bulletin of the Association for Business Communication, 50*(4), 11+.

[7]Williamson, M. (2008, June 11). Twittering the Internet. *TechnologyStory.com.* Retrieved from http://www.technologystory.com/2008/06/11/twittering-the-internet

[8]Keizer, G. (1992, August). Press one for Gregg. *Compute! 17*(7), 73–75.

[9]Kaye, S. (1999, March). Attitude adjustments. *Quality Progress, 32*(3), 28–33.

[10]Auerback, G. (2004, Winter). 10 ways to improve employee communication. *Society for Human Resource Management, EMA Forum*. Retrieved from http://www.shrm.org/ema/EMT/articles/2004/winter04auerbach.asp

[11]Meyer, J. (2005, February 25). E-mail ills delayed warrant. *Denver Post, p. A-6.*

[12]Mount, M. (2009, January 7). Army sorry for 'John Doe' letters to relatives of war dead. *CNN.com.* Retrieved from http://www.cnn.com/2009/US/01/07/john.doe.letters/index.html?iref=nextin

[13]Discarded hard drives prove a trove of personal info. (2003, January 16). *The Daily Sentinel*, p. 7A.

Chapter 7

[1]Memmott, M. (2006, January 4). Media forced to explain inaccurate reports on tragedy. *USA Today*. Retrieved from http://www.usatoday.com/news/nation/2006-01-04-mine-media_x.htm

[2]Porteus, L. (2006, January 4). Mine officials: 'We sincerely regret' mixed messages about miners. *Fox News.com*. Retrieved from http://www.foxnews.com

[3]Porteus, L. (2006, January 4). Mine officials: 'We sincerely regret' mixed messages about miners. *Fox News.com.* Retrieved from http://www.foxnews.com

[4]Sussman, S. W., & Sproull, L. (1999). Straight talk: Delivering bad news through electronic communication. *Information Systems Research, 10*(2), 150+. Retrieved from Business Source Premier database.

[5]Condotta, B. (2004, September 29). Just a miscommunication. *The Seattle Times*, p. D2.

[6]Intranet use—smart, fast, efficient. (2002, January). *Work & Family*, 7, 8.

[7]Stewart-Gross, B. (2008). Generational differences: Communication guidelines. *Ezine Articles*. Retrieved from http://ezinearticles.com/?Generational-Differences—Communication-Guidelines&id=859386

[8]Swisher, K. (2007, October 15). AOL layoffs letter from CEO Randy Falco. *All Things Digital*. Retrieved from http://kara.allthingsd.com/20071015/aol-layoffs-letter-from-randy-falco/

[9]Personality Test Center. (2005). Human relations test. Retrieved from http://www.personalitytest.net/funtest/index.htm

[10]Ethical workforce reflects honest management. (2008, June). *Internal Auditor*, 18–19.

[11]Advice from the pros on the best way to deliver bad news. (2003, February). *IOMA's Report on Customer Relationship Management,* 5–6.

[12]Purina on pet food recall 4-26-07. (2007). American Kennel Club. Retrieved from http://clubs.akc.org/brit/NEWS/07.PurinaPetFoodRecall.htm

[13]Workers get better at bearing bad news. (2005, October 11). *Personnel Today*, 46.

[14]Expert offers advice about how to lay off employees. (2008, October 9). *Immediate Care Business*. Retrieved from http://www.immediatecarebusiness.com/hotnews/laying-off-employees.html

[15]International Coal Group bungles crisis. (2006, January 4). *Fresh Glue*. Retrieved from http://www.freshglue.com/fresh_glue/2006/01/international_c.html

[16]International Coal Group bungles crisis. (2006, January 4). *Fresh Glue.* Retrieved from http://www.freshglue.com/fresh_glue/2006/01/international_c.html

[17]Chawki, M. (2006, July 9). Anonymity in cyberspace: Finding the balance. *Computer Crime Research Center.* Retrieved from http://www.crime-research.org/articles/2110/

Chapter 8

[1]Community involvement: Charities: Habitat for Humanity. (2008). *StoresOnline.* Retrieved from https://www.storesonlinepro.com/store/1234/page/1239546?sitecookie=d558c4da1961291b7c90d527b25e9d37

[2]Meet Habitat for Humanity chief executive officer: Jonathan Reckford, pastor and veteran Business leader. (2008). Official website of Habitat for Humanity, brief videocast from Jonathan Reckford. Retrieved from http://www.habitat.org/ceo/default.aspx

[3]McGinn, D. (2006, May 29). Building success: Habitat for Humanity's new CEO is aiming to modernize the nonprofit. *Newsweek*. Retrieved from www.accessmylibrary.com/coms2/summary_0286-15425022_ITM

[4]Put your faith into action: Online donation makes it easy! (2008). Habitat for Humanity official website. Retrieved from http://www.habitat.org/donation

[5]Battistelli, M. (2005, January 1). Building houses, building hope: Habitat for Humanity International focuses its energy on major gifts to fuel a global attack on substandard housing. *Fundraising Success Magazine.* Retrieved from http:///www.fundraisingmag.com/story/story.bsp?sid=32304&var=story

[6]Intrusive ads turn surfers away. (2008, July 24). *ITnews*. Retrieved from http://www.itnews.com.au/News/81023,intrusive-ads-turn-surfers-away.aspx

[7]Cody, S. (1906). *Success in letter writing: Business and social* (pp. 122–126). Chicago: A. C. McClurg.

[8]Cooper, T., & Kelleher, T. (2001). Better mousetrap? Of Emerson, ethics, and postmillennium persuasion. *Journal of Mass Media Ethics, 16*(2/3), 176+.

[9]Iwata, E. (2000, August 1). Gateway goes to extremes to empathize. *USA Today*, p. 3B.

[10]Treadmill HQ. (2009). Body Solid Endurance 8K Treadmill. Retrieved from http://www.treadmillhq.com/product-detail~pid~{F87B200B-4805-40A6-A9AE-204C99C10992}.htm

[11]GotoMeeting.com. Retrieved from https://www2.gotomeeting.com:443/en_US/m/g2mab_More2LMlp.tmpl

[12]Masur, S. (2008, July 19). Ready, handset, go: The rules of mobile marketing. *Billboard*, p. 8. Retrieved from General Businessfile database.

[13]Masur, S. (2008, July 19). Ready, handset, go: The rules of mobile marketing. *Billboard*, p. 8. Retrieved from General Businessfile database.

[14]Shields, M. (2008, June 16). Best use of mobile GSD&M Idea City. *Adweek*, *49*(20). Retrieved from Business Source Complete database.

[15]9 million U.S. consumers use mobile commerce, report says. (2008, June 20). *CardLine, 8*(25). Retrieved from Business Source Complete database.

[16]Papa John's rolls out text message ordering system. (2007, November 26). *Nation's Restaurant* News, p. 8. Retrieved from General BusinessFile database.

[17]Masur, S. (2008, July 19). Ready, handset, go: The rules of mobile marketing. *Billboard*, p. 8. Retrieved from General Businessfile database.

[18]Sinclair,B. (2003, July 20). Handle client complaints. *The Web design business kit.* Retrieved from http://www.sitepoint.com/article/handle-client-complaints/

[19]Steak and Ale. (1997). Signature style at Steak and Ale. Dallas, TX: Steak and Ale.

[20]McLean, J. (2009, July 10). Busted guitar blues is sweet YouTube revenge. *TheStar.com.* Retrieved from http://www.thestar.com/news/canada/article/663869 Star.com.

[21]Federal regulations. (2009). Call Compliance, Inc. Retrieved from www.callcompliance.com/regulations/federal-regulations.html

[22]Anti-Spam laws. (2009). *Email-Marketing-Reports.com.* Retrieved from www.email-marketing-reports.com/canspam/

[23]Walker, W. (2000, May 9). Junk mail, telemarketers, catalogs: How to get off the list. *Family Circle*, 40–43.

Chapter 9

[1]Capell, K. (2009, June 22). Novartis: Radically remaking its drug business. *BusinessWeek*, 30–35. Retrieved from Business Source Complete database.

[2]How Vasella interprets data—and the future. (2007, November). *Pharmaceutical Executive, 27*(11), 94. Retrieved from Business Source Complete database.

[3]Capell, K. (2009, June 22). Novartis: Radically remaking its drug business. *BusinessWeek*, 30–35. Retrieved from Business Source Complete database.

[4]Costanzo, C. (2005, April 19). How consumer research drives website design. *American Banker*, *170*(74), 4–5.

[5]Error had study subjects on wrong medications. (2002, August). *Bioresearch Monitoring Alert*, *2*(8), 10.

[6]Syllabus of Supreme Court Opinion for 96-511. (1997). Reno, Attorney General of the United States, et al. v. American Civil Liberties Union et al. Retrieved from http://supct.law.cornell.edu/supct/html/96-511.ZS.html

[7]Adams, D. (2000). Literacy, learning, and media. *Technos: Quarterly for Education and Technology*. Retrieved from http://www.findarticles.com

[8]Grimes, B. (2003, May 6). Fooling Google. *PC Magazine, 22*(8), 74.

[9]Michaels, S. (2009, April 8). Coldplay deny Joe Satriani plagiarism claims in court. *Guardian.co.uk*. Retrieved from http://www.guardian.co.uk/music/2009/apr/08/coldplay-deny-satriani-plagiarism-claims

[10]Gottlieb, J. (2008, December 10). Plagiarism charge puts Coldplay in hot water. *BostonHerald.com*. Retrieved from http://news.bostonherald.com/entertainment/music/general/view/2008_12_10_Plagiarism_charge_puts_Coldplay_in_hot_water/srvc=home&position=also

[11]Capell, K. (2009, June 22). Novartis: Radically remaking its drug business. *BusinessWeek*, 30. Retrieved from Business Source Complete database.

[12]Kinzer, S. (1994, August 22). Germany upholds tax on fast-food restaurants. *The New York Times*, p. 2.

[13]Kets de Vries, M. F. R. (1994). Toppling the cultural tower of Babel. *Chief Executive*, 94, 68.

[14]International marketing mistakes. (2009). *American Demographics*. Retrieved from http://wcthompson.com/funnies/mrktoops.htm

[15]Heath, R. P. (1996, October). Think globally. *American Demographics*, 48–54.

[16]SurveyMonkey.com. (2009, March). Quantcast. Retrieved from www.surveymonkey.com

[17]Mijailovic, J. (2009, January 21). Office workers send more than 160 e-mail messages daily and spend two hours to e-mail. Deloitte. Retrieved from http://www.deloitte.com/dtt/press_release/0,1014,cid%253D243722,00.html

[18]Email contributes to "Information Overload," claim UK managers. (2003, February). *Information Systems Auditor*, 8.

[19]Gordon, B. (2004, June 8). Remembering and forgetting in everyday life. NPR. Tavis Smiley Show. Retrieved from http://www.npr.org/templates/story/story.php?storyId=1943901

[20]Gilchrist, A., & Mahon, B. (2004). *Information architecture: Designing for information environments for purpose.* London: Facet Publishing.

Chapter 10

[1]Gannes, L. (2008, June 27). Chad Hurley: How we did it. *New TeeVee.* Retrieved from http://newteevee.com/2008/06/27/chad-hurley-how-we-did-it/

[2]Glaser, M. (2006, April 4). "Digging deeper: YouTube CEO hails 'Birth of New Clip Culture.'" Public Broadcasting Service. Retrieved from http://www.pbs.org/mediashift/2006/04/digging-deeperyoutube-ceo-hails-birth-of-a-new-clip-culture094.html

[3]YouTube audience ages. (2008). *Social Media Optimization*. Retrieved from http://social-media-optimization.com/2008/04/youtube-audience-ages/

[4]YouTube strikes content deals. (2006, October 9). *USATODAY.com*. Retrieved from http://www.usatoday.com/tech/news/2006-10-09-youtube-deals_x.htm

[5]Cullen, L. T. (2007, March 5). It's a wrap: You're hired! *Time*. Retrieved from http://www.time.com/time/magazine/article/0,9171,1592860,00.html

[6]Martin, M. H. (1997, November 27). The man who makes sense of numbers. *Fortune, 273–275.*

[7]Wright, P., & Jansen, C. (1998). How to limit clinical errors in interpretation of data. *Lancet, 352*(9139), 1539–1543.

[8]Ordinary Media. (2005, May 24). *Today Show*, MSNBC.com use wrong photo. Retrieved from http://www.regrettheerror.com/2005/05/today_show_msnb.html

[9]Simons, T. (2004). The multimedia paradox, *Presentations*, *18*(9), 24–25.

[10]Clark, R. C., & Mayer, R. E. (2007). *E-learning and the science of instruction* (2nd ed.). San Francisco: John Wiley and Sons.

[11]Hurley, C. (2008, September 16). Chad Hurley on the future of YouTube: We will conquer every screen. *TechCrunch*. Retrieved from http://www.techcrunch.com/2008/09/16/chad-hurley-on-the-future-of-youtube-we-will-conquer-every-screen/

[12]On pictograms. (2009, January 19). *This Material World.* Retrieved from http://thismaterialworld.wordpress.com/2009/01/19/on-pictograms/

[13]Kienzler, D. S. (1997). Visual ethics. *The Journal of Business Communication, 34*(2), 171–187. [p. 171].

[14]College Entrance Examination Board. (2006). Percentage and data interpretation. Retrieved from http://www.gomath.com/members/test/tutorial/section8/p1.html

[15]Gallo, C. (2008, December 10). Making YouTube work for your business. *Business Week Online*. Retrieved from http://www.businessweek.com/smallbiz/content/dec2008/sb2008129_398437.htm?campaign_id=rss_tech

Chapter 11

[1]Aflac takes next step in defining brand: Brand evolution of AFLAC. (2004, December 2). *PR Newswire US.* Retrieved from LexisNexis database.

[2]Aflac's annual report ranked first in *Chief Executive* magazine's listing of 10 Best. (1999, November 17). *PR Newswire, Financial News.*

[3]The annual report card. (2002, October 1). Treasury and Risk. Retrieved from http://www.treasuryandrisk.com/Issues/2002/October%202002/Pages/The-Annual-Report-Card.aspx

[4]Shoen, W. (2006, February). Corporate disclosure in a competitive environment. Social Science Research Network. Retrieved from http://papers.ssrn.com/sol3/papers.cfm?abstract_id=885961

[5]International Accounting Standards. (2006). *Investopedia.com.* Retrieved from http://www.investopedia.com/terms/i/ias.asp

[6]Hochhauser, M. (2001). Lost in the fine print: Readability of financial privacy notices. *Privacy Rights Clearinghouse*. Retrieved from http://www.privacyrights.org/ar/GLB-Reading.htm

[7]Moyer, L. (1999, December 2). Ads libs: Annual report guru ranks those that measure up, or don't. *The American Banker*, 4.

[8]Nunnemaker, J. F., Jr., Briggs, R. O., Mittleman, D. D., Vogel, D. R., & Balthazard, P. A. (1996/1997). Lessons from a dozen years of group support systems research: A discussion of lab and field findings. *Journal of Management Information Systems, 13*(3), 163–207.

[9]Emling, S. (2003, June 13). Patriot Act stirs concerns. *The Daily Sentinel* (Nacogdoches, TX), p. 4B.

[10]World Intellectual Property Organization. (2006). About WIPO. Retrieved from http://www.wipo.int/about-wipo/en/

[11]Niccolai, J. (2007, February 13). Google News guilty of copyright violation. *PCWorld*. Retrieved from http://www.pcworld.com/printable/article/id,128985/printable.html

Chapter 12

[1]Bridgwater, A. (2009, June 3). Oracle launches Java store. *Computer Weekly*. Retrieved from http://www.computerweekly.com/Articles/2009/06/03/236275/oracle-launches-java-store.htm

[2]Oracle to buy Sun. (2009). Retrieved from http://sun.com/aboutsun/media/presskits/2009-0420/

[3]Glinert, S. (1999, December). Presenting on the Web. *Home Office Computing*, 114.

[4]Kalytiak, T. (2008, October). Overcoming speaking anxiety: Toastmasters sculpt shy speakers into outstanding orators. *Alaska Business Monthly*. Retrieved from http://www.akbizmag.com

[5]Axtell, R. E. (1992). *Do's and taboos of public speaking: How to get those butterflies flying in formation.* New York: John Wiley.

[6]Britz, J. D. (1999, October). You can't catch a marlin with a meatball. *Presentations, 13*(10), A1–22.

[7]Hughes, M. (1990). Tricks of the speechwriter's trade. *Management Review, 9*(11), 56–58.

[8]Sommerville, J. (2003). Presentation tip: Stop the verbal spam. *About.com; Entrepreneurs.* Retrieved from http://entrepreneurs.about.com/cs/marketing/a/infodumping.htm

[9]Hughes, M. (1990). Tricks of the speechwriter's trade. *Management Review*, *9*(11), 56–58.

[10]Gallo, C. (2008, June 23). Making your points through numbers. *Business Week Online*, 22.

[11]Simmons, A. (2007). *Whoever tells the best story wins: How to use your own stories to communicate with power and impact*. New York: Amacon.

[12]Gallo, G. (2008, July 23). Making your point through numbers. *Business Week Online*, 22.

[13]Gallo, Carmine. (2009, April 8). Making your presentations relevant. *Business Week Online,* 15.

[14]Axtell, R. E. (1992). *Do's and taboos of public speaking: How to get those butterflies flying in formation.* New York: John Wiley.

[15]Zielinski, D. (2005, August). The speech trap; careful: What you say in a company presentation can be held against you in a court of law. *Presentations, 19*(8), 20–24.

[16]Decker, B. (1992). *You've got to be believed to be heard*. New York: St. Martin's Press.

[17]Hillary Campaign sends "docu-point" to House Dems. (2008, May 10). *Presentation Zen*. Retrieved from http://www.presentationzen.com/presentationzen/2008/05/hillary-campaig.html

[18]Earnest, W. (2007). Save our slides: PowerPoint design that works. Dubuque, IA: Kendall/Hunt.

[19]Earnest, W. (2007). Save our slides: PowerPoint design that works. Dubuque, IA: Kendall/Hunt.

[20]U.S. Copyright Office. (2000, September). What is copyright? Retrieved from http://www.copyright.gov/circs/circ1.html#wci

[21]Zielinski, D. (2001, July). Stop! Thief! The great web copyright crackdown. *Presentations, 15*(7), 50(9).

[22]Templeton, B. (2008, October). 10 big myths about copyright explained. Retrieved from www.templetons.com/brad/copymyths.html.

[23]Carson, E. (2009, April 19) DioGuaridi on being idol judge: It's not easy. *ABC News.com.* Retrieved from http://abcnews.go.com/Entertainment/wireStory?id=7374447

[24]Axtell, R. E. (1992). *Do's and taboos of public speaking: How to get those butterflies flying in formation.* New York: John Wiley.

[25]Decker, B. (1992). *You've got to be believed to be heard.* (p. 137). New York: St. Martin's Press.

[26]Wikipedia. (2006). Simplified English. Retrieved from http://en.widipedia. org/wiki/Simplified_English

[27]Hanke, J. (1998, January). Presenting as a team. *Presentations, 12*(1), 74–82.

[28]Hanke, J. (1998, January). Presenting as a team. *Presentations, 12*(1), 74–82.

[29]Hanke, J. (1998, January). Presenting as a team. *Presentations, 12*(1), 74–82.

[30]Hanke, J. (1998, January). Presenting as a team. *Presentations, 12*(1), 74–82.

[31]Davids, M. (1999). Smiling for the camera. *Journal of Business Strategy, 20*(3), 20–24.

[32]Connelly, M. (2006). Podcast tells Fusion owners about features. *Automotive News, 80*(6206), 33.

[33]Turner, C. (1998, February). Become a web presenter! (Really it's not that hard). *Presentations, 12*(2), 26–27.

[34]Ewers, J. (2006, January 23). A jolt of java. *U.S. News & World Report.* Retrieved from General Businessfile database.

[35]Nicholaus B., & Lowrie P. (1996). *The conversation piece: Creative questions to tickle the mind.* New York: Ballantine Books.

[36]Dudlicek, J. (2005, November). Team spirit: Yoplait strives to feel small but do things big through team work and leveraging the strengths of parent General Mills. *Dairy Field, 188*(11), 20(7).

[37]DeShields, O. W., Kara, A., & Kaynak, E. (1996). Source effects in purchase decisions: The impact of physical attractiveness and accent of salesperson. *International Journal of Research in Marketing, 13*(1), 89–101.

[38]Stern, D. A. (2005). Speaking without an accent. Dialect Accent Specialists, Inc. Retrieved from http://www.dialectaccentspecialists.com/accent_reduction.shtml

Chapter 13

[1]Container Store: 100 Best Companies to work for. (2009). *Fortune Magazine.* Retrieved from http://money.cnn.com/magazines/fortune/bestcompanies/2009/snapshots/32.html

[2]Earls, A. R. (2005, April 24). A new variety of retailer looks to lure, keep workers. *The Boston Globe,* p. G12.

[3]Roth, D. (2000, January 10). My job at The Container Store. *Fortune,* 74–78.

[4]Jackson, T. (2003). Find a job you love and success will follow. Career Journal (*The Wall Street Journal*). Retrieved from http://www.careerjournal.com/jobhunting/strategies/20030415-jackson.html

[5]Riley, M. F. (2009). *The Riley guide: Employment opportunities and job resources on the Internet.* Retrieved from http://www.rileyguide.com

[6]Tharp, P. (2006, February 21). Radioshack CEO lied about Bible school degree, quits. *New York Post* (online edition). Retrieved from http://www.nypost.com/business/63915.htm

[7]Can you spot the real resume? (2008). *Journal of Accountancy, 206*(4), 27.

[8]Gurchiek, K. (2008, August 14). Mensa membership, Kennedy kinship among outrageous resume lies. Retrieved from http://www.shrm.org/Publications/HRNews/Pages/OutrageousResumeLies.aspx

[9]Gurchiek, K. (2008, August 14). Mensa membership, Kennedy kinship among outrageous resume lies. Retrieved from http://www.shrm.org/Publications/HRNews/Pages/OutrageousResumeLies.aspx

[10]IOMA. (2006, June). How to ferret out instances of résumé padding and fraud. *Compensation & Benefits for Law Offices, 6*(6), 1, 4–12.

[11]Cullen, L. T. (2006, May 1). Getting wise to lies. *Time, 167*(18), 59.

[12]Elefant, C. (2008, March 11). Do employers using Facebook for background checks face legal risks? *Legal Blog Watch.* Retrieved from http://legalblogwatch.typepad.com/legal_blog_watch/2008/03/do-employers-us.html

[13]Ireland. S. (2002, July-August). A résumé that works. *Searcher, 10*(7), 98(12).

[14]Leonard, B. (2003, February). Study suggests bias against 'black' names on résumés. *HR Magazine, 48*(2), 29–30.

[15]Leslie, L. M. (2002, September 9). Muslims, Arabs say September 11 backlash has changed: Physical and verbal harassment have been replaced by subtle discrimination, related to jobs, for example. *Star Tribune* (Minneapolis), p. 8A.

[16]De Marcela, T.(2007). Getting to the top: Strategies for breaking through the glass ceiling. *The Multicultural Advantage.* Retrieved from http://www.multiculturaladvantage.com/leader/workplace-leadership/Getting-To-The-Top-Strategies-for-Breaking-Through-The-Glass-Ceiling.asp

[17]Harshbarger, C. (2003). You're out! *Strategic Finance, 84*(11), 46(4).

[18]Garone, E. (2009, March 18). Do references really matter? *WSJ.com*: Careers Q&A. Retrieved from http://online.wsj.com/article/SB123672074032087901.html

[19]Are you using the wrong resume? (2009). *Careerbulders.com.* Retrieved from http://www.careerbuilder.com/Article/CB-998-Cover-Letters-and-Resumes-Are-You-Using-the-Wrong-R%c3%a9sum%c3%a9/?ArticleID=998&cbRecursionCnt=1&cbsid=e34cc2cfa8dc4a94a2c1da7c6937807e301182628-JW-5&ns_siteid=ns_us_g_chronological_resume__

[20]Résumés you don't see every day. (2006). Retrieved from http://www.dummies.com/WileyCDA/DummiesArticle/id-1610.html

[21]Young, J. (2002). 'E-portfolios' could give students a new sense of their accomplishments. *Chronicle of Higher Education, 48*(26), 31(2).

[22]Sipper, R. A. (2007, October 15). Tips for creating a YouTube video résumé. Retrieved from http://www.associatedcontent.com/article/414702/tips_for_creating_a_youtube_video_resume.html?cat=3

[23]Cullen, L. T. (2007, February 22). It's a wrap. You're hired! *Business & Tech.* Retrieved from http://www.time.com/time/magazine/article/0,9171,1592860,00.html

[24]Duff, M. (2006, January 23). New president named at Container Store. *DSN Retailing Today, 45*(2), 3–4.

[25]Avoiding online job scams: Critical tips for job seekers. (2009). *Privacy Rights Clearing House.* Retrieved from http://www.privacyrights.org/fs/fs25a-JobSeekerPriv2.htm

[26]Holsman, S. (2009). The challenges of online recruiting. Search Express National, Inc. Retrieved from http://www.slideshare.net/scottholsman/Sourcing-In-Todays-Environment1

[27]EEOC addresses online recruiting. (2002, September 15). *Employee Benefit News*. Retrieved from http://www.accessmylibrary.com/coms2/summary_0286-25958382_ITM

Chapter 14

[1]General Electric Company. (2009). *GE Careers.* Retrieved from http://www.gecareers.com

[2]Top MBA Employers. (2009, May 27). *CnnMoney.com.* Retrieved from http://money.cnn.com/galleries/2009/fortune/0905/gallery.top_mba_employers.fortune/13.html

[3]General Electric Company. (2009). *GE Careers.* Retrieved from http://www.gecareers.com

[4]Diversity in action: GE wants to bring in diverse people and grow them. (2006, May 3). *Diversity Careers.* Retrieved from http://www.diversitycareers.com

[5]Hannon, K. (2005, April 14). Welch shows the "winning" side of business for all. *USA Today*, p. 5B.

[6]Stewart, G. L., Dustin, S. l., Barrick, M. R., & Darnold, T. C. (2008). Exploring the handshake in employment interviews. *Journal of Applied Psychology, 93,* 1139–1149.

[7]Vogt, P. (2006). Acing behavioral interviews. *Career.Journal.com.* Retrieved from http://www.careerjournal.com/jobhunting/interviewing/19980129-vogt.html

[8]Marion, L. C. (1997, January 11). Companies tap keyboards to interview applicants. *The News and Observer*, p. B5.

[9]Bhasin, R. (1997, January). The group interview: A new selection process. *Pulp and Paper*, 47.

[10]Thomson Learning announces name change to Cengage Learning. (2007, October). High Beam Research. Retrieved from http://www.highbeam.com/doc/1G1-169755193.html

[11]Art teacher in hot water over topless photos. (2006, June 17). CNN.com. Retrieved from http://www.cnn.com

[12]5 common interview blunders. *Classes & Careers*. Retrieved from http://www.classesandcareers.net/education-careers/2008/02/05/5-interview-faux-pas/

[13]Burns, D. (2009). *The first 60 seconds: Win the job interview before it begins.* Naperville, IL: Sourcebooks.

[14]Lai, P., & Wong, I. (2000). The clash of cultures in the job interview. *Journal of Language for International Business*, *11*(1), 31–40.

[15]Austin, N. K. (1996, March). The new job interview. *Working Woman*, 23, 24.

[16]Kennedy, J. L., & Morrow, T. J. (1994). *Electronic résumé revolution: Create a winning résumé for the new world of job seeking*. New York: John Wiley.

[17]Kleiman, P. (2003, May). Armed for a multitude of tasks. *The Times Higher Education Supplement,* p. 4.

[18]MIT Career Development Center (2008, September 16). STAR Method: Behavioral interviewing. Retrieved from **http://web.mit.edu/career/www/guide/star.html**

[19]Ryan, L. (2009, May 5). How do I prepare for a job interview? *Business Week Online*, 19.

[20]Stern, L. (2005, January 17). The tough new job hunt. *Newsweek*, 73–74.

[21]Interviews: Handling illegal interview questions. *JobWeb.* Retrieved from **http://www.jobweb.org/interviews.aspx?id=1343**

[22]General Electric, Inc. (2009). Diversity. Retrieved from **www.ge.com**

[23]General Electric, Inc. (2005). Our Actions: GE 2005 Citizenship Report. Retrieved from **http://www.ge.com**

[24]*Fortune*. (2000). America's most admired companies. Retrieved from **http://www.fortune.com/fortune/mostadmired/gat.html**

[25]Deloitte. (2007, June 8). Nonprofits to benefit from Deloitte's world-class business counsel and hands-on service on 8th annual Impact Day. *Corporate Social Responsibility Newswire.* Retrieved from **http://www.csrwire.com/press/press_release/21923-Nonprofits-to-Benefit-from-Deloitte-s-World-Class-Business-Counsel-and-Hands-On-Service-on-8th-Annual-Impact-Day**

[26]Deloitte. (2007, June 8). Nonprofits to benefit from Deloitte's world-class business counsel and hands-on service on 8th annual impact day. *Corporate Social Responsibility Newswire.* Retrieved from **http://www.csrwire.com/press/press_release/21923-Nonprofits-to-Benefit-from-Deloitte-s-World-Class-Business-Counsel-and-Hands-On-Service-on-8th-Annual-Impact-Day**

[27]Zimmerman, E. (2003, April). A subtle reference trap for unaware employers. *Workforce, 82*(4), 22.

[28]Smith, S. (2003, March 17). Rethinking your reference policy. *Westchester County Business Journal,* p. 4.

Index

A

B

C

D

E

F

G

H

I

J

K

L

M

N

O

P

Q

R

S

T

U

V

W

Y

Z